Encyclopedia of
Values
and Ethics

Encyclopedia of
Values
and Ethics

Joseph P. Hester

ABC-CLIO

Santa Barbara, California
Denver, Colorado
Oxford, England

Copyright © 1996 by Joseph P. Hester

All rights reserved. No part of this publication may be reproduced, stored in a retrieval system, or transmitted, in any form or by any means, electronic, mechanical, photocopying, recording, or otherwise, except for the inclusion of brief quotations in a review, without prior permission in writing from the publishers.

Library of Congress Cataloging-in-Publication Data

Hester, Joseph P.
    Encyclopedia of values and ethics / Joseph P. Hester
      p. cm.
    Includes bibliographical references and index.
    1. Ethics—Encyclopedias. 2. Values—Encyclopedias. I. Title.
  BJ63.H47   1996   170'.3—dc21   96-36928

ISBN 0-87436-857-X (cloth : alk. paper)

02 01 00 99 98 97 96 10 9 8 7 6 5 4 3 2 1 (cloth)

ABC-CLIO, Inc.
130 Cremona Drive, P.O. Box 1911
Santa Barbara, California 93116-1911

This book is printed on acid-free paper ∞.
Manufactured in the United States of America

CONTENTS

Encyclopedia of
Values
and Ethics

INTRODUCTION

Something of a taboo seems to have fallen over our discussions of ethics and values, not just in this decade, but in this decade in particular. Anticipated by Allan Bloom as "a closing of the American mind," we entered the 1990s ready to accept the dictum that truth is relative, the condition of a free society, and that relativism is necessary to openness. But Bloom warns us,

> Actually openness results in American conformism—out there in the rest of the world is a drab diversity that teaches only that values are relative, whereas here we can create all the life-styles we want. Our openness means we do not need others. Thus what is advertised as a great opening is a great closing. The point [in education] is to propagandize acceptance of different ways, and indifference to their real content is as good a means as any. Openness used to be the virtue that permitted us to seek the good by using reason. It now means accepting everything and denying reason's power.

This new openness has created a values shift in our society. We are now ready to accept any idea, any culture, any person on the grounds of openness, our new virtue, which also fuels its seductive postulate, political correctness. But in the 1990s, this has resulted in values confusion. What ethic other than openness is important for us to follow today? The proliferation of experiences and images each of us receives from the print, audio, and video media (the average person hears and sees over 300,000 commercials by age 18) serves this new openness to the extent that we find ourselves entrapped in a stereophonically televised ethnocentrism, and subsequently, in the morass of constant values conflict. Witness the efforts of a president trying to get a nominee confirmed by Congress and what we see and hear is a conflict over issues of ethics and values, first sexual harassment, next sex education in our schools, and then views on abortion.

Nothing is more central to a nation than its values and nothing is more important to the ordinary American's private and personal experience than the values of liberty and equality, respect for others, responsibility for one's behavior, and self-reliance. These values and those particular values predicated on them (and in conflict with them) comprise the content of this encyclopedia. It is the story of liberty and equality, of ethical transformation and accommodation, of values and value shifts in U.S. society, but not only in the United States. It will point to events, personalities, lifestyles, and laws that define ethics and values in other cultures as they have impacted on and become part of the fabric of American culture. It is the story of individualism and collectivism, of the one against the many, and, in our time, of the many (the corporation) defined as the one and given a value all its own. This story is found in song and poetry, in novels, plays, movies, books, magazines, academic literature, and advertisements; in any place we find human dialogue. For example, in the 1928 movie *The Crowd*, Mr. Anyman is engulfed in a mass society and loses his identity under the pressure of soul-destroying labor. In works such as Steinbeck's *The Grapes of Wrath*, Miller's *Death of a Salesman*, Riesman's *The Lonely Crowd*, Whyte's *The Organization Man*, and Matson's *The Broken Image*, the theme of the individual against big government, big business, nature, or the intrusions of science and technology is played out over and over again.

At the end of World War I, individualism dominated liberal thinking. This was the time when my parents came of age. My mother has told the story of how she and one of her sisters, girls in their late teens and early twenties, went against their parents' wishes and took a bus from North Carolina bound for the Chicago World's Fair in 1934. This was a far cry from the mother I came to know as a teenager in the 1950s. By 1955 the story was one of obedience to the church and to the authorities that ran the school, the small town where we lived, and the businesses where I found part-time work.

The 1920s was a decade defined by its search for individual freedom, but the desire to preserve freedom began to fence the alienated apart. After a war they did not fully understand, ordinary Americans were searching for answers, hoping to find some coherence beneath the world's disordered surface, while academia focused on science and technique. Even the abstruse social gospel emanating from theological seminaries said little to the person in the pew. In science and popular culture, in politics and religion, a comfortable obliviousness, an ignorant pretense, marked the Babbittry of those who governed. Prohibition became the hot button issue of the day, more important than the concern for civil liberties that led to the founding of the American Association of University Professors in 1914 and the American Civil Liberties Union in 1920. The rank and file, from the top to the bottom of the social scale, represented the un-

happy searchers for stability. They had voted for progressivism, but political reform had not restored order to the lives. They made connections in society and politics (by joining the KKK, the Communist Party, the American Bund, and the like) to protect and guarantee their freedoms, but in fact submerged the very individuality they wished to protect. The avant-garde that fled to France or England or to self-contained enclaves such as Greenwich Village hoping to find some coherence and self-understanding found little explanatory power in religion, myth, magic, or science.

The individualism that my mother displayed in her early years served for only a season to repel communal encroachments on personal freedoms. But, in truth, was anyone listening? By the mid-nineteen thirties, big government was promising relief from a depression that only World War II solved and demanded the relinquishing of basic liberties for resolutions "only" governments could bring. Even world philosophers, "keepers of the gate," had lost interest in the mundane, the common values and behaviors of ordinary individuals. They had drifted from issues of liberty and equality to problems of logic and epistemology incomprehensible to the uninitiated. By the early 1970s, the struggle for racial integration and the Vietnam War had brought the nation to the brink of destruction and departments of philosophy were struggling to find students who were interested in issues that had dominated the European Enlightenment but no longer seemed relevant to a world that had gone sour. Sociologists, interested in control, tinkered with social and educational reform, but behaviorism, which claimed to be beyond "freedom and dignity," offered little to the individual whose inner spirit had been scorched by years of demonstrations, violence, and death.

An encyclopedia of ethics and values cannot ignore the historical, the religious, the legal, the political, or the popular culture that defines our century and gives meaning to our lives. Neither can it ignore other world cultures; as transportation and communication have improved, the influence of other nations and new ideas, religions, beliefs, and values have impacted greatly on our lives.

The events and people and the ideas and movements of history tell us about the struggle, the shared sacrifices, and the uncertain future felt by Americans in every decade of our country's adolescence. From this history will be uncovered the foundational ethics and values for each generation. This will not be an abstract discussion of ethics and values. Rather, this reporting will be straightforward and factual. Where interpretation and metaphor are called for, those who lived and spoke about their era will be called upon to speak to us in the context of their own time.

To study our own culture objectively implies a detachment strong enough to make judgments. Criticism demands distance, it asserts difference, it entails discrimination. This will make our study difficult, for democracy, freedom, equality, and liberty—the values that define our personhood and nationhood—seem to impose compliance, acceptance of common norms and collective opinion, all that Tocqueville meant by the "tyranny of the majority." As we gathered ourselves for the 1990s, we found that "democracy" has been snubbed by "ingroups" in favor of gender, class, race, religion, and those particular terms that indicate our uniqueness and individualism. The rub of political correctness has had a tendency to erase those common values that bring people together and instead has separated us, emphasizing our differences and non-dependence on society, nation, and culture. At the same time, they have demanded that we have a concern for the collective whole and submerge our individualism under the cloak of the common good. The contradiction is obvious. Part of our task will be to chronicle these ideas and movements.

As we draw close to the end of the century, a new movement, character educa-tion, has today appeared on the horizon, ready to fill the values-vacuum felt by many . Values clarification—an educational program of the 1970s and early 1980s—left many educators and parents ethically empty as it emphasized clarifying and understanding one's most cherished values but offered no suggestions or recommendations about what values, what ethical principles, a person should promote in their own lives or for the well-being of the community at large. Values clarification lived and died by the values relativism that arose in the 1920s and perhaps was definitive of the past thirty years. On the other hand, the new movement, character education, defines a carefully formulated set of traditional and middle-of-the-road values called "virtues." Advocates of character education try to avoid such terms as "values," "morals," and "ethics," telling us that these words are philosophically loaded and carry too much negative baggage. Recent conversations with a proponent of character education revealed also that these programs wish to avoid controversy and stay with traditional, American-European "virtues" in their attempt to apply their curricula to the public schools. For example, in some character education programs, such terms as "tolerance" and "lifestyle" are omitted so that discussions of homosexuality and alternative lifestyles can be avoided. Hoping to avoid conflict with the religious and political extremes, character education may become more important for what it leaves out than what it includes in a curriculum designed for a pluralistic society. We should keep our eyes on this program as it becomes more widespread in our culture.

So many values have changed in our lifetime. An important cultural fact that we need to emphasize is that our philosophical and cultural roots are firmly planted in the Judeo-Christian understanding of history in terms of good and evil and damnation and salvation. We really cannot seriously understand concepts like morality and ethical life, person and individuality, or freedom and emancipation without appropriating the substance of this religious tradition. These concepts are perhaps nearer to our hearts than the conceptual overtones of Platonic thought, centering on order and revolving around the cathartic intuition of ideas. And in this encyclopedia we will also focus on these dictums, as well as the crust of custom that still holds them in place.

It is difficult to pinpoint when dramatic changes in the American character began. Some cite the end of World War II, others drop it back to the end of Reconstruction. There are those who point to the Depression of the 1930s, while others use the dropping of the atomic bomb on Japan as a point of departure. In my own generation, the years from 1954 to 1974—years of racial tension and change and, accompanying these events, the Vietnam War and the fall of Richard Nixon—is considered the watershed era when America and the world went through a major value-shift. But every era is important, for when they are taken together we are able to get a vision of the whole—the major and minor quakes that agitated the precarious and insecure values of every nation causing rifts, dips, and changes in what we believe and the way we behave.

Whatever the exact point of time, Americans no longer believe they are the chosen people, undefeatable in war, unparalleled economically, and immune from the corruption and vagaries of the rest of the world. Indeed, 1974 was an important year for us, for we can look back to that time and see a major realignment in our own values and ethical beliefs beginning to take place. In that year 58 percent of the American population was dissatisfied with the direction in which the nation was going. Roper pollsters reported that 65 percent of the nation believed that things had gotten off track in the country. In 1974, Daniel Yankelovich reported that 47 percent of Americans believed that unrest and ill-feel-

ing were leading to a real breakdown of the nation.

What a change! Just three generations before, nineteenth-century Americans believed they had escaped the fate of the "old world" and its feudal values. As Robert Heilbronner has pointed out, "we were permitted the belief that we were the sole masters of our destiny, and as few peoples on earth have been, we were." The Industrial Revolution came to America with the beginning of the railroad in 1835. After the Civil War, rail was able to open vast markets, which destroyed the cottage industries and local services that had dominated the economy. Although, at the turn of the century, most Americans were still involved in farming and were largely uneducated, large corporations in rail, steel, cotton, and tobacco (along with absentee owners and a new breed of middle managers) were beginning to dominate the economy. Shortly afterward came mass production techniques in the automobile industry, which further changed the concept of "craftsmanship" and redefined the value of work.

Underneath the social surface of the nineteenth century, major value changes initiated by new technologies were pushing America into an industrial age. The weak underbelly of the corporate world was later exposed during the Depression of the 1930s and major conflicts arose as workers now looked to their unions for security. After World War II, the corporation which achieved a personal identity, dominated by a few absentee owners, controlled by fluctuations in market prices, and run by a new team of middle managers, promised its workers security and a stable income in exchange for service and loyalty. As happened during the Depression and World War II, more and more the federal government became involved in private business. Through federal housing, the construction of highways (the Highway Act of 1944), the Tennessee Valley Authority, federal grants, contracts, and subsidies, the boundary between the public and private sectors became entangled, even blurred. Oscar and Lilian Handlin report:

> The regulatory agencies also defined their responsibilities narrowly, although the Interstate Commerce Commission, the Federal Trade Commission, the Food and Drug Administration, and the Environmental Protection Agency assembled vast bureaucracies remote from popular control or responsibility. Constant activity in Washington conveyed a sense of government's omnipresent role in the economy.
>
> The old barriers between public and private activities had collapsed during the war, and industrial concentration and the interrelations between business and government prevented their restoration. Political influences and the altered character of enterprise limited free competitive markets and modified the distinction between them and the public sectors.

Beginning in the 1970s, changes in technology (computers, telecommunications, fax, etc.) jolted America's economic forces, again causing major realignments in wealth and the skills required to enter the contemporary workforce. The American economy had become service oriented while Japan, Germany, and other Third World countries were dominating industrial production. This was a new age where machines ran other machines and a large proportion of the population (about 50 percent) devoted themselves to providing services to other people. Bankers, lawyers, teachers, waitresses, insurance salesmen, and clerks offered a variety of consumer services that the society wanted. National income increased and so did the size of cities and towns. Surrounding these cities were large suburbs, and more and more workers were entangled in bureaucracies. Between 1958 and 1973 service occupations increased by 2.7 percent. This category of workers together with the increased white collar group (from 42.6 percent to 47.8 percent of the work force in 1958 and 1973 respectively) provides evi-

dence that the majority of American workers were engaged in providing services to other Americans. During this period, market power, whether exercised by business or by labor (or by the growing number of lobbyists), affected the ordinary person's right to enjoy the hard earned attributes of life.

Were people happier? It is hard to tell, but the signs of distress—individual and corporate crime, divorce, alcoholism, and other forms of addiction—continued to rise in what has come to be called *the post-industrial age.* Sociologists William and Arline McCord chronicle the following results of these changes:

- *A growth in anonymity.* Urbanized societies tend to destroy the close emotional bonds that linked members of small towns and villages.
- *A growth in meaninglessness.* Because of exposure to a wide variety of lifestyles, the proliferation of new faiths, and the geographic mobility required by modern industrialism, there is little opportunity for the average family to "put down roots." One consequence of this continuous change is that Americans tend to become increasingly deprived of tradition. Exposure to many different ways of living and thought, although potentially enriching, is also a source of conflict and confusion.
- *A growth in electronic media.* The electronic media pervade our modern society. While hours of exposure to these media each day may lead to increased information, it may also well lead to increased frustration or even violence.
- *A disintegration of the family.* Industrial societies have no economic function for the extended family. Rather, nuclear families huddle together for comfort and protection. Economic demands, distance between work, home, and place of leisure, as well as increased mobility, place strains upon

the family. Also, the repercussions of economic independence are widespread. An economic base has now been created for the new custom of alimony and many retired persons are left to shift for themselves.

- *An extension of bureaucracy.* Work in an industrial society becomes increasingly specialized, routine, codified, and regulated. Initially conceived as a means of increasing efficiency, bureaucracies frequently serve to exaggerate conditions of impersonality and meaninglessness.
- *A new world view.* People in an industrial society commonly become imbued with secularism and a faith in technology; a tolerant, if not skeptical, point of view about human behavior; and a different sense of time, oriented to the future rather than the past.

In 1989, fifteen years after the McCords' observations, Joseph T. Plummer, writing in *The Futurist*, also examined the immense value changes still going on in American society. He commented:

Long-held beliefs about the meaning of work in one's life, relations between the sexes, expectations for the future—indeed, about many aspects of daily living and important relationships among people—are undergoing reexamination and reappraisal.

The changes cited by McCord and McCord earlier represent what Plummer calls a *paradigm shift:* a fundamental reordering of the way we see the world around us. Plummer says:

We are now gradually moving away from those traditional values that drove our societies through the first three-quarters of this century and toward the emerging new values being embraced on an ever-widening scare.

These characteristics of our time present us with a unique opportunity to focus on the ethical issues, values, and value shifts that characterize our time and place. These represent the parameters of the social arena where Americans live and work, and where they may find new, fresh solutions to the universal problems of human existence.

We can also turn to David Riesman's *The Lonely Crowd,* to further enhance our knowledge and understanding of people, their values, and changes in their frames of reference. Riesman identified three types of people, an understanding of which may also enlighten our understanding of ethics and values and changes in them. The first type, tradition-directed individuals and groups, value security and sustenance. They change little and see change as an enemy of basic values in the home, the school, the church, or the workplace. On the other hand, outer-directed individuals and groups value belonging and success. Status is important and is obtained by following rules and owning the material goods that society acknowledges as valuable. The last type Riesman identifies are those individuals who are inner-directed. These persons, while aware of the expectations of others, often decide not to behave in accordance with those expectations. They value personal experience and creativity and strive for self-actualization.

Citing Riesman, Joseph Plummer also points out that research in many markets around the world indicates that "more and more people in developed Western societies will exhibit inner-directed values in the future." This new paradigm shift is "showing up" in the following ways in Western societies:

- The new focus on individuality is favoring high levels of creativity, flexibility, and responsiveness by organizations rather than bigness and consistency.
- People increasingly expect high ethical standards of employees, political figures, and advertisers.
- The greater value being giving to experience is prompting the growth of travel, the arts, sports, and lifelong education.

- Health behavior is shifting from curing sickness to promoting wellness which is seen most dramatically in a decline in smoking and red-meat consumption.

With newspapers, magazines, and television chronicling values conflicts daily, and with other types of media and education promoting certain values and behaviors, the materials for this encyclopedia are readily at hand. This may be more of a curse than a blessing, because having so much to draw from, while living and working in its midst, makes understanding more difficult and selecting items to include in this book a fastidious task. Although this volume has been completed, an encyclopedia of ethics and values will never be finished. Change is constant and what people and societies deem of value never stays the same.

SOURCES

Bennett, William J. *The De-Valuing of America.* New York: Summit Books. 1992.

Bloom, Allan. *The Closing of the American Mind.* New York: Simon and Schuster. 1987.

Habermas, Jurgen. *Postmetaphysical Thinking: Philosophical Essays.* Translated by William Mark Hohengarten. Cambridge, MA: MIT Press. 1992.

Handlin, Oscar, and Lilian Handlin. *Liberty and Equality 1920–1994.* New York: Harper-Collins. 1994.

Heilbronner, Robert L. *The Future Is History.* New York: Harper & Row. 1960.

Lappe, Frances Moore. *Rediscovering America's Values.* New York: Ballantine. 1989.

Leinberger, Paul, and Bruce Tucker. *The New Individualists.* New York: HarperCollins. 1991.

McCord, William, and Arline McCord. *American Social Problems.* Saint Louis: C. V. Mosby. 1977.

Mead, Walter Russell. *Mortal Splendor.* Boston: Houghton Mifflin. 1987.

Packard, Vance. *Our Endangered Children.* Boston: Little, Brown. 1983.

Plummer, Joseph T. "Changing Values." *The Futurist.* January-February 1989.

Rorty, Richard. *Objectivity, Relativism, and Truth.* New York: Cambridge University Press. 1991.

Simon, S., and H. Kirschenbaum. *Values Clarification.* New York: Hart Publishers. 1972.

Simon, S., H. Kirschenbaum, and B. Fuhrmann. *An Introduction to Values Clarification.* New York: J. C. Penney, 1972.

Smith, Page. *Killing the Spirit, Higher Education in America.* New York: Viking Press. 1990.

Vincent, Philip F. *Character Education: A Primer.* Chapel Hill, NC: New View. 1994.

ABORTION

Abortion is the separation of the embryo or fetus from the mother before the organism is capable of extrauterine existence. There are three categories of abortion: *induced abortion*, the surgical termination of a pregnancy; *spontaneous abortion*, or miscarriage, the natural termination of a pregnancy during the first 20 weeks, usually because the pregnancy or the organism is biologically abnormal; and *therapeutic abortion*, the surgical termination of a pregnancy that endangers the life of the mother—the only legal form of induced abortion in most of the United States.

BACKGROUND

The reemergence of the abortion issue in the 1950s found the controversy remaining, in large part, a debate restricted to physicians and interested professionals. In 1958, 28 percent of the pregnancies in America were terminated by abortion, a figure comparable to the 33 percent in 1898. However, with the turbulent 1960s came an emphasis on new freedoms, often defined in terms of alternative lifestyles. It was a time when minorities asserted their rights—blacks, young people, the poor, and women. In the late 1960s, the right of a woman to choose abortion became a frequently debated topic,

and the U.S. Supreme Court *(Roe v. Wade)* ruled in 1973 that state antiabortion laws may interfere with an individual's freedom of expression as outlined in the First Amendment of the Constitution. The outcome of this ruling was that states could not forbid abortions during the first six months of pregnancy. After six months the fetus becomes viable or capable of living outside the mother's body; therefore, abortion was not permitted by law after the second trimester of pregnancy. We should note that in Canada, abortion is allowed only in a public hospital. At least three members of the hospital's staff must certify that the woman's life is in danger before the abortion may be performed.

The abortion debates since 1973 have little in common with the discussions among professionals that characterized abortion talk throughout the nineteenth century and through the 1950s. Instead of civility and collegiality, contemporary discussions have been marked by rancor and violence. Two major issues have emerged from these debates: (1) whether a woman should be permitted by law to have an abortion (pro-choice) and, if so, under what circumstances; and (2) whether, and to what extent, laws should protect the unborn child's right to life (pro-life). The crucial question, the question of ethics and value (and the question that must be answered before either of the above two issues can be effectively argued), is: "Is the embryo or fetus a person, or only a potential person?" This lifts the question from one of medicine and practicality or lifestyle to one of ethics and morality.

WHEN LIFE BEGINS

Although it is clear that a form of life begins at the instant of conception, there has always been legal, theological, philosophical, and biological disagreement as to precisely when the organism developing within the mother achieves the status of a person. Does the organism become a person prior to birth? If so, does it become a person as a zygote? As an embryo? As a fetus?

Historically, oriental cultures have considered a baby to be one year old at birth, reflecting a belief that the status of personhood is achieved at conception. Roman law, which forms the foundation for the European and American legal systems, considered the fetus not a human being but a part or possession of the mother; abortion was punishable as "property damage." Christianity brought with it the notion that the fetus was a human being, but the precise stage at which it became a human being remained a matter of speculation. Saint Augustine distinguished between a "formed" and an "unformed" fetus and believed that the soul does not enter the fetus until it is formed. Thomas Acquinas felt that life occurred only at the moment of *quickening*, the first perceptible movement of the fetus; this idea became part of the common law of England. Today the debate continues and has even been revitalized as a part of the controversy over liberalization of abortion laws.

We should note that until modern times humans lived close to the soil. One thing they knew how to do well was to scoop clay from the riverbank and shape it into vessels. Shards of pottery have been found wherever people have lit their fires and lived together. The Batek people of Malaysia tell of a supernatural being named Tohan who is "very big," but looks just like us. Tohan, the story goes, came to Earth, took some black soil, and molded it into the shape of a man and a woman. He shaped them into his own likeness, and from the western sky he brought them life-soul to bring them to life. The Toradjas of the Celebes tell how i Lai, the god of the upper world, and i Ndara, the goddess of the underworld, resolved to make man. They committed the task to i Kombengi, who made man and woman out of wood. The god Lai fetched eternal breath from the celestial mansion, but in the meantime, the Creator allowed the common wind to blow on the figures, and they drew their breath and life from it. That is why the breath returns to the wind when a man dies. In the earliest Hebrew account of creation, it is said that the god Yahweh molded the first man out of clay, just as a potter might do, and then animated it by breathing into the mouth and nostrils of the figure. To the Hebrews this derivation of our species from the dust of the ground suggested itself all the more naturally because, in their language, the word for "ground" (*adamah*) is in form the feminine of the word for "man" (*adam*). Thus both in language and myth, *ha-adam*, "the Man" (masculine), is created from *ha-adamah*, "the Earth" (feminine). And divine spirit/breath (in Hebrew, *ruah* and *nephesh* mean "spirit," "breath," "wind," and "soul") is breathed by Yahweh himself into the man's nostrils and pumped into his lungs. The man's body is from earth, but his spirit/breath is from Yahweh. Finally, the Shilluks of the White Nile ingeniously explain the different complexions of the various races by the differently colored clays out of which they are fashioned.

The Hebrew concept of *person* entered Western society through Christianity and is based on the idea of soul or spirit (*nephesh*). Unlike the Greek and Latin conceptualization, the Hebrew concept of person was "the inner self" and "the outer appearance"; i.e., what one is to oneself and what one appears to be to those who observe him. These cannot be separated. To the Hebrews, *nephesh* was the inner person, while the outer person was reputation, or *shem*.

Today we find that the major arguments against abortion are based on the belief that abortion is the unjustified killing of an unborn child—that the embryo is a person. This is the idea that reflects the Judeo-Christian tradition. Those who oppose abortion argue that human life begins when a sperm fertilizes an egg, and that the development of a human being continues from conception through birth and adulthood—there is no point when we can say that the embryo is not a person or becomes a person except at the moment of fertilization. John T. Noonan, Jr. (see *The Morality of Abortion*) argues that an embryo is a human being because it has a full genetic code and the potential capacity for rational thought. Western culture, based on Jewish and Christian theological ideas, supports Noonan's position, pointing to the embryo as "a living soul" and as being "God's creation."

We also find this idea expressed in the view of contemporary persons, especially those in the Judeo-Christian tradition. For example, when Mother Teresa of Calcutta, India, spoke at the National Prayer Breakfast in Washington, D.C., on February 3, 1994, she commented, "I feel that the greatest destroyer of peace today is abortion because it is a war against the child, a direct killing of the innocent child, murder by the mother herself. And if we accept that a mother can kill even her own child, how can we tell other people not to kill one another?"

The political and religious right in America point to abortion statistics as the major example of the decline of American culture, which they describe as a totally demoralized society. Jim Nelson Black comments:

Consider the slaughter of 1.6 million unborn infants every year since 1973 and the fact that 31 percent of Americans support the use of abortion "in any circumstance" to terminate pregnancy. . . . But we must ask ourselves, how is the murder of 30 million innocent children in America over the last twenty years any different? Isn't the rite of abortion our culture's sacrifice to the gods of materialism and greed? Unwanted pregnancies they're called today. Children who do not deserve to live. Evidence of our sin and our culture's insistence on "rights" and "choices" over God's gift of new life. Call it a cult of selfishness, of greed, or materialism. But call it what it is. The Phoenicians murdered many thousands of children. And, yes, they burned their young. But in the entire history of Carthage or Rome, they never killed 30 million in the name of "a woman's right to control her own body."

Black refers to this as a legacy of despair. He points to 1973, when Norma McCorvey won her suit against District Attorney Henry Wade and the courts of Dallas County, Texas, in the case now known as *Roe v. Wade*. There have been 31,460,374 legal abortions between January 1, 1973, and January 1, 1994. This is an average of 1.6 million abortions per year, 4,383 abortions per day, 182 abortions per hour, and 3 abortions per minute—every day of the year.

There is disagreement, however. Many people approve of abortion under certain circumstances. Some approve of abortion if a woman's life or health is endangered by her pregnancy or if the pregnancy results from rape. Others recommend abortion when there is a danger that the child will be born with a serious mental or physical defect. Latin American countries and many Western European countries allow abortion only to save the woman's life, but in Denmark, Sweden, Hungary, and Japan a woman can have an abortion for many reasons, including a simple request. All of these various practices fall under the broad heading of pro-choice, but the issues are much more complicated than they appear, especially if it is granted that the embryo is a human being. If the embryo is a human being, is it not entitled to basic human rights under the law, among those the right to life, liberty, and potential happiness? Judith Jarvis Thomson has provided excellent commentary on the issue of pro-life and pro-choice in *Rights, Restitution & Risk: Essays in Moral Theory.*

CAN LIFE BE DEFINED?

At present, we are able to define "life" with two fundamental qualities: self-replication and mutability. Any organism possessing these two qualities can be considered alive. In these two characteristics are contained the essential processes of evolution: continuity and adaptation. An organism must be able to replicate itself. If it can produce a likeness of itself, then it possesses the power to assure continuity of its species. But *mutability*—the ability to effect changes from one generation to another and adapt to a fluid environment—is essential. Without the ability to change and adapt, no species could long survive. Environmental conditions are forever changing; species must be able to change along with their environments.

Several other qualities have been suggested as essential to a definition of what it means to be alive:

- Mobility: the ability to move about.
- Metabolism: the ability to ingest materials, digest them, and excrete wastes.
- Growth: the ability to proceed through some sort of life cycle.
- Irritability: the ability to react to external stimuli, a first step in adaptation.
- Dynamic Equilibrium: the ability to maintain a stable internal condition within changing external conditions.

But even among the scientifically minded, there are those who still believe that life is "more than" matter in motion. Rene Dubos reflects, "In one form or another, the concept that life entails the operation of some principle of nature which is as yet ill defined seems to be gaining ground at the present time; and there is reason to believe that it is the fear of entrenched scientific orthodoxy which stills the voice of many who believe that life involves something more subtle than the latest chemical formulae for nucleic acids." Thus, in both scientific and religious circles, the conception of "life" as more than a perceptual matter affects the attitude of those who consider abortion a moral, if not a religious issue.

LANDMARKS

- In 1974, abortion became one of the dominant moral issues among Catholics in the United States. On March 4, 1974, four cardinals testified before the Senate Judiciary Constitutional Amendments Subcommittee in Washington, D.C., supporting amending the U.S. Constitution to provide due recognition of the right of the unborn child to life.
- On January 22, 1975, 50,000 Catholics demonstrated in Washington, D.C., in favor of a constitutional amendment to "undo" *Roe v. Wade.*
- On February 15, 1975, Kenneth C. Edelin, a Boston obstetrician, was convicted of manslaughter in an abortion operation and sentenced to a year's probation. Although flagged as a pro-life victory, this decision was overturned on December 17, 1975.
- On April 3, 1976, 30,000 women marched in Rome, demanding an end to restrictions on abortion.
- On July 1, 1976, the U.S. Supreme Court ruled that neither husbands nor parents of minors could legally veto a pregnant woman's decision to have an abortion. The Court also ruled that a state may not legally require a woman to have her husband's consent before she can undergo an abortion.

- In 1977, the U.S. Supreme Court ruled that while a woman did have a right to abortion, she had no right to ask the government to pay for it.
- In 1989, the U.S. Supreme Court narrowed the previous decision made in *Roe v. Wade* when it ruled that state governments could restrict women's rights to abortion and could forbid the use of public funds to pay for abortions.

ABORTION AND THE COURTS

Bradford Wilson (*Science News*, April 8, 1972) exhorts the scientific community "to come forth with a viable definition of exactly what constitutes a Person whom the 14th Amendment proscribes against depriving of 'life, liberty, or property, without the due process of law.'" Wilson questions whether "a fetus in utero is closer to the status of an internal organ than it is to that of a separate and discrete individual." He is concerned that a decision so important to the human condition and the quality of life might be left up to the courts rather than the scientific community.

SOURCES

Black, Jim Nelson. *When Nations Die.* Wheaton, IL: Tyndale House Publishers. 1996.

Christian, James L. *Philosophy: An Introduction to the Art of Wondering.* 4th ed. New York: Holt, Rinehart and Winston. 1986.

Dubos, Rene. *The Torch of Life.* New York: Pocket Books, 1962.

Kelley, Kathryn, and Donn Byrne. *Human Sexuality.* Englewood Cliffs, NJ: Prentice-Hall. 1992.

Luker, Kristin. *Abortion and the Politics of Motherhood.* Los Angeles: University of California Press. 1984.

Noonan, John T. *The Morality of Abortion.* Cambridge, MA: Harvard University Press. 1970.

Skolnick, Arlene S., and Jerome H. Skolnick, eds. *Family in Transition.* 8th ed. New York: HarperCollins. 1994.

Thomson, Judith Jarvis. *Rights, Restitution & Risk: Essays in Moral Theory.* Edited by William Parent. Cambridge, MA: Harvard University Press. 1986.

ABUNDANCE

"Abundance"—literally, "plenty, bountifulness, or ample sufficiency"—has been and is the goal of American capitalism in general and of individual Americans in particular. The quest for riches first brought Europeans to American shores and continues to be a major goal of Americans everywhere. The quest for opulency led to the enslavement of Africans and Native Americans, and for the latter, a gradual—but incomplete—extinguishing. For example, in 1862, 38 Sioux were hanged in the United States' largest legal execution. In the summer of 1865, General Patrick E. Connor marched into the Great Plains to deal with both the Sioux and the Cheyenne. In 1876, General George Armstrong Custer marched against the Sioux and Cheyenne and into history at the Battle of Little Big Horn. But all Americans did not agree with this search for richness, especially when it called for the enslavement and destruction of others. In 1893, 17 short years after Custer's last stand, the Columbia Exposition was held in Chicago to celebrate four centuries of white progress on the American continent. At the exposition, a young historian—Frederick Jackson Turner—proclaimed the impending decline of American national values.

Turner justified his remarks by saying: "This brief statement marks the closing of a great historic movement. Up to our own day, American history has been in a large degree the history of the colonization of the Great West. The existence of an area of land, its continuous recession, and the advance of American settlement westward, explain American development." For Turner, the uniqueness of America came from breaking the links with the Old World's conception of place. He believed that America was a place, a geographic space, in which European immigrants were allowed to reject the culture of the Old World and be reborn as free individuals. The religious overtones of Turner's remarks are obvious. He completes this thought by saying:

> American democracy was born of no theorist's dream. It came stark and strong and full of life out of the American forest and it gained new strength each time it touched a new frontier. Into this vast, shaggy continent of ours poured the first feeble tide of European settlement. European men, institutions, and ideas were lodged in the American wilderness, and this great American West took them to their bosom, taught them a new way of looking upon the destiny of the common man, trained them in adaptation to the conditions of the New World, and even as society on her eastern border grew to resemble the Old World in its social reforms, ever, as it began to lose faith in the ideal of democracy, she opened new provinces, and dowered new democracies in her most distant domains.

For Turner, America's wealth was tied to the abundance of land available for domestication. For Native Americans, the white man's western movement meant death. The mythological sources of rejuvenation for the Native American came from the natural cycle of birth, death, and rebirth. On the other hand, for the European pioneer, Turner saw the national mythology of cultural renewal dependent not on a fixed place, but upon the movement of man through space (land). He believed that as long as Americans moved west, they would remain young. The tragedy of 1890, at least in Turner's eyes, was that the free lands were gone. The material forces that gave vitality to Western democracy were passing away. With no new frontier to revitalize American democracy, Turner concluded that those uniquely American values that were tied to conquering new territories and converting its native people to the democratic ideal were going to decline. Turner concluded, "Never again can such an opportunity come to the sons of men. It was unique. The familiar facts of the massing of population in the cities and the contemporane-

ous increase in urban power, of the massing of capital and production in fewer and vastly greater industrial units, especially attest the revolution."

Seventy-seven years after Turner's prophecy, President Lyndon Johnson, remembering his own poverty-stricken youth and his labors on a road gang, and moved by heartbreaking descriptions of America's poor, trapped in misery without any capacity to act, considered the source of the problem not in the individual victims but in the surrounding society. In the midst of apparent plenty, the inability of the economy to employ at least one-fifth of the population at a livable wage led to terrifying riots in the cities during the early 1960s. Johnson then went about creating the Great Society, free of want, affording liberty to all.

With Johnson's Great Society programs, abundance was now defined as the ability to be employed at a livable wage and enjoy the abundance of this nation. Individual and national values in America have always been tied to property, wealth, and abundance. C. Wright Mills observed that the United States is "an overdeveloped society where the means of livelihood are so great that life is dominated by the struggle for status, based on the acquisition and maintenance of commodities." So, in March 1964, Johnson began to use the country's wealth to enrich and elevate national life—to eliminate poverty and racial injustice, improve the quality of urban existence, beautify the countryside, control pollution, and advance education—all for the common good. In his State of the Union address in January 1965, Johnson assumed that America was in the "midst of abundance." He said that individuals, free from the "wants of the body," could seek fulfillment of the "needs of the spirit." Johnson thereupon declared war on poverty and brought forth his Great Society to redress the legitimate grievances of minorities, achieving more in the decade of the 1960s (Medicare for 19 million, widening of Social Security, aid to education; air and water pollution control; help for Appalachia and for highway beautification) than in the whole time since the Emancipation Proclamation.

In 1982, Tom Peters published *In Search of Excellence*, which sold over 5 million copies in three years, including 15 translations. In *A Passion for Excellence*, which he published in 1985, Peters notes that the main goal of business hasn't changed: the achievement of sustainable growth and equity. What had changed since the industrial barons of the nineteenth century was the type of leadership required. According to Peters, "We got so tied up in our techniques, devices and programs that we forgot about people—the people who produce the product or service and the people who consume." Have American values changed? Hardly! The end—sustainable growth (profit)—is the same. The means to this end, according to Peters, has made a decided values shift with an emphasis on people—what he calls "values, vision, and integrity." The values shift, which began in the middle 1970s, was beginning to seep into business and industry by 1980. The new power words were *trust, integrity, care, quality,* and *imagination,* all of which would become a means to profit (abundance).

One key measure of abundance in America is how well the income of black Americans is improving when compared to the income of white Americans. Over the past two decades, record numbers of African Americans have graduated from high school, enrolled in college and entered the highly competitive professional work force. Still, the average real income of black families in 1993 hadn't changed since 1969. Those who have come the farthest are college-educated African-American women. Generally, reports from the Census Bureau show that one-third of all black families still live in poverty, and blacks on the average earn less than their white counterparts in all jobs at all levels. Consider these facts:

1. While incomes for blacks haven't budged since 1969, the income for white families rose 9 percent over the period.
2. Black children are three times as likely as white children to live in poor families headed by a single parent.
3. In 1995, six in ten black children lived in poverty. In 1970, four in ten black children were poor, and most lived in two-parent families.
4. Eighty percent of poor black families are headed by a single parent.

In February 1995, Commerce Secretary Ron Brown said that the above information provides further evidence that we are in danger of becoming a society of haves and have-nots, and that this is unacceptable. Considering the debates surrounding the Republican Contract with America in 1995, Brown said that for Democrats this information comes at an opportune time to challenge changes in welfare programs and in affirmative action. The facts point out that poverty is partly a result of the dramatic increase in the proportion of African-American children living in single-parent families—the rate has jumped from 32 percent to 58 percent from 1970 to 1993. But contrary to popular perception, about 62 percent of single parents were high school graduates and worked at least part time in 1990. Black earnings in 1993 still did not match white earnings. Black men earned 72¢ for every $1 earned by white men, up about a dime since 1969. And the income gap between young black and white men who are recent college graduates is widening, after reaching near parity in 1980. The greatest gains have been made by college-educated black women, who earn about 95¢ for every $1 earned by white college-educated women. But both groups of women earn far less than white men.

See also Capitalism and the Information Revolution; Consumerism.

SOURCES

Carroll, Peter N., and David W. Noble. *The Free and the Unfree: A New History of the United States.* 2d ed. New York: Penguin. 1988.

Handlin, Oscar, and Lilian Handlin. *Liberty and Equality 1920–1994.* New York: Harper Collins. 1994.

Jordan, Barbara C., and E. D. Roston, eds. *The Great Society.* Austin: LBJ School of Public Affairs, University of Texas. 1986.

Mills, C. Wright. *Power, Politics, and People.* Edited by Irving Louis Horowitz. New York: Balantine Books. 1963.

Peters, Tom, and Nancy Austin. *A Passion for Excellence.* New York: Random House. 1985.

Schulte, Brigid. Observer Washington Bureau. *The Charlotte Observer* (Feb. 23, 1995): Carolinas, 1C.

Schaefer, Richard T. *Racial and Ethnic Groups.* 3d ed. Boston: Scott, Foresman and Co. 1988.

ACTION, THEORY OF

Action, acting, and *doing* signify the intentional (and perhaps unintentional) movements and activities of individuals. Normally, when someone's actions affect us, we want to know what caused the behavior of the person or what reasons can be found to explain the behavior. Thus, for those investigating human behavior and ethics, *action* has come to have an enormous significance. Among philosophers trained in the tradition of Wittgenstein, the concept of action has become the focal point of investigation. Action, in the analytical context, has come to signify a complex web of issues in our understanding of such human behaviors as *intention, motive, purpose, reasons,* and *teleological (purposeful) explanation* that have dominated analytic philosophy since 1951.

The meanings of *praxis*—practice, action, and doing—and *action* are very close,

although when explored closely and subjected to comparative analysis (Marxist usage compared with analytic, existential, and pragmatic philosophies), significant differences are found. Actually, the focus on praxis and action is not unique to these traditions. John Dewey called for a philosophy that would "become a practical philosophy or rather a philosophy of practical activity." The pragmatic philosophers were preoccupied with the nature of human action and with practice. The pragmatic movement has been a distinctly American movement, but if we turn to Europe, we discover that among the phenomenological philosophers—especially the existentialists—the central issue again turns out to be the nature of human action. We find that Marxist usage reveals an undercurrent of humanism, while analytic philosophers remained interested in classifying language usage to clarify a theory of meaning. So they have concentrated on intentionalism (the speaker), the *use-theory* of meaning (the person who hears the speaker and responds), and *truth-semantics* (that something in the world being acted upon or spoken about—the object of one's intentions). In summary—although separated by proposed differences of emphasis, terminology, and purpose—Marxism, existentialialism, pragmatism, and philosophers with an analytical interest share a concern with humans as agents—intending, acting, doing, and developing meaning.

See also Praxis.

SOURCES

Bernstein, Richard J. *Praxis and Action.* Philadelphia: University of Pennsylvania Press. 1971.

Dewey, John. *Democracy and Education.* New York: Macmillan. 1916.

Hegel, Georg W. F. *Reason in History.* Translated with an introduction by Robert S. Hartman. New York: The Liberal Arts Press. 1953.

Marx, Karl. *Writings of the Young Marx on Philosophy and Science.* Edited by Loyd D.

Easton and Kurt H. Guddat. Garden City, NY: Doubleday. 1967.

Peirce, Charles Sanders. *Collected Papers of Charles Sanders Peirce.* Vols. I–VI. Edited by Charles Hartshorne and Paul Weiss. Cambridge, MA: Harvard University Press. 1931–1935.

Wittgenstein, Ludwig. "A Lecture on Ethics." *The Philosophical Review* 74 (January 1965).

ADAMS, HENRY

Henry Brooks Adams was an American historian and philosopher who placed himself at the fulcrum of change, facing large historic transitions. His moral roots were, as he said, in the eighteenth century. Adams was vividly responsive to the intellectual weather of the nineteenth century, and he prophesied with great accuracy for the twentieth.

Adams's best-known book, *The Education of Henry Adams,* won a Pulitzer in 1919. It is considered one of the most thoughtful of American autobiographies and contributes to the philosophy of history with ideas about power and order. His nine-volume *History of the United States* (1885–1891) demonstrated his fascination with the struggle of social forces, his deep respect for power in all its human and natural manifestations, and gave his writings a unity like the unity he longed for—and found missing—in the actual civilization he knew.

To understand what Adams wanted to communicate in his yearning for unity in the midst of multiplicity, we need to remember his premises, or theorems, which he liked to recite:

- "Man is a force; so is the sum; so is a mathematical point, though without dimension or known existence."
- "Man commonly begs the question again by taking it for granted that he captures the forces of nature. A dynamic theory, assigning attractive forces to opposing bodies in proportion to the law of man, takes for granted that the forces of nature capture man."
- "There is actually only one way that 'the feeble atom or molecule called man' can assert a form of control, and that is by identifying with the whole of which he is a part or by discovering 'the movement' of the forces [that] control the progress of the mind."

In the tradition of Marx, Spencer, Nietzsche, Bergson, Zola, and Sorel, Henry Adams adapted human values to naturalistic realities. Conflict—as in nature—was the locus, the driving force of history—a practical demonstration of power. Adams's story of history was thus a naturalistic ethic telling the story of civilization in terms of conflict relationships and power realities. What Adams teaches is submission to force in order to gain the residual power that comes from identifying with a larger collective energy. Like other nineteenth-century moralizing naturalists, he believed that history was in his favor. *The Education* has great resonance today because Adams's prophetic sensitivity to the politics of race, nation, class, and empire, and to the apocalyptic motifs of revolution and decadence, touch a reality that we all have experienced. The postindustrial system of America (or other countries) will attest to a historical confusion—if not contradiction—in values that has created a confused climate of ethical injunctions. The high crime rate and instability of the family attest to this cultural dysfunction. The urbanization and suburbanization of America has had a distinct rippling effect, creating a society that has broken into atomized, depersonalized groups in which traditional social controls are lacking.

Henry Adams made power abstract. When power conflict becomes so intense that moral judgments of it can no longer be made, Adams felt that it was almost certain that the shadow of paranoia will fall over it. And to talk about forces rather than men is to liberate rather than restrain the imagination of conspiracies. The depersonalization of moral judgments does not lead to their disappearance but to their magnification as political judgments. Nothing reveals the abstract moral ambiguity of this pattern of political thought better than Adams's close emotional involvement with the Dreyfus case. France was, at a time, Adams's alternate home, where he spent part of every year. What he saw in the Dreyfus campaign was a conspiracy directed against the entire social and national structure of France. Not only the army, but the people of France and the future of France would be condemned if Dreyfus were acquitted. Therefore, although he was able to admit that Dreyfus was probably innocent, Adams felt that the justice or injustice of the matter had no weight when France could be ruined as a corporate national entity. His choice for political survival rather than justice is instructive, for it suggests how far committed he himself was to the pragmatic use of power.

SOURCES

Kaplan, Harold. *Power and Order: Henry Adams and the Naturalist Tradition in American Fiction.* Chicago: The University of Chicago Press. 1981.

World Book Encyclopedia. Chicago: Field Enterprises Educational Corporation. 1993.

ADOLESCENCE

Adolescence, the time from the onset of puberty through teen age, is a period of growing and conflict. History suggests little difference between today's adolescent and those at other times. Adolescents, like adults, are struggling for their freedom and independence. They more often than not reject attempts of adults who demand conformity to traditional values and standards. Ruth Benedict (*Patterns of Culture,* 1948) reminds us: "The life history of the individual is first and foremost an accommodation to the patterns and standards traditionally handed down in his community. From the moment of his birth the customs into which he is born shape his experience and behavior. By the time he can talk, he is the little creature of his culture, and by the time he is grown and able to take part in its activities, its habits are his habits, its beliefs his beliefs, its impossibilities his impossibilities."

The view that "the younger generation is going to the dogs" is apparently held by each successive adult generation about those soon to enter adulthood. Conflict between generations is interpreted in many ways: some hold it to be essential to social development and the taking on of adult roles, and others regard conflict between adults and their children as evidence that the older generation is only partially successful in handing down its ideas, values, and solutions to the problems of life. There is another group of sociologists who suggest that this conflict reflects the dissatisfaction of youth with contemporary social life and our established social order. Apparently, the young in the United States have always been more willing than the old to reject the status quo and to challenge values accepted by the adult community member. The conflict between generations, while perhaps a necessary ingredient of a rapidly changing society, does produce casualties: the search for new experiences, the rebellion against family norms, and the testing of new ideas take their toll on both youth and their families.

Sociologists today recognize that the shift from agrarian to industrial society over the past 200 years has revolutionized parent-child relations and the conditions of child development. We have discovered that in medieval society, the idea of childhood did not exist, at least in the way childhood is perceived today. Parents in medieval times did not neglect their children; rather, they did not think of them as having a special nature that required special treatment. After the age of around five to seven, children simply joined the adult world of work and play. Childhood as we know it today is a relatively recent cultural invention. The same is true of adolescence. Teenagers, who are such a conspicuous and noisy presence in modern life, and their stage of life—known for its turmoil and soul-searching—are not universal features of life in other times and places.

Some variations are cultural and historical. In the past 100 years, the age of first menstruation in girls has declined from the mid-teens to 12, and the age young men reach their full height has declined from 25 to under 20. Both changes are believed to be due to improvements in nutrition and health care.

Adolescence, as we know it today, evolved in the late nineteenth century. It is a creature of the industrial revolution, and it continues to be shaped by the forces that defined that revolution: industrialization, specialization, urbanization, the bureaucratization of human organizations and institutions, and continuing technological development. A second condition leading to a distinct stage of adolescence was the founding of mass education systems. Compulsory education helped define adolescence by setting a precise age for it. In the nineteenth century, graded classrooms appeared in our schools to separate students according to perceived developmental stage. High schools brought large numbers of teenagers together to create their own society for a good part of their daily lives. In the final quarter of the twentieth century, a new innovation for recognizing these differences and segregating students accordingly—the middle school concept and the middle school—came into vogue.

Radical social change, a product of the twentieth century, helped make adolescence more psychologically problematic. With more options for teenagers to choose from, rapid social change made one generation's experience increasingly different from that of the next. At the turn of the twentieth century, a flood of immigrants were making their way into America and the generation gap became even more acute.

Further, the structure and emotional atmosphere of middle-class family life was changing also. Industrialization intensified at this time: Youngsters lived at home until they married, and depended more completely and for a longer time on their parents than in the past. The size of the family had been cut in half over the course of a century and mothers were encouraged to devote themselves to the careful nurturing of fewer children. Family conflict in general may have been intensified by this peculiar combination of teenagers' increased dependence on parents and their growing autonomy in making their life choices. Despite its tensions, the new emotionally intense middle-class home made it more difficult than ever for adolescents to leave home for the world outside.

In 1904, psychologist G. Stanley Hall defined adolescence as a turbulent transitional stage in the evolution of the human species: "Some ancient period of storm when old moorings were broken and a higher level attained." Hall's legacy, that adolescence is a time of stress and storm, outlived him. Adolescence continued to be a period of both great promise and great peril. The youth problem—whether the lower-class problems of delinquency, or the identity crises and other psychological problems of middle-class youngsters—has continued to haunt America and other industrial societies.

In the twentieth century, youth has had its own culture. Its transitional status is obvious, but while the young are young they create their own style characterized by dress, adornment, music, and slang—all used to assert independence from adult authority. During the 1980s, a distinctive youth culture emerged, built on the heavy metal and punk subculture of the prior decade. Hard core, thrash metal, skate punk, and death metal created their own unique followings. During the latter half of the 1980s, still another recapturing project was underway, which looked to the mythic past of the 1960s. Centering around the Grateful Dead, the music, clothing style, and drugs of choice (particularly LSD) of the counterculture found a new audience among young people in the upper middle class. Here the emphasis was embracing the final supernova of an attached youth culture. By the early 1990s, a new musical style emerged that has tried to speak to and for youth. Exemplified by groups such as Jane's Addiction and Nirvana, the style has been labeled "Alternative." These ready-for-prime-time, MTV-friendly bands play music with neopsychedelic elements over a guitar grunge and strong bass guitar and drum rhythm section.

In the summer of 1991, an explicit, self-conscious attempt was made to reinvoke the 1960s counterculture. A touring festival with a variety of Alternative music bands and political and artistic sideshows—called the Lollapalooza Festival—drew an avid audience of middle-class, college-aged youth. The tour was dubbed "Woodstock for a lost generation" by the *New York Times*. The adult reaction to these youth-cultural movements has been mixed. In 1986, the worldwide Live Aid concert excluded youth-specific musical styles. It was not until the 1990s that *Rolling Stone* magazine took any special interest in heavy metal or rap.

Much of this music cogently and emotionally articulates a sense of impending doom—ecological, economic, political, educational, and social. It was no accident, since adults have disapproved of rock music since the mid-1950s, that those who testified against heavy metal music at U.S. Senate hearings in 1985 were representative of parental interest groups—the PTA, fundamentalist ministers, and physician-owners of psychiatric hospitals specializing in the treatment of adolescents. Even more ominous than these reactions was the large increase in the number of adolescents sent to mental hospitals. *Newsweek* concluded that part of this was a response to youth behaving rebelliously. Therapy often included requiring the elimination of music and its associated sartorial styles. School officials began banning heavy metal T-shirts during this period as well.

Where does this leave youth today? Sociologists and psychologists who specialize in youth culture agree that the present situation results from two failures: (1) The youth culture of the 1960s, as an ideal and ideology of a specific age group, was unable to become culturally hegemonic; that is, youth did not become the leading social group of its time. Instead, the free-floating nature of "youth" became detached from a specific age grade and was made available to everyone; hence, the term *old hippie*. (2) This free floating signifies that "youth" was unable to displace the cultural expression of young people altogether. Genuine youth cultures have arisen that exist by marginalizing themselves from what society normally calls "youth." Thus, young people are now free to choose between an array of radically confrontational youth subcultures and the commercialized "youth" image.

SOURCES

Darnton, Nina. "Committed Youth: Why Are So Many Teens Being Locked Up in Private Mental Hospitals?" *Newsweek* 14, 5 (July 31, 1989): 66–72.

Le Vine, Robert, and Mary White. "The Social Transformation of Childhood." In J. B. Lancaster et al., eds. *Parenting Across the Life Span*. New York: Aldine de Grater. 1987.

Martin, L., and S. Kerry. *Anti-Rock: The Opposition to Rock'n'Roll*. Hamden, CT: Archon. 1988.

Rossi, A. "Transition to Parenthood." *Journal of Marriage and the Family* 30 (1968): 26–39.

Seliger, V. A. *Pricing the Priceless Child*. New York: Basic Books. 1985.

Simon, Reynolds. "Woodstock for the Lost Generation." *New York Times* (August 4, 1991): Section H, 22.

Skolnick, Arlene S., and Jerome H. Skolnick, eds. *Family in Transition*. 8th ed. New York: HarperCollins. 1994.

Weinstein, Deena. "Expendable Youth: The Rise and Fall of Youth Culture." In L.

Cargan and J. H. Ballantine, eds. *Sociological Footprints*. 6th ed. Belmont, CA: Wadsworth. 1994.

————. *Heavy Metal: A Cultural Sociology*. New York: Macmillan/Lexington. 1991.

ADULTERATION

Adulteration is the misbranding and misrepresentation of merchandise. An examination of the "Notices of Judgment in the FDA Papers" published by the Food and Drug Administration discloses the details and the wide variety of adulteration and misbranding or mislabeling of merchandise. Misrepresentation may also take the form of dummy bottoms in boxes and bottles or boxes that look larger but hold very little, and other gimmicks that deceive the unwary consumer. There is considerable agreement that the businessperson has not applied his or her stated ethical codes and ideals to business as fully as might be desired or expected.

Most legislation regulating food and drug manufacture has been passed in the twentieth century, although in ancient Greece and Rome there were laws forbidding the adulteration of wine, or the addition of impurities to it. In the nineteenth century Great Britain passed the Sale of Foods and Drugs Act of 1875 to prevent the addition of harmful ingredients, and the Food and Drugs Act of 1955 took into consideration the modern ways of processing food and drugs. The Food Safety Act of 1990 again restructured British food legislation.

In the United States, effective federal legislation was about a generation behind the British law of 1875. From 1906, various legislation has been passed to ensure food and drug safety. In the 1990s federal regulators targeted three important areas of label abuse: deceptive definitions, misleading health claims, and untrue serving sizes. They also proposed standard definitions for such terms as *high fiber* and *low fat*. Canadian legislation followed the legislation set in the United States and Great Britain. The nations of Western Europe also have strict laws regulating food processing. For international food quality control, the Codex Alimentarius Commission, under the auspices of the United Nations, has drawn up a set of standards aimed at protecting health and assuring fair trade practices.

See also Consumerism.

SOURCES

Dichter, Ernest. *The Strategy of Desire*. Garden City, NY: Doubleday. 1960.

World Book Encyclopedia. Chicago: Field Enterprises Educational Corporation. 1993.

ADULTERY

Adultery is having an extramarital sexual relationship. An extramarital relationship exists when someone who is married interacts sexually with an individual other than his or her spouse. Sexual involvement with a new partner raises numerous problems involving moral and emotional issues. Adultery may end the marriage, and in about half of the United States, it is a crime to engage in extramarital sex.

Extramarital sex may take three different forms:

1. Secret Extramarital Sex. Sixty to 80 percent of adults in the United States disapprove of sexual interactions outside of marriage for either men or women. Yet, in various surveys, 50 to 70 percent of American husbands and 45 to 65 percent of American wives report having one or more extramarital sexual relationships. Most of these relationships involve secrecy.

2. Sexually Open Marriages. Some married couples agree to having an

open marriage, in which each partner is free to establish sexually and even emotionally intimate relationships with others, though the spouses continue to live together. A study of over 3,500 heterosexual couples revealed that 15 percent of them found such an arrangement acceptable.

3. Comarital Sexual Activity. "Swingers" are couples who engage in sexual acts with someone other than their own spouse, most often as a couple interacting with other couples. Two to 5 percent of all husband-wife pairs exchange sexual behavior with other couples in this way as a recreational outlet for their sexual desires.

LEGAL GROUNDS FOR DIVORCE

Through the early twentieth century the "big three" grounds for divorce were desertion, adultery, and cruelty, with the latter gradually making inroads within the legal system. By the 1950s, some 60 percent of divorces were granted on the basis of cruelty, often mental cruelty. The history of divorce law until the 1970s was one of plaintiff and defendant, of establishing fault, of collusion and perjury. Love was increasingly the central fact of marriage, but its cessation was not a legal ground for divorce. The first major attempt to correct the inconsistencies in U.S. divorce laws was the 1970 California law abolishing divorce. Replacing divorce with *dissolution*, the legislature eliminated all fault-related grounds for divorce, such as adultery and extreme cruelty, and in their place substituted a no-fault standard, *irreconcilable differences*. Many believe the 1970 law has caused the irremediable breakdown of the marriage.

The change in legal grounds for divorce is consistent with cessation of love and companionship as central reasons for divorce. If the most important reasons for marriage today are love, companionship, emotional support, then the key reason for terminating marriage becomes the failure of marriage to meet these objectives. Thus, the *incompatibility* ground for divorce is the one that has become more commonly cited. Also, this has caused the value orientation of married couples to become increasingly important, both to the marriage and to changes in divorce laws. Attraction to other persons is based on perceived shared values and beliefs. Thus, no-fault divorce has been a central part of the change from a moral-legal problem definition of divorce to a clinical definition. The legal reforms that have accompanied these changing values include changes in alimony, support, and custody as well.

In 1995, realistic concerns about health hazards as well as a cultural shift toward more conservative values have produced a counterrevolution in sexuality that is affecting the family. Americans today increasingly favor monogamy and sexual restrictiveness. Many experts predict that marriage will become even more popular. Some even say that celibacy will increase, but total abstinence from sex seems unlikely to become an overwhelmingly desirable option.

SOURCES

Adams, Bert N. *The Family: A Sociological Interpretation.* 5th ed. New York: Harcourt Brace. 1995.

Ahrons, C. R., and R. H. Rogers. *Divorced Families: A Multidisciplinary View.* New York: Norton. 1987.

Eckland, B. K. "Theories of Mate Selection." *Eugenicu Quarterly* 15 (1968).

Kelly, Kathryn, and Donn Byrne. *Exploring Human Sexuality.* Englewood Cliffs, NJ: Prentice-Hall. 1992.

ADVERTISING, ETHICS IN

See Mass Media, Ethics of.

AESOP'S FABLES

Aesop's Fables are animal stories told to illustrate human faults and virtues. Aesop (about 620–560 B.C.) was a Greek slave and skillful storyteller. Although history has given Aesop credit for these stories, many came to Greece from India and others were Greek folktales long before Aesop was born. The tyrant Demetrius Phalereus of Athens made the first known collection about 300 years after Aesop's death. Some scholars doubt that Aesop ever lived, but he is mentioned by the Greek historian Herodotus. Socrates wrote poems about some of Aesop's fables, and Plutarch praised his wisdom.

SOURCES

Compton's Encyclopedia. Chicago: Compton's Learning Company. 1994.

World Book Encyclopedia. Chicago: Field Enterprises Educational Corporation. 1993.

AESTHETICS

Aesthetics (also spelled esthetics), or the philosophy of art, is the philosophical and scientific understanding of the arts in a broad but fundamental way. Aesthetics concerns all the arts from all countries and from all periods of history. A function of aesthetics is to organize our knowledge of art in a universal way. In their 1964 introductory anthology to aesthetics, Albert Hofstadter and Richard Kuhns locate aesthetics in the realm of metaphysics and the quest for a broad understanding of thought, word, and object. They comment:

> Somehow man participates in the ordering of the universe in his power to make and to respond to art objects. Thus, early philosophies of art and beauty are intermixed with cosmological inquiries and it is only relatively late in the development of philosophy that the philosophy of art can be thought of as distinct from ontology and theology. The greatest philosophies of art, then, are part of broader inquiries into man and nature.

Fundamentally, then, aesthetics is the study of how artists create, imagine, and perform/produce works of art; how others use, enjoy, and criticize such art; and what happens in thought and feeling when people are exposed to art—paintings, music, poetry, and so on—and understand what they see and hear.

Philosophers usually divide aesthetics into the following categories:

1. The Concept of Art is art considered as an end in itself, a significant form created by human beings that is emotionally significant to the artist or to another person as a work of art. Leo Tolstoy, the Russian writer, in his book *What is Art?* defines art as *the communication of feelings.* Other popular definitions include *beauty* and *form.* Skeptics ask if art can be defined at all. Is there any such thing as the essence of art or a set of properties common to all works of art and that are not found in anything else?

2. Beauty and the Aesthetic Experience or Aesthetic Appreciation is the second topic of focus by philosophers of art. *Beauty* is an especially difficult word, because we commonly use it in art as well as in nature. Of course, not all beautiful things are works of art. We can also ask, Who finds something to be beautiful, and under what conditions? Some philosophers have argued that genuine beauty is to be discovered in an object only when a person experiences it in a certain way, or under certain conditions.

Thus, not every response to an object is to be classified as an aesthetic experience, but when and under what conditions does this happen?

3. The Nature and Justification of Aesthetic Criticism and Evaluation is the third and final topic discussed by philosophers of art. They ask, "Can a work of art be a good work and yet not be beautiful?" Breaking this question apart, we wonder what it is that makes something like a work of art beautiful and not good or, on the other hand, good and not beautiful. While answering these questions, philosophers of aesthetics are concerned with the justification of a criteria of truth and falsity in the critical understanding and analysis of a work of art.

As a branch of philosophy, aesthetics was first given its own name in the 1700s. But philosophers from Plato to the present have discussed the philosophy of art. The Renaissance saw a revival of Platonic philosophizing about beauty that connects this period, especially in Italy, with the Plotinism and Augustianism of an earlier time. Ficino's translations of the dialogues of Plato and the Enneads of Plotinus did much to make the scholarly world aware of how much Christian theology had deviated from classical philosophy. They promoted the ideas that the aim of art is beauty; and beauty is itself a value of harmonious proportion, brought down from the cosmos to art. "Beauty," Alberti writes, "is a kind of harmony and concord of all the parts to form a whole which is constructed according to a fixed number, and a certain relation and order, or symmetry, the highest and most perfect law of nature demands."

Since the Renaissance, the Platonic interest in mathematics as the criteria for truth and beauty has given way to observation and more inductive methods. The history of the arts now accompanies theoretical approaches to develop a more universal aesthetics. Art is studied in relation to its physical, social, and cultural environments and is now broken into several important specialties: *aesthetic morphology*, which studies the forms and styles of art; *aesthetic value-theory*, which concentrates on the judging of art; and *aesthetic semantics*, which studies words and meanings in talking about art.

SOURCES

Hofstadter, Albert, and Richard Kuhns, eds. *Philosophies of Art and Beauty: Selected Readings in Aesthetics from Plato to Heidegger*. Chicago: University of Chicago Press. 1964.

Sprague, Elmer, and Paul Taylor, eds. *Knowledge and Value*. New York: Harcourt, Brace and World. 1967.

AFFILIATION, NEED FOR

The motivation to seek friendships and other close relationships is called affiliation. For most of us, having friends is a central part of our lives. We want to interact with others, share our feelings with them, and know that they like us. Though most people want to have friends, the need for affiliation varies in strength from person to person. The table below presents test items that differentiate people with high versus low affiliative needs.

How Strong Is Your Need to Affiliate?

These statements are part of a personality scale used to measure need for affiliation. Agreement with the first and third statements, and disagreement with the other three indicates a tendency to prefer affiliation to being alone.

*TEST ITEMS USED TO MEASURE
NEED FOR AFFILIATION*

1. I think that any experience is more significant when shared with a friend.
2. At parties, I prefer to talk to one person for the entire evening instead of participating in different conversations.

3. I like to make as many friends as I can.
4. I prefer the independence which comes from lack of attachments to the good and warm feelings associated with close ties.
5. If I had to choose between the two, I would rather be considered intelligent than sociable.

(*Source:* Mehrabian, 1970)

SOURCES

Mehrabian, A. "The Development and Validation of Measures of Affiliation Tendency and Sensitivity to Rejection." *Education and Psychological Measurement* 30 (1970): 417–428.

Research and Forecasts, Inc. "The Connecticut Mutual Life Report on American Values in the '80s: The Impact of Belief." Hartford, CT: Connecticut Mutual Life Insurance Company. 1981.

Wright, P. H. "Self-Referent Motivation and the Intrinsic Quality of Friendship." *Journal of Social and Personal Relationships* 1 (1994): 115–130.

AFFIRMATIVE ACTION

Affirmative action refers to positive efforts to recruit minority group members or women for jobs, promotions, and educational opportunities usually dominated by white males. The term *affirmative action* first appeared in an executive order issued by President John F. Kennedy in 1963. The order called for contractors to "take affirmative action to ensure that applicants are employed and that employees are treated during employment, without regard to their race, creed, color, or national origin." Four years later, in 1967, the order was amended to prohibit discrimination on the basis of sex.

Affirmative action became the most important tool for reducing institutional discrimination from the early 1960s to today. The Commission on Civil Rights has given some examples of institutional discrimination where affirmative action has been aimed:

- Height and weight requirements that are unnecessary for performing the job;
- Seniority rules such as "last hired, first fired";
- Nepotism that excludes those who are not relatives;
- Restrictive employment leave policies that prohibit part-time workers from taking part or denies them other fringe benefits;
- Rules requiring that only English be spoken at the workplace;
- Standardized academic tests or criteria geared to the cultural and educational norms of the middle class that are not relevant indicators of successful job performance;
- Preferences shown by law and medical schools in the admission of children of wealthy and influential alumni;
- Credit policies of banks and lending institutions that exclude minorities.

LEGAL DEBATES

In the Bakke case (*Regents of the University of California v. Bakke*) of 1978, the Supreme Court by a narrow margin ordered the medical school of the University of California at Davis to admit Allen Bakke, a white engineer who originally had been denied admission. The justices ruled that the school had violated Bakke's constitutional rights by establishing a fixed quota system for minority students. The Court added, however, that it was constitutional for universities to adopt flexible admissions programs that use race as one factor in making decisions.

In 1979 (*United Steelworkers of America v. Weber*), the Supreme Court ruled by a vote of 5 to 2 that the labor union did not have to admit white laboratory technician Brian Weber to a training program in Louisiana. They held that it was constitutional for the union to run a program for training skilled technicians that, in promoting affirmative action, admitted one black for every white person.

In 1984, the Supreme Court ruled in the case of *Firefighters Local Union No. 1784 v. Statts* that lower courts may not require an employer to protect the jobs of recently hired black workers at the expense of white employees with more seniority. By a vote of 6 to 1, the justices upheld the controversial principle of "last hired, first fired." The Court based its decision on Title IV of the 1964 Civil Rights Act, which explicitly protects seniority systems that were not set up for the purpose of discriminating.

In 1986 and 1987, there were four Supreme Court rulings that further defined the parameters of affirmative action. In *Local Number 93, International Association of Firefighters, v. City of Cleveland,* the Court upheld a lower court's decree in which the city of Cleveland agreed to settle a job discrimination suit by black and Hispanic firefighters by temporarily promoting them ahead of whites who had more seniority and higher test scores. Also, the Court required the local sheet metals union in New York City to meet a 29 percent minority membership by August 1987. In the same case, the Court held that judges may order racial preferences in union membership and other contexts if necessary to combat flagrant discrimination. Again in 1987, the Supreme Court in *United States v. Paradise* upheld a lower court decision requiring Alabama to promote one black trooper for each white state trooper promoted. Finally, in 1987, the Court ruled in *Johnson v. Transportation* that employers may favor women and members of minorities over better-qualified white men to achieve better balance in their work forces.

In 1995, affirmative action was back in the news. To its opponents, affirmative action programs meant to combat bias have become discriminatory themselves, setting up a rigid system of racial and gender preferences that have prompted unfair treatment of white males and even some minorities.

According to a 1995 national poll by the *Los Angeles Times,* there has been a sizeable increase in those who believe affirmative action in general has outlived its usefulness. In 1991, 2 percent of Americans said affirmative action had gone too far. By January 1995, support for that view had increased to 39 percent. Among men, the belief that affirmative action had gone too far jumped from 27 percent in 1991 to 43 percent in 1995. The poll also showed the following:

- Forty-six percent of whites said that affirmative action had gone too far.
- Eight percent of blacks felt that affirmative action had gone too far.
- Blacks, Hispanics, feminists, liberals, and public-employee unions support affirmative action.
- Affirmative action is unpopular among blue-collar whites known as "Reagan Democrats": 57 percent of white male voters went Republican in November 1994.

See also Feminism; Politics in the Classroom; Racism.

SOURCES

Becker, Gary S. *The Economics of Discrimination.* 2d ed. Chicago: University of Chicago Press. 1971.

Farrell, Warren. *The Myth of Male Power.* New York: Simon & Schuster. 1993.

Glazer, Nathan. *Affirmative Discrimination: Ethics Inequality and Public Policy.* New York: Basic Books. 1975.

Schaefer, Richard T. *Racial and Ethnic Groups.* 3d ed. Boston: Scott, Foresman and Co. 1988.

AFRICAN AMERICANS AND AFRICA

The importance of Africa to black Americans can be seen in the many ways that parts of African culture have become important aspects of their life in the United States. John and David Noss have noted that the religious rites and ceremonies of a people are a rich source of myths that establish their identity and thus add a needed sense of security in the present and continuity with the past. There is still a great deal of controversy over whether and how much African culture survived slavery. Black historians W. E. B. Du Bois and Carter Woodson, along with the respected white anthropologist Melville Herskovits, have all argued persuasively for the continued influence of the African heritage. They agree on the following:

- Africa not only produced cultures worthy of study, it produced cultures as glorious as those found in Europe.
- In Brazil and the Caribbean Islands, which also had slavery, it is much easier to recognize the continuity of African culture in the life of blacks today. Southern slave owners put more pressure on slaves to assimilate. Furthermore, there was a significantly higher proportion of U.S. slaves born in America and not in Africa. Thus, slaves in the United States had more limited awareness of African culture.
- The survival of African culture among black Americans can be most easily demonstrated in such cultural manifestations as folklore, religion, music, and some aspects of social organization. Many new cultures emerged from slaves drawing upon the older culture of Africa and adapting it to the American continent.
- Most of the distinctive aspects of black life today originate in the poverty and segregation created by slavery, not in Africa's rich cultural traditions.

The value of Africa for blacks in the Americas will always remain important. The significance of Africa to black Americans is one of the most easily identifiable themes in the black experience. The reality of African culture in America rests not in its scientific integrity in the traditional sense (as in the Sea Islands study along the coast of South Carolina and Georgia, which shows movement and dance among blacks similar to that of African folklife; but one should remember that the inhabitants of the Sea Islands have been isolated from the mainland, and therefore less acculturated to the rest of society), but in the extent to which it becomes real and significant to black Americans today and in the future.

SOURCES

Blauner, Robert. *Racial Oppression in America.* New York: Harper & Row. 1972.

Du Bois, W. E. B. *The Philadelphia Negro: A Social Study.* New York: Schucken Books. 1967.

Herskovits, Melville J. *The Myth of the Negro Past.* New York: Harper Brothers. 1941.

Noss, David S., and John B. Noss. *Man's Religions.* 7th ed. New York: Macmillan. 1984.

Patterson, Orlando. *Slavery and Social Death: A Comparative Study.* Cambridge: Harvard University Press. 1982.

Rawick, George P. *From Sundown to Sunup: The Making of the Black Community.* Westport, CT: Greenwood Press. 1972.

Toner, Robin. "Bible Is Being Translated into a Southern Coastal Tongue Born of Slavery." *New York Times* (March 1, 1987): 18.

Twining, Mary Arnold. "Movement and Dance on the Sea Islands." *Journal of Black Studies* 15 (June 1985): 463–479.

Woodson, Carter G. *The African Background Outlined.* New York: Negro Universities Press. 1968.

AGAPE

Interpreters of New Testament Christianity render the meaning of *agape* as "love, affection, and benevolence." Alternative interpretations include "to love in the social and moral sense," and its primary usage is to refer to God's love for humans and humanity's love for God. Originally, agape seems to have meant "satisfaction," "sympathy," or "a hospitable spirit." The adjective from which agape is derived is *agapatos*, which means "beloved." This is different from *filia*, which is used in the New Testament to mean "friendship."

In the teachings of Jesus, we find two commandments: "Love the Lord your God" and "Love your neighbor as yourself." We find in the explanations of these two commandments that the focal point is love that is patient, merciful, and generous. Whether in reference to God or to human beings, agape shares these qualities. Divine love in the Christian sense is, therefore, an active benevolence that will go to any length to do good for the beloved object and to secure its well-being. Jesus did not analyze love as theologians and philosophers might analyze it today. The mind of Jesus appears concrete rather than speculative. Nevertheless, it is consistent with his teachings to say that divine love is sovereign, spontaneous, and redemptive. In Mark 2:5, Jesus speaks the word of forgiveness and demands the utmost sacrifice for love's sake.

According to A. Nygren in *Agape and Eros*, "It is the Christian conception of fellowship with God that gives the idea of Agape its meaning." Hence, Jesus said that the second chief commandment was "like the first," for neighborly love is the will of God for his children. To love (agape) your neighbor or your enemies does not mean that you are pleased with their behavior or in agreement with their values and beliefs. Their present condition may be completely unappealing, even odious to you. But in the Christian sense of agape, you have a new relationship with God, which translates as a new moral relationship with your neighbor.

There was always an ethical meaning in the teachings of Jesus, corresponding to the gracious dealings of God the Heavenly Father with men and women. Agape is the new word for this relationship. Jesus demanded a righteousness that exceeded that of the scribes and Pharisees. The Samaritan—one should note that in the first century, Jews hated Samaritans—is to care for the "outsider" when the "outsider" is in trouble. The choice to care for one whom you despise is not merely a matter of emotion; on the contrary, it is much more a matter of mind and will (Matt. 7:21ff). Love gives, expecting no return (Luke 6:35). Love stoops to serve, like the master who waits on his laborers (Luke 12:37ff).

Agape has long been considered the "highest" form of morality, especially in Western societies, but not only in the West. Of the world's population, three-quarters have visualized love as a basic moral precept. The concept of love, generally thought of as The Golden Rule (and the usage appears similar to the Christian sense of agape), appears in a variety of versions in eight of the world's great religions. We should note that they all concur in demanding an identification between self and others, which is generally considered to be the foundation and the starting point of moral behavior:

- Christianity: *All things whatsoever ye would that men should do to you, do ye even unto them for this is the law of the prophets.*
- Brahmanism: *This is the sum of duty: do naught unto others which would cause pain if done unto you.*
- Buddhism: *Hurt not others in ways that you yourself would find hurtful.*
- Judaism: *What is hateful to you, do not to your fellow man. This is the entire law, all the rest is commentary.*
- Confucianism: *This is one maxim of loving kindness: do not unto others what you would not have them do unto you.*
- Taoism: *Regard your neighbor's gain as your own gain, and your neighbor's loss as your own loss.*
- Zoroastrianism: *That nature alone is good which refrains from doing unto another whatsoever is not good for itself.*
- Islam: *No one of you is a believer until he desires for his brother that which he desires for himself.*

From these various formulations of the conceptualization of "love," one is able to to learn—from the religious point of view—that ethics and value have a human base, certified by religious belief and founded on the idea of utilizing one's own needs and desires as a starting point for understanding and respecting the needs and desires of other persons. Philosophically and practically, other modern moral values can be derived from this primary and universal one.

SOURCES

Berry, George R., and James Strong. *Interlinear Greek-English New Testament with a Greek-English Lexicon and New Testament Synonyms and a Greek Dictionary of the New Testament*. Grand Rapids, MI: Baker Book House. 1981.

Kahn, Theodore C. *An Introduction to Hominology: The Study of the Whole Man*. Springfield, IL: Charles C. Thomas. 1972.

Nygren, A. *Agape and Eros*. Revised English Translation by P. S. Watson. Philadelphia: Westminster. 1953.

AGENT ORANGE

On May 28, 1980, Max Cleland, chief of the Veterans Administration (VA), announced that new studies by the U.S. Air Force and the Department of Health, Education, and Welfare would supplement a VA inquiry on the long-term effects of exposure to Agent Orange, a herbicide containing the poison dioxin. U.S. aircraft sprayed nearly 2 million acres of Vietnam jungle with Agent Orange between 1962 and 1970, trying to destroy Vietcong food and cover. The VA action came in response to complaints from hundreds of veterans who had filed claims alleging physical damage from exposure to the herbicide. In 1990, the Centers for Disease Control, a U.S. governmental agency, released a study that found no evidence that Agent Orange increased the risk of cancer among Vietnam veterans. That same year, a congressional committee declared the study flawed. In 1991, Congress passed a bill providing disability benefits for Vietnam veterans suffering from certain illnesses said to have been caused by exposure to Agent Orange.

SOURCES

World Book Encyclopedia. Chicago: Field Enterprises Educational Corporation. 1993.

World Book Encyclopedia Yearbook 1980. Chicago: Field Enterprises Educational Corporation. 1980.

AGGRESSION

Aggression is any action that is intended to hurt others. Intentions, according to social psychologists, have a central role in our judgments. People are particularly motivated to make causal attributions when others' actions are painful to them. People should therefore be especially likely to search for causes of actions when they are the victims of aggressive acts. One of the first attributions people make about aggression is of the person's intent—to hurt or harm, to cause pain, to do whatever has been done to them.

A second major distinction is also needed between antisocial and prosocial aggression. Normally we think of aggression as bad. If an aggressive act results from an intent to hurt another person, it must be considered as bad. But some aggressive acts are good: consider the aggressive way a University of North Carolina student stopped a gunman from killing more people on the streets of Chapel Hill in 1995 without killing the gunman. The question is whether the aggressive act violates commonly accepted social norms, or supports them.

Some aggressive acts, which might be called *sanctioned aggression*, fall somewhere between prosocial and antisocial. This includes aggressive acts that are not required by social norms, but that are well within their bounds. They do not violate accepted moral standards. Those who act in self-defense—even to the point of harming another person—and parents who discipline a disobedient child by sending the child to his/her room are usually thought to be well within their rights.

A third distinction is between aggressive behavior and aggressive feelings, such as *anger*. Our overt behavior does not always reflect our internal feelings. Someone may be quite angry inside, but make no overt effort to hurt another person. Society discourages and condemns most forms of aggressive behavior, and indeed can exist only if people control their aggressive feelings most of the time. Society places strong restraints on aggression that causes pain and that is antisocial.

Since anger plays such an important role in aggressive behavior, a consideration of the major sources of anger will illuminate our understanding of aggression even further. A first major source of anger is being attacked or bothered by someone else. When a person has been annoyed or attacked, it is extremely likely that the person will become angry and feel aggressive toward the source of the attack.

A second major source of anger is *frustration:* the interference with or blocking of the attainment of a goal. One of the basic tenets in social psychology is that frustration tends to arouse aggressive feelings.

Finally, for an event to produce anger and aggressive behavior, the key is that the victims must perceive the attack or frustration as intended to harm. This is easily understood in terms of attribution theory. If the victim attributes the frustration to unavoidable circumstances, then it will not create much anger. But if there are no such justifying external forces that come into play and an internal attribution is made, the anger is much greater.

SOURCES

Sears, David O., Letitia Anne Peplau, Jonathan L. Freedman, and Shelley E. Taylor. *Social Psychology.* Englewood Cliffs, NJ: Prentice-Hall. 1988. (See especially chapters 5–11)

AGING, SOCIALIZATION OF

Socialization is the process by which people acquire the beliefs, attitudes, values, and customs of their culture. The essential elements of socialization are human interaction, the mastery of language, and some measure of affectionate acceptance. The aged, when isolated by time and circumstance, have a need to renew this process in order to maintain and further develop the human side of their nature.

How difficult are the adjustments to old age? According to Bert N. Adams (*The Family: A Sociological Interpretation*), "They are most certainly made more difficult than they would otherwise be by the fact that roles and norms, or expectations concerning what the aged should do and be, are so poorly spelled out." Substantial reorientation on the part of individuals and married couples is required with the departure of children and retirement from one's occupation. The domestic-parental mother, who has poured body and soul into her children, can very easily shrivel up mentally and physically when her children achieve independence and she still finds herself attached to her absent children's apron strings. McGoldrick (*Women in Families*, 1989) recognizes this problem and observes:

> For some women, the period just after launching their children may be a time of special stress, since they often feel very much behind in the skills to deal with the outside world. Just when the children no longer need them and they are beginning to be defined by the male world as too old to be desirable, they must venture outward (217).

The problem is characteristic of what is commonly called "the empty-nest syndrome." Similarly, many men have died only a few months after retirement. The psychological and physical adjustments of retiring may be too much for the man whose entire life and well-being have been attached to working and earning a living. The family-oriented woman and the job-oriented man who have no alternative values and interests to fall back on are likely to be poorly prepared for positive disengagement from their major life roles.

Economics and health are two additional factors that have much to say about how the elderly adjust to that stage in life. Health is a major variable affecting not only life satisfaction, but kin interaction, residence, and financial situation. Research has discovered that a severe illness or disability of either spouse can create extreme and unexpected shifts toward unequal dependence. The disabled spouse normally loses in terms of his or her ability to provide rewards for the partner and gains in terms of needs that it is often the partner's lot to satisfy.

RETIREMENT STATISTICS
- Three-fifths of men and one-third of women between the ages of 60 to 64 were employed in 1980. This number is reduced by half between the ages of 65 and 69.
- Six percent of those over age 85 are still working.
- Income in retirement, on the average, declines by between one-third and one-half (in 1984 the average household under the age of 65 had a median income of $23,104, while those over 65 averaged $15,745).
- Social Security enables the elderly to live independently, but in poverty.
- Medicaid, Medicare, and Social Security are all partial determinants of the life change of the elderly.
- There are some differences of perception between black and white retirees: many blacks who are retired and do not have jobs do not consider themselves retired because they do part-time work.

In the problematic atmosphere of retirement and economics, negotiation and decision making are central to the life of the elderly. Decisions include the following four groups:

1. Residential decisions. Are the retirees to stay at home or change residence completely? If they change residence, are they to move into an apartment, a mobile home, a smaller house, a retirement or age-segregated community, or closer to or in with their children?
2. Activities. The elderly may continue to pursue the same activities as before or take up new ones. They may join age-related groups or continue their current group activities, or simply drop many old activities and organizations.
3. Social networks. How should the elderly relate—in terms of proximity and contact—to age companions, children, and other friends and kin? Should they simply disengage from social contacts, or continue normal relationships?
4. Marital relations. Couples who have gone their separate ways for many years must now decide on which activities to engage in as a couple and which as individuals. How should responsibilities be divided, now that the husband or the wife no longer goes off to work each morning?

There are still quite a lot of myths about kin relationships and the elderly. One of these is that older people are alienated from their children. Another is that older people, particularly those living alone, are isolated. Finally, research has shown that families are willing and able to care for their frail elderly members, and not the opposite. In fact, research shows that most elderly keep in touch with whatever kin they have; although they prefer to live alone, they see their children frequently. They do not tend to live in the same household unless either parents or children are in such poor health that they cannot take care of themselves or unless financial circumstances make it necessary. In addition to these, Cary Kart *(The Realities of Aging)* lists the following negative stereotypes about aging:

- *All elderly people are alike*. This stereotype puts the old into a distinct group, but in truth, there is no such thing as "the" young or "the" old. People do differ, but chronological age is a poor basis for grouping people who have attained biological maturity.
- *Most of the aged are disabled*. In 1985, 89 percent of all men and women over 65 lived in a community and were self-sufficient.
- *The aged are not capable of or interested in sexual activity*. Although this statement is essentially correct, it is correct for social, not physiological, reasons. Many of the elderly are widows without sexual partners. Approximately 60 percent of married couples remain sexually active to age 75.
- *As people age, their intelligence declines*. The fact is that mental faculties stay clear and sharp until very late in life. A minority of older people suffer from memory lapses, forgetfulness, and confusion, conditions that result from diseases such as hardening of the arteries.
- *The elderly are isolated, neglected, and sickly*. Studies show that the elderly do not become isolated and neglected and are not dumped into mental hospitals by cruel or indifferent children.

Although old age is a period of uncertainty and change with few positive compensations, there are some quite justifiable reasons to assume that a shift from mid-life to old age can be as significant a change as that from adolescence to adulthood, and the range of variations in the successful fruition of life in old age may really be much wider than it is for youth. The revolution in longevity that has been achieved in this century—life expectancy at birth has risen from less than 50 in 1900 to well over 70 in 1995—has produced configurations in kinship structure and in the internal dynamics of family life at every age that have never existed before and which we are just now discovering. In fact, we are approaching a "squared" mortality curve in which relatively few die before the end of the full lifespan. For the first time in history, we are living in a society in which most people live to be old.

The most striking feature about the aged in American society is their past and projected future growth in numbers and proportion. The Bureau of the Census has shown that the older population (using the arbitrary age of 65) has grown steadily as a share of the total U.S. population—from 3.1 million in 1900 to 28.5 million in 1985. The proportions have also shifted: those over 65 constituted 4.1 percent of the population in 1900 and 11.9 percent in 1985. The average life expectancy in 1900 was 49 years and in 1985 it was 74.7. Projections show that the proportion over 65 will grow steadily, to an estimated 16 percent in 2020 and 21.7 percent by 2050.

THE GREY PANTHERS

The Grey Panthers is a national organization founded in the early 1970s by Maggie Kuhn. With over 70,000 elderly activists, the Grey Panthers seek to bring together a political coalition of all age groups to fight against ageism in society (*ageism* is discrimination against persons on the basis of chronological age, depriving people of power and influence). They believe that the old and the young in our society have much to contribute to make our society more just and human, and that we need to reinforce each other in our goals, our strategy, and our actions. They point out that like racism, ageism is a destructive force that permeates all social institutions. The organization has set the following practices:

- They advocate participatory democracy and concern for all residents in institutional settings, educational institutions, and social service programs.
- They advocate adequate governmental and private support for mass transportation systems with minimal or no cost to consumers.
- They advocate the enactment of a national health care program through a public corporation rather than commercial insurance companies; an improved delivery system; and preventive care.
- They advocate the abolition of arbitrary and compulsory retirement and age discrimination in employment; adequate job training; and new career opportunities.
- They advocate a systematic approach toward the abolition of poverty.
- They advocate a renewed effort by the government and industry to encourage and support a national program of housing with a thorough cultural mix of all age groups, income levels, and racial backgrounds.
- They advocate the redirection of monies now earmarked for military programs into efforts to solve problems that concern people in their daily lives.
- Finally, they advocate a reform of our educational system to include programs and opportunities for people of all age groups at minimal or no cost to participants.

SOURCES

Adams, Bert N. *The Family: A Sociological Interpretation.* 5th ed. New York: Harcourt Brace. 1995.
"Battered Parents." *Society* 15, 5 (July/August 1978): 54–55.
Bureau of the Census. "Historical Statistics of the United States: Colonial Times to 1970." *Population Bulletin* 35 (January 1981): 4.
———. *Current Population Reports*, Series P-25, no. 704. "Projections of the Population of the United States: 1977–2050." *Statistical Abstract of the United States 1987*. Washington, D.C.: Government Printing Office. 1987: 34.
de Beauvoir, Simone. *The Coming of Age.* New York: Warner Paperback Library. 1973.
Eitzen, D. Stanley, and Maxine Baca Zinn. *Social Problems.* 4th ed. Boston: Allyn and Bacon. 1989.
Kart, Cary S. *The Realities of Aging.* Boston: Allyn and Bacon. 1981.
McGoldrick, Monica, et al. *Women in Families: A Framework for Family Therapy.* New York: Norton. 1989.
Parenti, Michael. *Democracy for the Few.* 5th ed. New York: St. Martin's Press.1983.
Skolnick, Arlene S., and Jerome H. Skolnick, eds. *Family in Transition.* 8th ed. New York: HarperCollins. 1994.

AIDS

AIDS, or acquired immune deficiency syndrome, is usually transmitted by blood or semen contaminated with HIV, or human immunodeficiency virus (also called HTVL-III or the Human T-cell Lymphotrophic Virus Type III). AIDS results when antibodies produced by the immune system fail to control the virus. The victim usually succumbs to cancer or any of several possible opportunistic infections that take advantage of the suppressed immunity. HIV attacks the helper T cells that signal the immune system to produce antibodies against infection. Moving from cell to cell, HIV destroys the body's capacity to produce antibodies and leaves it open to infection and death.

AIDS first appeared in the United States during 1981, in New York City. Similar cases appeared there as early as 1978, but they were not identified as AIDS at that time. By January 1983, 24 new cases of AIDS were being reported each week in the United States. So far, half of the victims have died, with death usually occurring within two years of diagnosis. By 1984, awareness of AIDS was sufficiently great that the rate of infections began to drop. As of February 1989, almost 90,000 AIDS cases and over 50,000 deaths had been reported to the U.S. Centers for Disease Control. By 1990, more young men had died of AIDS than were killed in the entire Vietnam War.

In 1990, the World Health Organization projected that because of increases in heterosexual transmission of the disease, 20 million people will have been infected by 2000, and estimates are that at least 3 million women and children will die of this disease during the decade of the 1990s.

One especially frightening characteristic of AIDS is that as many as eight years may pass between infection by HIV and the appearance of symptoms in the infected person. About one of every 200 persons in the United States is estimated to have antibodies to the virus causing AIDS.

FACTS
- Among college students, about one per 500 is infected.
- 61 to 73 percent of reported cases are in men engaging in homosexual or bisexual activities.
- 17 to 20 percent of those infected are intravenous drug users.
- 62 percent of homeless men are infected with AIDS.
- AIDS is now the leading cause of death among women aged 25 to 34 in New York City.

The threat of AIDS raises ethical question about taking responsibility and protecting yourself. A report in *Family Planning Perspectives* finds that about "one-third of sexually experienced, unmarried American women have changed their sexual behavior in response to the threat of AIDS; the most common change is limiting their number of sexual partners to one man."

Hobart's study in Canada reports that those "who know the most AIDS victims and so are most aware of the spread of the disease and note the seriousness of the AIDS threat most highly are the respondents who rate sex with briefly known partners as least risky and are least inclined to use condoms in sexual encounters with briefly known partners."

The following three points summarize the results, to this point, of the AIDS epidemic:

1. That much is known about AIDS, at least at a general level;
2. That a minority of women have restricted their behavior as a result of this knowledge; and
3. That many of the most sexually active are both knowledgeable and taking risks.

SOURCES

Bridge, T. P., A. F. Mirsky, and F. K. Goodwin, eds. *Psychological, Neuropsychiatric, and Substance Abuse Aspects of AIDS.* New York: Raven Press. 1988.

"Concern over AIDS Changed Sexual Behavior among One Third of Unmarried United States Women." *Family Planning Perspectives* 23 (1991): 234–235.

Hobart, C. "How They Handle It: Young Canadians, Sex, and AIDS." *Youth and Society* 25 (1992): 411–433.

Mandel, B., and B. Mandel. *Play Safe: How to Avoid Getting Sexually Transmitted Diseases.* Goster City, CA: Center For Health Information. 1985.

Roscoe, B., and T. L. Krugere. "Aids: Altering Adolescents' Knowledge and Its Influence on Sexual Behavior." *Adolescence* 25 (1990): 39–48.

AL-ANON

Al-Anon is a worldwide fellowship of the families and friends of alcoholics. Members learn that alcoholism is a disease and how it affects family life.

Through regular meetings that include professional speakers (counselors, physicians, ministers, and so on) and that provide professional reading/study materials, members of Al-Anon learn coping and conflict resolution skills, including strategies to help friends and family members recover from alcoholism.

Al-Anon cooperates with Alcoholics Anonymous. It was begun in 1954 and today has 500,000 members in 30,000 local support groups. The headquarters is: Al-Anon Family Group Headquarters, Inc., P.O. Box 862 Midtown Station, New York, NY 10018.

SOURCES

Compton's Encyclopedia. Chicago: Compton's Learning Company. 1994.

World Book Encyclopedia. Chicago: Field Enterprises Educational Corporation. 1993.

ALCOHOLICS ANONYMOUS (AA)

Alcoholics Anonymous is a fellowship of men and women who share their experiences to help each other solve their common problem of alcohol addiction. These people also work to help others recover from alcoholism. AA was founded in 1935. Today it has about 85,000 local groups in the United States and Canada, and groups in 130 countries. The fellowship is based on spiritual experiences and the dependence of each member on God, as the member understands a higher power. It is not directly connected with any religious body. The General Service office is: Box 459, Grand Central Station, New York, NY 10017.

See also Alcoholism.

SOURCES

World Book Encyclopedia. Chicago: Field Enterprises Educational Corporation. 1993.

ALCOHOLISM

Alcoholism is a disease in which the drinking of alcoholic beverages becomes a compulsion. Persons bothered with this urge to drink are called alcoholics. A form of alcoholism is called dipsomania, which comes from the Greek word meaning "thirst madness." Dipsomaniacs are bothered at times, rather than constantly, with a compulsion to drink. Over 6.5 million Americans are afflicted with alcoholism. Five of six alcoholics are men between 30 and 55 years old. Sociologists describe an alcoholic as a person who (1) orients his or her life to ingesting alcohol at whatever cost to himself or herself or others; (2) suffers withdrawal symptoms; and (3) has experienced a variety of social punishments (loss of job, of family, of friends, etc.) as a result of drinking.

SOURCES

Compton's Encyclopedia. Chicago: Compton's Learning Company. 1994.

McCord, William, and Arline McCord. *American Social Problems.* Saint Louis: C. V. Mosby. 1977.

World Book Encyclopedia. Chicago: Field Enterprises Educational Corporation. 1993.

ALIENATION

Alienation is the feeling of being isolated from certain aspects of one's environment. Alienation may occur when a person's emotional ties with another person, group, institution, or belief are disrupted, and he or she feels the attachment can never again be the same. Sometimes, entire groups become alienated. Causes of alienation include losing a group leader who represents one's dreams and hopes, as when a child discovers the shortcomings of an adult she or he has admired. Or it may result if a person believes that certain political, economic, or social institutions are impersonal and unresponsive to change. An alienated person may become disoriented or hostile, feel helpless, withdraw into himself or herself, or reject the values society has established. Social scientists have established a relationship between alienation and such behaviors as crime, mental illness, and voter apathy. But innovations (artistic creations, inventions, discoveries, etc.) have also resulted from a person feeling alienated.

SOURCES

Handlin, Oscar, and Lilian Handlin. *Liberty and Equality 1920–1994.* New York: Harper Collins. 1994.

Kafka, Franz. *The Complete Stories.* New York: Schocken. 1988.

Schaefer, Richard T. *Racial and Ethnic Groups.* 3d ed. Boston: Scott, Foresman and Co. 1988.

ALTERNATIVE MEDICINE

In the last quarter of the twentieth century, people the world over have turned to a phenomenon called alternative medicine. Alternative medicine is a vast field that encompasses many different treatments not normally prescribed by regular physicians, and a field where there are still too few careful scientific studies and where investigators haven't yet agreed on what rules of evidence should apply (*Consumer Reports,* January 1994). One of the emergent leaders in the alternative medicine arena is Deepak Chopra, M.D., whose books *Ageless Body, Timeless Mind, Quantum Healing,* and *Perfect Health* combine mind/body medicine-therapy to control the way we age, to harness the powers of awareness, and to give practical steps to experience timelessness.

In 1993, the National Institutes of Health (NIH) announced that it would fund research in the following areas:

- The use of acupuncture to treat depression.
- Biofeedback as a treatment for pain control and diabetes.
- *Ayurvedic* medicine—the traditional medicine of India—to treat Parkinson's disease.
- The benefits of hypnosis in healing broken bones.
- Massage therapy for patients with the AIDS virus, postsurgical patients, and people with bone marrow transplants.
- Yoga for heroin addiction and obsessive-compulsive disorder.
- The effects of prayer on health.

A survey published in the *New England Journal of Medicine* in 1993 showed that millions of Americans were using alternative medicine, whether their regular physicians were aware of it or not. The study of alternative medicine can be frustrating to the serious student. It is a field whose practitioners range from respected academic physicians to entrepreneurial faith healers. But despite the difficulties, the first steps have been taken by researchers toward defining what "alternative" medicine encompasses. David Eisenberg at Harvard Medical School defined "unconventional therapies" as "commonly used interventions neither taught widely in United States medical schools nor generally available in United States hospitals."

It is also interesting to note that Americans spent almost $14 billion on those therapies in 1990. These so-called unconventional therapies included such treatments as relaxation techniques, commercial weight-loss programs, and self-help groups. Others included chiropractic therapy, spiritual healing, and herbal medicine. Reluctantly, traditional U.S. medicine is beginning to take a serious look at many forms of unconventional medicine that it has ignored and criticized for decades. The NIH Office of Alternative Medicine began operations in 1992 under the direction of Joe Jacobs, a pediatric physician, and provides the opportunity for practitioners of alternative medicine to try to demonstrate that their practices are scientifically valid.

> Experience does not ever err, it is only your judgment that errs in promising itself results which are not caused by your experiments. Leonardo da Vinci (ca. 1510).

Another major player in this field is Dr. Wayne W. Dyer, a prolific author and psychologist. In 1992, Dyer offered up his version of alternative medicine in *Real Magic: Creating Miracles in Everyday Life*. His intent is to teach us how to achieve a new and higher level of consciousness. His is basically a mind-body technique that emphasizes spirituality, building relationships, self-improvement, and believing in miracles.

In the same vein, in *Love, Medicine & Miracles*, Bernie S. Siegel, M.D., says that "unconditional love is the most powerful stimulant of the immune system. The truth is: love heals. Miracles happen to exceptional patients everyday—patients who have the courage to love, those who have the courage to work with their doctors to participate in and influence their own recovery." Siegel practices surgery in New Haven, Connecticut, and teaches at Yale University. In 1978 he started ECaP (Exceptional Cancer Patients), a specialized form of individual and group therapy based on "carefrontation," a loving, safe, therapeutic confrontation that facilitates personal change and healing. This experience led to Siegel's desire to make everyone aware of his or her own healing potential.

> Whoever is to acquire a competent knowledge of medicine ought to be possessed of the following advantages: a natural disposition; instruction; a favorable position for the study; early tuition; love of labor; leisure. First of all, a natural talent is required; for, when Nature opposes, everything else is vain. Hippocrates, *The Law*.

THE ALTERNATIVE SPECTRUM

There are many differences among alternative treatments. These include the following:

- *Mind/Body Approaches.* Mind/body treatments include hypnosis, biofeedback, and relaxation training. These are based on well-established principles that stress and emotions can play a role in physical health.
- *Alternative Drugs.* This category lies outside accepted medical practice and includes a whole group of alleged cancer treatments, such as shark cartilage and herbal remedies such as those used in India's *Ayurvedic* medicine.
- *Acupuncture.* This 2,500-year-old form of Chinese medicine is probably the most widely used alternative medicine, yet the Chinese explanation for its mode of action has no connection whatsoever to Western science as we understand it today.
- *Homeopathy.* This form of treatment was developed by German physicians and uses herbal medicine. Homeopathy holds that remedies become more powerful when they are diluted to the point where virtually none of the original compound remains in solution—a position difficult for Western scientists to accept.
- *Chiropractic.* Chiropractic treatments come closer to Western medicine than any of the others. In manipulating the muscles and spine, chiropractors are able to treat muscular pain, but they claim to treat a wide range of disorders beyond muscular pain.
- *Jungian Therapy.* Practitioners help patients interpret dreams and impulses based on the theories of Carl Jung to discover their deeper feelings. In Jungian therapy, the patient does the talking. The centerpiece of treatment is interpretation of dreams. The therapy takes about two years.

- *Gestalt Therapy.* Developed by psychologist Fritz Perls at California's renowned Esalen Institute, this therapy approach heaves "thinking" out the window in favor of retuning the senses. In Gestalt, there's a lot of touching, hugging, tasting, and so on, not to mention the punching of pillows to "work off" anger. In Gestalt therapy, everybody talks, and the centerpiece of treatment is one's misplaced happiness. The treatment takes one week to one month.

- *Transactional Analysis.* The patient selects a "script" that helps define his or her role in the world. A "Poor Me" script, for example, has one offering oneself to the world as a victim. The "I Don't Care" script is a self-fulfilling guarantee one will never make friends or influence people. These scripts are supposed to help the patient realize that he or she can change unwanted behavior. The problem? One gets a speaking part in the epic movie that is one's life, but one does not necessarily get to direct. The centerpience of treatment is the "script," with the patient and the therapist talking. The treatment takes eight weeks to six months.

- *Graffito Therapy.* Patients are asked to draw their feelings as a therapist discusses their life with them. The therapist talks while the patient doodles. The centerpiece of treatment is, "It's right there on the page." The treatment takes one session.

- *Movement Therapy.* A relatively new approach, movement therapy encourages people to literally dance away their problems. With a therapist/instructor, the patient hits the dance studio to talk and pirouette away his or her worries. Sometimes gentle and flowing, sometimes hard-charging and aerobic, movement therapy seeks to "work off" problems or anxieties in a safe and relatively

sane way. The centerpiece of treatment is using movement to resolve the patient's repressed feelings as he or she talks to the therapist. The treatment takes from nine months to a year.

- *Psychopharmacology.* The antidepressant Prozac is so widely accepted that family doctors have been known to hand it out without benefit of any talk therapy. Evidence has shown that at least 20 percent and as high as 50 to 80 percent of Prozac users have problems with libido, ejaculation, or orgasm. In 1995, a similar antidepressant, Serzone, was approved that may have fewer side effects. Psychopharmacology generally requires some talk before symptoms are dissolved. The centerpiece of treatment is the drug, which the patient will take for from six months to life.

- *Aromatherapy.* This type of therapy uses smells to make associations that calm, invigorate, and counteract pain. It requires no talking—just sniffing. The centerpiece of treatment is one's nasal passages. The treatment can last as long as the patient wishes, or as Donovan Webster ("Shrink to Fit") says, "As long as it smells like a good idea."

The therapies above involve three basic approaches, with most therapists using them together and then tailoring them to each patient. These approaches are the following: Psychodynamic Therapy, which operates from the premise that in order to tackle problems in the here-and-now, one must first dredge up and resolve those nagging issues and conflicts from the past. This is the standard Freudian approach and can go on for years. A shorthand approach has been developed into something called POP *(psychoanalytically oriented psychotherapy).* The fast-track version of POP is called *short-term dynamic therapy* (STDT). It is designed to get to the root cause of the patient's anxieties, and do it fast. Behavioral Therapy is designed to help one start, or stop, doing something. It is based on the premise that behaviors like panic attacks, phobias, substance abuse, or sexual dysfunction can be unlearned and replaced with new, more productive traits. Cognitive Therapy seeks not to modify behavior, but to change the attitudes behind it. According to Webster, "Cognitive therapy helps the patient review his destructive thoughts and uses old-fashioned reason to alter them."

Proponents of alternative therapies say that there is no reason their treatments cannot be used side by side with regular medical treatment. Many prefer to call them "complementary" treatments rather than alternative ones. Harvard's David Eisenberg and Joe Jacobs of the NIH say that their primary interest is to find any practical treatments that may be of use to physicians, even if the way those treatments work is not understood for years. In Congress, the tide may just be turning for complementary medicine. In 1994, the Access to Medical Treatment Act was introduced and has gained support. It would grant permission to doctors and licensed practitioners to prescribe treatments not approved by the Food and Drug Administration (FDA), such as natural medicines, herbs, acupuncture, hydro- and phytotherapy, and stress management techniques. The act covers treatments that are not outlawed by the FDA, but neither are they sanctioned.

SOURCES

"Alternative Medicine." *Consumer Reports* 59, 1 (January 1994).

Chopra, Deepak. *Ageless Body, Timeless Mind.* New York: Harmony Books. 1993.

Dyer, Wayne. *Real Magic: Creating Miracles in Everyday Life.* New York: HarperCollins. 1992.

Jacobs, Leonard. *Holistic Health Directory and Resource Guide.* P.O. Box 869, Langley, WA 98260.

Leviton, Richard, ed. *Alternative Medicine Digest.* P.O. Box K, Milton, WA 98354.

Natural Health. P.O. Box 744o, Red Oak, IA 51591.

Siegel, Bernie S. *Love, Medicine & Miracles.* New York: Harper & Row. 1986.

Webster, Donovan. "Shrink to Fit." *Men's Health* (April 1995): 76–81.

ALTRUISM

Altruism is defined as unselfishness, or unselfish devotion to the interests and welfare of others, especially as a principal of action. Some have argued that selfishness is original in man's nature, while altruism is something artificial or added. But this fails to take into consideration that some human impulses are concerned with the safety and welfare of children or other members of the human group. Abraham Maslow has observed that all humans have a need for love and that "No psychological health is possible unless the *inner nature* of the person is fundamentally accepted, loved and respected by others." While feeling and emotion are personal, they are not always self-regarding.

Seeking one's self-interest is not always evil, and self-sacrifice is not always good. Moral philosophers argue that self-love may be morally good or morally evil, and the same is true of altruism. There are situations in which our first duty is to look after ourselves—especially in regard to health and reputation. To make a rigid separation between self-interest and altruism raises a false issue. Rather, we must inquire about the consequences of both. Our behavior is not good or right merely because it helps some other person, nor wrong or bad because it advances our personal well-being. Behavior is right or wrong according to whether it is fair or unfair, beneficial or harmful to those affected directly or indirectly, including ourselves, and according to whether it is consistent with the point of view of morality.

Looking back over our shoulders at the evolution of the human species, we should probably ask about the survival of altruism during evolution. In Darwin's group theory, in *The Descent of Man,* he wrote:

> When two tribes of primeval man, living in the same country came into competition, if (other circumstances being equal) the one tribe included a great number of courageous, sympathetic and faithful members, who were always ready to warn each other of danger, to aid and defend each other, this tribe would succeed better and conquer the others.

And again Darwin reported:

> Obscure as is the problem of the advance of civilization, we can at least see that the nation which produced, during a lengthened period, the greatest number of highly intellectual, energetic, brave, patriotic, and benevolent men, would generally prevail over less favored nations.

Darwin's theory is that devoted people propagate their own kind of personalities, not through their physical children, but through their ethical children, those who imitate the actions of the altruistic ones. The disciples that an altruistic person can create, even in a short lifetime, are a much larger number, Darwin says, than the children that a selfish man can father.

See also Ethics, Theory of; The Moral Point of View.

SOURCES

Hester, Joseph P., and Philip F. Vincent. *Philosophy for Young Thinkers.* 2d ed. Monroe, NY: Trillium Press. 1987.

Darwin, Charles. *The Descent of Man.* Princeton: Princeton University Press. 1981.

Maslow, Abraham. *Toward a Psychology of Being.* New York: Van Nostrand Reinhold. 1968.

Pollard, Spencer D. *Science News* (April 8, 1972): 228.

Titus, Harold H., and Morris T. Keeton. *Ethics for Today.* 5th ed. New York: Van Nostrand. 1973.

AMERICAN BAR ASSOCIATION

The American Bar Association (ABA) of lawyers, judges, and law professors of the United States and its territories was founded in Saratoga Springs, New York, in 1878. The major goals of the ABA are to advance jurisprudence, to promote the administration of justice and uniformity of laws, and to foster high standards of legal education and ethics. Its headquarters are at 1155 E. 60th Street, Chicago, Illinois.

SOURCE

World Book Encyclopedia. Chicago: Field Enterprises Educational Corporation. 1993.

AMERICAN CIVIL LIBERTIES UNION

The American Civil Liberties Union (ACLU) is a nationwide, nonprofit, nonpartisan organization dedicated to preserving and defending the principles set forth in the Bill of Rights. The ACLU functions in three primary ways: (1) through litigation, (2) through legislative advocacy, and (3) through public education. With the ACLU's network of affiliates and chapters in every state, it is the largest private law firm in the United States, claiming about 300,000 members.

The ACLU was founded in 1917 under the National Civil Liberties Bureau with the goal of protecting the free speech rights of citizens who spoke out against U.S. participation in World War I. It adopted its present name in 1920. A national board determines its policies. Some major goals of the ACLU are the following:

- To support fair treatment of conscientious objectors, people whose religious beliefs will not let them take part in war;

- To encourage the desegregation of schools and to support the black Civil Rights movement;
- To abolish capital punishment;
- To encourage separation of church and state;
- To support women who want to have abortions.

SOURCES

Compton's Encyclopedia. Chicago: Compton's Learning Company. 1994.
Encyclopedia Americana. Danbury, CT: Grolier Incorporated. 1993.
World Book Encyclopedia. Chicago: Field Enterprises Educational Corporation. 1993.

AMERICAN FEDERATION OF TEACHERS

The American Federation of Teachers (AFT) is a union of classroom teachers affiliated with the American Federation of Labor and Congress of Industrial Organizations. The AFT has about 2,200 local unions in the United States. The union's chief objectives are to secure a living wage, better working conditions, and job security for teachers. The union seeks to promote better school construction, smaller class size, and equal educational opportunities for all persons of all races. The federation upholds the rights of teachers to help form school policies and programs. The AFT was founded in 1916 and has its headquarters at 555 New Jersey Avenue, Washington, D.C.

SOURCES

Compton's Encyclopedia. Chicago: Compton's Learning Company. 1994.
World Book Encyclopedia. Chicago: Field Enterprises Educational Corporation. 1993.

AMERICAN INDIANS

See Native Americans.

AMERICAN LEGION

The American Legion works as the largest veterans' organization in the United States. Men and women who have served honorably in the U.S. armed forces may join the American Legion. The organization seeks to advance the aims and interests of veterans, to continue the friendships formed during military service, and to see that disabled veterans receive the care and help they need. The Legion takes part in programs that promote the American way of life at the local, state, regional, and national levels. It also sponsors patriotic community projects and educational and charitable programs. Its headquarters are at 700 North Pennsylvania Street, Indianapolis, Indiana.

SOURCES

Compton's Encyclopedia. Chicago: Compton's Learning Company. 1994.
The World Book Encyclopedia. Chicago: Field Enterprises Educational Corporation. 1993.

AMERICAN MEDICAL ASSOCIATION

The American Medical Association (AMA) is an organization of doctors of medicine founded in 1847 to promote the science and art of medicine and to improve public health. To be a member of the AMA, a doctor must belong to one of the state or territorial medical associations. The AMA is divided into groups by field of specialization. It publishes a weekly magazine, the *Journal of the AMA,* ten monthly specialty journals, a weekly newspaper, and *Today's Health.* Its headquarters are at 535 North Dearborn Street, Chicago, Illinois.

SOURCES

World Book Encyclopedia. A: Volume 1. Chicago: Field Enterprises Educational Corporation. 1993.

AMERICAN'S CREED

The American's Creed won a nationwide contest for William Tyler Page of Maryland in 1917 as "the best summary of the political faith of America." It follows:

> I believe in the United States of America as a government of the people, by the people, for the people; whose just powers are derived from the consent of the governed; a democracy in a Republic; a sovereign Nation of many sovereign States; a perfect Union, one and inseparable; established upon those principles of freedom, equality, justice, and humanity for which American patriots sacrificed their lives and fortunes. I therefore believe it is my duty to my country to love it; to support its Constitution; to obey its laws; to respect its flag; and to defend it against all enemies.

SOURCES

Encyclopedia Americana. Vol. 1. Danbury, CT: Grolier Incorporated. 1993.
World Book Encyclopedia. A: Volume 1. Chicago: Field Enterprises Educational Corporation. 1993.

AMISH

The Amish belong to a Protestant group that originated in Switzerland, but is now centered in the United States and Canada. The Amish teach separation from the world. Members are forbidden to go to war, swear oaths, or hold public offices. Their doctrine requires farming and personal simplicity as a way of life. Amish men wear beards and wide-brimmed hats and the women wear plain long dresses and bonnets. Members meet in their homes every two weeks for worship. They till the soil with horses, and their *ordnung* ("rules") forbid the use of electricity and telephones. They limit education to the eighth grade. Those who break with the Old Order usually join the Mennonites.

The Amish were named for Jacob Ammann, who led them in breaking away from the Swiss Mennonites in the 1690s because of disagreements over church discipline. The Amish were more strict and avoided completely excommunicated members. They first came to North America in 1728 and are part of the group called Pennsylvania Dutch. There is no longer a separate Amish group in Europe.

SOURCES

Encyclopedia Americana. Danbury, CT: Grolier Incorporated. 1993.
World Book Encyclopedia. Chicago: Field Enterprises Educational Corporation. 1993.

AMUSEMENT AND PURITANISM

While the Pilgrims separated themselves completely from the Church of England, the Puritans hoped to reform it from within. Because the Puritans were denied the freedom to worship as they pleased, many began to look toward the New World (America). By 1630, they had obtained a charter from King Charles to establish a colony in America. The colony in New England was not a pure democracy. Rather, the freely elected leaders felt it their duty to do God's will rather than the bidding of those who elected them. They wanted their colony to be a "Bible Commonwealth" and to be governed according to their interpretation of the Scriptures.

The New England Puritans tried to establish a society that would set an example for the rest of the Christian world. They placed great emphasis on education—especially religious education—and on worship and church organization. They tried to simplify life, decrying extravagance of any kind. Amusements or recreation were thought of as wasteful and evil. Puritan preachers stressed godliness in all human affairs and condemned worldliness and the search for material wealth and satisfaction. These so-called earthly benefits were thought to sidetrack a person from the more valuable treasures of heaven.

Seeking religious purity, the Puritans remained ideologically rigid. They sensed a drift away from spirituality toward secularism and materialism. Thus, they began to include hard work and labor as having both a spiritual and a secular side. They taught that God had summoned each person to a vocation to perform some secular task, thus bringing all of life under the rubric of spirituality. Idleness and recreational activities were discouraged as evil and unspiritual.

But we know today that exercise and recreation, which may take the form of play, amusements, or sports and competitive athletics, are basic needs of the human body. The play impulse grows naturally and spontaneously out of life itself. Play means doing things for the sheer joy and satisfaction the activity itself brings. For a child, play is preparation for adult life. For an adult, it is the renewing of life. It is one method of recreating body and mind and avoiding nervous exhaustion. A proper balance between work and play or recreation is the essential condition of health and efficiency. Recreation through play in one form or another may save many persons for high moral purposes.

Amusements have great potential both for good and evil. Among their values are the joy they add to living, the zest they give to life. There is a definite place in life for pleasures or amusements that have no immediate relation to the duties of life but contribute to one's capacity for enjoyment. On the other hand, the Puritan view is that amusements, because they add to mere bodily enjoyment and "waste" time, are evil and should be rejected. In the view of many, the Puritan attitude was too severe and one-sided, and it failed to do justice to the needs of both children and adults for play and recreation. Thus, we find in America—by the 1920s—a rejection of the Puritan view and an accompanying renaissance in the fine arts, music, dance, and many other "recreational" and social activities.

There is social value in many forms of recreation and amusement. There is nothing like play to break down reserve and artificial barriers, and to aid in the formation of friendships. With both children and adults, amusements, especially in the form of group games, help stimulate sociability and foster a spirit of cooperation and teamwork. Laughter and goodwill tend to draw people together. They also act as a means of release for emotional pressures that otherwise may express themselves in irritation or anger.

SOURCES

Arieti, Silvano. *The Intrapsychic Self: Feeling, Cognition, and Creating in Health and Mental Illness.* New York: Basic Books. 1967.

Jones, B. *Health of Americans.* Englewood Cliffs, NJ: Prentice-Hall. 1970.

Jones, Kenneth L., et al. *Health Science.* New York: Harper & Row. 1971.

Nozick, Robert. *The Examined Life: Philosophical Meditations.* New York: Simon & Schuster. 1989.

ANABAPTISTS

The Anabaptists were members of a Protestant religious group that flourished in the 1500s during the Reformation in Europe. Anabaptists held that infant baptism was invalid, and believed in baptizing believers only. People nicknamed them Anabaptists ("rebaptizers") because they rebaptized all who joined them. Anabaptists introduced such ideas as voluntary church membership and complete separation of church and state. Most were simple, pious, and claimed some gifts of prophecy. The Anabaptists were bitterly persecuted in Protestant and Roman Catholic countries. Their movement was active in Switzerland, Germany, and the Netherlands. Their beliefs survive today in the Mennonite and Huttenite faiths and, indirectly, in the Baptist faith.

SOURCES

World Book Encyclopedia. A: Volume 1. Chicago: Field Enterprises Educational Corporation. 1993.

ANARCHISM

Anarchism (from the Greek meaning "without government") is the belief that every form of government or regulation is immoral and that regulation of one person by another is an evil that must be destroyed. Pierre Joseph Proudhon of France, often called the father of anarchism, became the first to make it a mass movement. His philosophical, or individualistic, anarchism urged the willing cooperation of free men without any regulation or government. Terroristic anarchism began under the leadership of Mikhail Bakunin (1814–1876) in Russia. He believed in the destruction of government by violence and terror, and that land and other means of production should be owned in common. He and his followers murdered heads of government, including President William McKinley of the United States. Thereafter, the U.S. government passed a law barring anarchists from entering the country. Anarchism under the leadership of Prince Peter Kropotkin (1842–1921) of Russia, during the late 1800s, rejected the terroristic methods of Bakunin, but also exposed the authoritative type of communism. Under Kropotkin anarchism, the state would be eliminated and the future society would be built on the communes, or village communities, that had existed in feudal Russian society. Each commune would be a self-sufficient group. The strength of anarchism declined in the early 1900s, but anarchists played an important role in the Spanish Civil War of 1936–1939, and are still active in Spain today.

SOURCES

Compton's Encyclopedia. Chicago: Compton's Learning Company. 1994.
World Book Encyclopedia. Chicago: Field Enterprises Educational Corporation. 1993.

ANDROGYNY

Androgyny is a third gender category, in addition to masculinity and femininity that refers to those who possess both masculine and feminine traits, sometimes referred to as a gender-role alternative. The word *androgyn* originates from two Greek roots: *andro*, translated as "male," and *gyn*, translated as "female." The three gender roles—masculine, feminine, and androgynous—occur in almost equal proportion in the population. The androgynous individual blends the masculine and feminine gender roles together.

Androgyny does not mean that the person is bisexual, hermaphroditic, or an activist for economic/gender equality. Rather, this person, like those with traditional gender roles, has a strong gender identity of femaleness or maleness based on her or his biological sex. Androgynous persons develop some of the qualities characteristic of the opposite sex.

Some psychologists have tended to define androgyny as the ideal gender role for both sexes. A number of empirical studies support this view. For example, people like androgynous individuals better than masculine or feminine ones. Androgynous individuals are generally viewed as standard models for mental health. They also adapt to the demands of many kinds of situations better than primarily masculine or primarily feminine persons. Also, on many occasions, violence is more often a response of highly masculine men than of androgynous men.

Why do some people develop androgynous roles while others do not? For men, ego development seems to be an important factor. Men who are highly masculine tend to have a low level of ego development—which means they have little self-control and are dependent on others. In contrast, men with highly developed egos are flexible in considering options and in respecting the rights of others; they are generally androgynous. For women, ego development is a less important determinant of their behavior than the gender role adapted by their mothers. Women with androgynous mothers tend to become androgynous; traditionally feminine mothers also produce daughters like themselves. The evidence still does not tell us how androgyny develops in females in the first place.

Androgynous persons have relatively positive attitudes about sex, ranging from homosexuality to heterosexual relationships. They tend to be more comfortable with their sexuality than highly masculine or highly feminine persons. Androgyns express more satisfaction with their marriages than do traditional individuals. They are also more sexually satisfied than persons who are either especially masculine or feminine. Their self-esteem is usually higher, and grow-

ing evidence supports the idea that androgynous persons adjust to changing circumstances better than those who are more traditionally masculine or feminine.

SOURCES

Bem, S. L. "Sex Role Adaptability: One Consequence of Psychological Androgyny." *Journal of Personality and Social Psychology* 31: 634–643.

Cook, E. P. *Psychological Androgyny*. New York: Pergamon. 1988.

Williams, J. E., and D. L. Best. *Measuring Sex Stereotypes: A Multinational Study*. Newberry Park, CA: Sage. 1990.

ANGEL

Commonly, the word *angel* is used in two ways: (1) as a messenger from God, and (2) as a spiritual being. In the earlier portions of the Bible, however, the two are nicely distinguished: while every divine messenger is regarded as a spiritual being, not every spiritual being is a divine messenger.

The usual Hebrew word for angel means simply "messenger," or "envoy" (compare Ugaritic, Arabic, Ethiopic *l'k*, "send"). In the patriarchal and monarchic narratives, the principal functions of such messengers are: (1) to convey the mandates of God to men; (2) to harbinger special events; (3) to protect the faithful and punish their enemies; and (4) to serve as instruments of the divine displeasure against sinners and recalcitrants within Israel itself.

In the Near East, we find in the life of Zoroaster a series of miraculous visions where the archangel Vohu Manah ("Good Thought") appeared to him on the banks of the Daitya River. The archangel instructed Zoroaster to lay aside his material body and become a prophet. The story goes on to say that during the next eight years Zoroaster met in vision each of the six principal archangels and each conference made more and more complete the original revelation.

These conceptions of heavenly messengers have their roots in the earlier religions of the Near East. In the Canaanite mythology poems from Ras Shamra-Ugarit in the fourteenth century B.C., such prominent members of the pantheon as El, the supreme overlord; Baal, the controller of the rains; and Mot, the genius of death and aridity, communicate with one another by means of divine messengers *(ml'km)*, and the goddess 'Anat has at her service a special courier and henchman *(mhr;* compare Akkadian *mu-ar ili,* K. 3515, rev. 9). Nearly every major Mesopotamian and Hittite deity likewise possessed his subordinate *miniter (sukkalla)* and throne-barriers *(guzalu).*

Survivals in later Semitic folklore serve also to illustrate these concepts. The angel who accompanied the caravan of Israel on its journey through the wilderness has his counterpart in the deity *Shi'a-algum,* "a companion or protector of the people," mentioned in *Nabatean* inscriptions. The fact that angels appear especially at wells, beside oaks or broom trees, and in blazing thorn bushes is well illustrated by modern popular beliefs concerning the presence of *welis* and *jinns* at just such places.

Further illustration is found in comparative folklore. The idea that angels can serve their protégés in battle occurs in the *Iliad* (III. 381, v. 776; XVIII. 205) and is likewise associated with the Serbian *uily.* So too the idea of a personal guardian angel or genius may be readily paralleled from early Teutonic lore. In the Mesopotamian myth of Adapa, Ea cunningly prevents the mortal hero from partaking of such fare by pretending that it is lethal *(ANET* 101–102).

According to the *Iliad* (v. 341), the gods do not consume ordinary bread, but feed on ambrosia, which assures immortality (XIX. 38, 347). Broadly speaking, the New Testament adds nothing to the traditional conception of angels. They are harbingers of special births, they intervene in moments of crisis, and they surround the throne of God in heaven and chant his praises.

SOURCE

Buttrick, George Arthur, et al., eds. *The Interpreter's Dictionary of the Bible.* Vol. A–D. New York: Abingdon Press. 1962.

Noss, David S., and John B. Noss. *Man's Religions.* 7th ed. New York: Macmillan. 1984.

ANIMAL RIGHTS

Animal rights is the view that animals have legal, quantifiable rights. Animal rights advocates believe that we should leave the natural world strictly alone. Peter Singer, a leading authority on animal rights, challenges humans to find some ground, apart from arbitrary self-preference, for restricting the "sanctity of life" to *human* life. Singer, author of the widely read book *Animal Liberation: A New Ethics for Our Treatment of Animals* (1975), argues that if the requirements of morality are radically different in respect to our treatment of animals and our conduct toward our fellow human beings, it must be because there is some morally relevant difference between *all* individual animals on the one hand, and *all* individual humans on the other. But Singer says that we can find no such difference in every case. He believes that if rationality, intelligence, or sensitivity to anxiety and suffering are the morally relevant differences, then chimpanzees, for example, should have a claim against us not to be killed (when compared with severely and irreparably retarded human infants). And if the sheer fact of membership in the human species is what qualifies the retarded infants and excludes the developed apes, Singer cannot understand how species membership by itself, quite apart from any necessary correlation with other traits, could be morally relevant.

Singer calls discrimination on the basis of species alone *speciesism*, and condemns it as being as irrational and immoral as racism and sexism. He concludes his argument for animal rights by noting that if we are to continue to hold the doctrine of the sanctity of human life, we must extend it to members of the highest animal species; if, on the other hand, we deny sanctity to some (higher) animals for what we take to be good reasons, then we must withdraw our attribution of sanctity to particular humans where the same reasons apply.

SOURCES

E, The Environmental Magazine 6, 5 (Oct. 1995).
Singer, Peter. *Animal Liberation: A New Ethics for Our Treatment of Animals.* New York: Random House. 1975.

ANIMISM

Animism is the belief that all things in nature have spirits, even lifeless objects such as sticks or stones. An animist fears the spirits that reside in things; therefore the animist will try to please the spirits so they will not harm him or her. Animists believe that spirits can be transferred from one body or one object to another. Thus, a spirit may possess a person's body. Animism, which began in more primitive times, mainly survives today in Asia, Africa, and the Pacific Islands. Present-day "primitives" generally accept animistic beliefs, including the belief that the soul or souls leave the body temporarily during dreams and with finality at death. This notion of souls and spirits has a meaning quite distinct from that of *mana*, which is itself impersonal. Souls and spirits are usually given human characteristics: shape, mind, feelings, and will or purpose, along with moods and emotions. For these peoples,

all nature is possessed, pervaded, crowded with spiritual beings.

SOURCES

Compton's Encyclopedia. Chicago: Compton's Learning Company. 1994.
Noss, David S., and John B. Noss. *Man's Religions.* 7th ed. New York: Macmillan. 1984.
World Book Encyclopedia. Chicago: Field Enterprises Educational Corporation. 1993.

ANTI-SEMITISM

Anti-Semitism is a set of negative and sometimes hostile beliefs and prejudices directed at Jewish people. The term, however, is inaccurate, because the word "Semites" properly refers to persons who speak Semitic languages, and includes Arabs and other Near Eastern peoples. Anti-Semitism may have grown out of fear and distrust based on religious differences. It has lasted for hundreds of years, and has resulted in many forms of persecution, including the *pogroms* of eastern Europe and Nazi Germany's massive extermination of Jewish peoples during World War II. Anti-Semitism has also led to segregated living arrangements, called *ghettos,* in many European cities, and in a less obvious form in many American cities. Because many forms of anti-Semitism are subtle, its manifest discrimination is difficult to detect and thus to correct.

Historians have traced the roots of anti-Semitism to the following: (1) the role of some Jews in the crucifixion of Jesus Christ; (2) the belief that Jews use underhanded methods in business and finance; and (3) the knowledge that Jewish people tend to be clannish. The 1920s and 1930s were a period of extremely overt anti-Semitism, especially in Europe. During this time the myth of *international Jewry* took shape. A forged document, the *Protocols of the Elders of Zion,* said that Jews throughout the world were going to conquer all governments, and the major vehicle for this task was communism. Henry Ford published the *Protocols* in his Dearborn newspaper, but later gave a halfhearted apology for doing so. Groups like the Ku Klux Klan and the German-American Bund, plus radio personalities like the Catholic priest Charles E. Coughlin, preached about the Jewish conspiracy as if it were fact. This period reached its height in Hitler's effort to exterminate all European Jews. For the most part, until Hitler moved to take over other countries, little criticism was brought against his anti-Semitic efforts.

In 1913, the Anti-Defamation League of B'nai B'rith was founded to watch carefully any trends in disfavor for Israel. In the aftermath of the oil embargo of 1973, which was blamed on Israel, the United Nations General Assembly ignored American and Israeli objections and passed a resolution declaring that "Zionism is a form of racism and racial discrimination." Zionism refers to the old Jewish religious yearning to return to their biblical homeland. Because old hostilities seem never to die, the Jewish people of the United States have come together to form a minority group with a high degree of group identity, loyalty, and service to one another.

See also Discrimination; Prejudice; Racism.

SOURCES

Schaefer, Richard T. *Racial and Ethnic Groups.* 3d ed. Boston: Scott, Foresman and Co. 1988.

World Book Encyclopedia. Chicago: Field Enterprises Educational Corporation. 1993.

ANXIETY

Anxiety, which can be transformed into worry and fear, should be distinguished from both. Psychologist Mary Ainsworth found anxiety among infants when the primary caretaker did not respond consistently to the infant's needs. Rollo May and Paul Tillich provide an excellent summary of anxiety theories.

First, they distinguish anxiety from fear. Anxiety is an indefinite, pervasive, objectless apprehension that, unlike fear, lacks a logically identifiable source. It combines a feeling of being vaguely menaced from without with feelings of being subtly subverted from within. Anxiety attacks the whole pattern of one's being—the very core of one's beliefs and personality—and one's continued relationship to an environment on which life depends. Second, anxiety arises from existing between one's expectations and discrepant realities. It grows from the apprehension of social dilemmas and irresolvable contradictions.

In summary, anxiety is basic, normal, and necessary, although it may also have neurotic forms associated with irrational ideas. Alfred Adler saw anxiety in the striving of these inferiority feelings to be superior. Anxiety also arises from an empathic anticipation of disapproval from others. May reminds us, as does Tillich, that the self is formed by attempts to control such anxiety. Tillich says:

> Courage does not remove anxiety. Since anxiety is existential it cannot be removed. But courage takes anxiety of nonbeing into itself. . . . He who does not succeed in taking anxiety courageously upon himself can succeed in avoiding despair only by escaping into neurosis. . . . Neurosis is the way of avoiding nonbeing by avoiding being.

SOURCES

Hampden-Turner, Charles. *Maps of the Mind.* Edited and designed by Mitchell Beazley. New York: Macmillan. 1981.

May, Rollo. *The Courage To Create.* New York: Norton. 1975.

Sears, David O., Letitia Anne Peplau, Jonathan L. Freedman, and Shelley E. Taylor. *Social Psychology.* Englewood Cliffs, NJ: Prentice-Hall. 1988.

Tillich, Paul. *Perspectives on 19th and 20th Century Protestant Theology.* New York: Harper & Row. 1967.

APARTHEID

The word *apartheid* means "apartness" in Afrikaans, one of the official languages of South Africa. Apartheid was until 1991 the South African government's policy of rigid racial segregation. Its official goal was the separate development of the nation's several racial groups. Laws isolated these groups in education, employment, housing, politics, and recreation. Accordingly, every South African was classified by race as either black, white, colored (mixed race), or Asian. In South Africa the rights of nonwhites to own and occupy were limited; even their right to enter a white neighborhood was limited.

Apartheid not only segregated whites and nonwhites, but it also led to efforts to segregate South Africa's nonwhite groups from one another. Apartheid became the official policy of South Africa after the Nationalist Party gained control of the government in 1948. This party is dominated by Afrikaners, the descendants of the early Dutch settlers of South Africa. South Africa withdrew from the Commonwealth of Nations in 1961 after other member nations criticized its racial policies.

In the intervening years between 1948 and 1991, there were many protests against the apartheid policies of South Africa, including boycotts, demonstrations, and strikes. Many hundreds of blacks have been killed in South Africa as a result. From 1962, when the United Nations General Assembly urged its members to break diplomatic and economic ties with South Africa, the nation grew increasingly isolated. In response to these actions and subsequent internal pressures, South Africa began repealing apartheid laws in the 1970s and 1980s. Finally, in 1991, the government repealed the last of these laws. It will take much longer to repeal the racial attitudes among the various ethnic groups in the country.

SOURCES

Compton's Encyclopedia. Chicago: Compton's Learning Company. 1994.

World Book Encyclopedia. Chicago: Field Enterprises Educational Corporation. 1993.

AQUINAS, SAINT THOMAS

St. Thomas Aquinas entered the priesthood in 1252 at Cologne and returned to Paris to begin preparing for the doctorate in theology. As a philosopher, Thomas, writing during controversial days following the reintroduction of the Aristotelian corpus in the West, produced a philosophical system that has been called by many "the supreme synthesis." This system brought together elements of Platonism, Augustinianism, Aristotelianism, and even Averroism to express a total point of view that remained faithful to the brute facts of everyday experience and to the orthodox teachings of the Catholic Church.

St. Thomas was a prolific writer, but he is best known for his *Summa Theologica*, in which he substituted Christian Aristotelianism for Augustinianism. About this theology, Paul Tillich comments:

> In the Middle Ages Augustine's ideas were represented by the great Franciscan theologians, while the Dominican theologians represented Aristotle's ideas. The tensions between these two in the thirteenth century represent the high point in medieval thought. In the Franciscan school will precedes intellect. In the Aristotelian-Thomistic school, or Dominican school, intellect precedes the will. This is not a vague statement about man's psychology; it is always meant ontologically. That means that in God himself, in the creative ground of being, either will or intellect is the primary power. . . . Now in the thirteenth century Bonaventura was one of the great Franciscans in whom will was the decisive thing, that is, will as love. He was a great mystic and also an early general of the Franciscan order. This mysticism of love goes back also to Saint Francis. Standing in radical

opposition to Thomas Aquinas was Duns Scotus, himself a Franciscan, and the greatest critical mind of the whole Middle Ages and one of the most important philosophical minds of the Western world. Both Thomas and Scotus lived in the thirteenth century. Scotus defined God as will and nothing other than will.

On the other hand, different from the Franciscans, Thomas took two decisive steps to accomplish his theological purpose: the first was the separation of faith (will) from reason, and the second was to make the senses the source of all human knowledge. He said that he who knows anything knows something about God. For the Franciscans, if God is sheer will, there is no logos structure that would prevent him from doing what he wants; thus, the world is in every moment dependent on something absolutely unknown. But this is not true for Thomas, in whose doctrine reason supplemented faith rather than denying it. Thomas put knowledge to work in the service of belief. Its purpose was to prove the truth of revelation. Using reason to answer his critics, Thomas said:

> Objection 3. Further, evil cannot be a cause, save accidentally, as Dionysius declares. But every action has some effect which is proper to it. Therefore no action is evil, but every action is good.
>
> On the contrary, Our Lord said (Jo. iii. 20): Every one that doth evil, hateth the light. Therefore some actions of man are evil.
>
> I answer that, We must speak of good and evil in actions as of good and evil in things, because such as everything is, such is the act that it produces. . . .
>
> I answer that, As was stated above, the good or evil of an action, as of other things, depends on its fullness of being or its lack of that fullness. Now the first thing that belongs to the fullness of being seems to be that which gives a thing its species. And just as a natural thing has its species from its form, so an action has its species from its object, just as does movement from its term. Therefore, just as the primary goodness of a natural thing is derived from its form, which gives it its species, so the primary goodness of a moral action is derived from its suitable object; and

so some call such an action good in its genius, e.g., to make use of what is one's own. (Thomas Aquinas, *Summa Theologica*, Question XVIII *On the Goodness and Malice of Human Acts, In General*).

From sensible reality (in Thomas, "being"), he arrived at two very important consequences for ethics and value: the first is that from sensible reality we are able to arrive at certain guiding principles; and secondly, only through sensible reality can we come to knowledge. Like Aristotle, Thomas gave priority to reason and knowledge (the intellect) and conceived the intellect to be made up of potency and act. From the time of Parmenides the contradiction between the flux of the sensible world and the stability of our ideas had caused problems for both understanding and explaining (consistently) from first principles the world in which we live. For Thomas, potency was still undetermined being or sensible reality, which had not yet received a form. It was in a state of becoming—neither nothing nor imperfect being, but unrealized. "Form" transforms potential through activity into being, which is form and matter combined.

Using these abstract terms from Thomas' metaphysics, Man is viewed as both a material and spiritual being, composed of body and soul (matter and form). The soul, being form, is the "act" of his "being." The object of Man's will is to do good or the good as such. Man's reason is the cause of his free will, for only by the intellect can he act from free judgment. Accordingly, the cause of all liberty is reason, for in it lies Man's power to choose freely. But, in Thomas, there is a leap of faith, for to remain free from sin—to believe, to love God, and to achieve meritorious actions—it is necessary to be infused with grace, which does not abolish nature, but perfects it. Man in his state of sin can acquire certain natural habits for good, but is dependent upon supernaturally infused habits if he is to transcend the limits of this world.

SOURCES

Kenny, Anthony, ed. *Aquinas: A Collection of Critical Essays.* Garden City, NY: Doubleday. 1969.

Leff, Gordon. *Medieval Thought, St. Augustine to Ockham.* Baltimore: Penguin. 1958.

Pegis, Anton C., ed. *Basic Writings of St. Thomas Aquinas.* Vols. 1 and 2. New York: Random House. 1945.

Shapiro, Herman, ed. *Medieval Philosophy: Selected Readings.* New York: The Modern Library. 1964.

Tillich, Paul. *Perspectives on 19th and 20th Century Protestant Theology.* New York: Harper & Row. 1967.

ARISTIPPUS

Linked to Socrates are the Megarian school, founded by Eucleides of Megara; the Cynic school, led by Antisthenes; and the Cyrenaic school, associated with Aristippus of Cyrene. Whereas Plato stipulated a rigorous and scientific preparation for philosophers, Antisthenes and Aristippus turned their students away from astronomy and music, two sciences that they considered absolutely useless because they taught nothing about good and evil. They also rejected mathematics and dialectic (the use of discussion in establishing truth). They believed that teaching discussion and demonstration gave way to suggestion, persuasion through rhetoric, and reliance on direct, personal expression. Nothing could stand in sharper contrast to the methods of Plato, but to these two hedonists, pleasure and pain were the only criteria of truth.

Aristippus was a contemporary of Plato who was drawn to Athens by the desire to study with Socrates. Although it is difficult to reconstruct his doctrine, scholars agree that Cyrenaic hedonism differs from Epicurean hedonism. As a hedonist, Aristippus was thought of as a "pleasure-seeker." For the Cyrenaic school, pleasure was the highest good, but it differs sharply from the stable, flawless happiness envisioned by the sage. Pleasure is fleeting and mobile, and pleasure of the body always surpasses the pleasure of the mind, just as physical suffering is much more painful than moral suffering.

SOURCES

Brehier, Emile. *The History of Philosophy: The Hellenistic and Roman Age.* Translated by Wade Baskin. Chicago: University of Chicago Press. 1965.

Jones, W. T. *The Classical Mind: A History of Western Philosophy.* 2d ed. New York: Harcourt, Brace & World. 1969.

ARTIFICIAL INSEMINATION

In vitro fertilization—where ova are removed and combined with sperm (either from a sperm donor or a husband)—is called artificial because the natural sexual process has been bypassed. Artificial insemination takes place when a quantity of semen is injected into the vagina by a syringe at the time of ovulation. A common problem is blocked oviducts, which now can be overcome by women who wish to conceive their own offspring by turning to a new technique that involves fertilization in the laboratory rather than in the oviducts: in vitro fertilization. This procedure can be used if microsurgery cannot correct the problem. Despite the success of this technique, for many individuals it raises questions about how much—or even whether—medical science should experiment with the human reproductive process.

Reservations about in vitro fertilization and its newer variations center around moral and practical issues. The cost of this procedure is not typically covered by most insurance companies or by the government, making it available mainly to a select group that can afford it.

Simply because we possess the technology for the procedure, should it be used? Under what conditions? One Roman Catholic priest, a Jesuit, has pointed out the moral difficulties that arise when unneeded or defective embryos are discarded. The success rate of placing the embryo in the uterus averages about 15 to 20 percent, so most embryos do not survive the process. The counterargument to this objection is that about 15 percent of ordinary pregnancies end in a natural, spontaneous abortion. The ethical question can be raised: "Is one type of embryo loss less acceptable than another?"

SOURCES

Chartrand, S. "Experts Assess a Decade of In Vitro Fertilization." *New York Times* (April 11, 1989): C5.

Grobstein, C., M. Flower, and J. Mendeloff. "External Human Fertilization: An Evaluation of Policy." *Science* 222: 127–133.

ASSIMILATION

Assimilation is the process by which a subordinate individual or group takes on the characteristics of the dominant group and is eventually accepted as a part of that group. Sociologist Milton Gordon (*Assimilation in American Life: The Role of Race, Religion, and National Origins*) divided assimilation into the following subprocesses:

- For example, although a person might be assimilated into the culture of the dominant society, it would not necessarily mean he or she would be accepted into the social clubs and cliques of the host society.
- Integration is frequently advocated as preferable to racial, ethnic, or religious conflict. Usually integration is a form of assimilation. Unless the situation is very unusual, integrationists in the dominant group expect the minority group to conform. Even integrationists in the subordinate group are eager to shed their culture in exchange for acceptance.
- In the United States assimilation is encouraged by the dominant white society. The assimilationist perspective tends to devalue alien culture and prefer the dominant. Thus, the assimilationist's solution to black-white conflict is the development of a consensus around white American values. This is commonly referred to as "Americanization," implying that the immigrant assimilates to American culture. But what constitutes the American culture that they come to accept as theirs? This core is made up essentially of white, Protestant, middle-class values. [This is described] as *Anglo-conformity*, which demands complete renunciation of the individual's culture in favor of the behavior, attitudes, and values of the core group.

ASIAN AMERICANS: A RECORD OF ACHIEVEMENT

Asian Americans are a diverse group and one of the fastest growing segments of the U.S. population (for example, they grew from 1.4 million in 1970 to 5.1 million in 1985). Immigration is the primary source of this growth, especially among Koreans, Filipinos, and refugees from Indochina. All Asian groups, along with black and white Americans, coexist in unique Hawaii. Elsewhere in the United States, they are often viewed as a "model minority" that has successfully overcome discrimination. But this image doesn't tell the entire story about Asian Americans. There has been maltreatment that denies them the opportunities afforded other racial minorities.

In 1995, the Educational Research Service reported that "Asian students are the most successful racial group in American schools in spite of the fact that the great majority of the nation's Asian population are immigrants or children of immigrants who have come since 1965."

President Ronald Reagan called Asian Americans "our examples of hope and inspiration." *Time* and *Newsweek* articles have featured headlines such as "A Formula for Success" and "The Drive To Excel." There seems to be no end to the praise. Some observers see the existence of a model minority as reaffirmation that anyone can get ahead in the United States. Proponents of this view declare that because Asian Americans have achieved success, they have ceased to be a minority, and are no longer disadvantaged. The truth of the "model minority" ignores the diversity among this group.

FACTS TO CONSIDER

- Asian American school enrollment displays higher levels in high school and college than whites, blacks, and Hispanics.
- Asian American youth are more likely to be at work as well as in school.
- Some institutions adopt unofficial quotas to reduce Asian Americans' disproportionately high representation among college students.
- Asian Americans are found disproportionately in low-paying service occupations, although substantial proportions are also concentrated at the top in professional, managerial, and executive positions.
- Asian Americans have become middlemen in the economy, doing well in small businesses and modest agricultural ventures. This is a result of exclusion from other work, not of success.
- The 1980 census showed that the median family income of the six largest Asian American groups exceeded the comparable income for white Americans by nearly $3,000.
- On the other hand, sociologist Morrison G. Wong shows that with their high level of education, Asian Americans are actually $1,000 below where they should be compared to similarly trained white Americans.
- In 1980, 63 percent of Asian American families had two or more paid workers, compared to 55 percent for white Americans. Rates per worker show comparable earning power, though more recent figures show low incomes.

See also Politically Correct.

SOURCES

Broom, Leonard. *The Transformation of the American Negro*. New York: Harper and Row. 1965.

Educational Research Service. "Asian Students and Desegregation." *ERS Bulletin* (January 1995).

Gardner, Robert W., Bryant Robey, and Peter C. Smith. *Asian Americans: Growth, Change, and Diversity*. Washington, D.C.: Population Reference Bureau. 1985.

Gordon, Milton M. *Assimilation in American Life: The Role of Race, Religion, and National Origins*. New York: Oxford University Press. 1964.

Schaefer, Richard T. *Racial and Ethnic Groups*. 3d ed. Boston: Scott, Foresman and Co. 1988.

ATHEISM

Atheism is the belief that "God" does not exist and neither fact nor reason can prove otherwise. Atheism is not new, but Thomas Huxley (1825–1895) provides a clear modern example of this view. Huxley opposed all religious proofs for God's existence on essentially Kantian grounds. In his essay on agnosticism, he concluded, "But let him not delude himself with the notion that his faith is evidence of the objective reality of that in which he trusts. Such evidence is to be obtained only by the use of the methods of science, as applied to history and to literature, and it amounts at present to very little."

The term *atheism* has, unfortunately, functioned more as an epithet than as a description of a univocal position, and this serves merely to confound attempts to understand the varieties of atheistic belief with the proper degree of objective inquiry. It has been common in the Judeo-Christian Western culture to call anyone who believed in a god other than the *acceptable* one an atheist. But this confuses greatly the meaning of the concept. Generally, the term *atheist* refers to a class of persons who do not believe in the existence of any deity whatsoever. The atheist rejects all arguments for the existence of a deity and feels no necessity to assume the presence of a supreme deity to account for the existence of life or the universe.

Many persons who are committed to reason as the sole reliable source of truth are convinced that reason cannot prove that a god exists, that the soul is immortal, or that morality is absolute—that is, that the ground for all ethics and value lies in the nature and existence of an omnipotent deity. John Dewey (1859–1952) clearly stated the grounds for atheistic rationalism in his naturalistic worldview. For Dewey, the world of nature that we are able to understand through our sensory experience and rationalistic or scientific methods constitutes the sum total of reality. For Dewey our experiences take place within nature and will not carry us beyond nature to the supernatural. Consequently, he is of the opinion that there are no supernatural entities.

SOURCES

Edwards, Rem B. *Reason and Religion*. New York: Harcourt Brace Jovanovich. 1972.

Wells, Donald A. *God, Man, and the Thinker*. New York: Dell. 1962.

ATONEMENT

In Christianity, the root meaning of *atonement* is reconciliation, the recovery of "at-one-ment" of Man with God. Christians are convinced that Christ's life and death ef- fected an unparalleled rapprochement between God and Man. In the words of Saint Paul, "God was in Christ reconciling the world unto himself." In other words, atonement is an act of God for the salvation of Man. The Roman Catholic interpretation of this doctrine is expressed in legal language. By voluntarily disobeying God's order not to eat of the forbidden fruit in Eden, Adam sinned. As his sin was directed squarely against God, it was of infinite proportion. Sins must be compensated for—otherwise God's justice is outraged. As infinite sin demands infinite recompense, this could only be effected by God's vicarious assumption of our guilt and payment of the ultimate penalty it required— namely, death.

In Christ the disciples had caught a new vision of what Man might be, of the extent to which a love deeper than they had known might pervade his whole life. John Wesley brings out the difference in the quality of this Christian love when, in saying that we should love our neighbor as ourself, he catches himself immediately and adds, "Nay, our Lord hath expressed it still more strongly, teaching us to love one another as He hath loved us. 'As I have loved you, so love ye one another.' Now, herein perceive we the love of God in that He laid down His life for us."

In Judaism, in recognition of their historical journey, the Day of Atonement (Yom Kippur) preceded by the Day of Judgment (Rosh Hashana) and the Day of Repentance, called the faithful to repentance, prayer, and righteousness. On the Day of Atonement, Jews are called upon to participate in the fast and to exert their wills to turn from wrongdoing in true atonement for sin, as God wills them to do forever.

SOURCES

Toynbee, Arnold. *An Historian's Approach to Religion*. London: Oxford University Press. 1956.

Walhout, Donald. *Interpreting Religion*. Englewood Cliffs, NJ: Prentice-Hall. 1963.

ATTITUDES

Each of the traditional definitions of *attitude* contains a slightly different conception of what an attitude is or emphasizes a somewhat different aspect of it. For example, Gordon Allport proposed that "an attitude is a mental and neural state of readiness, organized through experiences, exerting a directive or dynamic influence upon the individual's response to all objects and situations with which it is related." Because this definition was much influenced by traditional psychology, it also emphasized how past experience forms attitudes in a cause-and-effect relationship. For the same reason, it viewed an attitude primarily as a set (of dispositions) to respond in a particular way, and thus drew upon its behavioral implications.

In contrast, Krech and Crutchfield, who were strongly committed to a cognitive perspective, defined an attitude as "an enduring organization of motivational, emotional, perceptual, and cognitive processes with respect to some aspect of the individual's world." No reference is made to the origins of the attitude (no cause/effect relationship is intended), and instead this view is committed to whatever current subjective experience the person is having. Thus, Krech and Crutchfield emphasize organization; they view the person as a thoughtful and actively structuring organism. In this view there is no mention of overt behavior; rather, the cognitive tradition strongly emphasizes the person's subjective experience.

Current definitions of attitude draw from both of these perspectives. An attitude toward any given object, idea, or person is an enduring orientation with cognitive, affective, and behavioral components. The cognitive component consists of all the cognitions the person has about that particular attitude-object—the facts, beliefs, and knowledge concerning the object. The affective component consists of all the person's affects or emotions toward the attitude-object, especially his or her evaluations of the object. The behavioral component consists of the person's readiness to respond or tendency to act regarding the attitude-object. The essential point to remember is that any attitude toward a particular attitude-object has these three different components. And what one should keep in mind is that these three components are not always found in equal measure in a person, nor are they always consistent with each other. Psychologists Sears, Peplau, Freedman, and Taylor have provided the following summary of attitudes:

1. Attitudes have a cognitive (thought) component, an affective (feeling) component, and a behavioral component.
2. People often have cognitively complex attitudes. However, like personality impressions, attitudes tend to be organized around the affective (or evaluative) dimension and to be evaluatively simple.
3. The learning approach views attitudes as learned by association, reinforcement, and imitation. The incentive approach views attitudes as the products of cost-benefit calculations by the individual. Cognitive consistency theories view people as attempting to maintain consistency among their various attitudes, between their affects and cognitions toward a given object, and between their attitudes and behavior.
4. It is usually assumed that behavior arises from attitudes, but considerable research questions how consistent the two are with each other. Now it appears that attitudes influence behavior most under certain conditions: strong, clear, specific attitudes, and with no conflicting situational pressures.

5. Dissonance is most commonly created by the individual's behavior. Dissonance arises following decisions and following behavioral acts contrary to the individual's attitudes.

6. Dissonance can be reduced in a variety of ways. If the behavior itself cannot be revoked, the most important alternative is attitude change to reduce attitude-behavior discrepancies.

7. Post-decisional dissonance is greatest when people remain committed to their decisions for a long time, if they have free choice in their decisions, if the consequences of the decisions are known in advance and are certain, and if they feel responsible for the consequences.

8. Dissonance following attitude-discrepant behavior depends upon barely sufficient incentives to commit the behavior. These incentives can be either minimal threat or minimal promised reward. The maximum dissonance following attitude-discrepant behavior occurs with minimum incentive, negative consequences of the act, and clear personal responsibility for the consequence.

9. Alternative explanations for these dissonance effects have been generated by attribution theorists. When people have rather vague, undefined attitudes, behavioral acts may lead to fresh self-perceptions of attitudes, thus leading to attitude-behavior consistency through an attribution rather than a dissonance-reduction process.

SOURCES

Allport, Gordon W. "Attitudes." In C. Murchison, ed. *A Handbook of Social Psychology.* Worcester, MA: Clark University Press. 1935.

Krech, D., and R. A. Crutchfield. *Theory and Problems of Social Psychology.* New York: McGraw-Hill. 1948.

Sears, David O., Letitia Anne Peplau, Jonathan L. Freedman, and Shelley E. Taylor. *Social Psychology.* Englewood Cliffs, NJ: Prentice-Hall. 1988.

AUGUSTINE, SAINT

Augustine was born in A.D. 354 in North Africa of a Christian mother and a non-Christian father and was thoroughly trained in rhetoric. He died as Bishop of Hippo in 430. Both his theology and philosophy are profoundly personal and denote his own search for wisdom. His early acceptance of the Manichean position, his flirtation with the skepticism of the New Academy, his subsequent contact with Neoplatonism, and his conversion to Christianity make up the menu of attitudes, dispositions, and ideas reflected in the problems he considered and many of the solutions he embraced.

Neoplatonism enabled Augustine to account for evil as an absence of good without adopting the dualistic solution of the Manicheans, who posited both good and evil as separate cosmic forces. It also freed Augustine from materialism and was foundational to his belief in the spiritual nature of the divine. After his conversion to Christianity his pursuit of wisdom became the struggle for Christian wisdom, reflected in his *Confessions.* His purpose in life was to seek a deep understanding of the soul and of God. Certain elements of his insightful journey are important to the history of Western philosophical and theological thought:

- His period of skepticism left him concerned with Man's capacity to know anything with certainty. Although he considered the senses unreliable, he was certain that he existed and he claimed that we can know that we exist. Thus, like Descartes, who followed him in this rational and spiritual quest some 1,300 years later, he claimed that the mind enjoys direct and immediate knowledge of at least one spiritual reality: itself.

- In turning within, the mind discovers certain truths, such as those of mathematics and other "eternal verities," that are necessarily and unchangeably true.
- By knowing ourselves and in knowing that we can know truth, we are led to affirm the existence of God.
- Divine illumination is not to be equated with mystical experience, nor is it to be equated with or reduced to the action of the intellect (as in Aristotelian philosophy). Augustine also rejects any theory of learning by recollection or by means of innate ideas. This seems to mean that in some way the eternal truths found in the divine mind are the source of truth in our minds, without thereby implying that we enjoy any direct vision of the divine ideas of God.
- Augustine's theory of *rationes seminales* ("rational seeds") further emphasizes the creature's dependence on God. All things were created by God in the beginning, but many were not created in perfect and completed form (or what we might call "mint" condition), but rather remain latent ("in seed") until their time comes to emerge into fully formed beings. No second cause can bring new form into being. Second cause can only aid a form already existing in its seminal principle to emerge.
- Augustine frequently describes man as a soul using a body. The soul is not related to the body as form is to matter; rather, the union is one of what he calls "vital attention." The soul watches over the body and is present as a whole in all parts of the body. Augustine has trouble accounting for sensory experience and the mode of the union of soul and body.

It makes no scruple to obey the laws of the earthly city, by which the things necessary for the maintenance of this mortal life are administered (St. Augustine, *The City of God*).

From these principles Augustine generates his theory of morals. He says, commenting on the concept of pleasure, "If you ask me, I think man's supreme good is in the mind." There you have his form of Platonism in one sentence. Like mathematics, the truths of morals are found in their pure form in the mind. These truths preside over our mind within us. Augustine's Christianity completed this ethic: It is Christ who lives in our inner selves and who provides the unchangeable power and eternal wisdom of God. This wisdom is given to every rational mind-soul as much as one is able to receive, according to one's own good and evil will.

SOURCES

Anderson, Robert T., and Peter B. Fischer. *An Introduction to Christianity*. New York: Harper & Row. 1966.

Augustine. *The City of God*. London: Everyman. 1945.

———. *Confessions*. London: F. J. Sheed. 1943.

Shapiro, Herman, ed. *Medieval Philosophy: Selected Readings*. New York: The Modern Library. 1964.

Wippel, J. F., and A. B. Wolter. *Medieval Philosophy from St. Augustine to Nicholas of Cusa*. New York: Free Press. 1969.

AURELIUS, MARCUS

What was great about Marcus Aurelius, the fourteenth emperor of Rome, was that he succeeded in living his life while refusing to compromise his ideals with the petty obsessions of lesser men; and what made this possible was his philosophy of life, which is outlined in *Things Written to Himself*. This philosophy was actually a set of convictions, rationally derived, about how he should run his life. These convictions are sometimes called the *Meditations*. His musings, an exercise in self-discovery, contain passages such as the following:

> Do not act as if you were going to live ten thousand years. Death hangs over you. While you live, while it is in your power, be good.

> Men seek retreats for themselves—houses in the country, by the seashores, in the mountains; and you too are apt to desire such things very much. But this is altogether a mark of the most common sort of men.

> Do you see me unhappy because thus-and-so has happened to me? Not at all. Rather, I am happy despite its happening to me. Why? Because I continue on, free from pain, neither crushed by the present nor fearing the future. For events such as this happen to every human being.

> [This wise man] will not go against the Divinity which is planted in his breast; but rather he will preserve his deepest inner self in tranquility. He will, above all, preserve his own autonomy and integrity, and not let anything alienate him from himself. [In fact, speaking of one's inner world, Marcus reminds us that each one of us is the sole and final caretaker of] this little plot that is thyself.

From his point of view, the major problem besetting men is finding a way to live in the world and not be destroyed by it. Although we wish to escape the tragedies of life, for Marcus escape was not a moral option. He reminds us that we are called to live the life of the social animal, and to be responsible to our fellow human beings, to whom our life belongs. Marcus comments: "This then remains, remember to retire into this little territory of the inner self—your own world (which is all there is)—and there be free, and, as a human being, observe the world passing by."

SOURCES

Christian, James L. *Philosophy: An Introduction to the Art of Wondering.* 4th ed. New York: Holt, Rinehart and Winston. 1986.

Noss, David S., and John B. Noss. *Man's Religions.* 7th ed. New York: Macmillan. 1984.

AUTHORITY IN ETHICAL DECISION MAKING

The first question we must answer in ethics is "Who is to make the ethical decision?" Ethicists have long agreed that any ethic is futile until someone decides to accept the point of view of morality and act on its precepts. We can assume, as many have, that only the individual person can make moral choices and act on them, but determining what action is moral may not have been decided at all. On the question regarding decision, there are two broad avenues of inquiry we can take, for we can speak of both *authoritarian decisions* and *autonomous decisions*.

In authoritarian ethics, decisions about right and wrong are handed down. These decisions are not the product of one's personal experience. They have already been made by another, either a person taken to be an authority or by society and its traditional givens (these givens include obeying the laws of a deity—Yahweh, Allah, Shamash, Ahura Mazda, etc.). The responsibility of the individual is to follow the law, obey the rules, and use them to resolve ethical problems or moral dilemmas in his or her daily life. In most authoritarian ethics we are obliged to cultivate the moral life so that we will be able to act morally (follow the commandments, rules, laws, norms, etc.) when called to do so. In an authoritarian ethic the individual takes no part in the first-order decision making about what constitutes the contents of morality and moral behavior. Laws and principles are given and cannot be changed.

An autonomous ethic arises from inside oneself, but among philosophers there is some doubt that this ever occurs in a pure form, without external (either cultural or authoritarian) influences. In autonomous ethics the individual is the decision maker regarding what is and what is not moral and what is and what is not a moral action. The word *autonomy* implies that the individual is self-determined and has freedom of choice. Actions flow from the decisions that one *freely* makes. Autonomous ethics come from one's own experiences and depend on the quality of the "inner self"—its ability to reason, to understand, and to assimilate moral principles. For the autonomous person, morality is deeply personal, reflecting the ability to function independently, to determine his or her own behavior and make decisions consonant with the moral conclusions he or she has reached.

Fundamentally, autonomous ethics "is a sincere goodwill and never empty conformity to prevailing customs" (Christian 1986), but it presupposes several things. First it requires an awareness of one's needs, and this comes only from experience. It means being able to recognize one's own feelings and sort out one's own needs. Second comes the courage of self-affirmation, to accept all that one is despite serious flaws. Finally, an autonomous ethic presupposes an understanding of the cultural patterns within which a person has lived his or her life. Without a recognition of the beliefs and values that one has unknowingly followed, it is difficult to separate autonomous behavior from conformity. The satisfaction of these three categories is what is meant by being autonomous or free.

In summary, the differences between an ethic based on authority and one based on the decision-making and reasoning ability of the autonomous self raises an interesting issue—the issue of the problem of authority—and not just metaphysical, but authority in everyday life. Sociologists tell us, and experience bears this out, that we cannot have society without some structure, some authority. They remind us that every society must inculcate a habit of obedience in its citizens. But what roles does the autonomous self play in "the habit of obedience"?

Authority may manifest itself in the impersonal dictates of law, the internalization of these principles by persons, the externalization of conscience in a deity, and in the example and council of persons whom we respect and admire. According to moral philosopher Harry K. Girvetz, "the essence of reliance upon authority in an ethical situation consists of a willingness to accept dictates or suggestions of authority not directly because of what is proposed, but because of a belief in the integrity and insight of the authority him- or herself. If we are responsive to the suggestions of the authority, it is not the merit of the proposal which we consider but the merit of the authority."

Is there a middle ground? The balance between blind obedience to authority, the rational acceptance of what the authority says to us, and individual initiative is voluntary, tentative, and experimental. Because any authority is subject to our own personal assessment concerning its trustworthiness, heeding the authority does not necessarily mean prejudging the values at issue—hence it does not arrest mental growth, it encourages it. Obedience unrestrained by reason or by conscience may in fact inhibit moral growth. In addressing this problem, Abraham Edel distinguishes five different cases in which there is an interplay of authoritarian considerations and those of a more autonomous nature:

1. Must-rules carry a mandatory quality, brimful of necessity, with a bitter "woe unto you" taste.
2. Always-rules have a universality and are a reliable dependency rather than a menace; they tell you exactly the right thing to do. Herein moral quality is derived from the importance of the enterprise and the values they support, or the seriousness of the dangers they avoid.
3. Break-always-with-regret rules have an exalted status, but they do not have an absolutely compelling power over the individual situation.

4. For-the-most-part rules carry a certain authority, but when you find them inapplicable, you feel no qualms in departing from them.
5. The complex singular situation is the limiting case in which no rule may introduce a binding element. This case underscores the uniquely creative character of Man in moral decision making.

From Edel's point of view, the conception of moral law (moral authority) does not entail moral absolutism, nor does it lead to moral relativity as many religionists claim. Edel says, "for it might turn out to be desirable to employ each of the five types in different areas of human life under a value scheme that can yield definite and correct answers."

SOURCES

Christian, James L. *Philosophy: An Introduction to the Art of Wondering.* 4th ed. New York: Holt, Rinehart and Winston. 1986.

Edel, Abraham. *Ethical Judgment: The Use of Science in Ethics.* London: Free Press of Glencoe. 1955.

Girvetz, Harry K. *Beyond Right and Wrong.* New York: Free Press. 1973.

AXIOLOGY

See Ethics, Theory of; Values.

AYER, A. J.

A. J. Ayer was Wykeham Professor of Logic, Oxford University. At the age of 26 (1936) he published *Language, Truth, and Logic,* which is regarded as a classical defense of logical positivism with widespread appeal in the 1930s and 1940s. Ayer, having revised his earlier version, later published *The Foundations of Empirical Knowledge* (1940), *Philosophical Essays* (1954), *The Problem of Knowledge* (1956), and *The Concept of a Person and Other Essays* (1963).

Positivists did not wait long to extend their ideas from language, truth, and logic to ethics and values. They assimilated ethical and other valuations into positivist theory in two ways: on the one hand, they considered ethics as empirical statements about valuations considered as facts, or, on the other hand, they treated ethical statements as noncognitive. M. Schlick adopted the first approach in his *Problems of Ethics:* "Values, the good, are mere abstractions, but valuation, approbation, are actual psychic occurrences. . . . The problem which we must put at the center of ethics is a purely psychological one." A similar approach was also put forth by J. A. Irving: "Our analysis suggests that the proper method of ethics would be to study the undeniable moral consciousness." This version of positivism viewed ethics as factual, psychological statements about valuations and their moral efficacy in moral and social conduct.

Ayer took the second approach to the problem of ethics, according to which ethical and other valuational statements are viewed as noncognitive. Thus, Ayer asserts that one class of ethical statements—exhortations to moral virtue—"are not propositions at all, but ejaculations or commands which are designed to provoke the reader to action of a certain sort." On this account, the statement "Stealing is wrong" expresses nothing but a disapproval of theft; the sentence "You ought to tell the truth" is tantamount to the command, "Tell the truth!" The function of ethical words in these cases is purely emotive. A highly suggestive and original version of the emotive theory of ethics was developed by C. L. Stevenson in *Ethics and Language.* Stevenson's linguistic analysis of ethical statements testifies to the versatility of the positivistic theory and the fruitfulness of positivistic analysis in clarifying noncognitive as well as cognitive statements.

SOURCES

Ayer, A. J. *Philosophical Essays*. New York: St. Martin's. 1954.

Hospers, John. *Human Conduct: An Introduction to the Problem of Ethics*. New York: Harcourt, Brace & World. 1961.

Irving, J. A. "Towards Radical Empiricism in Ethics." In *American Philosophy: Today and Tomorrow*. Edited by H. M. Keller and S. Hook. New York: L. Furman. 1935.

Schlick, M. *Problems of Ethics*. New York: Prentice-Hall. 1939.

Stevenson, C. L. *Ethics and Language*. New Haven, CT: Yale University Press. 1944.

B

BABY BOOM GENERATION

Soaring population after World War II fueled a population boom (demographers place the Baby Boom from about 1945 to 1965) as well as economic growth and expansion. In the 1930s, the number of residents in the United States had grown by only 7 percent, the lowest increase in history. The census of 1950 counted 151 million persons, an increase of 14 percent over 1940; in 1960 the numbers rose to 179 million, an increase of 18 percent; in 1970 they revealed 203 million, up 13 percent, and the trend showed every sign of continuing.

Growth stemmed not from world events, but from a change in the native birthrate, which moved upward until 1970. The Baby Boom did not subside but generated an expanding population eager and able to consume the goods being produced by industrialization. The increase in population was not a drag on the economy, but was used to create more wealth. The total labor force grew from 63 million in 1950 to 72 million in 1960 and to 85 million in 1970. Productivity was more efficient than ever before and wages were higher. The rise in per-capita income, although unequally distributed, expanded purchasing power. Some 20 percent of the population in the 1960s lacked enough for

necessities without assistance; another 20 percent, somewhat better off, used their income for rent and food, with little left over. But a full 60 percent enjoyed enough to make discretionary purchases. With a large disparity between low and middle/high incomes, Americans in 1960 seemed more committed to political than economic equality. But a system utterly committed to fostering political equality left the question of economic equality in abeyance.

Despite the Depression of the 1930s and a second world war in the first half of the 1940s, the economy had acquired a new structure. As a result, the realignment of productive forces in the 1950s and 1960s brought affluence, and an unprecedented abundance of goods poured into the markets, offering a vision of a great society providing enough to all. The unexpected outcome of this growth was a new and confusing expansion of liberty, challenging inherited ideas of freedom and rights. A sense of uneasiness persisted as parents reminded their children of the Depression's effects. Social turbulence exploded into disorder toward the end of the 1960s. Many Americans confronted the contradictions inherent in the country's political and economic systems: one promising that the "one man, one vote" formula assured equality of results, and the other promising only equality of opportunity.

The results of the economic upsurge of the 1950s slowly penetrated consciousness.

Talk was about a new frontier and beyond it a great society. Americans experienced social mobility and felt better off financially than their parents and grandparents. These changes strengthened the core values of growth, and the belief in equality—the universal ability to act. In the twentieth century, industrialization and technological know-how replaced the older imagined sources of wealth and had perhaps provided a fresher vision of a world in which all people, including minorities, would have the freedom to grow economically and socially.

What the New Deal had failed to achieve, the forced mobilization of combat in World War II succeeded in doing. During the war, the U.S. Navy had to build 750 housing units in Norfolk, Virginia, and build them quickly. It asked William J. Levitt to do the job. Afterward, in 1946, Levitt constructed 17,000 single-family homes for returning GIs that sold for $7,990 each. Similar mass-production techniques—along with standardized kitchen appliances and heating, plumbing, and electrical fixtures—were used in building such homes throughout the country.

The booming economy and the booming population prepared the way for a revival of feminism. With historical roots in the suffragette and temperance movements, the contemporary revival of feminism could be said to have begun with the publication of Betty Friedan's *The Feminine Mystique* in 1963. Using the expressive self as the ground of value, Friedan's brand of feminism brought expressive values into the public arena. Like other movements of the period, feminism generated both a rational reform movement and a pitiless critique of rationalism. Moving toward rational reform, many feminists pursued legislative, regulatory, judicial, and constitutional remedies for sex discrimination.

The Baby Boom was over by 1965 and its effects by 1970. After 1970, realizing that there were too many people for the good jobs and few economic opportunities available, a stampede to business began and steadily gained momentum through the 1980s. The big loser during the 1971–1985 period was education, which awarded only half as many bachelor's degrees in 1985 as in 1971. As the Baby Boomers passed out of the public school system, there was a narrowing of opportunity in education and a national decline in education majors. Social science suffered a similar decline, dropping from almost one-fifth of all bachelor's degrees in 1971 to one-eleventh in 1985.

The winner was business. In 1960, only about 5,000 MBAs were awarded. By 1971 that figure had increased to 26,500 and by 1985 to 67,000, an increase of 154 percent during a time (1971–1985) when all master's degrees increased by only 24 percent. Three-fourths of that increase was accounted for by the increase in MBAs.

In the 1950s and 1960s, the number of workers aged 25 to 34 ranged from 14 million to 17 million; by 1985 the number had increased to 30 million. From the end of World War II to 1973, real wages grew at an average of 3 percent a year; after 1973 the growth stopped. The Baby Boomers had caught a glimpse, as children, of the kind of life that had once been possible on one income from almost any kind of middle-class job. But because of the sheer quantity of Baby Boomers and the long-term stagnation of the American economy, financial and retirement security grew even more elusive. Older Baby Boomers found they could not simply secede from the economy. The more ambitious found a crowded career ladder and experienced a slow but perceptible widening between their prospects and their expectations. Younger Baby Boomers, squeezed by the enormous numbers of their older siblings and coming of age in an economy that had been sour longer, felt the impact more directly and moved quickly to swell the ranks of business majors.

In many ways, times were tough for the younger Baby Boomers. Their liberal arts professors wrote them off as materialistic, unimaginative, and incurious. Businesspeople thought them less educated and less prepared than the preceding generation. The media exploited them, falsely assuming that all young people were affluent, contributing to feelings of inadequacy in the overwhelming majority who were not. Middle-aged moralists simply called them selfish.

These younger members of the Baby Boom generation gave the moralists ample ammunition. According to surveys conducted by the Higher Education Research Institute, 83 percent of incoming freshmen in 1967 had identified "developing a meaningful philosophy of life" as an essential goal. In all but two of the next 21 years, the percentages dropped steadily, reaching an all-time low of 39 percent in 1987. Meanwhile, the percentage of freshmen who identified "being very well off financially" as an essential goal climbed steadily from a low of 39 percent in 1970 to an all-time high of 76 percent in 1987.

In the face of such evidence—the increases in business majors and MBAs and the dramatic shift of personal goals—the Baby Boomers brought with them a values shift much different from the generation who came before them. But in the 1980s, the same economic forces that had driven so many young people to seek the security of business careers had turned business upside down as businesses failed or disappeared into the maw of predatory takeovers, leveraged buyouts, mergers, and calculated bankruptcy. Stagnant incomes and the demographic squeeze sent even more Baby Boomers scurrying for jobs in larger organizations where they had to get used to being bought and sold.

In *The New Individualists*, Paul Leinberger and Bruce Tucker take a careful look at the generation after the "organization man" (William H. Whyte, Jr., *The Organization Man*, 1956). In the following steps they recall some of the more startling measures of the long-term decline of the generations' economic prospects as against the expectations that the postwar period of affluence had inculcated in them:

- During Eisenhower's two terms of office, the average family's income, adjusted for inflation, rose by 30 percent; during the Kennedy-Johnson years, it also rose 30 percent. But from 1973 to 1980, the prime years of the "Me Decade" and the search for self-fulfillment, the average family's income, adjusted for inflation, *declined* by 7 percent. During Ronald Reagan's first term, it grew by only 5 percent.
- An average 30-year-old man in 1956, when *The Organization Man* was published, could carry the mortgage on an average-price home for about 14 percent of his gross pay. By 1984 the figure was 44 percent.
- Before 1973, a 30-year-old man would have already been earning 15 percent more than his father was earning when the young man left home at age 20. But by 1983, a young man who left his parents' home in 1973 was earning 25 percent less (rather than 15 percent more) than his father had earned in the early 1970s.
- In 1975 the median income of 40-year-old men exceeded the median income of 30-year-old men by 21 percent, but by 1984 that figure was 34 percent, which indicates that Baby Boomers were experiencing a wage gap relative to the generation that immediately preceded them, a generation that benefited from its small size, as well as from the head start that the postwar boom afforded them.
- Wages stagnated in all occupations, including those in business and related fields, as formerly high-paying jobs became oversupplied. For example, the average 30-year-old white male lawyer earned $39,304 in 1969, but only $34,821 in 1979.

The reality of what had happened was slow to dawn on the average worker. As

Frank Levy observed, "The dream expands in good times, and in bad times it is slow to contract." Leinberger and Tucker conclude: "But as the American Dream receded from the grasp of people who had thought of it as their birthright, the new reality could be glimpsed not only in the complicated frustration that went into Yuppie bashing, but in the subtle changes that occurred in the meaning of the term *middle class* and in the significance of consumption. . . . After 1973, a middle income no longer guaranteed the ability to purchase what has been thought of as a middle-class life. As one of our interviewees astutely and ruefully observed: 'To be middle class now means that your parents can afford to help you buy a house.'"

SOURCES

Handlin, Oscar, and Lilian Handlin. *Liberty and Equality 1920–1994.* New York: Harper Collins. 1994.

Leinberger, Paul, and Bruce Tucker. *The New Individualists.* New York: HarperCollins. 1991.

BACON, FRANCIS

Francis Bacon (Baron Verulam, Viscount St. Albans, 1560–1626) was educated at Trinity College, Cambridge, later studied law, and in 1584 was elected to Parliament. He became an important civil servant and rose to be solicitor general in 1607, attorney general in 1613, and lord chancellor of England in 1618. In the struggles between Parliament and the Crown, Bacon was usually on the king's side. In 1621, he was convicted of taking bribes, was briefly imprisoned, and his political career ended. While active in Parliament and the government, Bacon wrote *Essays or Counsels* (1597), *The Advancement of Learning* (1605), *The New Atlantis* (1617), and *Novum Organum*, part of *Instauratio Magna* (1620). In his last years, in disgrace, he continued writing scientific and philosophical works and died as a result of bronchitis.

Bacon's ethics are revealed most clearly in his philosophy of Man. In human philosophy Bacon thought of Man as a separate individual, and in civil or political philosophy as a member of society. He thought that the philosophy of Man studies body and soul and their relation. Among its topics are the miseries and the prerogatives or excellencies of the human race, physiognomy and the interpretation of natural dreams, the effect of bodily states on the mind, the influences of mind on body, the proper seat and habitation of each faculty of the mind in the body and its organs, and also medicine.

Bacon embraces in his human science a knowledge of Man as a psychophysical individual. His philosophy of Man is a comprehensive philosophical anthropology, and his envisaging of a comprehensive science of man was the foundation of scientific humanism, which was later revived in the twentieth century by John Dewey. For Bacon, the human soul has a divine, or rational part, and an irrational part. All problems relating to the former must be handed over to religion. Logic treats understanding and reason; and ethics focuses on the will, appetite, and affections. Reason produces resolutions; ethics produces actions. The logical arts include inquiry, judgment, memory, and delivery. Ethics describes the nature of the good and prescribes rules for conforming to it. Bacon distinguishes between individual good—self-preservation and defense—and social good—duty, government, justice, and the public good. He says that because man is prompted by selfish and social impulses, he needs ethics or rules for conforming to the nature of good.

Although Bacon did not offer a universal system of philosophy, he did believe that philosophy is founded on the just, pure, and strict inquiry into all subjects. His purpose was "to lay more firmly the foundations and extend more widely the limits of the power and greatness of man."

SOURCES

Popkin, Richard H. *The Philosophy of the 16th and 17th Centuries.* New York: The Free Press. 1966.

Thilly, Frank. (Revised by Ledger Wood in 1941.) *A History of Philosophy.* New York: Henry Holt. 1914.

BAN THE BOMB

In 1964, Jacob Bronowski wrote: "The gravest indictment that can be made of our generalized culture is, in fact, that it erodes our sense of the context in which judgments must be made. . . . As it is, I leave *Science and Human Values* at the point which its last page reaches: the demonstration that values are not rules, 'but use those deeper illuminations in whose light justice and unjustice, good and evil, means and ends are seen in fearful sharpness of outline.'"

In Bronowski's 1953 lecture "The Creative Mind," he tells the story of inspecting the atomic ruins in Nagasaki in November 1945. He tells of driving into the center of the city but not realizing he was in a town: "I did not know that we had left the open country until unexpectedly I heard the ship's loudspeakers broadcasting dance music. Then suddenly I was aware that we were already at the center of damage in Nagasaki." Bronowski remembered that the dance tune being broadcast that moment was called "Is You Is or Is You Ain't Ma Baby?" In that hour he conceived the essays that would be published eight years later. He reflects, "For the moment I have recalled was a universal moment; what I met was, almost as abruptly, the experience of mankind. On an evening like that evening, some time in 1945, each of us in his own way learned that his imagination had been dwarfed." And Bronowski reminds us of our new dilemma, born of an atomic blast and characteristic of the Cold War. He concludes: "Nothing happened in 1945 except that we changed the scale of our indifference to man; and conscience, in revenge, for an instant became immediate to us. . . . Let us acknowledge our subject for what it is: civilization face to face with its own implications."

From the end of World War II and the dropping of the first atomic bomb on Japan, science became eternally connected to war, and together science and war brought humans the world over to the verge of a new frontier where the potential for violence, for world destruction, evoked a mixture of fear and anticipation. The use of the atomic bomb ushered in a new reactionary era resulting in another lost generation (the first being after World War II) as dropouts, hippies, and Beat poets reacted to the Cold War and the potential for destruction on a massive scale, and ordinary American citizens built bomb shelters with their new ranch-style houses, not knowing the futility of their own acts.

Allen Ginsberg, one of a group of poets centered in San Francisco, wrote of his America as

Moloch! Solitude! Filth! Ugliness!
Ashcans and unobtainable dollars!
Children screaming under the stairways!
Boys sobbing in Armies! Old men weeping
    in the parks!
Moloch whose mind is pure machinery!

(Handlin and Handlin, 1994)

From 1950, a slowly growing number of physical scientists—including Jacob Bronowski—and social scientists were willing to listen to members of the American counterculture, as was evidenced by a conference in 1955 on "Man's Role in Changing the Face of the Earth." Norman Podharetz of *Commentary* magazine summed up the liberal establishment's view of the Beat poets when he wrote, "In America, we are witnessing the revolt of all the forces hostile to civilization itself." But the liberal establishment's view was

being challenged by a youth counterculture that reached its zenith in 1970.

The experience of atomic fallout had
startled many scholars who were beginning, in the 1960s, to accept the idea of life
as a chain of interrelationships. Atomic
bombs had been tested in the Pacific, but
much to the dismay of the government,
Strontium 90 had been carried across the
ocean, across the United States, brought to
the ground by rain, absorbed by grasses,
eaten by cows, and finally drunk in milk
by infants, in whose bones it had caused
degeneration.

The bomb had helped to produce a
counterculture and, by 1962, the ecology
movement. In that year, Rachel Carson's
Silent Spring showed how DDT had entered the food chains and threatened the
health of all humankind. *Time*, reflecting
the establishment's view, identified
Carson's concept of a "chain" with unsci-
entific mysticism and emotionalism. By
1970, however, the scientific community's
old linear cause/effect metaphor had dramatically given way to such concepts as
chains, and balance and interdependence.
Twelve years later, the physicist Fritjof
Capra wrote *The Turning Point*, whose
major thesis is the interrelatedness of all
of life. He says:

> The new concepts in physics have brought
> about a profound change in our world view;
> from the mechanistic conception of Des-
> cartes and Newton to a holistic and ecologi-
> cal view, a view which I have found to be
> similar to the views of mystics of all ages
> and traditions.
>
> The new view of the physical universe
> was by no means easy for scientists at the
> beginning of the century to accept. The ex-
> ploration of the atomic and subatomic
> world brought them in contact with a
> strange and unexpected reality that seemed
> to defy any coherent description. In their
> struggle to grasp this new reality, scientists
> became painfully aware that their basic con-
> cepts, their language, and their whole way
> of thinking were inadequate to describe
> atomic phenomena. Their problems were
> not merely intellectual but amounted to an
> intense emotional and, one could say, even
> existential crisis. . . .

The basic thesis of this book is that these
are all different facets of one and the same
crisis, and that this crisis is essentially a crisis of perception. Like the crisis in physics in
the 1920s, it derives from the fact that we are
trying to apply the concepts of an outdated
world view—the mechanistic world view of
Cartesian-Newtonian science—to a reality
that can no longer be understood in terms of
these concepts. We live today in a globally
interconnected world, in which biological,
psychological, social, and environmental phenomena are all interdependent. To describe
the world appropriately we need an ecological perspective which the Cartesian world
view does not offer.

In 1972 Garrett Hardin declared: "I am
convinced a time will come when the
physiologists, the poet, and the philosopher will speak the same language and
mutually understand each other. That language is proving to be the language of ecology." Hardin had just written a science
fiction fable, *The Voyage of the Space Ship
Beagle*, whose moral was the need for humans to recover the sense of the earth as
the center of their existence and meaning.
Citing the first Earth Week as an example
in his 1970 book, *The Closing Circle*, Barry
Commoner echoed Hardin's message and
stated that "the environment had just been
discovered by the people who live in it."

From 1945, the problems associated
with the atomic age created many new and
far-reaching challenges. If humans were to
live safely with the atom, they must meet
these challenges successfully: atomic
weapons, radiation, and the disposal of
atomic waste (in 1995, these problems have
as yet to be ethically resolved). On November 15, 1969, in a paper read before the fall
meeting of the Middle Atlantic States Philosophy of Education Society at the
Belmont Plaza Hotel in New York City,
Thomas B. Caldwell, Jr. pointed out that
the limits of nature have been transgressed,
and then said: "Thus, it is imperative to
see that formulating the problems of community as an ecological problem, instead
of a merely social one, makes a profound
difference to its solution. For making the
problems of community turn on the issue

of what is good for the system of nature as a whole, rather than man and then nature, opens doors to ways of conceiving of community life, its organization and its values, that differ radically from present community designs."

Reaction to atomic weapons thus led to a chain of events, lasting for 50 years, that together proved to be a turning point in our conception of humans, human communities, and the interconnectedness of all life. It produced a counterculture, the feminist movement, and what was then called "the most subversive of the sciences," ecology. And society waits to see what other institutions (educational, political and governmental, religious, etc.) are brought into this circle. Don McLean summed up the feelings of this generation of Americans and this period in American life in his 1971 song, "American Pie": "Now for ten years we've been on our own / And moss grows fat on a rolling stone, But that's not how it used to be."

SOURCES

Bronowski, Jacob. *Science and Human Values*. New York: Harper & Row. 1965.

Capra, Fritjof. *The Turning Point*. New York: Bantam Books. 1982.

Halberstam, David. *The Fifties*. New York: Villard Books. 1993.

Handlin, Oscar, and Lilian Handlin. *Liberty and Equality 1920–1994*. New York: Harper Collins. 1994.

BEAUTY

See Aesthetics.

BEHAVIORISM

Behaviorism is the view that human beings can profitably be studied only by a rigorous scientific examination of human action. The most famous contemporary behaviorist, B. F. Skinner, offers the following hint as to the foundations of behaviorism *(Beyond Freedom and Dignity)* :

> Unable to understand how or why the person we see behaves as he does, we attribute his behavior to a person we cannot see, whose behavior we cannot explain either but about whom we are not inclined to ask questions. . . . The function of the inner man is to provide an explanation which will not be explained in turn. Explanation stops with him . . . he is a center from which behavior emanates. . . . The inner man has been created in the image of the outer . . . something like an inner man had been invented to convert a stimulus into a response . . . but it was a false scent from which a scientific analysis is only now recovering. The environment not only prods or lashes, it selects. . . . Behavior is shaped and maintained by its consequences.

A radical behaviorist is one who believes that humans are nothing but the entire range of their behavior. However, upon closer inspection, it has proven difficult to specify precisely what is meant by a "behavior," and as a result there are many different types of behaviorism. Skinner is one of only a few behaviorists who has developed a comprehensive behaviorist account of the nature of human beings and society. Skinner defends the view that a "behavior" is some movement of an organism where the causes of the movement are other than physiological. He understands behavior in this way because he is interested in causes that substantially contribute to making us individual entities. Skinner notes that we all have genes, muscles, and internal organs that affect our responses to stimuli. We all are physically similar and therefore react similarly on a physiological level.

What makes us interestingly different is our different individual behaviors, which Skinner believes are the inevitable results of the different environments in which we are raised. The notion of *environmental control* is at the heart of Skinner's thought about human beings. As a psychologist, he sets out to determine through precise experimental means how behavior is controlled by exposure to an environment. Skinner accepts three basic principles: (1) behavior is far more important for the study of humans than consciousness, because only behavior can be precisely measured and controlled in an experimental way, while consciousness is scientifically unobservable; (2) environmental influences control us more than does heredity; and (3) scientific laws can be discovered that relate environmental causes to the control of human behavior.

From these three assumptions, Skinner generalizes a philosophical theory of human beings. He says:

> There are two important results. One concerns the basic analysis. Behavior which operates upon the environment to produce consequences ("operant" behavior) can be studied by arranging environments in which specific consequences are contingent upon it. The contingencies under investigation have become steadily more complex, and one by one they are taking over the explanatory functions previously assigned to personalities, states of mind, feelings, traits of character, purposes, and intentions. The second result is practical: the environment can be manipulated. It is true that man's genetic endowment can be changed only very slowly, but changes in the environment of the individual have quick and dramatic effects.

Skinner is convinced that behavioral psychology can tell us what controls should be instituted for reform and which reinforcers are the most powerful inducements to change. He argues that we will have to give up such outdated and illusory notions as "human freedom and dignity," which have no place in a scientific psychology, but he thinks this price is a small one to pay for a more satisfying life.

SOURCES

Compton's Encyclopedia. Vol. B. Chicago: Compton's Learning Company. 1994.

Skinner, B. F. *Beyond Freedom and Dignity*. New York: Alfred A. Knopf. 1972.

World Book Encyclopedia. Chicago: Field Enterprises Educational Corporation. 1993.

BENEVOLENCE

Benevolence (altruism, brotherly love, or good will toward others) lies near the heart of the moral point of view and the ethical treatment we show others, for it is the uncoerced giving of help, friendship, and love (prosocial behavior) to others when there is no expectation of receiving a reward in any form. To say that someone acted benevolently toward another we must understand their intentions (not to gain reward and recognition in the case of benevolence) before passing judgment.

For example, John Rawls distinguishes a beneficent from a benevolent action in the following way: "We can now define a good act (in the sense of a beneficent act) as one which we are at liberty to do or not do, that is, no requirements of natural duty or obligation constrain us either to do it or not to do it, and which advances and is intended to advance another's good (his rational plan). Taking a further step, we can define a good action (in the sense of a benevolent action) as a good act performed for the sole purpose of the other person's good. A beneficent act promotes another's good; and a benevolent action is done from the desire that the other should have this good."

Benevolence, or benevolent behavior, is an essential part of moral goodness, since it is behavior not only performed for the sole purpose of another's good, but with the sincere desire that a person should have this good. In his well-known sermon, "Upon the Love of Thy Neighbor," Bishop Joseph Butler (1692–1752) refutes the old cynical saying that men act only from a motive of self-love, that beneath the surface of generosity, sympathy, or benevolence, there always lurks the egoistic thought: *Will I get pleasure from this act?* Butler's lengthy analysis of egoism and altruism turns on a single fundamental distinction. It is one thing to say that a man gets pleasure from accomplishing the end of his action, and quite another to say that the expectation of that pleasure is his reason for action. That is, when I do something to help a friend or an associate (or to help one of my children), I may get pleasure from the fact he or she appreciates it and feels positive about my action. But my reason for helping was to give my friend (or another) pleasure. My act can be said to be a benevolent act because its purpose was to make sure my friend received his or her good.

Again, Butler summarizes the concept of benevolence:

> The short of the matter is no more than this. Happiness consists in the gratification of certain affections, appetites, passions, with objects which are by nature adapted to them. Self-love may indeed set us on work to gratify these: but happiness or enjoyment has no immediate connexion with self-love, but arises from such gratification alone. Love of our neighbor is one of those affections. This, considered as a virtuous principle, is gratified by a consciousness of endeavouring to promote the good of others: but considered as a natural affection, its gratification consists in the actual accomplishment of this endeavour. Now, indulgence or gratification of this affection, whether in that consciousness, or this accomplishment, has the same respect to interest, as indulgence of any other affection; they equally proceed from, or do not proceed from, self-love; they equally include, or equally exclude, this principle. Thus it appears, that "benevolence and the pursuit of public good have at least as great respect to self-love and the pursuit of private good, as any other particular passions, and their respective pursuits."

See also Character; Ethics, Theory of; Values.

SOURCES

Butler, Joseph. "Sermon XI, Preached on Advent Sunday, from Fifteen Sermons upon Human Nature." London, 1726. Printed in Robert Paul Wolff. *Philosophy: A Modern Encounter.* Englewood Cliffs, NJ: Prentice-Hall. 1971.

Rawls, John. *A Theory of Justice.* Cambridge, MA: Belknap Press of Harvard University Press. 1971.

BENNETT, WILLIAM

William J. Bennett served as director of the Office of National Drug Control Policy under President George Bush and served as secretary of education and chairperson of the National Endowment for the Humanities under President Ronald Reagan. In his 1992 book *The De-Valuing of America*, Bennett offers insightful and provocative discussion of some of the hot-button domestic and social issues of our time, including education, drug control, cultural policy, race relations, politically correct thinking, and the failures of contemporary liberalism. He also addresses problems in government, the role religion plays in our public life, the importance of character and culture, and affirmative action and quotas.

This forceful and passionate polemic is best characterized in the following:

> The battle over culture reaches beyond art, music, poetry, photography, literature, cinema, and drama. The broader issue has to do with a growing realization that over the past twenty years or so the traditional values of the American people have come under steady fire, with the heavy artillery supplied by intellectuals. This all-out assault has taken its toll. In our time, too many Americans became either embarrassed, unwilling, or unable to explain with assurance to our children and to one another the difference between right and wrong, between what is helpful and what is destructive, what is enobling and what is degrading. The fabric of support that the American people—families especially—could traditionally find in the culture at large became worn, torn, and unraveled.

In particular, Bennett believes that American society and culture have been deconstructed, notably by the liberal left. His mission is to reclaim American institutions (churches, schools, the legal profession, colleges, Congress, and universities). Bennett comments: "Somebody's values will prevail. In America, 'we the people' have a duty to insist that our institutions and our government be true to their time-honored tasks. . . . The debate has been joined. But the fight for our values has just begun."

SOURCE

Bennett, William J. *The De-Valuing of America*. New York: Summit Books. 1992.

BENTHAM, JEREMY

Jeremy Bentham, inventor of what is now known as utilitarianism, was a child prodigy who read Latin and Greek and studied philosophy when other boys his age were still enjoying fairy tales. He spent his youth in the company of distinguished scholars and social reformers instead of the company of the eligible young ladies of his own generation. At the age of 13, Bentham was offended and his mind troubled by doubts when he was required to affirm his belief in the 39 Articles of the Anglican Church before being allowed to enroll in Oxford University. He did enter Oxford and upon his graduation, proceeded to study law in London. Because of his marked ability, his father had hopes that Jeremy would become a distinguished jurist, but Jeremy took little interest in the practical side of his profession.

Bentham spent almost the whole of his life in London. He soon gathered around him a group of devoted friends who accepted his views and were eager to help in spreading his philosophy. His outstanding book, *The Principles of Morals and Legislation* (1789), was written as a background for a new penal code he was advocating. He promoted this program at heavy expense to himself, but it was finally rejected by the British government.

Although his friends called Bentham's philosophy "practical utilitarianism," Bentham preferred a somewhat more cumbersome phrase, "the greatest happiness principle." In time, utilitarianism became the accepted name for Bentham's philosophy as well as for that of John Stuart Mill. It was Bentham's hope that he could make ethics as exact and precise as the physical sciences. At the heart of his ethics was the idea that pleasure and pain are forces at work in controlling our lives: "It is for them alone to point out what we ought to do, as well as determine what we shall do."

Upon reading, one discovers that the moral philosophy of Bentham contains little more than a careful restatement of the major points of Epicureanism, an ancient Greek moral philosophy. By *utility*, Bentham means those objects or actions that tend to produce more good and pleasure than other objects and actions. If choosing a particular action (or behavior) would give you an advantage in the marketplace, then—on Bentham's account—you should choose it over those actions or behaviors that would not give you the same monetary advantage. No philosophy can be more simple and direct. All choices, when clearly analyzed, are really of this sort: the advantage, the satisfaction for us, in each case determines our choice. Therefore, the right action in any circumstance is the one that on the whole produces the best approximation to the desired results for all concerned. It is not our motives, but the consequences of *what we do* that count. The only moral problem is that of determining what conduct produces the greatest pleasure or brings the least pain. Bentham, interested in producing an exact standard for measuring pleasure, developed a hedonistic calculus in which the following seven factors have to be taken into account:

1.   the intensity of the pleasure and pain involved;

2. their duration;
3. their certainty or uncertainty;
4. their propinquity or remoteness;
5. their tendency to produce other pleasures or pains;
6. their purity, that is, the freedom of pleasure from attendant pains, and pains from pleasures; and
7. their extent or the number of persons whom they affect.

According to Bentham, right and wrong are based on the calculated amount of pleasure or pain of a given behavior. If more pleasure is to be gained, this will give the good tendency of the act. If more pain is to be gained, this will give the bad tendency of the act. It was Bentham's application of these principles to social and legal philosophy that has made the most lasting impact. He was convinced that good government must promote the greatest happiness of the greatest number, not the interest of the privileged few. He felt that all men are naturally egoistic or selfish and need to be made to think also of the good of others if a stable society is to be possible. Hence, it is the function of the law to see that a man does consider the good of others as well as his own good.

SOURCES

Hester, Joseph P., and Philip F. Vincent. *Philosophy for Young Thinkers: Beat Him When He Sneezes.* Middle Grades, Book Two. Monroe, NY: Trillium Press. 1990.

Thilly, Frank. (Revised by Ledger Wood in 1941.) *A History of Philosophy.* New York: Henry Holt. 1914.

Wolff, Robert Paul. *Philosophy: A Modern Encounter.* Englewood Cliffs, NJ: Prentice-Hall. 1971.

BERGSON, HENRI

The most interesting and popular figure in the antirationalistic movement of the first half of the twentieth century is Henri Bergson (1859–1941). With the romanticists, pragmatists, and mystics, Bergson proclaimed the incapacity of science and logic to explain ultimate reality. He noted that in the presence of life and movement, conceptual thinking (reason) stands helpless. Conceptual thought is well adapted for employment in a dead, static world, the world of inert matter that is both physical and mechanistic. Bergson argued that where there is no individuality, no inwardness, nothing but dead surface, science and logic have both practical and theoretical worth. When, however, science and logic are applied to the living world, they mutilate and falsify the real.

According to Bergson, life and consciousness cannot be treated mathematically, scientifically, or logically. The scientific intellect translates the flux and flow of real people moving through time into space relations: for it, duration, movement, life, and evolution are mere illusions; it mechanizes them all. Bergson says that the philosopher must keep a direct vision of reality, a *Weltanschauung*, a "world-intuition." Intuition is life, real and immediate—life envisaging itself. It is a creative spirit, a living, pushing force, an *elan vital*, that eludes the mathematical intelligence and that can be appreciated only by a kind of divine sympathy, a feeling that approaches nearer to the essence of things than does reason. The real, the "becoming," the inward *duree*, life and consciousness, we can apprehend only through the faculty of intuition.

The moral and religious nature of humans is described with penetrating insight in Bergson's last important work: *The Two Sources of Morality and Religion*. The opposition between the static and the dynamic, which appeared in Bergson's theory of knowledge as the antithesis between the intellect and intuition, and in his metaphysics as the contrast between the mechanical and the vital, likewise pervades his treatment of morality and religion:

Static ↔ Dynamic
Intellect ↔ Intuition
Mechanical ↔ Vital
Repose ↔ Movement

Bergson concluded that morality has two fundamental sources: the first rests on obligations resulting from the structure of society and its pressures; the second source is a creative morality, the expression of our moral genius and insight. The first is reflected by the left-hand column and the second by the right-hand column above. Thus, for Bergson, moral genius and insight are dynamic, intuitive, vital, and alive with movement, whereas reason is not.

SOURCES

Bergson, Henri. *The Two Sources of Morality and Religion.* Garden City, NY: Doubleday. 1935.

Bochenski, I. M. *Contemporary European Philosophy.* Berkeley: University of California Press. 1966.

BETTER BUSINESS BUREAU

The Better Business Bureau is a nonprofit corporation organized to protect the public from unfair advertising and business methods/practices. More than 200 cities in the United States and Canada have Better Business Bureaus. There are also bureaus in Israel, Mexico, Puerto Rico, and Venezuela.

Each year the bureau handles more than 6 million calls for information and assistance on routine business-consumer problems. Its agents also investigate and act on false and deceptive advertising and selling practices. Bureaus do not take direct legal action, but if they cannot convince a business to adopt fair practices, they may refer the case to a governmental agency. Better Business Bureaus are supported by thousands of business firms. They are members of the Council of Better Business Bureaus Incorporated, at 4200 Wilson Boulevard, Arlington, VA 22203.

SOURCE

World Book Encyclopedia. Chicago: Field Enterprises Educational Corporation. 1993.

BIAS

See Discrimination; Prejudice; Racism.

BIBLE

The Bible (the term originates from the Latin *biblia*) is the collection of writings to which the Christian Church attaches canonical authority. The limits of this collection have varied considerably at different periods, and there are profound differences within the Church over the degree of authority that is to be attributed to the collection and to particular books within it.

The English Bible originally contained 80 books—39 of the Old Testament, 27 of the New Testament, and 14 of the Apocrypha. Since early in the nineteenth century when the British and Foreign Bible Society decided against including the Apocrypha in editions published under its sponsorship, it has become the general custom to publish Bibles of 66 books, containing only the "canonical" scriptures of the Old Testament and New Testament.

The *Greek Bible* includes the same 27 books of the New Testament and a much more extensive Old Testament: (a) Greek versions of all the books of the Hebrew Old Testament, chiefly from the LXX (the oldest Greek version of the Old Testament based on the tradition that 70 elders completed the translation between 285–247 B.C.) but in part from the later translations; (b) additional works originally composed in Greek; (c) Greek versions of Hebrew works that are no longer extant in Hebrew; and (d) Greek supplements to the books of Esther and Daniel.

The Hebrew Bible contains 39 books of the Old Testament that the Christian churches, accepting in this the judgment of the rabbis, have acknowledged as canonical. Jewish writers frequently refer to the collection alone as "the Bible." The Old Testament reached its present formulation in the second century B.C. and was not officially accepted by Christians until the sixteenth century A.D.

The Latin Bible, or Vulgate, according to the decision of the Council of Trent, contains 72 books—45 of the Old Testament and 27 of the New Testament. The 45 Old Testament books correspond with some differences of arrangement to the 39 Old Testament books in the English Bible with the Apocrypha. These are held to be "sacred and canonical," on the ground that "having been written by inspiration of the Holy Ghost, they have God for their author, and as such have been handed down by the church" (Buttrick 1962). This is generally the view of the Christian Church in the West, and "the Bible says" is usually meant as "God says," so that the Bible has authority over faith and practice for Christians.

The Bible has now been translated into more than 1,000 languages, and the work of translation into other languages and dialects is still going on. Also, hundreds of paraphrased or "modern" editions have been published. No other literature has ever been rendered into any remotely comparable number of versions, and no book

has ever approached the Bible in world-wide circulation.

SOURCE

Buttrick, George Arthur, et al., eds. *The Interpreter's Dictionary of the Bible.* Vol. A–D. New York: Abingdon Press. 1962.

BILL OF RIGHTS

The first ten amendments to the U.S. Constitution are often called the Bill of Rights. We read in the First Amendment that no one may be restrained from merely talking and expressing a point of view: "Congress shall make no law respecting an establishment of religion, or prohibiting the free exercise thereof; or abridging the freedom of speech, or of the press; or the right of the people peaceably to assemble, and to petition the Government for a redress of grievances." In the Fifth Amendment, which deals with prosecution and imprisonment and private property taken for public use, there is a due process clause. Certain things are not to be done "without due process of law." The First Amendment, however, contains no such clause; it simply says "no law." When it comes to thoughts, ideas, and opinions, a person is free to express himself or herself. The opinion of others is not to be forced on a person, and there is to be no coercion or repression by state, church, or other groups on the mere expression of opinions. One's freedom to speak does not depend on what one says being true or right as others view it. According to this tradition of freedom, the only opinion established by the Constitution is the opinion that a person is free to hold any opinion. The principle here seems to be that the important thing is the person, the person's worth, uniqueness, and individuality. Americans believe that individual uniquenesses will be damaged or lost if attempts are made to enforce uniformity.

Thomas Jefferson, in many statements and actions, reinforced this tradition of freedom. Jefferson believed in the freedom of speech so strongly that he felt the government should not interfere with human expression unless civil disorder was the result. He said, "It is time enough for the rightful purposes of civil government for its officers to interfere when principles break out into overt acts against peace and good order."

In 1947, President Harry S. Truman, addressing a newly appointed committee on civil rights, said, "I want our Bill of Rights implemented in fact. We have been trying to do this for 150 years." The committee report, *To Secure These Rights,* is one of the outstanding documents of American society. This report dealt with a wide range of civil liberties, pointed out various flaws in the nation's record, emphasized the heritage and the dream not fully attained, and made recommendations for actions. These actions took place between 1957 and 1965 in a series of civil rights acts. These acts made it possible for minority groups to begin making progress in the age-old struggle for civil rights. Many excellent books and articles dealing with these issues have been written. They have sensitized the public, which has become more concerned with them. The American Civil Liberties Union stated in 1962:

> The civil rights issues are among the "great issues" of our times, not because of their novelty—the century since the Emancipation Proclamation belies that possibility—nor because of their complexity, but because of their relationship to our national purpose. . . . Today's civil rights test has become the proving ground on which to demonstrate whether we can use our rights and our machinery of self-government to resolve the first of these great issues to which the nation has turned its attention.

From 1960, the struggle for freedom of thought and expression has continued in five areas:

1. In the field of education, both in the public schools and in the colleges, teachers have been censored and dismissed for discussing openly such topics as civil liberties, race relations, labor relations, the United Nations, and religion. In certain localities, teachers fear to discuss many sensitive topics and questions, even to this day, and so free inquiry and free discussion (requirements for a liberal education) become impossible. During the 1970s, young people, and especially students in some high schools, were censored or suspended for talking openly about the Vietnam War or in any way protesting the war, such as by wearing an armband on which had been inscribed a peace symbol. The U.S. Supreme Court or circuit courts of appeal have handed down decisions declaring, among other things, that a student has a right to express his or her opinions in the classroom or on the campus if he or she does not interfere with appropriate discipline or interfere with the rights of others; that the wearing of an armband is "symbolic speech" and is protected under the First Amendment; that students may not be suspended for wearing buttons; that school officials may not claim that the wearing of long hair is "inherently distracting" to other students; and that students may publish and distribute their views.

2. Freedom of thought and expression have been violated by banning certain speakers on school campuses. "Black lists" and "gray lists" have been circulated of persons whose views were not approved by the group circulating the lists.

3. The issue of censorship has been a persistent one since 1960. Both obscene and antiestablishment literature can be inspected in bookstores

in some states. A disturbing wave of textbook and reading-list censorship has threatened not only to ban the writings of political revolutionaries, but to eliminate many controversial issues (evolution, sex education, etc.) and some important classics from public school teaching. These include works by Plato, Shakespeare, Thoreau, and Mark Twain.

4. Freedom of thought and expression in the area of security clearance has presented many problems during cold and hot wars. Security regulations are set up for those who serve the nation in either a civil or military capacity. No thoughtful person will deny the need for protecting the national security, but this protection may call at times for some limitation of our traditional values.

5. Finally, during the Cold War the investigating committees of various governmental agencies have tended to ignore the important principle of the separation of powers and functions and to act as prosecutors, juries, and judges as well as investigators. Among the safeguards for our freedoms are the following: that a person is innocent until proven guilty; that a person has a right to know the charges made against him or her; that one should be confronted by one's accusers and have a right to cross-examine them; and that a person has a right to a speedy and public trial, with counsel.

These five areas by no means exhaust the types of attacks on the principles of a free society, the principles embodied in the Bill of Rights. Today, the religious right has become publically connected and appears to be attempting to break down the traditional separation of church and state and label as socialist any person or group that has a concern for social justice. Evidence for this situation is found on such television shows as the "700 Club," with group members running for boards of education in many states, and the continuous pressure to put Christian prayer back into the public schools.

John Rawls, in his *A Theory of Justice*, comments:

There are firm constitutional protections for certain liberties, particularly freedom of speech and assembly, and liberty to form political associations. The principle of loyal opposition is recognized, the clash of political beliefs, and of the interests and attitudes that are likely to influence them, are accepted as a normal condition of human life. A lack of unanimity is a part of the circumstances of justice, since disagreement is bound to exist even among honest men who desire to follow much the same political principles. Without the conception of loyal opposition, and an attachment to constitutional rules which express and protect it, the politics of democracy cannot be properly conducted or long endure.

See also Inalienable Rights.

SOURCES

American Civil Liberties Union. "Freedom through Dissent." In *42nd Annual Report, July 1, 1961 to June 30, 1962*. New York: ACLU. 1963.

———. "To Secure: To Use: These Rights." In *43rd Annual Report, July 1, 1962 to June 30, 1963*. New York: ACLU. 1964.

Douglas, William O. *Freedom of the Mind*. Chicago: American Library Association in cooperation with the Public Affairs Committee. 1962.

Knight, Harold V. *With Liberty and Justice for All: The Meaning of the Bill of Rights Today*. Rev. ed. Dobbs Ferry, NY: Oceana Publications. 1968.

The National Council of Teachers of English. "The Students' Right to Read." Champaign, IL: NCTE. 1962.

President's Committee on Civil Rights. *To Secure These Rights*. Washington, D.C. 1947.

Rawls, John. *A Theory of Justice*. Cambridge, MA: Belknap Press of Harvard University Press. 1971.

Schwartz, Bernard, ed. *The Roots of the Bill of Rights.* 4 vols. New York: Chelsea House. 1971.

BIOETHICS

Bioethics is a broad field of inquiry encompassing medical ethics and the ethical critique of technology and its effects on human life, including human engineering and environmental ethics. The purpose of bioethics is not to remove disagreements altogether, but to illuminate vital questions for responsible choice. Fundamentally, bioethics pushes our preferences back to fundamental convictions about what is real and worthwhile and thus requires us to acknowledge the implications of our choices.

We must admit that society is moving with unrelenting swiftness into a future with which we have no heritage, as we do with the past. Some have said that the bombing of the World Trade Center in New York City and the Alfred P. Murrah Federal Building in Oklahoma City has brought America into a world of terror that other countries have been experiencing for some time. The world of science—of bomb making and terror making—that is now open to us all calls into question the values and institutions that have in the past controlled our erstwhile tendencies and actions. As new knowledge keeps piling up onto new knowledge, our ability to know, understand, and evaluate is diminished. In some subtle but dramatic ways we are inventing the future with no script or props. Improvements in science and technology have enriched the quality of our lives and, since 1970, have initiated a knowledge revolution that has moved from mainframes to personal computers and from research facilities to the nearest phone line in our homes. Refinements in health care, living conditions, medical science, and nutrition have increased the lifespan of the average human, but the downside is that they have decreased our ability to make sound ethical judgments due to a proliferation of choices.

As far back as 1954, J. Robert Oppenheimer saw this more closely than most: "One thing that is new is the prevalence of newness, the changing scale and scope of change itself, so that the world alters as we walk in it, so that the years of man's life measure not some small growth or rearrangement or moderation of what we learned in childhood, but a great upheaval." During the past 50 years, traditional ethical codes—secular and religious—have quickly become outdated as we faced new problems, especially in medicine, the use of disposable nuclear energy/waste, and the use of and disposal of other cancer-producing chemicals in business and industry. Only in the last 10 to 15 years have we begun building up a knowledge base in these sensitive areas, a knowledge base that is fast becoming a part of our reflective ethical judgments. Ethicists remind us that we are required to become students of change, but we also need to recognize our accountability for future consequences stemming from present actions. There is an urgent need for us to recognize our essential biological nature, that we live in a physical world in which our inner needs and goals will be balanced against an outer reality. This task is enormous and difficult, but it must be carried out if our humaneness is to grow and achieve full stature.

The survival of humankind as a humane and ethical species is at stake. V. R. Potter calls this future ethos *bioethics.* Julian Huxley refers to it as *evolutionary humanism,* and Thomas Dobehansky has labeled it *the biology of ultimate concern.* Regardless of what we call it, the development of this ethic is crucial and overdue. Two broad areas with which bioethics is concerned are *medical ethics* and *environmental ethics.*

MEDICAL ETHICS

With improvements in the medical sciences, contemporary ethicists face problems that individuals in the past have not faced, problems not covered in traditional secular or religious value codes, problems about which we are just now receiving enough information to make sound, reflective judgments. These problems include the following:

- Heart and organ transplants: From whom should they be taken and to whom should they be given?
- Kidney machines: Since they are limited in number and very expensive, who shall live and who shall be left to die?
- Artificial insemination: Should we build up sperm and ova banks? What is to be done with unused fertilized zygotes?
- Biological engineering to control heredity: What danger is there in the manipulation of the DNA molecules and our probable control of human future development?
- Use and control of outer space and the oceans: Who should own or control what?
- Automation, cybernation, and computers: Should we guarantee an income for those who cannot find work because machines have replaced them, and is this creating a new class system—those who can use computers and have access to them and those who cannot and do not have access to them?

In a rapidly changing world, human values also are in evolution. There is a need, according to ethicists, to bring our morals up to date and to close the gap between principles and practices. When controversies arise over what is good for health, the best type of marriage regulation, the effect of television and video games on children, fair trade practices in industry, and accessibility to technology and information, ethical principles by themselves do not provide all the answers or all the evidence on the basis of which decisions should be made.

Those who wish to come to reasonable conclusions about what is right and what is wrong in human conduct need to consult the moral experience of the past as well as the findings of the sciences and other disciplines that shed light on such subjects. The steps in thinking in science and morality may be similar—careful observation, analysis and classification, setting forth hypotheses, and testing those hypotheses—but the purpose to be achieved is different. The purpose of a revised moral code goes beyond the collection, analysis, and application of information to solve some human physical problem. Rather, a moral code is designed for the purpose of guiding human conduct into practices that are fair, just, and reflect a respect for human life and the environment.

Although moral codes are less than perfect, we have developed them as human guidelines for improved behavior toward others. When we encase our moral codes in stone and fail to revise them as needed, we are, as Alfred North Whitehead says, "shocked, or amused, by the sight of saintly old people hindering in the name of morality the removal of obvious brutalities from a legal system" (*Adventures of Ideas* 1933).

Experimentation was originally sanctioned by the natural sciences, but as soon as animate, feeling beings became the subject of experiments, as they did in the life sciences and especially in the medical arena, the innocence of the search was lost and questions of conscience arose. One difference between human experiments and physical (nonhuman) ones is this: the physical experiment employs small-scale, artificially devised substitutes for that about which knowledge is to be obtained, and the experimenter extrapolates from those models and simulated conditions to nature at large. For the most part, no such substitution is possible in the biological (including the human) sphere. We here must operate on the original self—the *real thing* in the fullest sense—and perhaps affect it irreversibly. Especially in the human sphere, experimentation loses entirely the advantage of the clear decision between vicarious model and true object. Up to a point, animals may fulfill the proxy role of the classical physical experiment, but in the end humans themselves must furnish knowledge about the human species, and the comfortable separation of non-committed experiment and definitive action vanishes.

There is in human experimentation always present a responsible, nonexperimental, definitive, person value when dealing with a subject. Not even the noblest purpose abrogates the ethical obligations this involves. By an appeal to "the common good," experimenters have been encouraged to use humans as their "guinea pigs." The ethical issue in bioethics is between the long-range interests of society, science, and progress on the one hand, and the moral rights of the individual on the other.

Bioethics brings to us the problem of the rights of the individual versus the rights of society. We concede, as a matter of course, to the common good some pragmatically determined measure of precedence over the individual good. In terms of rights, we let some of the basic rights of the individual be overruled by the acknowledged rights of society—as a matter of right and moral justice and not of mere force or dire necessity. But to make this concession, we must define the so-called common or public good and its potentially superior claims, to which the individual good must or might be sacrificed. It seems that *consent* is the most emphasized and examined concept in discussions of this issue. But if *society* has a right, its exercise is not contingent on volunteering. On the other hand, if volunteering is genuine, the public has no right over it. The question turns on the issue between the moral claims of a common good and society's right to that good and to the means of its realization. A moral claim requires consent; a right can do without it! Where consent is present anyway, the distinction may become im-

material, but without consent an uneasy situation exists for both sides.

ENVIRONMENTAL ETHICS

Bioethics also includes the environment. This may sound redundant, for medical ethics also includes the environment of humans and animals. In this section we turn to a specific ethical problem: environmental *quality*. A major issue is the use of fossil fuel for energy. Will any fossil fuel be left for future generations if humans continue using such fuels at the present rate? Some natural resources are today becoming scarce at a time when the disposal of wastes is an ever-increasing problem. What will be the results of recycling and recovering materials in wastes? In some cases, failure to conserve resources is not reversible. For example, the conversion of farmland to urban development is not a readily reversible process. Nor can we easily reverse the destruction of ecologically significant wetlands.

Purdom and Anderson encourage us to use zoning and land-use planning based on natural physical and ecological factors following the guidelines below:

- Determine environmentally sensitive areas and plan to protect and preserve them.
- Determine geophysical characteristics of soil and reserve prime agricultural land for that use.
- Identify naturally hazardous areas and restrict human settlement there or take special precautions to cope with hazards.
- Develop plans for extracting minerals and other natural deposits for the benefit of society.
- On the basis of terrain and geology, select suitable and efficient transportation corridors. These plans may have to be modified to avoid disrupting the social life of communities and to minimize environmental impact.
- On the basis of foundation conditions, select areas that are suitable for

construction of offices, residences, and factories.

- Determine the area's carrying capacity for human population and activity, considering water supply and its capacity to receive air and water pollution and solid wastes.
- Identify and reserve areas that are able to bear the impact of significant operations like electric power stations, heavy industries, and landfills for solid wastes.
- Examine all decisions to judge their combined impact on the area's ecology. Consider any related actions to a proposed plan, such as energy systems to sustain the population, transmission lines, and the like.
- Consider how natural resources and energy will be committed to the development plan.
- When planning for the amenities of life in the living environment, determine whether they are socially and culturally satisfying and necessary to an acceptable quality of life.

Considerations of individual freedom often arise when we ask such questions as "Should individuals be allowed to build homes in flood plains or where they are subject to earthquakes and mudslides?" "Should meats containing cancer-causing nitrites be allowed in our stores?" "Should industries be allowed to expose workers to toxic substances or to discharge pollutants of ill-defined toxicity into the environment?" An environmental ethic would require that individuals, corporations, and government agencies assume a responsibility to know the consequences of these actions and prevent any diverse results from ill-considered practices.

In 1965, a Gallup poll asked people in the United States to identify three national issues from a list of ten to which the government should give most of its attention. Air and water pollution ranked ninth. In a similar poll conducted after Earth Day in 1970, the environmental issue was sec-

ond. The group, Resources for the Future, repeated the survey in 1980. Unemployment was now in second place and the environment was sixth—still an important issue in the minds of people.

Although many people no longer view environmental protection as a crisis issue, surveys by the National Opinion Research Center revealed that 48 percent think we are spending too little on environmental concerns and 31 percent think we are spending about the right amount. As programs introduced in the 1970s resulted in improvements in environmental quality, the percent who believe we are spending "too little" declined. A new word—*ecology*—was coined to describe these programs, and today it is the term we most often use to refer to the relationship of an organism or a group of organisms to its environment. Ecology is one of the disciplines constituting the core of environmental science, and ecologists are interested in how organisms use resources, how living things interact, and the limits and possibilities of life. We might say that ecology is the study of these processes, while *environmental science* is the application of this knowledge to managing the environment. Another term often used is *deep ecology*, which spells out the moral/ethical nature of environmental protection.

Human behavior, and thus human ethics and values, is the cause as well as the solution of many environmental problems. For a person to have a satisfying quality of life and to exercise options to enhance that quality, several interrelated preconditions are necessary: adequate income, knowledge and skills, personal health, a healthy environment, positive social adjustment, and a code of ethics and values that support the attainment and maintenance of these factors. When individuals establish and then live by an environmental ethic that reflects their needs as well as the needs and satisfactions of others, a high quality of environment will be embodied in the culture.

See also Cyberspace.

SOURCES

Council on Environmental Quality. In *Environmental Quality—1980*. Washington, D.C. 1980.

Odum, E. P. *Fundamentals of Ecology*. Philadelphia: W. B. Saunders. 1971.

Purdom, P. Walton, and S. H. Anderson. *Environmental Science*. 2d ed. Columbus, OH: Charles E. Merrill. 1983.

U.S. Department of Health, Education, and Welfare, 1968. "Proceedings: Symposiums on Human Ecology." Washington, D.C. 1968.

U.S. Environmental Protection Agency, 1973. "The Quality of Life Concept." Washington, D.C. 1973.

BIOLOGICAL WARFARE

See Chemical-Biological-Radiological Warfare.

BIRTH CONTROL

In 1962, one of the important biological discoveries affecting the future of the family was "the pill," which women could take to prevent pregnancy. The pill set in motion a contraceptive revolution. Prior to the introduction of the pill, more than three-quarters of all fertility control was by one of three methods: the condom, the diaphragm, or rhythm—which means avoiding intercourse during a portion of the menstrual cycle. By 1970, two-thirds of all women in the United States had tried the pill, with half of all women and two-thirds of younger women still using it. Other prevalent methods of birth control include the intrauterine device (IUD) and sterilization. Some people use abortion as a "backup" strategy. Sterilization is the fastest-growing contraceptive method among couples who have had all the children they want. In 1965, 12 percent of such couples in the United States had been sterilized, and by 1970 the percentage was 18. Only three years later it had risen to 29 percent, and by 1982 it was 41 percent of contracepting couples (39 percent of married couples). Of interest is the fact that this is not a female phenomenon: the sterilized were about half women and half men. Thus, one can safely say that changes in fertility (birth control) have been revolutionary, not just evolutionary. Kathryn Kelly and Donn Byrne (*Exploring Human Sexuality*) remind us that the statistics on unwanted and unplanned pregnancies are alarming. They comment: "Of the babies born each year in the United States, over 13 percent are born to young women in their teens, including .3 percent under age 15. An average of 3,231 women have abortions each day. Every twenty-four hours, 2,740 adolescent pregnancies begin. Our country spends over $16 billion yearly on teenage mothers and their offspring in the form of welfare payments and other benefits." This information suggests that a great many maladaptive decisions are being made, which, as Kelly and Byrne point out, makes the emotions and experiences of persons as important as the statistical data.

TRENDS

- The number of births per family has dropped dramatically over the course of U.S. history. From a high of eight children per mother in colonial days, fertility dropped to two per mother by the 1920s, and other than a slight upturn in the 1950s, the birthrate has continued to drop to about 18 births per 1,000 people (on average).
- Between 1830 and 1870, information about contraceptive devices circulated widely.
- In 1900, fertility for U.S. women stood at 3.34 children on average,

half of what it was a century earlier. However, that same year, among professionals, half had two or fewer children, and ten years later that figure was almost two-thirds.

- Between 1940 and 1960 there was a rise in birthrates; from World War II, one additional child per family, on average, would continue for some 15 years (they were called the *Baby Boomers*).
- During the 1980s there was another small rise *(boomlet)* in birthrates. This is explained by the number of Baby Boomers passing through their childbearing years at that time. Perhaps more important is to explain why the rise was as small as it was, from about 13 children per 1,000 population in the 1970s, to 16.6 per 1,000 in 1990. Among other things this means that, while a larger proportion of the U.S. population was of childbearing age, there was no apparent rise in the number of children per fecund woman.

ISSUES

1. *Nonmarital pregnancy.* In 1981, a study of sexually active women revealed that 28 percent used no contraception, 26 percent used the condom, 21 percent used withdrawal, 20 percent used the pill, and 5 percent used other methods. Only 13 percent said they used some form of protection every time they had sex. Today, it is estimated that perhaps 1 million teenagers become pregnant each year in the United States, 80 percent of them unmarried at the time and some 30,000 under the age of 15. If the current trend continues, 40 percent of all women will become pregnant before they reach 20.

2. *Nonmarital births.* In 1940 there were 100,000 births in the United States outside of marriage. By 1973 this figure was 400,000, and by 1980 a full million. Part of this is due to the fact that during this period the number of fecund women almost doubled. In the 1985 *Current Population Survey,* 62 percent of nonmarital births for white women were to never-married women, and 84 percent for black women.

On an August 24, 1971, television program, the interviewer asked his guest, a woman newspaper columnist, to comment on the saying that "This is the last married generation." This question signaled that a sexual revolution was in high gear in the United States. So far we have talked about trends and social issues, about changing attitudes and practices among certain population segments. But what *should* they be? This is a question calling into consideration both ethics and values. Perhaps the best way to address the "should" question is to spell out the type of issues that require choice making. These will involve assumptions about what is right and good.

The first type of issue is about what is right and good. Consider the Catholic view that marriage is a sacrament that creates a sacred union of husband and wife. The central function of this union is procreation, and the enjoyment of sexual relations is to serve that end, not the pleasure of the partners for its own sake. Only in that relationship are sexual relationships considered right. Attempts to prevent conception are therefore prohibited because they interfere with the purpose of marriage. Attempts to end pregnancy after conception are viewed as murder—as morally wrong—for the fetus is a living human being. The ideals and values of the Roman Catholic religion are a matter of spiritual law to which they consider temporal authority subordinate.

A quite different example of the sources of controversy about the correct or best ways of regulating sexual and marital relationships is the activity of Christian and political conservatives. As far back as 1969, in a Christian Crusade, the John Birch Society adopted the slogan, "Is the schoolhouse the proper place to teach raw sex?" The Reverend Billy James Hargis commented to a rally of conservative Americans in Boston that "I don't want any kid under 12 to hear about lesbians, homosexuals, and sexual intercourse. They should be concerned with tops, yo-yos, and hide-and-seek." He, too, saw the drive to provide sex education as "part of a gigantic conspiracy to bring down America from within." He claimed that being for sex education in the public schools was the same as advocating free love, loose morals, and liberal permissiveness.

There are other points of view. For example, in 1967 Harriet Van Horne felt that the sexual revolution was given too much good press and not enough searching analysis. Conceding many changes resulting from higher education for women, higher incomes, urbanization, growing slums, low-quality schools, the pill, and the decline of parental and church authority, she asked why we do not also mention the "increasing vulgarization of sex by the mass media and the wanton misreading of Freud" on the dangers of repression. She complained that the media promotes sex for sex's sake, for pleasure without responsibility. She also felt that there are false prophets who argue that there are no immoral persons or amoral societies, but only different moral systems. She commented that many who appear happy and free are, in fact, lonesome and lost; "they need love desperately and sex is not doing anything for them."

These reports and commentaries, coming at the peak of the sexual revolution and tied to the sexual freedom provided by the pill, raise many questions still important today: whether unconcern for others may play a larger role in the sexual revolution than the concern for more meaningful relationships; whether promiscuity rather than more meaningful mating relationships may be more widespread than is admitted by the researchers; whether the researchers have injected their own value biases into their surveys; whether the plea for respect for divergent moral systems may actually be a plot to undermine the strength of society; whether the preoccupation of mass media with the sensations of the sexual revolution may be having the effect of promoting irresponsible faddism; and what the actual consequences of these changes will be when we really begin to understand them adequately.

Current debates on issues of abortion, contraception, and modes of fertilization are not viewed as a sign of a breakdown in U.S. society or the family as strongly as they were 25 years ago. Many today view dialogue as a valuable tool for strengthening society and the family for they bring with them a promising reevaluation of institutions, a gradually growing clarity as to the many values that are affected and must be given consideration and attention, and a capability in our society for struggling with these problems while we go forward, acting upon divergent postulates and conflicting opinions concerning the facts. Ours is a multiethnic, multireligious, multivalue based society and, as Martin Buber said, dialogue is the connecting link, the common ground, between ourselves and the many others who may or may not share our point of view. To build a common value and ethical base requires a searching and a sharing of ideas and beliefs, a seeking of points of agreement, and a certain tolerance for difference. Ethics does not imply sameness or total agreement with the actions and beliefs of others.

SOURCES

Hechinger, Fred M. "Storm Over the Teaching of Sex." *New York Times* (September 1969): Education Section, 7.

Kelley, Kathryn, and Donn Byrne. *Exploring Human Sexuality.* Englewood Cliffs: Prentice-Hall. 1992.

Rubin, Lillian B. *Erotic Wars: What Happened to the Sexual Revolution?* New York: Harper Collins. 1990.

Skolnick, Arlene S., and Jerome H. Skolnick, eds. *Family in Transition.* 8th ed. New York: Harper Collins. 1994.

Van Horne, Harriet. "A Commentary by Harriet Van Horne: The Sexual Revolution—in Living Color." *McCalls* 95 (October 1967): 46.

BLACK MUSLIM

See Nation of Islam.

BLACK POWER

Black Power is essentially black consciousness, an umbrella term that when set against the backdrop of riots in the North in the 1950s and 1960s signaled to many that the Civil Rights movement was over. Black Power was born not of black but of white violence. On June 6, 1966, James Meredith was carrying out a one-person march from Memphis, Tennessee, to Jackson, Mississippi, to encourage fellow blacks to overcome their own fears and vote now that the Voting Rights Act was law. During that march an unidentified assailant shot and wounded Meredith. This was a call to blacks throughout the country, many of whom immediately continued the march, being led by Martin Luther King, Jr., of the Southern Christian Leadership Conference, Floyd McKissick of CORE, and Stokely Carmichael of the Student Nonviolent Coordinating Committee. Responding to King's pressure, the march was opened to whites. This was the last integrated effort by all the major civil rights organizations.

Of course, frustration had set in among blacks, and King had noticed that they had begun quarreling among themselves. But unity came to black consciousness and it was the aching feet of a Negro woman (Rosa Parks) that fused black consciousness into Black Power. Why did the phrase *Black Power* frighten whites and offend so many blacks? It was not really new. The National Advisory Commission on Civil Disorders correctly identified it as old wine in new bottles. Black consciousness was not new, even if the phrase was. A survey of Detroit blacks in 1967 showed many confused or vague about the concept. But to many whites, the meaning was crystal clear: Black Power signaled to many that the Civil Rights movement was over. In a 1966 interview, Carmichael declared:

> We've got to fight separately now because we've never done anything on our own. . . . Things have been all white too long. . . . Integration has always been Negroes going to white schools because the white schools are good, and black schools are bad. . . . If integration means moving to something white is moving to something better, the integration is a subterfuge for white supremacy.

Carmichael went on to say: "Before a group can enter the open society, it must first close ranks. . . . Group solidarity is necessary before a group can operate effectively from a bargaining position of strength in a pluralistic society."

Eventually, Black Power was accepted among blacks and whites. The phrase implied endorsing black control of the political, economic, and social institutions in black communities. Black Power presented to the Civil Rights movement a restructuring of society as the priority item on the black agenda.

Of course, there were differences of opinion even in the black community. Black Power clearly operated outside the conventional system with the organization of the Black Panther Party in October 1966 in Oakland, California. The organizers were Huey Newton, age 24, and Bobby Seale, age 30. Their purpose was to protect blacks from police abuse. Controversial from the beginning—1969 to 1972

—internal problems, trials involving most of its leaders, and several shootouts with police combined to bring the organization to a standstill. Newton admitted in 1973 that the party had alienated blacks and had become too radical to be a part of the black community. The militant Black Panther Party encountered severe difficulties during the 1970s and fell victim to both internal political problems and external surveillance. Finally, their former outspoken leaders moved in new directions.

See also Civil Rights Movement.

SOURCES

"Attack on the Conscience." In *Bridges and Borders: Diversity in America. Readings from Time Magazine, 1923–1994.* New York: Time Warner Books. 1994.

Cross, Theodore. *The Black Power Imperative.* New York: Faulkner Books. 1984.

Killian, L. M. *The Impossible Revolution, Phase 2: Black Power and the American Dream.* New York: Random House. 1975.

Wilson, William J. *The Declining Significance of Race: Blacks and Changing American Institutions.* 2d ed. Chicago: University of Chicago Press. 1980.

BLUE-COLLAR WORKER

Blue-collar worker refers to those who execute a work order rather than to those who plan the work. Owners and managers normally wore white shirts and ties. Speaking of the class of "white-collar" managers, Robert B. Reich said: "Those specialized thinkers were to be sharply distinguished from the rest of the work force. Planning was to be distinct from execution, brain distinct from brawn, head from hand, white collar from blue collar." On the one side stood the professional managers who were responsible for developing, implementing, and monitoring the scientific-management principles that governed the production process. On the other side stood the workers, supervisors, and foremen who were responsible for the day-to-day operation of the plant.

Between 1870 and 1920, the United States was transformed from an agrarian society to the most powerful industrial economy in the world. As U.S. industry increased, the small craft shops and family-run businesses of the nineteenth century disappeared. Such rapid growth over such a short time created a crisis: trained blue-collar labor was now in short supply. With such rapid growth, corruption began to creep into the production process, while productivity lagged far behind the demand for products. There was a need for new technologies and new work arrangements to make the most of the abundance of untrained workers and machines.

The breakthrough came when industrialists discovered that they must simplify the tasks of individual workers while increasing the power and control of a relatively small number of managers. This simple solution, carried to its logical extreme by Frederick Winslow Taylor, the father of U.S. "scientific management," proved to be one of the most consequential organizational discoveries of the century. Taylor said, "In the past man has been first; in the future, the system must be first." In 1990, Peter Senge carried the system-model to completion in his best seller, *The Fifth Discipline.* Returning to Taylor's theories for the moment, we find that he advocated dividing all jobs into small, discrete tasks, each one easy to learn and none dependent upon the workers' skills. Workers were to be provided with detailed instructions from which they were forbidden to deviate. Once jobs had been subdivided into their smallest possible components, it would be possible to determine "the one best way" to perform a task. Jobs would be standardized and routinized according to "scientific" principles.

In 1914, at the height of his popularity, Taylor spoke to an estimated 69,000 people attending an efficiency exposition at the Grand Central Palace in New York City. Taylorism catapulted the United States into the second stage of the Industrial Revolution—the era that divided the work force into management and workers, the latter becoming known as blue-collar workers.

On May 10, 1876, the tolling of the bell in Independence Hall sounded the beginnings of the nation's centennial celebration. Unlike the 1776 celebration, the theme in 1876 had turned from "freedom" to "progress." In the central exhibition hall of the Centennial Fair in New York City was the gigantic Corliss machine, 30 feet high and weighing 700 tons, which was able to release 1,400 horsepower units of energy to provide power for all the fair's exhibits. This engine symbolized the spirit of the centennial, which focused upon a future of unlimited power and energy. In 1876, the Industrial Revolution ideal was of a productive national economy, smoothly and efficiently integrating the physical power of the machine with the social power of a machinelike institution, the corporation. By 1914, Taylorism had effectively divided the work force into managers and blue-collar workers. In 1956, the number of managers (white-collar workers) in middle-class occupations surpassed for the first time in U.S. history the number of blue-collar workers.

SOURCES

Bravermon, Harry. *Labor and Monopoly Capital: The Degradation of Work in the Twentieth Century.* New York: Monthly Review Press. 1974.

Carroll, Peter N., and David W. Noble. *The Free and the Unfree: A New History of the United States.* 2d ed. New York: Penguin. 1988.

Leinberger, Paul, and Bruce Tucker. *The New Individualists.* New York: HarperCollins. 1991.

Reich, Robert B. *The Next American Frontier.* New York: Times Books. 1983.

Senge, Peter. *The Fifth Discipline.* New York: Doubleday. 1990.

BRADLEY, F. H.

The most subtle and best known of the English idealistic thinkers, F. H. Bradley (1846–1924), presented his metaphysical system in his book *Appearance and Reality* (1893) and his ethics in his book *Ethical Studies* (1876). Bradley's ethics is one of self-realization formulated in the metaphysical context of absolute idealism. With this he remains within the Platonic domain. According to Bradley, the ethical end or purpose is not only the realization of the self, but of the self as a *whole*. The individual can only fulfill himself or herself by relating his/her finite ends to ever wider and more inclusive ends, which ultimately are embraced in the infinite absolute whole. With Bradley we find metaphysical consistency: the ultimate end of morality coincides with the ultimate reality and there ethics and metaphysics are convergent. Bradley tells his readers, "Realize yourself as an infinite whole," which means, says Bradley, "realize yourself as the self-conscious member of an infinite whole, by realizing that whole in yourself."

In any sort of metaphysicalism there is mystery, intuition, and abstractness. So in Bradley we discover the *infinite whole* referred to as the *absolute* and the absolute as *the ideal toward which we direct our moral activities*. To bring concreteness to his ethics, Bradley says that there are also intermediate wholes that promote the moral development of the individual and social groups of which the individual is a member, such as the family, community, or the society to which one belongs. Every person can voluntarily and consciously pursue activities that promote the interests and well-being of the group to which he/she already belongs. In so doing, the person realizes a larger self than the self of his or her own personal or private interests, and at the same time promotes the welfare of the communal group. Membership in these groups embodies a system of duties and concomitant rights.

One will note the apparent relativism in Bradley's ethic: one's moral obligations are relative to the group or society into which he/she was born and to which he/she now belongs. His ethic is not an individualism, but a defense of an aristocratic, caste-type system of morality reflective of one's "station" in life. In the 1950s and 1960s, the adoption of a particular society's or culture's moral point of view and then making it the criteria by which all other ethics are to be judged was called *ethnocentrism* by ethical philosophers. Ethnocentrism may be embodied in the rules and regulations definitive of a particular social caste, as in Bradley, or in a particular religion when that religion is held up as the judge of all morality to the exclusion of other criteria and/or points of view. In the 1960s and 1970s, the writings of Kurt Baier and Kai Nielsen were focused on discovering a more widely acceptable or universal criteria upon which to build the point of view of morality. The serious student of contemporary ethics will need to read these two philosophers, as well as the many others to whom they reacted and who reacted to them. Nielsen's conceptualization of *wide reflective equilibrium*, which seeks a broad, rational base for ethics, and Baier's conceptualization of *the moral point of view* represent excellent starting places for this study.

See also Ethics, Theory of.

SOURCES

Bradley, F. H. *Ethical Studies*. London: Oxford University Press. 1970.

Frankena, William K., and John T. Granrose, eds. *Introductory Readings in Ethics*. Englewood Cliffs, NJ: Prentice-Hall. 1974.

Hudson, W. D. *Modern Moral Philosophy*. Garden City, NY: Doubleday & Company. 1970.

BROWN V. BOARD OF EDUCATION

Before 1954, for the majority of black children living in the United States, public school education meant attending segregated schools, most of which were inadequate. Southern school districts assigned children to school by their race, rather than their neighborhood, a practice that constitutes *de jure* segregation. It was this form of legal humiliation that was attacked in the landmark decree of *Linda Brown et al. v. Board of Education of Topeka*.

Seven-year-old Linda Brown was not permitted to enroll in the grade school four blocks from her home in Topeka, Kansas. She was required to attend the black school almost two miles from her home. This denial led the National Association for the Advancement of Colored People (NAACP) Legal Defense and Educational Fund to bring suit on behalf of Linda Brown and 12 other black children. The NAACP argued that the Fourteenth Amendment to the U.S. Constitution was intended to rule out segregation in public schools. This suit was supported by briefs filed by labor, Jewish organizations, and the solicitor general of the United States, who represented the federal government. The NAACP brief contained statements by 32 social scientists describing the harm of segregated education. Thereafter Chief Justice Earl Warren presented the unanimous opinion that "in the field of public education the doctrine of separate but equal has no place. Separate educational facilities are inherently unequal."

Twenty years later, Linda Brown (now Linda Brown Smith), looking back on that 1954 decision, correctly recorded its significance: "After 100 years of bondage, this was the key to the beginning of freedom."

See also Civil Rights Movement.

SOURCES

Commission on Civil Rights. *Twenty Years after Brown: The Shadows of the Past.* Washington, D.C.: U.S. Government Printing Office. 1974.

Franklin, John Hope. *From Slavery to Freedom: A History of Negro Americans.* 5th ed. New York: Alfred A. Knopf. 1980.

BUBER, MARTIN

Martin Buber's long life of 87 years (1878–1965) spanned a time in world history that suffered extraordinarily violent upheavals and changes. Not only the devastating wars of the twentieth century, but the immense revolutions in thought and in technology—which introduced terror as well as possibilities whose results can scarcely be exaggerated—painted the backdrop of Buber's life and intellectual achievements. The most decisive personal meeting of Buber's life took place in the early 1920s. This was with Franz Rosenzweig, the leader of the Free Jewish Academy in Frankfurt am Main (Germany). Rosenzweig was a Jew to the core of his being, and at the same time, a precursor of what was to become *existentialism.* He and Buber worked together to translate the Jewish Bible into modern German, which left a lasting mark on of the whole of German Jewry.

Brought up in the Jewish tradition in central Europe, Buber experienced the last phase of the Enlightenment, endured the violence of the antihuman Nazi regime in Germany, and spent the last 27 years of his life in Palestine. From 1916 until 1924 Buber edited the journal *Der Jude,* which he established in order to further the spiritual and cultural realities underlying the political aspirations of Zionism. From 1926 until 1930 he edited, along with Joseph Wittiz and Viktor von Weizsacker, a journal, *Die Kreatur,* which was devoted to problems common to all different religions.

In 1923, Buber was appointed professor for Jewish History of Religion and Ethics at Frankfurt University. This was later enlarged to include the History of Religions. In 1933, his professorship was taken from him by the Nazis. From that time until 1938 Buber lived in the village of Heppenheim in Germany. In 1938, he went to Palestine to accept the call to be professor of sociology at the Hebrew University of Jerusalem. He was 60 years of age.

Now began the time of Buber's greatest intellectual activity. Fighting incessantly for true Hebrew humanism, which included Arab-Jewish cooperation in Palestine, Buber struggled to redirect the Jewish Diaspora to its one true and common source in the Bible. His greatest work lay beyond the schools and universities and focused on a life of trust in God: "God is to be seen in everything, and reached by every pure deed." Thus he summarized the teaching of Hasidism. In 1953, Buber made the following comment:

> I believe, despite all, that the people in this hour can enter into dialogue, into a genuine dialogue with one another. In a genuine dialogue each of the partners, even when he stands in opposition to the other, heeds, affirms, and confirms his opponent as an existing other. Only so is it possible for conflict, though not to be eliminated from the world, yet to be subject to human arbitration, and so led to the point where it is overcome.

In Maurice Friedman's 1958 biography of Buber, *Martin Buber: The Life of Dialogue,* Buber himself says in the foreword to the first volume of the German edition that there is not much in his writings that might be called a "work" in the sense of something "complete and not pointing beyond itself." This meant for him that his thought is bound up with his actions, being molded by them, and in turn molding them and illustrating them. It also means that his writings form an interlocking unity. For Buber, this unity is found in God. He says, "True address from God directs man into the place of lived speech, where the voices of the creature grope past one another, and in their very missing of one another succeed in reaching the eternal partner."

Also, leaving aside for the present the profound complexity of Buber's thought about God, we may note also that he looks for an understanding of man in and through the limitations of everyday life. Buber's view is that it is only in the manifold concreteness of existence, and precisely in its ordinariness, that reality is disclosed—that is, as lived reality. He comments: "I possess nothing but the everyday out of which I am never taken. The mystery is no longer disclosed, it has escaped or it has made its dwelling here, where everything happens as it happens. I know no fullness but each mortal hour's fullness of claim and responsibility."

SOURCES

Buber, Martin. *Good and Evil*. New York: Charles Scribner's Sons. 1953.
———. *I and Thou*. 2d ed. New York: Charles Scribner's Sons. 1970.
———. *Between Man and Man*. Boston: Beacon Press. 1955.
Friedman, M. *Martin Buber: The Life of Dialogue*. New York: Harper & Row. 1960.

BUSINESS ETHICS

Capitalism is the economic system in the United States, Canada, most of Europe, and in many Asian countries. It is based on the belief that emphasizes the private ownership of the instruments of production, distribution, and exchange, and their operation under a plan of open competition and individual initiative, for private profit, with a minimum of governmental interference. Capitalism rests on four main doctrines: free enter-

prise, competition, the profit motive, and the right to private property.

In the twentieth century the changes within the industrial system have taken place so rapidly and have been so far-reaching that older terms, such as *capitalism* and the *free enterprise system*, do not apply very accurately anymore. As the Industrial Revolution has gone through successive stages, orthodox capitalism has given way to liberal capitalism, regulated capitalism, and the welfare state. The curious thing is that while the system and its operations have changed drastically, the doctrine of capitalism has remained relatively unchanged for many years—the desire for profits. In the nineteenth century, Adam Smith's rigorous economic theory succeeded in systematizing the tradition that brought forth modern capitalism. According to Smith, self-interest is "the basis rather than the nemesis of moral ends and hence of legitimate political rule; embodied labor no longer distinguishes natural from unnatural economic pursuits but characterizes all economic life; far from indicating an unstable government, credit and national debt are shown to presuppose political stability; the standing army is proven to ensure the liberty of all propertied owners." Finally, in Smith's system, the lack of constraint that conservatives feared as a sign of political decline becomes the opportunity for economic growth. Allen Kaufman observes that "for Smith, the true impetus of social life is the human being's propensity to 'truck, barter, and exchange'; sociopolitical activity is both economic and historical" (*Capitalism, Slavery, and Republican Values: American Political Economists, 1819–1848*).

In the United States, the idea developed that business must observe a high standard of ethics. High standards of responsibility to the community such as truth in advertising, giving the customer his/her money's worth, fair pricing, and quality products and services have become standards for ethical practice—"or your money back"—that have replaced the ancient business principle, "Let the buyer beware."

In spite of the advantages of capitalism—never have so many had so much—there is considerable dissatisfaction with modern industrial society. The four major criticisms are the following:

- Extreme and unjust inequality concerning the unequal distribution of wealth results in the unequal distribution of power; the control of avenues of opinion (radio, newspapers, television, magazines, etc.), which are business enterprises first, whose policies are determined in part by monetary considerations; the unequal distribution of risks to life, limb, and health; and the unequal distribution of physical labor.
- Waste and lack of planning from a human point of view results in an abundance of food, clothing, and other good things for some and not for others. A part of the answer to this problem is that the purpose of the economy—to supply human needs—has been obscured by the desire to make money.
- Overemphasis on the acquisitive motive often results in an emphasis on the profit motive to the neglect of other values. A pressing ethical problem is to discover the conditions under which the profit motive may serve the enrichment of personality and not just the acquisition of more wealth.
- One criticism of the Industrial Revolution is that it has produced a lopsided society, not only of haves and have-nots, but also an abundance of those who have a technological mentality, created by the industrial-scientific-military complex, as opposed to the emotional and personal needs of individuals that must be expressed or met. When the drive for profit, power, and acquisition become the dominant goals of a society, the soci-

ety becomes indifferent to human need; it builds up a great deal of resentment; many of its people become alienated from common and important values and events; and there is a defiance of authority and an extension of the area of violence.

Specific unethical practices leading to the four characteristics above are the following:

- Adulteration or the misrepresentation of merchandise;
- Creating false values through misleading advertising;
- Bribery in business and politics;
- Price-fixing and market rigging;
- Planned obsolescence; and
- The opposition, by business, of effective legislation intended to protect the public good.

Frances Moore Lappe (*Rediscovering America's Values*) asks, "Does capitalism embody moral values?" She then reminds us that democratic capitalism doesn't deny the existence of moral qualities in people, it just doesn't depend on them in economic life. As Smith saw it, self-interest is the best economic guide. Although establishing a common set of moral values is the goal of other economic systems, capitalism is different in allowing morality to remain the province of individual persons.

Since the beginning of this century, there has been a constant demand on the part of enlightened business leaders and the public for improvements in business standards. This movement has expressed itself in such diverse ways as Theodore Roosevelt's campaign against corruption, the emphasis on the "social gospel" in churches, and the development of ethics for business and professional groups. Organizations like the Better Business Bureau, the Federal Trade Commission, and service clubs like the Rotarians have been active in promoting higher ethical standards. Rotarians have, for example, developed "The Four-Way Test" as a simple measuring device that may be applied to find out whether any proposed plans, policies, statements, or actions are right or wrong. This test is stated in four questions: Is it the truth? Is it fair to all concerned? Will it build good will and better friendship? Will it be beneficial to all concerned?

Writing in the fifth edition of their *Ethics for Today*, Titus and Keeton comment: "Institutions do not exist as ends in themselves; they derive their value from their contribution to human welfare." Accepting this perspective, business ethics function to bring a sense of fair play and justice to the capitalist system. In the United States there has been an uneasy marriage between democracy, as a system of moral/political control, and capitalism, as an aggressive economic system based on greed and human desire. At least the idea of ethics in business gives us pause for thought and cautions us to make our decisions not merely from the motive of profit, but out of a genuine concern for the welfare of others as well.

See also Adulteration; Capitalism and the Information Revolution; Consumerism.

SOURCES

Bellah, Robert N., et al. *Habits of the Heart: Individualism and Commitment in American Life.* Berkeley: University of California Press. 1985.

Galbraith, John Kenneth. *The New Industrial State.* 2d ed. Boston: Houghton Mifflin. 1971.

Muller, Herbert J. *The Children of Frankenstein: A Primer on Modern Technology and Human Values.* Bloomington, IN: Indiana State University Press. 1970.

Titus, Harold H., and Morris T. Keeton. *Ethics for Today.* 5th ed. New York: Van Nostrand. 1973.

CALVIN, JOHN

John Calvin (1509–1564) was born in Nayon in Picardy, France, where it has been said citizens were known for their independence of mind. Calvin studied theology and law, and was early acquainted with Renaissance humanism. He continued his studies of humanism and literature in Paris, where he joined a humanistic society that spent its time discussing the doctrines of Luther. These associations led to an early departure from Paris and travels in Italy, Germany, and Switzerland. It was at Basel, in 1536, that he published the *Institutes of the Christian Religion*, which was probably the greatest Protestant document ever written. This led to a rise in Bibliocracy, which enabled theologians to study the Divine Word and led to vindications of Protestant doctrine against the calumnies of the Catholic Church and the persecutions of kings.

Calvin was called to Geneva, a Protestant stronghold, to bring some religious order. He appealed to the New Testament for doctrine, discipline, and church organization. He asserted that both church and state were divine and were to serve divine purposes on earth. The state was not to meddle in church affairs, but since the state did exist to serve divine ends, it was bound to bring its force to bear on securing of

proper worship and the maintenance of public morality. It was the church, however, that decided what was true, so that in practice the state became the servant of the church. Calvin believed that he saw in the Bible a blueprint for a new society and set out, in the sixteenth century, to establish that society in Geneva. The teachings of Calvin are strongly represented in the teachings of both the Presbyterian and Baptist churches and are found sprinkled through much of Protestantism throughout the world.

SOURCES

Kaufmann, Walter, ed. *Religion from Tolstoy to Camus*. New York: Harper Torchbooks. 1961.

Wells, Donald A. *God, Man, and the Thinker*. New York: Dell. 1962.

CAPITAL PUNISHMENT

A major problem about the morality of killing is whether the state can ever be justified in imposing the death penalty on criminals, and if so, on what grounds and for which crimes. Another way of asking this, perhaps more philosophically, is whether any nonreversible action is ever right, and if so, what reasons can be given to support it. For the utilitarian, the death penalty is like all punishment, at best a "necessary evil" justified by what it does rather than by what it is. Thus capital punishment, for the utilitarian, can be justified only on the grounds that of its total consequences for society in general, the good outbalances its immediate evil—the pain, suffering, and anxiety of the criminal and any loved ones, and the deprivation of whatever happiness the criminal's future life might have held in store.

What punishment does when it works is: (1) keeps dangerous criminals off the streets and deprives them, at least for a time, of all opportunity to repeat their crimes; (2) persuades them, either through fear of repeated punishment or by means of genuine repentance and moral reform, not to repeat their crimes; and (3) makes credible the threat of punishment to other would-be transgressors and thus deters them from committing the crimes they might otherwise be tempted to try. But this is the ideal situation: by means of incapacitation, reform, and deterance, the total number of crimes is reduced, and the great amounts of suffering caused to the victims of crimes diminished. This is the ideal utilitarian point of view.

Capital punishment is, of course, the ultimate in incapacitation; on the other side, it is a total failure as a reforming treatment for the criminal, since one cannot improve people by killing them. Almost all of the disagreement over the consequences of capital punishment is over the extent to which it succeeds in performing its third utilitarian function—that of deterring others. Some have argued, and reasonably so, that imposing capital punishment on convicted murderers can be justified if and only if it seems necessary to save the lives of innocent human beings. In this view, the more lives saved the better, since all human life, after all, is sacred. And if circumstances force us to choose between the innocent and the lives of guilty murderers, then reluctantly we must choose to save the innocent. Consistently, we are forced to make this choice only if we believe that killing the murderers we have in our clutches now will deter other potential murderers and thus save innocent lives. If we hold this belief in the deterrent efficiency of capital punishment and still refuse to execute murderers, then we are deliberately saving some known guilty lives at the cost of permitting a larger number of (still unknown) innocent lives to be lost. This, too, would violate the principle of the sanctity of human life. Even so, it hasn't been established that the death penalty succeeds in deterring potential murderers.

Another consideration, other than the pragmatic and sociological reasons, is the problems associated with the morality of killing that involves guilt and desert. A *retributivist* is a person who argues that the primary justification for any punishment is that the criminal *deserves* it and not for any future benefit or advantage. Thus, a deliberate murderer deserves to be killed, whatever the effect on deterrence. James Fitzjames Stephen, the eminent Victorian jurist, argued strongly in favor of capital punishment because vengeance deserves its "legitimate satisfaction," and because the murderer should be exterminated.

On the other hand, the American judge Curtis Bok opposed capital punishment because he believed that to execute is not to punish. Punishment, he argued, expresses a stern moral judgment; it implies that the criminal could have avoided the evil deed; and it is typically accompanied by dread and anguish, if not guilt and remorse. It would be unfair to execute a person suffering from "moral illness or deficiency."

The moral problem comes to this: the uncertainty of moral principles themselves and our definition of *person*. We may be confident, for example, that it is wrong to kill a certain kind of being in a certain set of circumstances *if* that being is a person, *but* we may be quite bewildered about how to go about deciding whether it is a person or not. So, our confusion may not be about the content of the moral principle so much as about whether any of the principles *apply at all*. We see this in cases about killing animals and fetuses, but in the case of a living human being who has been convicted of murder, we are not always certain. Thus, we appeal to such reasons as utilitarian considerations, personal freedom, and the sanctity of life. The relative "weights" we give to each of these considerations, whether we hold to one of them or espouse a mixed moral theory, are variables in our decision to kill or not to kill as in capital punishment.

SOURCES

Bedau, Hugo, ed. *The Death Penalty in America*. Garden City, NY: Doubleday. 1964.

Marx, Karl. "Capital Punishment." In *Marx and Engels: Basic Writings on Politics and Philosophy*. Edited by F. Feuer. Garden City, NY: Doubleday. 1959.

Sellin, T., ed. *Capital Punishment*. New York: Harper & Row. 1967.

CAPITALISM AND THE INFORMATION REVOLUTION

Capitalism is an economic system in which individuals and businesses develop, own, and control much of a country's physical capital. It has been and is the major economic system in the United States and the other top industrial nations in the world. Ironically, capitalism, based on the profit motive, and democracy, based on principles of equality and fairness, coexist in a tentative and uneasy relationship. Out of this relationship has come the development of suburbia and a new-found individualism.

In a landmark study of suburbia, *Crabgrass Frontier*, urban historian Kenneth Jackson argues that the suburbanization of the United States is largely the result of the interaction of market dynamics, governmental policies, and certain values among America's middle class, including racial prejudice and a pervasive fondness for grass and solitude. Jackson identifies six key factors that encourage this growth:

1. Americans enjoy one of the highest standards of living in the world, possess unprecedented per capita wealth, and therefore can afford the relative wastefulness of suburban sprawl.
2. Cheap and plentiful land around American cities encourages large-scale speculative developments.
3. Inexpensive transportation, most notably the automobile, enables Americans to commute between their place of work and their homes in suburbia.
4. Balloon-frame construction dramatically lowered the material and labor costs of home building.
5. Mortgage insurance programs of the Veterans Administration and Federal Housing Administration; federal tax policies; federal financing of public works projects; the placement of public housing in central city locations; and the development of the interstate highway system all contributed to the promotion and expansion of suburbia.
6. Finally, the capitalist system itself, in which land speculation, real estate firms, mortage bankers, developers, and the housing industry were able to take advantage of the unique market conditions created by post–World War II prosperity and pent-up demand for housing, was a major player in the growth of suburbia, which took advantage of changing American values.

Paul Leinberger and Bruce Tucker (*The New Individualists*) point out the decentralizing power of capitalism:

In a sense, the decentering of organizations, especially corporate ones, seems almost inevitable, for after language itself the most general and pervasive centerless system is capitalism. Located everywhere and nowhere, this economic system endlessly circulates capital and power. And it is also the most notoriously unsettling: it uproots communities, it eradicates essential values, and it fragments the identity of individuals. Just as language operates on the principle of identity as difference, capitalism depends on the exchange relations of commodities, rather than on anything intrinsic to them. Much as any signifier derives it significance from all the signifiers that are not present, the value of any commodity, including one's labor, is found not in what it is, but in its relation to all the other absent commodities for which it may be exchanged, including money.

In the 1990s, *information* entered the capitalist picture as never before. Information has become the new raw material of capitalist economics, the postindustrial equivalent of what iron ore was to the industrial age. This new value has become the most significant resource for nearly every kind of organization. As a capitalist resource, information has the following properties:

- *Information is expandable*. It is a synergistic resource—the more we have and use, the more useful it becomes. And the more we have, the more it must be managed and manipulated if it is to be useful and form the basis for the expansion of knowledge.
- *Information is compressible*. It can be summarized, combined, and recombined in various ways to create new insights; it can be integrated and concentrated.
- *Information is substitutable*. It can replace capital goods, labor, and physical materials. For example, companies using computer-assisted design and manufacturing can actually replace physical materials and people with information.
- *Information is instantaneously transportable*. It can travel at the speed of light and it can defy the attempts of authorities to prevent its dissemination.
- *Information is diffused*. It has an almost inherent tendency to leak. "Information," according to Harlan Cleveland, "is aggressive, even imperialistic, in striving to break out of the unnatural bonds of secrecy in which thing-

minded people try to imprison it. Monopolizing information is very nearly a contradiction in terms that can be done only in more and more specialized fields, for shorter and shorter periods of time."

With the information revolution, capitalism has changed. Organizations have learned that they are not only manufacturing goods or providing services, but that they are also creating social and organizational change. They have also learned that the nature of information as a factor of production does not operate the way land, labor, capital, or raw materials do. Information has brought a peculiar change to organizational structure—the *network*. The network, as an organizational form, is perhaps the first important change in organizational design since the creation of functional hierarchies.

See also Business Ethics.

SOURCES

Cleveland, Harlan. *The Knowledge Executive: Leadership in an Information Society.* New York: E. P. Dutton. 1985.

Jackson, K. *Crabgrass Frontier: The Suburbanization of the United States.* New York: Oxford University Press. 1985.

Leinberger, Paul, and Bruce Tucker. *The New Individualists.* New York: HarperCollins. 1991.

CARGO CULTS

A great pioneering study that brought attention to and defined the cargo cult was F. E. Williams's report published in 1923, "The Valilala Madness." The cargo cult arose among colonial New Guinean natives who needed to explain to themselves just why they had to work so hard, whereas the idle and powerful white elite commanded great wealth. Somehow this situation was mysteriously connected with the great cargo ships that took away native products like copra and came back filled with many mysterious items like machines and radios that made the white men so powerful. The cargo cultists preached that all these objects were actually made by their own native ancestors in some far-off volcano, and were intended to be sent to them but were intercepted by whites. If only the New Guineans would throw away their old native cult objects and ceremonies and imitate the behaviors of the whites, such as sitting solemnly and speechlessly around tables, then the cargoes would come to their rightful owners.

An example of the cargo cult is the Kekesi cult of northwest Papua that Bia, a notorious sorcerer and a most plausible rogue, began in 1914. Bia was possessed by the spirit of Kekesi, who controlled the growth of food and lived at Mitre Rock near where Bia had his vision. *Kesi* was the name of Kekesi's steamboat, which would mysteriously bring them many white goods from overseas. This last feature—also present in Manau, the "Guman Wislin" (Wesleyan) and other cults—has led to these New Guinea movements being called in general the *cargo cults*, forms of which continue in the present day.

The importance of cargo ships in the Pacific islands cannot be exaggerated, for they are the main link with the outside world. Every person becomes excited on the remote islands when at rare times a ship ties up at the sleepy ports to break the endless monotony of labor.

The great wealth and power of the white race was a mystery to Melanesians. As far as the islanders could see, whites did no work at all and made no artifacts, and yet got great stores of goods merely by sending out bits of paper, and meanwhile blacks had to labor. The beings who made these goods became "the secret of the cargo," for surely they could not be idle white men—perhaps the spirits of their ancestral dead in some unknown land. The cargo ships were their link to that mysterious country and the obvious secret of their power.

THE FUNCTION OF PRIMITIVE RELIGIONS

By examining the ten basic functions of primitive religions, we begin to understand the function of the cargo cults in the daily lives of the people of New Guinea. David and John Noss *(Man's Religions)* define these functions as follows:

> The religious beliefs and practices of "primitive" individuals and groups try to deal practically with the mysteries surrounding life and death. The Cargo Cults reduced the mysteries and provided both a rationale and a way of dealing with surrounding realities, helping individuals and groups to act with some confidence when otherwise there would be fear and insecurity.
>
> In these circumstances religion fits the community and its individuals into a certain geographical-cosmological space or locality. Myths emerge going back to the beginnings of things, thereby settling questions concerning the origin of the world and the place of the community in it. The cargo ships link the Melanesians to the mysterious country of the whites and the obvious secrets of their power.
>
> Religion not only provides individuals with the assurance that they belong in a certain locality and should ordinarily stay where they are, but it also helps to fix the role they are meant to play in the social scene, a role that is ordained, not only by the community, but also by the ancestral spirits, and the invisible realities. The New Guineans began to imitate the whites so that the cargoes would come to their proper recipients.
>
> Religion provides a year-round schedule of rituals and activities that help to maintain community cohesion by filling the days and weeks with specific things to do. The regularity of the ships and their link to the outside world; the whites sending out their white paper and the blacks laboring to produce gold and copra; and the goods that came by ship told of the power of the whites and regulated life on the islands.
>
> Religion dispels anxiety caused by adverse circumstances and conditions, such as otherwise unexplainable events, haunting fears, bad dreams, illness, lack of success in hunting, fishing, gardening, and stockraising, fearsome natural occurrences, ominous signs of retribution imposed by greater or lesser spirits, and

the like. Religious and magical rites placate threatening powers and render them harmless. The great wealth of the whites that came by ship eventually became the object of worship, the secret of white power.

Religious rites and their magical accompaniments assure individual and group survival; the fertility of the soil, cattle, and human beings; rain, good harvests, success in hunting and fishing, individual and community well-being, and the like; they also, at a time of death, assure the survivors that the dead have safely departed to the place ordained for them and will return only to do good and not evil.

Religious rites give scope to gratitude, especially toward ancestors and supernatural powers; they thus insure continuation of supernatual favors, now and in the future.

Religious rites enable individuals to fulfil or realize their inner powers: physical potentialities, sexual fertility, special mental capacities, individual skills, leadership, and so on. The Cargo Cults enabled the islanders to explain why they had to work so hard, whereas the idle whites commanded great wealth and respect.

Religion enables individuals to have moments of vision that give them insight into realities ordinarily not seen nor understood. Exceptional individuals may experience divination or spirit-possession and become diviners, shamans, magicians, sorcerers, priests, prophets, and prophetesses.

When religious rites and ceremonies clearly prove their worth, they become sacred and more or less unalterable. They may also become a rich source of myths that establish their far-off origin and unquestionable authority. They thus add a needed sense of security in the present and continuity with the past.

Some cargo cult revelations were hostile to whites, as in the Sepik River region around 1935. Here there arose an anti-mission cult, with apocalyptic rumors of a Black King in the interior who had many hands and a skin of iron and stone. In a dream, one Marafi went to Satan in the bowels of the earth and saw the spirits there. He concluded that they should worship Satan, for he would send an earthquake and a rain of burning kerosene to destroy his enemies, the whites. The blacks should build large refuge houses, for after the holocaust they would find their own dead who would have returned with many cases of canned meat, tobacco, loin-cloths, lamps, rice, and rifles bigger than the whites'. No more gardening needed to be done. Marafi's Satanism smoldered as late as 1936.

SOURCES

La Barre, Weston. *The Ghost Dance*. Garden City, NY: Doubleday & Company. 1970.

Noss, David S., and John B. Noss. *Man's Religions*. 7th ed. New York: Macmillan. 1984.

Williams, F. E. "The Valilala Madness." Port Moresby, Territory of Papua: Anthropology Report #4. 1923.

Worsley, Peter. *The Trumpet Shall Sound: A Study of "Cargo" Cults in Melanesia*. London: Macgibbon and Kee. 1957.

CARING, ETHIC OF

Carol Gilligan's *In a Different Voice: Psychological Theory and Women's Development* launched the ethic of care as a field of study in 1982, and after a decade of commentary, Mary Jeanne Larrabee's *An Ethic of Care: Feminist and Interdisciplinary Perspectives* brings together key contributors to the extensive debate that has arisen about Gilligan's work. *An Ethic of Care* examines a wide range of views and brings together in discussion moral philosophy, empirical studies within psychology that examine allegations of sex differences in moral reasoning, and challenges to Gilligan's work that claim it leaves African Americans and other cultures out of the discussion.

In her book, Gilligan claimed that there is a moral orientation—a "different voice"—that she discovered in the women she investigated, but a voice that could also belong to men. This voice was one of care and responsibility, of concern and connection with other people. Gilligan claims that this voice stems from a self that is intrinsically related to other people. It is a voice that was underrated by Lawrence Kohlberg, because his theory of moral reasoning accentuates and therefore limits investigations to a voice of justice, and by implication considers a mature self to be autonomous and capable of abstract reasoning. Gilligan thus points to a serious oversight in Kohlberg's paradigm of human development: the failure to take seriously a moral orientation based on care that would display a type of moral reasoning as mature as the one based on the voice of justice. She also claims that her evidence shows that this mode of moral concern typically dominates the moral reasoning of women, whereas a moral system of rights and formal reasoning that uses a universalizable, abstract, and impersonal style dominates men's moral decision making and development.

See also Feminism.

SOURCES

Gilligan, C. *In a Different Voice: Psychological Theory and Women's Development.* Cambridge: Harvard University Press. 1982.

Kohlberg, L. *Essays on Moral Development: The Psychology of Moral Development.* Vol. 1. San Francisco: Harper & Row. 1981.

———. *Essays on Moral Development: The Psychology of Moral Development.* Vol. 2. New York: Harper & Row. 1984.

Larrabee, Mary Jeanne, ed. *An Ethic of Care: Feminist and Interdisciplinary Perspectives.* New York: Routledge. 1993.

CARSON, RACHEL

The serious environmentalist—whose values and ethics include not only human beings but all living things—will be disposed to listen to the words of Rachel Carson (1907–1964), whose 1962 classic *Silent Spring* called public attention to the wasteful and destructive use of pesticides. Carson, a marine biologist, worked for the U.S. Fish and Wildlife Service for most of her adult life. In her writings, Carson points to the dependence of human life on natural processes and focuses on the interrelation of all living things. She warned that pesticides poison the food supply of animals, birds, and fish, killing them in large numbers. Her writings and work with the government helped lead to restrictions on the use of pesticides in many parts of the world.

SOURCES

Carson, Rachel. *Silent Spring* (1962). New York: Houghton Mifflin. 1987.

———. *Under the Sea Wind.* New York: Dutton. 1991.

THE CATEGORICAL IMPERATIVE

The idea of everyone deciding moral issues on the basis of his or her own feelings, desires, or preferences enjoys much popularity today. "Everyone doing his or her own thing" seems a reasonable and tolerant approach to morality. It has an understandable appeal to the young people who are inclined to challenge their parents' moral code, and to those of all ages who are disenchanted with traditional views. The April 1995 bombing of the federal building in Oklahoma City and subsequent reactions by the "militant right"—or those who are disenchanted with the American government—reflect this point of view. Basing one's values on personal feelings and desires also harmonizes well with the prevailing concern with individuality espoused by the so-called *me generation* that is now in its 20s and early 30s. The philosophical claim is that if each person is an individual, different from all others, then his or her morality—like fingerprints— should reflect his or her individual uniqueness. Those who take this view emphasize making one's lifestyle and moral perspective reflect personal needs and wants rather than some prefabricated set of principles that "society" sanctions. They value subjective validity more highly than external norms. The conclusion that follows from this reasoning is that no one person's view is preferable to another's. Each is good in its own way. This, they claim, allows for more personal freedom and less social or governmental interference with one's chosen way of life.

The first thing to note about this view of morality is that it's not very new. Two centuries ago Jean Jacques Rousseau wrote, "What I feel is right is right, what I feel is wrong is wrong." There is no question, of course, that a concern for individuality is legitimate. There do seem to be strong forces at work in the best and purest of human societies that, when unchecked, stifle the uniqueness of persons, promote conformity, and lead to artistic, intellectual, and social sterility.

The individualist shares the position of *contextualism*, which holds that there can be no moral rules one can memorize ahead of time and apply meaningfully to a particular situation. The contextualist holds that relevant criteria for making a meaningful ethical decision can be found only within the context of each concrete ethical problem. Every ethical situation is in fact unique and each person makes the best decision he or she can, using the best knowledge available. There are no moral rules that can guide us in every situation. Meaningful ethical judgments can be made only after the problem situation surfaces, not before.

The moral position that is contrary to contextualism and individualism is *formalism*. The formalist believes that the criteria to be used in making ethical decisions are universal laws that apply to all persons alike. Our responsibility is to be informed about these rules before we find ourselves caught up in the ethical complexities of life. The views of the German philosopher Immanuel Kant are in this tradition. Kant held that universal moral laws do exist and they are to be found within the structure of the human mind: just as 8 + 4 is always 12—it is a priori knowledge yet applied to the concrete world (a priori and synthetic)—there are moral "rules of thought" that are known by reason alone, universal, and applicable to the real world. Kant says that ethical rules "must not be sought in human nature or in the circumstances of the world . . . but [must be sought] a priori simply in the concepts of reason."

Kant formulated his famous *categorical imperative* to be such an a priori rule. It categorically applies to all rational people and is imperative as an absolute "ought" that binds individuals to the moral law. In part, Kant's formula stated, "Act only on the maxim whereby thou canst at the same time will it should become a universal law." He reasoned that if any kind of action can be universalized, then it is ethical. For example, can I universalize stealing? Hardly. I may think stealing is expediently justifiable in some particular case, but I can't recommend stealing as a matter of course—as a universal form of behavior. Human interaction would become chaotic if stealing were the norm and we couldn't trust one another. Therefore, prohibiting stealing is a categorical imperative. The categorical imperative is a normative law, logical and axiomatic. It is meant to apply universally to all ethical decisions we make.

See also Ethics, Theory of; Golden Rule.

SOURCES

Kant, Immanuel. *Critique of Practical Reason.* Translated by Louis White Beck. New York: Bobbs-Merrill Library of Liberal Arts. 1956.

Muelder, Walter G. *Moral Law in Christian Social Ethics.* New York: John Knox. 1966.

CATHOLICISM AND THE MODERN WORLD

The word *catholic* was first applied to the Christian Church in its meaning of "universal." Descriptively, this was an apt designation for a religious faith that now reached into all provinces of the Roman Empire and into every class of society. It became, in fact, part of the name of the single organized institution that expressed the

Christian religion after the middle of the second century.

To keep both its outer and inner integrity, the ancient Catholic Church developed two things: (1) a system of doctrine, clarified, purged of error, and declared to be orthodox; and (2) an ecclesiastical organization characterized in its own eyes by apostolicity, catholicity, unity, and holiness.

MODERN LANDMARKS

- 1854: Pius IX proclaimed the Immaculate Conception of the Virgin to be a dogma of the Catholic Church. The meaning of this was that all Catholics must believe that Mary, in order to be fitted to conceive Christ while still a virgin, was freed from original sin by immaculate purity in which her parents conceived her.
- 1864: Pius IX issued a *Syllabus of Errors* in which he condemned socialism, communism, rationalism, naturalism, the separation of church and state, and freedom of the press and religion. "The Roman pontiff," he said, "cannot and should not be reconciled and come to terms with progress, liberalism, and modern civilization." This pronouncement stunned Catholic liberals without totally silencing them.
- 1870: Pius IX issued a declaration of the infallibility of popes under certain conditions: *not all plain utterances of the pope are without error, but only those that he pronounces ex cathedra in exposition of "the revelation or deposit of faith delivered through the Apostles" and the Catholic tradition.* The declaration affirms:

> The Roman pontiff, when he speaks *ex cathedra,* that is, when in discharge of the office of pastor and doctor of all Christians, by virtue of his supreme apostolic authority, he defines a doctrine regarding faith or morals to be held by the universal church, by the divine assistance promised to him in blessed Peter, is possessed of that infallibility with which the divine Redeemer willed that His church should be endowed.

- ca. 1900: Toward the end of the nineteenth century many thoughtful Catholics saw the need to take into account theories based on modern historical and biblical criticism and the discoveries of modern science. This short-lived movement, called Catholic Modernism, sought the reconciliation of Catholicism with modern scientific knowledge and critical methods. A group of Catholic scholars tried to come to terms with the theories of biological and geophysical evolution, while others adopted the methods of biblical criticism current among Protestant scholars, and went so far as to question the historicity of the Virgin Birth. Leaders in this movement included George Tyrrell in England, Alfred Loisy in France, and Hermann Schell in Germany.
- 1907: Pius X found the modernists dangerous and condemned them with a number of excommunications in 1910. This brought the movement to an end. During this time, Jacques Maritain and others created a different movement, *Neo-Thomism,* as an attempt to put Catholic doctrine into current thought-forms. They expressed the philosophy of Thomas Aquinas in modern terms and applied it to modern issues.
- 1950: Pius XII proclaimed as a dogma of the Church the assumption of the uncorrupted body of the Virgin Mary to heaven after her death.
- 1959: Pope John XXIII summoned delegates from the entire Catholic world to Rome in an ecumenical council known as Vatican II. The first session began in 1962 with additional sessions in 1963, 1964, and 1965 at the call of Pope Paul VI, the successor of Pope John, who died in 1963.

Vatican II sought adjustments to the twentieth-century world and promotion of Christian unity. Its decisions included the following:

- Authorization of a more extensive use of vernaculars in the celebration of the sacraments and in public worship.
- Endorsement of *collegiality*, or the principle that all bishops as successors of the Apostles share with the pope in the government of the Church.
- Provision for greater lay participation in Church administration by creating a permanent separate order of deacons, to include married mature men and not merely celibate youth preparing for the priesthood.
- Approval of a declaration that no man should be forced to act against his conscience and that nations should neither impose religion nor prohibit freedom of religious belief and association.
- Authorization of worship by Catholics with non-Catholics in special circumstances.
- Recognition of the possibility of salvation outside the Catholic Church.
- A declaration that Jews are not to be held collectively responsible for the death of Christ.

In opening the second session of the council (1963), Pope Paul said that the long-range goal of the council was the complete and universal union of all Christians.

- 1967: Pope Paul organized a Synod of Bishops, representing national hierarchies from all over the world, to advise him in doctrinal matters and administrative decisions.
- 1968: Pope Paul issued an encyclical on birth control (*Humanae vitae*) that reiterated the Church's previous stand against all forms of artificial birth control; but it met with considerable resistance throughout the Catholic world, not only among laity but also among priests and nuns.
- 1978: Pope Paul died and was succeeded by Pope John Paul I, who at once affirmed that he would follow his two predecessors in confirming the decisions of Vatican II. He was succeeded by a non-Italian (Polish) cardinal, John Paul II, who is similarly committed to Vatican II.

SOURCES
Denzinger, H. J. D. *The Sources of Catholic Dogma*. B. Herder. 1957.
Kelley, J. N. D. *Early Christian Doctrines*. New York: Harper & Brothers. 1958.
Rouse, R., and S. C. Neill, eds. *A History of the Ecumenical Movement, 1517–1948*. New York: Westminster Press, 1954.

CENSORSHIP

Censorship is the control of what people say or hear, write or read, see or do. In most cases, censorship comes from governments or private groups. When the issue of censorship comes up, we usually want to know how free we are anyway and under what circumstances. Censorship affects books, newspapers, motion pictures, magazines, radio, speeches, advertisements, and television programs. Public school textbooks are often the target of censorship groups or state legislatures, especially science books that teach evolution, health education or family living texts that talk about such topics as birth control and AIDS, literature that has "foul" language in it, and history texts that teach about religion. Censorship also involves the arts, especially in such areas as uses of the human body or religious icons. Censorship may even affect such things as the clothing we wear.

Freedom of thought and expression are basic rights that lie at the heart of a democratic society, but even in a democratic society a government may turn to censorship if it feels threatened or when it thinks that censorship will benefit the entire nation. The strict control and limitation of information and expression occurs in dictatorships and during wartime. There is a difference between dictatorships and democracies. Democracies—such as the United States—have checks on unlimited censorship through courts and by having a Bill of Rights; dictatorships do not.

MORAL CENSORSHIP

Aristotle defined human beings as persons who have the ability to think and reason. Reflective intelligence is usually listed among the unique qualities of persons. Moral censorship may occur when some people believe they have the right to force their values on others—to limit their right to freedom of thought and expression. Many governments or groups try to preserve their standards of morality by preventing people from learning about or following other standards. Governments, state and national, have obscenity laws; they ban books and regulate what movies are shown and what type of magazines are sold within their jurisdiction.

Elizabeth Noll talks about "the ripple effect of censorship" within the public school classroom. She quotes a high school teacher who said, "I constantly self-censor literature and related materials. . . . No complaints have been lodged against me, but the administration in our district has made it apparent that it will not support teachers' legitimate choices." Noll finds that censorship challenges—defined as efforts to ban materials and methods to all children—are on the rise and are limited to no one geographic region or to a particular level of instruction or area of the curriculum. Between 1992 and 1993, People for the American Way documented 395 incidents of censorship in schools across the country. Forty-one percent of those cas-

es resulted in the removal or restricted use of materials. But Noll sees an undocumented ripple effect in our nations' schools. She asks, "How do these often widely publicized incidents of censorship influence classroom teachers and instructional methods?"

Many teachers view the threat of censorship as coming from fundamental religious groups—what are today collectively called "the religious right"—and from public school administrators afraid of that group. Joan Delfattore notes that "challenges initiated by people who identify themselves as fundamentalists not only outnumber the protests of all other groups combined, but also involve more topics." Research conducted by People for the American Way shows a correlation between an increase in challenges since 1980 and a rise in activism in the schools by far-right and religious-right groups.

SUMMARY FROM THE MORAL POINT OF VIEW

Moralists count intellectual freedom as important for four reasons: (1) freedom of expression is a basic condition for the development of mature persons and the creation and enjoyment of human values; (2) intellectual freedom is a necessary condition for the discovery of truth and new ideas, and for creativity; (3) freedom of expression is the basis for democracy; and (4) to defend freedom of the mind is to defend a way of life rooted in the Western political and religious heritage. Metaphysically, philosophers also claim the necessity of freedom. Harold Titus and Morris Keeton argue:

> Man's freedom or need for freedom is grounded in his very nature and in the nature of the relationships in the midst of which he lives. . . . Freedom of thought and speech are not privileges granted by the state or by any group in society. We may call them natural rights or God-given rights. At least they are based on the nature of Man and the conditions necessary for his moral, intellectual, and spiritual development.

Although other types of censorship are often mentioned—military censorship, which protects battle plans, troop movements, weapons data, research, and other information that could help the enemy; political censorship, which is used by governments that fear the free expression of criticism and opposing ideas; and religious censorship, when a government promotes one religion above all others—most arguments for basic freedoms and civil liberties are founded on the moral issues involved. Noll recognizes this perspective when she says that freedom of expression and freedom in education in general mean "creating opportunities for honest and open dialogue for all of us, at every teaching level, who struggle with censorship and self-censorship." She points to three questions that should be asked and discussed for those wishing to expose the grounds of intellectual freedom or the need for censorship:

1. What are our responsibilities in advocating our students' intellectual freedom?
2. In what ways do we support and silence our colleagues' freedom of expression?
3. What are our beliefs about the roles and responsibilities of schools as institutions of a democratic society?

These questions get to the heart of the matter very quickly, take on the concrete or practical problems involved in censorship, and uncover the philosophical issues as well. Such questions place our individual responses to the question of censorship in a broader philosophical context that supports a proactive, rather than a reactive, stance.

See also Civil Rights.

SOURCES

Delfattore, Joan. *What Johnny Shouldn't Read: Textbook Censorship in America.* New Haven, CT: Yale University Press. 1992.

Noll, Elizabeth. "The Rippling Effect of Censorship: Silencing in the Classroom." *English Journal* 83 (December 1994).

People for the American Way. "Attacks on the Freedom to Learn: Report." Washington, D.C. 1994.

Titus, Harold H., and Morris T. Keeton. *Ethics for Today.* 5th ed. New York: Van Nostrand. 1973.

Weil, Jonathan S. "Dealing With Censorship: Policy and Procedures." *Education Digest* 53 (January 5, 1988).

CHARACTER

When we talk about a person's character, we are trying to capture something of the person's essence as a human being, the major traits or characteristics of the person, what the person typically does or says, the person's major beliefs, and the person's values or ethical principles. If we probe deeply enough, we find the self-concept at the core of a person's character. By *self-concept* we mean what a person thinks of himself or herself when the facade of social living has been removed. The person's character develops out of a complicated interaction between self-concept and environment as the person tries to develop a meaningful existence. The bridge between meaning and character, therefore, is *value,* and the key to understanding a person's self-concept, or the meaning he/she places on life, is the person's *value system*—the scale of values that is followed as a guide or framework for ordering his or her behavior. So to understand character is to understand the interplay between meaning, self-concept, and value in terms of human moral sensibility.

James Q. Wilson, professor of Management and Public Policy at UCLA, examines human character in terms of *moral sense.* He says: "[To] say that there exists a moral sense (or, more accurately, several moral senses) is to say that there are aspects of our moral life that are universal, a statement that serious thinkers from Aristotle to Adam Smith had no trouble in accepting." By "moral sense" Wilson is not referring to universal moral rules (as found among different societies of individuals), but rather universal dispositions. He comments: "To find what is universal about human nature, we must look behind the rules and the circumstances that shape them to discover what fundamental dispositions, if any, animate them and to decide whether those dispositions are universal. If such universal dispositions exist, we would expect them to be so obvious that travelers would either take them for granted or overlook them in preference to whatever is novel or exotic."

Wilson believes that the moral dispositions that define human character begin in the home:

> They are the affection a parent, especially a mother, bears for its child and the desire to please that the child brings to this encounter. Our moral senses are forged in the crucible of this loving relationship and expanded by the enlarged relationships of families and peers. Out of the universal attachment between child and parent the former begins to develop a sense of empathy and fairness, to learn self-control, and to acquire a conscience that makes him behave dutifully at least with respect to some matters. Those dispositions are extended to other people (and often to other species) to the extent that these others are thought to share in the traits we find in our families. That last step is the most problematic and as a consequence is far from common; [for] many cultures, especially those organized around clans and lineages rather than independent nuclear families based on consensual marriages and private property, rarely extend the moral sense, except in the most abstract or conditional way, to other people. The moral sense for most people remains particularistic; for some, it aspires to be universal.

For Wilson, character comes to this: a distinctive combination of personal qualities by which someone is known (that is, a personality), and moral strength or integrity by which a person strikes a balance between his or her moral senses and prudent self-interest.

The tenor of our age is skepticism, especially about morality. Science has rendered morality to mere opinion, and *political correctness* has followed by claiming that one set of customs, one set of rules, one way of expressing virtue and morality is as equally appealing as another way and must be given equal merit. Thus, we linger in moral confusion and are governed only by immediate impulse or calculating self-interest. We have talked ourselves out of having a moral sense or any inner disposition that we can label *character* because we do not wish to prejudice ourselves against another culture or ethnic group. By focusing on the expressions of character through differing rules and procedures, we have lost sight of the inner dispositions and experiences from which character flows.

Contemporary educators, interested in developing character in their students, understand the concept of balance between self-interest and one's moral senses, but they have found another word to describe it: *virtue*. The trouble is, among many young people, virtue has acquired a bad name. It seems to be the opposite of having fun; to older adults it is a symbol of lost values that politicians now exploit; and to others virtue is a set of rules that well-meaning but intolerant people impose on others. But virtue is more than any of these: it is not simply about human relationships, but what those relationships ought to be. Virtue is about striking that moral balance between genuine self-interest and the moral disposition acquired through love and affection. Thus, virtue is about morality and moral choices. The daily discourse of ordinary people is permeated with moral references, and these concerns derive from their shared moral sense, a character-base, which is shaped by the basic realities and experiences they endure. Because they share a moral sense, individuals with widely divergent perspectives are able to address common problems. Understanding the nature of character as involving an expansion of our moral sensibilities has led to the gradual expansion of the imagination of those in power and their gradual willingness to use the term *we* to include more and more different sorts of people. Our ideal of character, although culture-bound and local, because it produces a consideration of others and a balance between the needs of others and one's own self-interests, nevertheless may be our best hope for the development of a widely accepted human-moral base.

SOURCES

Geertz, Clifford. "The Uses of Diversity." *Michigan Quarterly Review* 25 (1986).

Rorty, Richard. "On Ethnocentrism: A Reply to Clifford Geertz." In *Objectivity, Relativism, and Truth.* Edited by Richard Rorty. New York: Cambridge University Press. 1991: 203–210.

Vincent, Philip F. *Character Education: A Primer.* Chapel Hill, NC: New View. 1994.

Wilson, James Q. *The Moral Sense.* New York: Free Press. 1993.

CHARISMATICS

Working within the main churches of both Catholicism and Protestantism, and also independently of them, are the so-called charismatics. These individuals experience religion as ecstasy, or even as a kind of possession. They are convinced that these experiences are "gifts of Divine grace" or a "baptism of the Holy Spirit" by which they become new persons with extraordinary powers and a new persuasiveness over others. But charismatics are not limited to modern religions. In ancient times and among primitive cultures, a charismatic leader was one who responded to stress (a *ghost dance* is a society of individuals responding to stress). The mystery of charisma is a kind of supernatural, omnipotent compulsion streaming out from an individual like animal magnetism.

Weston La Barre provides the following comment about charismatic leaders and religion:

Perhaps charisma comes merely from awe before a leader's functional fatherhood? Moses was a messiah to the Hebrews long before and above any other—for all that he may have borrowed his monotheistic god from the tradition of Ikhnaton; beloved like an Egyptian prophet on the Mount, like an African snake-shaman with Aaron before the Pharaoh, and a Pharaoh-like African rain king in the Wilderness; and like a Pharaoh wrote his edicts on stone, and was prophet to a shaman's and smith's god of fire—for like a sheikh-patriarch he did lead his chosen people out of bondage to the borders of a Promised Land.

We can conclude that enormous charisma is required of a new prophet for retrospective rewriting of history, of being able to manipulate information and people. From Moses to Jesus, and with Caesar and Hitler, we discover this ability. Commonly though, in a crisis-cult the charismatic obtains credence more among the dispossessed and ignorant than among those with sufficient education and knowledge.

See also Ghost Dance Movements.

SOURCES

La Barre, Weston. *The Ghost Dance: The Origins of Religion..* Garden City, NY: Doubleday. 1970.

Noss, David S., and John B. Noss. *Man's Religions.* 7th ed. New York: Macmillan. 1984.

CHAUVINISM

Chauvinism comes from the French *chauvin*, a name applied to any old soldier of the first French Empire who professed an idolatrous admiration for Napoleon and his achievements. The word came to mean "any person who has a blind and extravagant admiration or enthusiasm for his or her country's military glory." Thus chauvinism means "unreasoning enthusiasm for the military glory of one's country"—a boastful, warlike patriotism. It was quite natural that feminists would appropriate this term to refer to men who treat women unequally and relegate them to subordinate status. When used in this way the term is usually *male chauvinism*, referring to any male or part of the male-created civilization—including laws, beliefs, and customs—that considers women more emotional, weak, irresponsible, or inferior to males simply because they are of the opposite gender.

See also Feminism; Politics in the Classroom.

SOURCES

Boetcher, Ruth-Eller, et al., eds. *Signs, Journal of Women in Culture and Society* 20 (Winter 1995).

Freeman, Jo. *The Politics of Women's Liberation.* New York: David McKay. 1975.

CHEMICAL-BIOLOGICAL-RADIOLOGICAL WARFARE

Chemical-Biological-Radiological Warfare (CBR) is war waged with chemicals, biological agents, or radioactive materials. Development of CBR weapons and protection from these weapons are normally considered together in military training and strategy. These weapons have the purpose of killing large numbers of people, temporarily disabling them, or destroying their food supply. These weapons are usually effective without destroying property. Although war itself is considered an immoral choice to resolving conflicts, biological weapons were banned in 1971 by the United Nations General Assembly as an acceptable practice. There is some evidence that such weapons were used against United Nations forces in the short war with Iraq in 1990 and 1991.

SOURCE

The World Book Encyclopedia. C–Ch: Volume 3. Chicago: Field Enterprises Educational Corporation. 1993.

CHILD CARE

The issue or problem of child care gained importance when the men went off to war and their wives went off to work in 1942. In the 1960s, child care again became an issue for the feminist movement with the publication of *The Feminine Mystique* by Betty Friedan. From a practical point of view, mothers and fathers want child care that is safe, nonabusive, and affordable. From the view of some in the feminist movement, child care must be nonsexist, or as Susan Douglas reflects when commenting on the media, "Then they get off the hook for doing what they do best: promoting a white upper-middle class, male view of the world that urges the rest of us to sit passively on our sofas and fantasize about consumer goods while they handle the important stuff, like the economy, the environment, or child care." Three important feminist goals, shared by many men, are the following: (1) equal opportunities in employment and education, (2) abortion on demand, and (3) child-care centers.

More and more, as both husband and wife have been required to work to meet subsistence needs or as women have entered the professions (especially since the early 1970s), provision of adequate child care has grown in importance. Since the early 1980s, with the new emphasis on education—from the cradle to the grave—and the recognition that American education is lagging far behind other industrial powers, a new emphasis has been placed on child care. Not only in our nation's inner cities is adequate child care before school age seen as a problem. Today, the problem is universal. Throughout the country, "smart start" programs for three-, four-, and five-year-olds are being established to prepare students for the social and academic requirements of a technology-centered nation.

Fundamentally, there are two major types of child care: family day care and group day care. *Family day care* is hiring some person, a relative or not, to care for the child in his or her home. While interviewing possible family day-care proprietors, Vance Packard reminds us to keep the following questions in mind:

- Does she (or he) have children herself? How do they look as samples of her mothering ability?
- Does she seem to have a cheerful or affectionate disposition, or is she putting on an act? How do she and your children interact?
- How many children will she be tending, including her own, and what are their ages?
- What kind of a report does she get from a mother who already is using or has recently used her services?
- Does she seem to have a nice, clean home?
- How busy is she going to be with housework, television, or with neighbors coming in for coffee?
- Does she have play facilities at least as good as your own and have access to a safe outdoor area?
- If she has a husband who is going to be in the home for part of the day, check his disposition and attitude.
- Are there books or serious magazines in the home? In short, does she seem to be a reasonably literate, articulate person?
- Since she will presumably have a television set on the premises, what is her policy about using it as a child pacifier? How much time will she sit in front of it herself?

If *group day care* is considered, there are some more variables to weigh. Here are some pertinent questions to keep in mind:

- How many caretakers (or substitute mothers) will be having regular contact with your child? In general, the fewer the better. A small child has an urgent need for continuity of relationship, especially if the child is under three. The Princeton Center for Infancy has concluded that "nothing is worse than a series of caretakers."
- What is the total size of the group of children that will be mingling with, or circulating in sight of, your child? Again, the fewer the better. According to a federally sponsored study by the Abt Associates of Cambridge, "group size" is the most significant factor in determining the quality of care provided by day care centers.
- How many children are there per staff member? This is usually referred to as "the ratio." Once again, the fewer children per staff member, the greater the likelihood of achieving quality day care.
- What are the qualifications of the staff person who will have direct contact with your child? Don't settle for anything less than a high school graduate with some formal training in child care and the psychological needs of children at each age level as the primary caregiver of your child.
- What is the center's real attitude toward parent involvement? Two early childhood specialists at the University of Minnesota call parent involvement "a key ingredient in any pre-school program and one notoriously hard to come by."
- Will the center help your child's overall development? That is, do the center's staff, facilities, and programs combine to provide a congenial, cheerful, stimulating place for your child to grow? Or is it oriented to being simply custodial? Is the daily program appropriate for each age level? Is the atmosphere homelike or institutional? Will your child have a variety of materials to work with?

See also Feminism; Politics in the Class-room.

SOURCES

Boetcher, Ruth-Ellen, et al., eds. *Signs, Journal of Women in Culture and Society* 20 (Winter 1995).

Friedan, Betty. *The Feminine Mystique.* 10th Anniversary ed. New York: Norton. 1974.

Packard, Vance. *Our Endangered Children.* Boston: Little, Brown. 1983.

CHOICE

What is the essence of human freedom—a fundamental value for both Eastern and Western cultures? Western thinkers have been the pioneers in articulating the freedom that humans can achieve through reason, while Eastern sages have led the way in realizing the freedom that needs to be achieved due to the contrived limitations.

THE WESTERN IDEAL

The conviction of people in Western Europe and North America is that humans have the liberty they seek when they can make their own choices and proceed, it is hoped, to satisfy their own desires. Most philosophical theories of freedom imply this conviction; whatever blocks the liberty to choose and/or the liberty to pursue one's goals and ideals must be overcome if a person is to be truly free. Western ideals recognize that some constraints are necessary for the sake of social order, but these are, in the opinion of many, limitations on their freedom to choose. The black scholar Orlando Patterson, raised in a Third World nation, praises the West for recognizing the merits of freedom for all people and of claiming that certain social constraints such as slavery are morally wrong. He comments:

> At its best, the valorization of personal liberty is the noblest achievement of Western civilization. That people are free to do as they please within limits set only by the personal freedom of others; that legally all persons are equal before the law; that philosophically the individual's separate existence is inviolable; that psychologically the ultimate human condition is to be liberated from all internal and external constraints in one's desire to realize one's self; and that spiritually the son of God made himself incarnate, then gave up his life in order to redeem mankind from spiritual thralldom and to make people free and equal before God—all add up to a value complex that not only is unparalled in any other culture but, in its profundity and power, is superior to any other single complex of values conceived by mankind.

Freedom, equality, and their implications were most visibly explored in Europe during the eighteenth century as part of the movement that we call the Enlightenment. The Enlightenment meant many things—an enthusiasm for science, a desire to master nature, a belief in progress, a commitment to reform, and a faith in reason—but at its root was, as Immanuel Kant put it, "man's release from his self-imposed tutelage" (In German: "*Aufklarung ist der Ausgang des Menschen aus seiner selbstverschuldeten Unmundigkeit*"). By *tutelage* Kant meant having one's understanding directed by another; by *self-imposed* he meant a lack of courage to assert and rely on one's own reason. Tutelage came from unthinking or cowardly obedience to authority—the authority of revealed religion, ancient custom, received wisdom, or hereditary monarchs. In no other place has a modern culture undergone an Enlightenment where the ideas of a few philosophers became the common understanding of the populace at large, and, in time, the general practice of reconstituted governments.

THE EASTERN IDEAL

According to the dominant orientation of the East, one who is merely free from external constraints is by no means really free; for this the person must be liberated from the internal forces that drive him or her to make wrong claims or are revealed in unrealistic and ego-centered desires. When an inquirer asked Sri Ramakrishna,

"When shall I be free?" the saint replied, "When the 'I' shall cease to be." He meant the ego that is in bondage to these forces; only when liberated from this bondage is a person truly free. In Eastern thought, human sociopolitical or religious constraints or the lack thereof have no bearing on what is meant by freedom. Freedom is internal, not external, and can occur despite human circumstances.

From both the Western and Eastern points of view, freedom poses a theoretical and practical problem. These take different forms in the East and in the West. In general, the *theoretical* problem for each consists of showing that a person has by nature the capacity for or an intrinsic right to freedom. The *practical* problem consists of overcoming whatever obstructions prevent a person from achieving it. When philosophers have concentrated on the theoretical problem, freedom naturally presents itself as an absolute: humans either have freedom or lack the capacity that the concept is believed to involve. When one is concerned with the practical problem, freedom is always a matter of degree—under any given set of conditions a certain measure of freedom is realized, which with a change in those conditions would be increased or diminished.

This is the case because thinkers on both sides realize that ignorance means bondage, whereas knowledge spells freedom. From the Western viewpoint as to what is important, scientific knowledge brings humans greater freedom in their relationship to the physical world; instead of being in bondage to its forces, humans are able to partially control nature to benefit whatever purposes they have. Likewise, knowledge of the political and social forces around us brings greater freedom as a citizen; when we gain this understanding, instead of remaining in bondage to institutions that unjustly suppress our power of action, we can change them so that they serve our needs.

From the Eastern viewpoint, it is knowledge of oneself that brings true liberation. Nothing else can achieve this result, for the bondage the Eastern philosopher is concerned about is bondage to one's own inner drives and emotions. While ignorant of them one is inevitably their captive, but as one becomes aware of their presence and nature one no longer needs to express them compulsively in thought and action. The freedom from external constraints emphasized by the West can plausibly be sought under the guidance of reason, while freedom from inner bondage cannot be achieved by reason alone—this faculty itself easily falls captive to the subconscious urges from which liberation is needed. The pervasive conviction of Western philosophers has been that humans realize the best life by fulfilling their present desires as far as their goals appear justifiable; he or she must then have freedom to do so. "The best," says George Boas, "is that the future will satisfy our present desires." On the other hand, Eastern sages have strongly maintained—and religious thinkers in the West have done so too—that even the desires that seem most reasonable are not unqualifiedly good. They need to be transformed through clearer awareness of their true place in our growing experience as a whole; only the aspirations of the self that is achieving unity through such awareness can be wisely and safely satisfied.

See also Free Will.

SOURCES

Bergson, Henri. *The Two Sources of Morality and Religion*. Garden City, NY: Doubleday. 1951.

Boas, George. *The Limits of Reason*. New York: Harper & Row. 1961.

Champion, Selwyn Gurney, and Dorothy Short, eds. *Readings from World Religions*. Greenwich, CT: Fawcett. 1951.

Moore, Charles A., ed. *Philosophy and Culture: East and West*. Honolulu: University of Hawai'i Press 1962.

CHRISTIAN ETHICS

Christian ethics, like the Christian religion, is based on interpretations of the teachings of Jesus beginning with the New Testament. Also important to the early interpretation and formulation of Christian ethics were the letters of Saint Paul and the teachings of the early Christian Church, especially its formulation of doctrines, beliefs, and creeds. Because Christianity and Christian ethics have been so pervasive in Western civilization, we discover many interpretations and practices, some of them seemingly contradictive of others. Jurgen Habermas has remarked that because Christianity has dominated thinking and practice in the West, he does not believe that we can seriously understand concepts like morality and ethical life, personality and individuality, or freedom and emancipation, without "appropriating the substance of the Judeo-Christian understanding of history in terms of salvation."

Indeed, the religious consciousness of Jesus carried over into his ethical teaching. He spoke with the authority of moral assurance, calling for self-commitment and asking his followers to put their moral obligations above social, legal, or ceremonial demands. It was at this point that Jesus was the most critical of the Pharisees. They were guilty of certain obvious faults: complacency, the desire for honor and applause, spiritual pride, and hypocrisy. But their gravest shortcoming was that they substituted ceremonial practices for a creative and faithful regenerating morality: justice, mercy, and integrity. For Jesus, good and evil originate in the heart; thus, of great importance was the person's inward motivation, spirit, and attitude—in modern terms, a truly Eastern philosophic point of view.

Before the application of Christian moral principles is discussed, we should understand that Jesus linked application with a twofold demand: concern for one's own inner integrity and concern for the inner health of others. According to Jesus, who echoed Hebrew teaching, we are not to hurt others at the center of their moral being! The importance of the spiritual and inward parts of morality reached its most significant form in Jesus' teaching about love. The absolute principle of love is contained in the following:

> You have heard that [the men of old] were told, "You must love your neighbor and hate your enemy." But I tell you, love your enemies and pray for your persecutors, so that you may show yourselves true sons of your Father in heaven, for he makes his sun rise on bad and good alike, and makes his rain fall on the upright and the wrong doers. . . . You are to be perfect as your heavenly Father is (Matthew 5:43–48).

> You must always treat other people as you would like to have them treat you, for this sums up the Law and the Prophets (Matthew 7:12).

> "You must love the Lord your God with your whole heart, your whole soul, and your whole mind." That is the great, first command. There is a second like it: "You must love your neighbor as yourself." These two commands sum up the whole of the Law and the Prophets (Matthew 22:39–40).

Jesus only states the central principle of morality; the application of it at any juncture is left to the conscience of the individual who espouses it. But there is some clear guidance given by Jesus: one should not resist with violence evil done to one's own self; retaliation is embittering and futile; rash and ill-considered criticism of another's conduct is warned against. Rather, Jesus says that it is always best to be generous and thus call forth love from others:

> But I tell you that anyone who gets angry with his brother and anyone who speaks contemptuously to his brother and anyone who says

to his brother "You cursed fool!" will have to answer for it.

> Pass no more judgments upon other people, so that you may not have judgment passed upon you. . . . You must be merciful just as your Father is. Do not judge others . . . . Give, and they will give to you; good measure, pressed down, shaken together, and running over, they will pour into your lap. For the measure you use with others they in turn will use with you.

The Apostle Paul has been called "the second founder of Christianity." It was Paul who developed certain basic theological concepts for stating the spiritual effects of Jesus upon the lives of his followers, concepts that enabled Christianity to win the gentile world. Two great spiritual beliefs animated Paul and gave him his dynamic faith: the "Lordship of Christ Jesus" and "the freedom of the spirit." Thus, mysticism and ethics were in Paul's teaching one and inseparable. To follow Christ meant not only "salvation," but even more; it meant doing as Jesus did, living as Jesus did. Paul says:

> If I can speak the languages of men and even of angels, but have no love, I am only a noisy gong or a clashing symbol. . . . I want you all to speak ecstatically . . . but in public worship I would rather say five words with my understanding so as to instruct others also than ten thousand words in an ecstasy.

This was an important teaching for Christian ethics. Herein Paul saved Christian ethics from nonethical mysticism and the legalism of the Judaizers.

Christians today—Catholic, Protestant, and nondenominationalist—share the conviction that God continually reveals himself in history, and recent trends in theology are quite naturally responsive to contemporary historical events and to social upheavals over war, racism, sexism, the widening gulf between the rich and poor, and over such issues as sex education, marriage and divorce, birth control, and abortion. Since 1950, U.S. theologians such as Harvey Cox, William Hamilton, Paul Van Buren, and Thomas Altizer have

responded to the widespread experience of alienation felt by many persons and perhaps reaching a political high in the counterculture of the 1960s. For Altizer his "death of God" theology meant the death of transcendence. Christianity for him was about men, not about God; after the cross God was born again as here-and-now immanence.

In Europe, theologians like Jurgen Maltmann and Wolfhart Pannenberg have responded to secularism and the collapse of traditional values by reinterpreting the eschatological dimensions of the Gospels as *the Coming One, who is also present, offers the power and hope of the future.* Aspects of this theology of hope anticipated and paralleled some new developments in the Americas where particular aspects of oppression came to the focal points of black theology, liberation theology, and feminist theology. Richard Niebuhr categorized the various Christian ethical positions as the following: "Christ Against Culture," which represents all the groups who believe that this world is essentially evil and man must withdraw from it in order to purify himself; "The Christ of Culture" group, which sees religion and culture as essentially the same (this is predominant among many Americans who equate the American way of life with the Christian way of life); and finally, "The Christ Above Culture" group, which agrees that religion and culture interact, but also claims that there is an area into which culture cannot reach. This symbolic life is beyond all secular concerns, which Niebuhr claims is the majority position within Christanity.

All ethical questions rest on a basic dilemma that is expressed particularly in ethical controversies involving religion. In Christianity there are those who emphasize faith and those who focus on works or the day-to-day living of the Christian life as an ethical response to the world. The former emphasizes salvation that is determined by the will of God, and the latter emphasizes the fulfillment of Christian ethical obligations as evidence of one's faith. Another of these dilemmas is the continuing controversy between the spirit of the law and the letter of the law. The spirit of the law may be impossible to legislate. Paul states, "Against these [love, joy, peace, patience, kindness, goodness, faithfulness, gentleness, and self-control] there is no law."

Free will, salvation by works, and legalism define the parameters of Christian ethics. Every person, says Gordon Allport, "whether he is religiously inclined or not, has his own ultimate presuppositions. He finds he cannot live his life without them, and for him they are true. Such presuppositions, whether they be called ideologies, philosophies, notions, or merely hunches about life, exert creative pressures upon all conduct." In Christianity, like other religions, religious beliefs are the foundation stones to a person's self-concept, the meaning he or she places on life, his or her value system, and his or her character. Each person has a value hierarchy, a scale of values, an ethic that he or she follows as a guide for ordering behavior. The highest value for the religious person may be called *unity*, for it is one's religious beliefs and practices—the mystical that seeks to comprehend the cosmos as a whole and to relate oneself to its embracing totality—that provide meaning and motivation for living in the world. The point is that faith gives meaning to life and provides the religious truth that fuels the ethical experience.

SOURCES

Anderson, Robert T., and Peter B. Fischer. *An Introduction to Christianity*. New York: Harper & Row. 1966.

Cone, James. *Black Theology and Black Power*. New York: Seabury Press. 1969.

Daly, Mary. *The Church and the Second Sex*. Rev. ed. New York: Harper & Row. 1975.

Royce, Joyce R. *The Encapsulated Man*. Princeton, NJ: Van Nostrand. 1964.

Walker, Williston. *A History of the Christian Church*. New York: Charles Scribner's Sons. 1918.

Zachner, R. C., ed. *The Concise Encyclopedia of Living Faiths*. New York: Hawthorn Books. 1959.

CHURCH AND STATE, SEPARATION OF

Sidney Mead, the eminent U.S. church historian, has described the United States as "a nation with the soul of a church." Perhaps this description alone best typifies the relationship between religion and government in the United States. The U.S. Constitution states that there will be no law establishing a particular religion. The results have been—in the United States—not only *religious pluralism*, but also, as Peter Berger notes, *moral pluralism*. This factor has resulted in moral conflicts because certain religious moral ideas have become secularized in law, as the First Amendment institutionalized religious liberty itself.

Within the American national character, such as its deep-rooted sense of historic mission and its inveterate moralism, we discover the "soul" of religious belief. Historians have made it clear that the men who drafted the First Amendment had quite different things in mind. They remind us that in view of the historical evidence it is difficult to sustain the later interpretation that the two clauses of the First Amendment, the "establishment" clause and the "free exercise" clause, implied a balanced theory of church-state relations. For example, James Madison was a relaxed deist comfortable in the Anglican Church, an advocate of "republican virtue" in the spirit of the American Enlightenment. On the other hand, Roger Williams was born of the fanaticism of English Protestant dissent. He was a cantankerous Puritan who also concluded that religious liberty was a desideratum in this world. The main concern of those who drafted the First Amendment—and by the way, it was a hurried affair in order to get on to more important matters—was not to formulate a positive statement about the rights of religion but to make sure that the new national government would not usurp rights and powers in the several states, most of which illustrated a variety of different religious practices. Thomas Curry says:

> The passage of the First Amendment constituted a symbolic act, a declaration for the future, an assurance to those nervous about the federal government that it was not going to reverse any of the guarantees for religious liberty won by the revolutionary states. . . . Congress approached the subject in a somewhat hasty and absentminded manner. To examine the two clauses of the amendment as a carefully worded analysis of church-state relations would be to overburden them.

Historians present a vivid picture of the bewildering variety of the colonies in the matter of religious arrangements. New England was dominated by the powerful Puritan presence. There was Virginia with its Anglican establishment, which was tolerant of a sort of mellow deism that characterized Jefferson, Madison, and Washington. Maryland experienced a short-lived attempt at Catholic libertarianism, and Pennsylvania, rooted in Quaker ideology, had a motley collection of religious eccentrics. And New York, perhaps the center of capitalism in the colonies with its tradition of Dutch mercantilism, demonstrated that religious liberty could be the fruit as much of commercial pragmatism as of lofty ideas. Berger comments:

> It is one of the miracles of American history that the representatives of these discrepant political entities could agree on anything; possibly the First Amendment was one of their less miraculous arguments, since no one desired to see the new nation institutionalize church-state relations along the lines of the English establishment.

From the United States's colonial past grew a set of particular political and ecclesiastical attitudes, perhaps fueled by the skepticism of the Enlightenment, that gave birth to the idea that since no certainties were available in the area of religion, tolerance was the only reasonable position. And the Protestant churches in the United States were amenable; that is, they possessed a strong sense of theological certitude, including the conviction that since the state and any state-established church would always misuse its power, the church that was faithful to the truth of the gospel must also be politically independent.

CHURCH-STATE RELATIONS

These ideas combined, at a particular time and place, to create a unique fabric of church-state relations. The variety of ethnic and cultural groups in the colonies gave way to too many religio-political interests for any one of them to become dominant. They learned to live with one another and later legitimized their religious freedom in the First Amendment. Although the Constitution, as it came to be interpreted, might have set up a wall of separation between church and state, it did not and could not separate religion from politicians. As we gather our intentions and review the major events in U.S. history, we find religion and politics mingled and intertwined with each other. From the antislavery and temperance campaigns of the nineteenth century, to the Civil Rights movement, the antiwar movement, and the antiabortion movement of our own time, we find each group defining its adversary as an illegitimate intrusion of religion into politics. Although the Constitution prevented Protestantism from becoming the established religion of the nation, it did not and could not change the fact that U.S. society was crucially shaped by Protestant beliefs and values.

But, from the middle 1970s and early 1980s, the Protestant character of U.S. civilization has become less distinct as masses of non-Protestants—Catholics, Jews, Buddhists, and Muslims—began moving into the country and effecting a change in society. Perhaps we are living in "post-Protestant" America. If so, this may be the reason we have seen a Protestant reaction to these changes, changes that the religious right considers immoral and devastating to its way of life. We have also witnessed a proliferation of Protestant television shows, some high-profile Protestant ministers campaigning for president, a new age of violence wrapped in both the "flag and the Bible," and the political right embracing these values as they too struggle to control America's destiny. The majority of Americans are as religious today as ever and whatever Americans are, they are not "secular humanists." Some have expressed the feeling that they are fighting for their values, their beliefs, and their country as they believe it should be morally and socially configured.

Modernization and secularization in the United States, different from Western Europe and Japan, have not killed her religious spirit, especially at the grassroots level. There has been a Western European type of secularization in the United States, but with a difference: It tends to be class-specific. It is mostly found among the college-educated upper middle class—the *New Class*—who derive their living from the production and distribution of symbolic knowledge rather than goods. Today, the evangelical upsurge that wishes to reinstate traditional religion in schools and other public places is more of a rebellion against the culture of the secularized New Class than against some subversive metaphysical evil. The phrase *born-again Christian* serves to separate the New Class from the noncollege-educated class who put religion and faith out front and who have yet to secularize or institutionalize religion—or recognize that, in the United States, it has been already done.

Within the New Class we find a secularization of certain religiously based moral issues about which they are perhaps unaware. Two basic positions are now emerging in American politics: those who advocate a strict separation of church and state, religion and politics, and those who

would somehow accommodate the religious character of the American people. This dual perspective flies in the face of reality, for most Americans remain persistently religious. Thus, the political turmoil of the middle 1990s can be interpreted as a religiously based political conflict with one side openly and unreservedly religious, and the other espousing the separation of church and state, keeping their religious convictions concealed—perhaps even from themselves.

The best example of this collision is the argument engendered by the Supreme Court decision on prayer in the public schools in June 1985. Many Americans view that decision as a solemn declaration that their country has become godless, that their deeply held beliefs and values have been disenfranchised by the government. But there is a deeper problem: every society—especially a democratic one—requires legitimation. Its beliefs and laws must be morally justified! Such legitimation cannot be pulled from thin air; it must be credible in terms of the beliefs and values that people actually hold. The strict interpretation of the First Amendment—the separation of church and state—has thus contributed to a crisis of legitimation in the United States. And yet, as American society has become more diverse, its own dedication to freedom, fraternity, and equality creates a "catch-22" situation. If we want to display our religion in public places, just which religious symbols are we to accommodate in the "public square"? This problem is likely to surface over such questions and issues as abortion and prayer in the public schools as a diverse people seek common ground in a rapidly changing society.

SOURCES

Berger, Peter L. *The Noise of Solemn Assemblies.* Garden City, NY: Doubleday. 1961.

Birnbaum, Jeffrey H. "The Gospel According to Ralph." *Time* (May 15, 1995).

Cargan, Leonard, and Jeanne H. Ballantine, eds. *Sociological Footprints: Introductory*

Readings in Sociology. 6th ed. Belmont, CA: Wadsworth. 1994. (See especially chapter 8, "Religion: The Supernatural and Society.")

Curry, Thomas. *The First Freedom: Church and State in America to the Passage of the First Amendment.* London: Oxford University Press. 1986.

Kessler, Gary E., ed. *Voices of Wisdom: A Multicultural Philosophy Reader.* Belmont, CA: Wadsworth. 1992. (See especially chapter 4, "What Makes a Society Just?")

CIVIL DISOBEDIENCE

Are there times when disobeying the law is morally justified? What are the responsibilities of a citizen? In one way or another we have been asking these questions whenever the issue of government authority has arisen. In 1995, were the violent acts of right-wing militia groups acts of civil disobedience? Can they ever be justified? In the *Dialogues* of Plato, Crito raised these issues; we read about the Confucian recommendation for rule by moral example; and Henry David Thoreau went to jail for refusing to pay his taxes to a government that supported slavery. He argued that conscience constitutes a higher law than the law of any land. We all have a moral duty to obey our consciences. However, Thoreau allowed that the person who commits civil disobedience must pay the legal penalty.

Many, of course, believe that the rule of law is both good and necessary. Laws protect people, create social stability, and provide opportunities to create rights that people might not otherwise enjoy. The right to life, liberty, and the pursuit of happiness needs to be protected and defined by laws. In pluralistic societies, we cannot depend on customs and traditions to unite people. Nor can we depend on the virtue and goodwill of our leaders. Only the rule of law can prevent abuse of power.

But how can we tell the difference between good laws and bad laws? Should we add that the right of civil disobedience be granted, or would such a right undermine entirely the rule of law? In the twentieth century, civil disobedience has played and continues to play a major role in effecting political and legal change. It became a political strategy in many nations. Gandhi used it to liberate India from British colonial rule. He carried a copy of Thoreau's *On Civil Disobedience* with him and used it as a blueprint for nonviolent resistance. Nelson Mandela also symbolized the use of civil disobedience to change the apartheid system of South Africa. Unlike Gandhi, however, Mandela and the National African Congress did not renounce the use of force. Morally, we must face the questions: When does civil disobedience become political revolution? When violence is used? Must one be willing to suffer the consequences of breaking the law in order to engage in a morally justifiable act of civil disobedience?

In 1963, the belief that individuals have the right to disobey the law under certain circumstances was not new. Under the leadership of Martin Luther King, Jr. (1929–1968), however, civil disobedience became a widely used tactic and even gained a measure of acceptability among some whites. King, a Baptist minister and winner of the Nobel Peace Prize, devoted his life to the struggle for racial justice in the United States. In his "Letter from the Birmingham Jail," King clearly distinguished between the laws to be obeyed and disobeyed: "A just law is a man-made law of God. An unjust law is a code that is out of harmony with the moral law." Like Thoreau and Gandhi, he argued for nonviolent methods. King also said, "Injustice anywhere is a threat to justice everywhere."

King's strategy of civil disobedience included the following tactics:

- Active nonviolent resistance to evil
- Not seeking to defeat or humiliate the opponent, but to win his friendship and understanding

- Attacking the forces of evil rather than the people who happen to be doing the evil
- Willingness to accept suffering without retaliation
- Refusing to hate the opponent
- Acting with the conviction that the universe is on the side of justice

King, like other blacks before him and since, made it clear that passive acceptance of injustice was intolerable. By emphasizing nonviolence, he hoped that Southern blacks would display their hostility to racism but minimize violent reaction by whites. By the end of 1963, the pattern was established and a method devised to confront racism—but civil disobedience did not work quickly. The struggle to desegregate buses in the South took seven years. The success of the Civil Rights movement rested on a dense network of local groups. Organized tactics were crucial to dismantling racist institutions that had existed for generations.

See also Civil Rights; Civil Rights Movement.

SOURCES

Gaines, James R., et al., eds. *Bridges and Borders: Diversity in America.* New York: Time Warner. 1994.

Knefel, Don, ed. *100 Essays from Time.* Boston: Allyn and Bacon. 1992.

Morris, Aldon. *The Origins of the Civil Rights Movement: Black Communities Organizing for Change.* New York: Free Press. 1984.

Rigden, Diana W., and Susan S. Waugh, eds. *The Shape of This Century: Readings from the Disciplines.* New York: Harcourt Brace Jovanovich. 1990.

CIVIL RIGHTS

The struggle for freedom goes back many centuries and embraces many people in different parts of the world. This struggle also involves many different issues, from freedom of speech to censorship and women's rights. For example, in 1643, the two houses of the British Parliament drew up a law providing that no book or other publication should "from henceforth be printed or put to sale, unless the same be first approved of and licensed by such persons as both or either of the said Houses shall appoint for the licensing of the same." This measure prompted John Milton to write one of the great defenses of free speech, entitled *Areopagitica,* which states the intellectual and moral case against censorship and for freedom of expression. Milton said, "Who kills a man kills a reasonable creature, God's image; but he who destroys a good book, kills reason itself." Milton was of the opinion that we could not know what is good unless we know what is evil, or recognize truth except as we can distinguish it from falsehood. For him, a free discussion of all social problems—including the abuses of government power—is needed. Human nature and morals, he reminds us, cannot be improved by repressive measures.

Another historic defense of freedom of expression was made by John Stuart Mill (1806–1873) in his essay "On Liberty." Mill believed that any attempt to limit freedom of speech, even among minority groups, is to be condemned. He comments: "If all mankind minus one were of one opinion, and only one person were of the contrary opinion, mankind would be no more justified in silencing that one person, than he, if he had the power, would be justified in silencing mankind." The one opinion may be right, says Mill, but even it if is clearly wrong, society gains by "the clearer perception and livelier impression of truth produced by its collision with error."

The first ten amendments to the U.S. Constitution are often called the "Bill of Rights": no one may be restrained from merely talking and expressing a point of view; Congress will make no laws respecting an establishment of religion or prohibiting the free exercise thereof; or abridging the freedom of speech, or the press; or the right of the people to assemble peaceably, and to petition the government for a redress of grievances. From other amendments we learn that certain things are not to be done "without due process of law." According to the tradition of freedom established by the U.S. Constitution, the "only opinion established by the Constitution is the opinion that a man is free to hold any opinion." The principle espoused by civil rights laws seems to be that the important thing is the individual person, the person's worth, uniqueness, and individuality, and that this uniqueness will be damaged or lost if attempts are made to enforce uniformity. Jefferson said, "It is time enough for the rightful purposes of civil government for its officers to interfere when principles break out into overt acts against peace and good order."

Fundamentally, civil rights refers to legal protection (under the law) against discrimination in terms of intentional behavior treating an individual differently on account of race, color, religion, sex, or national origin. Federal intervention had roots in the Fifteenth Amendment, and its reaffirmation led to a gradual transfer of political power to the formerly underprivileged. Active enforcement of civil rights legislation (the Twenty-fourth Amendment to the Constitution [1964] banning the poll tax as a requirement for participation in national elections and the Voting Rights Act [1965] provided blacks the assurance of full rights that enabled them to act as citizens) and the assignment of federal registrars to secure equal voting rights in the South led to substantial advances for minorities.

Early in 1947, Harry S. Truman, addressing a newly appointed Committee on Civil Rights, said, "I want our Bill of Rights implemented in fact. We have been trying to do this for 150 years." The committee report "To Secure These Rights" is one of the outstanding documents of our free society. From 1957 to 1965, a number of civil rights acts, a series of Supreme Court decisions, and various executive orders and legislative enactments indicate that progress was made in America in the age-long struggle for freedom of expression—the right to vote, to work, to live where one wished to live, and equality in general.

The American Civil Liberties Union (43rd Annual Report) states:

> The civil rights issues are among the "great issues" of our times, not because of their novelty—the century since the Emancipation Proclamation belies that possibility—nor because of their complexity, but because of their relationship to our national purpose. It is in this sense that they differ from the host of lesser but important questions that have prior to 1963 occupied the forums of national debate. But the 1960s promise to pose for us other "great issues"—issues which will "test whether [our] nation, or any nation so conceived and so dedicated can long endure"—and many of these issues will in addition be both novel and complex. The world-wide revolution of rising expectations will test the premises of our conduct of foreign affairs. The accelerating growth of the world's populations, and of our own, will test that and much more. The technology of production will test the premises of our economic order. And the technology of destruction will test the premises of both foreign policy and national defense. Today's civil rights test has become the proving ground on which to demonstrate whether we can use our rights and our machinery of self-government to resolve the first of these great issues to which the nation has turned its attention.

TRENDS

During the past 35 years, the struggle for freedom of thought and expression has continued in the following major areas:

- *Education.* Teachers have been dismissed for discussing such topics as civil liberties, race relations, the Vietnam War, the United Nations, and various topics related to abortion and sex education. In the 1990s, various state legislatures have been discussing whether and what type of sex education curriculum will be allowed in the public schools and at what grade levels various topics may be discussed. Another often debated issue involving freedom of expression is prayer in the public schools.

- *Freedom of thought and expression.* This issue came to the forefront in the 1950s and 1960s during the McCarthy Senate hearings and the banning of speakers on college campuses. "Blacklists" were frequently circulated, even through the Nixon era, that included not only "dangerous radicals" but persons whose views were not approved by the groups circulating the lists. Freedom of thought and expression in the area of security clearance and monitoring of individuals who are considered dangerous to society presents many problems, especially now that militant groups in the United States have expressed a disdain for governments of any kind. No thoughtful or loyal person will deny the need for security in a time no longer characterized by muskets, but by weapons of mass destruction. The protection of governments from such groups may call at times for some limitation of traditional liberties. The question of how far the government can go to limit the freedoms or civil liberties of its citizens depends, in the long run, on the severity of the situation or the crisis that presents itself.

- *Censorship.* The issue of censorship has been a persistent one in recent decades. Both obscene and antiestablishment literature has been banned from schools, libraries, and bookstores. A disturbing wave of text and reading-list censorship hit the country in the mid-1960s and has resurfaced through political pressure from the religious right. A statement by President Dwight D. Eisenhower should be kept alive and remembered, because it is still applicable today. He said: "Don't join the book burners. Don't think you are going to conceal faults by concealing evidence that they ever existed. Don't be afraid to go in your library and read every book as long as any document does not offend our own ideas of decency. That should be the only censorship."

Recently, in the wake of the Oklahoma City bombing (April 19, 1995), President Bill Clinton has called for self-censorship of those he referred to as talk show "hate mongers." Immediately, the censorship issue (freedom of speech and freedom of the press) was being debated on radio and television and written about on editorial pages across the country. Although Clinton's remarks and the reactions to them may have been overcharged with the reaction to the many deaths in Oklahoma City, free people—from both sides of the political spectrum—have spoken openly about the constitutional right to freedom of speech and the press, and some have spoken about the responsibilities such freedom carries.

- *The right to privacy.* The problem national security presents leads quite logically to a discussion of the right to privacy. The U.S. Constitution, especially as stated in the Fourth Amendment, recognizes the right to privacy: "The right of the people to secure in their persons, houses, papers, and effects, against unreasonable searches and seizures, shall not be violated, and no Warrant shall issue, but upon probable cause, supported by Oath or affirmation, and particularly describing the place to be searched, and the persons or things to be seized."

With the development of new technology and other instruments of surveillance, privacy has become a matter of great concern. Wiretapping, secret files, and computerized national data banks have given the "Big Brother" name new meaning in the United States. Using income tax returns, social security records, passports, and other documentation, the private lives of men and women can be accessed through computer networks. Although in a complex, high-tech society privacy will never be an absolute condition, the central question of how to maintain effective law enforcement and to retain our human and constitutional liberties at the same time is one that needs to be addressed. Fear and suspicion tend to destroy the human personality and disrupt the intercommunication that is the basis of a free nation. The contemporary world now faces a crisis over the question of the direction in which we should move on the issue, and the presence of extremist groups makes the preservation of safety and freedom more difficult. While civil liberty is not an absolute, the maintenance and enrichment of the democratic ideal is an important ethical goal for the protection of human freedom and values.

See also Bill of Rights; Censorship; Church and State.

SOURCES

American Civil Liberties Union. "To Secure: To Use: These Rights." In *43rd Annual Report, Jul 1, 1962 to Jun 30, 1963*. New York: ACLU. 1964.

Dewey, Robert E., and James A. Gould. *Freedom: Its History, Nature, and Varieties*. New York: Macmillan. 1970.

Eisenhower, Dwight D. (Address at Dartmouth College, June 14, 1953.) Quoted in *The Freedom to Read*. Chicago: American Library Association. 1953.

Knight, Harold V. *With Liberty and Justice for All: The Meaning of the Bill of Rights Today*. Rev. ed. Dobbs Ferry, NY: Oceana. 1968.

Mill, John Stuart. "On Liberty." In *The Range of Philosophy*. Edited by Harold H. Titus and Maylon H. Hepp. New York: American Book. 1964.

National Council of Teachers of English. "The Students' Right to Read." Champaign, IL: NCTE. 1962.

President's Committee on Civil Rights. "To Secure These Rights." Washington, D.C. 1947.

CIVIL RIGHTS MOVEMENT

To many rational individuals, the black-and-white images that appeared on their 12-inch Philco television sets in 1957 caused a moral awakening. Little Rock perhaps ushered in a sort of moral enlightenment, a regurgitation of a heretofore undigested moral disposition that was now longing to extend itself beyond small-town traditions, beyond the negligence of white Anglo-Saxon Protestant churches, beyond the big-city ghettos—to tear down the walls of separation distinguished by "white only" and "black only" signs of indignation. Many whites (especially males, as feminism and the equal rights movement for women grew in importance) who supported the cause of blacks—and later, the cause of women—felt the intense pressure of an inner moral dilemma as they struggled with the conflicting moral and social forces swelling inside of them, pulling and pushing, pulsating and subsiding, and urging them to express their own moral sensibilities.

It is difficult to say exactly when a social movement begins or ends. Usually a movement's ideas or tactics precede the actual mobilization of people and continue long after the movement's driving force has been replaced by new ideals and techniques. This description applies to the Civil Rights movement and its successor, "the continuing struggle of the oppressed for freedom, dignity, and equality." The Civil Rights movement gained its momentum with a Supreme Court decision in 1954 and ended as a major force in black America with the civil rights disorders of 1965 through 1968. But to point to a beginning and an end to this struggle is misleading, for even prior to 1954 there were some confrontations against white supremacy, including the CORE sit-ins of 1942 and efforts to desegregate buses in Baton Rouge, Louisiana, in 1953. And the movement for black rights evolved into a continuing moral struggle for the rights of children, of women, and of all oppressed people.

Although *Brown v. Board of Education* (1954) is a landmark and perhaps the most significant post–World War II beginning of the Civil Rights movement, the reaction to it demonstrated just how deeply held prejudice was in the South—but not only the South. Resistance to desegregation occurred on a number of levels: Some people called for the impeachment of all the Supreme Court justices; others petitioned Congress to declare the Fourteenth Amendment unconstitutional; cities closed public schools rather than comply with the law; the National Guard was used to block black students from entering a previously all-white school; there were sit-ins, demonstrations, and marches in towns and cities and on college campuses. Perhaps the stiffest resistance to segregation came from the White Citizens' Councils founded in Mississippi, which opened all-white schools as a means of evading the Supreme Court edict. These "freedom schools," as they were called, enrolled 300,000 white children by 1970. Gradually, school districts practicing *de jure* segregation complied. In those states bordering the South, desegregation occurred without court order. *Brown* was important as a contemporary beginning to the Civil Rights movement and for raising our moral sensibilities, but in the minds of some it did not resolve the school controversy, and today questions remain unanswered.

See also Brown v. Board of Education; Civil Rights.

SOURCES

Du Bois, W. E. B. *The Philadelphia Negro: A Social Study.* New York: Schocken Books. 1967.

Franklin, John Hope. *From Slavery to Freedom: A History of Negro Americans.* 5th ed. New York: Alfred A. Knopf. 1980.

Handlin, Oscar, and Lilian Handlin. *Liberty and Equality 1920–1994.* New York: HarperCollins. 1994.

COMMON GOOD

James Q. Wilson says, "To find what is universal about human nature, we must look behind the rules and the circumstances that shape them to discover what fundamental dispositions, if any, animate them and to decide whether those dispositions are universal." The roots of these *fundamental dispositions* are found, says Wilson, in the affection that a parent bears for a child. He comments, "Our moral senses are forged in the crucible of this loving relationship and expounded by the enlarged relationship of families and peers." Herein we discover the framework of what is normally called the *common good.*

Philosopher E. A. Burtt expands this notion in his own conceptualization of love. He finds that love is "freedom from self-centeredness" and, as such, possesses an "outreaching sensitivity." In both Wilson and Burtt, the expression of love is foundational to human societies. Says Burtt, "Love has its inherent implications for the guidance of action, and complete support of the person loved is not necessarily implied." One who loves will act so as to bring about the condition under which love will be able to realize itself more fully. To love is to seek the common good, a concept indispensable and assumed in legal and political thought; one that gains its meaning through the existence and intrinsic universality of love. And ethicists agree that a common good cannot arise except where there is effectively present a concern for the well-being of every person in the community.

Frances Moore Lappe, noting the conflicts that exist in society, believes that references to "the common good" may be overstated and even gloss over true differences, making it easy for someone to portray as some general interest what is really one's own version of truth. That is, what is in the "public interest" may in fact be the tale of government bureaucrats and politicians. As John Locke observed in 1664, "Whenever either the desire or the need of property increases among men, [and] there is no extension, then and there, of the world's limits. [I]t is impossible for anyone to grow rich except at the expense of someone else."

So is there really a "common good," or have we been misled? It seems to some, at least, that if there is a "common good" and if we have "common interests," then we would all have the same definition of the concept. Lappe says that the common good is what emerges in the healthy competition of interests. She comments: "Yes, there is a common good if by that you mean personal security, liberty under the law, and hope of increasing prosperity for those who apply themselves. Beyond that, to idealize a common definition of the good is dangerous." We should put ourselves on guard, especially when listening to politicians and those who seek power, because they are prone to tell us what the common good is and then set out to convince us that we should seek it.

SOURCES

Burtt, E. A. *In Search of Philosophic Understanding*. New York: New American Library. 1965.

Lappe, Frances Moore. *Rediscovering America's Values*. New York: Ballantine. 1989.

Wilson, James Q. *The Moral Sense*. New York: Free Press. 1993.

COMMON LAW

A major source of rules in English-speaking countries is common law. These common law rules are made by judges who enforce the customs of the community as each understands them. Once a court decides on a rule that it considers just, and that court and the other courts enforce the rule established in the first place, we have the makings of common law. The particular case in which a rule of this kind is first established is called a *precedent*. When this rule has been uniformly applied in a number of cases, it becomes a solid part of common law. A precedent is not rejected until a court feels that the rule no longer reflects the beliefs of the community. When a court rejects a precedent, it is said to *overrule* the earlier judgment. Thereafter, when rules are written in the form of statutes, difficulties sometimes arise in deciding exactly what the statute means, or to whom it applies. Such questions are decided by the courts in accordance with common law traditions.

A good example of the instability of common law is found in opinions about abortion. It has been over 22 years since the Supreme Court, in *Roe v. Wade*, established a constitutional right to abortion—yet abortion opponents are still active through various organizations, including the religious conservative political action groups that now have the ear of the Republican Party. David O'Steen, the executive director of the National Right to Life Committee, commenting on the 1994 congressional election, responded, "It was a good election for the pro-life movement." He then added that the movement had to contend with a president who is committed to a woman's right to abortion. In addition, in 1994, 52 percent of the abortion clinics surveyed by the Feminist Majority Foundation said they had experienced one or more types of violence, including death threats, stalkings, bombings, and arsons. The Rev. Flip Benham, the director of Operation Rescue National, a militant group that protests outside abortion clinics, said his group had no intention of scaling back.

Those who support a woman's right to abortion said the increase in violence, along with increased regulations on clinic providers, had contributed to a decrease in the number of doctors willing to perform abortions. Kate Michelman, president of the National Abortion and Reproductive Rights Action League, said, "It's a very difficult picture out there for women—politically, medically and in terms of safety. Access to abortion is in very serious jeopardy. Twenty-two years after the court handed down a landmark decision, we find ourselves really going backward rather than forward."

Will the law be changed? The law could be changed by the Supreme Court if it feels that *Roe v. Wade* is now out of step with common opinion. In 1990, in one Gallup poll, 73 percent of the public favored a law that would prohibit abortions after the first three months of pregnancy, and 69 percent favored restrictions on the use of abortion for the purpose of birth control. One observer noted that about 60 percent of the public is opposed to about 90 percent of the abortions that are carried out under *Roe v. Wade*. As the public speaks its mind on such topics as abortion, prayer in the schools, censorship, and the like, the majority-rules principle interpreted in terms of the "common wisdom" could find itself a part of the common law.

SOURCES

Arkes, Hadley. *Abortion Politics: Principle and Paradox.* New York: The Wall Street Journal. 1995.

Rawls, John. *A Theory of Justice.* Cambridge: Harvard Paperback. 1971.

COMMUNISM, ETHICS OF

Communism is the view that the modes of production determine the social and political institutions of society, and these in turn influence the ethical, religious, and philosophical notions that prevail in the society. Communism, as formulated by Karl Marx and Friedrich Engels, said that humans should be treated as persons and not as commodities. This idea we find in communism was formulated by Marx as the idea of the classless society, which included state ownership of industry and property. This, said Marx, is the beginning of freedom, equality, and abundance. The formula to be achieved is "from each according to his abilitiy, to each according to his needs." Thus, communism is an ethical system in which one must restrict his or her personal morality and conscience to the Communist Party and cause—the classless society.

Turning to Marxism, we learn that theories about the meaning of life, the sanctity of personhood, the nature of mind, proper moral behavior, the equality of persons, social reform, and religious belief—what we mean by *ethics* and *values*—are all nestled in a particular view of the nature of what it means to be a human being. The Marxist view of the nature of human life is no exception, but one should take note that it stands in sharp contrast to more religious or spiritual views found in Western civilization. This philosophy originated in the nineteenth century with the work of Marx, a committed atheist. In his ethics, Marx argued that social arrangements, not God, make us what we are. He and his collaborator, Engels, provided a distinctive philosophical view of human beings. This view is developed within the framework of their *historical materialism*, according to which human belief and behavior are determined by "the material conditions of life" (most notably, the economic modes of production needed to sustain existence). That is, Marx believed the only way to understand humans is to examine the social conditions that lead to their beliefs and behaviors, rather than by studying the beliefs and behaviors themselves.

From this frame of reference, Marx generates his well-known view of humans. More than anything else, it is *toolmaking* that distinguishes the human creature; that is, humans have a capacity to use what they produce to produce something else, while supposedly improving the conditions of life. This thesis fits comfortably with his view that the primary human social activity is economic production, as created from the work of laborers. In turn, economic production and technological change also change human lives and even whole societies, creating various ethics and values by which to live. In the *Manifesto of the Communist Party*, Marx and Engels connect their materialistic view of human beings to a communist vision of past and future society. In it, capitalist socialism is differentiated from the communist ideal, the central thesis being that society under capitalist domination has been merely a "history of class struggles" between the bourgeois class, which controls the means of production, and the proletarian or "working" class.

"Karl Marx has had more impact on actual events, as well as on the minds of men and women, than any other intellectual in modern times," says Paul Johnson. The reason for this gigantic influence is the fact that his views were institutionalized in two of the world's largest countries, the former Soviet Union and China, and their many satellites. And although there has been a radical shift of thought in Russia, the philosophy of Marx still lives in many of its people.

Marx was born in Trier (then Prussian territory) on May 5, 1818, one of nine children but the only son to survive into middle age. The family was middle class, and following a Prussian decree of 1816 that banned Jews from the higher ranks of law and medicine, the family converted to Protestantism in 1824. He attended Bonn University and from there he went to Berlin University, then one of the best in the world. Essentially, Marx became a classical scholar, specializing in Hegelian philosophy. He took his doctorate from Jena University and in 1842 became a journalist with the *Rheinische Zeitung*. The paper was banned a year later, and thereafter he wrote for the *Deutsche-Französische Jahrbucher* and other journals in Paris until his expulsion in 1845. In Brussels he organized the Communist League and wrote its manifesto in 1848. After the failed revolution, he moved to London until his death on March 14, 1883. He spent 34 years researching material for a massive study of capital and trying to get it into publishable shape. He saw one volume through the press (1867), but the second and third were compiled from his notes by Engels and published after his death.

According to Johnson's analysis, Marx was not interested in finding truth but in proclaiming it. He was a poet, journalist, and moralist; each was important, and taken together they made him a formidable writer and seer. Perhaps his greatest gift was as a polemical journalist. He made use of epigrams and aphorisms, many of which were not his own invention. Marat produced the phrases "The workers have no country" and "The proletarians have nothing to lose but their chains." Heine wrote the famous joke about the bourgeoisie wearing feudal coats-of-arms on their backsides and the phrase "Religion is the opium of the people." Louis Blanc provided "From each according to his ability, to each according to his needs." From Karl Schapper came "Workers of all countries, unite!" and from Blanqui, "the dictatorship of the proletariat." Of course, Marx produced many of his own ideas. The last three sentences of the *Manifesto* are perhaps his greatest: "The workers have nothing to lose but their chains. They have a world to gain. Workers of the world, unite!" Marx believed that a world crisis was building up. Throughout his life he had an apocalyptic vision of an immense, impending catastrophe on the existing economic system, and was fond of quoting Mephistopheles's line from Goethe's *Faust*, "Everything that exists deserves to perish." Some have said that Marx's communism was bound to fail because it was based not on scientific facts nor information about workers and their conditions, but on his poetic imagination and his vision, which was eschatological and laced with religious imagery.

SOURCES

Johnson, Paul. *Intellectuals*. New York: Harper & Row. 1988.

Marx, Karl. *A Contribution to the Critique of Political Economy*. Translated by N. I. Stone. Chicago: Charles Kerr. 1904.

Marx, Karl, and Friedrich Engels. *Manifesto of the Communist Party*. Revised (English Edition). Moscow: Foreign Language Publishing House. 1888.

COMMUNITY

Social scientists tell us that there is a community movement growing in the United States. Although it may only be a fleeting phenomenon on the social scene, it is important enough for us to take a look and define its major characteristics. Real community is connectedness. It is a place or an ideal that expresses and symbolizes our equal human dignity, our autonomy, and our powers of self-direction. Shaffer and Anundsen remind us that the requirements of real community are personal commitment, honesty, and vulnerability, as opposed to old notions of "rugged individualism." The community Shaffer and Anundsen write about—community with integrity—is a current social frontier. For them, community is a dynamic whole that emerges when a group of people:

- participate in common practices
- depend upon one another
- make decisions together
- identify themselves as part of something larger than the sum of their individual relationships, and
- commit themselves for the long term to their own, one another's, and the group's well-being.

They comment: "Certain timeless qualities epitomize every type of community, whether traditional or newly emerging. Chief among these is commitment. Commitment as a group—whether to family, place, clear communication, or the healthy working out of conflict—requires that community members embody such other timeless values as trust, honesty, compassion, and respect."

The Hopi Indians used to say that we all began together; that each race went on a journey to learn its own road to power, and changed; that now is the time for us to return, to put the pieces of the puzzle back together, to make the circle whole. In the United States today, perhaps it is the vast numbers of a selfish, narcissistic "me generation" and their language of individualism that limits the way we think about community. According to Tom Atlee, the editor of *Thinkpeace*, community has three fundamental dimensions:

- *Length:* How long your group has shared experience and how committed you are to continue that sharing.
- *Breadth:* How many facets of your life you share, and how wide a range of people and experiences you include.
- *Depth:* How deeply, thoroughly, or intimately you share.

The towering moral problem of our age is the problem of community lost and community regained. A true community is inclusive and its greatest enemy is exclusivity. Groups who exclude others because of religious, ethnic, gender, or more subtle differences are not communities. We live with heterogeneity and must design communities to handle it.

SOURCES

Atlee, Tom. *Thinkpeace*. 6622 Tremont, Oakland, CA, 94609.

Nozick, Robert. *The Examined Life: Philosophical Meditations*. New York: Simon & Schuster. 1989.

Shaffer, Carolyn R., and Kristin Anundsen. *Creating Community Anywhere*. New York: Putnam. 1993.

CONFLICT RESOLUTION

Conflicts of interest exist when the behavior of one person attempting to maximize his/her advantages or benefits prevents, blocks, interferes with, injures, or in some way makes ineffective the actions of another person attempting to maximize his/her advantages or benefits. Conflict resolution will be defined as conduct informed by reason, intelligence, and a fair-minded disposition, including the selection of appropriate strategies and behaviors that are able to bring resolution to troubling and inappropriate situations. This is a deliberate and critical process of self-control built upon self-understanding. Self-understanding largely controls our images of others, the values we believe are important, and the relationship between our thinking, our conduct, and the development of our character.

METHODS OF CONFLICT RESOLUTION

The first step is building positive human relationships. We can connect with other people in positive or negative ways. Effective conflict resolution depends on our ability to connect with family, friends, co-workers, and classmates in ways that promote the interest of all involved persons and in ways that are growth producing.

Building positive human relationships will have three different but interconnected parts: self-understanding, understanding why people like each other (our images of others), and isolating and understanding important internal values. As Stephen David Ross reflects: "The indefinable character of the self within the world-process is not simply an assemblage or even a sequence of events within that process, but is unified by a direction, an order, a focus, or point of view, from which and within which we assert a person to have a particular character."

The second step is learning methods for resolving conflicts effectively without hurting someone else or being hurt ourselves. These methods will include, but are not limited to, learning effective communication skills, responding to others in positive ways, building strategies for constructive conflict and controversy, learning problem-solving and decision-making skills, and channeling change into growth. After all, the Socratic quest for self-knowledge was nothing other than the quest for the conditions under which responsible choices can be made by human beings. Associated with these skills are such processes as addressing alternative perspectives and being fair minded. These are essential elements of resolving conflicts in ethically defensible ways.

VALUES, CONDUCT, AND REASONING

Conflict resolution connects values, conduct, and reasoning with the assumption that we all are responsible for our behavior. These ideas form the concept of critical self-control and will be applied to examples of ordinary human relationships and to those special aspects of behavior that are causes of concern in the contemporary schoolroom. A traditional goal of education is that of developing citizenship in a complex democracy. It provides a justification for the rules, principles, practices, and norms that we actually employ in our day-to-day activity of resolving personal and intrapersonal conflicts.

The ideas embodied in this inquiry reflect those of Charles Sanders Peirce, who provides the theme of rationality as critical self-control, and John Dewey (1916) who has provided an even richer conception of the nature of human action. Dewey's ideal of a self-critical community of inquirers has significant consequences for education, social reconstruction, and a revitalization of democracy. He advocated an ideal of shared intelligent activity in the life of a democratic community by which persons can eliminate social evils, enrich their experiences, and achieve desirable goods. Dewey's idea was that of developing and cultivating habits of creative intelligence so that we will not allow ourselves to become misshapen and dehumanized by social forces. He saw humans as "craftsmen" making selective responses to their environment. These responses would characterize their individuality. He reminds us that in acting we are always choosing, and our choices can be blind, motivated by impulse, convention, or rigid habit, but our choices and actions can also be intelligent. Dewey says: "A choice which intelligently manifests individuality enlarges the range of action, and this enlargement in turn confers upon desires greater insight and foresight, and makes choices more intelligent." For Dewey, the paradigm of a moral situation is one in which there are conflicts, and our task is to decide what is to be done. In such situations, we are called upon to make a practical judgment.

From Peirce's idea of *the growth of rationality as self-control,* to Dewey's notion that self-hood is an active process, we can generate the following educational themes:

- Education is a continuous process of reconstruction in which there is a progressive movement away from the child's immature experience to experience that becomes more pregnant with meaning, more systematic and controlled.
- The goal of education is the development of creative intelligence, which consists of a complex set of flexible and growing habits that involve sensitivity, the ability to understand the complexities of situations, imagination that is exercised in seeing new possibilities, fairness and objectivity in judging and evaluating conflicting values and opinions, and the courage to change one's views when it is demanded by the consequences of our actions and the criticism of others.

- The image of human behavior that emerges from this point of view is that we are "craftsmen," active manipulators advancing our own ideas, actively testing them, always open to ongoing criticism, and reconstructing ourselves and our environment.

Building on these themes, and recognizing that humans live and work with each other and their environment in dynamic and fundamentally connected relationships, we realize that all of life is organically connected. Through these relationships are created understanding and meaning. Conflict resolution incorporates understanding and meaning and the dynamics of human interaction into a multilevel and meaningful network of relationships. Our lives are continually created and renewed through this interactive process. The conjunction of these relationships is the most exciting experience of human living.

Defined as conduct informed by reason and intelligence, conflict resolution will be infused into this network of relationships. This infusion will give meaning, value, and a depth of human concern to our critical reasoning, thereby reducing conflict and helping create a peaceful, cooperative environment. Strategies such as negotiation, compromise, apologizing, sharing, problem solving, and decision making will help us keep alive the spirit of human communication and rejuvenate dialogue about issues and behaviors that matter the most. As we teach ourselves and our children constructive conflict management, we will be learning to deal with our lives in fruitful and productive ways. These practical strategies are based on the idea that humans are important and valuable and our lives should, ethically, reflect this frame of reference.

SOURCES
Hester, Joseph P. *Bridges: Building Relationships and Resolving Conflicts.* Carrboro, NC: New View. 1995.

————. *Teaching for Thinking.* Durham, NC: Carolina Academic Press. 1994.

Ross, Stephen David. *The Nature of Moral Responsibility.* Detroit: Wayne State University Press. 1973.

CONFUCIANISM

When we speak of Confucianism, we mean all the ancient writings and books dating from the time of the master, Confucius. Confucius noted that he was merely a transmitter, not a creator. In many ways this is true, for the religion that bears his name is based not only on his own teachings, but has a long history and eclectic nature. Yet, Confucius did provide ethical principles in a day when China was disturbingly corrupt. And he did believe that the moral condition of the country was not beyond redemption.

Twelve years after the Buddha was born in India, Confucius (551–479 B.C.) was born in the state of Lu in China. *Confucius* is the Latinization of *Kong Fuzi,* which means "Master Kong." He lived in a time when Chinese society had disintegrated into social and political chaos. Living during a time of social and political upheaval, Confucius became interested in the question of how the well-being of society can best be achieved.

Tradition tells us that Confucius was born a nobleman (upper class). His father died when he was 3, and at age 19 he married and went to work in the government. In the end, he made his career and reputation in education, not as a politician. Confucius provided what we today call a *humanistic* education to both nobleman and commoner. His concern was for achieving a good social order and to cultivate the humane qualities in the human spirit. Thus, he taught a humanistic social philosophy. His reputation in China became so great that among the common people he was deified, while among scholars he was venerated as a great sage.

Perhaps to understand the teachings of Confucius more fully, we can turn to *The Golden Mean of Tze-sze* (tr. Ku Hungming) for enlightenment and understanding. Lin Yutang has said, "The Golden Mean (Chungyung) represents probably the best philosophical approach to Confucian moral philosophy." In this teaching we learn that *"Truth means the fulfillment of our self; and moral law means following the law of our being."* Because truth is indestructible it is eternal. Being eternal, it is self-existent. Being self-existent, it is infinite. Being infinite, it is vast and deep. Being vast and deep, it is transcendental and intelligent. We learn also that human nature is God-given and that to fulfill the law of our human nature is what we call the *moral law.* The cultivation of the moral law is what we call *culture.* All is connected, related through absolute truth, and eternal. Confucius taught that wisdom, compassion, and courage are the three universally recognized moral qualities of man. It matters not in what way men come to the exercise of these moral qualities, the result is one and the same. These teachings come from Tze-sze (ca. 335–ca. 288 B.C.), a Chinese philosopher and grandson of Confucius.

Central to the teachings of Confucianism are the following:

- *Ren* (the Pinyin spelling for *jen*) is central to Confucius' teaching. It has been translated as "human excellence," "virtue," "humanity," "love," "benevolence," "humanism," and "human heartedness." *Ren* is humanity at its best, the "ideal human nature." It is humanity having realized its full positive potential— the source of moral principles and the outcome of a life lived doing the right things. When assessed for its implications, *Ren* gives rise to the principles of conscientiousness *(zhong)* and altruism *(shu)*—the golden rule, or, "Do unto others as you would have them do unto you."

- *Li* (pronounced "lee") refers to order, ritual, rite, custom, manners, ceremony, appropriateness, or propriety (conformity to establish standards of behavior and manners). The meaning of this teaching is that humans should behave appropriately, the models for which come from rites and customs handed down from the past Golden Age. Confucius thought of himself as a traditionalist and spent much of his time teaching and interpreting the cultural classics (called the *six disciplines*). Tradition is important in his view because it provides an external check on our present dispositions to act in one way or another.

- A major traditional virtue in China is *xiao* (the Pinyin spelling of *hsiao*, pronounced "shee-ow"). *Xiao* is familial love and involves the practice of kindness, honor, respect, and loyalty among family members. Confucius believed that a strong family is the basis of a strong society and, ultimately, familial love should be extended to the whole human community.

- *Yi* (pronounced "yee" and sometimes spelled *i*) is translated as "righteousness." Rightness is both a virtue and principle of behavior. It prescribes a pure motive and states that one should do the right thing because it is right. Tradition tells us that it is right to follow *li*, to practice *xiao*, or to seek *ren*. *Yi* says one should do what is right (follow tradition) because it is right.

The Confucian concern for balance, harmony, and appropriateness also reflects aesthetic values. Ethics has to do with moral values; aesthetics with artistic value and beauty. Confucius did not separate them because, for him, to call an action right was not merely to pass a moral judgment, but an aesthetic judgment as well. Morality is aesthetic order; the good and beautiful are one.

SOURCES

Ames, Roger T. *Thinking Through Confucius.* New York: State University of New York Press. 1987.

Koller, John. *Oriental Philosophies.* 2d ed. New York: Charles Scribner's Sons. 1985.

CONSCIENTIOUS OBJECTOR

See Civil Disobedience.

CONSUMERISM

Consumerism is a movement that promotes the interests of those who buy goods and services. Its main purposes are to protect consumers from unsafe products, fraudulent advertising, labeling, or packaging, and business practices that inhibit fair competition among businesses. Consumerism is active in many countries other than the United States. It includes private as well as government action and provides information about products and services. A valued part of these services includes information for consumers about effective means of obtaining compensation for damage or injury caused by defective products.

Consumer groups insist that consumers have several basic rights, including (1) the right to products that are consistent with their prices and the claims of manufacturers, (2) protection against unsafe goods, (3) truthful, adequate information about goods or services, and (4) a choice among a variety of products. Buyers also have a responsibility to use a product for the purpose intended by the manufacturer, and they should follow the instructions provided with the product.

Warranties and money-back guarantees provide assurances that a product will live up to the claims of the manufacturer. The Magnuson-Moss Warranty Act of 1975 provides the regulation for warranties. This law requires that warranties be written clearly and gives the consumer the right to an implied warranty if the manufacturer does not provide a written one. The right to safety is provided through a number of federal agencies: the Food and Drug Administration enforces laws concerning the safety of food, drugs, and cosmetics; the Consumer Product Safety Commission sets safety standards for many household products; the National Highway Traffic Safety Administration sets and enforces safety requirements for automobiles and related products; and the Federal Trade Commission (FTC) regulates advertising and administers several programs that handle deceptive claims. Such laws as the Consumer Credit Protection Act of 1968, often called the Truth in Lending Act, requires sellers to state clearly the charge made for loans and installment purchases and to express the interest rate as an annual rate. The Fair Packaging and Labeling Act of 1966, also known as the Truth in Packaging and Labeling Act, requires that the package used for a product provide certain information: the identity of the product, the manufacturer's name and address, and the net quantity of the contents. The U.S. Department of Agriculture requires that the grade of meat and dairy products appear on those items for the benefit of consumers. Consumer organizations such as Consumers' Research, Inc. and Consumers Union test a wide variety of products and publish the results.

The U.S. government regulates business in order to promote free and fair competition. The Sherman Antitrust Act of 1890 forbids monopolies and price fixing. The U.S. Justice Department and the FTC enforce the Sherman Act. The FTC also enforces the Clayton Antitrust Act of 1914 and the Celler-Kefauver Act of 1950, which are designed to prohibit businesses from forming combinations that would reduce competition.

SOURCES

Mayer, Robert N. *The Consumer Movement: Guardians of the Marketplace.* Twayne, 1989.

Reader's Digest. "Consumer Adviser: An Action Guide to Your Rights." Rev. ed. 1989.

Schmitt, Lois. *Smart Spending: A Young Consumer's Guide.* New York: Charles Scribner's Sons. 1989.

COOPER, ANNA JULIA

In 1892, Anna Julia Cooper, a Washington, D.C., educator, published *A Voice From the South,* her collection of essays considering questions of race, gender, education, and other related topics. Cooper's book has been praised as "the most precise, forceful, well-argued statement of black feminist thought to come out of the nineteenth century" (Mary Helen Washington, 1988). By 1892, most of the major African American higher educational institutions—Howard, Tuskeegee, Hampton, and Fisk—had been founded. The Fisk Jubilee Singers had traveled to Europe and raised $150,000, much of which went to further construction of the university, and Thomas Fortune had founded the self-help-oriented African-American League. The General Federation of Women's Clubs, which expressly excluded African American women, was established in 1890; 4 million women participated in the 1890 American workforce, a million of whom were African American. This was the age of reform in the post–Civil War United States; by the end of the decade, U.S. imperialism would be the norm.

The depression of 1893, the first-of-its-kind Conference of Black Women in Boston (1895), and *Plessey v. Ferguson* (1896) were just ahead. The year 1892 was one of intense contradictions for women activists of the emergent African American elite. Lynching was at its highest point that year. The year in which the black women's club movement was born, the following were all published or at press: Frances Ellen Watkins Harper's novel, *Shadows Uplifted* (1892); Ida B. Well's *Southern Horrors: Lynch Law in All its Places* (1892) and *Oak and Ivy* (1893); and Paul Lawrence Dunbar's first book of poems. Booker T. Washington was nine years away from publishing *Up From Slavery* (1901) and W. E. B. Du Bois was a graduate student at Friedrich Wilhelm University in Berlin—his *The Souls of Black Folk* was 11 years ahead.

This was the social, educational, political, and literary climate in which Cooper wrote *A Voice From the South,* her collection of essays written between 1886 and 1892, which examines questions of race and gender separately and as they intersect. Cooper critiques the burgeoning white women's movement for its racist exclusion as well as African American male "race-leaders" for their neglect of both the potential and actual contributions of women. She observed: "While our men seem thoroughly abreast of the times on almost every subject, when they strike the woman question they drop back into sixteenth century logic." Cooper's analysis examines images of African peoples in literature by white writers and evaluates the ethics behind a growing U.S. expansionism. She felt that grassroots and elite echelons of politics and society needed to hear African American women's voices in order to survive. "Lifting As We Climb," the motto of the National Association of Colored Women, would be a credo.

Elizabeth Alexander observes:

> Looking at *A Voice* as a whole, rather than in its parts, reveals a textured strategy taken by Cooper to find a new form in which to house the contemplations of an African-American female intellectual, and, by extension, a nascent African-American women's intellectual movement. The essays are at once allegory, autobiography, history, oratory, poetry, and literary criticism, with traces of other forms of address. Only such a diverse structure could encompass the tension of forging an African-American, female, demonstrably thinking self from whatever intellectual material was at hand. In *A Voice,* Cooper creates an unprecedented self: the African-American female intellectual at the end of the nineteenth century, little more than a generation beyond slavery and two generations before the unimaginable changes to come.

Cooper wrote out of the impulse to present a unified, serviceable vision of the future for African Americans as well as out of a resistance to a static, monolithic view of what it was to be black, and to be a black woman. She articulates a philosophy that works in service to her race and gender. Her best-known statement, which gives voice to this philosophy, is the following: "Only the BLACK WOMAN can say 'when and where I enter, in the quiet, undisputed dignity of my womanhood, without violence and without suing or special patronage, then and there the whole *Negro race enters me.*' "

SOURCES

Alexander, Elizabeth. "'We Must Be About Our Father's Business': Anna Julia Cooper and the Incorporation of the Nineteenth-Century African-American Woman Intellectual." *Signs, Journal of Women in Culture and Society* 20 (Winter 1995).

Cooper, Anna Julia. *A Voice From the South.* (Introduction by Mary Helen Washington.) New York: Oxford University Press. 1988.

Culp, D.W., ed. *Twentieth Century Negro Literature.* Atlanta: J. L. Nichols. 1902.

COOPERATION

Cooperation is based on the ability of persons to get along—to attach significance to a larger social entity than themselves and their immediate families. Cooperation, as an attitude or disposition to behave in certain ways, begins within the nuclear family and is there developed, advanced, and expanded so that as a child matures it can be extended outward to humankind as a whole. To say this is to point out that cooperation is based on collaborative thinking and decision making that helps one organize his or her self-centered desires by taking other people into consideration. This is why ethicists normally include cooperation among humans' moral dispositions. It is the ability to exercise self-control and restraint, and to work out problems with others while improving relationships. Some cultures emphasize the virtues of duty and self-control, some sympathy and fairness, but sociability is more complex: it involves both the desire to love and be loved, and to please others and to be pleased by them. These are powerful sources of sympathy, fairness, conscience, and cooperation.

One should understand that cooperation, as a moral behavior, will involve the idea of building reciprocal relationships. Reciprocal relations, the idea of reciprocity, are built on a foundation of mutual exchange, a mutual giving and receiving. This interchange is a form of interdependence and, when based on reciprocal affection, becomes critically important to the development of moral character. To understand these characteristics of cooperation is also to understand that cooperation is of the essence of community, of human dialogue and interaction, and of recognizing one's interdependency with others and the environment.

See also Ethics, Theory of.

SOURCES
Buber, Martin. *Between Man and Man*. Boston: Beacon Press. 1955.

Schutz, William C. *FIRO: A Three-Dimensional Theory of Interpersonal Behavior*. New York: Rinehart and Winston. 1958.

Wilson, James Q. *The Moral Sense*. New York: Free Press. 1993.

CORPORAL PUNISHMENT

Corporal punishment refers to physical discipline, usually an issue in public and private schools and day-care centers. But is corporal punishment ever right? This is the moral issue, and the pragmatic question is: Are its effects negative or positive? Fredric H. Jones, in his *Positive Classroom Discipline* (1987), says: "Of all the discipline techniques in existence, corporal punishment distinguishes itself as having the fewest assets and the greatest number of liabilities." Jones considers corporal punishment to be a quick, short-term cure for negative behaviors that places the adult and child into a series of coercive cycles and negative reinforcers.

Terry Rose describes the multiplicity of reinforcers and reinforcement errors that cause many educators to be consistently deluded into thinking that corporal punishment has caused something effective to happen in discipline at their school. The bogus reinforcers occur during the four phases of a typical student's trip to the office to receive corporal punishment: (1) disruption in the classroom, (2) the trip to the office, (3) arrival at the office, and (4) return to the class. These reinforcers are bogus because the negative behaviors soon reappear in the student and the only solution is the "trip to the office." The research on corporal punishment shows nothing: whether it works or does not work. There is no scientific literature of consequence to serve as the basis of scientific debate. Thus, the argument is usually a moral one: from the ethical point of view, corporal punishment is thought of as a primitive discipline rather than a positive and humane course of action because it depends on coercion and pain control in its purest form.

SOURCES

Jones, F. H. *Positive Classroom Discipline.* New York: McGraw-Hill. 1987.

Patterson, Gerald R. *Coercive Family Practices.* Eugene, OR: Castilio. 1982.

Rose, T. L. "The Corporal Punishment Cycle: A Behavioral Analysis of the Maintenance of Corporal Punishment in the Schools." *Education and Treatment of Children* 4 (1981): 157–169.

CORRUPTION

See Crime.

COURAGE, MORAL

Courage is usually considered to be the ability of an individual to sacrifice safety and comfort and to endure hardship (either physical or mental) for the sake of some noble cause. It may be physical courage or moral courage. The person with moral courage stands for what he or she believes to be right in the face of ridicule and unpopularity and even though it may mean personal loss. Of course, the courage that is displayed by a person may be the means to the attainment of a worthy or an unworthy goal. Thus, courage, loyalty, and intelligence by themselves do not make a person good. These must be considered in the light of the motives and the consequences to which they are related and evaluated by accepted ethical criteria.

SOURCES

May, Rollo. *The Courage to Create.* New York: Norton. 1975.

Riesman, David, and N. Glazer. *Faces in the Crowd: Individual Studies in Character and Politics.* New Haven, CT: Yale University Press. 1952.

COURTSHIP AND ROMANTIC LOVE

There is some history to the social habits of human beings. What today we perceive as acceptable courtship and romantic love practices were not always considered so, and they are by no means universally accepted in different societies even today. Of course, to think about love is not to think about a singular disposition or emotion. Love is much more complex. For example, in Robert Sternberg's triangle theory, love has three main components: intimacy, passion, and decision/commitment. An analysis of these three components leads Sternberg to identify eight kinds of love, depending on the presence or absence of each component: nonlove (all three components absent), liking (passion and decision/commitment absent), infatuated love (intimacy and decision/commitment absent), empty love (intimacy and passion absent), romantic love (decision/commitment absent), companionate love (passion absent), fatuous love (intimacy absent), and consummate love (all three present).

Although Sternberg's varieties are based on contemporary studies, there is some indication that in our past history, individuals and cultures understood enough about love and courtship to fix its importance to society and thus regulate its practices. For example, in the early Middle Ages, in the upper strata of society, parents commonly arranged the marriage of their offspring to members of appropriate kin groups—a practice still used today in certain societies. During this period, codes of etiquette and chivalry became highly developed in the courts of European nobles. Chivalry and arranged marriage were not, however, sufficient to produce the idea of romantic love as something different from the ordinary love resulting from sharing and companionship.

In the late medieval period in Europe among those of high status, romantic love came to be a technique of rebellion against familial control of mating. In short, the historical factors most immediately responsible for the development of courtship and romantic love as something unique or different from ordinary love included the practice of arranging marriages, the courtly games and etiquette codes developed in medieval times, and the increasing separation of the nuclear family from other societal groups, in accordance with the official morality of the day. During this period, romantic love and courtship could be found, distinguishable primarily in the upper strata of society, but they had little direct relation to either marriage or the selection of a mate.

Romantic love is not unique to the Western world. Given the opportunity, it can "break out" in any society. Variations from one society to another are a matter of definition and control. In kin-centered societies, love is an inadequate basis for mating and sex relations, and is therefore defined negatively and controlled by the kin group. A love relationship may develop between mates, but this is not the basis for, nor even a necessary concomitant of, their marriage.

In the colonial American family, in which the nuclear family dominated many functions and vied with the kin group for solidarity, choice of mate was individual but greatly restricted by the nuclear family and kin influences. In the contemporary U.S. family, in which individualism dominates values, the young and their peers compete with both the nuclear family and kin solidarity; mate selection is by choice and not normally prearranged, and it is therefore based on love. Taking this into consideration, the nuclear family and various kin relationships still use various methods, often successful, to influence the courtship process.

Love, therefore, is an emotional potential that is controlled to varying degrees by different societies. The amount of control varies directly with the degree to which institutional functions and individuals are embedded within the kin group. But when the mating process is participant-run, it is highly correlated with romantic love as a selection criterion. In modern U.S. society, love has been institutionalized, through the mass media and the rise in popularity of and access to the automobile, as the basis for individual choice of a mate, but even in the United States diverse means are used by family and kin to restrict the opportunity for love to develop. Normally, people in the United States will cite love as the reason for their marriage, but are unable to define the disposition itself.

SOURCES

Adams, Bert N. *The Family: A Sociological Interpretation.* New York: Harcourt Brace. 1995.

Quale, G. A. *A History of Marriage Systems.* Westport, CT: Greenwood. 1988.

Sternberg, Robert. "A Triangular Theory of Love." *Psychological Review* 93 (1986): 119–135.

CREATIONISM

Creationism is the belief that the world and what is in it were created by God and given in the account in the first chapter of Genesis in the Old Testament. Isaac Asimov commented in 1981: "However much the creationist leaders might hammer away at their 'scientific' and 'philosophical' points, they would be helpless and a laughingstock if that were all they had. It is religion that recruits their squadrons. Tens of millions of Americans, who neither know nor understand the actual arguments for—or even against—evolution, march in the army with frightening force, impervious to, and immunized against, the feeble lance of mere reason." Creationism then, as juxtaposed with theories of evolution, recalls the Enlightenment debate between science and reason, belief and fact, faith and hypothesis.

ARGUMENTS

Scientists tell us that a hypothesis requires more than plausibility to be adopted; it requires evidence. Evolution, according to scientists, bears the status of "fact" because of the amount of verifiable evidence that supports it. The best scientific education encourages skepticism, questioning, independent thought, and the use of reason. Discoveries in science, therefore, are not always simple, clear, and certain. Facts are contingent, based on available evidence. New evidence may change what is thought of as fact.

Modern-day evolution theory begins with Charles Darwin (1809–1882), one of the greatest scientists of all time, who came only slowly to an evolutionary position. He brought biology out of the Middle Ages with his *The Origin of Species*, and gave evolution a material cause—*natural selection*—which was the adaptation of organisms to their environment. Although today there are conflicts within evolutionary science, especially between the geneticists and the Darwinians (neither side doubts that evolution is a fact; it is the "how" of evolution that is being questioned), a "New Synthesis" has been reached. We now know that populations contain very extensive genetic variation that continually arises by mutation of preexisting genes. Scientists know what genes are and how they become mutated. As of 1982, the historical existence of evolution was viewed as fact by biologists. To explain how the fact of evolution has been brought about, a theory of evolutionary mechanisms—mutation, natural selection, genetic drift, and isolation—has been developed.

But not everyone is convinced by the claims of biological science. Claiming evolution to be ill-conceived are the creationists. Creationism is primarily a theistic movement motivated by a belief in God and the literal interpretation of the Old and New Testaments. In the fourth century A.D., St. Augustine declared that "nothing is to be accepted save on the authority of scriptures, since that authority is greater than all the posers of the human mind." "Moses opened his mouth," affirmed St. Ambrose, "and poured forth what God had said to him." And so the fathers of the church established one of the most powerful, lasting beliefs in Judeo-Christian civilization: the literal truth of the Bible's every word. Although church scholars have established that the story of creation with which the Bible opens was developed by the Hebrews from even more ancient Babylonian and Chaldean myths, devoted believers still hold to its literal, God-inspired truth.

For these creationists, Darwin's theory of evolution (1859), like Galileo's astronomy (1615), has become a symbol of atheistic materialism. It was as late as 1925 that high school teacher John Scopes was found guilty of violating the Tennessee law against teaching evolution, and today fundamentalist religion and evolutionary biology are still fiercely at odds.

In 1981, two states passed laws requiring creation to be given "equal time" with evolution in textbooks and teaching in the public schools. Similar bills have been proposed in other states. Creationists represent only one facet of a movement that is dedicated to extinguishing "secular humanism," under which they include all attitudes and educational programs that do not explicitly include their theological doctrines. As leading creationist Nell Segraves has put it, "We have a lot to undo. Creation/evolution is only the beginning."

SOURCES

Asimov, Isaac. "The 'Threat' of Creationism." *New York Times Magazine* (June 14, 1981).

Cloud, P. "Scientific Creationism—A New Inquisition Brewing." *The Humanist* 37:1 (1977).

Creation/Evolution (P.O. Box 5, Amherst Branch, Buffalo, New York 14226) is a quarterly publication dedicated to promoting evolutionary science and covers current creationist political activities. See especially Issue 7 (Winter 1982).

Futuyma, Douglas J. *Science on Trial.* New York: Pantheon Books. 1983.

CREATIVITY

Creativity is the highest expression of humanity's giftedness. It involves the synthesis of all cognitive functioning, and yet it is still more. Creativity includes a "spark" from another dimension, as E. Paul Torrance concludes in his *Search for Satori and Creativity.* Although there is no agreement as to the precise definition of creativity, most scholars agree that it is "effective intelligence" involving the ability to solve problems, to be open to experience, to be free from crippling restraints and impoverishing inhibitions, to have an aesthetic sensitivity, to possess cognitive flexibility, and to have acquired independence of thought and action.

CREATIVITY: A MULTIFACETED PHENOMENON

It is probably most productive to view creativity as a multifaceted phenomenon rather than a single unitary constant capable of precise definition. In 1950 psychologist J. P. Guilford, one of the early pioneers in creativity research, pointed out that as creativity research expands so will the number of definitions used for the concept. In 1959, Calvin Taylor found more than 100 definitions of creativity in literature. These definitions were varied and some could be considered conflicting. For example, in 1977 Guilford found that problem solving and creative learning are often linked together. He defined problem solving as facing a situation with which you are not fully prepared to deal. Problem solving occurs when there is a need to go beyond the information given—thus there is a need for new intellectual activity. Guilford remarked: "Problem solving and creative thinking are closely related. The very definition of those activities show[s] logical connections. Creative thinking produces novel outcomes, and problem solving involves producing a new response to a new situation which is a novel outcome."

This definition is closely related to a framework for describing the process of creative learning put forth by Torrance and Myers in 1970. They describe the creative learning process as "Becoming sensitive to or aware of problems, deficiencies, gaps in knowledge, missing elements, disharmonies . . . bringing together available information; defining the difficulty or identifying the missing element; searching for solutions, making hypotheses, and modifying and retesting them; perfecting them; and finally communicating the results."

In 1961, Mel Rhodes set out to find a single definition of creativity. He examined 56 different definitions of the word and found in them interconnecting strands: *the person* (stages of thinking people go through when overcoming an obstacle or achieving a goal); *the product* (characteristics of artifacts or outcomes of new thoughts, inventories, designs, or systems); and *the press* (the relationship between people and the environment, the situation, and how it affects creativity). Each of these strands operates as an identifier of some key components of the larger, more complex concept of creativity. Although creativity research may not always be conclusive, there does appear to be sufficient evidence to warrant the consideration of its various implications.

SOURCES
Clark, Barbara. *Growing Up Gifted.* 2d ed. Columbus, OH: Charles E. Merrill. 1983.

Isaksen, Scott G., ed. *Frontiers of Creativity Research.* Buffalo, NY: Bearly. 1987.

Guilford, J. P. "Creativity." *American Psychologist* 5:444–454. 1950.

Torrance, E. Paul, and R. E. Myers. *Creativity Learning and Teaching.* New York: Dodd-Mead. 1970.

CRIME

Crime is defined variously by different groups of people. Some equate crime with all antisocial behavior. Others say that crimes are actions associated with racism, sexism, and imperialism—behaviors that violate basic human rights. Similarly, some use moral rather than legal criteria to define what is or is not a crime. For example, Martin Luther King, Jr., and his followers believed that the laws enforcing racial segregation were morally wrong, so to violate them (civil disobedience) was not a crime but a virtue. There are also religious people who believe any sinful behavior is a crime, regardless of what the formal law decrees. Thus, two unmarried or same-gender people living together in a sexual relationship would be a crime for many religious people because they believe such behavior to be sinful, even though in many states there are no laws against these behaviors.

The most common definition of crime—the breaking of a law—officially labels people and separates society into criminal and noncriminal categories. Accordingly, criminality is a social status determined by the way in which an individual is perceived, evaluated, and treated by legal authorities. Generally, the law designates as criminal any behaviors that violate the strongly held norms of society. Among these are theft, murder, vandalism, rape, and assault. Although there may be consensus in society on certain laws, because law is an inherently political phenomenon, a violation of law means that the crime is ultimately an expression of group conflict of interest. Individuals and groups in power determine what behaviors violate their interests and thus are criminal. The following observation of Emile Durkheim (*The Division of Labor in Society*), definitely personalizes the definition of "crime" and lends credence to crime's amoral aspects: "We must not say that an action shocks the common conscience because it is criminal, but rather that it is criminal because it shocks the common conscience. We do not reprove it because it is a crime, but it is a crime because we reprove it."

CATEGORIES OF CRIME

The Uniform Crime Reports of the Federal Bureau of Investigation (FBI) concentrate on traditional types of crime, which tend to be concentrated among the young and the poor. To focus only on traditional crimes and ignore other types that may actually be more costly to society in terms of lives and property is a mistake. The major categories of crime are the following:

- *Traditional Street Crime.* These are serious crimes against property or violence against people. People accused of these crimes are the ones who typically clog the courts and jails.
- *Victimless Crimes.* To enforce the morality of the majority, legislation has made criminal certain acts that may offend an individual but do not harm others. Laws prohibiting Sunday sports, gambling, sex between consenting adults, and drug use create such "victimless crimes." The argument for such laws is that the state has a right to preserve the morals of its citizens in the interest of promoting social stability and consensus.
- *White-Collar Crimes.* Traditional street crimes such as assault and robbery, while legitimate concerns, are much less significant in cost and social disruption than crimes committed by middle-class and upper-class citizens in their business and social activities. These crimes include theft of company goods, embezzlement, tax evasion, forgery, passing bad checks, and fraudulent use of credit cards.
- *Corporate Crimes.* Businesses are also guilty of crimes. The list of illegal acts committed in the name of corporate

good includes fraudulent advertising, unfair labor practices, noncompliance with government regulations regarding employer safety, price-fixing agreements, stock manipulations, copyright infringement, theft of industrial secrets, marketing of adulterated or mislabeled food or drugs, bribery, and swindles. The magnitude of such crimes far surpasses the human and economic costs from other types of crime.

- *Political Crimes.* Any illegal act intended to influence the political system is a political crime. The operant word is "illegal." Political crimes are nothing new. The Credit Moluler scandel during Grant's administration and the Teapot Dome scandal under Harding rival Watergate under Nixion. For sheer depraved corruption, perhaps nothing can rival the nefarious regime of William "Boss" Tweed, who controlled New York City from 1859 to 1871. Tweed and his cronies controlled the decision making and used their influence to stay in power and become wealthy. For example, Tweed bought 300 church benches for $5 each and resold them to the city for $600 apiece, for a profit of $178,500 on an investment of $1,500. It is estimated that Tweed's corrupt government cost the city approximately $200 million from 1865 to 1871.

- *Organized Crime.* Organized crime is a business operation that seeks profit by supplying illegal goods and services: drugs, prostitution, pornography, gambling, loan sharking, the sale of stolen goods, cigarette bootlegging, and even the disposal of hazardous wastes. In short, persons can and do organize to provide what others want even if it is illegal. In fact, the illegality of what people want ensures that someone will supply the goods or services because the profits are so high.

See also Capital Punishment.

SOURCES

Eitzen, D. Stanley, and Maxine Baca Zinn. *Social Problems.* 4th ed. Boston: Allyn and Bacon. 1989.

Etzioni, Amitai. *Capital Corruption: The New Attack on American Democracy.* New York: Harcourt Brace Jovanovich. 1984.

Quinney, Richard. *The Social Reality of Crime.* Boston: Little, Brown. 1970.

CROSS-RACE ADOPTION

The 1995 movie *Losing Isaiah* explores whether adoptive parents can successfully rear children of another race. But parents of one race adopting children of another is an issue playing out in real life as well. There is a growing trend toward interracial adoption: a 1991 survey found that 64 private adoption agencies placed 53 percent of children cross-racially; for 23 public agencies, the figure was 15 percent.

The ethical issues involving cross-race adoption arise in relation to the question, "How difficult is it for a black child reared in a white world?" or vice versa, a white child reared in a black world? How will the child adjust to having a foothold in two cultures but a full stake in neither? Can good parenting overcome racial and cultural differences?

Although the easiest path to an adoptable infant for 40-something parents is cross-racial or foreign adoptions, will white couples seeking to adopt black infants be taking a child away from a black couple seeking to adopt? This is perhaps a sociological rather than a moral question, but one that is fraught with value issues as well. In 1972, the head of the National Association of Black Social Workers condemned the practice of white couples adopting black infants as "racial genocide." And how about the child's future? How will the child feel about being a black child of white parents or a white child of black parents? How will the child adjust to having to live in two seemingly different worlds?

Recently, researchers who followed 204 adoptive families for 20 years found that cross-racial adoptions in the group were successful. Black kids adopted by white parents had problems no different from those of children reared by their biological parents. Yet, there are concerns being expressed quite universally: Will there be prejudice from both whites and blacks? Although separatism is still a growing issue in the black community, perhaps the single most important value issue in cross-racial adoption is the parents' ongoing cultural awareness of likenesses and differences in the black and white cultures.

Rebecca Carroll, a black person who grew up in a white family in an all-white town, says she "invented" her black identity. She says: "Love is important, and family bonds certainly can cross racial boundaries, but not without a fierce compromise, invariably rife with mental and emotional strain. It's no cakewalk. Not if the adoptive parents intend to encourage their child to explore what it means to be black, to learn his or her history—the good, the bad, and the ugly."

Carroll continues: "Loyalty to two often opposing cultures has forced me to develop an unequivocal humanistic bottom line in terms of my personal code of ethics. Further, what my parents did provide me with was, and is, invaluable. And that is a sense of limitless creativity, willful integrity and lucid vision all of which have given me the tools I've needed to self-invent my identity as a black woman. From scratch. Everyday, I am grateful to them for that."

SOURCES
"Cross-Race Adoption: Not a Black and White Issue." *USA Weekend* (March 17–19, 1995).
Skolnick, Arlene S., and Jerome H. Skolnick, eds. *Family in Transition.* 8th ed. New York: HarperCollins. 1994.

CULTS

The word *cult* is a general word referring to any system of religious worship, especially with reference to its rites and ceremonies. It also refers to having a great admiration for a person, thing, idea, etc. to the point of worshipping it. Although religion is perhaps best defined as the human attempt to achieve the highest possible good by adjusting life to the strongest and best powers in the universe, some would argue that the mainstream religions of today should not be called "cults." They argue that this word should be left to those marginal faiths that seem mysterious, different, and nontraditional. Rather than being merely descriptive, *cult* has become loaded with value and is usually perceived by mainstream religions in a negative light.

See also Religion and Morality.

SOURCES
La Barre, Weston. *The Ghost Dance: Origins of Religion.* Garden City, NY: Doubleday. 1970.
Toynbee, Arnold. *An Historian's Approach to Religion.* London: Oxford University Press. 1956.
Walhout, Donald. *Interpreting Religion.* Englewood Cliffs, NJ: Prentice-Hall. 1963.

CULTURAL RELATIVISM AND ETHICS

Relativism is the theory of knowledge or ethics that holds that criteria of judgment are relative, varying with the individual, time, and circumstance. In the case of cultural relativism, the view is that knowledge and value vary from culture to culture and find their justification within the culture itself. No cross-cultural evaluation of knowledge or ethical values is possible or necessary. Important to world peace and the workings of humans with humans all over the globe is the development of some principles of value for guidance. But is this possible? That is, can we discuss some uniformity in human nature that could be reflected in universally accepted moral standards?

Some maintain that with the striking differences between cultures, there exists some basic identity manifesting itself in human societies independent of time and place. Some scholars have argued that the actual range of difference between cultures is enormous, too great for the development of a universal moral code. They point to the fact that the same kind of act is praised in one culture and condemned in another. Robert Redfield says, "Sometimes, when we look at all that ethnography and history have recorded about customs and institutions, it seems as though there had developed varieties of moral judgment so different from one another as to force the conclusion that there is no common human nature but only a multitude of human natures."

Another opinion represented in the works of anthropologists is that people are in fact the same everywhere. Mary and Abraham Edel comment: "Birth and death, love and sorrow and fear are the lot of all men; all are capable of desires and dreams, and use symbolic thinking, identification, reaction-formation." And Redfield writes, "All people feel shame or guilt or, probably, some combination of them; all take satisfaction in or feel dissatisfaction with regard to their enterprises and productions; all dislike, under some conditions, public humiliation and enjoy recognized success; and so on." From the point of view of these writers, there seems to be some range of psychic disposition common to all people that could be recognized as a component of human nature. This range of dispositions is of special interest to the ethicist, since he or she relates these dispositions to the sphere of morality. The metaprob-

lem for the ethicist is to explain how these dispositions fit into and support a universal conception of morality.

Besides common dispositions, Edel and Edel also mention some basic facts: birth and death, to be exact. They comment, "Common needs, common social tasks, common psychological processes, are bound to provide some common framework for the wide variety of human behavior that different cultures have developed." But does this show that all human communities the world over share the same moral principles? Edel and Edel argue that it only shows that they have worked out some rules of conduct, that they have some morality; but it does not support the claim that there is a genuine identity of people of different cultures with respect to their moral principles. Morris Ginsberg agrees that morality is universal, but only in the *formal* sense that everywhere we find rules of conduct prescribing what is to be done or not to be done. But behind this similarity of form there is considerable diversity of content—the content of these moral rules themselves.

In more recent times, Richard Rorty and Clifford Geertz have reopened the discussion of moral relativism through a discussion of ethnocentrism, the view that "my" (whoever is doing the speaking) and the ways of "my" community are the highest and best, and all other ways, because they differ from "mine," are perhaps immoral. Holding firmly to this view negates any possibility of a cross-cultural or universal morality. The antiethnocentric position, similar to that of the Edels, has given hope for a universal moral view that can be developed into rules and procedures acceptable to all and is perhaps the foundation of contemporary attempts to place multiculturalism in the public school curriculum. Rorty takes a different and third position, which he calls "anti- anti-ethnocentrism," a position that Geertz fears. If a person is ethnocentric, which we all are to some degree or another, then the person will hold on to certain values learned as a child that are culture-dependent. On the other hand, if we negate these values and search for more universal ones, we perhaps will throw out some of the very values we seek. The antiethnocentric view says throw them out and let the search begin. On the other hand, Rorty argues that the anti-antiethnocentric view should be looked upon as a protest against the persistence of the Enlightenment view that there is something called a common human nature, "a metaphysical substrate in which things called *rights* are embedded." "It is," Rorty says, "just a bit of ad hoc philosophical therapy, an attempt to cure the cramps caused by the idea that you are being irrational, and probably viciously ethnocentric, whenever you cannot appeal to neutral criteria." Rorty argues that we should take with full seriousness the fact that the ideals of procedural justice and human equality are parochial, recent, eccentric cultural developments, and then to recognize that this does not mean they are any the less worth fighting for. He says that our ideals may be local and culture-bound, but nevertheless be the best hope of the species.

To investigate this issue at length, one should perhaps review the classical arguments for and against relativism found in philosophy, anthropology, and sociology, and then begin a thorough study of *postmodernism*, some of which is found in Rorty, to pick up the argument through thinkers who are striving to escape their mental and cultural connections to the European Enlightenment up through Kant.

SOURCES

Edel, Mary, and Abraham Edel. *Anthropology and Ethics.* Springfield, IL: Charles C. Thomas. 1959.

Geertz, Clifford. "The Uses of Diversity." *Michigan Quarterly Review* 25 (1983): 661–683.

Ginsberg, Morris. *On the Diversity of Morals: Approaches to Ethics.* London: Heinemann. 1962.

Redfield, Robert. *Human Nature and the Study of Society.* Chicago: University of Chicago Press. 1962.

Rorty, Richard. *Objectivity, Relativism, and Truth.* New York: University of Cambridge Press. 1991.

CYBERSPACE

In the 20 years since 1975, the intersection of computers, telephones, and cable television, as well as electronic services by which information travels across these networks, has created a new world in which traditional notions of truth, fact, meaning, and value must be reinterpreted, if not reinvented. This is the world of the information highway known simply as cyberspace. Within seconds in this cyberworld, billion-dollar Pentagon spy satellites can deliver detailed photographs to ground stations. The National Security Agency's supercomputers can sort through intercepted phone calls with lightning speed, or a young student can bring the sounds and moving images of a rainforest or a porno flick into his or her bedroom. And if this is not enough, electronic images (*virtual reality*) can be used to train a fighter pilot or a brain surgeon without either leaving the classroom, or put the youngster in "virtual" touch with various sexual partners. The information is out there, but you have to know what to look for and how to look for it.

Jurgen Habermas's *Postmetaphysical Thinking* reminds us that four themes characterize the break with traditional Enlightenment philosophy that ended with Immanuel Kant's *Critique of Pure Reason*, published in 1776. These are postmetaphysical thinking, the linguistic turn, situation reason, and reversing the primacy of theory where possible. The implication of this movement for ethics and values is the move from an emphasis on semantics and the understanding of sentences to a pragmatic orientation—to both an understanding of meaning and the relationship of speakers and hearers. Habermas says: "The reciprocal interpersonal relations that are established through the speaker-hear-er perspective make possible a relation-to-self that by no means presupposes the lonely reflection of the knowing and act-ing subject upon itself as an antecedent consciousness. Rather, the self-relation arises out of an *interactive* context."

It took approximately 200 years for philosophical thinking to make this tran-sition—from a traditional mind-body, sub-ject-object context where meaning and truth are to be measured and rendered in terms of the inductive-deductive truth-value context (because the Enlightenment mind believed that truth existed, immuta-ble, outside the self and was knowable and measurable) to one in which meaning and truth are inherently subjective and inter-active, situational and practical.

And what ethic can be developed for those who travel in cyberspace? In the past decade dozens of anonymous *remailers* have sprouted up who provide a conduit by which users can ship data around the world in complete anonymity. Hundreds of thousands of people on the Internet (the program that connects a personal comput-er to the outside world via phone line) use remailers to transmit the most sensitive and explosive information, secure in the assurance that it could never be traced back to them.

But while anonymity can be liberating, it can also abet illicit activity. The Internet can be used to send all sorts of contraband, from copyrighted articles to stolen soft-ware, to hard-core pornography. U.S. businesses have been on the frontier of cy-berspace, but setting up shop on the com-puter network has, in many cases, turned out to be terminally insecure. When utili-ty programs (programs that allow a person to access another's computer pro-gram—the electronic equivalent of a lock-smith's toolbox) are stolen, the computer hacker has a new set of burglar's tools that allows other programs to be opened and information stolen.

Among the most common ways to at-tack via the Internet are the following:

1. *Password Sniffers:* These tiny pro-grams are hidden in a network and instructed to record passwords and other information that are stored in a file.
2. *Spoofing:* This is a technique for getting access to a remote computer by forging the Internet address of a trusted or "friendly" machine. This allows a person much easier access to exploit security holes from inside a system than from outside the system.
3. *The Hole in the Web:* Thousands of businesses are setting up on the World Wide Web—the fastest grow-ing zone on the Internet. In Febru-ary 1995, an alert was posted that there was a "hole" in the software that ran most Web sites. This entry point allowed an intruder to do any-thing that owners of the site could do. For example, a Web site could have been a credit card company; if their numbers were accessed by an intruder, transactions could be made and the theft be virtually un-detectable.

The ethical issues arising from cyber-space range from outright theft to access to pornography by preteen youngsters. Perhaps the greatest value problem is that access to the information highway itself may determine the basic ability to function in a democratic culture. As we have moved from a subject-object orientation to one that is personal and interactive, our children have developed a belief that there is a kind of actual space behind the screen that you can't see, yet you know it is there. In cy-berspace a new paradigm for ethics is be-ing forged by its users, while those who do not have knowledge or access are quick-ly becoming second-class citizens, disen-franchised by a lack of something that is almost indefinable.

Changes are occurring daily because of this technology. Telephones lines are being strung throughout the world, and with satellite technology, entire libraries can pass, virtually undetected, through cyberspace. The fax, the ATM, and the credit card business have been frontline movers and shakers in this new world. Now, through the Internet, we all can get a piece of the action. And more changes are coming. Those with computer knowledge and the income to purchase a computer and get on-line will be the users of this new world of information. Even today, those workers with computer knowledge can make 15 percent more than those who have none. As this field grows even more complex and the applications become available to more and more people, the ethical implications grow even more problematic.

SOURCES

Desmond, Edward W. "Playing Catchup in Cyberspace." *Time* (March 6, 1995).

Habermas, Jurgen. *Postmetaphysical Thinking: Philosophical Essays*. Cambridge, MA: MIT Press. 1992.

Quittner, Joshua. "Cracks in the Net." *Time* (February 27, 1995).

———. "Unmasked on the Net." *Time* (March 6, 1995).

Time Magazine. Special Issue (Spring 1995).

Waller, Douglas. "Spies in Cyberspace." *Time* (March 20, 1995).

Wolgast, Elizabeth. *Ethics of an Artificial Person*. Stanford, CA: Stanford University Press. 1992.

D

DEHUMANIZATION

Dehumanization means to deprive one of human character, values, and virtues. It means that decisions and choices are made, either personally or on a larger scale, without taking the human qualities of individuals into consideration. As Paul Tillich *(The Courage To Be)* notes: "Twentieth-century man has lost a meaningful world and a self which lives in meanings out of a spiritual center. The man-created world of objects has drawn into itself him who created it and who now loses his subjectivity in it. He has sacrificed himself to his own productions."

We all wish to think the best of our society and its culture, but many social commentators are today telling us that the culture produced in Western civilization is weighted against the human species; that is, they warn that we have produced a lopsided culture with an emphasis on the fabrication of machines, the rapid exploitation of nature and the environment, and the drive for power and profits. Surely there is evidence of this onesidedness. As far back as Henry Adams, in post–Civil War America, we find the view that education is essentially a Darwinian process of adaptation and a post-Darwinian strategy of seizing a degree of control over natural power. The mood of Adams in bowing down to scientific power in a half-mock worship of the Dynamo is fully expressed by D. H. Lawrence, who said, "that which is and that which moves is twice godly." Since 1975, this power mentality (now transposed into technology), created by the industrial-scientific-military complex that emerged half-grown in 1945 but achieved full maturity in the decade of the 1990s, has perhaps destroyed the emotional and collective life of the whole of society because of its quest for riches and power and its disregard for the unique.

This situation is labeled "dehumanization" by those who are senstive to more personal and spiritual needs. They say that humans have some basic emotional and personal needs that must be expressed or met. Among these are control over their own lives, fellowship with those around them, a sense of the sacred, and a sense of mystery that escapes mechanization. When these needs are repressed and the drive for power, profit, speed, and standardization become dominant goals, the outcome is dehumanization, savage wars, revolutions and riots, and widespread mental disorder. This withdrawal of allegiance to the system, to society as it is, is seen in indifference, resentment, alienation, defiance of authority, the extension of violence, and unabashed greed.

SOURCES

Cohen, Jerry S. *America, Inc.: Who Owns and Operates the United States.* New York: Ideal Press. 1971.

Dichter, Ernest. *The Strategy of Desire.* Garden City, NY: Doubleday. 1960.

Kaplan, Harold. *Power and Order.* Chicago: The University of Chicago Press. 1981.

Mumford, Lewis. *The Pentagon of Power.* Volume 2: *The Myth of the Machine.* New York: Harcourt Brace Jovanovich. 1970.

DEITY

Sooner or later, most individuals come to believe that their lives depend on forces in the world more powerful than themselves. They give names to these powers, provide them with human attributes and qualities, regard them with awe, and seek good relations with them. These forces become their gods or *deities*. Some people do not believe in a deity and are usually called *atheists*, from *theist* (the Greek word for "god"); an atheist is a nontheist. Others, called *agnostics*, do not deny the existence of a deity, but say that it is impossible for humans to know whether there is a deity and a spiritual world.

Many indigenous peoples believe that a vague, general, powerful, living, but impersonal force exists in the world. Others believe that all of nature—stones, trees, rivers, mountains, and storms—is alive with spirits and each has its own form. Some worship the basic powers of nature, including storms or heavenly bodies. We call this *animism*, and to those who subscribe to it, these are their deities. Of course, some people believe in many deities; this is called *polytheism*.

In what is labeled "civilized culture," most individuals are today *monotheistic*— they believe in a single deity. We find this belief in Christianity, Judaism, Islam, and Zoroastrianism. The single deity of these religions is thought of as all-good, all-powerful, and all-wise, and rules the universe with a conscious purpose. Thus, these religions express a seemingly contradictory or at least inconsistent belief in both the freedom to believe and worship, and in a vague predestinationism. Some of the great religions of the world—Taoism, Buddhism, Hinduism, and Confucianism—teach that personality traits of any sort ascribed to a deity suggest man rather than God.

SOURCES

Noss, John B., and David S. Noss. *Man's Religions.* 7th ed. New York: Macmillan. 1984.

Walhout, Donald. *Interpreting Religion.* Englewood Cliffs, NJ: Prentice-Hall. 1963.

DEVIANCE

Deviance is a noun describing behavior that wanders, or deviates, from what is considered to be the desirable, the traditional, or the approved ways of acting. We should be cognizant that behavior that is labeled "deviant" by one group or person is their way of expressing certain social expectations—and perhaps disappointments. That is to say, deviance is a social creation. Societies create right and wrong by originating norms and saying that failure to follow the rules constitutes deviance. Whether or not a behavior is deviant depends on how others react to it or what social conventions have been created to govern this specific action. As Kai Erikson has remarked, "Deviance is not a property inherent in any particular kind of behavior; it is a property conferred upon that behavior by the people who come into direct or indirect contact with it."

Most of us conform to the norms of society most of the time, but on occasion many of us violate minor social norms, violations that are usually tolerated or even ignored. When we do breech these norms, such as with bad etiquette, participation in a riotous celebration after an important sports victory, or loud chatter in a theater, we may meet with social disapproval but no serious punishment. These are not serious deviant behaviors. There are of course more serious kinds of deviance, such as criminal behavior and adolescent delinquency.

What we must understand is that deviance is a relative norm, not an absolute one. It is not a property inherent in any particular kind of behavior. Evidence for its relativism is found in the wide variation of definitions of deviance from society to society, and from one historical period to another. For example, in the United States homosexuality is generally thought of as a deviant behavior, but homosexuality is not considered to be deviant worldwide. One anthropological study of 190 societies found that two-thirds of them accept homosexuality for certain individuals or specific occasions. Among the 225 Native American tribes, over half accepted male homosexuality and 17 percent accepted female homosexuality prior to the influence of Western Christian culture. In ancient Greece, homosexual relationships between men were considered the supreme intellectual and spiritual expression of love. Men in ancient Greece and Rome were regarded as naturally bisexual.

Important to our understanding is that deviance is an integral part of all societies. According to Emile Durkheim, deviant behavior actually has positive consequences for society, because it gives the nondeviants a sense of solidarity. By punishing the deviant, the group expresses its collective indignation and reaffirms its commitment to the "rules."

The negative sanctions applied to the deviant (gossip, avoidance, exclusion, etc.) serve to enforce conformity in the group by restraining others from deviating. Durkheim explains:

> We have only to notice what happens, particularly in a small town, when some moral scandal has just been committed. They stop each other on the street, they visit each other, they seek to come together to talk of the event and to wax indignant in common. From all the similar expressions which are exchanged, for all the temper that gets itself expressed, there emerges a unique temper which is everybody's without being anybody's in particular. That is the public temper.

Whoever holds the power determines who or what is deviant. Power is a crucial element in this decision for it reveals the dominant and nondominant status of the members of the group. Master status is given to the one who controls all the rest. Going back to the example of homosexuality, sexual orientation is a master status-determining trait because it goes to the very heart of social and personal identity. Normally, violators of important social norms are merely stigmatized, but this can run the gamut from being set apart to being socially disgraced. Before the 1960s, extremely negative reactions to deviants kept them invisible and out of the public eye, as in the case of retarded or physically handicapped individuals; this behavior drove some into ghettos, and may have caused extreme personal distress in many individuals.

SOURCES

Durkheim, Emile. *The Division of Labor in Society.* Translated by S. A. Solovay and J. H. Mueller. Glencoe, IL: Free Press. 1960.

Eitzen, D. Stanley, and Maxine Baca Zinn. *Social Problems.* 4th ed. Boston: Allyn and Bacon. 1989.

Erickson, Kai T. *Wayward Puritans: A Study in the Sociology of Deviance.* New York: Wiley. 1966.

DEVIL WORSHIP

Devil worship is not a twentieth-century phenomenon, although it has been resurrected in nontraditional religious groups since the 1960s. In the religion of Zoroastrianism, dating from 660 B.C., Ahura Mazda is the one supreme great God and wise Lord. But opposing Ahura Mazda is the Evil Spirit, Angra Mainyu—literally, "the Bad Spirit." It is characteristic of the *Gathas* (devotional hymns) to lay continual emphasis on the fundamental cleavage in the world of nature and in human life between right and wrong, good and evil, the true religion and the false. This cleavage began when Ahura Mazda created the world and established freedom of choice for his creatures:

> Now the two primal Spirits, who revealed themselves in vision as Twins, are the Better and the Bad in thought and word and action. And between these two the wise once choose aright, the foolish not so. And when these twain Spirits came together in the beginning, they established Life and Not-Life, and that at the last the Worst Existence (Hell) shall be to the followers of the Lie, but the Best Thought (Paradise) to him that follows Right. Of these twain Spirits he that followed the Lie chose doing the worst things; the holiest Spirit chose Right (Noss and Noss 1984).

Although good and evil are not clearly defined, they give us an indication of the practical differences between right and wrong. The good people accept the true religion, whereas the evil are those who reject it. Zoroaster believed that the good religion of Ahura Mazda would eventually defeat evil.

Theologians have summarized this ancient Middle Eastern dichotomy between good and evil, right and wrong, into "the doctrine of evil," which approaches an almost complete ethical dualism. The problem associated with this doctrine is the origin of evil. That is, if the one supreme God is both all-good and the creator of all things, whence cometh evil? One way to solve the problem is to say that all good comes from God, all evil comes from the Devil. But consistency demands that the Devil, if he is the true author of evil, be coeternal with God from the beginning of time; otherwise, God created the Devil and evil in the beginning.

Edward H. Madden and Peter H. Hare remind us of the difficulty of either evading or denying the problem of evil. The question "If God is unlimited in power and goodness, why is there so much prima facie gratuitous evil in the world?" challenges us either to deny the unlimitedness and goodness of God and accept the power of evil or to deny the existence of God altogether, for we can't, in all honesty, deny that evil exists in the world. This inability to explain the existence of both God (good) and evil has caused the personification of evil as an object of worship.

SOURCES

Madden, Edward H., and Peter H. Hare. *Evil and the Concept of God.* Springfield, IL: Charles C. Thomas. 1968.

Noss, David S., and John B. Noss. *Man's Religion.* 7th ed. New York: Macmillan. 1984.

Pike, Nelson. *God and Evil.* Englewood Cliffs, NJ: Prentice-Hall. 1964.

DEWEY, JOHN

John Dewey (1859–1952) labels his version of pragmatism (a method of determining the truth or falsity of propositions according to whether they do or do not fulfill our purposes and satisfy our biological and emotional needs) "instrumentalism," or "experimentalism," and describes its fundamental purpose as follows:

> Instrumentalism is an attempt to constitute a precise logical theory of concepts, of judgments and inferences in their various forms, by considering primarily how thought functions in the experimental determination of future consequences.

The essential feature of this idea in its instrumentalist version is its reference to consequences. The term *pragmatism* means only the rule of meaning and test. The meaning of a judgment consists of its anticipated consequences and its truth is established by the actual verification of these.

The instrumentalist theory was advanced by Dewey's early logical essays, *The Quest for Certainty* (1929) and *Logic: The Theory of Inquiry* (1938). In the first of these works, the instrumentalist position is cast in the language of the operational theory of meaning of scientific concepts advanced by P. W. Bridgman. Bridgman contends that "we mean by any concept nothing more than a set of operations; the concept is synonymous with the corresponding set of operations." Combining the operational technique of conceptual definition with the pragmatic emphasis on consequences, Dewey proposes a definition of the nature of ideas in terms of operations to be performed and the test of the validity of ideas by the consequences of these operations.

Using this methodology, Dewey says that philosophy must become a method of moral and political diagnosis and prognosis—"the world is in the making, and we must help in the process." For Dewey, this charge calls for new thinking, thinking that he labeled *inquiry*. Thinking, Dewey reminds us, is an instrument for the removal of collisions between what is given and what is wanted, a means of realizing human desire, of securing an arrangement of things that satisfy, fulfill, and bring happiness. This harmony is the ultimate test of thinking: success in this sense is the goal of thought. Successful ideas are true ideas. As Dewey says: "The distinctively intellectual attitude which marks scientific inquiry was generated in efforts at controlling persons and things so that consequences, issues, outcomes would be more stable and assured. The first step away from oppression by immediate things and events was taken when man employed tools and appliances for manipulating things so as to render them contributory to desired objects" (Gouinlock, *The Moral Writings of John Dewey* 1994).

Dewey has been called the national philosopher of the United States. Indeed, with his emphasis on life as *in the making*, he believed that we shape it to our ends, and in the process the thinking and beliefs of conscious personal beings play an active part. The ethical community is thus mentally active and self-critical, as well as creative. All things are what they are experienced as being, and every experience is something known: aesthetically, morally, economically, and technologically; hence, to give an account of any objective and empirical experience is simply to tell what that experience is. The individual is both knower and an emotional, impulsive, willing being; the reflective attitude is evolved by the will, the basal or primal side of the self. Thus, for Dewey, values are functions of natural processes. As such they are in principle open to scientific investigation and control as much as any other event in nature. This conclusion is a major achievement for Dewey, and from it flows much of his thought and contribution to ethics and epistemology. In general terms, the role of scientific inquiry is to determine how we can interact with nature in a consummatory way. Science is conceived as an instrument of human liberation and enrichment.

SOURCES

Dewey, John. *Democracy and Education*. New York: Macmillan. 1916.

———. *Reconstruction in Philosophy*. New York: Henry Holt. 1920.

Gouinlock, James, ed. *The Moral Writings of John Dewey*. Rev. ed. Amherst, NY: Prometheus. 1994.

DIGNITY

The concept of human dignity is of great ethical importance because it recognizes each person as precious and having intrinsic worth/value. Thus dignity, when applied to humans and the various ethical principles it generates, is the foundation of human discourse, the creation of communities and institutions, and the maintenance of the human family.

In his *Natural Law and Human Dignity*, European philosopher Ernst Bloch connects human dignity with the best of the Enlightenment tradition, which expresses a deep and lasting concern for the welfare of human life in all its dimensions: cognitive, physical, moral, political, religious, and economic. Bloch says: "The will is the generic character of mankind, and reason itself is only its eternal rule. For this reason, there is no greater indignity for man than to suffer violence, because violence cancels him. One who commits violence does nothing less than contest humanity; one who cowardly suffers violence throws away his humanity."

Correctly, Bloch links human dignity to happiness and to the end of misery and all forms of subjugation. Like Kant, Bloch agrees that justice is the ground of human dignity: "Justice is therefore the aggregate of those conditions under which the will of one person can be united with the will of another person in accordance with a universal law of freedom." It is not surprising that the modern conception of human dignity comes to the forefront of thought and discussion during the seventeenth and eighteenth centuries. This was a time of renaissance, a time when feudalism and despotism in both politics and religion were gasping their final breaths, and a time when humanity was beginning to awaken from its self-imposed tutelage. This was the age that gave birth to modern science, when the stirrings of freedom and democracy were beginning to move societies and cultures east and west, north and south, in exploration, discovery, and settlement.

Thomas Jefferson, Ben Franklin, and John Adams brought this tradition to the United States and planted it deeply within the conscience of those who would claim this country as their own. Jefferson set the tone for U.S. politics when he said, "It does me no injury for my neighbor to say that there are twenty Gods or no God." For Jefferson, politics can be separated from beliefs about matters of ultimate importance—those shared beliefs among citizens on such matters are not essential to a democratic society. Jefferson, like many other figures of the Enlightenment, assumed a moral faculty common to both atheist and theist upon which civic virtue can be constructed. It is on this moral faculty that human dignity is built.

Jefferson did not wish to discard religion as many of his contemporaries did. He thought it enough to privatize religion, to view it as irrelevant to social order but relevant to, and possibly essential for, individual perfection—to human dignity. There are two sides to Jefferson's view: Its absolutist side says that every human being, without the benefit of special revelation, has all the beliefs necessary for civic virtue. These beliefs come from a universal human faculty, the conscience, possession of which constitutes the specifically human essence of each person. This is the faculty that gives the individual human dignity and rights. But there is also a pragmatic side. This side says that when a person finds his or her conscious beliefs are relevant to public policy but incapable of defense on the basis of beliefs common to his or her fellow citizens, he or she must sacrifice these beliefs on the altar of public expediency.

The tension between these two sides—the absolutist and the pragmatist—is resolved in the Enlightenment idea of *reason*, which claims that there is a relation between the ahistorical (unaffected by time and change) essence of the human soul and the moral truth, a relation that ensures that free and open discussion will produce "one right answer" to moral as well as scientific questions. Such a theory guarantees that a moral belief that cannot be justified to the mass of mankind is "irrational," and thus is really not a part of the moral faculty at all.

In the twentieth century, this rationalist justification of the Enlightenment compromise has been discredited and, since the early 1970s, a postmodern conceptualization of values and knowledge, of truth and meaning, has been discussed. Contemporary intellectuals have forfeited the notion that religion, myth, and tradition can be opposed to something ahistorical, something common to all humans *qua* humans. Anthropologists and historians alike have blurred the distinction between innate rationality and the products of acculturation. Philosophers such as Heidegger have provided ways of seeing human beings as historical through and through. Quine has also obscured the distinction between permanent truths of reason and truths of scientific, objective fact. Psychoanalysis has blurred the distinction between morality and prudence. The result is to ease the picture of the self common to Greek metaphysics, Christian theology, and Enlightenment rationalism: the picture of an ahistorical (mind, soul, reason) natural center, the locus of human dignity. The distinctly modern notion of human dignity is tied to Hegel's and Heidegger's sense of the self's historicity rather than the Enlightenment, Christian, Greek idea of self, which develops undisturbed in and by history. Dignity, in the contemporary world, is being linked more to human interdependence and less to autonomy, less to the notion that dignity is to be defined in terms of the ability to act on one's own without interference or subordination to outside authority.

The Enlightenment tried to free us from tradition with its historically developed institutions and beliefs, and thereby give us a view of self and human dignity that is disengaged, ahistorical, and universal. The focus on universals was not on rules and principles that are found to be held in common among humans the world over, but on innate ideas and their virtual stability within the mind and reason. The twentieth century, influenced by the pragmatism and historicism of John Dewey and the matter-of-factism of nineteenth-century existentialists, has forced us to think of dignity, of morality, and of human freedom and justice in terms of community. Both Jefferson and Dewey described America as an "experiment" within which the concept of human dignity as a "centerless web of historically conditioned beliefs and desires" is sufficient to allow fairmindedness, cooperation, and justice without embodying a universal and ahistorical order.

SOURCES

Bloch, Ernst. *Natural Law and Human Dignity.* Translated by Dennis J. Schmidt. Cambridge, MA: MIT Press. 1986.

Lyotard, Jean-Francois. *The Post Modern Explained.* Translated from the French by Don Barry, Bernadette Maher, Julian Pefanis, Virginia Spate, and Morgan Thomas. Minneapolis: University of Minnesota Press. 1992.

———. *The Postmodern Condition: A Report on Knowledge.* Translated from the French by Geoff Bennington and Brian Massumi. Minneapolis: University of Minnesota Press. 1993.

Toulmin, Stephen E. *Cosmopolis: The Hidden Agenda of Modernity.* Chicago: The University of Chicago Press. 1990.

Vogel, Lawrence. *The Fragile "We" Ethical Implications of Heidegger's "Being and Time."* Evanston, IL: Northwestern University Press. 1994.

DISCRIMINATION

Prejudice is an attitude; discrimination is a practice, a practice of unequal treatment of groups of people, especially racial, ethnic, or religious groups. It seems clear that prejudice leads to discrimination and discrimination can lead to increased and prolonged prejudice. For example, as a general rule, black Americans have been discriminated against—because of their race—in education, keeping many if not most blacks poor and ignorant. The fact that so many were poor and ignorant became a reason for keeping them poor and ignorant. Gunnar Myrdal spoke of the relationship between prejudice and discrimination as *cumulative causation*, or a vicious circle, with discrimination barring job opportunities and education, and these shortcomings creating additional prejudice and renewed discrimination.

Fundamentally, discrimination is the denial of opportunities and equal rights to individuals and groups because of prejudice or other arbitrary reasons. To understand discrimination, one must understand the forms that it takes:

RELATIVE VERSUS
ABSOLUTE DEPRIVATION

It is crucial that although minority groups may be viewed as having adequate or even good incomes, housing, health care, and educational opportunities, it is their position *relative* to some other groups that gives evidence of discrimination. The term *relative deprivation* is defined as the conscious feeling of a negative discrepancy between legitimate expectations and present activities. It may be characterized by a scarcity rather than a lack of necessities. *Absolute deprivation*, on the other hand, implies a fixed standard based on a minimum level of subsistance below which families should not be expected to exist. Discrimination does not necessarily mean absolute deprivation.

INSTITUTIONAL DISCRIMINATION

Discrimination is practiced not only by individuals in one-to-one encounters, but also by institutions in their daily operations. Institutional discrimination has more profound results than discrimination by prejudiced individuals. *Institutional discrimination* refers to that denial of opportunities and equal rights to individuals and groups resulting from the normal operations of a society.

TOTAL DISCRIMINATION

Social scientists, and increasingly, policy makers, have begun to use the concept of *total discrimination* to refer to current discrimination operating in the labor market and also to the effects of *past* discrimination. Past discrimination includes those practices—relatively poorer education and job experiences received by racial or ethnic minorities compared to white Americans—that have occurred in the past and that, perhaps, are still ongoing, that discriminated against the person or the group.

AFFIRMATIVE ACTION

Affirmative action has become the most important tool for reducing institutional discrimination. Federal measures under the heading of *affirmative action* have been aimed at procedures that deny equal opportunities even if they were not intended to be overtly discriminatory. The term itself first appeared in the executive order issued by President Kennedy in 1963, which called for contractors to take "affirmative action to ensure that applicants are employed, and that employees are treated during their employment without regard to their race, creed, color, or national origin." Four years later, the order was amended to prohibit discrimination on the basis of gender, but affirmative action was still vaguely defined and is being debated by political figures today.

See also Affirmative Action; Feminism; Gender Equity; Racism.

SOURCES

Becker, Gary S. *The Economics of Discrimination.* 2d ed. Chicago: University of Chicago Press. 1971.

Glazer, Nathan. *Affirmative Discrimination: Ethnic Inequality and Public Policy.* New York: Basic Books. 1975.

Weinberg, Meyer. *A Chance to Learn: A History of Race and Education in the United States.* Cambridge, MA: Cambridge University Press. 1977.

DIVORCE

Divorce is the ending by law of a valid marriage. It is usually distinguished from an annulment, which is a declaration by a court that a marriage is invalid (not legally binding) because of some defect at the time of the marriage ceremony. A divorce also differs from a legal separation, which does not actually dissolve a marriage. Instead, it authorizes the parties to live apart, usually with a provision of financial support for the wife.

One of the major social problems in the United States today is divorce and the breakdown of family life. In 1975 over 3 million men, women, and minor children were involved in a divorce. Today, one-third to one-half of all adults in the United States, and close to one-third of the minor children under the age of 18, will be affected by a divorce or dissolution. While divorce may have been considered a "deviant family pattern" in the past, it has become in the 1990s accepted as a possible outcome of marriage. The social problems linked to divorce are poverty, alcoholism, and the psychological effects on children.

Since 1970, there has been a major reform in divorce law that reflects the growing acceptance of divorce as a social pattern and attempts to institutionalize fundamental social change in family patterns. Referred to as *no-fault divorce*, this new legislation seeks to alter the definition of marriage, the relationship between husbands and wives, and the economic and social obligations of former spouses to each other and to their children after divorce.

The state of California brought forth the first no-fault divorce law in the United States in 1970. Since then, 14 other states have adopted "pure" no-fault divorce laws and an additional 13 states have added no-fault grounds to their existing reasons for divorce. Some have praised no-fault divorce as the embodiment of "modern" and "enlightened" law and heralded it as the forerunner of future family law in the United States. The political and religious right have attacked these no-fault provisions and claimed that they have helped to "destroy the family" and caused irreparable harm to women and children.

TRADITIONAL LEGAL MARRIAGE

The origins of Anglo-American family law may be traced to the tenth or eleventh century, when Christianity became sufficiently influential in Britain to enable the church to assert its rules effectively. Traditionally, we can say a legal marriage was a Christian marriage in a "holy" union between a man and woman. Marriage was a sacrament: a commitment to join together for life. The nature of this marital relationship and the legal responsibilities of the spouses were specified by law—by statute, case law, and common law. Accordingly, a legal marriage has five important features: (1) it was limited to a single man and a single woman—bigamy, polygamy, and homosexual unions were prohibited; (2) legal marriage was monogamous—the spouses were to remain sexually faithful to each other and adultery was explicitly prohibited; (3) marriage was for procreation and one of the major objects of matrimony was the bearing and rearing of children; (4) legal marriage established a hierarchical relationship between the spouses in which the husband was the head of the family, with his wife and children subordinate to him (according to common law, a married woman became a *femme covert*, a legal nonperson, under her husband's arm, protection and cover, and although most of the disabilities of coverture were removed by the Married Women's Property Acts in the nineteenth century, the common law assumption that the husband was the head of the family remained firmly embodied in statutory and case law in the United States); and (5) the most important feature of traditional legal marriage, its sex-based division of family roles and responsibilities. The woman was to devote herself to being a wife, homemaker, and mother in return for her husbands' promise of lifelong support. The husband was given the sole responsibility for the family's financial welfare, while he was assured that his home, his children, and his social-emotional well-being would be cared for by his wife. This attitude persisted into the late 1950s and early 1960s as evidenced by such television shows as "Father Knows Best," "Leave It to Beaver," and "Ozzie and Harriet."

TRADITIONAL DIVORCE LAWS

Since marriage was regarded as an indissoluble union, it could be ended only by the death of one of the parties. Divorce, in the modern sense of a judicial decree dissolving a valid marriage, and allowing one or both partners to remarry during the life of the other, did not exist in England until 1857. A rare exception, originating in the late seventeenth century, allowed divorce on the sole ground of adultery by special act of Parliament. The church also permitted divorce *a mensa et thoro,* literally a divorce "from bed and board," which allowed the parties to live apart but not to sever the marital bond. The Ecclesiastical Courts retained their exclusive jurisdiction over marriage and divorce in England until 1857, when divorce jurisdiction was transferred to the Civil Court System and divorces were authorized for adultery.

Divorce laws in the United States were heavily influenced by the English tradition. In the middle and southern colonies, divorces were granted by the legislature and were rare. However, New England allowed divorce more freely. Influenced by the Protestant church, divorces were authorized, either by the courts or an act of the legislature, for adultery, desertion, and cruelty. Historically, traditional legal divorce in the United States (1) perpetuated the sex-based division of roles and responsibilities in traditional legal marriage; (2) required grounds (reasons) for divorce; (3) was based on adversary proceedings that tried to prove which party was guilty or responsible for the divorce; and (4) linked the financial terms of the divorce to the determination of fault.

NO-FAULT DIVORCE

No-fault divorce law began in 1970 in California, which abolished completely any requirement of fault as the basis of marital dissolution. The no-fault law provided for a divorce upon one party's assertion that "irreconcilable differences have caused the irremediable breakdown of the marriage." In establishing the new standards for marital dissolution, the California State Legislature sought to eliminate the adversarial nature of divorce, and thereby to reduce the hostility, acrimony, and trauma characteristic of fault-oriented divorce.

The year 1970 marked the beginning of a nationwide trend toward legal recognition of "marital breakdown" as a sufficient justification for divorce. New laws not only eliminated the need for evidence of misconduct; they eliminated the concept of fault itself. These new laws thereby abolished the notion of interpersonal justice in divorce. With this seemingly simple move, the California Legislature dramatically altered the legal definition of the reciprocal rights of husbands and wives during marriage and after dissolution.

See also Family; Marriage.

SOURCES

Carter, Hugh, and Paul C. Glick. *Marriage and Divorce: A Social and Economic Study.* Cambridge, MA: Harvard University Press. 1970.

Clark, Homer. *Domestic Relations.* St. Paul: West. 1968.

Skolnick, Arlene S., and Jerome H. Skolnick, eds. *Family in Transition.* 8th ed. New York: HarperCollins. 1994.

DRUGS AND DRUG ADDICTION

A drug is any chemical that affects the structure or function of a living organism. This definition includes aspirin, caffeine, nicotine, and alcohol as well as many drugs considered to be illegal, unacceptable, or dangerous. The labeling of some drugs as *licit* and others as *illicit* is not merely a matter of the chemical makeup of the drug and what it does to human beings, but involves religion and politics as well. Moreover, because of the religious and political involvement in the labeling of drugs, we should understand that it is not merely the intrinsic makeup of the drug that is the problem. Important to understanding drugs in society is understanding the "politics of drugs."

DRUGS IN SOCIETY

Drugs, as we know, are used for pleasure as well as for medical purposes. The average American has about 30 different drugs in the medicine cabinet and numerous alcoholic beverages in the liquor cabinet. Over 80 percent of Americans are regular caffeine users, and two-thirds of adults use alcoholic beverages. Without question, America is a society where psychoactive drugs are very important because they influence behavior by altering feelings, moods, perceptions, and other mental states. Drugs can get us started, keep us going, or slow us down. As one alcoholic said, "I don't drink because I like the taste of liquor; I drink to get drunk."

The 11 categories of psychoactive drugs are the following: caffeine, marijuana, inhalants, tranquilizers and antidepressants, psychedelics, narcotics, cocaine, amphetamines, barbiturates, nicotine, and alcohol.

DRUG USE

For whatever reason—perhaps increased awareness of the danger of drugs, renewed health consciousness, or monitoring in the workplace—drug use is declining in the 1990s. This decline, however, is not uniform. The middle and upper classes have reduced their drug use, but the poor have not. This also is delineated along educational lines, with the better-educated young people having reduced their drug use of marijuana and cocaine, and the least educated having no reduction in their usage of these two drugs. With the introduction of "crack" a few years ago, the consumption of cocaine has increased among the poor and less educated, especially the inner-city poor.

Intravenous drug users continue to be found predominately among the inner-city poor. This practice places them at great risk of exposure to the AIDS virus from the sharing of needles. In 1987, it was estimated that about 40 percent of diagnosed AIDS cases were blacks and Hispanics, who constitute the majority of intravenous drug users. One devastating consequence is that black babies are 25 times more likely to get AIDS than are whites. It may seem that drug use and abuse is a lower-class phenomenon; it is for cocaine and heroin, but other drugs are more commonly used by the affluent classes. For example, white college graduates with household incomes over $40,000 a year consume alcohol more than any other group. There are more than 1 million barbiturate and tranquilizer addicts in the United States, and they are generally middle- and upper-class whites. The more affluent tend to use legal and prescription drugs rather than illicit drugs, and they are treated by private physicians. Thus their addiction is typically protected and hidden from public awareness.

MEDICAL AND SOCIAL PRESSURES

Since World War II, chemists have created numerous synthetic substances that have positive health consequences. Vaccines have been developed to fight illnesses such as polio, mumps, smallpox, diphtheria, and measles. Many contagious diseases have been eliminated by the wonders of science, the miracle of chemistry. Similarly, antibiotics have been created as cures for many infectious diseases. The public has accepted these drugs and the industry that created them as beneficial to the health and welfare of all people.

By the end of the 1950s, chemists made breakthroughs in drugs for treating mental disorders such as depression, insomnia, aggression, hyperactivity, and tension. These drugs (tranquilizers, barbiturates, and stimulants) are today widely prescribed by doctors for these problems. Consequently, about 11 percent of the adult population uses barbiturates each year. Pharmaceutical firms manufacture more than 300 tons (3.5 billion doses) of barbiturates each year.

The pharmacological industry works very hard to convince the public to use their products and to convince physicians to prescribe them. But this encouragement is only a part of the reason Americans buy drugs. Many find life so stressful, boring, competitive, and frustrating that they seek drugs for a change in mood or to repress what they do not want to think about. These pressures cause anxiety, stress, and other symptoms for some persons. Also, the pressure to succeed in competitive situations has also encouraged some to take drugs.

In this pressure-filled environment, drugs are used to enhance performance. Amphetamines generally increase alertness, respiration rate, blood pressure, muscle tension, heart rate, and blood sugar. These drugs normally abolish a sense of fatigue. The pressure to use these drugs is unrelenting. Doctors, coaches, parents, advertising, and even friends often encourage drug use. For people who want to succeed or to impress others, the pressure to enhance ability, to get ahead, and to perform without fear is enormous.

SOURCES

Anderson, Patrick. *High in America: The True Story Behind NORML and the Politics of Marijuana.* New York: Random House/Viking. 1981.

Goode, Erich. *Drugs in American Society.* 2d ed. New York: Alfred A. Knopf. 1984.

Hills, Stuart. *Demystifying Social Deviance.* New York: McGraw-Hill. 1980.

Kerr, Peter. "Rich vs. Poor: Drug Patterns Are Diverging." *New York Times* (August 30, 1987).

Levine, Art. "The Uneven Odds." *U.S. News & World Report* (August 17, 1987).

Stengel, Richard. "The Changing Face of AIDS." *Time* (August 17, 1987).

DU BOIS, W. E. B.

W. E. B. Du Bois was a positive and intellectual leader in the black protest movement in the United States. By 1950, he was considered the leading black spokesperson against racial discrimination in this country and elsewhere. Du Bois was also a notable historian and sociologist. Interestingly, he was the first African American to earn a doctorate from Harvard University. Although he didn't coin it, Du Bois was one of the first scholars to use the term *Pan-Africanism*—the belief that all people of African descent have common interests and should work together to conquer prejudice and discrimination. In 1900, Du Bois predicted that man's chief problem in the new century would be "the color line." Vigorously promoting black culture, he espoused the view that art should be earnest, beautiful, and above all didactic; that is, art for Du Bois was propaganda and, in his view, an essential race-building tool. Insightfully, in 1920, Du Bois sounded the inspiring call to arms: "A renaissance of American Negro literature is due; the material about us in the strange, heart-rending tangle is rich beyond dreams and only we can tell the tale and sing the song from the heart" (Watson, *The Harlem Renaissance* 1995).

From 1887 to 1910, Du Bois taught history and economics at Atlanta University. Soon after attending the first Pan-African Conference in London in 1900, he organized a Pan-African Conference in Europe and one in the United States. Du Bois strongly opposed the noted black educator Booker T. Washington, who believed that blacks could advance themselves faster through hard work than by demands for equal rights. Du Bois said that blacks should continue to speak out against racial discrimination in all of its forms. He believed that college-educated blacks must lead the fight against prejudice. He founded the Niagara Movement in 1905 and in 1909 helped to found the National Association for the Advancement of Colored People (NAACP). From 1910 to 1934, Du Bois was the chief editor of the NAACP magazine, the *Crisis*.

In 1934, Du Bois left the NAACP and returned to Atlanta University, but from 1944 to 1948 he again worked for the NAACP. Then after 1948, he became increasingly dissatisfied with the slow progress of race relations in the United States and came to think that even communism might be a solution to the problem. His books include the following: *The Souls of Black Folk* (1902), *The Autobiography of W. E. B. Du Bois* (1968), and *Black Reconstruction in America* (1935).

SOURCE

Watson, Steven. *The Harlem Renaissance*. New York: Pantheon Books. 1995.

DUTY

Duty—being faithful to our obligations—will sometimes require us to tell the truth even when telling the truth is not advantageous and to keep our promises even when it may not be advisable. Duty is the inner disposition, felt by some, to honor obligations even without hope of reward or fear of punishment. A person reveals himself or herself to be a moral person not merely by honoring obligations but by being disposed to honor them even when it is not in one's interest to do so.

We normally tell the truth and keep our promises not out of a sense of honor, but because it is useful to do so. Honesty in ourselves causes others to trust us. If we are disloyal or lie to others then we will lose their respect and friendship. Of course there are other motives involved: religious belief and fear of hell, a sense of moral integrity, or the rewards and recognition that we get when our honesty—being a valued trait—is recognized by others. Actually, we work hard because of the rewards we receive. We discharge many of the duties of citizenship—obeying the law, paying taxes, responding to a call to arms, observing the military code of honor—because fail-

ing to do so exposes us to punishment and certain negative labels: coward, criminal, traitor, etc.

Some have claimed that duty is among the weaker of the moral senses. They point out that excessively dutiful people—those who are bluntly candid, narrowly rule abiding, or relentlessly reformist—are often regarded as difficult and uncooperative. In the extreme case we depict them as obsessed personalities. On the other hand, a sense of duty can be a powerful moral ally if, in certain circumstances, it becomes autonomous and independent of the consequences of certain actions. In either case, a person's duty will never be duty unto itself, but duty in relation to other values that we hold. For example, in the 1960s and early 70s, young men were being drafted into the military for the purpose of serving in the Vietnam War. Most entered the lottery, signed up for the draft, and took their chances. Others protested the war, burned their draft cards, and when called into the military, either failed to show up and were arrested or left the country and sought amnesty after the war. Both groups felt they were doing their duty: one to their country, right or wrong, and the other to a "higher" moral sense that was antiwar. James Q. Wilson reminds us that when duty is placed "in competition with our natural sociability, it often loses out." Most of us want to be popular and have a tendency to be swayed by the crowd, usually our in-group—the group we want to be in with. At work, home, and school we will tell "little white lies" to protect our friends—duty be damned.

So we wonder if duty is in fact a "moral" responsibility, a moral obligation. Moral obligations (duties) confront everyone everywhere and equally. Our moral world has indefinite and constantly expanding boundaries and cannot be ignored. Stephen David Ross writes that "the concept of responsibility is like other moral concepts in being fundamentally instrumental in character. Its primary meaning resides in the act of making a judgment about the person in question. It makes no reference to an absolute property of the agent or his deed. . . . What is necessary is to discover the grounds for the legitimacy of statements of responsibility." But upon examination, we discover that pervasive responsibility and the power to act are separate and distinct. We have a duty, a responsibility in the moral sense, for the welfare of all human beings everywhere. Even though we cannot fully and completely act on this responsibility, it is still ours—from the moral point of view. We cannot confront the world in detail at every turn, but there are collective responsibilities that will forever remain nameless and faceless. This is often the source of our anguish when we know a part of the world suffers and we personally are powerless to carry out any action that would help.

When we turn from pervasive responsibility—duties so big they seem impossible to fulfill—we are still confronted with personal responsibilities. Pervasive responsibility means that we are obligated as human beings to face the world morally, choosing and acting on our choices. Complete or personal responsibility may be thought of as being able to answer duty's call. A responsible and dutiful person is one whose responsiveness to things, persons, and events is as great as humanly possible. Being ready to answer the call

of duty and being ready and able to answer the call are entirely different. In the latter case, "able" implies being able to act on our duty. A dutiful person is one who has weighed himself or herself before the world and its obligations, has responded to the depths of his or her being to them, and is willing and able to stand by his or her choices as they define what he or she can and will do to answer them.

When one is completely responsible for an action and has a duty to carry it forward, it will be an action that cannot be laid to anyone else's responsibility in quite the same way. It differs markedly from the pervasive duties that are everyone's. Complete or personal responsibility varies, as we say that one person is more completely responsible than another. Here duty, as a fact of moral responsibility, will bear the marks of being both pervasive and complete. The critical point is the recognition that we have two kinds of duties related to moral obligation in an intrinsic and intimate way, but distinguishable from each other.

SOURCES

Ross, Stephen David. *The Nature of Moral Responsibility*. Detroit: Wayne State University Press. 1973.

Wilson, James Q. *The Moral Sense*. New York: Free Press. 1993.

E

EAVESDROPPING DEVICES, ETHICS OF

Audio surveillance, wiretapping, bugging, and video surveillance are electronic devices for listening to and viewing—undetected and secretly—private conversations and meetings. Sophisticated methods and devices permit such eavesdropping in almost any situation.

In most countries the right of people to speak freely in their homes and businesses and in public places, without eavesdroppers, is thought of as extremely important and vital, especially to a nation that promotes freedom and democracy for its citizens. Usually, in "free" countries eavesdropping is conceived of in the negative, as the invasion of privacy. Although democratic nations have passed laws restricting or prohibiting certain types of eavesdropping, much illegal eavesdropping continues, both by individuals and by governments.

In the United States, the problem has been both a moral and a complex legal issue. Most Americans believe that eavesdropping on private individuals by governments or by anyone else should not be permitted. Disagreements among lawmakers focus on two issues: (1) the constitutionality of electronic surveillance by law enforcement agencies, and (2) methods of controlling government eavesdropping if it is permitted.

The controversy began in 1928, when the U.S. Supreme Court ruled that wiretapping did not violate the Fourth Amendment to the Constitution. This amendment sets forth the restrictions of search and seizure:

> The right of the people to be secure in their persons, houses, papers, and effects, against unreasonable searches and seizures, shall not be violated, and no Warrant shall issue, but upon probable cause, supported by Oath or affirmation, and particularly describing the places to be searched, and the persons or things to be seized.

In 1934, Congress passed the Federal Communications Act, which prohibits the interception and public disclosure of any wire or radio communication. On the basis of this law, the Supreme Court ruled in 1937 that evidence obtained by wiretapping may not be used in federal courts. Following this ruling, federal officials argued that the 1934 law did not prohibit wiretapping by the government so long as the evidence was not used in court. Since 1940, U.S. presidents have claimed constitutional power to order wiretapping in matters of national security.

In 1968, Congress passed a law permitting federal, state, and local government agencies to use wiretapping and bugging devices in certain criminal investigations. Before undertaking such surveillance, an agency would have to obtain a court order. The law stated that nothing in it was intended to limit the president's constitutional authority to order eavesdropping without court warrants in national security cases. In the late 1960s and early 1970s, the executive branch broadly interpreted the national security provisions of the 1968 law. It conducted electronic surveillance without court approval on a number of domestic radicals it considered subversive. In 1972, the Supreme Court ruled that such surveillance without a court warrant was unconstitutional.

The issue of privacy has become an important moral as well as legal issue in the United States as governmental agencies, with the aid of computer technology, are reported to be compiling data on individuals who file income tax returns, receive Social Security benefits, apply for a passport, are arrested, or participate in antigovernment demonstrations. Some private agencies such as credit associations have created vast computerized data banks reflecting the credit history of almost every citizen of the United States.

Our privacy seems to be "up for sale." The loss of privacy will mean the loss of individuality, the marks of a police state, and the death of freedom and democracy as we know it. On this issue, Harold H. Titus and Morris Keeton comment: "We do not believe that in a complex society privacy can be an absolute condition. The central question is how to maintain effective law enforcement and to retain our human and constitutional liberties at the same time. Fear and suspicion tend to destroy the human personality and disrupt the intercommunication that is the basis of a free society. We have been warned that the growing espionage and the invasions of privacy are threatening to undermine the mental health of the country."

SOURCES

"Eavesdropping Devices." Grolier Electronic Publishing. 1992.

Titus, Harold H., and Morris T. Keeton. *Ethics for Today.* 5th ed. New York: Van Nostrand. 1973.

ECOLOGY AND ENVIRONMENTAL ETHICS

Ecology is a branch of biology that deals with the relationships living things have to each other and to their surroundings. Many people view ecology and environmental science as synonymous; thus, environmentalists are frequently considered ecologists. Ecology, in the strict sense, is one of the disciplines constituting the core of environmental science, and within ecology there are many subdisciplines such as *aquatic ecology* and *radiation ecology* that focus on particular kinds of substances and their environmental requirements and relationships.

The word *ecology* is derived from the Greek word *oikos*, meaning "a place to live." Most ecologists therefore define ecology as the study of the relationship of an organism or group of organisms to their environments. The ecologist Eugene Odum points out that ecologists are concerned with the biology of groups of organisms and with functional processes. He defines ecology as "the study of the structures and the functions of nature." Ecologists are also concerned about the limits of life, how living things use resources such as minerals and energy, and how living things interact. Strictly, ecology is the study of these processes; environmental science is the application of this knowledge to managing the environment.

Arne Naess, Norwegian philosopher and alpinist extraordinaire, coined the term *deep ecology* as a symbol for the vision of a world in which we protect the environment as a part of ourselves, never in opposition to humanity. Deep ecology has profound moral implications: David Rothenberg, in his conversations with Naess, comments that Naess "imagined the individual self as something to be realized outward into the world, such that it is enlarged and deepened the more universal experience it is able to contain. . . . One approaches fulfillment through empathy with the world beyond the ego."

The moral aspect of ecology—treating the environment as moralists have normally recommended that we treat each other—has not been fully accepted (especially in industrial and political circles), perhaps because it breaks with the Western (Greek-Roman, Christian-Enlightenment) idea of the "unchanging, ahistorical self," which has heretofore been thought of as the "depository" of value and belief. To transfer the idea of intrinsic value to nature and then to say that humans are a part of that environment, and to clearly articulate a "gestalt view" of humanity's place in nature, reinforces a deep (moral) ecological mentality. But this is not a traditional view, anchored in the spiritual and rational self; rather, it is a naturalist view, based on change, experience, and expansion.

SOURCES

Odum, Eugene P. *Fundamentals of Ecology.* Philadelphia: W. B. Saunders. 1971.

Rothenberg, David. *Is It Painful to Think? Conversations with Arne Naess.* Minneapolis: University of Minnesota Press. 1993.

ECUMENICAL MOVEMENT

Ecumenical, from the Greek *oikoumenikos,* "the inhabited world," is a general or universal movement among both Protestant and Catholic churches promoting unity. During the past 50 years, many of the fissions and separations within Protestantism have slowed down and unity among the Protestant churches has grown. There has also been a turn to active ecumenism by the Roman Catholic Church that has broadened the effort to include the prospect of the reunion of all Christians.

According to David and John Noss:

The century-old Protestant trend toward rapprochement has been due, not only to the attitude of the liberals in all denominations who have stressed agreement on essentials as a basis for unity, but also to many other factors, e.g., the change that an economy marked by rapid communication and general interdependence has brought about; the fact that scientific skepticism and widespread secularism have tended to drive adherents of religion together; the very expansion of the Christian effort into all the world; the growing interchange between denominations of helpful literature, such as hymns, lesson-materials, and devotional aids; the meeting and intermingling of ministers and laymen from many different denominations on interdenominational boards and committees and at conferences and camps; and, not least, the realization that a divided Protestantism is a weakened Protestantism.

In Catholic circles worldwide, there is also a sense of union. In 1959, Pope John XXIII issued a summons embracing the entire Catholic world. He asked that delegates be sent to an ecumenical council, to be known as Vatican II. It met in Rome for its first session in 1963 and met again in 1963, 1964, and 1965, at the call of Pope Paul VI. Official observers from Protestant and Orthodox churches (including the Russian but not the Greek) and selected lay "auditors" were present. The second council sought adjustment to the twentieth-century world and the promotion of Christian unity.

Among other things, the Catholic council recognized the possibility of salvation outside the Catholic Church; authorized worship of Catholics with non-Catholics in special circumstances; promoted religious freedom worldwide; and declared that Jews are not to be held collectively responsible for the death of Christ. The council's declaration on the relation of the Catholic Church to non-Christian religions contains these highly significant passages:

From ancient times to the present, there is found among various peoples a certain perception of that mysterious power abiding in the course of nature and in the happenings of human life; at times some indeed have come to the recognition of a Supreme Being, or even of a Father. This perception and recognition penetrates their lives with a profound religious sense.

Religions, however, that are bound up with an advanced culture have struggled to answer the same questions by means of more refined concepts and a more developed language. . . . Likewise, other religions found everywhere try to counter the restlessness of the human heart, each in its own manner, by proposing "ways," comprising teachings, rules of life, and sacred rites.

The Catholic Church rejects nothing that is true and holy in these religions. She regards with sincere reverence those ways of conduct and of life, those precepts and teachings which, though differing in many respects from the ones she holds and sets forth, nonetheless often reflect a ray of that Truth which enlightens all men. . . .

The Church therefore exhorts her children to recognize, preserve and foster the good things, spiritual and moral, as well as the socio-cultural values found among the followers of other religions.

Among European Protestants, the first great achievements in unity were in the area of foreign missions. The problems of interdenominational comity on the mission fields led to the calling of the great Edinburgh Missionary Conference of 1910, which resulted in the formation of the International Missionary Council in 1921, a body that has since merged with the World Council of Churches.

The World Council of Churches itself emerged from the Church of England (Episcopal) with hopes of serving as a mediator between the Protestant and Catholic worlds. This goal led in 1937 to two Protestant world conferences, one on Faith and Order, and the other on Life and Work. From these conferences came the World Council of Churches, designed to parallel—on a worldwide scale—the National Council of Churches of Christ in the United States. The first assembly of the World Council of Churches was held in Amsterdam, Holland, in 1948. Since that time it has met in countries all over the world. Also, it has admitted to membership all of the Eastern Orthodox churches, and has invited observers from the Roman Catholic Church, members of which now serve on its Commission on Faith and Order. This was a historic breakthrough for unity, made in Uppsala, Sweden.

Two separate methods of union have emerged from these efforts: (1) a federal union of churches without abolishing the members' own denominations, and (2) complete organic union through merger; for example, in Canada, of Presbyterians, Methodists, and Congregationalists into the United Church of Canada (1925). Along denominational lines, separate branches of the Lutheran and also of the Presbyterian churches in the United States have merged. Ecumenically, more significant was the organic union in 1961 of the Congregational-Christian church and the Evangelical and Reformed churches under the name of the United Church of Christ.

SOURCES

Noss, David S., and John B. Noss. *Man's Religions.* 4th ed. New York: Macmillan. 1984.

Walhout, Donald. *Interpreting Religion.* Englewood Cliffs, NJ: Prentice-Hall. 1963.

Toynbee, Arnold. *An Historian's Approach to Religion.* London: Oxford University Press. 1956.

EDELMAN, MARIAN WRIGHT

Marian Wright Edelman (1939–) is a leading advocate for children's rights and the founder and president of the Children's Defense Fund (CDF). Growing up in rural South Carolina in the 1940s, she learned early on that "If you don't like the way the world is, you change it. You have an obligation to change it. You just do it, one step at a time." For most of her life, changing the world—especially the treatment of children in the United States—has been her mission. Citing statistics about infant deaths, divorce, poverty, teenage pregnancy, lack of adequate day care in the United States, and school dropouts, she said in 1973 that her goal was to turn these statistics around. She called them a national tragedy.

Growing up in Bennettsville, South Carolina, Edelman says that because of the potential hurts of the segregated world outside the black community, her parents, teachers, and preachers took great care to try to instill in her and her contemporaries a strong sense of self-respect and self-confidence. She comments: "They believed in us, and we, therefore, believed in ourselves." When she was 14 her father died after suffering a heart attack. "The last thing he said to me before he died was, 'Don't let anything get between you and your education,'" Edelman reflects. Four years later she entered Spelman College in Atlanta, the nation's largest liberal arts college for black women. She won a Merrill Scholarship to go abroad for her junior year and, in preparation for a career in the foreign service, studied for one summer at the Sorbonne, in Paris, and during the academic year at the University of Geneva, in Switzerland. Supported by a Lisle Fellowship, she spent the following summer in Moscow. "That year gave me a sense of confidence that I could navigate in the world and do just about anything," she said.

When Edelman returned to Spelman for her senior year, the Civil Rights movement was just heating up. With memories of racial injustices from her childhood now combined with a maturing social conscience, she abandoned her plans to join the foreign service and entered the Civil Rights movement as a participant by joining the sit-ins in Atlanta's City Hall. After graduating with a B.A. degree in 1960, she entered Yale Law School. She chose law to better prepare herself to help black people, and law was a tool she needed.

Shortly before receiving the LL.B. degree from Yale in 1963, Edelman signed on with the National Association for the Advancement of Colored People's Legal Defense and Educational Fund. After a year of civil rights law training in New York City, she went to Jackson, Mississippi, to work. She chose Mississippi because the state had some 900,000 blacks and just three black lawyers. During the four years Edelman stayed in Mississippi, she became the first black woman admitted to the Mississippi state bar. Her activities were broadened to include civil rights litigation, aiding community efforts directed at improving the economic condition of the state's blacks, helping to restore federal funding to Mississippi's Head Start program, and becoming an advocate for children's rights.

It was during her years in Mississippi that she met her future husband, Peter B. Edelman, a Harvard Law School alumnus, a former Supreme Court law clerk, and, in 1967, a legislative assistant to Senator Robert F. Kennedy of New York, who visited the Mississippi Delta that year in connection with his work on the Senate Subcommittee on Employment, Manpower, and Poverty. He gives Edelman credit for bringing the plight of Mississippi blacks to his attention. Marian Wright and Peter Edelman were married on July 14, 1968. Afterward, she moved to Washington partly to be with her husband and partly to expand her work for Mississippi's poor to the political arena. She served as counsel to the Poor People's Campaign, which came to Washington later that summer, and established the Washington Research Project, a public interest research and advocacy organization. She concentrated on lobbying congressional support for re-funding and expanding the services of Head Start to cover more children. In 1971, the Edelmans moved to Boston, where Peter served two years as vice president of the University of Massachusetts and Marian directed the Center for Law and Education at Harvard University while continuing to oversee the activities of the Washington Research Project. She was named that year one of the nation's top 200 young leaders by *Time* magazine.

In 1973, Edelman spun off the Children's Defense Fund from the Washington Research Project to provide a voice for America's voiceless and voteless millions, the group that she believes is the true "silent majority." Part think tank, part lobbying group, the nonprofit, nonpartisan organization cuts across race and class lines. According to the CDF's entry in the *Encyclopedia of Associations*, among the activities in which it engages are research, public education, monitoring federal agencies, assisting with the drafting of legislation, and providing testimony before lawmakers. It works with individuals and groups to change policies and practices resulting in neglect or mistreatment of millions of children and advocates a strong parental and community role in decision making. As Edelman has reminded us, "it takes a whole community to raise a kid." Her goals are caring adults, a caring community, a caring government, and a caring private sector.

Over the past two decades, the CDF has grown to a staff of 100 in its Washington headquarters and a $4.6 million budget. Its purpose is to advocate for our nation's children. Edelman still believes that our children are not getting a fair deal from the richest nation on earth. In her book *Families in Peril: An Agenda for Social Change* (1987), she points out that the priorities of a world that permits 40,000 children to die quite legally each day from malnutrition and infection cannot go unchecked. In her most recent book, *The Measure of Our Success: A Letter to My Children and Yours* (1992), Edelman pleads passionately for action on behalf of the children of the United States.

In an advertisement that appeared in newspapers during the week of the 1992 Democratic presidential convention, CDF provided a summary of its primary goals for U.S. children: a healthy start (children need basic health care to grow into healthy, productive adults), a head start through quality preschools (only by getting children ready for school can we begin to achieve other national education goals), and a fair start ensuring families a minimum level of economic security. She said, "All told these investments will prevent thousands of taxpayer dollars in later medical, education, and welfare costs."

Marian Wright Edelman disclaims all personal ambition and has no desire to run for political office or to be a judge or a Cabinet secretary. Her many awards include a John D. and Catherine T. MacArthur Foundation Fellowship and a Rockefeller Public Service Award for her contributions toward solving important problems facing the nation, as well as honorary degrees from upwards of 50 U.S. colleges and universities. She has said that her greatest personal concern is the possibility that she hasn't lived up to the highest moral standards, that she has not lived as purposefully as she could, and that she will not do what she was sent here to do.

SOURCE
Current Biography 53:9 (September 1992).

EDUCATION AS A RIGHT

In 1642, the Massachusetts Bay Colony passed a law requiring parents to teach their children to read. A Massachusetts law passed in 1647 established the first public schools in the United States. The law required every town with at least 50 families to start an elementary school, and every town of 100 families or more to have a Latin grammar school. The elementary schools were open to all children and the grammar schools were attended mainly by boys preparing for college.

By the early 1800s, many Americans believed that something was needed to give the American people common goals and a sense of national unity. The answer, they felt, lay in public education. Legislators proposed that each state set up a system of free, compulsory, tax-supported schools. The schools were to be free of religious control but devoted to building character and patriotism. The *McGuffey Readers* taught patriotism and played an important role in forming literary tastes in America, while Noah Webster's famous *Blue-Backed Speller* helped standardize spelling and pronunciation in the United States. Although a free and public education is today thought of as a basic right in the United States, less clear are answers to the questions What should be taught? Who should attend school and for how long? and Who should control education?

WHAT SHOULD BE TAUGHT?

Most debates in state legislatures and school board meetings concern both the purpose and context of public schooling. These debates have included: (1) the acquisition of knowledge, (2) skill versus content, (3) education for citizenship, (4) vocational training, (5) individual development, and (6) character education. In recent years debates have surged forth over censorship issues of certain books and other materials, the so-called new math, sex education, grouping practices—including gifted and handicapped education—phonics versus whole language or literature-based instruction, and the inclusion of expensive technology in schools, such as hookups to the Internet.

Traditionalists usually emphasize knowledge and skills. They believe that education should be an organized process with measurable results. After 1957, when Russia launched its first man-made satellite, U.S. education was criticized for being too "soft" and not training enough scientists and engineers. In response, Congress passed the National Defense Education Act of 1958, which provided funds to improve educational programs. New studies emphasized learning the structure of a discipline rather than merely memorizing facts. Receiving renewed interest were early childhood education, testing, and programmed learning. Since 1983 and the publication of *A Nation at Risk,* schools have experimented with accountability systems such as outcome-based education and the effective schools concept, and today many have turned to locally controlled systems of schooling and site-based management to find ways to improve the quality of learning.

Those who hold nontraditional views generally emphasize acquiring self-knowledge and personal development as education's chief goals. Believing that education should be less formally structured, they desire that students find their own path of self-development and encourage them to acquire a social conscience and become involved in community affairs. Nontraditionalists accept many of the ideas developed by innovative and "progressive" educators. Among these is an increased emphasis on multiculturalism and giving students a voice in making decisions. Believing that education is a fundamental right, people holding nontraditional views have started hundreds of schools outside the established public and private school systems. These have variously been called *alternative schools, free schools,* and *storefront schools.* This last group was started mainly for minority students in poor sections of larger cities.

EDUCATION FOR WHOM?

Most educators and most states agree that all children should attend school for a certain number of years. Some say attendance laws are too strict. They argue that many high school students would benefit more from on-the-job training than sitting in a classroom all day. Although there are express differences among state legislatures, prominent educators and parents almost all agree that every American student should have an equal opportunity for an education.

WHO SHOULD
CONTROL EDUCATION?

Traditionally laced committees and boards of education have had considerable control over education. Constitutionally, however, control of education belongs to state legislatures and state boards of education. There has been a long history of give-and-take between local boards and state boards of education over who should control education and how much control each body will have.

With rising costs and the demand for accountability, more and more state and federal agencies have exerted their power and control over various parts of the educational system. The rising cost of education has made it more difficult for parents to choose private or religious schools, or even educate their children at home. Some have suggested a voucher system of school support in which the state and/or the local government or both would pay a share of a student's private schooling.

To make schools better educationally and to have them more effectively respond to community needs, there has been a 30-year trend of schools being managed by elective neighborhood councils of parents. In New York City and in many other large cities, and now in the state of Kentucky, community-based schools have been established to meet local needs. The entire public school system in the state of Kentucky has reconstructed its public school system so that qualified members of the community, the professional teaching staff, and administrators work jointly to micromanage the schools. To date, the experiment is showing positive results.

Because education is the process by which people acquire knowledge and skills, as well as habits, values, and attitudes that help a person become a useful member of society, it will always be important to a community and to a nation. A modern society cannot survive without education, and in democratic societies the benefits of education are held in high regard—not only for the skills needed for the workplace, but for what it provides for people individually. Education, by helping individuals develop moral and spiritual values, and by providing healthy attitudes and emotions, is a necessary prerequisite to the modern democratic society. Thus, in the mid-1990s, character education, or as some say, citizenship training, is slowly finding its way back into the public school curriculum. This will be a trend that will bear much watching in the years ahead to see just what values, skills, or other personal and social dispositions are emphasized by these programs.

SOURCES

Adler, Mortimer J. *The Paideia Proposal: An Educational Manifesto.* New York: Macmillan. 1982.

American Association of School Administrators. "Teaching Thinking and Reasoning Skills: Problems and Solutions." *AASA Critical Issues Report* no. 20. Arlington, VA: American Association of School Administrators. 1987.

Beene, K., and S. Tozer, eds. *Society as Educator in an Age of Transition: Part II.* Chicago: National Society for the Study of Education. 1987.

Brown, Rexford G. *Schools of Thought.* San Francisco: Jossey-Bass. 1991.

Carnegie Forum on Education and the Economy. *A Nation Prepared: Teachers for the 21st Century.* New York: Carnegie Corporation. 1986.

Goodlad, J., ed. *The Ecology of School Renewal: Part I.* Chicago: National Society for the Study of Education. 1987.

National Commission on Excellence in Education. *A Nation At Risk.* Washington, D.C.: U.S. Government Printing Office. 1983.

Schlechty, P. C. *Schools for the 21st Century: Leadership Imperatives for Educational Reform.* San Francisco: Jossey-Bass. 1990.

EHRLICH, PAUL RALPH

Paul Ralph Ehrlich (1932–) is a U.S. biologist, a leader of the international movement for population control. In his book *The Population Bomb* (1968), Ehrlich claimed that the world's population was growing faster than man's food supply. He predicted that hundreds of millions of people would starve to death during the 1970s. Many scientists criticized some of Ehrlich's statements as exaggerations. Although he agrees that other factors are involved, Ehrlich continues to stress that overpopulation is the most important cause of hunger and environmental problems. Ehrlich has called for an end to population growth and in 1968, helped the organization called Zero Population Growth, which urged every family to have no more than two children.

SOURCES

Ehrlich, Paul Ralph, and Anne H. Ehrlich. *Population/Resources/Environment: Issues in Human Ecology.* 2d ed. San Francisco: W. H. Freeman. 1972.

Ehrlich, Paul Ralph, et al. *Human Ecology: Problems and Solutions.* San Francisco: W. H. Freeman. 1973.

THE ELECTRONIC REPUBLIC

Lawrence K. Grossman says, "As we approach the twenty-first century, America is turning into an electronic republic, a democratic system that is vastly increasing the people's day-to-day influence on the decisions of state." Richard C. Leone, president of the Twentieth Century Fund, observes: "Technology is making mass participation possible in previously unimaginable ways. The electronic town hall, instant public-opinion polls, citizen juries, and other breakthoughs based, in part, on new communication technologies are touted as solutions to bad government and public cynicism. We seem to be in the early stages of a major shift away from our republican form of government. If this is the case, it is important to ask if direct 'electronic' democracy is either workable or desirable in a country like America."

CHARACTERISTICS

1. The distance between the government and those who govern is actually shrinking. Incessant public-opinion polling and sophisticated interactive telecommunications devices make government instantly aware of, and responsive to, popular will.

2. In the 200-year-long march toward political equality for all citizens and the explosive growth of new telecommunications media, the remarkable convergence of television, telephone, satellites, cable, and personal computers, this is the first time citizens can see, hear, and judge their own political leaders simultaneously and instantaneously.

3. The emerging electronic republic will be a political hybrid. Citizens will be able to select those who govern them, but also will be able to participate directly in making the laws and policies by which they are governed. With the use of two-way digital broadband telecommunication networks, citizens are turning themselves into the new fourth branch of government. With the ability to respond quickly to every ripple of public opinion, some of our most cherished constitutional protections against the potential excesses of majority impulses may be undercut.

4. Telecommunications technology has reduced the traditional barriers of time and distance. In the same way it can also reduce the traditional constitutional barriers of checks and balances and separation of powers. Observed James Madison: "Extend the sphere, and you take in a greater variety of parties and interests; you make it less probable that a majority of the whole will have a common motive to invade the rights of other citizens." However, as distances disappear and

telecommunications shrinks the sphere, and as the executive and legislative branches of government become more intertwined with public opinion and popular demand, only the courts may be left to stand as an effective bastion against the "tyranny of the majority."

5. *Direct democracy*, which originated in fifth-century Greece, and toward which we seem to be heading, was the earliest form of democracy. By contrast, representative government is a relatively recent phenomenon, originating in the United States a little more than two centuries ago. But our Constitution, unlike the Greek model, specifies a government that separates the rulers from the ruled. Constitutional "space"—which distances the government from the people by making the elected the ones who actually enact the laws and conduct the business of government—is the genius of America. It keeps the process of democratization under control and prevents our democracy from running itself by carrying itself to extreme.

6. Telecommunications technologies such as computers, satellites, interactive television, the telephone, and the radio are breaking down the age-old barriers of time and distance that originally precluded the nation's people from voting directly for the laws and policies that govern them. Interactive telecommunications now make it possible for millions of people to receive information at home or at work and act upon it, giving them some power over their own lives.

In conclusion, we now can see that the electronic republic has already started to redefine the traditional roles of citizenship and political leadership. Lobbyists in the next century may turn to the people, as well as the elected, and lobby public opinion. Sven Birkerts remarks: "The advent of the computer and the astonishing sophistication achieved by our electronic communications media have together turned a range of isolated changes into something systematic. The way that people experience the world has altered more in the past fifty years then in the many centuries preceding ours." Grossman concludes by reminding us that there is now a need for new thinking, procedures, policies, and even political institutions to ensure that in the century ahead "majoritorian impulses will not come at the expense of the rights of individuals and unpopular minorities."

See also Cyberspace; Protestantism.

SOURCES

Birkerts, Sven. "The Advent of the Computer." In *The Gutenberg Elegies*. Boston: Faber and Faber. 1994.

Grossman, Lawrence K. *The Electronic Republic*. New York: Viking. 1995.

Leone, Richard C. "Foreword. " In L. K. Grossman. *The Electronic Republic*. New York: Viking. 1995.

Madison, James. "Extend the Sphere": The Federalist No. 10. In *The Federalist Papers by Alexander Hamilton, James Madison, and John Jay*. New York: Bantam. 1982.

EMANCIPATION PROCLAMATION

President Abraham Lincoln issued the Emancipation Proclamation on January 1, 1863, a historic document that led to the end of slavery in the United States. This proclamation declared freedom for slaves in those Confederate states that had seceded from the Union and were now at war with the United States. The proclamation also provided for the use of blacks in the Union army and navy.

It should be pointed out that Lincoln agreed with the abolitionists who called slavery evil. He once declared that "If slavery is not wrong, nothing is wrong." But early in the Civil War, Lincoln believed that if he freed the slaves, he would divide the North. He feared that the four slave-owning border states—Delaware, Kentucky, Maryland, and Missouri—would secede if he adopted such a policy.

In July 1862, with the war going badly for the North, Congress passed a law freeing all Confederate slaves who came into Union lines. At about the same time, Lincoln decided to change his stand on slavery. But he waited for a Union military victory, so that his decision would not appear to be a desperate act. So, on September 22, 1862, five days after Union forces won the Battle of Antietam, Lincoln issued a preliminary proclamation. It stated simply that if the rebelling states did not return to the Union by January 1, 1863, he would declare their slaves to be "forever free." The South ignored Lincoln's warning, and so he issued the Emancipation Proclamation on New Year's Day, 1863.

The Emancipation Proclamation, Lincoln argued, attacked the core of Southern society and would expedite a military victory. "Without slavery the rebellion could never have existed; without slavery it would not continue," Lincoln maintained. He also reaffirmed his willingness to compensate former slave owners for the loss of their chattel.

Affected by the issuance of the Emancipation Proclamation was the institution of slavery in only those 11 Confederate states fighting against the Union. It did not touch slavery in the loyal border states, nor did it apply even in federally controlled areas of the South, such as New Orleans. As Secretary of State William Seward remarked, "We show our sympathy with slavery by emancipating slaves where we cannot reach them, and holding them in bondage where we cannot set them free." In his first inaugural address, Lincoln had indicated his willingness to accept a Thirteenth Amendment that would have guaranteed slavery in the Southern states. Now, he urged a different Thirteenth Amendment: to eliminate slavery in the Confederate states. A Republican Congress, more radical than the president, went beyond this request and endorsed an amendment prohibiting slavery throughout the United States. Ratified in December 1865, eight months after Lincoln's death, it represented a fundamental alteration of the Constitution of 1789.

The doctrine of national loyalty, so vigorously denied within the Southern Confederacy, emerged in the North as a central tenet of Union ideology. In rejecting the constitutionality of secession, the North also repudiated the doctrine of states' rights and with it the institution of slavery. Although Lincoln reversed his position on Southern slavery, he remained ambivalent about the problem of race. "I am not, nor ever have been in favor of bringing about in any way the social and political equality of the white and black races," he asserted in 1858. "There must be the position of superior and inferior, and I am in favor of having the superior position assigned to the white race." As Lincoln repeated these sentiments to a delegation of free blacks, hoping to convince them to support colonization, he said: "On this broad continent not a single man of your race is made the equal of a single man of ours. . . . I cannot alter it if I would. It is a fact, about which we all think and feel alike, I and you. It is better for us both to be separated."

Although the Emancipation Proclamation did not actually free a single slave, because it affected only those states/territories under Confederate control, it did strengthen the North's war effort and perhaps the resolve of many to end slavery in the United States forever. More than 500,000 slaves had fled to freedom behind Northern lines. Many of them joined the Union army and navy or worked for the armed forces as laborers. The 200,000 black soldiers and sailors, most of them former slaves, helped the North win the war.

SOURCE

Carroll, Peter N., and David W. Noble. *The Free and the Unfree: A New History of the United States.* 2d ed. New York: Penguin. 1988.

ENDANGERED SPECIES ACT OF 1973

In the United States, at least 500 species and subspecies of plants and animals have become extinct since the 1500s. Natural causes appear to have claimed just one of the animals, a marine snail that used to live off New England's shores. We who live today barely knew the others, but in the 1950s almost all of us heard about the passenger pigeon, the last one of millions dying alone in a cage a few decades earlier. The bison, whooping crane, and southern trumpeter swan are all but gone. Some are making a recovery, but none too soon. During the 1960s and early 1970s, with a newfound environmental awareness—this age gave birth to the field known as *ecology*—the nation was ready to try. Congress responded with the Endangered Species Act (ESA) of 1973. This act was based on the assumptions that each life form may prove valuable in ways we cannot yet measure and that each is entitled to exist for its own sake as well. ESA gave the federal government the powers to prevent extinction. Some have called this a bill of rights for nonhumans, or an attempt to guarantee a future for as many as possible. In 1973, the list of threatened and endangered species in the United States had 109 names on it; the total in 1995 is well over 900 in this country and 1,400 worldwide. There are 3,700 more species whose names may well appear on this list.

See also Ecology and Environmental Ethics.

SOURCE

Chadwick, Douglas H. "Dead or Alive: The Endangered Species Act." *National Geographic* 187:3 (March 1995).

ENTROPY, LAW OF

Entropy, from the Greek "a turning in," is a measure of the degree of disorder of a system (such as a family, a group, a school, a nation, etc.). An increase in entropy with change signifies a reduced amount of energy available to the system.

Systems theory has been introduced as a way of analyzing the function of groups by reducing dependence on cause-effect relations and emphasizing the relationship of the parts to the whole. Most systems, such as families, corporations, and classrooms, are a collection of interdependent parts and are also parts of larger systems in which they are necessary units or subsystems. For example, a school system (an organized group of schools that normally serve a definite geographical area) is made up of individual schools in the area, and each school is made up of classrooms with teachers and students. The system has no function or existence apart from its teachers and students. The interrelationships among these multiple systems can be complex and, to outsiders, confusing. One primary purpose of management is to create a workable and utilitarian structure in which these various subsystems can operate smoothly, harmoniously, and efficiently.

Some systems are open, which means that they are responsive to the larger environment. Open systems maintain a constant flow of information, keep its production free-flowing, and function with a clear, goal-directed emphasis. Open systems are dynamic, have the ability to communicate within their structures and with the outside world, and their members give mutual support, accept each other, and show increasing productivity.

On the other hand, closed systems tend to exhibit low levels of energy and to be static, lack innovation, and be highly resistant to change. In theory, closed systems eventually shut down and die because the ability to adapt—which they lack—is crucial whether in nature, business, or social systems. The concept of *adaptability* is useful, since we know that nonadaptive human organizations become restrictive, inflexible, and resistent. Closed systems have decreasing productivity and low morale.

When a system is closed, there is a tendency for a certain degree of entropy (chaos and disorder) to occur. In human systems, this results in the breakdown of communication, loss of information, role confusion, and a general increase in organization. This is called a *state of entropy*. Entropy, therefore, defines a negative condition in which systems have decreasing energy and few new ideas or healthy adaptations. It is of great value for organizations to avoid entropy if possible, but entropy tends to increase naturally. In organizations where tenure is prevalent and personnel turnover rare, intellectual stagnation is common and individuals tend to isolate themselves and pay increasingly less attention to the needs of the whole system. In such a context, entropy becomes a sort of "noise" that reduces the system's ability to function efficiently with optimum morale.

SOURCES

McLeod, A. *Management Information Systems* (Casebook). Chicago: Science Research Associates. 1987.

Wilden, A. *Systems and Structure: Essays in Communication and Exchange*. 2d ed. London: Tavistock. 1980.

ENVY

Envy implies resentment, jealousy, or even hatred directed toward others. It is the feeling of ill will at another's good fortune because one wishes it had been one's own good fortune. Envy is a negative value and can lead to unethical behaviors, because when one is envious, one normally dislikes the person who has what one wants and covets the other's fortune or good luck.

SOURCES

Nozick, Robert. *The Examined Life: Philosophical Meditations*. New York: Simon & Schuster. 1989.

Peck, M. Scott. *The Road Less Traveled*. New York: Simon & Schuster. 1978.

EPICUREANISM

Most humans have asked about the meaning of life. Epicurus (341–270 B.C.) taught that we are here to cultivate the pleasures of the mind, wisdom, and understanding. Opposing this view was the Cyrenaic philosopher Aristippus, who advocated the cultivation of physical pleasures—the more the merrier. Those of the mind were to be cultivated as a last resort. Because of Aristippus, Epicureanism is known in terms of gluttony, debauchery, and bacchanalian orgies. Epicurus himself led a life of sobriety and simplicity, eating bread, cheese, and olives, drinking a bit of wine, napping in his hammock, and enjoying conversation with his friends while strolling through his garden. He died with dignity and courage after a painful, protracted disease.

Epicureanism was grounded in the atomic theory of Democrites, but like most post-Alexandrian philosophers, Epicurus does not seem to have been interested in science. His major interest was finding out about the good life. He believed that the goal of life was happiness, but happiness he equated simply with pleasure. No act should be undertaken except for the pleasures in which it results, and no act should be rejected except for the pain that it produces.

This simple idea provoked Epicurus to analyze the different kinds of pleasure. He said that there are two kinds of desires, hence two kinds of pleasures as a result of gratifying these desires: *natural desire* and *vain desire*. There are two kinds of natural desire: (1) the *necessary* desire for food and sleep, and (2) the *unnecessary* desire for sex. An example of vain desire is the desire for decorative clothing or exotic food.

Natural necessary desires must be satisfied and are easy to satisfy. They result in a good deal of pleasure and in very few painful consequences. Vain desires do not need to be satisfied and are not easy to satisfy. Because there are no natural limits to them, they tend to become obsessive and lead to very painful consequences.

One should notice that Epicurus's definition of pleasure is negative; that is, pleasure is the absence of pain. The truly good person, the one who experiences the most pleasure, is the one who, having overcome all unnecessary desires, gratifies his necessary desires in the most moderate way possible, leaves plenty of time for physical and mental repose, and is free from worry. Some of Epicurus's Roman followers interpreted "pleasure" quite differently, defining it as a positive titillation. It is because of these extremists that today Epicureanism is often associated with sensualistic hedonism.

SOURCES

Palmer, Donald. *Looking at Philosophy.* Mountain View, CA: Mayfield. 1988.

Thilly, Frank, and Ledger Wood. *A History of Philosophy.* New York: Henry Holt. 1959.

EQUALITY, PRINCIPLE OF

Theoretically and practically, the most misunderstood ethical concept is that of equality. Equality is an ideal that, if misinterpreted, can destroy a nation, a community, or an organization. Most communities—especially if, all things being equal, they are communities of friends—operate on the unspoken assumption that all members have equal amounts of power. Members of some groups that include management-staff hierarchies feel uncomfortable about power differences, so they downplay these differences and create the impression that, beneath the titles, everyone is equal. Problems usually arise when the gap between the ideal and the real widens to the point of creating resentment or disillusionment among community leaders. This is a practical problem and one that has to be worked out in the daily intercourse of men and women living in a community, whether or not the community is a city, a school, or a place of employment.

But no matter how complex the working out of human relationships, equality remains as a moral and social ideal. In Western societies the fundamental moral axiom has been formulated as a universal rule and, in Christianity, is called the *Golden Rule.* Immanuel Kant explicitly interprets this axiom as a universal law of reason that embodies the principle of equality: "So interpreted, its meaning is that every man, just because he is a man, is always to be treated as an end, never merely as a means to another's end." This maxim is embodied in legal principle as impartial justice, as the right of every human being, whatever his or her station in society. As a political principle embodied in Western civilization's religious history, equality clearly revealed the democratic insight of Europeans and, later, Americans. Every human being, simply by virtue of being a human being, has a right to participate with others in the processes and institutions that determine the conditions under which his or her life is lived. And when the moral implication of this universal ideal is examined, we discover that the concept of equality lies embedded within its core. Thus, the ideal of equality is foundational to the political ideal of democracy.

But why are humans equal? Or, what makes us believe that all humans are equal? Some might say it is because all of us are created by God. Others, especially those heavily influenced by Enlightenment thought, will claim it is because humans have the power of reason. Some will say that we all possess a soul and it is the soul in us that creates equality. In the nineteenth century, pragmatists, utilitarians, and instrumentalists insisted that equality was more practical than metaphysical, that truth in any matter is what produces desired results.

How to define and support the ideal of equality has always been perplexing, and in the history of mankind there have been and are differences of opinion. No matter—this handicap has not prevented equality from exercising a strong and persistent appeal from ancient times until today. Increasingly, moral philosophers have defined the concept not in terms of possessions or talents, nor even in terms of opportunity. Rather, its basic meaning is to be found in the idea of the dignity and worth of individuals: All humans are equal in their human dignity and worth. Associated with the idea of dignity and worth is the right to be respected because one is a human, and to be treated on the basis of that dignity. On the negative side it means the rejection of all condescension in human relations, of every hint of self-righteousness, superiority, or aloofness. Equality not only implies dignity, respect, and worth, it also implies true freedom from external constraint—freedom from all forces whose expression is irreconcilable with this equality of worth.

See also Ethics, Theory of; Dignity.

SOURCES

Burtt, E. A. *In Search of Philosophic Understanding.* New York: New American Library. 1965.
Harvard University Press. "Perspectives on Inequality." Harvard Education Review Reprint Series No. 8. Cambridge, MA: Harvard University Press. 1976.
Nozick, Robert. *Philosophical Explanations.* Cambridge, MA: Harvard University Press. 1981.

EROS

In attempting to understand human behavior, observers over the centuries have speculated about several different kinds of love. The ancient Greeks probably described the different kinds of love more completely than any other group. According to the Greeks, there are four types of love: *Storge* indicates affection and caring, the way a parent might feel about an offspring; the way we can love a pet animal or an inanimate object, expecting nothing in return. *Philia* refers to the feeling between friends and seems to be what is described as an interpersonal attraction. *Agape* is a charitable or concerned feeling toward others. Goodness and decency result from agape, and it sometimes seems to be in short supply in modern societies. In the Christian New Testament, agape is the word used to describe the love of God for humans and is recommended as the type of love humans should give to each other (sometimes referred to as "Christian love"). *Eros*, the subject of this essay, differs significantly from the above three types of love, but shares many of their qualities. Eros is romantic love, usually characterized by a person's total preoccupation with the loved one.

Hendrick and Hendrick (in Hendrick 1989) present a similar system that outlines six types of love: passionate, game-playing, friendship, logical, possessive, and selfless. On tests that measure these kinds of loving, Hendrick and Hendrick show that men score higher than women in passionate and game-playing love, while women outscore men in friendship, logical, and possessive love.

Abraham Maslow, in contrast, suggested that there are only two kinds of love: *B-Love* (Being-love) is his term for love that is unselfish, healthy, and concerned with the needs and successes of the other person rather than oneself; whereas *D-Love* (Deficiency-love) is a selfish kind of love whose primary goal is to satisfy one's own interests and needs. Maslow believed that relationships suffer when one or both partners are narcissistically centered on themselves rather than being truly concerned about the best interests of the other person.

Without minimizing the importance of these varieties of love, a great deal of current interest centers on the emotional state of passionate love—of eros. Passionate love often is illogical and impractical, where obsessive thoughts about that person occupy much of one's attention. Other activities and relationships are usually abandoned in favor of interacting with the lover. We call this "being head over heels in love." Passionate love is clearly different from liking. Liking refers to a positive evaluation of the other person and a desire to spend time with him or her, while passionate love involves much more intense feelings, as well as sexual desires.

The three-factor theory of passionate love may throw some light on the meaning of eros. The three-factor theory states three conditions that must precede the development of passionate love: (1) the culture or society must convey the message that romantic love is expected and desirable; (2) an appropriate love object must be present for passionate love to occur; and (3) an intense emotional arousal that is interpreted as love must be present. Because passionate love is intense and based partially on unrealistic expectations and misinterpreted emotions, couples are unable to continue indefinitely in this emotional state. They either lose interest and the love affair dies, or they move on to a more realistic kind of love that can endure, one normally based on companionship.

SOURCES

Bloom, Allan. *Love and Friendship*. New York: Simon & Schuster. 1993.

Breham, S. S. *Intimate Relationships*. New York: Random House. 1985.

Hendrick, C., ed. *Close Relationships*. Newberry Park, CA: Sage. 1989.

Maslow, Abraham. *Toward a Psychology of Being*. New York: Van Nostrand Reinhold. 1968.

Sternburg, R., and M. L. Barner, eds. *The Psychology of Love*. New Haven: Yale University Press. 1988.

ETHICS, THEORY OF

Most of us pay lip service to the principle of the sanctity of life, which is the foundation of ethics and ethical theory. This principle reminds us that life is sacred and the taking of a life, except perhaps for the most weighty reasons, is morally wrong. But people do not agree on what it means to attribute "sanctity" to life, the grounds for such an attibution, or the nature of the reasons that are "weighty" enough to override it in specific exceptional cases. Hence, in practice many persons participate in good conscience in the slaughter of animals, the abortion of fetuses, the withdrawal of life-support systems for the terminally ill, the killing of enemy soldiers or civilians in war, or the capital punishment of criminals, while others respond to these acts with moral outrage.

Ethical theorists take as their role finding general principles, amid all this confusion, that allow one to take a reasoned and consistent stand on all these different questions. They search for universal or even instrumental principles that point to the morally relevant differences between cases that allow for consistent and reasoned decision and practice. These sought-for moral principles, moreover, must not have unnoticed logical consequences that would be unacceptable when applied to actual or hypothetical situations.

THREE FAMILIES OF
MORAL CONSIDERATION

At least three different types of reasons have been advanced by theorists to guide our moral judgments. The first of these is often called *utilitarian considerations*. They refer to the effects of actions, or contemplated actions, on the happiness or unhappiness of the person likely to be affected by them. The person who does the action, of course, will be affected—as in the case of killing someone. The victim is also affected. Then there are the "third parties"—spouses, siblings, children, friends and dependents, colleagues, customers, neighbors, and the like. Insofar as these persons have love for the victim, or interests in his or her continual existence, they are harmed by the victim's death, and will be saddened by it.

Finally, there are many "distant" groups of persons—the neighborhood, professional groups, or community in general—who are deprived of the victim's services, or threatened by the example of the killing. Some of these effects are immediate and direct, and some are rather indirect. One can see that in the overwhelming proportion of cases of killing, doing harm to another person, and so on, both the direct and indirect effects on human welfare and happiness will be very bad indeed. This fact constitutes the utilitarian case against such acts and renders them immoral.

A second class of reasons are considerations of *personal autonomy*. In cases such as killing, there are situations where people choose to kill themselves or ask another person to kill them, or there are cases where there appears to be a strong utilitarian case for killing oneself and yet one chooses not to do so. A truly autonomous person is one who is rightly in control of his or her life; just as a truly sovereign political state is one that is legitimately in control of its own territory. Some people claim that insofar as the conduct of autonomous people does not violate the autonomy of other people's personal sovereignty, they are free to do as they wish, to determine their own lot in life, to be their own boss, to risk mistakes, to take responsibility, or to "go to hell on their own" if that's how it turns out.

A third and quite distinct kind of reason can be called a consideration of *the sanctity of life*. This sort of reason is usually advanced as an independent value and a constraint on the use of utilitarian and personal autonomy considerations that might otherwise apply. What makes certain actions—like killing—morally wrong is simply *that they are acts of killing*, whatever their effects on happiness or personal autonomy. The sanctity of life so construed is not derived from considerations of utility or autonomy. Like them, it is basically underived, a basic moral consideration in its own right.

There are, of course, various interpretations of the sanctity of life principle. Albert Schweitzer's "reverance for life" was unrestricted, applying to all living things, not only human beings, and is a principle definitive of *deep ecology*. Likewise, the teachings of Buddhism attach sanctity to the whole animal kingdom. The Christian tradition emphasizes the unique importance of human life, but not of other living things. Some sanctity of life theorists ground their moral principle in theological doctrine; others hold it to be independent of theology, a kind of moral ultimate, ungrounded in anything beyond itself, thus making it the foundation assumption or postulate of all moral value.

RIVAL MORAL PRINCIPLES

Much of the controversy among moralists over the morality of certain actions—killing, stealing, lying, etc.—can be traced to disagreements over the relative "weights" (degrees of stringency) to be ascribed to the three types of moral considerations above. For some theorists, only one type of reason will have application to such problems, and if more than one type applies, there is a clear and invariant order of priority among them.

Utilitarianism can be defined as the view that ultimately only utilitarian considerations have relevant application to moral decisions. When another kind of reason appears to be relevant, it is only because that reason points to a feature of actions in virtue of which they tend, in the vast majority of cases, to have an effect on human happiness. Utilitarians might condemn killing or robbery on the ground that it is a deliberate act of taking human life or depriving a person of something that is rightfully theirs, but only because they believe that such actions tend on balance to have very adverse effects on human happiness. In the very case where utilitarians think that killing or stealing or cheating will lead to a net gain in happiness over unhappiness, they will—in all consistency—approve of the act.

We can attach the label *libertarianism* to the view that personal autonomy is the weightiest of moral considerations. The libertarian never tires of emphasizing the moral importance of voluntary choice and consent. That which is truly within the domain of a person's autonomy can be disposed of as the person voluntarily chooses or voluntarily consents to another party's disposal, whatever considerations of happiness or sanctity of life may say about the matter. Some moral problems, for sure, do not seem to involve autonomy or consent at all, at least not in a clear, nonproblematic way. For example, fetuses make no choices of their own; nor do newly born brain-damaged infants, or irreversibly comatose adults. Libertarians would probably argue that in these cases "sovereign control" belongs to other parties, perhaps parents or guardians whose informal consent is morally required and morally sufficient, or that testamentary directions in the form of "living wills" made at an earlier date should control the situation. Other libertarians might concede that in cases of these sorts, personal autonomy is not involved, and that either utilitarian considerations or considerations of the sanctity of life should govern. But where all three considerations do apply, and personal autonomy conflicts with the other two, personal autonomy must triumph.

The third leading moral position already mentioned ranks considerations of the sanctity of life, when it applies, above considerations of the other two kinds. There are two leading versions of this position. The *absolutist version* holds that acts such as the intentional killing, robbing, or beating of human beings, whether born or fetal, healthy or sick, allies or enemies, conscious or comatose, innocent or guilty, are absolutely impermissible morally. The *weaker version* holds that killing or otherwise harming another person are permissible if and only if it seems on reasonable grounds to be necessary to save the lives of (other) innocent human beings. An absolutist sanctity of life position would endorse unconditional pacifism in "just" as well as "unjust" wars; it would condemn capital punishment; it would forbid abortion even when necessary to save the life of the mother, and would reject self-defense as a moral excuse for homicide. The weaker version, on the other hand, is consistent with killing combatants in just wars, using the death penalty (but only as a deterrent), and killing or harming another in self-defense.

Both versions of the sanctity of life principle agree that where sanctity of life considerations conflict with utilitarian or libertarian considerations, the latter must be subordinate in authority. We can kill animals to put them out of their misery, but killing suffering human beings is always a greater evil in this view. And when the sanctity of life seems to conflict with personal autonomy, they argue that the latter has been misinterpreted. Personal autonomy is important, but—as the argument goes—the decision to live or die falls outside its boundaries. That is because our lives do not belong to us, but rather are the property of our Creator, or because, in the language of Kant, the "humanity in each individual's person" commands categorical respect and hence cannot be destroyed.

There is, finally, a *mixed theory*, which allows room for considerations of all three kinds, but does not put them into any fixed order of priority. In this view, the situation of the individual dictates which of these principles, or which aspects of more than one of these principles, a person takes. All one can do in these difficult situations is become sensitive to *all* points of view and make decisions on those considerations that seem the most important at the time. In the end the decision rests with informal but fallible *intuition*, rather than elaborate reasoning or deduction from fixed principles. This view is therefore sometimes called *intuitionism*.

To understand these differing frames of reference and how they impact ethical decision making, one need only consider three questions. If asked sincerely and explored carefully, they will carry one a long way toward understanding ethical problems and deciding what moral action to take regarding the human dilemmas in which we find ourselves. These questions are the following: (1) Who actually makes an ethical decision? (2) What criteria should one use in making a relevant and meaningful ethical decision? and (3) To whom or what do one's moral obligations apply?

We can also devise a fourth question that logically follows these three: Can one in fact do what one decides is right? That is, having decided what is right, can a person will it to happen and do what he or she wills? So much of becoming an ethical person in both word and deed is linked to developing a mature self, for the more mature we are, the better are the chances that we will be able to will and do what is right. There will always be a close correlation between personal autonomy, the choice of ethical criteria, and the willingness and ability to act.

SOURCES

Edel, Abraham. *Ethical Judgment: The Use of Science in Ethics.* London: Free Press of Glencoe. 1955.

Hudson, W. D. *Modern Moral Philosophy.* New York: Anchor Books. 1970.

Lamont, Corliss. *The Philosophy of Humanism.* New York: Frederick Ungar. 1971.

Niebuhr, Reinhold. *Moral Man and Immoral Society.* New York: Charles Scribner's Sons. 1932.

Toulmin, Stephen E. *Cosmopolis: The Hidden Agenda of Modernity.* New York: Free Press. 1990.

ETHNIC PRIDE IN AMERICA

Minority groups who are designated by their ethnicity are differentiated from the dominant group on the basis of cultural differences such as language, attitudes toward marriage and parenting, food habits, etc. Ethnic groups in the United States include a grouping that is referred to collectively as Hispanics or Latinos, including Chicanos, Puerto Ricans, Cubans, and other Latin Americans. White ethnics are also included in this category—Irish Americans, Polish Americans, Norwegian Americans, and so on.

The cultural traits that make groups distinctive usually originate from the "homeland" or, for the Jewish people, from a long history of being segregated and prohibited from becoming a part of the host society. Once in the United States, an ethnic group may maintain distinctive cultural practices through associations and clubs. Ethnic enclaves such as Little Italy or Greektown in urban areas also perpetuate cultural distinctiveness and ethnic pride.

Racial groups may have cultural traditions that are truly different, as we can readily see in the many Chinatowns throughout the United States. Because physical and language differences generally prove to be barriers to acceptance by the host society, individuals of the same ethnic group tend to live in close proximity to one another. Recognition of different ethnic groups has led to the creation of white ethnic studies programs at as many as 135 colleges in the United States. The 230 foreign-language papers and periodicals published in the United States are joined by 708 English or bilingual publications aimed at ethnics and having a total circulation of over 6 million.

Interestingly, once coming to the United States, a place many have dreamed about, ethnics seldom forget their heritage, and society reminds them of their strangeness in numerous, not always subtle ways. The mass media has today discovered the white ethnics, but as early as 1913 some argued that a second generation of white ethnics in America could not be distinguished. Even in the 1940s, sociologists said that the future of U.S. ethnic groups seems to be limited. They felt that these groups would be absorbed quickly. Oscar Handlin's *The Uprooted* (1951) told of the destruction of immigrant values and their replacement by U.S. culture. Assimilation was the dominant theme of his work. Many scholars have felt that ethnicity should vanish in the United States. Ethnicity was treated as dysfunctional, for it meant continuation of old values that interfered with allegedly superior new values. Ethnicity was expected to disappear because "higher" social class and status demanded that it vanish.

The principle of "third generation interest," developed by historian Marcus Hansen, flew in the face of these conclusions. He theorized that among white ethnic groups in the third generation—the grandchildren of the original immigrants—ethnic interest and awareness would actually increase. Hansen said, "What the son wishes to forget the grandson wishes to remember." His principle has been tested several times since it was first put forth, and with Irish and Italian Catholics ethnicity was found more important to members of the third generation than it was to the immigrants themselves.

Nathan Glazer and Daniel Moynihan admitted in the second edition of *Beyond the Melting Pot*, which appeared in 1970, that perhaps they had been too hasty in concluding in the first edition that "religion and race define the next stage in the evolution of the American people." Minimizing the importance of ethnicity had started with the social scientific dismissal of ethnic awareness by blue-collar workers. It was viewed as merely another aspect of white ethnics' alleged racist nature. Ironically, these same scholars bent over backwards to understand the growing solidarity of blacks, Hispanics, and Native Americans. In the 1960s and 1970s, white ethnics saw that solidarity and an unapologetic self-consciousness was helping with blacks' upward mobility and asked, "Why not us?" The black movement pushed other groups to reflect on their own past. The increased consciousness of blacks and their positive attitude toward African culture has even been labeled by some writers as "emergent ethnicity" or "ethnogenesis." Thus, by the middle 1970s, the mood was set for the country to be receptive to ethnicity. By legitimizing black cultural diversity, along with that of Native Americans and Latinos, the country's opinion leaders legitimized other types of cultural diversity as well. Ethnic pride or ethnicity gives continuity with the past, an affective or emotional tie. The significance of this sense of belonging cannot be emphasized enough. Community building, no matter what the locus or chief interests, provides a foundation of friendships, of pride, a sense of personhood, and is the primary source of cohesion.

A vast amount of evidence points to the revival of ethnicity in the United States. Beginning in the mid-1960s, non–English language publications, churches, radio stations, and television programs grew throughout the decade and into the next. Even the conventional media seemed more sensitive to ethnic interests, although this may have been for commercial reasons. By the decade of the 80s, however, the ethnic revival seemed to have subsided considerably, perhaps not to the levels of the 50s, but the emergent ethnicity had peaked. Perhaps a revival of ethnicity has begun again, for in the 90s we have witnessed a new emphasis on *multiculturalism* as a valid topic for study in public schools and colleges. Even the movement to *political correctness* in speech and print connects with and supports this emphasis.

Recently, a new problem has arisen involving ethnicity. Thallieus Massey (of African and Native American descent) and his wife Melissa Meyer (who is white) of Miami want their son, Jordan, to appreciate all three of his heritages. In August 1995, just before the school bells were about to ring, they won a partial victory. The state agreed to add "multiracial" to Florida's school registration forms. And the multiracialist movement is gaining ground. Almost a dozen states have passed or are considering similar legislation, and the U.S. Census will test a new "multiracial" category in a minisurvey in 1996 in preparation for the next national count in 2000.

The National Association for the Advancement of Colored People flatly denounces the proposed change. African Americans cannot afford to stop identifying as black people, it is reasoned, as long as they are struggling against discrimination based on their identification as black people. Clarence Page, writing for Tribune Media Services, observes that "It is here, ironically, that the multiracialist movement exposes the fundamental myth of race: it is less a physical fact than what Baldwin called it, a political fact." Page continues:

> Physically, there is no single characteristic—not brown skin, not curly hair, not thick lips, not brown eyes—that is either universal among all black people or unique only to us. It is only the "one-drop rule"—the uniquely American notion that one drop of black blood in your family tree makes you black—that holds the rainbow of African-American people together as a people. It is the ultimate irony that this notion, invented by slave masters to increase the numbers of their slaves, is now embraced most fiercely by African-Americans, mainly to boost our numbers in a country where numbers translate into political clout.

This problem calls into question the entire notion of ethnic pride, political correctness, multiculturalism, and the political program known as *affirmative action*.

See also Racism.

SOURCES

Fishman, Joshua, ed. *The Rise and Fall of the Ethnic Revival*. Berlin: Mouton. 1985.

Page, Clarence. "Counting by Race." *The Charlotte Observer* (September 13, 1995): 13A.

Schaefer, Richard T. *Racial and Ethnic Groups*. 3d ed. Boston: Scott, Foresman and Co. 1988.

ETHNOCENTRISM

Ethnocentrism, literally "to focus or lift one's own values above all others," compels each race, each culture, each nation to exaggerate the importance of its own folkways, values, morals, and practices, and to depreciate those of others—especially those who are radically different. Whether ethnocentrism is natural or sociocultural has yet to be determined. This we know: each significant human group—and perhaps each person—considers itself the center of mankind. It judges all others by its own standards, and not necessarily by a higher standard than is determined by data that are representative of the best interests of all peoples. For example, the Greeks and Romans called all outsiders "barbarians"; the Jews considered themselves "the chosen people" and all others heathens or pagans, especially the Romans and the Greeks.

In the nineteenth century, Nietzsche put forth the idea of Nordic superiority. However, it was DeGobineau (1816–1882) who laid the foundations for the doctrine of Aryan and Nordic superiority. In 1855 he published his *Essay Upon the Inequality of the Human Races*, in which he developed the hypothesis that the racial question is the most important one in history. He went on to construct a thorough doctrine of racial determinism based on natural heredity and environment. For DeGobineau, heredity is the key to social advancement.

Racial determinism is but one implication of ethnocentrism, but it is not a necessary or sufficient condition for ethnocentrism. One must accept other hypotheses as well before one can logically infer racial determinism from ethnocentrism. These hypotheses include the following and have yet to be proven: the passing of cultural traits genetically from one generation to another, and the idea that cultural development and character are limited by race and genetic endowment.

But ethnocentrism does exist. The Europeans who settled America felt themselves superior to the Native Americans found here. The Europeans spoke some variant Indo-European language; had a common religious tradition—Judeo-Christian; and their political and social conventions reflected their Greco-Roman heritage. The newly arrived Europeans also shared a belief in what they considered the international law of the right of discovery, which held that the European nation first landing on and claiming the right to territory not formerly held by other Europeans had the exclusive authority to negotiate with the natives for the absolute ownership of that land. This "official" ethnocentric idea was supported and sanctioned by both government and religious institutions and was further buttressed by the European's belief that they represented the highest level of civilization. They were convinced of their superiority to the natives of the New World, as well as those in Africa and Asia, whom they considered to be not only infidels, but inferior beings.

The sociological fact of the existence of ethnocentrism poses quite a problem for ethical theorists, especially those in the Greek, Christian, and European-Enlightenment tradition who also posited the existence of an ahistorical, uncorruptible self (mind, soul, *nous*, etc.) that is the depository of universal moral values. In the 1950s and 1960s, there arose a group of antiethnocentrists who mainly argued, from the linguistic point of view, that it was a logical fallacy to judge other people's morals by one's own unless one's personal moral creed or national moral creed had been evaluated by objective criteria. Of course this was impossible, for all of us are ethnocentric.

Today, with the emphasis on multiculturalism and antiracism, another group, the anti-antiethnocentrists, have promoted the claim that we must not be too relative in our moral evaluations or we will lose the very best in our own moral traditions. The ethnocentrists held themselves higher than other cultures and claimed racial-cultural superiority; the antiethnocentrists found their moral worth based on their tolerance for diversity; and the anti-antiethnocentrists—although they had no desire to be identified with the ethnocentrists of the first part—felt that we have become so open-minded and tolerant that our morals and other cultural values have become entangled in witless relativism, where all values are given equal merit.

The anti-antiethnocentrist position is a recent phenomenon in ethics and is not an attempt to change the habits of our culture, or to block the windows up again and grind our values into prejudice and discrimination. Rather, it is an attempt to overcome pseudoliberalism (where all values are relative) by correcting our culture's habit of giving its desire to be accepting of all people a philosophical foundation. There is no claim that we are trapped in our own cultural biases, but only that if we remain open to the world around us and forget our own traditions and morals, we are no more close to the nature of humanity or the demands of rationality than the close-minded ethnocentrists who surround us.

See also Discrimination; Prejudice; Racism.

SOURCES

Bogardus, Emory S. *The Development of Social Thought*. 4th ed. New York: David McKay. 1960.

Geertz, Clifford. "The Uses of Diversity." *Michigan Quarterly Review* 25 (1986): 525–534.

Rorty, Richard. *Objectivity, Relativism, and Truth*. New York: Cambridge University Press. 1994.

EUTHANASIA

Euthanasia is mercy killing for the terminally ill, especially those enduring intense and hopeless suffering. Of course, we must realize that those who cannot end their own lives, even with outside help, are virtually all aged and/or physically helpless. Hence, the problem of *voluntary* euthanasia (killing another at his or her request and for his or her own sake) is almost entirely a problem of medical ethics, about what is or should be acceptable hospital practice. In ethics this would be considered a pragmatic problem, but the consideration of the sanctity of life—of what is and what is not ethical—also plays a huge part. Ethics is concerned with what ought to be and with the improvement of persons and conditions for living full and positive lives. When a professional group, business, or trade association formulates a code or set of standards, it deals, as a rule, not with the moral standards of the society at large, but with the problems that are characteristic of that field of service or work. In the profession of medical ethics, the physician's code embodies ideas that have been in the process of formulation since ancient times. The laws of Hammurabi—from about 2500 B.C.—dealt with fees to be given a physician and with punishment when injury was done. During the fifth century B.C. in Greece, the "Oath of Hippocrates" set forth the duty of the medical person.

The American Medical Association (AMA) was organized in 1847 and immediately became concerned with a code of ethics and with setting minimum standards for medical education and practice. The code of the AMA, "Principles of Medical Ethics," states that "the principal objective of the medial profession is to render service to humanity with full respect for the dignity of man." It affirms the "patient's right to choose his physician" and "the physician's right to choose whom he will serve," which supports an individualism in the practice of medicine and free competition among doctors.

The "Principles of Medical Ethics" clearly condemns certain practices as unethical. Among these are the secret division of fees among doctors for referring patients to them; "ghost surgery," in which one doctor passes his patient over to another in the operating room to perform the operation; advertising or the solicitation of patients; and acceptance of rebates on prescriptions. Historically, there have been changes in these principles. The question to ask is: Do the standards embodied in recent pronouncements by the AMA and changes in its "Principles" express the highest ethical ideals, or do they in the main protect the self-interests of the physicians?

Nowhere is this question more important than over the issue of euthanasia. The question, May euthanasia ever be justified? begs moral analysis, discussion, and debate. It remains an important ethical and legal concern for doctors and families who have family members, or perhaps close friends, who are terminally ill. Another issue associated with euthanasia—but slightly different—is *physician-assisted suicide*. Argued is the point that legal euthanasia would permit the ending of life for merciful release when all efforts to save the life have failed. Those who oppose euthanasia under any conditions say that it is the doctor's task to save life, that there are now effective pain-relieving drugs, that where there is life there is hope, and that *incurable* is a very tricky word. They point out that mercy killing can lead to abuses, and that to sanction this practice weakens respect for life. Those who favor mercy killing point out that the law requires people to put seriously wounded animals to death, that doctors routinely decide to save a mother and sacrifice the life of a fetus, and that with proper safeguards abuses may be prevented.

At bottom, the question "Is killing ever right?" when "right" is thought of in moral terms—that is, respect for the dignity and soundness of human life—is the question we must answer. Absolutists argue that killing is always wrong, even a mercy killing. Others disagree and are of the opinion that when all efforts to save a life have been expended and there is no hope for recovery, with the permission of that person—or if the person is not coherent, with the nearest kin—mercy killing is the "best" moral solution. They will argue that in life there are no absolute rights and wrongs, no situations that are clearly black and white. What we are morally required to do in any situation is to make the best moral decision possible.

Marvin Kohl urges the legalization of active voluntary euthanasia for those who are in intense and hopeless suffering. Refusing euthanasia in some cases, he charges, is to treat a fellow human being with exquisite cruelty. Where kindness and personal autonomy pull in the same direction, he says, consideration of the sanctity of life has very little countervailing force.

On the other side, members of the Study Group on Euthanasia set up by the Catholic Union of Great Britain in 1968 warn that a legalization of euthanasia would be a threat to the lives of all of us. They distinguish between (1) direct killing and not using extraordinary measures to save a life, and (2) between producing another's death as a means or an end and permitting it as a foreseen by-product of the pursuit of an acceptable end. They point out the difficulties of determining the voluntariness of a purported statement of consent and the effects of euthanasia on the doctor-patient and patient-family relationships. The study concludes with a version of the fa-

mous "slippery-slope" argument that legalizing voluntary euthanasia would be just the first step on the inevitable downward path to involuntary euthanasia and eventually to the mass murder of "misfits" as a society policy.

To understand the position of the AMA more fully, we must review the many varieties of euthanasia. Defined as "the killing of another person for what is thought to be his or her own good," euthanasia can be distinguished as follows: *Voluntary euthanasia* is euthanasia performed at the request of the person who is killed, or failing that, with presumed consent. *Involuntary euthanasia* is euthanasia performed without the consent of the person who is killed, because he or she is incompetent—that is, legally incapable of giving consent to anything, being either an infant, brain damaged, senile, or comatose. Cutting across this distinction are *active euthanasia*, in which the patient is directly killed by some positive act such as injecting a substance into the blood, and *passive euthanasia*, in which the patient is left to die, although positive steps might have been taken to keep the person alive for an extended period of time.

The official position of the AMA is that active euthanasia of patients is strictly forbidden, but that it is permissible to allow them to die by withholding treatment that would merely prolong their lives. Some have argued that these two forms of euthanasia are morally equivalent, that either is acceptable or unacceptable on moral grounds. In other words, there is no moral difference between killing and letting die.

Euthanasia is perhaps one of the most poignant dilemmas involving morality and the sanctity of life. One of the major problems in medical ethics is that philosophers interested in this issue are able to give doctors, whose training and time are devoted to medicine rather than to moral philosophy, considerable assistance; yet, with few exceptions, this has not been the case. Doctors discuss their ethical dilemmas in the medical journals, and philosophers keep to the philosophy journals. Information and debate, problems and theories in each case remain within the circle of the author's colleagues.

See also Ethics, Theory of.

SOURCES

Beauchamp, Tom L., William T. Blackstone, and Joel Feinberg. *Philosophy and the Human Condition.* Englewood Cliffs, NJ: Prentice-Hall. 1980.

Christian, James L. *Philosophy: An Introduction to the Art of Wondering.* 4th ed. New York: Holt, Rinehart and Winston. 1986.

EXISTENTIALISM, ETHICS OF

Existentialism is a reaction against some features of Enlightenment philosophy and some trends in modern society. Specifically, existentialism is a protest in the name of individuality against classical concepts of reason and nature emphasized during the eighteenth-century Enlightenment in Europe. It is a revolt against the impersonal nature of the modern technological age and against scientism, positivism, and the mass movements of our time. It is also a protest against totalitarian movements, whether fascist, communist, or others, which tend to crush or submerge the individual in the collective and impersonal society.

On the positive side, existentialism stresses the uniqueness and privacy of human existence—the inner, immediate experience of self-awareness. Reality or being is existence, the personal "I" rather than the impersonal "it." The center of thought and meaning is the existing individual thinker. The individual's fundamental drive is to live, to exist, and be recognized as an individual in his or her own right. From this struggle for recognition a person is likely to gain meaning and significance in life.

We can further explain the term *existentialism* by distinguishing the terms *essence* and *existence. Essence* is that which distinguishes a thing from other types of objects. In classical Greek philosophy (and in Christian theology and in the Enlightenment) the concept of *human being,* for example, had more reality than the individual human being. Plato thought that the participation in the idea, or essence, of *humanness* is what makes a person what he or she is. Christian theologians called this essence the *soul,* and the Enlightenment philosophers dubbed it *mind* or *reason.* Fundamentally, existentialists reject these ideas and insist that there is something that cannot be conceptualized, and this is the personal act of *existing.* Personal existence must be experienced or lived to be actually known; it cannot be described in its fullness by propositions alone. *Existence* means the state of being actual, of occurring within space and time—something given here and now.

While not a clear system of philosophy, existentialism does have several clear implications in the area of ethics. For one, it is a protest against many of the movements and things that neglect or threaten the person in his or her most private, separate, individual life. On this basis it can approve of some actions and condemn others. Existentialists observe that with the modern emphasis on science and technology, only the physical and quantitative seem to be of importance in business, industry, and education. This renders the person and his or her uniqueness and individuality of secondary importance to other things that are impersonal. When this outlook is carried to extremes, life becomes hollow and meaningless. Thus, existentialism represents the human rebellion against all attempts to ignore or suppress the uniqueness of one's subjective experience—to depersonalize life.

Existentialists emphasize a person's moral freedom and freedom of choice, as well as one's civil liberties and responsibility for one's own life. Soren Kierkegaard

(1813–1855), the Danish thinker who perhaps founded existentialism, devoted much of his time to personal introspection. As a religious man, his main concern was what it means to be a Christian or to become a whole person. The two great enemies that depersonalize humanity were, in his view, Hegelian philosophy with its abstract speculation, and the unreflective Christian. There is, he says, an "unbridgeable gulf" between God and the world. When we find ourselves in anguish, our only salvation is to abandon reason and take a "leap of faith." Ethics for Kierkegaard is not a matter of discovering the good in the "essence" of man; it is a matter of obedience and the making of a decision.

Other major existentialists include the theologian Paul Tillich, Martin Buber, Friedrich Nietzsche, Karl Jaspers, Gabriel Marcel, Martin Heidegger, Nicolas Berdyaev, and Jean-Paul Sartre. In the areas of literature and art, existentialism has made its widest appeal. The sense of the human predicament and the spirit of revolt have been expressed in the novels and plays of Kafka, Sartre, and Camus; in the poetry of Eliot and Auden; in the paintings of Cezanne, Van Gogh, Picasso, Chagall, and de Chirico. The broad theme we find in these creative works is an attempt to restore the person and his or her inner strivings to a place of respect and dignity.

See also Ethics, Theory of.

SOURCES

Grene, Marjorie. *Introduction to Existentialism.* Chicago: Phoenix Books. 1963.

Lawrence, Nathaniel, and Daniel O'Connor. *Readings in Existential Phenomenology.* Englewood Cliffs, NJ: Prentice-Hall. 1967.

FACING HISTORY AND OURSELVES CURRICULUM

At the center of debates about moral thinking and social responsibility curricula for precollege-age students is the Facing History and Ourselves (FHAO) curriculum developed in 1976 by middle school teachers in Brookline, Massachusetts. FHAO seeks to provide a model for teaching history so that youngsters are challenged to think critically on a variety of contemporary social, moral, and political issues, such as the Nazi rise to power in depression-era Germany and the Jewish Holocaust. It also seeks causes and consequences of present-day prejudice, intolerance, violence, and racism.

FHAO reaches nearly half a million students a year in rural, urban, and suburban settings in public, private, and parochial schools. Through its national headquarters in Brookline and its satellite offices in Chicago, Los Angeles, Memphis, and New York, the FHAO organization has trained a nationwide network of some 30,000 educators to teach the program. The FHAO curriculum's complex intellectual content is undergirded by a pedagogical imperative: to foster developing perspective, critical thinking, and moral decision making among students. It is specifically geared toward adolescents who are devel-

opmentally engaged in a fierce struggle to become distinct individuals and to fit in with their peers.

The FHAO curriculum has become a target of New Right activist Phyllis Schlafly. With the assistance of Ronald Reagan's political appointees within the Department of Education, the FHAO organization was repeatedly denied federal funding to disseminate the curriculum between 1986 and 1988. The funding denials sparked congressional hearings and heated debate among public policy makers, educators, and other concerned citizens. The public controversy surrounding funding for FHAO reveals how different groups have different understandings of what should be taught in U.S. schools and who should make that decision. More significantly, it demonstrates a lack of social consensus about how public education should address the fact of differences in U.S. society.

See also Politics in the Classroom; Rainbow Curriculum.

SOURCES

ASCD Panel on Moral Education. "Moral Education in the Life of the School." Report. Alexandria, VA: ASCD. 1988.

Fine, Melinda. "Collaborative Innovations: Documentation of the Facing History and Ourselves Program at an Essential School." *Teachers College Board* 94:4 (1993).

Schlafly, Phyllis. *Child Abuse in the Classroom.* Illinois: Pere Marquette Press. 1980.

———. *The Phyllis Shlafly Report* (*See* June 1983 and September 1984).

Strom, Margot S., and William S. Parsons. *Facing History and Ourselves: Holocaust and Human Behavior.* Watertown, MA: Intentional Educations. 1982.

FAIRNESS

Young children know when things are fair; that is, when they are receiving equitable treatment from parents, teachers, their friends, or their brothers and sisters. Perhaps the first moral judgment uttered by a young child is, "That's not fair!" James Q. Wilson calls our attention to the concept of fairness: "It is quite astonishing that at an early age children not only can express notions of preference, property, entitlement, and equity, but can do so in ways that in fact alter the behavior of other children." According to philosopher Richard Paul, the fair-minded critical person needs to be distinguished from the self-serving critical person. A fair-minded critical person is one who internalizes the skills of reason and critical thinking in the service of balanced truth, rationality, autonomy, and self-insight. He comments:

> Children enter school as fundamentally non-culpable, uncritical and self-serving thinkers. The educational task is to help them to become, as soon as possible and as fully as possible, responsible, fairminded, critical thinkers, empowered by intellectual skills and rational passions. . . . If we want children to develop into adults with a passion for clarity, accuracy, and fairmindedness, a fever for exploring the deepest issues, a propensity for listening sympathetically to opposition points of view; if we want children to develop into adults with a drive to seek out evidence, with an aversion to contradiction, sloppy thinking, and inconsistent applications of standards; then we need to unite cognitive and affective goals.

Fair-mindedness involves the following behaviors:

1. Sharing and sociability based on mutual respect and solidarity. Children learn early, and from one another, ways of establishing friendly relations even before they are able to talk, and this tendency to share increases with age and is accompanied by a rapid growth in the sense of what rules ought to govern play and contact. Out of ordinary play and interaction there emerges a fairly clear sense of rules and justifications, of principles of ownership, justice, and excuses based on incapacity or lack of intention.

2. Fairness means equity. A vast amount of research on adult behavior provides compelling evidence for the importance of fairness as a guide to how we behave. In these studies fairness means equity, reciprocity, and impartiality.

3. Fairness also implies self-control and etiquette. We cannot overlook the values of etiquette and courtesy as part of being a fair-minded person. Although determined by convention and social norms, the prevalence of rules governing self-control and etiquette are universal to human societies. In every person there is a parliament of instincts set forth by genetics and the environment. Self-control competes with self-expression; the desire for immediate pleasure competes with the attraction of more distant ones; the lure of what is novel contends with the comfort of what is familiar.

In summary, being fair-minded is based on the equality principle involving justice, impartiality, and fairness. In religion this is known as the Golden Rule; in philosophy, the *Categorical Imperative* or *principle of universality*, which was given voice by Immanuel Kant: "Act only on that maxim whereby thou canst at the same time will that it should become a universal law"; or, "So act as to treat humanity, whether in thine own person or in that of any other, in every case as an end withal, never as means only." Thus, the law of moral equality, or fairness, says that there shall be no law for one person that is not the law for all, unless there are circumstances that clearly justify different treatment. Herein fairness extends sympathy and concern to other persons, which is an important value in community and in society.

See also Ethics, Theory of.

SOURCES

Cloninger, C. Robert. "A Systematic Method for Clinical Description and Classification of Personality Variants." *Archives of General Psychiatry* 39 (1987): 1242–1247.

Damon, William. *The Moral Child.* New York: Free Press. 1988.

Eibl-Eibesfeldt, Irenaus. *Human Ethology.* New York: De Gruyter. 1989.

Paul, Richard. *Critical Thinking Handbook, K–3.* Rohnert Park, CA: Center for Critical Thinking and Moral Critique. 1986.

Wilson, James Q. *The Moral Sense.* New York: Free Press. 1993.

FAITH

Although generally associated with religion, faith has also a cognitive function that has two aspects: (1) *reason*, understanding truth and reality through the natural powers of the mind, and (2) *faith*, a trust in one's abilities, or in the case of religion, grasping truth through the supernatural deliverance of its propositions through *revelation.* Concerning the importance of faith in the first sense of its meaning, those who advocate the cultivation of mental health say that we need a faith as a set of consistent ideals or as a philosophy of life that is life-affirming, because there is a deep tendency in human nature to become like what we imagine ourselves to be. The second meaning attributed to faith is that the religious experience of faith is not devoid of

cognitive elements, but is, on the contrary, an avenue of religious truth.

In either case, the locus of faith is that part of the personality that is morally significant and that concerns decision making, attitude, and character—the domain we broadly call the *will*. Emotion and intellect are both present in faith, for we cannot isolate portions of our personality. A person's faith is essentially the basic orientation of his or her will, which sets the direction and inclinations of his or her character. Faith, in ourselves or in a supernatural being, forms a steady and enduring disposition as the volitional background for daily action and choices.

SOURCES

Schedler, Norbert O. *Philosophy of Religion.* New York: Macmillan. 1974.

Walhout, Donald. *Interpreting Religion.* Englewood Cliffs, NJ: Prentice-Hall. 1963.

FAMILY

In the election campaign of 1992, then Vice President Dan Quayle set off a serious debate with a remark denouncing a fictitious television character for choosing to give birth out of wedlock. Quayle said that the "Murphy Brown" show was mocking the importance of fathers. He commented that it reflected the "poverty of values" that was responsible for the nation's ills. From these comments, arguments began—and in 1995, continued on welfare payments to unwed mothers—in the media and across dinner tables, about the meaning of family and motherhood.

Certainly, as much as anything we know, the family is a central institution in our society, an institution that brings instant community to husbands and wives, and to fathers, mothers, and their children. But is it the only legitimate form of "family" that is valid? We should remember that family, like other social institutions and conventions, is always changing; thus what we see as the family today was not always here, and will change in the future. The vision of the family put forth by Quayle is shared by many, but for others it may be more myth than reality. Some believe that the family is doing fine in meeting people's needs for love and belonging, and that it doesn't have to have a traditional structure with father, mother, and siblings. As a matter of fact, some believe that where there is support, love, and solidarity, there is family. They define family in terms of community and spirit rather than the "kinds" of people that compose its membership. Of course, many think that the family is in serious trouble; some because the traditional model of family has changed and others because, regardless of composition, the family's values and support system have been eroded.

No one will deny that the primary institutions of the United States are the community, home, church, and school. These institutions are assumed to involve some important subsections of social life: politics, economics, and religion. They are defined by certain important structures, activities, and values. Thus, the family as an institution is an organized aspect of society that is perpetuated by various norms and rules. We live in, experience, alter, and have attitudes about our important institutions, and this goes for the family. Because of its importance, it is the alteration of our attitudes toward the family that gives rise to our present confusion regarding it.

Basic to governmental institutions concerned with social control and mobilization, economic institutions that regulate the production and distribution of goods and services, and religious institutions that seek to relate us to the supernatural and to ultimate values has been the family—that institution pertaining to sexual relations, marriage, reproduction and childbearing, socialization or child rearing, and to relating the individual to the other institutions of society. In recent history the so-called traditional family has been the form against which all other relationships have been judged. This is clearly a value judgment and one that ignores the history of the development of family itself. We must guard against intermingling value judgments with descriptions. Also, in scientific studies of family we are warned of the ideology-laden nature of family studies. The sociology of the family is noted for its normative and moralistic tone mixed in with social policy and the social objectives of various groups.

About the universal core we have usually called "family," we can ask the following questions: (1) Has the family's core always been the traditional family as defined by having a married father and mother with two to three children, going to work regularly, eating meals together, attending church, obeying the law, and getting an education? (2) Does this core capture the character of the traditional family or are there other variables that need exploration, such as patriarchy, conflict, and coercion? (3) How quickly is this core giving way to a variety of other arrangements of intimate life that may or may not be called "family"?

The characterisitics and changes in the nature of the family can be treated scientifically, but we cannot ignore the commentaries and interpretations that abound in both popular and social science literature. Is the family today still important? Is it dominant? Is it specializing and adapting to the contemporary world? Or is the family disintegrating? These topics should be explored fully and completely.

SOURCES

Adams, Bert N. *The Family: A Sociological Interpretation.* 5th ed. New York: Harcourt Brace. 1995.

Foucault, Michel. *The History of Sexuality: An Introduction.* Vol. 1. Translated from the French by Robert Harley. New York: Vintage Books. 1990.

Skolnick, Arlene S., and Jerome H. Skolnick, eds. *Family in Transition.* 8th ed. New York: HarperCollins. 1994.

FASCISM

A symbol of authority in ancient Rome was the *fasces*, consisting of a bundle of birch or elm rods bound together by a red strap. The blade of an ax projected from the bundle. Servants called *lictors* carried these bundles ahead of magistrates, governors, and emperors. The fasces stood for the official's power to punish or put to death, and for unity. By the twentieth century, governments based solely on the arbitrary power and authority of rulers were deemed *fascist*.

Fascists—for the most part—are a far-right, reactionary, ultraconservative group, dogmatic and intolerant of those who disagree with them and exhibiting what is often called "black-and-white" thinking. They assume things are all good or all evil, with no middle ground—that they have all the truth and virtue, and of course that other groups have all the error and evil. They have a strong distrust of democratic processes and tend to be authoritarian and to support some minority, elite group, or leader. They want to control the institutions in our society and suppress criticism, at least of their programs and tactics.

As a form of government, fascism centers all power in a single party headed by an absolute dictator. Twentieth-century fascist governments controlled Italy from 1922 to 1943, headed by Benito Mussolini, and Nazi Germany from 1933 to 1945, under Adolf Hitler. Fascism depends upon the police to crush all opposition or dissent and is highly nationalist. It tries to identify its principles with the country so that disagreement will look like treason. Some other country or some group within the country is usually picked out as the "enemy" and made to appear as the cause of all evils and misfortunes. For example, the Nazis in Germany represented their movement first as a crusade against the Jews and then as a fight against communism.

To maintain the consent of a large part of the population, fascism must cultivate ignorance by controlling the media and education. Travel to other countries must also be controlled and freedoms of speech and assembly rigorously suppressed. Fascism maintains among the people a permanently warlike frame of mind. The dictator usually comes to power during a period of economic crisis and employs his citizens in the making of armaments, thus giving the illusion of prosperity. From a sociological perspective, fascism is an extreme form of ethnocentrism and a reason why ethnocentrism has been thought of by some as an immoral behavior, one with a racist attitude.

See also Ethnocentrism; Racism.

SOURCES

Rawls, John. *A Theory of Justice*. Cambridge, MA: Harvard University Press. 1971.

Struhl, Karsten J., and Paula R. Struhl, eds. *Ethics in Perspective*. New York: Random House. 1975.

"The Familiar Faces of Fascism." *Utne Reader* 72 (November-December 1995).

FATALISM

Fatalism is the belief that events are irrevocably fixed so that human effort cannot alter them, although sometimes things appear otherwise. It is the idea that "what is to be, will be." More specifically and significant for ethics, fatalism espouses the view that at least certain events in life are determined independently of human choices and actions, so that the future is removed from one's personal control. Fatalism seems to have its origin in human weakness or helplessness in the face of specific eventualities, especially death.

SOURCES

Ayers, M. R. *The Refutation of Determinism*. London: Methuen. 1968.

Blanshared, Brand. "The Case for Determinism." In *Determinism and Freedom in the Age of Modern Science.* Edited by Sidney Hook. New York: New York University Press. 1958.

Taylor, Richard. "Fatalism." *The Philosophical Review* 71 (January 1962): 56–66.

FEMINISM

Feminism refers to the advocacy of women's rights to full citizenship, including political, economic, and social equality with men. Its widely divergent views include those advocating female separatism. Modern feminism, born in the United States and France in the eighteenth century, was an outgrowth of the human rights movement and the movement toward democracy. In mid-century America, this included the abolition of slavery. For women it meant the application to women of those same citizenship rights that were provided to men. Abigail Adams asked her husband John to "remember the ladies in framing the Constitution"; and Mary Wollstonecraft drafted the first feminist treatise, "A Vindication of the Rights of Women," in 1792.

BACKGROUND

In 1848, at the Seneca Falls Convention, women in the United States began a serious fight for women's rights, especially the right to control their own property, persons, and earnings, and for the right to vote. At this convention, Elizabeth Cady Stanton's "Declaration of Rights and Sentiments" established a blueprint for the women's rights movement. Although women would not gain the right to vote until 1920, many other feminist goals were gradually realized, specifically the rights of married women to control their own property.

The major personalities in the early feminist movement were the following (adapted from "Women Win the Vote," published by the National Women's History Project, in *Women of Power* 24 [1995]: 6):

- *Susan Brownell Anthony* (1820–1906) was a Quaker, a teacher, a temperance and abolition organizer, and an outstanding women's rights leader with sharp political instincts. Anthony took suffrage petitions door-to-door in 1854, published *The Revolution* from 1868 to 1870, lectured throughout the country for 30 years, and became an internationally respected symbol of the women's movement.

- *Lucretia Coffin Mott* (1793–1880), a Quaker minister and leading women's rights pioneer, was called a "spitfire" for her tart tongue, and was a leading Philadelphia abolitionist. Mott called the first women's rights convention in Seneca Falls, New York, in 1848, and was president of the American Equal Rights Association in 1866.

- *Ida Bell Wells-Barnett* (1862–1931), born to slave parents, was an inspirational and passionate teacher, journalist, and lecturer, and led a national antilynching campaign. She founded the Alpha Suffrage Club of Chicago with other black suffragists, and marched in the suffrage parades in Washington, D.C., in 1913 and in Chicago in 1916.

- *Lucy Stone* (1818–1893) led the call for the first national women's rights convention in Worcester, Massachusetts, in 1850. Stone converted Susan B. Anthony to suffrage, pressed for both black and women's suffrage, and published and edited the influential weekly *Woman's Journal* for 47 years. Her dying words to her daughter, Alice Stone Blackwell, were: "Make the world better."

- *Alice Stone Blackwell* (1857–1950), daughter of Lucy Stone, was a leading suffrage writer and journalist. Alice edited the *Woman's Journal* for 35 years, helped merge rival suffrage groups into the National American Woman Suffrage Association in 1890, and urged women to become an autonomous moral force in politics.

- *Alice Stokes Paul* (1885–1977) was a chief strategist for the militant suffrage wing. She was the founder of the Congressional Union for Woman Suffrage, the author of the Equal Rights Amendment, the organizer of the 1913 suffrage parade in Washington, D.C., and she influenced the charter of the United Nations. Paul waged a hunger strike while imprisoned and was force-fed and treated as insane.
- *Carrie Lane Chapman Catt* (1859–1947) was a pacifist, journalist, and lecturer. She led state, national, and international organizations for women's rights, worked for world peace, organized a successful 14-month campaign for ratification of the Woman Suffrage Amendment, and founded the League of Women Voters.
- *Elizabeth Cady Stanton* (1815–1902) was a brilliant women's rights leader. She believed that a woman should not submerge her identity in marriage and omitted the word "obey" in her marriage ceremony. She was a forceful speaker, ran for the U.S. Congress in 1866, agitated for the suffrage amendment from 1878 onward, and was the author of *The Woman's Bible*, which decried the Bible's derogatory treatment of women.

In the nineteenth and twentieth centuries the women's movement was a white middle-class values movement, while the goals of black women and white working-class women remained inseparable from their racial and class oppression. Middle-class women wanted the opportunities available to the men of their own class, such as education or reforming society as a whole. Many used the temperance movement to engage in social reform and lobby for protective legislation for working women. In 1920, after women had won the right to vote, the women's movement waned, and the first Equal Rights Amendment (ERA), introduced by Alice Paul in 1923, failed to pass. The women's movement reemerged in the 1960s among college-educated women and found focus in Betty Friedan's *The Feminine Mystique* in 1963. In 1965, the founding of the National Organization for Women provided the women's movement a national focus that was inclusive. In 1973, the ERA was reintroduced but was again defeated during the 1980s. Since the passage of the Civil Rights Act of 1964, women have won the right to abortion and some guarantees for equal opportunity and pay in employment. By 1992 and the election of President Bill Clinton, the right to abortion had come under attack by the political right and the Christian Coalition. The decline in alimony and child support, combined with the rising divorce rate, have focused additional attention on fathers who refuse to support their ex-wives and children. As Friedan's *The Second Stage*, published in 1981, suggested, many feminists were also interested in building a new kind of family life.

There are differences within the feminist ranks, but most seek equal economic rights; support reproductive rights, including the right to abortion; criticize traditional definitions of gender roles; and favor raising children of both genders for similar public achievements and domestic responsibilities. Many wish to reform language so that it does not equate man with humanity (referred to as being *politically correct*), and campaign to stop violence against women, sexual harassment in the home and the workplace, and the denigration of women in the media.

SOURCES

Freeman, Jo. *The Politics of Women's Liberation*. New York: David McKay. 1975.

Giddings, Paul. *When and Where I Enter*. New York: William Morrow. 1985.

"Feminism." Grolier Electronic Publishing. 1992.

Kramarae, Cheris, and Paul Treichler. *A Feminist Dictionary*. Boston: Pandora Press. 1985.

Pearson, Carol, and Catherine Pope. *The Female Hero in American and British Literature*. New York: R. R. Bowker. 1981.

Richardson, Laurel W. *The Dynamics of Sex and Gender: A Sociological Perspective*. Boston: Houghton Mifflin. 1981.

Women of Power: A Magazine of Feminism, Spirituality, and Politics. Charlene McKee, ed. Orleans, MA (published biannually).

FIRST AMENDMENT RIGHTS

No sooner had the Constitution of the United States been ratified and the first Congress begun its work than changes were made in the document to ensure individual rights. It was possible to consider amendments to the Constitution because an amendment process had been incorporated into the final document. At the time of ratification the framers of the Constitution knew the document must be flexible enough to adjust to unforeseen conditions. The Constitution provided that an amendment could be proposed at any time by either a two-thirds majority vote of Congress or by a special convention called by two-thirds of the state legislatures. Any amendment would become part of the Constitution when it had been ratified by three-fourths of the states.

The first series of amendments involved individual liberties. Several delegates to the Constitutional Convention wanted to clearly specify a list that the government could not violate. Despite arguments against a separate bill of rights, pressure continued by North Carolina and Rhode Island for such a bill. Massachusetts and Virginia ratified the Constitution with the understanding that the new Congress would incorporate a bill of rights into the Constitution.

James Madison drafted the new rights document himself. Congress took Madison's draft and passed it as the first ten amendments to the Constitution. These amendments, known as the Bill of Rights, were then submitted to the states for ratification. Over the next two years, the necessary three-fourths majority of the states accepted the amendments, and the Bill of Rights became part of the Constitution in December 1791.

The First Amendment guarantees individual liberties, including freedom of speech and religion, the right to peaceful assembly, and the right to petition the government. It also protects freedom of the press. It reads:

> Congress shall make no law respecting an establishment of religion, or prohibiting the free exercise thereof; or abridging the freedom of speech, or of the press; or the right of the people peaceably to assemble, and to petition the government for a redress of grievances.

The subject of the First Amendment is freedom. It prohibits the government from limiting freedom of expression; it protects the press from government control or censorship; and allows citizens to peaceably gather to express a point of view. Citizens are granted the freedom to petition the government to set right or correct problems that might occur.

Freedom of religion has been a ticklish issue since the establishment of public schools in the United States. Schools that are public—that receive state and federal dollars—are prohibited from promoting any single religion over another, such as devotional Bible reading. On the other hand, the government is not allowed to restrict the free exercise of religion. Thus, it may not penalize a citizen for the exercise of his or her religious beliefs.

Over the years the U.S. courts have been instrumental in determining the range of conduct protected by the free speech clause. In *Schenk v. United States* (1991), the

Supreme Court upheld Schenk's conviction for distributing antidraft pamphlets during World War II. It ruled the Schenk actions presented a "clear and present danger" to the United States.

William Pitt, Earl of Chatham, perhaps anticipating the American Bill of Rights, speaking to the British House of Commons on the American reaction to the Stamp Act on January 14, 1766, remarked:

> I have been charged with giving birth to sedition in America. They have spoken their sentiments with freedom against this unhappy act, and that freedom has become their crime. Sorry I am to hear the liberty of speech in this house, imputed as a crime. But the imputation shall not discourage me. It is a liberty I mean to exercise. No gentleman ought to be afraid to exercise it. It is a liberty by which the gentleman who calumniates it might have profited, by which he ought to have profited. He ought to have desisted from his project. I rejoice that America has resisted (Schwartz 1980).

Throughout the twentieth century the issue of freedom, of liberty, has been in the forefront of U.S. history and a lively project for the American Civil Liberties Union. By 1922, an article in *Harper* explained that liberty had become "a mere rhetorical figure," with the United States no longer free in the old sense. Walter Lippmann explained that the world had become too complicated for human understanding; thought had become hazardous and rights insecure. The Supreme Court gingerly asserted that some restraint on personal liberty violated the Fourteenth Amendment, and Justice Brandise argued, in *Whitney v. California* in 1927, that the spread of political truth depended on freedom to think and speak.

From prohibition in the decade of the 1920s to the Civil Rights movement of the 1960s, to flag burning and feminism, and in the 1990s to newly opened debates about affirmative action and the new wave of multiculturalism and political correctness, Americans have stood for a set of enduring values: freedom, democracy, fair play, and equality. These values have given them a common identity in the midst of incredible diversity and cultural change, and have made them one people. In the future, as the United States changes, what will be crucial is reaching a consensus about what these values mean. Each generation must not only understand what these values meant in the past and the history of their reinterpretations, but, based on this knowledge and understanding, exercise a common wisdom in their interpretation and application to their own time and place.

See also Affirmative Action.

SOURCES

Handlin, Oscar, and Lilian Handlin. *Liberty and Equality 1920–1994*. New York: HarperCollins. 1994.

Hofstadter, Richard, ed. *Great Issues in American History*. Vol. 2. New York: Vintage Books. 1958.

Lappé, Frances Moore. *Rediscovering America's Values*. New York: Ballantine. 1989.

Schwartz, Bernard, ed. *The Roots of the Bill of Rights*. Vol. 5. New York: Chelsea House. 1980.

FORGIVENESS

In Western civilization one has difficulty understanding the meaning of forgiveness—the act of absolving, pardoning, or giving up the wish to punish, or giving up all claims to, or not demanding a payment for—without some knowledge and understanding of the Judeo-Christian conception of the term. In the Bible, forgiveness is primarily the act of God by which He graciously takes away the obstacles or barriers that separate man from His presence, thus opening the way to reconciliation and fellowship (or salvation). The ethical implications of this religious tradition for humans in relationship to other humans are significant. Forgiveness is a way of reconciling differences with our friends and neighbors. It is essential for friendships to flourish and community to grow among neighbors.

The common word in the LXX (Greek Old Testament) for forgiveness is *afihmi*—"to send away"—which is also interpreted as "to be merciful." Forgiveness is an expression of the religious relationship between God and humans: when sins are forgiven, reconciliation is possible and humans may experience again the blessings of fellowship with God. Likewise, on the human scale, forgiveness—even in secular circles—is an expression of the ethical relationship between individuals. When negative (evil, immoral, hurtful, or unethical) acts are forgiven, we may experience again the joys of fellowship and community with our friends. Forgiveness removes the barriers between humans and God, and forgiveness removes those barriers that make community impossible. Forgiveness renews and regenerates the moral life of humans in their natural communal relationships.

SOURCES

Buttrick, George Arthur, et al., eds. *The Interpreter's Dictionary of the Bible*. Volume E–J. New York: Abingdon Press. 1962.

Shaffer, Carolyn R., and Kristin Anundsen. *Creating Community Anywhere*. New York: Putnam. 1993.

FOUCAULT, MICHEL

Michel Foucault (1926–1984) was a French philosopher and historian whose theories have been widely influential in the study of culture, literature, history, and sociology. His books include *In the Order of Things* (1966), in which he divided European history into three distinct *episteme*, meaning a set of relations used to organize and produce whatever counts as knowledge in that era. The three episteme are the late Renaissance (1500s), the classical era (mid-1600s to late 1700s), and the modern era (early 1800s to the present). *The Archaeology of Knowledge* (1969) describes the language and ideas used by a particular profession or that define a particular field of knowledge. His final work, *The History of Sexuality* (1976, 1984), traces the ways of talking about sexuality and of attempts to channel, control, or regulate it. This last book has been and is influential in the study of gender, especially feminism, by serious scholars.

SOURCES

Information Finder. World Book. 1994.

Signs: Journal of Women in Culture and Society 20:2 (1995).

FREE WILL

Free will is the idea that people are unlimited and unconstrained in their ability to make decisions and act. Whether this is true or not—from a psychological, cultural, religious, or genetic (physical) point of view—constitutes the philosophical problem of free will and determinism. This problem symbolizes one of our deepest human dilemmas. On the one hand, we feel free; our lives are founded on the assumption that normal people are able to make genuine choices and should be responsible for them. We in fact blame others for their mistakes and feel guilty about our own. Throughout history humans have come to believe that there are capricious forces that lie inside us, directing us to do countless acts against our wills. Premodern thinkers interpreted these forces as good or evil spirits. Today we are better able to account for the causes of our behavior in empirical terms—in terms of sociological and psychological conditions or by physical explanations. The result is the same: we have a dual experience of both freedom and determinism. Both experiences feel real to us and we have never quite understood how to reconcile the apparent contradiction.

Western Christian theology has symbolized this problem very clearly. It points to the Bible, where there is abundant support for two basic beliefs: (1) that God is omnipotent and therefore determines every event in our lives, and (2) that we possess free will (freedom of choice) and are therefore responsible for our own sins. Therefore, in this view, humans can justly be condemned to hell for making wrong decisions and God can be blamed for evil that is in the world. Saint Thomas Aquinas explained the paradox in this way:

I. Man is predestined.

It is fitting that God should predestine men. For all things are subject to His Providence.... As men are ordained to eternal life through the Providence of God, it likewise is part of that Providence to permit some to fall away from that end; this is called reprobation.... As predestination includes the will to confer grace and glory, so also reprobation includes the will to permit a person to fall into sin, and so impose the punishment of damnation on account of that sin.

Summa Theologica, I, 23, 1, 3
Summa contra Gentiles, III, 163

II. Man is free.

Man has free choice, or otherwise counsels, exhortations, commands, prohibitions, rewards and punishments would be in vain. If the will were deprived of freedom, no praise would be given to human virtue; since virtue would be of no account if man acted not freely: there would be no justice in rewarding or punishing, if man were not free in acting well or ill: and there would be no prudence in taking advice, which would be of no use if things occurred of necessity.

Summa Theologica, I, 83, 1
Summa contra Gentiles, III, 73

III. Can man be both predestined and free?

The predestined must necessarily be saved, yet by a conditional necessity, which does not do away with the liberty of choice.... Man's turning to God is by free choice; and thus man is bidden to turn himself to God. But free choice can be turned to God only when God

turns it.... It is the part of man to prepare his soul, since he does this by his free choice. And yet he does not do this without the help of God moving him.... And thus even the good movement of free choice, whereby anyone is prepared for receiving the gift of grace, is an act of free choice moved by God.... Man's preparation for grace is from God, as mover, and from free choice, as moved.

Summa Theologica, I, 23, 3; I–II, 109, 6; I–II, 112, 2, 3

Since both of these doctrines originated in biblical authority and Catholic theology was called upon to explain them, Western Christianity had no alternative but to accept both as absolutely true despite their apparent contradictions. For almost 2,000 years no two theologians have resolved this problem in exactly the same way, and of their solutions, none is free of logical difficulties. Yet, there is a solution, or could be. If either doctrine—free will or determinism—is softened, then they can possibly be reconciled. If God does not predetermine every event of our lives, then we can claim to have some free will; or, if we admit that we are not completely free, then some predetermination can be accepted; but neither free will nor determinism can be accepted (logically) if both are taken as absolutes. Whatever the solution, however, the theological formulation of the problem is an accurate portrayal of a real human dilemma, whether we accept the theological motif or a natural one. We are both free and determined; and somehow we must work at the dilemma until we understand how both views bear some truth.

From the moral perspective, if there is no freedom of choice, there can be no moral, legal, or any other kind of responsibility, praise, blame, or punishment. The fact of personal responsibility is a crucial assumption of morality: we blame others and give them praise; we hold ourselves responsible and feel guilt for our misdoings; we indict alleged lawbreakers, hold trials, and convict or free them. All the while we operate on the assumption that human beings can be morally and legally responsible; that is, *free*. If this assumption is wrong, legal and moral responsibility is lost and the so-called choices we make are illusory—and life loses its meaning.

According to behavioral psychologist B. F. Skinner, freedom is a myth; it is not a fact of human experience. *All* of our responses—the impulses that lie behind so-called free choice—are the result of unique past contingencies of conditioning and reinforcement that have shaped us into what we are. For Skinner, what we call *freedom* is merely the successful avoidance on the part of any organism of some aversive feature in its environment. He theorized that organisms are manipulated and controlled by the dynamic features of their environment.

On the other side of this view, Jean-Paul Sartre writes that we are living in an antinomian world without guidelines, cultural norms are relative, and societies are humorously absurd. There is no God and therefore no absolute mandates to give life order. There is no meaning to human life as such. Nor is there any past conditioning that we can blame for making us what we are. There is not even a "human nature" that might help us to define ourselves. For Sartre, we are "condemned" to be free and this freedom entails tragic choices with formidable consequences. Out of our freedom we do not make decisions for ourselves alone, but for others, and sometimes for all of mankind.

In a new volume of philosophical papers, *Making Sense of Humanity*, Bernard Williams wrestles with this problem anew. Although these papers are somewhat technical, a patient reading will bring the reader up to speed with contemporary ethics and the many nuances of the determinism problem.

See also Ethics, Theory of.

SOURCES

Aquinas, Saint Thomas. *Summa Theologica, I–II*. New York: Random House. 1944.

Rogers, Carl R. *On Becoming a Person: A Therapist's View of Psychotherapy*. Boston: Houghton Mifflin. 1961.

Skinner, B. F. *Beyond Freedom & Dignity*. New York: Alfred A. Knopf. 1971.

Williams, Bernard. *Making Sense of Humanity*. New York: Cambridge University Press. 1995.

FREEDOM OF CHOICE

The struggle for freedom colors human history as no other issue of value or ethics. Even today, on every continent, among all races and ethnic groups and cultures, there is a struggle for freedom and freedom of choice—among feminist groups, racial and ethnic minorities, the poor, and alternative lifestyle groups. There is a strong Anglo-Saxon tradition of civil liberties, based on English common law and practice and on U.S. constitutional law and practice. From the Magna Carta to the Bill of Rights, on to the Civil Rights movement during the 1960s, and among those who feel disenfranchised, people desire freedom and seek it with passion; they also want order and security. Order is necessary for the enlargement and maintenance of freedom, but freedom often conflicts with order and security. Values do not come to us in neatly organized "black" and "white" packages. Values can be and usually are sociologically and politically messy. The problem is to maintain a balance that will protect the rights of the individual and of the community and at the same time allow order and security to unfold, as they are valued as well.

Since the fourteenth century, Western society has changed from one dominated by the church and a moral and religious ideal to one dominated by commerce and industry primarily interested in production and profits. When the Industrial Revolution began in England in the eighteenth century, there were in existence many antiquated laws and regulations that prevented the free movement of labor and merchandise. Some of these restrictions had originated under agrarian feudalism, and they were defended by the landed interests. The merchant and manufacturing classes demanded freedom for the acquisition of markets and raw materials, the hiring and firing of labor, and the movement of labor from one area to another.

The first cry for freedom of choice was "Let us alone"; "Hands off"; *Laissez-faire.* This slogan has been heard since the constitutional stirrings of the nation's founders: "Men must be free to pursue their self-interest"; "There must be free enterprise"; "The economic man must have freedom from interference"; "There should be a minimum of governmental control." These same slogans have been heard again in battles with state and federal governments over gun control, environmental laws, abortion, and protecting endangered species. In other areas of life the same kind of separation and demand for freedom of choice is taking place: artists are asking for freedom of art from moral and religious ends, proclaiming "art for art's sake"; scientists are demanding freedom for objective and disinterested inquiry; religion for the inclusion of creationism and prayer in the public schools; and some women for pro-choice, while others call out for pro-life.

This tendency toward independence and separation of functions in society was reinforced by an economic theory that developed in the eighteenth and nineteenth centuries in connection with the rise of the new industrial system. This theory took slightly different forms, known variously as *individualism, laissez-faire individualism,* and *economic liberalism.* Social philosophers in France known as the Physiocrats, and a group of writers in Great Britain, among them Adam Smith (1723–1790), Thomas Malthus (1766–1834), and David Ricardo (1772–1823), were leaders in advancing this view. They argued that social, political, and economic phenomena are governed by natural laws and any attempt to regulate

or control them is not only useless but harmful. Natural law, it was argued, would regulate prices, wages, and hours in the most equitable way. Consequently, there must be no interference with the laws of competition and of supply and demand. In the nineteenth century, Jeremy Bentham and John Stuart Mill gave voice to individualism, which was now supported by the theory of evolution: Herbert Spencer held that man should let nature take its course and should not interfere in most areas.

Individualism also was manifest personally in the doctrine of self-interest. The individual, it was said, should be free to pursue his or her own interests as long as that individual keeps the peace and does not demean the rights and freedoms of others. The individual should have freedom of choice to make as much money as possible and spend it as he or she sees fit. This definition of personhood in terms of economics makes the ideal individual one who manages his or her own affairs, consulting only self-interests and guided by the profit motive.

In its political application, individualism is the doctrine of noninterference, the view that the government should confine itself to the suppression of fraud and violence, to the protection of property, and to the enforcement of contracts. The government policy is one of laissez-faire, or let people act economically as they please. Proponents of this doctrine believe that if a person seeks his or her own interests through free competition, the result will be both material and social progress.

Although laissez-faire and freedom of choice were popularized in the eighteenth and nineteenth centuries, since the 1930s a social-service view of society and government has been promoted with a considerable degree of governmental control of the economy through public housing, food subsidies, and health and welfare programs. From the point of view of morality, governmental control, like individualism, can become destructive. The individualist and the supporters of the social-service view are concerned primarily with somewhat different values. The individualist wishes to protect individuality, initiative, and self-reliance; hence, freedom of choice. These character traits have genuine value and are among those being touted by character educators with a more conservative bent. The person who supports a greater degree of community or government control wishes to achieve the values that come through sharing, cooperation, and group action. One can compare these two different views to the feminist separation of vertical and lateral thinking, with lateral thinking representing the feminist perspective and the values embodied in community—sharing, cooperation, and group interaction.

See also Civil Disobedience; Civil Rights Movement; Free Will.

SOURCES

Arendt, Hannah. *Crises of the Republic.* New York: Harcourt, Brace, and Jovanovich. 1972.

Boorstin, Daniel J. *The Americans: The Democratic Experience.* New York: Random House. 1973.

Cohen, Edmond. *The Predicament of Democratic Man.* New York: Macmillan. 1961.

Commoner, Barry. *The Closing Circle.* New York: Knopf. 1971.

Goldwin, Robert A., ed. *Left, Right and Center: Essays on Liberalism and Conservatism in the United States.* Chicago: Rand McNally. 1967.

FRIEDAN, BETTY

Betty Friedan (1921–) is a writer and a trained psychologist. In 1963, with the publishing of her book, *The Feminine Mystique,* she became the "founding mother" of contemporary feminism in the United States. In this book she isolates the "housewife syndrome" and says that, contrary to what contemporary research from the social sciences has shown, women must have opportunities for fulfillment beyond those provided by marriage and motherhood. Friedan argues that in the years following World War II women were permitted but one career: that of housewife and mother. The result was a tremendous boredom among middle-class women that often translated into a neurosis harmful to both themselves and their families. Social scientists, she observes, had generally misdiagnosed this problem as one of individual adjustment rather than a social malady with important implications for sexual equality. Friedan has campaigned for reforms that would end both subtle and overt discrimination against women. In 1966, she helped found the National Organization for Women, and since then has been active in the formation of other feminist groups. Her book *It Changed My Life* (1976) is an account of her years in the women's movement. *The Second Stage,* which was published in 1981 and revised in 1986, represents a major shift in her thinking that emphasizes the importance of the family and the necessity of male participation in feminist movements.

See also Feminism.

SOURCES

"Friedan, Betty." Grolier Electronic Publishing. 1992.

Larrabee, Mary Jeanne, ed. *An Ethic of Care: Feminist and Interdisciplinary Perspectives.* New York: Routledge. 1993. (See also the *Thinking Gender* series edited by Linda J. Nicholson and published by Routledge.)

FRIENDSHIP

A friend is someone who knows and likes another. As Shakespeare said, "A friend should bear his friend's infirmities." Likewise, friendship is liking between persons; based on liking, we call two people *friends.*

The role of friendship was a noticeable theme with the Stoic philosophers, such as Seneca, Aurelius, and Epictetus. Who would not agree, "That is not loss which a friend gets"? A list of sound advice is also given: "A man who has friends must show himself friendly"; "The shortest road is when the company is good." And a true and vital test of friendship is suggested: "A friend is never known till a man have need."

The word *friend* expresses a special moral relationship between persons characterized by trust, honesty, companionship, and a willingness to help the one in need. Most American proverbs that explain the value of friendship, passed from one generation to the next in colonial days, had European origins. Benjamin Franklin gave his voice to many of these proverbs and is credited with many more himself. Nearly all were practical and expressed a close observation of basic social relationships, such as "A man is known by the company he keeps," and "One good turn deserves another," or "Many hands make light work," and "People who live in glass houses mustn't thrown stones."

From primitive times the need for and value of friendship found in maxims, proverbs, and prose testify to the uniformity of human experience and human social needs, irrespective of race, religion, or place of origin. Primitive thought, like contemporary moral philosophy, testifies to the need for friends and the importance of friendship. Moral philosophers and social scientists also support the virtue of friendship. In 1962, W. T. Stace observed: "And if there is any condition which can rival the exercise of special gifts as the chief source of man's happiness, I would say that it lies in the affection of friends and in the love for one another as members of a family. . . . Friendship is the poor man's riches; and it is a happier lot to be rich in human affection though poor in gold than to be king of half the world but without a

friend." The concept of friendship found in Aristotle's ethics, elaborated upon by Cicero, and understood for centuries in the context of the Christian conception of personhood was well known to colonial Americans, and it continued into the nineteenth century. It is worth noting this traditional idea of friendship, because in the twentieth century there has been a shift in meaning to a more therapeutic attitude and conceptualization. The traditional view had three essential components: (1) friends must enjoy one another's company; (2) they must be useful to one another; and (3) they must share a common commitment to the good.

The contemporary conception of friendship differs in that it is based on "the enjoyment of one another's company," and "the necessity of being friendly to those who may be of use to us." In a world dominated by expressive and utilitarian individualism, it is easy to understand the components of pleasure and usefulness, but as Robert Bellah and his associates reflect in *Habits of the Heart*, "We have difficulty selling the point of considering friendship in terms of common moral commitments." For the ancients and into the Enlightenment of Europe and colonial America, it was precisely the moral component of friendship that made it the indispensable basis of a good society.

By the 1830s, Alexis de Tocqueville had noticed certain features of American life that endangered traditional relationships, traditional ideas of friendship. He wrote, "Democracy does not create strong attachments between man and man, but it does put their ordinary relations on an easier footing." In the complexities of an "emerging" consciousness, the people of the United States were becoming easier to meet and their daily interactions more flexible and open, but the ties between them were also becoming more casual and transient. The country was on the move and so were her values. It was inevitable that the idea of friendship would be affected by the changing social nature of humans and human groups. De Tocqueville wondered, as we also wonder, how such a restless, competitive, and anxious people could sustain enduring relationships, especially when "they clutch everything and hold nothing fast."

SOURCES

Bellah, Robert N., et al. *Habits of the Heart: Individualism and Commitment in American Life.* Berkeley: University of California Press. 1985.

Bogardus, Emory S. *The Development of Social Thought.* 4th ed. New York: David McKay. 1960.

Stace, W. T. *The Concept of Morals.* New York: Macmillan. 1962.

G

GAUTAMA, SIDDHARTHA (BUDDHA)

Siddhartha (Pali, Siddhattha) was the given and *Guatama* (Pali, Gotama) the family name of the founder of Buddhism. He was probably born in 563 B.C. in northern India, some 100 miles from Banaras (Benares), in a fertile tract of country among the foothills of the Himalayas. His father was a chieftain of the Sakya clan and his mother reportedly died when he was a few days old; an aunt became his stepmother through marriage with his father.

Rather than pursuing politics, as it is believed his father wanted, Gautama—who possessed a clear, analytic mind and sensitive spirit—left his home sometime during his 20s to "go out from the household life into the homeless state" of the religious mendicant, and when, in his late 20s, his wife bore him a son, he felt free to follow his secret inclination.

The Buddhist legends tell of the inner struggle of the young Gautama as he made his decision to renounce his high status in life and take up the place of a monk. In his 20s he began a six-year period of intensive struggle for realization of salvation. The legends imply he was not anxious to reject the Brahmin philosophy until he had tested it. He turned to teachers to instruct him. The first teacher, the ascetic Alara Kalama, taught him of "the realm of nothingness," which a man might attain if he followed "the stages of meditation." But Gautama, being too objective and practical, rejected this way. So he went on to the second teacher, the ascetic Uddaka Ramaputta, who talked about "the states of neither-ideation-nor-non-ideation," with no better results. In the end, convinced that these teachers would not conduct him to the true way of enlightenment, he withdrew and resolved to test the extreme bodily asceticism that Jainism, among other sects, was advocating.

After a short period of wandering, he entered a grove of trees at Uruvela, past which flowed a clear river with, "hard by, a village for sustenance." There, sitting under the trees, he undertook for five years such rigorous self-discipline that he almost died. He became extemely thin and emaciated. He thought to himself, "with all these severe austerities, I fail to transcend ordinary human limits and to rise to the heights of noblest understanding and vision. Could there be another path to enlightenment?" Having come close to death, he resumed the life of a wandering mendicant. Six years of search along the two most widely recognized roads to salvation known to India—meditation and bodily asceticism—had yielded no results. But he did not give up the struggle.

In his wanderings, Gautama turned into a place called Bodh-gaya, into a grove, and sat down at the foot of a fig tree (which came to be known as the *Knowledge* or *Bodhi tree*) and there entered upon a process of meditation that was to affect the thinking of millions of people after him. He concluded that his inability to experience release from his suffering was due to desire, but to eliminate misery-producing desire he must determine its causes and prevent them from controlling his life. By resisting temptation, Gautama escaped evil and entered into full enlightenment. He realized that desire arises in the context of a 12-linked chain of causation, but that he had escaped from it into a new life, a higher form of consciousness, freed of desire and its suffering. The Buddhist book says he then passed into a state of "awareness" or "wakefulness" culminating in the realization that "knowing neither satisfaction nor dissatisfaction, is the consummate purity of poised equanimity and mindfulness." It seemed to him that "ignorance was destroyed, knowledge had arisen, darkness was destroyed, light had arisen." Buddha was convinced that "rebirth is no more; I have lived the highest life; my task is done; and now for me there is no more of what I have been." This was the early foretaste of *Nibbana* or *Nirvana*. From now on he was the Buddha, the Enlightened One. He rose and went back into the world to communicate to others his saving truth.

SOURCES

Bouquet, A. C., ed. *Sacred Books of the World.* Baltimore: Penguin. 1967.

Champion, Selwyn Gurney, and Dorothy Short, eds. *Readings from World Religions.* Greenwich, CT: Fawcett. 1951.

Ch'en, Kenneth K. S. *Buddhism: The Light of Asia.* Woodbury, NY: Barron's Educational Series. 1968.

Noss, David S., and John B. Noss. *Man's Religions.* 7th ed. New York: Macmillan. 1984.

GAY RIGHTS AND THE ISSUE OF LEGAL MORALISM

Gays, like other minority groups, have significantly less control over their own lives than the members of society's majority groups. With fewer persons and a lifestyle that is significantly different from the majority culture, gays are discriminated against in terms of power, status, and privilege. The term *pervert*, commonly used to describe homosexual persons, has a pejorative connotation. It, like the slang expressions *fag, queer,* and so on, express the contempt of the majority for gay people. In part, as a response to community pressures, gays have developed their own social organizations that support and order the lives of the sexually different in their struggle against community norms that ignore their needs as well as their rights.

William J. Helmer has remarked:

> As might be expected, the common view of homosexuality we find in recent novels, plays, and films is often very limited. Even the more "understanding" studies of the problem seem to consider homosexuals as a definable group—distinct from heterosexuals—whose chief concern in life is to satisfy their sexual desires while shamefully concealing them from friends and associates. In fact, homosexuality is a condition which takes so many forms that the word is of little use in describing any single group of people. And many homosexuals insulate themselves from hostile heterosexual society, taking refuge in a separate homosexual community which possesses its own customs, social structure, ethics, argot, organizations and even business establishments.

When we apply moral principles and principles of moral legalism to homosexuals, or any group that significantly differs from the majority, how do we determine who is equal and who is not? What are the relevant differences? These questions are especially important when developing laws that function to safeguard individual and societal rights and liberties. They are also extremely important for the application of moral rules and procedures. All laws have two sides. By ensuring liberty to one set of persons, the law may restrict the liberty of others. A law by its very nature is coercive because it places a limit on what was formerly an open option. The acceptability of these liberty-limiting laws ultimately depends upon the adequacy of the justification offered for them, and when an adequate justification is not forthcoming, the law can easily become an instrument of oppression.

In the history of these discussions, four "liberty-limiting principles" have been advanced that form the organizing scheme for discussing equality and rights, liberty and justice: (1) the Harm Principle: A person's liberty is justifiably restricted to prevent harm to others; (2) the Principle of Paternalism: A person's liberty is justifiably restricted to prevent harm to self; (3) the Principle of Legal Moralism: A person's liberty is justifiable restricted to prevent that person's immoral behavior; (4) the Offense Principle: A person's liberty is justifiably restricted to prevent offense to others.

The application of these principles to legal moralism and sexual liberties has an uneven and argumentative history. We are all opposed to having a moral view that is alien to our own forced on us by an external authority. Hence, when we approach discussions of legal moralism, or the legal enforcement of morality as such, we are immediately inclined to be skeptical that it can be justified. On the other hand, the justification of many laws in our society is based on some form of moral belief, and this fact indicates that there is moral content already in our laws. For example, the Harm Principle itself is a moral principle that provides the primary basis for massive numbers of laws, and certainly immoral conduct is no trivial matter. Perhaps,

then, it is legitimate to enforce moral views as such if they are overwhelmingly important to moral stability in a society. Perhaps what are known as "moral offenses" or "offenses against human decency and morality" should be subject to legal sanctions even though they do not actually produce physical or psychological harm to the individuals involved.

These are questions concerning what kinds of moral content and what degree of moral content should be allowed in our laws. The issue is whether, in a pluralistic society, deviant moral conduct of any sort, however serious and controversial, is sufficient justification for limiting freedom by making such behavior illegal. This issue is especially troublesome when certain sexual acts are widely regarded in a society as sexual perversions, and yet are also purely private affairs involving only consenting adults. Homosexuality is the most frequently mentioned example, but the ethical problems involving sanctions of sexual activity extend far beyond this single issue.

Many complex and confusing issues plague legal moralism. Among these are the following: (1) First, there is the question of whether the morality of any human action can ever—solely because it is immoral—provide a sufficient justification for making that type of action illegal. (2) Then there is the problem of freedom of choice, especially with regard to homosexuality. The issue is this: if a person doesn't choose to be homosexual, then it is as natural as heterosexuality, even though the number of homosexuals in the population is minute when compared to the number of heterosexual persons. Natural behaviors, especially those that are predetermined (genetically), are not immoral. (3) Finally, when rules are established that prohibit the actions of certain kinds of people—women, minorities, homosexuals, etc.—such as the right to work in certain places, then we have extended the Harm Principle to encompass the principles of legal moralism and the Offense Principle, in which a person's liberty is restricted to prevent immoral behavior and offenses to others.

An example of this came in 1995 when Senator Jesse Helms introduced legislation that could limit the ability of homosexuals who work for the federal government to form employee associations. This measure would ban the spending of federal money to promote or carry out any programs for government employees that "would compel, instruct, encourage, urge or persuade employees or officials to embrace, accept, condone or celebrate homosexuality as a legitimate or normal style."

Supporters of gay rights say the measure, which they call the first such bill to be introduced in the new Republican-controlled Congress, would sharply curtail the activities of groups made up of gay or lesbian federal employees. Leaders of these organizations, which exist in 22 federal agencies, say the measure would ban them from meeting in federal offices, using interoffice mail for communications, or posting notices on bulletin boards. Such activities are permitted for other groups, including black or Hispanic employee organizations.

SOURCE

Freeman, Howard E., and Norman R. Kurtz, eds. *America's Troubles: A Casebook on Social Conflict*. Englewood Cliffs, NJ: Prentice-Hall. 1969.

Helmer, William J. "New York's 'Middle-Class' Homosexuals." *Harpers Magazine* (March 1963), 85–92.

GEMEINSCHAFT

Ferdinand Tonnies (1855–1936) conceived of social relations in terms of *Gemeinschaft* (community) and *Gesellschaft* (society). *Gemeinschaft* is characterized by *wesenwillen*, or the actions of basic life-forces or urges. On the other hand, *Gesellschaft* is motivated by *kurwillen*, or action based on deliberation and conscious choice. Community emphasizes natural processes; society, artificial ones. Community is a form of primary grouping, and society of secondary grouping.

Tonnies, a descendant of peasant farmers who had known something of a real community spirit and genuine cooperation, expressed universal feelings in his social theories. His ideas of community and society are strongly influenced by Karl Marx's economic materialism, which showed that our early social relations are normal expressions of satisfying the need for food and other material necessities; and Thomas Hobbes, whose theory of society was motivated by the *kurwillen* or artificial will. Tonnies concluded that moving from *Gemeinschaft* to *Gesellschaft*, and then to a combination of the two types of social relations governed by a rational ethic, will be the cause of social evolution, a logical process in a vast historical sequence. Justice is therefore natural rather than arbitrary, law is based on morals, and society becomes socialistic.

See also Community.

SOURCE

Tonnies, Ferdinand. *Community and Society*. East Lansing, MI: Michigan State University Press. 1957.

GENDER EQUITY

Gender equity means simply to provide equal opportunities, equal pay, equal status (all that is meant by equal rights) to both males and females as if gender did not matter. It means that gender, like race, is not a basis for discrimination. Yet, the history of womanhood is the history of discrimination against the female gender. Today, women are an oppressed group; they are a social minority in the United

States and have been pushed to minority status throughout Western society. Although women do occupy positions of power, those who do are a rare exception. Many people find it difficult to conceptualize women as a subordinate group; after all, they do not live in ghettos nor do they attend inferior schools. They freely interact and live with their alleged oppressors, men. How then are they a minority? Consider the following:

1. Women do experience unequal treatment. Although they are not residentially segregated, they are victims of prejudice and discrimination.
2. Women clearly do have physical and cultural characteristics that distinguish them from the dominant group (men).
3. Membership in sexual classification is involuntary.
4. Women are being made increasingly aware of their subordinate status through "rap" sessions, consciousness-raising groups, and special-interest groups, all of which leads to stronger group solidarity.
5. The rule of endogamy does not apply to women, but it is in marriage that many women feel their subordinate role is most irrevocably defined.

See also Feminism; Inalienable Rights.

SOURCES

The National Women's History Project has published a 16-page gazette, *Women Win the Vote.* The gazette includes a history and analysis of the woman suffrage movement, biographies of the movement's activities, a timeline, information on the 75th anniversary celebration events throughout 1995, and many other resources. The NWHP also offers a Suffrage Anniversary Party Kit. The address is: The National Women's History Project, 7738 Bell Road, Dept. S, Windsor, CA 95492.

Freeman, Jo. *The Politics of Women's Liberation.* New York: David McKay. 1975.

Giddings, Paul. *When and Where I Enter.* New York: William Morrow. 1985.

Kramarae, Cheris, and Paul Treichler. *A Feminist Dictionary.* Boston: Pandora Press. 1985.

Pearson, Carol, and Catherine Pope. *The Female Hero in American and British Literature.* New York: R. R. Bowker. 1981.

Richardson, Laurel W. *The Dynamics of Sex and Gender: A Sociological Perspective.* Boston: Houghton Mifflin. 1981.

Women of Power, A Magazine of Feminism, Spirituality, and Politics. Charlene McKee, ed. Orleans, MA (published biannually).

GENOCIDE

Genocide is the systematic extermination of an entire political, racial, national, religious, or ethnic group of people. Three contemporary documents: "To Secure These Rights" (1947), "Goals For Americans" (1960), and "The Universal Declaration of Human Rights" (1949), express the values and hence the rights that are fundamentally opposed to genocide, in any form and against any living species. Many nations have today ratified conventions to outlaw genocide, abolish slavery, and promote equal rights for women. The fundamental rights, expressed in these documents, are rights that all people demand and are the claims made by individuals on the state or the social group of which they are a part. Human rights grow out of the mutuality of individual and social relations, and they express a position that is neither extreme individualism nor extreme statism.

SOURCES

Schaefer, Richard T. *Racial and Ethnic Groups.* 3d ed. Boston: Scott, Foresman and Co. 1988.

Schermerhorn, R. A. *Comparative Ethnic Relations: A Framework for Theory and Research.* New York: Random House. 1970.

GHOST DANCE MOVEMENTS

Reinhold Niebuhr defines religion as "the implicit sense of life's meaning." Surely all humans have some sense of the meaningfulness of existence and cannot live or think or act without it. In that sense, all humans are religious. According to anthropologist Emile Durkheim, the function of religion is that of strengthening society, maintaining its institutions, and generally assuring stability and coherence to the social body. In essence then, religion is the beliefs, behaviors, and feelings of people about the mystery of life and the mystery of the universe, but there is no mystery about religion per se.

Of interest to the study of religion is the part ghosts have played in religious belief and ceremony. For example, many Native Americans and tribe members in Africa and the Pacific Islands believed in powerful spirits that influence the living world. These people performed rites to please these spirits (ghosts) in order to assure success in daily life. Many of them greatly feared the dead and observed special funeral customs to make sure that the ghosts did not return to haunt them. In the Americas, the basic sameness of Ghost Dance movements everywhere is quite remarkable. The repeated similarities in New World movements may be ascribed to four causes: (1) contact-borrowing of the same European elements of belief (there was explicit identification of the shaman-prophet with Christ, or at least the colorings of the prophets' doctrines by Christianity); (2) old culture traits common in both Americas (a striking parallel to the Ghost Dance is found in South Africa, with of course no possible suggestion of influence by Native Americans); (3) a diffusion of traits of specific cults (a major motif of the early movement was a tremendous interest in the dead, where the

chief ritual was the making of mortuary feasts for them; these feasts are obligatory to cultists, lest the ghosts visit sickness on them); and (4) the general psychic characteristics of human nature.

In the United States the two Ghost Dance movements of 1870 and 1890 represent the final catastrophe of Native American cultures. Both were part of a returning wave of crisis cults spreading eastward from the Prophet Dance of the Far West. It was the Great Ghost Dance of 1890 that provided the crashing climax to the collapse of Native American culture. Tavibo, the messiah of the Ghost Dance of 1870, had a son named Wovoka, "The Cutter." As a boy, Wovoka is thought to have witnessed the ceremonies in Tavibo's tule reed *wickiup,* and he saw the many visitors who came from all over the West to hear the prophet's revelations. Like many other Paiute, Wovoka worked for the white ranchers of Mason Valley in Nevada. There he learned more about Christian theology and the English language. He also acquired the name Jack Wilson from the family of David Wilson, on whose ranch he worked. Under this name he achieved legendary fame all over the West. Even far-off tribes knew he was omniscient, spoke all languages, was invisible to white men, and was a direct messenger from the Great Spirit.

The story goes like this: while a young man, Wovoka became sick with fever in 1899, and at this time "the sun died" in total eclipse, and in a delirium or trance Jack was taken to see God. All the people who had died long ago were there in heaven, busy with the games and occupations, happy and forever young. God told him to preach goodness to his people and to practice war no more. They should dance a ceremony that God taught him, to hasten the reunion with the dead. God gave him charge of the West, while "Governor Harrison" would take care of the East, and God looked after heaven. In effect, Wovoka was the new messiah. Jesus, he told the Arapaho and Cheyenne, was now back on earth.

His command was exact and exacting: Do no harm to anyone; do right always.

At the news of the messiah, various tribes reacted variously. In 1890 the Sioux, under the influence of the medicine man Sitting Bull, were greatly excited at the coming "return of the ghosts." The Great Spirit had sent the white man to punish the Indians for their sins. The Indians had now been punished enough and deliverance was at hand, but the whites had been bad ever since they had killed Jesus. Dancing would preserve the Indians from sickness, and the white man's bullets would no longer penetrate Indian skulls.

Ghost Dance movements continued among Native Americans until the Battle of Wounded Knee. Parallel movements occurred in South Africa in 1856 and New Zealand as late as 1934. Scholars who have studied this phenomenon point out striking similarities in Muhammadanism, Joan of Arc, the dancers of St. John, the Flagellants, the Ranters, Quakers and Fifth Monarch Men, the French Prophets, the Jumpers, Methodists, English Shakers, Kentucky Revivalists, Adventists, Beekmanites, Patterson-and-Brownites, Wilderness Worshipers, and the Heavenly Recruits. No time and no culture has been without its Ghost Dance phenomenon. A. F. C. Wallace early argued that, in fact, "all organized religions are relics of old revitalization movements, surviving in routinized forms in stabilized cultures, and that religious phenomena per se originated in visions of a new way of life by individuals under extreme stress."

SOURCES

La Barre, Weston. *The Ghost Dance, Origins of Religion.* Garden City, NY: Doubleday. 1970.

Moorehead, W. K. "Ghost-Dances in the West." *Illustrated American* 5:48 (1891).

———. "The Indian Messiah and the Ghost Dance." *American Antiquarian* 13 (1890).

Wallace, A. F. C. "Revitalization Movements." *American Anthropologist* 58 (1956).

GIDEON V. WAINWRIGHT

In the case of *Gideon v. Wainwright* in 1963, the U.S. Supreme Court, speaking through Justice Hugo Black, overruled *Betts v. Brady* (1942), in which an earlier majority had held that the Sixth Amendment's guarantee of the right to counsel applied only to trials in federal courts, that it was not essential to a fair trial, and that it was not incorporated into the Due Process clause of the Fourteenth Amendment.

Clarence Earl Gideon had been charged with breaking and entering a poolroom in Florida, was found guilty by a jury, and had been sentenced to five years in prison. Gideon had not been represented by counsel even though he had requested that the state appoint a lawyer for his defense. Justice Black argued that the Fourteenth Amendment's guarantee of due process embraced the Sixth Amendment's right to counsel. The case was significant in that it made one provision of the Bill of Rights that had previously applied only to the federal government apply also to state criminal proceedings. Prior to the decision in *Gideon*, the Supreme Court had used the Fourteenth Amendment to apply to the states only the rights guaranteed in the First Amendment (freedom of speech, press, religion, assembly, and petition) and in the Fourth Amendment (freedom from unreasonable search and seizure).

SOURCE

Lewis, Anthony. *Gideon's Trumpet.* New York: Random House. 1964.

GOLDEN RULE

Morality in its highest form is inclusive and thus applicable to both the entire human species, and as deep ecology reminds us, to the very environment of which humans are so important a part. Morality is not only personal—directed at self-commitment and self-interests—but is also by definition other-directed. An essential part of the "other" to which and for which morality is directed and formulated is the living environment upon which all living things depend. This is the meaning of the Golden Rule: to treat others fairly, equitably, and with respect for their dignity as human beings—just the way each of us wishes to be treated ourselves.

Four categories of moral behavior are assumed in and implied by the Golden Rule. These are (1) the *Graces*, which include good manners, politeness, neatness, courtesy, and adherence to prescribed patterns of dress and speech; (2) the *Virtues*, generally the ability to repress instinctual drives and aggressive emotions, including sex, fear, anger, pride, and greed; (3) the *Duties*, which represent expressed or implied contracts between people, including obligation, social cooperation, and reciprocity—the assumption that if you are honest in your dealings with me, and if in return I am honest with you, we shall both benefit and so will society; and (4) the *Dedications*, which go beyond cooperation and obligation to doing something to help comfort others because they need your help and because they are more important, at that time, than anything else. If the *Dedications* represent the highest level of morality, those who dedicate themselves must do so freely; dedication cannot be demanded. This kind of morality has been visualized by three-quarters of the world's population and is generally referred to as the *Golden Rule*. The Golden Rule reflects the transcendent nature that sets one moral behavior apart and above our biological and cultural natures.

In Western societies one cannot fully understand ethics and moral values without a distinct and full comprehension of the impact and influence of Judeo-Christian theology on its mores, legal system, and moral practices. Like it or not, the secular view of values in the West is cultural-ly tied to and a part of religious views in many significant and meaningful ways. Upon examination, we can also say that this assumption holds true—that the religion of a society significantly influences secular habits and practices—for nations and societies the world over.

The Golden Rule has been formulated in the following ways:

- Christianity: *"All things whatsoever ye would that men should do to you, do ye even unto them for this is the law of the prophets."*
- Brahmanism: *"This is the sum of duty; do naught unto others which would cause pain if done unto you."*
- Buddhism: *"Hurt not others in ways that you yourself would find hurtful."*
- Judaism: *"What is hateful to you, do not to your fellow men. That is the entire law, all the rest is commentary."*
- Confucianism: *"There is one maxim of loving kindness: do not unto others what you would not have them do unto you."*
- Taoism: *"Regard your neighbor's gain as your own gain, and your neighbor's loss as your own loss."*
- Zoroastrianism: *"That nature alone is good that refrains from doing unto another whatsoever is not good for itself."*
- Islam: *"No one of you is a believer until he desires for his brother that which he desires for himself."*

According to Theodore Kahn, the Golden Rule means that humans' moral values stem from using our own needs and desires as a foundation for understanding and respecting the needs and desires of others. Other modern moral values can be derived from this primary and universal one.

Robert Nozick refers to this as the "push and pull" of moral interaction:

Value or preciousness of persons has a dual role in my interpersonal actions. Your value generates a moral claim or constraint on my behavior toward you; because of your value, others (including me) ought to behave toward you in some ways, not in others. Also, my value is expressed in how I am best off behaving, in the kind of behavior that should flow from a being with my value, in how that value is shown or maintained in action. My value fixes what behavior should flow from me; your value fixes which behavior should flow toward you. Value manifests itself as a push and as a pull. . . . Ethics is harmonious when the push is at least as great as the pull, when the person's own value leads him to behave toward another as the value of that other requires.

See also The Categorical Imperative; Ethics, Theory of; Judeo-Christian Ethics.

SOURCES

Kahn, Theodore C. Hominology: The Study of the Whole Man. Springfield, IL: Charles C. Thomas. 1972.

Leuba, C. The Natural Man. Garden City, NY: Doubleday. 1954.

Lisitzky, G. Four Ways of Being Human. New York: Bantam. 1963.

Nozick, Robert. Philosophical Explanations. Cambridge, MA: Harvard University Press. 1981.

GOOD

See Common Good; Ethics, Theory of.

THE GREEN REVOLUTION

The Green Revolution has been compared to other major developments in history, such as the advent of tool making or the beginning of domestication and cultivation as agricultural practices. It was essentially the development of fast-growing, high-yield crops from more than 20 years of agricultural research that was the revolution's foundation. Because of major crop failures in 1965 and 1966, China, India, the Soviet Union, and other countries had to import huge quantities of grain to prevent famine. In 1968, Paul Ehrlich, a population biologist, stated (in his new book The Population Bomb) that the world had nine years to find a solution to the food-population crisis. At the same time that Erlich's book appeared on the bookstands, the "famine" had turned into surpluses. By 1970, countries like the Philippines and Malaysia, formerly on the brink of starvation, were talking of food self-sufficiency in several years. This dramatic change in a few short years was the product of a major agricultural breakthough—the Green Revolution.

But in 1972, food production in the world fell and food prices rose once again. Production continued to fall for several years, shattering the hopes many had in the Green Revolution. Wholesale starvation seemed imminent. During 1977, 1978, and 1979, U.S. farmers staged strikes to obtain greater support for their products. Tractors paraded around Washington, D.C., and protest groups marched on the Capitol steps, while other farmers held back beef and dairy products to increase their incomes. In 1982, U.S. legislators debated the distribution of surplus cheese to the poor. Meanwhile, consumers balked at the high grocery prices. During this time, one-third of the people in the world suffered from malnutrition.

The Green Revolution or Green Movement ranks alongside the movement for social justice and the peace movement as one of the three impact movements of the past 50 years. Within the Green Movement we also find the seeds of the deep ecology movement, which views all life as fundamentally one. Together, these movements are highly moral in that they are connected to the essential needs and welfare of all humanity.

See also Ehrlich, Paul Ralph.

SOURCES

Purdom, P. Walton, and S. H. Anderson. Environmental Science. 2d ed. Columbus, OH: Charles E. Merrill. 1983.

Rothenberg, David. *Is It Painful to Think? Conversations with Arne Naess.* Minneapolis: University of Minnesota Press. 1993.

GREENPEACE

Greenpeace is an international organization dedicated to preserving endangered species, preventing environmental abuses, and heightening environmental awareness through direct confrontation with polluting corporations and governmental authorities. The organization was founded in 1971 in British Columbia to oppose U.S. nuclear testing at Amchitka Island in Alaska. This loose-knit organization quickly attracted support from ecologically minded private individuals and began undertaking campaigns seeking, among other goals, the protection of endangered whales and seals from hunting, the cessation of the dumping of toxic wastes and radioactive wastes at sea, and the end of nuclear-weapons testing.

On July 10, 1985, the Greenpeace ship *Rainbow Warrior,* which was due to sail to Moruroa Atoll to protest French atmospheric nuclear-weapons tests there, was sunk by a two-bomb explosion while berthed in Auckland Harbour, New Zealand. Upon discovering that the bombs were the responsibility of French intelligence agents, the French defense minister and the head of France's intelligence service were forced to resign.

SOURCES
Encyclopaedia Britannica. Chicago: Encyclopaedia Britannica. 1990.

GROUP MORALITY

There are those who claim that a distinction must be made between individual moral standards and conduct on the one hand, and the behavior of professional and social groups and organizations on the other hand. We are told that these are elements in human collective behavior that cannot readily be brought under the guidance of reason and conscience. Relations between groups will be more ruthless than relations between individuals, especially where self-preservation is at stake.

Group selfishness is an exceedingly dangerous kind of selfishness, for while masquerading under the cloak of loyalty to one's group, one may do much harm to others and to the social welfare in general. Sociologists have gone to great effort to make a distinction between the *in-group* (we-group) and the *out-group* (other-group). We quite naturally have sympathy and affection for members of our we-group and show attitudes of cooperation, loyalty, and mutual aid toward them, while harboring attitudes of avoidance, suspicion, hatred, or even—in extreme cases—actual warfare toward the out-group.

The relations between groups is as important morally as the relations between people, and perhaps more so. The loyal attitudes of individuals toward groups may blind them to the antagonistic attitudes of groups toward one another. Part of the problem of ethics is to help individuals free themselves from the biases caused by narrow self-interest and the pressures caused by group opinion, and to develop a concern for the welfare of the larger communities of which they are a part. Of course many see a dangerous decline in the condition of Western morality as reflected in our groups (families, schools, businesses, etc.). James Warburg comments: "Our civilization has for centuries practiced neither the Jewish teaching of justice under moral law nor the Greek teaching of rational thought and behavior, and least of all the Christian teaching of love, compassion, and human brotherhood."

Many of our ideals and principles—such as treating people as ends, not as means—appear to be unimpeachable. The real problems seem to be the gap between principles and practice, and our "double morality," which limits the application of our principles when it comes to certain areas of human life and relationships. Improvement in public morality as distinct from private morality must wait until a proportionately larger number of persons attain the level of reflective morality and until individuals are made to feel a sense of individual responsibility for the acts of the groups to which they belong. Growth is a law of life—of individual life and of collective, social life. The problem of bringing our morals up to date is a continuous one and we should be cognizant of the need to apply them to a growing population of groups and of persons.

See also Community; Ethics, Theory of.

SOURCES

Ernest, J. F. *Patterns of Ethics in America Today.* New York: Collier. 1962.

Larrabee, Mary Jeanne, ed. *An Ethic of Care: Feminist and Interdisciplinary Perspectives.* New York: Routledge. 1993.

Toulmin, Stephen E. *Cosmopolis: The Hidden Agenda of Modernity.* Chicago: University of Chicago Press. 1990.

Warburg, James. *The West in Crisis.* Garden City, NY: Doubleday. 1959.

H

HABITS OF THE HEART

In the 1830s, the French social philosopher Alexis de Tocqueville offered the most comprehensive and penetrating analysis of the relationship between character and society in the United States that, perhaps, has ever been written. In his book *Democracy in America*, he described the mores of Americans, which he called "habits of the heart." De Tocqueville singled out family life, our religious traditions, and our participation in local politics as helping create the kind of person who could sustain a connection to a wider political community and ultimately support the maintenance of democratic institutions. He went on to point out that "individualism" might eventually destroy America by isolating individuals and further separating the "haves" from the "have nots." He commented on the way to develop moral habits: "At first it is of necessity that men attend to the public interest, afterward by choice. What had been calculation becomes instinct. By dint of working for the good of his fellow citizens, he in the end acquires a habit and taste for serving them" (*Democracy in America*, 1835).

In their book, *Habits of the Heart*, Robert N. Bellah et al. begin their own study of U.S. values with de Tocqueville's observation and pose the question of how to preserve or create a morally coherent life in America. They note that the kind of life we want depends on the kind of people we are—on our character or habits of the heart. In their 1991 study of Baby Boomers (*The New Individualists*), Paul Leinberger and Bruce Tucker show contemporary American life to be filled with paradoxes. Pointing out that World War II drastically altered the life course of millions of young Americans, they note a shift to an organizational ethic in the 1950s and 1960s, but for their children—the Baby Boomers—a shift back to a new individualism, a self-ethic in which the moral imperative is the duty to express the authentic self. As our loyalties shift, from the family to the organization and then to the self, a radical new individualism has been brought forth that is perhaps redefining our values—and our habits of the heart.

SOURCES

Bellah, Robert N., et al. *Habits of the Heart: Individualism and Commitment in American Life*. Bekeley: University of California Press. 1985.
Leinberger, Paul, and Bruce Tucker. *The New Individualists*. New York: Harper Collins. 1991.

HAMMURABI

The great Semitic king and law-giver, Hammurabi of Babylon (1728–1686 B.C.), united the northern and southern regions briefly into a Sumero-Akkadian Kingdom. But this kingdom was overthrown by the Kassites, probably an Indo-European people invading from the northeast in about 1600 B.C. They in their turn could not prevent the rise of the Assyrian Kingdom in the north, based at Nineveh, which rose to world power in about 1100 B.C. and then began a slow decline. Assyria fell before the Babylonians in 612 B.C., and the latter succumbed to Cyrus the Persian in 539 B.C.

With Hammurabi's coming to power, we also saw the rise in importance of the god Marduk. Hammurabi, the sixth king of the first dynasty of Babylon, made Babylon the capital of a powerful kingdom stretching from the Persian Gulf to the central provinces between the Tigris and Euphrates rivers. It was an achievement of permanent significance, for Babylon thus became and was to remain through 20 centuries of change one of the great cities of the world. And with the rise to power of Babylon, Marduk, its god, rose to greatness and absorbed the surrounding gods into himself.

From this rich tradition and a growing mythology came the creation stories that eventually found their way into Hebrew and Christian scripture. And the great law code of Hammurabi, when examined carefully, is found to embody the major laws encoded in the Hebrew Ten Commandments. One can thus, by historical connection and similarity, trace the ethics and values of Western civilization—as pertains to origins—to the mythic pantheon of Sumeria and Akkadia and the rich library of laws left by Hammurabi.

SOURCES

Kamer, Samuel N. *Sumerian Mythology*. New York: Harper Torchbooks. 1961.

Murray, Gilbert. *The Five Stages of Greek Religion*. Oxford: Clarendon Press. 1925.

Pritchard, James B. *Ancient Near Eastern Texts Relating to the Old Testament*. 3d ed. Princeton: Princeton University Press. 1969.

HAN FEI

Han Fei (d. 233 B.C.) is known for his book, the *Han-fei-tzu*. Here we discover that he acquired a deep admiration for the *Tao Te Ching*, which he studied under the Confucian scholar Hsun Tzu, and that these influences appear in his writings and give them a richness and depth not found in other legalist treatises.

Han Fei believed that every man is naturally selfish and materialistic. Man's religion, obedience to the ruler, his relations to parents, wife, and children, and his dealings with his fellow men are all permeated by his desire for advantage. That people love each other Han Fei did not deny, but such love, he maintained, was secondary to the desire for advantage. He says:

> There is nothing like the warm feelings between sons and fathers; and anyone who wants to act on the basis of public morality and issue prohibitions to those under his jurisdiction must needs take into account the intimacy of the flesh-and-blood relation. But there is something more [than love] in the relationship of fathers and mothers with their sons. If a son is born, then they congratulate each other. If a daughter is born, they (may) kill it. Both these have come out of the mother's womb, and when it is a boy, congratulations, when it is a girl, death! The parents are thinking of convenience later on. They calculate on long-term profit. Thus it is that even fathers and mothers in their relation to their children have calculating minds and treat them accordingly.

SOURCE

Noss, David S., and John B. Noss. *Man's Religions*. 7th ed. New York: Macmillan. 1984.

HAPPINESS

John Dewey observed, "Happiness is fundamental in morals only because happiness is not something sought for, but is something now attained, even in the midst of pain and trouble, when even recognition of our ties with nature and with fellow men release and informs our action. Reasonableness is a necessity because it is the perception of the continuities that take action out of its immediateness and isolation into connection with the past and future." This concentration on "happiness" and the pleasure principle in morals has a long-standing place in the history of philosophy. Among teleologists—those who place emphasis on the end results of behavior—there have been differences of opinion about the decisive features of consequences. Self-realizationists treated the end (happiness) as the fullest actualization of the individual's potentials. *Hedonism*, as this ethic was called, thought pleasure or happiness the defining mark of values.

Hedonism dates back at least to Aristippus (ca. 435 B.C.–356 B.C.) and Democritus (ca. 460 B.C.–362 B.C.) Aristippus, a pupil of Socrates, named pleasure the one and only good. The most intense pleasure, he said, is the highest good and one at which life should aim. One need seek his own pleasure, and the pleasure of the moment should not be subordinated to the uncertain pleasure of the future. Epicurus (c. 342 B.C.–270 B.C.) sharply modified the views of Aristippus. In genuine Epicureanism we are counseled to seek not the most intense pleasures, but those most likely to produce long-term satisfaction. Epicurus identified these, on the basis of experience, as pleasures of the mind and spirit rather than physical pleasures. Self-control, friendship, and wisdom are recommended as the avenues to the greatest personal happiness.

Hedonism was revived during the Renaissance and was popular in England during the seventeenth century, when it was made famous by Thomas Hobbes (1586–1679) and John Locke (1632–1704). Later exponents of a pleasure standard were Jeremy Bentham (1748–1832) and John Stuart Mill (1806–1873). We find in all of these scholars that hedonism has taken a number of differing forms:

1. *Psychological hedonism* is the view that every person does in fact seek personal pleasure in life. The only motive that is effective in conduct is the desire to get pleasure and avoid pain.

2. *Ethical hedonism* does not claim that we do always seek to gain pleasure and avoid pain, but that we ought to do so. We should choose our actions so as to bring about the most happiness or the least unhappiness as possible. The pleasure principle is not one among many competing moral principles; it is itself the most important human value.

3. *Egoistic hedonism* refers to those who accept pleasure as a standard of enlightened self-interest based on the pleasure-pain criterion. Thus, if there is a conflict between ourselves and others, our sole duty is to ourselves.

4. *Altruistic hedonism* seeks the greatest happiness for the greatest number and stresses a community ethic that may or may not be based on self-interest.

SOURCES

Clark, John, ed. *The Students Seek an Answer.* Waterville, ME: Colby College Press. 1960.

Gouinlock, James, ed. *The Moral Writings of John Dewey.* Amherst, MA: Prometheus. 1994.

Jones, H. M. *The Pursuit of Happiness.* Ithaca, NY: Cornell University Press. 1953.

HARLEM RENAISSANCE

During the 1920s, black literature began to flourish in Harlem, a district of New York City. This movement is known by two names: the *Harlem Renaissance* and the *New Negro*, the latter after the title of an anthology collected by educator and writer Alain Locke. The major writers of the Harlem Renaissance were James Weldon Johnson,

Claude McKay, Langston Hughes, Sterling Brown, Countee Cullen, Jean Toomer, Zora Neale Hurston, and Alain Locke.

Johnson's *God's Trombones* (1927) has inspired many ministers and lay persons, as he set seven black sermons in verse. The dramatic and musical qualities of his poetry reflect his experience writing songs for the musical theater. McKay wrote powerful poems in dialect and later, highly formal but emotional verse on explosive topics. We find in Hughes, Cullen, and Brown not only the dialect and rhythmic tones found in black music and poetry, but an expression of pride in their distinctive cultural traditions and a protest against discrimination and other racist practices.

Many black prose writers grew to prominence and flourished during the Harlem Renaissance. Toomer's *Care* (1923) provides a sophisticated mixture of short stories, sketches, poetry, and a play. Hurston collected black folktales and became known as a skillful storyteller. Her best-known novel, *Their Eyes Were Watching God* (1937), traces a black woman's steady growth in insight and spiritual strength. Her characters come alive with strength, vitality, and even weakness.

SOURCES

Rigden, Diana W., and Susan S. Waugh, eds. *The Shape of This Century: Readings from the Disciplines*. New York: Harcourt Brace Jovanovich. 1990.

Watson, Steven. *The Harlem Renaissance*. New York: Pantheon. 1995.

HATE

Hate is normally defined as a strong dislike for a person, suggesting hostility and the desire to hurt or harm him or her. Because morals are the application of principles of truth, honesty, equality, and fairness to individuals based on a belief in the worth of persons, the attitudes and resultant behaviors flowing from hate have a negative impact on actualizing the moral ideal. The worth of persons further accentuates their dignity and compels us to respect who and what they are. These values are also tied to a reverence for life; the right and the good. Evil is that which denies the good, or impairs or destroys persons or human welfare. As such, hate is a corollary of evil and a basic immoral attitude.

SOURCES

Adler, Mortimer J. *Six Great Ideas*. New York: Collier. 1981.

Margolis, Joseph. *Values and Conduct*. New York: Oxford University Press. 1971.

HEAVEN

It is hazardous to draw conclusions about who influenced whom and what impact one culture has had on another, but the Jewish people came to know Zoroastrianism from observations near at hand in Babylon in the seventh and sixth centuries B.C., and certain Persian beliefs about Satan, angels, the afterlife, and the messianic deliverance supplied what must have been missing elements in older Jewish beliefs. Before they met the Satan of Zoroastrianism, the Jewish people had thought about the old stories involving the serpent in the Garden of Eden and the fallen angels who had taken wives from among the daughters of men before Noah.

There was also an Adversary among the heavenly beings surrounding Yahweh who obtained permission to afflict Job and make him curse God. These stories antedated the exile, and in some of them there is the suggestion that the Spirit of Evil is a cosmic being, manifested from the beginning of time, and of a strength and creative power almost equal to that of the Spirit of Good (God). But after the exile the Adversary among the heavenly beings became an evil and malicious power, wholly in opposition to God, with attendant devils to match the angels who stood before God himself. She'ol, the shadowy land of the dead, was replaced by a heaven or paradise and a hell, and some Jewish people began also to speak of a resurrection from the dead at the last day of judgment, a final reward of the good and condemnation of the evil.

From the coming of the Romans in 40 B.C. to the time of the destruction of Jerusalem in A.D. 70, the messianic expectation increased its hold on thousands of suffering Jews. The ardent hope of a supernatural deliverance from their pain and suffering and everlasting life in heaven—a life of perfection—was fed by apocalyptic literature. The central belief was that divine intervention would bring about a radical change in the world order. Through his Messiah, God was going to gather together "his own," both living and dead, and live with them in blessedness (heaven) forever.

THE IDEA OF "HEAVEN" IN OTHER RELIGIONS

The Teutons, who were of somewhat purer Indo-European stock and appeared in time later than the Celts, began to press westward from the southern shores of the Baltic as Anglo-Saxons and Jutes; southward as Saxons, Alamanni, Lombards, Frisians, and Franks; northward as Scandinavians; and southeastward as Goths and Vandals. Teutonic tradition comes from two Icelandic works, the *Poetic Edda,* an anthology of hymns to the gods and heroic poems, said to have been assembled by Saemundr the Wise (A.D. 1056–1133); and the *Prose Edda,* the work of Snorri Sturleson, a thirteenth-century Christian scholar who tried to provide a practical guide for young poets who would wish to draw upon the traditional myths of Iceland for their material.

From these sources we get a rather crowded picture of a score of gods and goddesses—gods of law and war—traveling through the heavens and visiting the wider world. For example, Odin was popular with the common people as one who would protect them. In heaven he surveyed the world from the windows of his home. Other Teutonic gods represented fertility, death, and the end of the world, important watersheds or periods of crisis and emergency in human life. They were believed to rule over man and his world.

Hinduism also contains ideas about heaven. Above all other gods, morally speaking, stood the deity Varuna, originally the god of the high-arched sky, who was assigned the function of directing the natural forces in order to create natural and moral orderliness. Here lay the domain of natural laws and the force of keeping humans obedient to the moral law. Varuna was the discloser of sin and the judge of truth and falsehood. It was natural that Varuna would be associated with Mitra, the god of loyalty, honor, and promise keeping; and also with the mysterious abstract principle called *Rita,* the indwelling principle in everything in the universe that shows regularity and order of action.

Out of the complex matrix of early Hinduism came two religions with alternate answers to the central problems of life: how to find release from karma and the ever-lengthening round of rebirths entailed by it. One of them, Jainism, was destined to win adherents in India only. The other, Buddhism, spread throughout India and Southeast Asia.

The philosophy of Jainism followed a distinct philosophical and ethical course in which the doctrine of karma is interpreted strictly: the consequences of one's deeds are literally deposited in and on the soul. The soul's chief problem is ridding itself of karma-matter, and the ethical activity of the soul annihilates the old karmas more swiftly. From Jainism emerges an inherent duality: soul and flesh, mind and matter. All things were divided into two categories: (1) the *jiva,* or living beings in the universe, to be defined more precisely as the infinite multitude of individual souls composing the real life of the spirit; and (2) the *ajiva*, or lifeless things in the universe, especially the realm of dead matter. The *jiva* are eternal and are of infinite value. They contain all good, for souls are indestructible and infinitely precious. In their pure state, when liberated from matter, all souls are perfect, possessing infinite perception, knowledge, power, and bliss. When liberated they rise through the universe and come to live in an umbrella-like place—"the home of the perfect ones."

In Buddhism, especially in the Mahayana schools of thought in China and Japan, we find differing views of heaven: (1) In the Pure Land school the motive is one that appeals to the commoner, that of getting to heaven. The chief interest and ultimate goal of Pure Land Buddhists is the Western Paradise of Amitabha Buddha. (2) In the meditative schools of Ch'an and Zen, the goals change. In the Ch'an school the goal is immediate insight and enlightenment. The method of salvation is meditation, but through insight or awakening. Zen is primarily an attempt to experience the unitary character of reality: "I" and "Not-I" are one; both are aspects of Buddha-reality. This becomes clear when one "sees into one's own nature," in a moment of "awakening" or *satori*. Both the Taoists of China and Zen Buddhists of Japan agree that to contemplate nature is to pass into the True *(Tatha)*, the void; but this is misleading, for Nature is "nothing but one's own true mind," and therefore the Void is within. Truth is therefore to be found in the heart—the wisdom that has gone beyond, to the beyond that is also within.

SOURCES

Bouquet, A. C., ed. *Sacred Books of the World.* Baltimore: Penguin. 1967.

Champion, Selwyn Gurney, and Dorothy Short, eds. *Readings from World Religions.* Greenwich, CT: Fawcett. 1951.

Ch'en, Kenneth K. S. *Buddhism: The Light of Asia.* Woodbury, NY: Barron's Educational Series. 1968.

Noss, David S., and John B. Noss. *Man's Religions.* 7th ed. New York: Macmillan. 1984.

HINDUISM, ETHICS OF

The history of Hinduism represents an originality and diversity of thought as rich and complex as Judaism or Christianity in Western civilization. It would be quite impossible in this space to give due consideration to the astonishing variety and amount of literature, opinion, and range of disagreement that has accompanied the unfolding of this religion. Few Hindu doctrines have ever stood for long without being challenged. This is true even of the essentials of Hinduism—that the beliefs outlined in the Vedas and Upanishads, properly interpreted, are true, and that the caste system represents what is right and just according to the law of karma.

During the past 100 years, reactions to Western religion and science and resultant social reforms have changed not only the intellectual outlook of Hindus, but initiated changes in the caste system and marriage laws, regulations that from the start have constituted major sources of social and religious difficulty. Informed by other cultures, Hinduism has witnessed one attempt after another, by persons who have gained fresh insight, to get around untouchability and other restrictions imposed by the caste system, or to get rid of the caste system altogether. Jainism and Buddhism are the best examples of this attempt to deal with caste by saying "Come ye from among them." Some tried to form new sects in which all beliefs were equal in the sight of God no matter what their previous caste affiliations. But because they could not marry outside the sect, the new sect became in time just another caste. The best example of these castes are the Shiva-worshipping Lingayats of Bombay and southern India and the Baishtams of Bengal.

A second type of assault on the caste system sought its reform from within. Motivated by high social idealism, directly or indirectly influenced by Christianity and studies of Western social organizations, leaders should, as Mahatma Gandhi believed, let occupations be hereditary but drop all other caste restrictions. Especially, untouchability should be abolished. Late in 1948, Hindu India's Constituent Assembly abolished untouchability and forbade its practice in any form.

From Jawaharlal Nehru to his daughter, Indira Gandhi, change has come slowly to Hindu India. Sarvepalli Radhakrishman, late president of India, defended Hinduism against criticism that it is "nonethical." He emphasized the moral growth that is necessary preparation for mystic union with the ultimately real, and by pointing to the duty of applying the spiritual lessons of religion in social and political activity.

SOURCES

Kessler, Gary E., ed. *Voices of Wisdom: A Multicultural Philosophy Reader.* Belmont, CA: Wadsworth. 1992.

Radhakrishman, S., and Charles Moore, eds. *Source Book in Indian Philosophy.* Princeton, NJ: Princeton University Press. 1957.

HIPPOCRATIC OATH

Hippocrates (460?–377? B.C.) is thought of as the father of modern medicine. His principles of medical science and ethics laid down 2,400 years ago formed the basis for the medical theory as well as medical practice developed in the 1800s. The Hippocratic Oath, named for him, gave the medical profession a sense of duty to mankind, which some have come to question in the modern era of rising costs and medical malpractice. In a time when superstition ruled men's minds, Hippocrates believed only in the facts. He noted, "Life is short and the art long; the occasion fleeting; experiment dangerous, and judgment difficult." He thought that men could find out the laws of nature by studying facts and reasoning from them; therefore, he applied logic and research to medicine, which made the practice of medicine workable.

Physician's Oath

I swear by Apollo Physician, by Asclepiades, by Health, by Panacea, and all the gods and goddesses, making them my witnesses, that according to my ability and judgment I will carry out this oath. . . .

To hold my teacher in this art equal to my own parents; to make him partner in my livelihood; when he is in need of money to share mine with him; to consider his family as my own brothers, and to teach them this art, if they want to learn it, without fee of indenture. . . .

I will give no deadly medicine to anyone if asked, nor suggest any such counsel. . . . I will use treatment to help the sick according to my ability and judgment but never with a view of injury or wrong doing. . . . I will keep pure and holy both my life and my art. . . .

Into whatever houses I enter I will go into them for the benefit of the sick, and will abstain from every voluntary act of mischief or corruption, further, from the seduction of females and males, of freemen and slaves. . . .

Whatever, in connection with my professional practice, or not in connection with it, I see or hear, in the life of men, which ought not to be spoken of abroad, I will not divulge, as believing that all such should be kept secret....

The *Encyclopaedia Britannica* (11th ed., vol. XIII, p. 518) adds skeptically, "Perhaps also the Oath may be accepted as genuine." Hippocrates, it states, "was the first to dissociate medicine from priesthood." In several translations there is also included the line: "I will not give to any woman the instrument to procure abortion."

SOURCES

Hall, Thomas S. *Ideas of Life and Matter, Studies in the History of General Physiology 600 B.C. to*

1900 A.D. Vols. 1–3. Chicago: The University of Chicago Press. 1969.

Thilly, Frank, and Ledger Wood. *A History of Philosophy.* New York: Henry Holt. 1959.

HOLOCAUST

The injustices to the Jewish people have continued for centuries, but not all non-Jewish people are anti-Semitic. At certain times and in particular places anti-Semitism was an official government policy, and in other situations it was the product of a few bigoted individuals and sporadically emerged for brief periods as a mass movement. By 1870, most legal restrictions aimed at the Jewish people had been abolished in Western Europe. Since then, however, the Jewish people have been used as scapegoats by opportunists who blamed them for every misfortune befalling a nation. The most tragic example is that of Adolf Hitler, whose "final solution" to Germany's problems led to the Holocaust—the extermination of 6 million Jewish civilians during the 1930s and 1940s. During World War II, two-thirds of Europe's Jewish population was killed, and in Poland, Germany, and Austria, the proportion killed reached 90 percent.

See also Genocide; Racism.

SOURCES

Dawiclowicz, L. S. *The Golden Tradition: Jewish Life and Thought in Eastern Europe.* New York: Holt, Rinehart and Winston. 1967.

———. *The War Against the Jews.* New York: Holt, Rinehart and Winston. 1975.

Hertzler, J. O. "The Sociology of Anti-Semitism Through History." In Isacque G. Raeber, ed. *Jews in a Gentile World.* New York: Macmillan. 1942.

HONESTY

Morally right conduct is characterized by honesty—fair dealing, reasonable self-control, and personal honesty. Honesty is a moral behavior because it is an action that is favorable to the welfare of persons and groups of persons; it is community producing. In a society there are advantages to having a reputation for honesty. For people to be impressed by one's honesty, the person must either be honest all the time or be honest in some very conspicuous, highly dramatic fashion, such as telling the truth even when it costs or when it hurts. No one likes a dishonest person—even the dishonest person prefers that everyone else be honest—because no one likes to be hurt or taken advantage of. Expressing genuine indignation at an injustice and acting to right the situation at considerable cost to self are not merely ways we signal to others our sense of duty or enculturated honesty; they are ways by which we live.

See also Ethics, Theory of.

SOURCES

Shaffer, Carolyn R., and Kristin Anundsen. *Creating Community Anywhere.* New York: Putnam. 1993.

Wilson, James Q. *The Moral Sense.* New York: Free Press. 1993.

HONOR

Honor usually means credit given for acting well, for sticking to actions that are right and just, and for respecting the welfare of others. Honor cannot be understood by referring to duty and obligation only. Duty is honoring an obligation to behave in a certain way, even under duress. Prisoners of war who resist becoming collaborators with the enemy or betraying their country show how much they honor or value their comrades and how little they value their captors. The capacity of people in the most extreme circumstances to express and act upon conceptions of duty and honor suggests deep social attachments to family, to friends, and to country. But what about normal, everyday cases such as keeping promises and fulfilling one's job responsibilities? In the absence of coercion, what happens to duty, honor, and obligation? Free riders usually feel little obligation to others. They break promises, cheat on their taxes, take shortcuts in their work, and so on. Those who give it their best, who are honest, who feel an obligation to employer and to country, and who have a sense of duty should be given credit for sticking to actions that are considered right and what is usual and expected—they should be honored for their actions.

See also Duty.

SOURCES

Fine, Melinda. *Habits of Mind: Struggling over Values in America's Classrooms.* San Francisco: Josey-Bass. 1995.

Nozick, Robert. *The Examined Life: Philosophical Meditations.* New York: Simon & Schuster. 1989.

Peck, M. Scott. *The Road Less Traveled.* New York: Simon & Schuster. 1978.

HUMANISM

Humanism is a life-affirming philosophy that emphasizes a life devoted to one's own improvement and the service of all mankind. Corliss Lamont begins his *Philosophy of Humanism* (1949) with a reference to Francis Bacon's *Novum Organum*, which "urged men to depart from scholasticism and 'pursue science in order that the human estate may be enhanced'." Scientific humanism, as Lamont refers to this philosophy, moves away from supernaturalism to naturalism, from concern with the next world to the life of this world, from revelation and magic to science and reason.

This "new" synthesis is called both evolutionary and naturalistic humanism. It has several characteristics: (1) it builds on the scientific spirit and method; (2) it accepts the ethical ideal of concern for all people; (3) it embraces the democratic view of the worth of the individual; and (4) it seeks the welfare of all humanity. This principle has taken many forms:

NATURALISTIC HUMANISM

Naturalistic humanism is basically a "this-wordly" movement that proceeds from the assumption "that man is on his own and this life is all and that we are responsible for our own life and the life of mankind as well." Naturalistic or philosophic humanism's major theme is self-determination, for persons, for groups and societies, for mankind together, and a rejection of responsibility to "God" or any "higher" authority. This is also sometimes called "literary humanism" and "scientific humanism." It draws its strength from the European rediscovery of Greek and Latin literature during the Renaissance and the beginnings of rationalism and science with Galileo, Descartes, and Newton. More recent versions of naturalistic humanism are found among existentialists represented by Sartre and Marcel, and anthropologists led by Sir Julian Huxley. H. J. Blackham comments: "Assumption-responsibility-response: these three natural roots of humanism involve the three sides of human nature usually spoken of as intellect, will, and feeling. All three sides are equally important to humanists as to others. But the humanist is a rationalist, who puts reason first; and he stresses the open mind, dedication to a disinterested search for truth."

RELIGIOUS HUMANISM

Religious humanism proceeds from the assumption that God exists and accepts the myths, rituals, and symbols traditionally associated with the Christian Church to support their practice of the "humanist's" ethical life. Blackham, in his analysis of humanism, says: "The humanist who chooses to call himself a Christian and practice the Christian way of life without the Christian faith is an extreme case, but the name 'Christian humanist' has meaning in [that it] gives full value to human life in this world and allows it a relative autonomy, and who does so because in his belief it is God's world and a God-given autonomy. The contrast is with a fundamentalist preoccupation with salvation or with an other-worldly force of interest."

ETHICAL CULTURE SOCIETIES

Ethical culture societies are very close to religious humanists in their worldview and ethics. They consider themselves religious fellowships, and several adherents of these societies were signatories of the "Humanist Manifesto." The oldest and strongest of the ethical societies is the Society for Ethical Culture of New York City, founded in 1876 by Dr. Felix Adler, a teacher of philosophy at Columbia University. The society is "dedicated to the ever-increasing knowledge and practice and love of the right." Its purpose, like the many other ethical societies and fellowship groups making up the American Ethical Union, is "To assert the supreme importance of the ethical factor in all relations of life—personal, social, national, and international—apart from any theological or metaphysical considerations."

SOURCES

Blackham, H. J. *Humanism*. Baltimore: Penguin. 1968.

Lamont, Corliss. *The Philosophy of Humanism*. New York: Frederick Ungar. 1971.

I

IDEALISM

Idealism is the position that the mind is not simply an instrument of perception and understanding, but the entire range of human conscience. If we cannot know without a mind, then who is to say we know anything except that mind? The extreme idealist position is that if there is a world beyond mind it is unreachable. All idealists insist on the permanent significance and reality of the mind. No one embodies the classical position of the moral idealist more than Johann Gottlieb Fichte (1762–1814). Fichte's moral system begins with Immanuel Kant's moral imperative and ends with an emphasis on the universal moral purposes of God. The idealistic tradition is one made famous by Plato's dualism—the reality of the material and nonmaterial worlds—because for Plato the most "real" type of reality is the nonmaterial. One hundred years before Fichte, Baruch Spinoza (1634–1677), the Dutch-born Jewish philosopher, in the idealistic tradition, accepted René Descartes's idea that "in truth, there can be but one substance which is absolutely independent, and that is God;" but he also equated infinite substance with Nature. The equation "Nature=God" makes Spinoza a pantheist.

Like Spinoza, and in the tradition of Plato and among the Continental rational-ists, Fichte's idea of moral law is connected to and embodied in reason and in the infinite, perfect substance: God. The law commands freedom from the objective, scientific world. Like other idealists, Fichte comes to his position through reason rather than the senses or pure intuition. Using reason, he says that the moral law implies freedom, freedom implies overcoming obstacles, and this implies a sensible world and a life of struggle. For Fichte, it also meant that there must be a universal purpose or a God. This is the essence of his idealism. It is God who provides a moral order to the universe that lies beyond our sensory knowledge that gives meaning to human life. For Fichte, morality and religion are synonymous; our role is to discover and do God's duty, to work for the realization of the highest good, to work toward the universal moral end.

We can compare and contrast Plato's theory of knowledge with that of Descartes by looking at their models of reality: how they compartmentalized and prioritized the various kinds of knowledge from their own assumptions (see charts on page 216).

For Plato and Descartes, the most real tier of knowledge/reality is the nonmaterial, where we discover the essence of their idealism (see Donald Palmer's *Looking At Philosophy*, Mountain View, CA: Mayfield Publishing Company, 1988).

From Fichte we can easily understand the trail of German idealism as it moved through Schleiermacher, Humboldt, and

PLATO'S "SIMILE OF THE LINE"

Knowledge	Pure Reason Understanding	The Forms Concepts	The Intelligible World
Opinion	Belief Conjecture	Particular Objects Images	The Visible World

Knowledge   *Existence*

Hegel. The *ideal* in idealism was to construct a System; it was a project of totalization through which unity would be restored to learning, which had settled into separate sciences and departments. The System would become a rational narration, a universal "history" of the spirit and the mind. Thus, German idealism finds comfort in the principle called *divine life* by Fichte and *life of the Spirit* by Hegel. In idealism, knowledge becomes speculative and true knowledge is always indirect, composed of reported statements and assumptions rather than inductive and factual propositions. Humans, according to this idealism, are both historical and spiritual, and our historic mission is to realize the true world of the spirit. Upon careful study and reflection, one can see in post-

moderism a hint of idealism, especially in Jurgen Habermas—but there is a difference. As William Mark Hohengarten says of Habermas, "He thus defends the view that genuinely postmetaphysical thinking can remain critical only if it preserves the idea of reason derived from the tradition while stripping it of its metaphysical trappings. In order to steer between the twin dangers of a nostalgic return to or a radical critique of metaphysics, we must transform our inherited conceptions of reason and the rational subject." He comments that Habermas "contributes to this task by further developing his intersubjectivistic approaches to meaning and validity and, especially, to subjectivity and individuality." To understand the trail from the Enlightenment to postmodernism, one must

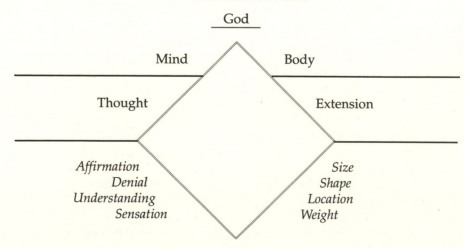

DESCARTES'S SYSTEM

God

Mind   Body

Thought   Extension

Affirmation   *Size*
Denial   *Shape*
Understanding   *Location*
Sensation   *Weight*

travel the course through nineteenth-century idealism and its earlier roots in Fichte and Spinoza.

SOURCES

Habermas, Jurgen. *Postmetaphysical Thinking: Philosophical Essays*. Translated by William Mark Hohengarten. Cambridge, MA: MIT Press. 1992.

Lyotard, Jean-Francois. *The Post Modern Explained*. Translated from the French by Don Berry, Bernadette Maher, Julian Pefanis, Virginia Spate, and Morgan Thomas. Minneapolis: University of Minnesota Press. 1992.

———. *The Postmodern Condition: A Report on Knowledge*. Translated from the French by Geoff Bennington and Brian Massumi. Minneapolis: University of Minnesota Press. 1993.

IMMIGRATION

The legacy of immigration in America is the rich and full diversity of the ethnic and racial backgrounds of its population. Most people in the United States today, with the exception of Native Americans and Africans, brought to this country enslaved, are the product of those who chose to leave their homes (emigrate) and come to a new country. Oscar Handlin has written, "Once I thought to write a history of the immigrants in America. Then I discovered that the immigrants were American history."

The causes of emigration include financial failure in their home country, perceived higher standards of living in the new homeland, dislike of the present government leadership, racial or religious bigotry, and the desire to reunite families. All these factors push individuals from their homeland and pull them to other nations such as the United States. Except during the 1930s and 1940s, when immigration was tightened in the United States, the country has been open to a sizable flow of immigrants, especially during the nineteenth century when immigration was mostly unregulated and naturalization was easily available.

In the early years of the country, immigration was encouraged. The nation needed population and fixed the residence requirement for naturalization at five years. Briefly the Alien Land Act (1913, 1920) in California slowed immigration, but this was repealed by the Supreme Court of California in 1952. Immigration has always been controversial in the United States. The absence of federal legislation from 1790 to 1881 does not mean that all new arrivals were welcomed. *Xenophobia* (fear of strangers) led naturally to *nativism* (beliefs and policies favoring native-born citizens over immigrants). Roman Catholics, especially the Irish, were among the first Europeans to be ill treated. Anti-Catholic feelings originated in Europe and were brought by the early Protestant immigrants. The Catholics of colonial America were subject to limits on civil and religious rights. Even Samuel Morse, inventor of the telegraph, wrote a strongly worded anti-Catholic treatise in 1834 entitled "A Foreign Conspiracy against the Liberties of the United States." Originally directed against the Irish, it warned that the pope planned to move the Vatican to the Mississippi River Valley. Even poet Ralph Waldo Emerson wrote of "the wild Irish . . . who sympathized . . . with despotism." From 1834, antagonism, harsh words, and mob violence characterized the treatment of Catholics in the United States.

Nothing typifies the American attitude toward non-European immigrants more than the dealings of the United States with China. From 1831 to 1881, more than 200,000 Chinese immigrated to America, lured by the discovery of gold and the opening of job opportunities. Overcrowding, drought, and warfare in China encouraged many citizens to take a chance in the United States. During the 1860s, railroad work provided the greatest demand for Chinese labor. Ninety percent of the Central Pacific labor force was Chinese, but these workers were physically prevented from witnessing the driving of the "golden spike" at Promontory, Utah, in 1869.

The anti-Chinese movement was dualistic, involving legislators restricting the rights of Chinese immigrants and citizens using violence against them. Americans found their customs and religion difficult to understand, and *sinophobia* (the fear of anything associated with China) began appealing to the latent racism of many left over from slavery days. Americans were beginning to be more conscious of biological inheritance and disease, and so it was not hard to come up with a fear of alien genes and germs. The fear of the "Yellow Peril" overwhelmed any desire to know more about Oriental people and their customs.

In 1882, Congress enacted the Chinese Exclusion Act, which prevented Chinese immigration for ten years. No allowance was made for spouses and children to be reunited with their husbands and fathers in the United States. Only Chinese government officials, teachers, tourists, and merchants were exempted. The balance of the nineteenth century saw the remaining loopholes to Chinese immigration closed. Two years later the Statue of Liberty was dedicated. The poem inscribed on its base welcoming "your tired, your poor, your huddled masses," must have seemed a hollow mockery to the Chinese. In 1892, Congress extended the Exclusion Act for another decade and added that Chinese laborers had to obtain certificates of residence within a year or be forcibly deported.

For four years the U.S. Immigration Commission, known as the Dillingham Commission, studied the effects of immigration. The findings, presented in 1911 in 41 volumes, were preordained by the commission's assumptions about types of immigrants. The two types were the "old" immigrants, mostly Anglo-Saxons, who were characterized as hard-working pioneers, and the "new" immigrants from southwestern Europe, who were branded as opportunists. Not surprisingly, the pres-sure for a more restrictive immigration policy resulted in a literacy test, the result of hostility against "new" immigrants that was passed by Congress in 1917. The act also prohibited immigration from parts of Asia and the South Sea Islands.

THE NATIONAL ORIGINS SYSTEM

Beginning in 1921, a series of measures marked a new era in U.S. immigration policy. The isolationists' policies after World War I, fueled by anti-immigration sentiments, caused Congress to restrict entry privileges severely, not just for the Chinese and Japanese, but for Europeans as well. The national origins system was begun in 1921 and remained the basis of immigration policy until 1968. This system used the country of birth to determine whether an person could enter as a legal alien, and the numbers of previous immigrants and their descendants were used to set the quota of how many individuals from a country could enter annually. In 1929, the permanent system went into effect, based on the 1920 census. This quota system was deliberately weighted in favor of immigration from northern Europe, which continued unrestricted. With statistical manipulation, 70 percent of the quota for the Eastern Hemisphere went to Great Britain, Ireland, and Germany.

With World War I, the economic depression of the 1930s, and then World War II, Atlantic immigration was almost ended. The Immigration and Nationality Act of 1952 retained the quota system with minor changes: Japanese were for the first time allowed to become citizens and families were able to reunite. Also significant, following the Immigration Reform and Control Act of 1986, communists and so-called subversives were barred entry to the United States.

THE 1965 IMMIGRATION AND NATURALIZATION ACT

The National Origins System was abandoned with the 1965 Immigration and Naturalization Act, signed into law by

President Lyndon B. Johnson at the foot of the Statue of Liberty. The primary goals of the act were reuniting families and protecting the U.S. labor market. Hemispheric quotas replaced nationality quotas. The Western Hemisphere was limited to 120,000 entrance visas annually; an additional 170,000 visas were allocated to the rest of the world. About three-fourths of these were reserved for dependents of U.S. citizens and resident aliens. Any remaining visas went to individuals and their families who possessed job skills needed in the United States.

There have been four continuing criticisms of the immigration policy during the past 30 years: (1) *Brain drain* refers to the immigration to the United States of skilled workers, professionals, and technicians who are desperately needed by their home countries. Conflict theorists see the current brain drain as yet another symptom of the unequal distribution of world resources. (2) With the birthrate in the United States near zero, the contribution of immigration to population growth has become more significant. Legal immigration accounted for 20 percent of the nation's growth during the 1970s, and 30 percent by 1981. (3) Illegal immigration is the most bitterly debated aspect of U.S. immigration policy. These immigrants and their families come to the United States in search of higher paying jobs than are available in their home countries. In 1986, the Census Bureau estimated that 4.7 million illegal aliens were in the United States, with the number growing by 200,000 per year. The number today is closer to 12 million, and the situation has become a political issue. Nearly half the aliens reside in California, with Texas, Illinois, New York, and Florida accounting for most of the rest. Some 95 percent of "deportable aliens" are persons crossing the United States–Mexico border. An estimated 50 to 60 percent of illegal aliens are Mexicans and a sizable proportion of the remainder were born in other Latin American countries. Since the Immigration Reform and Control Act of 1986, hiring illegal aliens in the United States is illegal, a fact that has ruined several political appointees of the U.S. president. This marks a historic change and values shift in immigration policy. The act also extended legal status to illegal aliens who entered the United States before January 1, 1982, and have lived here continuously since. The 1986 plan to deal with a complex problem was a compromise. It provided monies for local governments to supply increased public assistance, health care, and education to the millions of newly legal immigrants. In signing the Immigration Reform and Control Act, President Ronald Reagan hailed it as "the most comprehensive reform of our immigration laws since 1952." (4) Finally, the plight of refugees has become a hotly debated topic in U.S. politics. Since World War II and the advent of the Cold War, the United States has allowed three groups of refugees to enter in numbers greater than regulations would routinely allow: Hungarians, Cubans, and Indochinese. Despite periodic public opposition, the U.S. government has officially committed itself to accepting refugees from other nations. According to the United Nations treaty on refugees, which the government ratified in 1968, countries are obliged to refrain from forcibly returning people to territories where their lives or liberties might be endangered. About 23 percent of people who apply for political asylum receive it.

A symbol of the frustration surrounding refugees is the growing Sanctuary Movement. Begun in 1982, a loosely connected organization offers asylum, often in churches, to those seeking refugee status but who are classified as illegal aliens. *Asylees* are persons who fear persecution if forced to return to their homeland, but unlike refugees they are already in the United States. This category was created by the Refugee Act of 1980. The Sanctuary Movement has concentrated on immigrants from Central America, Haiti, and Cuba. The influx of Cubans into south Florida since 1960 has caused many difficulties, essentially changing the ethnic makeup of that region. Bilingualism in the workplace and the "Latinization" of many housing areas are emotional issues to many who are native to that area.

What about the future? What will be the effect of continual immigration? Projections show the Hispanic population of the United States increasing dramatically in the next 100 years. By 2080 it is estimated that Hispanics will outnumber blacks and will account for 23 percent of the nation's population. The Asian population will also increase, perhaps to as much as 12 percent of the population. Because of population shifts, the proportion of white, non-Hispanic Americans will decrease significantly. By 2080, the combined black, Hispanic, and Asian populations in the United States may be approximately equal to the number of whites. This suggests that the United States of 2080 will be a vastly different society than that of today.

SOURCES

Boswell, T. D., and J. R. Curtis. *The Cuban-American Experience.* Totowa, NJ: Rowman and Allanheld. 1984.

Kennedy, John F. *A Nation of Immigrants.* New York: Harper & Row. 1964.

Schaefer, Richard T. *Racial and Ethnic Groups.* 3d ed. Boston: Scott, Foresman and Co. 1988.

Periodicals: *Center for Migration Studies; International Migration Review; Migration Today; The Journal of Refugee Resettlement; Refugee Reports.*

INALIENABLE RIGHTS

In 1776, the Declaration of Independence did not simply rehash traditional politics; rather, in justifying separation from England, it appealed to "self-evident" truths and the "unalienable rights" of "all men"— rights that cannot be taken or given away. Here we have the revolutionary premises: Jefferson explained that the principles of revolution did not lurk in the mysteries of constitutional law and were not obscure or scholarly. He said they were "intuitive," within the capacity of most people, and they legitimated bold acts in defense of "life, liberty, and the pursuit of happiness." These "rights" did not exist in American society in 1776. Of course, Jefferson's statement never claimed to be descriptive of social conditions in America. He was merely asserting the fundamental principles that justified political revolution. Governments, he declared, derive their power "from the consent of the governed," and when governments threaten the basic rights of the people—those that cannot be taken or given away—"it is the right of the people to alter or to abolish it." In 1776, those rights validated the destruction of monarchy and the institution of the republican form of government, and not just in America alone, but some years later in France as well. For Jefferson, inalienable rights possessed a universal quality that "in the course of human events" justified other revolutions throughout the world. These powerful ideas, alarming as they were in 1776 to monarchs throughout the world, were the colonists' legacy to those who would come after them.

See also Ethics, Theory of.

SOURCES

Dworkin, Ronald. *Taking Rights Seriously.* Cambridge, MA: Harvard University Press. 1978.

Schwartz, Bernard, ed. *The Roots of the Bill of Rights.* Vols. 1–5. New York: Chelsea House. 1971.

Thomson, Judith Jarvis. *Rights, Restitution, and Risk.* Cambridge, MA: Harvard University Press. 1986.

ISLAM, MORAL CODE OF

The teaching of Muhammad became after his death the basis of faith *(iman)* and practice—right conduct or duty—(din) of Islam. Ultimately, Muslim authorities added a third pillar to their religion: religious duty, or *ibadat*. Faith and good conduct were set forth in the Qur'an (Koran); religious duty came later.

ARTICLES OF FAITH

One cannot fully understand the moral code of Islam without knowledge of the Islamic faith. In the famous Muslim creedal formula, the first part reads, "There is no god but God." No statement in Muslim theology is more fundamental than the declaration that *God is One*, and no sin seemed to Him as unpardonable as associating another being with God on terms of equality. God stands alone and supreme. God existed before any other being or thing, is self-subsistent, omniscient, and omnipotent. This is the foundation of morality in Islam because God is the creator, and in the awful day of judgment He is the sole arbiter who shall save the believer from the dissolution of the world and place him in paradise.

In reference to God's "guidance," the Qur'an is varied, opening to differing interpretations. Does God "guide" men by challenging them to choose freely between right and wrong conduct, or by determining their choices in advance? Some passages imply free will: "Say: 'The truth is from your Lord; so let whosoever will believe, and let whosoever will disbelieve'"; or, "If you do good, it is your own souls you do good to;" and, "Whoever does evil, or wrongs himself, and then prays God's forgiveness, he shall find God all-forgiving, all-compassionate."

But many other passages say God not only has perfect foreknowledge of man's actions, but controls human choices as well: "Very well He knows you, when He produced you from the earth, and when you were yet unborn in your mother's womb;" and "whosoever God will, He leads astray, and whomsoever He will, He sets him on a straight path;" and God declares: "We elected them, and We guided them to a straight path."

Two additional articles of faith are essential to Muslims and fundamental to Islamic moral codes. The first is that "Muhammad is the messenger (or prophet) of Allah." Muhammad is the last and greatest of the prophets, including Jesus—man at his best—and God is still the Wholly Other. With Him Muhammad was united in will but not in substance. The second is that the Qur'an is the undistorted and final word of Allah (God) to mankind.

RIGHT CONDUCT

The Qur'an has supplied Muslims with such comprehensive guidance for everyday life that their schools of the law have been able to prescribe a wide range of acts for Muslims. These laws prohibit wine and gambling, as well as the regulations concerning the relations of sexes and granting a higher status to women. Consider the following passage: "It is not piety, that you turn your faces to the East and to the West. True piety is this: to believe in God, and the Last Day, the angels, the Book, and the Prophets, to give of one's substance, however, cherished, to kinsmen, and orphans, the needy, the traveller, beggars, and to ransom the slave, to perform the prayer, to pay the alms. And they who fulfil their covenant when they have engaged in a covenant, and endure with fortitude misfortune, hardship and peril, these are they who are true in their faith, these are the truly godfearing." And the passage continues at length to enumerate moral duties or right conduct toward parents, orphans, marriage, and in war.

RELIGIOUS DUTY

We come next to that part of Muslim religious practice that, except for the fact of the month of Ramadan, which is prescribed in the Qur'an, took some time to fix in tradition. It is summed up as the five pillars and, like "right conduct," is essential to defining Islamic morality. These pillars are the following:

1. Repetition of the creed, or *Shahada,* "There is no god but Allah, and Muhammad is the prophet of Allah." Accepting this confession of faith is the first step in becoming a Muslim.

2. Five acts of prayer, or *Salat,* is what the faithful Muslim reserves time for each day. The Muslim's Lord's Prayer or *Fatiha* reads: "Praise belongs to God, the Lord of all Being, the All-merciful, the All-compassionate, the Master of the Day of Doom. Thee only we serve, to Thee alone we pray for succour. Guide us in the straight path, the path of those whom Thou hast blessed, not of those against whom Thou art wrathful, nor of those who are astray."

3. Almsgiving, or *Sakat,* is a freewill offering of gifts to the poor, the needy, debtors, slaves, wayfarers, beggars, and various charities.

4. The fast during the sacred month of Ramadan, except for the sick and ailing or those on a journey; this fast is laid upon all as an obligation.

5. The pilgrimage, or *Hajj,* is a once-in-a-lifetime journey to Mecca that every Muslim is expected to make. The pilgrim should be in Mecca during the sacred month of *Dhu-al-hijja,* so as to join thousands of others in the annual mass observance of the circumambulation of the *ka'ba,* the lesser and greater pilgrimage, and the Great Feast.

The rapid spread of Islam confronted Muslims with other crucial and even more complex decisions concerning Muslim behavior. Outside of Arabia the injunctions of the Qur'an proved insufficient and inapplicable. The first step is to appeal to the *sunna*—the behavior—of Muhammad in Medina or to the *hadith* that reported his spoken decisions or judgments. If this doesn't work, the next step is to ask what the consensus of opinion of the Medina community was during Muhammad's time. Finally, if no information is available, analogies are to made from the principles embodied in the Qur'an or in Medinan precedents, and then applied or followed. The Muslims who take this way of solving their behavioral problems are called *Sunnis.* They do not distinguish between law and religion because Islam espouses a solid, religiously oriented ethical code. As Islam spread, four schools of Islamic law arose to interpret the theological and legal practices within the faith. These schools developed in Iraq, Medina, Baghdad, and Persia. They have given meaning to such moral concepts as justice, the public good, public advantage, and the relation of law and God.

SOURCES

Andrae, Tor. *Mohammed: The Man and His Faith.* Translated by Theophil Menzel. London: George Allen & Unwin. 1936.

Arberry, Arthur J. *The Koran Interpreted.* (Combined in one volume). New York: Macmillan. 1955.

Bell, R. *Introduction to the Qur'an.* Edinburgh: Edinburgh University Press. 1953.

Watt, W. M. *Islam and the Integration of Society.* London: Routledge & Kegan Paul. 1961.

JIM CROW

The term *Jim Crow* appears to have its origin in a dance tune, but by the 1890s it was synonymous with segregation and referred to the statutes that kept blacks in an inferior position. It was in the political sphere that Jim Crow exacted its price soonest. In 1898, in *Williams v. Mississippi*, the use of poll taxes, literacy tests, and residential requirements to discourage blacks from voting was declared constitutional. In Louisiana in that same year, 130,000 blacks were registered. Eight years later only 1,342 were registered to vote. These measures did not deprive all blacks of the vote, and so a final obstacle was erected. By the turn of the century, the South had a one-party system, making the primary the significant contest and the general election a mere rubber stamp. Beginning with South Carolina in 1896 and spreading to 12 other states within 20 years, statewide Democratic primaries were adopted, but the Democratic Party explicitly excluded blacks from voting; this was constitutional because the party was interpreted as a private organization free to define its membership. The white primary and Jim Crow brought a virtual end to the political gains made during Reconstruction.

See also Racism.

SOURCES

Lacy, Dan. *The White Uses of Blacks in America.* New York: McGraw-Hill. 1976.

Lewinson, Paul. *Race, Class, and Party: A History of Negro Suffrage and White Politics in the South.* New York: Universal Library. 1965.

Woodward, C. Vann. *American Counterpoint: Slavery and Racism in the North-South Dialogue.* Boston: Little, Brown. 1971.

———. *The Strange Career of Jim Crow.* New York: Oxford University Press. 1974.

JOHN BIRCH SOCIETY

The John Birch Society is a U.S. organization founded in 1958 by Robert Welch, a retired business executive, to "promote less government, more responsibility, and a better world." In the *Blue Book of the John Birch Society* (1961), Welch writes: "Our enemy is the Communists, and we do not intend to lose sight of that fact for a minute. We are fighting the Communists—nobody else." The society is named for John M. Birch, a Baptist missionary and World War II U.S. Army Air Forces officer who was shot by Chinese Communists in 1945 while serving as a U.S. intelligence officer in China. A monthly magazine, *American Opinion*, is published for the general public.

SOURCE

World Book Encyclopedia. Chicago: Field Enterprises Educational Corporation. 1993.

JUDAISM, ETHICS OF

One important theme dominates the course of Jewish history and religion: that a single, righteous God is at work in the social and natural order. Only morally and socially sensitive minds conceive of history in terms of a covenant relationship with a whole group of people or develop a group consciousness of such a God. The early Hebrews (or "wanderers"), and later Jews, were consistent and steady in their sociotheocratic interpretation of the God of history. Hebrew scriptures provide a theological and moral interpretation of history. This was a religious, not a secular history; the facts they cited and the traditions they invoked no longer have quite the value for us that they had for them because the narratives contain hidden meanings and significance that are time-relevant and that are still being unraveled today.

The Hebrew scriptures, known in the Christian world as the Old Testament, are regarded as "God's word" for both faith and practice. To the devout Jew, these writings are a revelation of the will of God not only to the Jews, but to all mankind. These verses form a sacred canon—which means they have been accepted as standard texts of the Jewish faith, have passed tests of their authenticity, and been pronounced inspired (although modern historical and textual scholarship differs with the ancients on many points of authenticity).

The Jewish religion and morality is based on the history of God's covenant with the Children of Israel, his deliverance of them from slavery—first from Egypt and then from Babylon—his giving them a "promised land," and the promise of a future Messiah who would deliver them finally into the hands of God in heaven. The high ethical code of this people is called the Ten Commandments (Exodus 20), although what has survived of this code is the elaborated form of later days, when it was finally the general conviction among Israelites that God (*Yahweh*) was not just Israel's god but the creator of the entire physical world, the maker of sky and earth and sea and all that they contain.

Another list of commandments, found in Exodus 34, is largely ritualistic in character. Scholars generally agree that it is an earlier list. It is very interestingly introduced in the following way:

> The Lord said to Moses, "Cut two stone tablets, and in the morning ascend Mount Sinai, and present yourself there to me on the top of the mountain. No one is to ascend with you, nor is anyone to be seen anywhere on the mountain, nor must the flocks and herds graze in front of that mountain." So Moses cut two stone tablets, and rising early next morning, he ascended Mount Sinai, as the Lord had commanded him, taking the two stone tablets in his hand. Then the Lord descended in a cloud, and took up a position with him there, while he called upon the name of the Lord. The Lord passed in front of him proclaiming, "The Lord, the Lord, a God compassionate and gracious, slow to anger, abounding in kindness and fidelity, showing kindness to the thousandth generation, forgiving iniquity, transgression, and sin, without leaving it unpunished however, but avenging the iniquity of fathers upon their children and grandchildren down to the third or even the fourth generation." Then Moses quickly bowed his head to the ground, and made obeisance.

This passage is followed by Yahweh's announcement that he wishes to make a compact or covenant with the Israelites in the following specific terms:

> You must not make any molten gods for yourselves. You must keep the festival of unleavened cakes, eating unleavened cakes for seven days, as I commanded you. . . . Whatever first opens the womb belongs to me, in the case of all your livestock that are male, the firstlings of oxen and sheep; a firstling ass, however, you may redeem with a sheep, but if you do not redeem it, you must break its neck; any first-born son of yours you may redeem. None may visit me empty-handed. Six days you are to labor, but on the seventh day you must rest, resting at ploughing-time and at harvest. You must observe the festival

of weeks, that of the first-fruits of the wheat harvest, and also the festival of ingathering at the turn of the year; three times a year must all your males come to see the Lord God, the God of Israel. . . . You must not offer the blood of a sacrifice to me with leavened bread. The sacrifice of the passover feast must not be left over night until morning. The very first of the first-fruits of your land you must bring to the house of the Lord your God. You must not boil a kid in its mother's milk.

Like other religions, Judaism has gone through prophetic protests and reforms and reinterpretation—God's love and purpose is meant not only for Jews, but non-Jews as well; He means to "save" all mankind or bring all people into a moral relationship with Himself and their fellow creatures. During and after the nations' Babylon exile, Deutero-Isaiah brought forth the idea that to bring saving knowledge of God and His holy will to all mankind, God needs a messenger, a servant. Israel is that servant. The nations of the earth are heard saying of the Suffering Servant:

He was despised, and rejected of men; A man of sorrow, and acquainted with grief: And as one from whom men hide their face he was despised, And we esteemed him not. Surely he hath borne our griefs, And carried our sorrows: Yet we did esteem him stricken, Smitten of God, and afflicted. But he was wounded for our transgressions, He was bruised for our iniquities: The chastisement of our peace was upon him; and with his stripes we are healed. All we like sheep have gone astray, We have turned every one to his own way: And the Lord hath laid on him The iniquity of us all.

Thus, Deutero-Isaiah justified the ways of God to the Jews. But he not only looked into the past, he also saw into the future. The next phase of God's redemptive plan, he declared, was a glorious restoration of the Jews to Jerusalem, where the work of redemption could proceed into all the world. But not only would the world come to Jerusalem; Israel would reach out into the world: "Thus says the Lord God: 'Behold! I will lift up my hands to the nations, And they shall bring your sons in their bo-

soms, And your daughters shall be carried on their shoulders. And kings shall be your foster fathers, and their queens your nursing-mothers.'"

The God who saved Israel will reach out to all mankind through them. One cannot understand the morality of this people in particular, nor of Western civilization in general, without a thorough grasp of their history and of such events as covenant, deliverance, sin, and salvation. Some understood the high moral idealism of Deutero-Isaiah; some did not. His prophecies have been searched time and time again for those who waited expectantly for the coming of a Messiah. The Suffering Servant—Israel by early interpretations—became personalized, humanized, and identified with the coming Messiah who would one day redeem (make moral in relationship to God) the world through his suffering. The early Christians found in Jesus of Nazareth one who, in their eyes, fit these descriptions perfectly, and thus for the almost 2,000 years since the birth of Christianity, the distinctly Christian Western culture has brought forth and carried with it, accentuating its finer points, the morality of the Jewish faith as was incorporated within the Christian message.

Contemporary Jewish philosopher Hans Jonas sees a crisis in contemporary ethical theory. He points out that reason, triumphant through science, replaced revelation and God's covenant in the office of guiding our moral choices, then disqualified itself when it claimed ultimate status in matters of truth. Because reason and science have been so successful in physical matters, a whole range of other matters was omitted from its domain. "This situation," notes Jonas, "is reflected in one failure of contemporary philosophy to offer an ethical theory, i.e., to validate ethical norms as part of our universe of knowledge."

According to Jonas, there are three interrelated determinants of modern thought that have a share in this nihilistic situation: (1) the modern concept of nature, which denies God's creative work; (2) the modern concept of man, which is valueless, neither good nor bad, and without purpose; according to the scientific frame of reference, this is a world of facts alien to value, which renders intentions and purposes meaningless; and (3) the fact of modern technology supported by both. Jonas comments:

> If it is true that both religion and morality originally drew sustenance from a sense of piety which cosmic mystery and majesty instilled in the soul—a sense of being excelled in the order of things by something not only physically beyond our reach but also in quality beyond our virtue: if the wonder and humility before nature had something to do with a readiness to pay homage also to norms issued in the name of an eternal order—then there must be some moral implication in the loss of this sense, in the nakedness of things without their noumenal cloak, offered up for our conquering rape. If reverence or shame has no share in the hold which moral laws may have on us, then the experience of technological power, which expunges reverence and shame, cannot be without consequences for our ethical condition.

The contemporary Jewish ethic, as espoused by Jonas, begins not with human wisdom, but human wisdom as filtered through the voice of divine revelation. In this way Jonas connects contemporary morality with a religious tradition begun over 4,000 years ago. He says, "The simple attentiveness of such a stance may help us realize that we are not completely our own masters, still less those of posterity, but rather, trustees of a heritage. If nothing else, the tempering of our presumed superiority by that injection of humility will make us cautious, and caution is the urgent need for the hour. It will make us go slow on discarding old taboos, on brushing aside in our projects the sacrosanctity of certain domains hitherto surrounded by a sense of mystery, awe, and shame."

SOURCES

Albright, W. F. *From the Stone Age to Christianity*. 2d ed. New York: John Hopkins Press. 1957.

Finkelstein, L., ed. *The Jews: Their History, Culture, and Religion*. New York: Harper & Brothers. 1960.

Jonas, Hans. *Philosophical Essays: From Ancient Creed to Technological Man*. Englewood Cliffs, NJ: Prentice-Hall. 1974.

JUDEO-CHRISTIAN ETHICS

We normally distinguish between the Judeo-Christian and the Greco-Roman strains in the Western tradition. Western civilization, including the American culture, is a part of this tradition. Essentially our Judeo-Christian inheritance provides us with our faith, beliefs about salvation and punishment, and the uniqueness of our moral code. On the other hand, the Greco-Roman traditions give us our humanistic qualities, including our emphasis on reason, science, law, and government. It is the blend of these two strains in our cultural history—and perhaps their conflict (separation of church and state, prayer in the public schools, and the contemporary political issues revolving around values)—that defines who we are. It is a unique feature of the civilization that evolved in Europe in postclassical times that it encompassed within its very constitution this dual bequest from Mediterranean antiquity. This cultural duality has profoundly shaped our culture—its symbols, institutions, and values. But the inner tensions it created, the enormous polarity it had to span, and its various competing commitments may well account for some of the uniqueness that today sets apart "Western Man," the heir of this historic collision and resultant mutation. Without knowledge of either of them as integral to our heritage, our present could not be understood.

This duality is further complicated by being composed of other dualities: Jewish and Christian, Greek and Roman; tensions within tensions. Understanding the Jewish and Christian theological motifs is essential to understanding their ethical principles. Also important is speaking of them as one side of contemporary ethics as distinguished from the others—the Greco-Roman motif. Because Christianity almost alone transmitted the Jewish share—simply by what it contained of Judaism in its own, original constitution, or by what it later appropriated from it into its own memory when both had their encounter with the Greco-Roman philosophy—we tend to refer to the Jewish and Christian motifs as one: Judeo-Christian.

The claims of revelation to be the "highest" truth, and to be the most important truths with which philosophy itself is concerned, touches the Greco-Roman civilization at its core. Revelation forced philosophy to think about the scope and limits of its rational discourse as rational knowledge, and revealed "truth" came into contact. The history of the Enlightenment in Europe—the sixteenth, seventeenth, and eighteenth centuries—made the relations of faith and reason, religion and science, and philosophy relevant. This did not make the Judeo-Christian ideas themselves elements in the history of philosophy, except as an irritant in its discourse.

But something more important took place in the Western philosophical tradition. Since philosophy is the work of living beings, the humanity of these individuals, insofar as it includes a common heritage of faith, asserts itself in their research and writing. As a result, certain ideas and continuing motifs of revealed religion passed—concealed—into the central themes of philosophy and, eventually, lost their connection from their origin in revelation and its authority. They then became genuine parts of the modified philosophical landscape—the Western intellectual tradition. This happened despite the agonizing effort of René Descartes to strip his thought of all presuppositions; it is the legacy of Western ethnocentrism, but one that is laced with the efforts of generation after generation to seek a broader, more inclusive, multicultural view without losing sight of its Judeo-Christian heritage and the values that it undergirds.

Historically, when Western Europe and the Americas constituted themselves a Christian world, Christianity gained something of a monopoly in mediating the Jewish theocentric morality through its own derivative Jewishness. Once this situation prevailed, authentic Judaism was unable to exert its influence in the Western hemisphere independently and directly. But, on occasion, Judaism was able to come forth. When this happened, as in the marked influence of Arabic-Jewish thinkers on Latin Schoolmen, or in the brief spurt of Cabbalistic interests in the Renaissance, it was a Christian choice that determined its reception, and a Christian amalgam in which it resulted. Thus, "Judeo-Christian" ideas and values entered the orbit of Western literature, science, and philosophy. This is why it is difficult to separate the Jewish and the Christian influences on Western civilization, for the Jewish depended on the Christian for its entrance. They were indivisible—and we do violence to the consciousness of a past age when we try to separate them.

From the sacred truths of this heritage we discover the origins of our own values and moral themes. The Jewish half of Christianity provided a natural theology with which philosophers dealt. The Christian half tended to defy philosophical assimilation and to compel its recognition of a supernatural mystery. The doctrine of creation has had an obvious bearing on natural theology and even on the concepts of nature and man. When we recognize the central motifs and assumptions of deep ecology, we intuitively also feel the tug of creationism, its spirituality and wholeness with reference to humans and the environment. On the other hand, in Christianity, the doctrines of the Trinity, incarnation, and salvation were more alien to natural philosophy, and since they defied rational discourse, could be considered to lie beyond the pale as mysteries of faith.

The rational status of the two components of the Christian theology—the Jewish and the Christian—and their suitability for philosophical assimilation were *intrinsically unequal*. The propositions of the one were more germane to philosophy than those of the other. It is therefore paradoxical that in a Christian intellectual universe it was the Jewish component that had the major philosophical impact. It was not before Hegel's theory of the Absolute Spirit that the theme of incarnation found major expression in philosophy and psychology—and then only by the boldest transmutation.

See also Judaism, Ethics of.

SOURCES

Brehier, Emile. *The History of Philosophy: The Hellenistic and Roman Age.* Translated by Wade Baskin. Chicago: University of Chicago Press. 1965.

Edwards, Paul, and Richard H. Popkin, General eds. *Readings in the History of Philosophy.* (An eight-volume paperback series.) New York: Free Press. 1969.

Jonas, Hans. *Philosophical Essays: From Ancient Creed to Technological Man.* Englewood Cliffs, NJ: Prentice-Hall. 1974.

Jones, W. T. *The Classical Mind: A History of Western Philosophy.* 2d ed. New York: Harcourt, Brace & World. 1969.

Williams, Bernard. *Making Sense of Humanity.* New York: Cambridge University Press. 1995.

JUDICIAL ACTIVISM AND RESTRAINT

Ronald Dworkin (*Taking Rights Seriously*) compares and contrasts two very general philosophies of how the courts should decide difficult constitutional issues. Legal literature labels these the problems of "judicial activism" and "judicial restraint." Dworkin warns us that these names may be misleading.

Judicial activism promotes the idea that courts should accept the directions of the "so-called value constitutional provisions" to work out (or interpret) principles of legality and equality, revise these principles from time to time in the light of what seems to the court fresh moral insight, and judge acts of Congress, the states, and the president accordingly. On this ground, the Constitution is not treated as a binding text. Judicial activism requires the court to face issues of moral principle that the logic of the text demands.

Judicial restraint, on the contrary, argues that the courts should allow the decisions of other branches of government to stand, even when they offend the judges' own sense of the principles required by the broad constitutional doctrines, "except when these decisions are so offensive to political morality that they would violate the provisions on any plausible interpretation, or perhaps, when a contrary decision is required by clear precedent."

Looking back, we should note that the Supreme Court followed the policy of *activism* rather than *restraint* in segregation cases and the like because the language of the Constitution's Equal Protection clause left it open whether the various educational practices of the states involved should be taken to violate the Constitution. No clear precedent held that they did, and reasonable persons might differ on the moral issue involved. For example, if the Supreme Court had followed judicial restraint, it would have held in favor of the North Carolina statute in *Swann v. Charlotte-Mecklenburg Board of Education*, 402 U.S. 1 (1971), not against it.

Understanding that the policy of judicial activism presupposes a certain objectivity of moral principle—that citizens do have certain moral rights against the states—one can conclude that a person has a moral right to equality of public education and to fair treatment by the policy. Only if these moral rights exist, at least in some sense, can activism be justified as a program and rest on something beyond the judge's personal preferences. Political skeptics say that in fact individuals have no such moral rights against the state. They have only such *legal* rights as the Constitution grants them, and these are limited to the plain and uncontroversial violations of public morality that the framers of the Constitution must have had actually in mind, or that have since been established in a line of precedent.

An alternative to restraint is a theory of "judicial deference," which assumes that citizens do have moral rights against the state beyond what the law expressly grants them, "but it points out that the character and strength of these rights are debatable and argues that political institutions other than courts are responsible for deciding which rights are to be recognized" (Dworkin). The skeptical theory and the theory of deference differ in the kind of justification they bring to the table, and in their implied moral applications. The skeptical theory may or may not assume that rights "exist." All the skeptic has to do is assume—in a restricted sense—what is right or wrong for governments to do. This view may be based on a general-interest theory—that what is moral is consistent with what benefits the community generally—or on a totalitarian view that merges the interests of the individual with the good of the general community and denies the two conflict.

The theory of deference, on the other hand, holds that one might argue that judicial deference is required because democratic institutions, like legislatures, are in fact likely to make sounder decisions than courts about the underlying issues that constitutional cases raise; that is, about the nature of an individual's moral rights against the state. As Dworkin says, "one might argue that it is for some reason *fairer* that a democratic institution rather than a court should decide such issues, even though there is no reason to believe that the institution will reach a sounder decision."

See also Gideon v. Wainwright.

SOURCES
Bickeo, Alexander. *The Supreme Court and the Idea of Progress.* Cambridge, MA: Harvard University Press. 1970.

Dworkin, Ronald. *Taking Rights Seriously.* Cambridge, MA: Harvard University Press. 1978.

Rawls, John. *A Theory of Justice.* Cambridge, MA: Harvard University Press. 1973.

JUDICIAL VIRTUES

The study of the history of legal theory and justice reveals certain judicial virtues, namely impartiality and considerateness. These are thought of as those excellent virtues of cognitivity and sensibility that enable human beings to construct objective moral principles and develop moral convictions. By reviewing the history of this development, we discover that moral principles are objective to the extent that they have been arrived at and tested, and by assuming a person possesses the general frame of reference defined by these two virtues.

John Rawls comments: "The veil of ignorance prevents us from shaping our moral view to accord with our own particular attachments and interests. We do not look at the social order from our situation but take up a point of view that everyone can adopt on an equal footing. In this sense we look at our society and our place in it objectively: we share a common standpoint along with others and do not make our judgments from a personal slant."

SOURCES
Aiken, H. D. *Reason and Conduct.* New York: Alfred A. Knopf. 1962.

Hester, Joseph P. "Subjective Commitment and the Problem of Moral Objectivity." *Philosophy and Phenomenological Research* 25:4 (June 1975).

Rawls, John. *A Theory of Justice.* Cambridge, MA: Belknap Press of Harvard University Press. 1973.

Terrell, Huntington. "Moral Objectivity and Freedom." *Ethics* 76 (1965).

JUSTICE

Justice is the first virtue of social institutions and should not be considered a property of individuals and their actions but as a predicate of societies. Simply put, justice is fairness, the idea that human rights are not subject to political bargaining or to the calculus of social interests. Justice is a virtue of national societies, of nations, both formal—their laws—and informal—their cultural institutions, conventions, moral rules, and moral sanctions. For a society to be fully just, it must be just in its informal as well as its formal aspects. From a religious perspective, justice is also associated with love. Reinhold Niebuhr and Emil Brunner argue that social and legal justice are a political application of the law of love and that, as such, love is the fulfillment of justice.

CRITERIA OF JUSTICE

Support for the conception of justice as a social value rests on the answers to two questions: (1) What are the criteria or principles of social justice—or, what features make or render a society just or unjust? and (2) What are we saying when we say of a society that it is just or unjust? Defenders of a theory of justice say that a society is just if it renders to its various members what is due to them. But what is it that is due to them? This is answered by the development of legal theory and in the laws of the state. That is, the laws of a state prescribe, legally, what is a person's due and what their right may be. One

could respond that a society may be unjust and its laws unfair. If this is so, it follows that social justice cannot consist wholly of observing these laws, because social justice includes moral as well as legal justice. Therefore, one might say that a society is just if its laws and actions conform to moral standards. Of course, what is and what is not moral is a matter not completely settled.

We can add to this the idea that moral principles must be *valid*. A person's due or right is that which is his/hers by virtue not merely of the law or of prevailing moral rules, but of valid moral principles. Also, a society is just if it operates by valid moral principles. Social justice in this view is any given system of distribution and retribution that is governed by valid moral principles. Of course, we can still go on to ask what moral principles are valid. But this view does indeed simplify matters: justice, or what is right, is defined in terms of valid moral principles.

Richard Brandt argues that not all moral principles are "principles of justice" even if they are valid. For example, principles of generosity and beneficence, although valid moral principles, are not principles of justice because justice is not simply the greatest possible balance of pleasure over pain or goodness over evil. Rather, justice has to do with the process of distributing and retributing—*just-making* considerations are only one kind of *right-making* considerations. To understand the difference between "right" and "just," examine the following passage from John S. Mill, who says that in order to save a life,

> it may not only be allowable, but a duty" to do something which is contrary to the principles of justice—for example, "to steal or take by force the necessary food or medicine, or to kidnap and compel to officiate the only qualified medical practitioner.

Mill continues:

> In such cases, as we do not call anything justice which is not a virtue, we usually say, not

that justice must give way to some other moral principle, but that what is just in ordinary cases is, by reason of that other principle, not just in the particular case. By this useful accommodation of language, the character of indefeasibility attributed to justice is kept up, and we are saved from the necessity of maintaining that there can be laudable injustice.

The point for us to think about is that *just* and *unjust* seem to play a double role. They refer to certain kinds of right-making considerations as against others—involving power, oppression, fairness, and equality—and they seem to have the same force as do the general terms *right* and *wrong*. Thus, we can conclude that justice and morality are connected but that morality has more to do with love and altruism; justice begins as a principle of restraint. It is at first mainly useful for curbing disorder and limiting the use of power. As Adam Smith pointed out, "Society flourishes and is happy" when the cooperation indispensable to human life is based on love and friendship. But though society can manage without affection, it cannot survive when hurt and injury are unrestrained. Smith (*The Theory of Moral Sentiments*) explains:

> Beneficence, therefore, is less essential to the existence of society than justice. Society may subsist, though not in the most comfortable state, without beneficence; but the prevalence of injustice must utterly destroy it. . . . [Beneficence] is the ornament which embellishes, not the foundation which supports the building, and which it was, therefore, sufficient to recommend, but by no means necessary to impose. Justice, on the contrary, is the main pillar of the edifice.

Mill had much the same idea in mind when he spoke of justice as "a name for certain classes of moral rules, which concern the essentials of human well-being more clearly, and are therefore of more absolute obligation, than any other rules for the guidance of life." For Mill, "justice implies something which it is not only right to do and wrong not to do, but which some individual person can claim from us as his moral right."

Finally, a theory of justice must be grounded in historical experience; that is, it should take its departure from principles that have received recurrent recognition. These include: *entitlement*—claims of right must be based on what has already been granted by law or custom; *justification*—when deprivations are imposed, reasons must be given or tacitly understood, and some form of consent is presumed; *equality*—at a minimum, like cases must be treated alike, and the intrinsic worth of every member must be recognized; *impartiality*—bias and self-interest must be excluded from rule making and administration; *proportionality*—relevant differences must be considered when allocating benefits or burdens; *reciprocity*—a balance of giving and taking must be maintained, especially in determining mutual obligations; *rectification*—injured parties must be compensated for the losses they have suffered; *need*—allocations must be based on what people are thought to require for survival or for a minimally acceptable standard of existence; *desert*—comparative worth, merit, or blame must be weighed; and *participation*—every person must be recognized as a member of the community, especially in respect to basic rights and having a voice in decisions that affect vital interests.

We can impose some order on these principles by recognizing that some of them—entitlement, proportionality, need, and desert—speak mainly to justice in the *distribution of opportunities, benefits, and burdens*. Other principles, such as impartiality, are concerned with *governance*; that is, with the way rules are made and implemented, especially where coercion is involved and where fairness and mitigation of arbitrariness are primary concerns. Still other principles—reciprocity, rectification, participation—make *social justice* their chief concern, which includes the obligations and claims that arise from transactions, interdependence, injury, and group membership. In this form of relational justice, people are compensated for unjustified losses, and their legitimate expectations are vindicated. In closing, when considering justice and morality, we should understand that some principles, notably equality and justification, are pervasive; they are common threads in every kind of just or moral relationship.

SOURCES

Barry, Brian. *Theories of Justice.* Berkeley: University of California Press. 1989.

Brandt, Richard B., ed. *Social Justice.* Englewood Cliffs, NJ: Prentice-Hall. 1962.

Brunner, Emil. *Justice and the Social Order.* London: Lutterworth Press. 1945.

Dworkin, Ronald. *Law's Empire.* Cambridge, MA: Harvard University Press. 1986.

McCallum, R. B., ed. *On Liberty, Considerations on Representative Government.* London: Oxford University Press. 1946.

Miller, David. *Social Justice.* Oxford: Clarendon Press. 1976.

Plamenatz, J. D., ed. *Mill's* Utilitarianism, *Reprinted with a Study of the English Utilitarians.* London: Oxford University Press. 1949.

Smith, Adam. *The Theory of Moral Sentiments.* London: Bohn. 1853.

JUSTIFICATION OF ETHICAL PRINCIPLES

In ethics there are, broadly speaking, two types of questions: (1) questions about what is morally right or wrong, good or bad, which are called *normative* questions; and (2) questions that ask if normative answers can be justified—and if so, how—which are called *metaethical* questions. Metaethical reasoning involves the question of ethical justification, and thus the following questions are of importance to metaethical reasoning: (a) Aren't the answers to questions about what is morally right or good relative or even arbitrary? (b) Can answers to normative questions ever be justified? and (c) Why should one be moral or do what is morally right at all?

JUSTIFICATION

We usually justify ethical judgments by giving reasons for them. If we say that "keeping promises is right or good," then we must be prepared to give facts to support this normative assertion, facts about humans and their social and cultural relationships, and facts about the world. Epicurus did this (and so did Mill) when he argued that pleasure is the good because it is what we all seek. In another way, the author of I John 4:7–11 (in the Christian New Testament) did this when he wrote: "Beloved, let us love one another: for love is of God . . . if God so loved us, we ought also to love one another." To quote William Frankena and John Granrose, "Not only is it natural to make such an appeal to psychological, metaphysical, or theological premises in defending ethical goals and principles, it seems impossible to justify our basic ethical beliefs without the use of such factual premises."

Kurt Baier observes that in asking for the case for morality, one is asking "Are moral reasons superior to reasons of enlightened self-interest?" and "What reasons could there be for being moral?" These questions, he maintains, are meaningful. There is no attempt here to derive a moral value from a fact—an ought from an is. Rather, one is merely exploring which types of normative behavior will lead to a better life—reasons of morality or reasons of self-interest, and facts about humans in society can be provided to show that moral rules would produce a state of affairs that would serve everyone's interest. By examining these two alternative worlds, we can see that the moral world is the better of the two.

Like Baier, Kai Nielsen has no doubts about the benefit of morality as a social institution. Nielsen contends that a practical choice is involved in choosing either to live morally or to live selfishly, and this choice need not be arbitrary. He comments: "But need we despair of the rationality of the moral life once we have dug out and correctly placed this irreducible element of choice in reasoning about human conduct? If one is willing to reason morally, nothing need upset the objectivity and rationality of moral grading criteria." And Michael Scriven concurs that "if a rational justification of morality is to be given, it apparently must show that unselfishness is a rationally superior pattern of behavior in comparison with selfishness. That is, it must show that a selfish man has good reason for being unselfish—if he can be by choice—for else it preaches only to the converted."

The necessity of justifying ethical principles reminds us of the stubborn fact that we do offer factual information, or reasons for moral rules and conclusions, and that some reasons are better than others. Baier and Nielsen have successfully argued this point. Perhaps the clearest statement of this approach to justifying moral norms was given by S. E. Toulmin in his 1950 book, *The Place of Reason in Ethics*. He too approached ethical justification by providing good reasons for being moral as opposed to being immoral as he addressed the moral extremist theories of subjectivism and emotivism, which rendered moral life arbitrary, relativistic, and without foundation. In Toulmin's view, practical judgment replaces goading, commanding, and subjective knee-jerk reactions as one approaches the moral life from a reasonable and calm, prudent, and objective judgment.

See also Metaethics.

SOURCES

Frankena, William K., and John T. Granrose, eds. *Introductory Readings in Ethics*. Englewood Cliffs, NJ: Prentice-Hall. 1974.

Pahel, Kenneth, and Marvin Schiller, eds. *Readings in Contemporary Ethical Theory*. Englewood Cliffs, NJ: Prentice-Hall. 1970.

Toulmin, Stephen E. *The Place of Reason in Ethics*. Cambridge: Cambridge University Press. 1950.

K

KANT, IMMANUEL

It is said of Immanuel Kant (1724–1804) that his failures are more important than most people's successes. Kant lived by routine and, although he had many friends, he never married and never ventured more than 40 miles from Königsberg (now Kaliningrad), East Prussia, the city of his birth and death. The Kant family belonged to the lower middle class and was devoutly religious. His father recognized Immanuel's academic ability and sent him to the local Pietistic College to prepare for the ministry. He continued his studies at the University of Königsberg and became increasingly interested in natural science and philosophy. Between 1746 and 1755, he supported himself as a private teacher. He was then appointed to an instructorship at the university and finally, in 1770, was promoted to a full professorship.

Kant wrote five important books: *General Natural History and Theory of the Heavens* (1755); *Critique of Pure Reason* (1781); *Critique of Judgment* (1790); *The Fundamental Principles of the Metaphysics of Morals* (1785); and *The Critique of Practical Reason* (1788). The direction of his philosophical interests is revealed in his reflection that "two things fill the mind with ever new and increasing admiration and awe—the starry heavens above and the moral law within." His concern was with nature and morality. This naturally led Kant to assert that reason is the only ground for certainty. He argued that reason guaranteed the certainty of scientific knowledge. Reason is not limited to specific sensory experiences, but is universally applicable to all experiences, including the moral life.

In his search for the grounds of the validity of ethics, he used the same method by which he established the grounds of the certainty of science. A valid moral principle, he says, must be independent of experience and binding on all people. In short, a genuine morality, one that is objectively and universally binding, requires a rational foundation. The universal basis of morality lies in the human's rational nature, since this alone is the same in everyone. For Kant, the rational tests for a valid ethic lie in universality and consistency. Thus, he developed the *categorical imperative* as a moral principle that embodies these two rational principles. It says those actions are right that conform to principles one can consistently will to be principles for all persons, and those actions are wrong that are based upon maxims that a rational person could not will that all men should follow. For Kant, the categorical imperative enables us to tell right from wrong. However, Kant says that it is not only the test but it is also the unconditional directive for behavior. It is binding upon everyone because each rational person acknowledges this obligation to follow reason. Reason prescribes duty, and the moral law holds whether or not men actually follow it.

See also The Categorical Imperative.

SOURCES

Beck, Lewis White, ed. *18th-Century Philosophy*. New York: Free Press. 1966.

Wolff, Robert Paul, ed. *Kant: A Collection of Critical Essays*. Garden City, NY: Doubleday. 1967.

KEVORKIAN, JACK

Jack Kevorkian is a Michigan doctor who has (as of February 5, 1995) assisted in 21 suicides and plans to take the case of doctor-assisted suicide to the U.S. Supreme Court. Three terms are commonly used in the debate over the legality and/or morality of this issue: *active euthanasia, passive euthanasia,* and *assisted suicide.*

A good deal of controversy about euthanasia—or mercy killing—involves the decision-making process. Who is it that decides if a patient lives or dies? Some believe that those doctors like Kevorkian seem to lack the clinical and perhaps even the moral judgment to fully comprehend the implications of what they are doing. This issue has not been established legally in the United States, and its ambiguity has allowed the physician in charge to suggest the option of death to a patient's relatives, especially if the patient is brain-dead. Some terminally ill patients, in an attempt to make decisions about when their own lives should end, used a controversial suicide device, developed by Kevorkian, to end their lives. *Suicide* means literally "self-killing," but in the early 1990s the controversial topic of assisted suicide—in which terminally ill people are aided in committing suicide by physicians, loved ones, or others—was examined as a legal topic. Voters in Wash-

ington State in 1991 rejected a proposition to legalize physician-assisted suicide. Nevertheless, Derek Humphry's book *Final Exit*, a guide for terminally ill people who want to comit suicide, became a best seller that same year. Kevorkian himself has remained active throughout the 1990s in assisting terminally ill people to kill themselves. This topic needs more examination, both from a legal point of view and from the point of view of morality, and in conjunction with it more discussion on the right-to-die principle, because medical advances in recent decades have made it possible to keep terminally ill people alive far beyond any hope of recovery or improvement.

See also Euthanasia.

SOURCES

Compton's Online Encyclopedia. (See euthanasia, suicide.) Compton's Learning Company. 1995.

KINDLINESS

Being kind means doing good, being friendly, and showing a generous, sympathetic, considerate attitude toward others. Kindliness is the quality of being kind and implies moral integrity and personhood. In ordinary language, *integrity* suggests both honesty and coherence. Integrity properly denotes both wholeness and soundness; thus, to have integrity is to be unmarred by distortion, deception, or other forms of disharmony and inauthenticity. John Rawls identifies the "virtues of integrity" as "truthfulness and sincerity, lucidity and commitment, or, as some say, authenticity."

The concept of kindliness not only implies moral integrity but goes to the heart of what is meant by *person* and *personhood*. In Western philosophy, theology, and social thought, *person* embodies a core of meaning that is inseparable from moral thought. We certainly find this in such concepts as human dignity and worth. Thus, *person* suggests both a particular person of dignity and worth, but also that such a person will lead a life of coherence and responsibility. The lesson learned by examining the historical use of "person" and "personhood" should give full weight to self-affirming participation in a moral order defined by its respect for persons with the implication of how we are to regard and act toward other individuals in their own concrete specificity, that we take full account of their specific aims and purposes and of their own definitions of their life situations. In other words, the person as an object of moral concern requires our moral consideration or kindness. This is a *ground-zero project*, or a set of activities and commitments that, taken together, construct a moral identity and give meaning to life.

SOURCES

Maritain, Jacques. *The Person and the Common Good*. New York: Scribner's. 1947.

Williams, Bernard. *Moral Luck*. Cambridge: Cambridge University Press. 1981.

KU KLUX KLAN

The Ku Klux Klan is a secret terrorist organization that first appeared in 1866. It led underground resistance against the civil rights and political power of newly freed slaves during the Reconstruction period after the U.S. Civil War. The Klan's goal was to reestablish the dominance of the prewar plantation aristocracy. In the twentieth century the Klan has been revived with a goal of white supremacy. The Klan was reorganized in 1915 (after being officially disbanded in 1869) near Atlanta, Georgia, and peaked politically in the 1920s with over 4 million members nationally. From the 1920s, the Klan began to persecute Roman Catholics, Jews, foreigners, communists, and organized labor. Stressing white supremacy, the Klan was revived once again in the mid-1960s in reaction to the Civil Rights Act of 1964, but faded after President Lyndon B. Johnson denounced the organization in 1965. In the late 1970s, the Klan revived with renewed vigor and fragmented into several separate and competing groups, some of which allied themselves with neo-Nazi and other right-wing extremist groups. By the early 1990s, after being prosecuted for illegal activities, the Klan was estimated to have between 6,000 and 10,000 active members, mostly in the Deep South.

See also Ethnocentrism; Racism.

SOURCES

Carroll, Peter N., and David W. Noble. *The Free and the Unfree: A New History of the United States*. 2d ed. New York: Penguin. 1988.

Handlin, Oscar, and Lilian Handlin. *Liberty and Equality 1920–1994*. New York: HarperCollins. 1994.

LAISSEZ-FAIRE

Modern national sovereignty at first meant absolute internal authority, as well as freedom from external control. The state was regarded as a law unto itself. It made the laws but, in the early days, was above law and morals. After the Industrial Revolution of the eighteenth and nineteenth centuries and the rise of the mercantile class, commercial and business groups wanted to be free even from government restrictions on the right to make money as they saw fit. The demand was "leave us alone"—*laissez-faire*—or "business is business." The mercantile class felt that business ought to be free to make decisions on the basis of financial considerations alone.

History has taught us that a civilization is a set of ideas, ideals, values, and loyalties that act as the cohesive force or the cement that holds the various parts of society together. When they are weakened or lost, society tends to break up into conflicting groups, humans seek other and less worthy ends, and civilization tends to decline. The doctrine of laissez-faire, also known as *free enterprise*, played an important role in the transition from a feudal economy to the modern industrial state and its market economy. Although the conditions for modern life were established by the decline of the feudal economy, the true break into the modern world was the revolutionary process initiated by the American and French revolutions. Here the modern political economy took root in the same merchant capital as the European mercantilist policies that preceded the revolutions. From its inception, the doctrine of laissez-faire was a part of this revolutionary process, especially when combined with other social and political norms—among them the doctrine of national sovereignty.

The idea of free enterprise, which arose during the seventeenth and eighteenth centuries, is sometimes called *individualism* or *classical liberalism*, and assumes a minimum interference by the government in economic and social affairs. In its origin, the doctrine was a part of the reaction against the excessive and irritating restrictions placed on trade and business by the monarchs of seventeenth- and eighteenth-century Europe. Some of these restrictions were relics of the guild system of feudal days. By 1600, the doctrine of *natural law* had won the day, and with it came *natural rights*. People believed that there were natural laws that, if left to themselves, would work to the best interests of all, and that nature would regulate wages, prices, and supply and demand in the most equitable way.

Across the globe, politics lies in such deep disrepute that almost anyone who holds or aspires to a hopeful view of humanity's future will either attempt to ignore politics in describing the unfolding of that future, or will put the burden of its unfolding on some other, nonpolitical (and therefore, I believe, mythical) way of ordering human affairs. . . . By attending to the health of the body politic, we are reminding ourselves of the ancient wisdom that individuals cannot be fully healthy physically and mentally, in isolation, but only as meaningful players in a meaningful community. Or again, the attention to the potential of our cities is reminding us that children cannot realize their own full potential except in the context of a well-functioning community (Daniel Kemmis, *The Good City and the Good Life: Renewing the Sense of Community* [Boston: Houghton Mifflin] 1995).

During the latter part of the nineteenth century, this belief seemed to receive biological sanction in the doctrine of *natural selection* and the *survival of the fittest*. In the United States, especially, individualism was fostered by pioneer conditions. *Rugged individualism* was thought to be indispensable in conquering a continent. And although laissez-faire has been questioned for its ability to deal with the problems of the intricate industrial-technological society of the second half of the twentieth century, we today find the neoconservative movement in politics and the emergence of right-wing militant groups and the religious right seemingly giving lip service to some hybrid forms of this doctrine.

See also Natural Law; Survival of the Fittest.

SOURCES

Kaufman, Allen. *Capitalism, Slavery, and Republican Values: American Political Economists, 1819–1848.* Austin: University of Texas Press. 1992.

Leinberger, Paul, and Bruce Tucker. *The New Individualists* New York: HarperCollins. 1991.

Selznick, Philip. *The Moral Commonwealth.* Berkeley: University of California Press. 1992.

Titus, Harold H., and Morris T. Keeton. *Ethics for Today: Social Theory and the Promise of Community.* 5th ed. New York: Van Nostrand. 1973.

LAO-TZU

Some scholars believe that only one man, Lao-tzu, wrote the most translated work in all the literature of China, the *Lao-Tzu* (also called *Tao-te Ching*). This book is the earliest document in the history of Taoism (the Way), one of the major philosophical and religious traditions that, along with Confucianism, has shaped Chinese life and thought for more than 2,000 years. It is a viewpoint that emphasizes individuality, freedom, simplicity, mysticism, and naturalness. We know of Lao-tzu only through legends. He perhaps lived in the district of Hu during the Chou Dynasty (1122–256 B.C.). He presumably worked in astrology and divination at the court of the emperor. After his death, he was worshipped as an imperial ancestor during the T'ang Dynasty (A.D. 618–907).

See also Confucianism; Taoism, Ethics of.

SOURCE

Noss, David S., and John B. Noss. *Man's Religions.* 7th ed. New York: Macmillan. 1984.

LIBERALISM

For many citizens in the United States the "L-word" has become a term of contempt, but this was not always true. By *liberalism* is meant the values, views, and policies that people who consider themselves liberals or progressives generally support. As Daniel Yankelovich reflects: "From Franklin Roosevelt to Lyndon Johnson, liberalism has meant greater concern for the problems of poor people and workers than with the interests of rich people and employers. Since the

1960s, liberalism has also emphasized environmental protection, expanding individual rights based on need, and advancing the interests of women and minorities."

Yankelovich, best known as an interpreter of public opinion and values, as an analyst of American society, has attained a reputation for prescient insight. In the 1960s and 1970s, his firm evaluated the Great Society for strengths and weaknesses. He has written eight books, including *New Rules*, an analysis of America's changing social morality, and *Coming to Public Judgment*, which describes a new social theory for understanding American public opinion.

Yankelovich notes that the greatest strengths of liberalism lie in three core values:

1. *Inclusiveness.* Liberals extend their world beyond their own family, community, and ethnic group to include a wide range of "others," including the environment itself.
2. *Social Justice.* Liberals believe a civilized and humane society ensures its weaker and poorer members are treated fairly.
3. *A Positive Role for Government.* Liberals see a strong government as a counterbalance to special interests and as a restraint assuring that an economy based on maximizing profits does not trample fundamental human rights.

Liberals have traditionally translated these values into legislation through many programs and policies, including entitlement programs that guarantee benefits to all who qualify; regulations covering everything from clean air and water to protecting the rights of people with disabilities; and affirmative action programs designed to give an edge to women and minorities to compensate for existing prejudices and past wrongs.

It is the policies of liberalism that are troubling an ever-widening number of Americans. Most Americans do not reject liberalism's underlying values. Almost two-thirds of the American public continues to believe the government should take care of people who cannot take care of themselves (*New York Times*/CBS, February 1995). According to Yankelovich, "It is the values of liberalism, in contrast to specific policies, that gave liberalism its moral authority with the electorate and enabled it to exercise a powerful political hegemony for so many years."

Today, we find these conditions:

1. Liberalism's moral authority has waned, and its proponents seem unclear on how to regain it.
2. Priorities such as a balanced budget, health care costs, and/or improved transportation systems communicate no special moral authority.
3. Voters do not weigh policies on their technical merits; they judge ideas and policies by their moral worth: Are they practical and are they *right*—meaning fair, decent, and humane?

From 1932 to the mid-1970s, those who said they were liberal rarely accounted for more than one out of three voters. Yet during that period, the liberal agenda dominated U.S. politics and was advanced by conservative Republicans because liberal ideas blended moral authority with common sense in ways that appealed to the moderate-conservative majority. Yankelovich seems to believe that if the liberals are to rebuild their moral authority, they must understand and become more sympathetic with the public's quarrel with their policies, give top priority to offsetting the harmful effects of today's lopsided economy, reduce the federal government's role in social policy while strengthening its role in economic policy, and rebuild institutions helping teachers, doctors, lawyers, and unions to restore the public confidence they once enjoyed.

SOURCES

Kimball, Bruce A. *Orators and Philosophers: A History of the Idea of Liberal Education.* New York: College Entrance Examination Board. 1995.

Yankelovich, Daniel. "Restoring Public Trust." *Mother Jones* (November/December 1995).

LIBERTY

See Civil Rights.

LOVE

See Agape; Eros.

MACHIAVELLI

With the growth of secular nationalism in modern Europe, war came to be regarded by many as necessary and inevitable. The more extreme view is sometimes called "Machiavellianism" because Machiavelli (1469–1527) wrote in *The Prince* that the state not only rests on force, with material prosperity its conscious aim, but the ordinary rules of morality do not apply to affairs of the state. From Machiavelli to contemporary fascists, the state for Machiavellians has been seen as rightly resting on power and force. For some it was an end in itself. For others, the sole purpose of the state is material prosperity. For still others, the purpose of the state is to glorify their race, ethnic group, religion, or way of life. Again, for those committed to a totalitarian state, unlimited in its power, the end is so important that statecraft is exempted from the ordinary rules of morality: individuals and groups are of worth only as they serve the ends of the state.

SOURCES
Ardvey, Robert. *The Territorial Imperative*. New York: Atheneum. 1966.
Montagu, Ashley, ed. *Man and Aggression*. New York: Oxford University Press. 1968.

MAGNA CARTA

History is about time—changes, passages, processes—as it hinges on sequence and chronology. But history is also about place—setting, environment, context. *Where* events happen and *when* they happen are as important and informative as *why* they happen. For example, James Madison wrote to a correspondent in 1834, "You give me a credit to which I have no claim in calling me 'the writer of the Constitution of the United States.' This was not like the fabled goddess of wisdom the offspring of a single brain. It ought to be regarded as the work of many heads and many hands." Madison could draft the Bill of Rights and participate in constitution-making only because of the precedents furnished by centuries of Anglo-American constitutional development. Madison, Jefferson, and their colleagues could draw up a bill of rights and a working constitution based on their rights because they were the heirs of the constitutional struggles waged by their English forebears.

The roots of American freedom are found in English constitutional history. In particular, the federal Bill of Rights was based directly upon the great "Charters" of English liberty, which began with the Magna Carta. In the Magna Carta we see for the first time in English history a written organic instrument—exacted from a sovereign ruler by the bulk of the politically articulate community—that purports to tie down binding rules of law that the ruler himself may not violate. In the Magna Carta is to be found the germ of the root principle that there are fundamental rights above the state, which the state—otherwise sovereign power that it is—may not infringe.

The Magna Carta was the result of a bargain struck between the king and the nation at Runnymede in A.D. 1215. This document enumerated what were deemed the basic liberties of Englishmen of the day. In 63 short chapters, this legal form set forth the irrevocable rights of Englishmen. It is a feudal grant steeped in the technicalities of feudal law and appears, for the most part, to deal with the mundane and petty aspects of the relations between the king and his barons. There is in it no broad statement of principle or defined political theory. It was a practical document to remedy current feudal abuses.

Yet, when we look closely at the Magna Carta, we discover much that is noble. The custom of feudal tenure is stated as a defined component of English law, with precise limits set to royal claims in strict terms of money, time, and space. The question of scutage (a tax), feudal reliefs, wardships, and the like are regulated in legally enforceable terms against a king who had claimed to be a law unto himself. The Magna Carta can be interpreted as being directed against specific feudal abuses committed by the king, but more importantly, its key provisions are cast in broader terms that allowed it to fit the needs of later generations (e.g., when the original Articles of the Barons were being refined, the words "any baron" were changed to "any free man" (liber homo), and although "free man" was a technical feudal term with a limited meaning, it turned out to give the Magna Carta the widest application in future centuries). For this reason, the Magna Carta should not simply be analyzed and summarized, but savored for the foundation in freedom that it provided the founders of the United States.

SOURCES

Schwartz, Bernard, ed. *The Roots of the Bill of Rights.* Vol. 1. New York: Chelsea House. 1971.

Ver Steeg, Clarence T., and Richard Hofstadter, eds. *Great Issues in American History.* Vol. 1. New York: Vintage. 1969.

MANIFEST DESTINY

By linking geography with nationalism in an apocalyptic vision, special responsibilities were placed on the American people. In the words of John L. O'Sullivan, editor of the *Democratic Review,* this was our "Manifest Destiny"—to stretch the influence of the United States until "the whole boundless continent is ours." Central to this ideal was a belief in American superiority—including the uniqueness of republican governments and the blessings of political liberty. It was believed that by stretching this political idea from sea to sea, U.S. expansion would broaden the foundations of liberty, extend freedom geographically, and elevate those who live under inferior forms of government.

One cannot disconnect Manifest Destiny from the missionary impulse found in the Protestant religions. By taking the Protestant Gospel into the "virgin" lands west of the Mississippi River, American evangelicals would protect these areas from Spanish Jesuits and convert the "heathen devils" who lived there. Thus, Manifest Destiny reinforced the idea that a republican government and the Protestant religion would preserve the purity of the continent.

Peter Carroll and David Noble comment: "Despite pervasive materialism, the popular image of the American West continued to emphasize its antimaterialistic purpose. For Thomas Jefferson and his proselytes, the unsettled wilderness symbolized the boundless possibilities of national regeneration. Free from corrupting institutions, open to all settlers, the vast spaces represented the land of innocence, a veritable Garden of Eden. Thus, in a timeless place of purity, the American nation would fulfill its destiny."

But Manifest Destiny had decidedly ethnic and racial overtones. Washakie, a Shoshone forced from his land by the white invasion, said: "The white man kills our game, captures our furs, and sometimes feeds his herds upon our meadows. Every foot of what you proudly call America not very long ago belonged to the red man. The Great Spirit gave it to us. But the white man had, in ways we know not of, learned some things we had not learned; among them, how to make superior tools and terrible weapons; and there seemed no end to the body of men that followed from other lands beyond the sea."

And we find a racial-ethnic response to the suggestion that the United States annex Mexico after the defeat of General Santa Anna. Annexing Mexico was logical to many expansionists in light of the concept of Manifest Destiny or U.S. continentalism, but it soon floundered on another, less obvious problem. John C. Calhoun objected, and explained: "To incorporate Mexico would be the very first instance of incorporating an Indian race; for more than half of the Mexicans are Indians, and the other is composed chiefly of mixed tribes. I protest against such a union as that! Ours, sir, is the government of a white race." Manifest Destiny is perhaps the most destructive ethnocentric and racial response made by America's European forefathers to the indigenous people (Native Americans) who were living on this continent when they began their settlement.

SOURCES

Carroll, Peter N., and David W. Noble. *The Free and the Unfree: A New History of the United States.* 2d ed. New York: Penguin. 1988.
Ver Steeg, Clarence T., and Richard Hofstadter, eds. *Great Issues in American History.* Vols. 1 & 2. New York: Vintage. 1969.

MAO ZEDONG

Mao Zedong (1893–1976) led the long struggle that made China a communist nation in 1949. He then became the ruler of China and one of the world's most powerful people, controlling China's artistic, intellectual, military, industrial, and agricultural planning and policies. Mao was a communist who believed himself to be the true interpreter of Marx, Lenin, and Stalin. He believed that poor nations would inevitably revolt against richer nations and, in fact, rule the world. But all did not work to a perfect script for Mao. In 1958 his Great Leap Forward program failed, and in the 1960s his relationship with the Soviet Union collapsed. Suffering a series of diplomatic defeats in the same decade, Mao launched a campaign against so-called revisionists (those favoring changes) to maintain revolutionary enthusiasm. But, after his death in 1976, China reversed many of Mao's policies, ended the emphasis on his personality, and began to rebuild its relationships with the other great industrial powers of the world.

SOURCES

Lawson, Don. *The Long March: Red China Under Chairman Mao.* New York: Harper. 1983.
Ver Steeg, Clarence, and Richard Hofstadter, eds. *Great Issues in American History.* Vol. 3. New York: Vintage. 1969.

MARRIAGE

Marriage provides the formal basis for stable heterosexual relations and for the formation of nuclear families. In order to encourage and benefit from the social order provided by marriage, all societies control and regulate the marital institution by putting it into a legal and/or religious framework that (1) makes it a liaison of expected permanence; (2) formalizes the reciprocal rights and obligations of the married couple; (3) requires the nurture, protection, and socialization of children; and (4) provides formal kinship relations and establishes property rights and stable lines of inheritance.

For many people, the current state of marriage seems to provide the clearest evidence that the family is falling apart. In the past 30 years, marriage rates have declined, divorce rates have risen, and increasing numbers of couples have come to live together without being married. What has occurred in this historical change is not that people no longer want long-term commitments, but rather that in the contemporary world marriage has increasingly become a personal relationship between two people. Over time, fewer and fewer reasons tie couples to unsatisfactory relationships. As the need for emotional fulfillment in marriage has arisen, so have the levels of discontent.

Before the industrial revolution, the least important aspect of marriage was the emotional relationship between husband and wife. A marriage was an exchange between kin groups, a unit of economic production, and a means of replenishing populations with high death rates. In those (traditional) societies, parents many times selected their children's mates. Parents were more interested in the practical outcomes of the marriage than in romantic considerations.

In modern societies, people are supposed to marry for love. Of course, there are other reasons people get married, such as money; nevertheless, they often follow their culture's rules and decide they are "in love." People today may also decide they're in love and want to live together but do not care to formally "get" married, either by the state or by the clergy. We therefore discover that marriage relationships are influenced by social norms and

behaviors—our reactions to them and perceptions of them. Before 1960, a relationship between a man and woman could be categorized as either "honorable" or "dishonorable" depending on whether the relationship followed a traditional or alternative pattern. An honorable relationship went through stages of dating, keeping company, going steady, agreeing to be married, announcing the engagement, and finally getting married, presumably for life. Divorce was thought of as a personal tragedy and social disgrace. Sexual relations before marriage were also thought of as shameful, especially for the woman, although the shame decreased as the marriage drew nearer.

In the 1990s, the system of courtship has dramatically changed. Relationships today are less permanent, more flexible, more experimental. What makes for a happy or—more important—an enduring marriage includes the ability to change and tolerate change, to share values, to share good luck—life stability, job stability, good health—all contributing to the longevity of the marriage. John F. Cuber and Peggy B. Harroff (*The Significant American*) have discovered five distinct marriage styles. Their research conclusions are based on interviews with 211 persons: 107 men and 104 women. The styles they have found are the following:

- *The Conflict-Habituated*. This is the most prevalent of the styles. In this association there is much tension and conflict, although it is largely controlled. At worst, there is some private quarreling, nagging, and "throwing up the past" of which members of the immediate family and close friends have some awareness.
- *The Devitalized Style*. This style is best understood by noting the clear discrepancy between middle-aged reality and earlier days. These couples say that they were "deeply in love" during the early years, spent a great deal of time together, enjoyed sex,

and had a clear identification with one another. In middle-age, with some variations from case to case, they spent little time together, the sexual relationship became far less satisfactory, and interests and activities were not shared, at least not in the deeper and meaningful way they once were. Most of their time together now is "duty time"—entertaining together, planning and sharing activities with children, and participating in various kinds of community responsibilities.

- *The Passive-Congenial.* This style has a great deal in common with the devitalized marriage, the essential difference being that the passivity that pervades the association has been there from the start. The devitalized have a more exciting set of memories; the passive-congenial give little evidence that they had ever hoped for anything much different from what they are currently experiencing. Therefore, there is little suggestion of disillusionment or compulsion to make believe to anyone. Relationships are comfortable and adequate; there is little conflict. They remind themselves that they have many common interests that they enjoy. Research tells us that couples make their way into the passive-congenial mode by two quite different routes—by default and by intention. Perhaps in most instances they arrive at this way of living and feeling by drift, or there is so little that they have cared about deeply in each other that a passive-congenial mode is a deliberately intended arrangement for two people whose interests and creative energies are directed elsewhere than toward the pairing.

- *The Vital Relationship.* This stage or mode stands in extreme contrast to the first three. The vital pair can easily be overlooked as they move through their worlds of work, recreation, and family activities. Publicly at least, they may appear as the other couples, but when a close, intimate, confidential look is taken, the essence of their vital relationship becomes clear: they intensely bond together psychologically in important life matters. Their sharing and togetherness are genuine. It provides the life essence for both man and woman.

- *The Total Relationship.* This mode is like the vital relationship with the addition that it is more multifaceted. The points of vitality are more numerous—in some cases all of the important life foci are vitally shared. There is practically no pretense between persons in this total relationship environment or between them and the world outside. There are few areas of tension, because the items of difference that have arisen over the years have been settled as they arose. There often were differences of opinion but they have been handled, sometimes by compromise, sometimes by one or the other yielding; but these outcomes were of secondary importance because the primary consideration was not who was right or who was wrong, only how the problem could be resolved without tarnishing the relationship. When faced with differences, they can and do dispose of the difficulties without losing their feeling of unity or their sense of vitality.

Frances Klaysbrun points out the following characteristics of the long, satisfying, happy marriage: (1) an ability to change and tolerate change; (2) an ability to live with the unchangeable; (3) an assumption of permanence; (4) trust; (5) a balance of dependencies; (6) an enjoyment of each other; (7) a shared history that is cherished; and (8) luck. Klaysbrun adds: "There is no formula, no single recipe that when used in the right proportions will produce the perfect marriage, or even a working one. Rather, there are certain abilities and outlooks that couples in strong marriages have, not all of them at all times, but a larger proportion a good part of the time."

Like families, marriages have been in dramatic transition since the 1950s, and, historically, have probably always been in a state of evolution that has moved in an unsteady and somewhat herky-jerky fashion. Families and marriages have always struggled with outside circumstances and inner conflict. The problems and issues today are in part unique, for in the past people didn't live quite as long; they died before they got old; and before 1850, most women died in childbirth at the average age of 35. We today face conditions unknown to our ancestors, and we must find new ways to cope with them.

SOURCES

Cuber, John F., and Peggy B. Harroff. *The Significant American*. New York: Hawthorn. 1965.

Klaysbrun, Frances. *Married People: Staying Together in the Age of Divorce*. New York: Bantam. 1985.

Skolnick, Arlene S., and Jerome H. Skolnick, eds. *Family in Transition*. 8th ed. New York: Harper Collins. 1994.

MARSHALL, THURGOOD

Thurgood Marshall (1908–1993) was the first black justice of the Supreme Court of the United States and served as an associate justice from 1967 until his retirement in 1991. Marshall was appointed by President Lyndon B. Johnson. As a justice, Marshall took the liberal position on a wide variety of issues, including capital punishment, free speech, school desegregation, the rights of welfare recipients, and affirmative action. His background included serving as the chief counsel for the National Association for the Advancement of Colored People (NAACP) from 1938 to 1950; director and chief counsel for the NAACP Legal Defense and Educational Fund from 1940 to 1961; and presenting the legal argument that resulted in the 1954 Supreme Court decision that racial segregation in public schools is unconstitutional. He was appointed to the U.S. Court of Appeals in 1961, and in 1965 he was appointed solicitor general of the United States.

SOURCE

Fiss, Owen M. *Information Finder*. World Book. 1994.

MARXISM, ETHICS OF

Karl Marx was born in Trier, in the Rhineland province of Prussia, in 1818. His parents were Jews who had converted to Christianity when he was a child. He studied history, law, and philosophy at Bonn, Berlin, and Jena. In 1841, he received the doctorate in philosophy at Jena. Two years later he married and became a socialist. His radical views made him suspect with the authorities of his day, and perhaps prevented his employment as a university teacher. He threw himself into radical journalism, and, being expelled from Prussia, engaged in conspiratorial activities in France and Belgium from 1843 to 1849. *The Communist Manifesto*, written jointly with Friedrich Engels, was a product of these years, being published in January 1848. Having been expelled from France in 1849, he went to London where he spent the remainder of his life. During an exile that amounted to more than half his life, most of his energy was spent accumulating notes that were eventually published as *Das Kapital (Capital)*.

In Marx's writings, we are able to summarize his ethical teaching in the following major headings:

POLITICAL PHILOSOPHY

Communism was offered as a set of principles, action on which would realize once and for all the avowed objectives of the Great French Revolution—liberty, equality, and fraternity. With the realization of economic equality, to which communism furnished the key, real liberty and real brotherhood would be automatically attained. The basis for the communist protest was the appalling degradation that accompanied uncontrolled industrialism in the middle of the nineteenth century, an example of which is child labor. Marx wrote (in *Das Kapital*):

> There [is] an amount of privation and suffering among that portion of the population connected with the lace trade, unknown in other parts of the kingdom, indeed, in the civilized world. Children of nine or ten years are dragged from their squalid beds at two, three, or four o'clock in the morning and compelled to work for a bare subsistence until ten, eleven, or twelve at night, their limbs wearing away, their frames dwindling, their faces whitening, and their humanity absolutely sinking into a stone-like torpor, utterly horrible to contemplate. We declaim against the Virginian and Carolina cotton-planters. Is their black-market, their lash, and their barter of human flesh more detestable than this slow sacrifice of humanity which takes place in order that veils and collars may be fabricated for the benefit of capitalists?

Lane W. Lancaster remarks:

> We misconceive the nature of the communist appeal unless we understand that the moral impetus of that appeal came from the bitter indignation that Marx felt when he contemplated the injustice implied in these figures. As a social scientist, however, he tried to look at this waste of life and thwarting of hopes quite impersonally. In his view of history the accumulation of capital necessarily involved these consequences, since the profits of capitalists amounted to the difference between the wages paid to the worker and the price which the entrepreneur was able to exact in the market. It was this differential that he called surplus value, and he devoted a good part of his work, *Capital*, to developing this conception in what he believed was a scientific manner.

BASIC PRINCIPLES

We discover three basic principles in Marx's writings and the development of the communist ethic. The first is the *materialistic conception of history*, which represents the special "twist" Marx and Engels gave to the ideas of Hegel. Hegel believed that the only real thing about actual events was their rational aspect. This struck Marx and Engels as simply a reflection of the class interest of the bourgeois intellectuals. For them the moving force of history was not ideas or thought or spirit, but rather the relations in which men stood to each other in the process of production. For them history moves by contradiction and conflict in the affairs of men in real events. Engels comments:

> According to the materialistic conception of history the factor which is in the last instance decisive is the production and reproduction of actual life. More than this neither Marx nor I have ever asserted. But when anyone distorts this so as to read that the economic factor is the sole element, he converts the statement into a meaningless, abstract, absurd phrase. The economic condition is the basis, but the various elements of the superstructure—the political forms of the class contests, and their results, the constitutions—the legal forms, and also all the reflexes of these actual contests in the brains of the participants, the political, legal, philosophical, the religious views, all these exert an influence on the development of the historical struggles, and in many instances determine their form.

The second principle of importance is that of *class struggle*. The materialistic conception of history asserts that development takes place through a confrontation of opposites in a series comprising thesis, antithesis, and synthesis. Each of the manifestations of this unfolding of history produces its opposite; the resulting contradiction is transcended in a new synthesis, which itself becomes a new thesis. Thus in reality, any given system of production embodies itself in two contending classes, each of which exhibits patterns of thought as well as social, legal, and political institutions appropriate to its place in the production process. The end of this process for Marx and Engels is the classless society. Marx and Engels comment:

> We see then: the means of production and of exchange, on whose foundation the bourgeoisie built itself up, were generated in feudal society. At a certain stage in the development of these means of production and of exchange, the conditions under which feudal society produced and exchanged, the feudal organization of agriculture and manufacturing industry, in one word, the feudal relations of property became no longer compatible with the already developed productive forces; they became so many fetters. They had to be burst asunder; they were burst asunder.
>
> Into their place stepped free competition, accompanied by a social and political constitution adapted to it, and by the economical and political sway of the bourgeois class.
>
> A similar movement is going on before our own eyes. Modern bourgeois society with its relations of production, of exchange and of property, a society that has conjured up such gigantic means of production and of exchange, is like the sorcerer who is no longer able to control the powers of the nether world whom he has called up by his spells. . . .
>
> The essential condition for the existence and for the sway of the bourgeois class is the formation and augmentation of capital; the condition for capital is wage-labour. Wage-labour rests exclusively on competition between labourers. The advance of industry, whose revolutionary promoter is the bourgeoisie, replaces the isolation of the labourers, due to competition, by their revolutionary combination, due to association. The development of modern industry, therefore, cuts from under its feet the very foundation on which the bourgeoisie produces and appropriates products. What the bourgeoisie therefore produces, above all, are its own gravediggers. Its fall and the victory of the proletariat are equally inevitable.

The final major principle we find in Marx and Engels is the goal of the *classless society*. The many laborers of the proletarian dictatorship are preliminary to the classless society of the future. Until that society is a reality a very powerful and ruthless state will be necessary, but its function will render any state at all unnecessary. Once the dictatorship has succeeded in this enterprise, the working class will be the only class. There is no other to be opposed, and the state, which is by definition the organ of a class, disappears. Marx and Engels comment: "Society, thus far based upon class antagonisms, had need of the State, that is, of an organization for the purpose of preventing any interference from without with the existing conditions of production, and therefore, especially, for the purpose of forcibly keeping the exploited classes in the condition of oppression corresponding with the given mode of production (slavery, serfdom, wage-labour). When at last it becomes the real representative of the whole of society, it renders itself unnecessary."

This materialistic dialectic was offered by Marx and Engels, and later by Lenin, as the only true description of the historical process. In the twentieth century, Mao Zedong would provide a similar philosophy for Chinese communism. The political ethics involved in such a system stand in direct contrast to those implicit in democratic systems. Democratic views do not assume that there are any final answers to political and social questions, and are based on the belief that society survives by compromise hammered out from the conflicting views of individuals, views that they believe they are morally entitled to express and to which their transient rulers are morally bound to listen. The communist dialectic is based on the belief that there are political certainties that are scientifically inevitable and, therefore, ethically right. All who assist this historical process are found to be good, while those who impede it are evil. Physical power to reward the good and punish the evil becomes the only test of legitimacy and morality.

See also Communism, Ethics of.

SOURCES

Berlin, I. *Karl Marx: His Life and Environment.* London: Oxford University Press. 1948.

Lancaster, Lane W. *Masters of Political Thought.* Vol. 3. Boston: Houghton Mifflin. 1966.

MASS MEDIA, ETHICS OF

Mass media are the instruments by which mass communication takes place in modern societies. The four major categories of mass media include print media, recordings, motion pictures, and radio and television broadcasts. Because mass media communications are primarily one-way—audience members are rarely able to use the media to send their own messages; audience feedback is infrequent, indirect, and delayed; the communicators are physically separated from their audience; and the individuals and groups that make up the audience are separated from one another—this capacity to influence has made the mass media the subject of intensive study, criticism, and debate.

Another problem associated with propaganda and control is the fact that much of the world's media is controlled by a handful of international companies. As these media companies compete for advertising dollars, more and more control is given over to those retailers as they supply both the content of the mass media and support them financially. The mass media's dependence on advertising can force it to concentrate on attracting larger audiences rather than providing better books, programs, news coverage, or magazine articles. The influence of the media's content by advertisers is in opposition to media claims of "freedom of the press" in covering events and personalities, and seems to be an ethical dilemma. For in a democratic society where there are checks and balances for government organizations, there

appear to be no checks on the media. Hence, in both the print and broadcast media we find both "tabloid" journalism and far-right and -left political and religious "news" shows using the platform of freedom of the press to put forth their side of things with little concern for facts and truth, but, when pushed on the issue, claiming to be a part of the "entertainment" industry. The public's inability to verify news reports, technical information, and guarded "facts" makes it vulnerable to propaganda. Although a free and democratic society wishes to use censorship only sparingly, there seems to be an ethical dilemma or dilemmas involved in the mass media of today: control by only a few major companies, the infusion of advertiser dollars, the separation of audience from the source of the news or information, and the rise of tabloid journalism are causing serious ethical problems. A society that has tried to free itself from the tyranny of the majority may now be in serious jeopardy from the tyranny of the minority (it is tyranny of the majority if we substitute dollars for people).

SOURCES

Bagdikian, Ben H. *The Media Monopoly.* 4th ed. Boston: Beacon Press. 1990.

Boorstin, Daniel J. *The Image.* New York: Macmillan. 1961.

DeFleur, M. L., et al. *Understanding Mass Communication.* 4th ed. New York: Scholastic College Division. 1991.

McLuhan, Marshall H. *Understanding Media.* Cambridge, MA: MIT Press. 1994.

MATERIALISM

Materialism is a term used to refer to a broad spectrum of beliefs that give a primary place in the universe to matter and that attribute a secondary, dependent place to mind—or perhaps no place at all to mind. A material thing is something that has only physical properties such as size, shape, solidity, and hardness. Since such items as consciousness, purpose, and dreams do not seem to be physical, the materialists must either explain how they are physical, or at least how they are derived from the physical.

The thing most consistently unifying materialists of different types is that humans and everything else in nature must be explained in terms of causal laws based exclusively on observations of matter and motion. This approach to the study of humankind has been embraced with special enthusiasm in the physical sciences and among many behavioral psychologists. It is the desire to provide a comprehensive, unified, and scientific account of nature and the human's place in nature that continues to motivate scholars to embrace materialism.

The classical materialist Thomas Huxley was one of Charles Darwin's closest friends, and was a defender of Darwin against clergymen who attacked the theory of evolution, itself a view based on materialism. Moreover, Huxley began an explicit comparison of humans with the anthropoid apes, and he zealously pursued antievolutionists with challenges of public debate. As a biologist, Huxley believed that animal and human bodies are best understood as purely mechanical physical systems. Yet he was aware that states of consciousness do not appear themselves to be physical, and he set himself the task of discovering the relation between the mechanical body and the mind. Huxley never argues that the mind is the body, but he does contend that the mind is entirely controlled by the body. His materialism led him not only to determinism, but also to atheism, and to a strong denunciation of the religious view of human beings.

SOURCES

Beauchamp, Tom L., William T. Blackstone, and Joel Feinberg. *Philosophy and the Human Condition.* Englewood Cliffs, NJ: Prentice-Hall. 1980.

Hunt, Morton. *The Universe Within: A New Science Explores the Human Mind.* New York: Simon and Schuster. 1982.

Jaynes, Julian. *The Origin of Consciousness in the Breakdown of the Bicameral Mind.* Boston: Houghton Mifflin. 1976.

MATERNITY AND MOTHERHOOD

Women have played important economic roles in many societies, while suffering under overt patriarchy. During the past 150 years, separation of economic production from family has made the homemaking wife-mother role normative, and has subordinated these roles to the life and roles of the husband. But this situation is beginning to change, as noted by M. McGoldrick:

> Women have always played a central role in families, but the idea that they have a life cycle separate from their roles as wife and mother is relatively recent, and still not widely accepted in our culture. The expectation has been that women would take care of the needs of others, first men, then children, then the elderly. They went from being daughters, to wife, to mother, their status defined by the male in the relationship and their role by their position in the family's life cycle.

Bert N. Adams observes that "the notion of an independent life cycle is still not a reality for most women, and when it is real it is often out of necessity, not choice." Of course, there are negative elements in life-cycle expectation and even in the word *feminine,* which seems to connote deference to males, emotionality, and a lack of assertiveness, rather than the more positive qualities that facilitate interpersonal interactions (Gill, et al., 1987).

However, feminists provide "new thoughts" on maternity and motherhood. Upon inspection, we find that the subjects of maternity and motherhood are as deeply rooted in feminist scholarly discussion as they are in the feminist movement and for women in general. They are, as the editors of *Signs* remind us, "topics that connect all feminist scholars in their own lives—we may not all be mothers, but we are all the daughters or sons of mothers."

Keeping in mind both the positive and negative elements associated with maternity and motherhood, there are three broad role choices available to women that are important to mention: (1) In the first place, research shows that among college women, both careers and childbearing are expected (Baber and Monaghan, 1988). For most of these women, home/mother roles were not an option, but an assumption. (2) This idea is broadened as we discover that a daughter's identification with her mother's role as a mother transcends their generic identity as females and involves social and cultural norms. (3) Finally, the complexity of examining women's roles is further muddled because some women freely choose a "two-earner" family arrangement as a preferred lifestyle. Thus, it is childbearing that is added on to work, rather than vice versa. The decision is not whether or not to work, but whether or not to have a child.

To examine the complexity of women's role choices we must go beyond the simple dichotomy of employment versus nonemployment. Some women see motherhood as the most basic element in women's roles; others see employment and career as the basic self-identity force. These complexities, therefore, include which—parenthood or career—is subordinated, the difficulty in trying to "have it all," the continuing preeminence of male roles and lack of male role sharing, and choice versus nonchoice.

EMPLOYED WIVES: CONSENSUS, MOTIVES, SOCIAL CLASS, AND WAGES

In 1890, when the labor force of the United States was one-sixth female, few women worked and it was unmarried daughters who composed a majority of the female labor force, while today it is mothers and wives. Women's employment can be divided into four patterns:

1. *Conventional*—those who left the labor force at marriage or first birth and never returned;
2. *Interrupted*—those who left at marriage or first birth and returned after last birth;
3. *Double-track*—those who returned to the labor force before the birth of the last child; and
4. *Unstable*—those who have been in and out of the labor force several times.

Women's labor-force participation has dramatically changed in the past 50 years. Breadwinner-homemaker married couples have dropped from over two-thirds of all families to one-fifth. At the same time, dual-earner couples have risen from under 10 percent to over 40 percent. Four sets of issues, which overlap but are analytically separable, will bring the concept of maternity and motherhood into clearer focus:

Role Consensus

Marital adjustment is likely to be good if both spouses are doing what they prefer to be doing and what their spouse prefers them to be doing. Recent research (Vannoy-Hiller and Philliber, 1989) shows that the more traditional the wife believes her husband's expectations to be, the lower the quality of marriage experienced by both partners. Hochschild (1975) identifies three bases for marital tension: (1) between the husband's idea of what he and his wife should do at home and work, and his wife's idea about that matter; (2) tension to live the old-fashioned breadwinner-homemaker life, and the economic realities that make that life impossible; and (3) the tension between the family's need for care and the devaluation of the work required to provide such care—the care once provided by the homemaker.

Motives

Research finds "the negative consequences of wives' employment are concentrated among couples with traditional values who find it necessary for the wife to work" (Garfinkel and McLanahan, 1986). The psychological benefits of employment depend almost entirely on the mother of a young child feeling that she chooses to work, rather than working out of necessity or obligation. Paula Avioli (1985) studied white and black employed and unemployed wives with a child under three years of age. She found the following: (1) white employed wives work because of interest in participating in the labor force; (2) black employed wives work out of financial need, and usually work full time; (3) white housewives have little attachment to the labor force, and their husbands don't want them to work; and (4) black housewives have financial need, but cannot find work. When studying maternity and motherhood, issues of race and class cannot be ignored.

Social Class

More women than men hold to an egalitarian ideology, and more middle-class than working-class couples hold an egalitarian ideology. Because of class, religious, and ethnic differences, the studies that focus on this subject are quite vast and show many nuances and subtle differences. One would perhaps be advised to carefully examine feminist literature on this subject for a more complete perspective; namely, Langer's *Motherhood and Sexuality*; Johnson's *Mothers of Incest Survivors*; Rosenzweig's *The Anchor of My Life: Middle-Class American Mothers and Daughters*; Boyer, et al., *Apache Mothers and Daughters: Four Generations of a Family*; and Oakley's *Social Support and Motherhood*.

Wages

The highest marital adjustment scores are often reported when both couple members are satisfied with their jobs and the husband is high and the wife is low on job salience. Even with consensus, the husband may not want his wife's work to "get in the way" of other things—especially activities that involve the family or "his" work. In terms of consensus, regardless of social class, couples in the United States are still a long way from the goal of either women's or men's liberation.

SOURCES

Adams, Bert N. *The Family: A Sociological Interpretation*. 5th ed. New York: Harcourt Brace. 1995.

Avioli, P. S. "The Labor-Force Participation of Married Mothers of Infants." *Journal of Marriage and the Family* 47 (1985).

Baber, K. M., and P. Monaghan. "College Women's Career and Motherhood Expectations: New Options, Old Dilemmas." *Sex Roles* 19 (1988).

Boyer, R. W., et al. *Apache Mothers and Daughters: Four Generations of a Family*. Norman: University of Oklahoma Press. 1992.

Garfinkel, I., and S. S. McLanahan. *Single Mothers and Their Children*. Washington: Urban Institute. 1986.

Gill, S.. et al. "Measuring Gender Differences: The Expressive Dimension and Critique of Androgyny Scales." *Sex Roles* 17 (1987).

Hochschild, A. R. "Disengagement Theory: A Critique and Proposal." *American Sociological Review* 40 (1975).

Johnson, J. T. *Mothers of Incest Survivors*. Bloomington: Indiana University Press. 1992.

Langer, M. *Motherhood and Sexuality*. Translated by Nancy C. Hollander. New York: Guilford Press. 1992.

McGoldrick, M. "Women through the Family Life Cycle." In McGoldrick et al., eds. *Women in Families*. New York: Norton. 1989.

Oakley, Ann. *Social Support and Motherhood*. Cambridge: Blackwell. 1993.

Rosenzweig, L. W. *The Anchor of My Life: Middle-Class American Mothers and Daughters, 1880–1920*. New York: New York University Press. 1993.

MATRILINEAGE

Since the publication of Alice Walker's *In Search of Our Mothers' Gardens* in 1974, black feminist literary critics have recurrently used the metaphor of matrilineage to authorize their development of a black feminist literary tradition. Writers such as Dianne Sadoff, Marjorie Pryse, and Joanne Braxton posit the mother as the origin of the black woman's literary tradition, as well as the guarantor of its temporal continuity. The black feminist conversation on matrilineage seeks to unwrite a brutal history of rupture and dislocation and to write an alternative story of familial and cultural connection.

See also Feminism.

SOURCES

Braxton, Joanne M. "Afra-American Culture and the Contemporary Literary Renaissance." In *Wild Women in the Whirlwind: Afra-American Culture and the Contemporary Literary Renaissance.* Edited by Joanne M. Braxton and Andree N. McLaughlin, xxi—xxx. New Brunswick, NJ: Rutgers University Press. 1990.

Pryse, Marjorie. "Zora Neale Hurston, Alice Walker and the 'Ancient Power' of Black Women." In *Conjuring: Black Women, Fiction and Literary Tradition.* Edited by M. Pryse and H. Spellers. Bloomington: Indiana University Press. 1985.

Sadoff, Dianne F. "Black Matrilineage: The case of Alice Walker and Zora Neale Hurston." *Signs* 11 (1985).

Walker, Alice. *In Search of Our Mothers' Gardens.* New York: Harcourt Brace Jovanovich. 1984.

MEANING OF LIFE

The confusion that prompts the question, "What is the meaning of life?" can be expressed in a number of different ways, and it is the responsibility of the reader or hearer to interpret or understand each one: Does life have any significance or importance? Does it all add up to anything in the end? Or is it pointless, senseless, empty, unimportant, insignificant, or absurd? Of course, we can respond to the first of these questions by asking, "Whose life?" Plainly—and we should understand this point clearly—questions about "meaningfulness" make much more sense when asked about particular individuals than when asked about "life" in general. According to common sense, at least, some lives do have meaning, purpose, and/or significance. Some have more, some less, some none at all. This—and we should be clear about this, too—is a judgment call, because meaning is inherently personal and one whose life may appear to be relatively insignificant to the community at large may in fact be thought of—by the person himself or herself or by significant relatives and friends—as extremely significant and vital.

We can distinguish two broadly different ways of interpreting our original question, "What is the meaning of life?": (1) What is it that in fact confers meaning on the careers of those whose lives are (relatively) meaningful, at least by ordinary standards? and (2) What, if anything, is the meaning of human life in general? If this second question is answered negatively—that life in general has no meaning in the cosmic or ultimate sense—it leads quickly to a third: (3) If human life has no meaning, why is that the case? Exactly what is missing? What would it take to confer meaning on human life?

MEANING

When we inquire into the meaning of *meaning,* we discover two senses of the word that are applicable to questions about the meaning of life. First, we sometimes speak of "the meaning" of a particular work of art—novels, plays, paintings, sculpture, dance (but rarely musical compositions). For example, when we speak of "the meaning" of a particular work of art, we normally refer to the artist's intentions, what meaning he or she intended to convey, or we refer to something outside the work of art that it "points to" or "stands for." No matter which direction we take, its "meaning" is the key to its understanding, what one has to grasp about it in order to apprehend and admire it fully as a work of art.

Second, we sometimes speak of the actions or activities of human beings as having a meaning. Often when we do so, we do not apply arbitrary symbolic conventions or interpret natural signs, nor infer the person's intentions (for the meaning of the person's actions may not be anything he or she intends to convey to others), nor display the key to a sympathetic appreciation of what is observed. Rather, we describe what we take to be the actor's *purpose* in acting, the organizing play, or aim, or goal behind his or her actions that render them coherent, as opposed to merely random. It may be a *good* purpose or a *bad* one, but because it brings order and continuity to a person's activities in life, it can be called their "meaning."

PURPOSE

The word *purpose* also needs clarification. A person's purpose is his or her conscious goal, aim, or end—what the person wishes to produce as a consequence of the action. Often the answer to the question, "Why did you do so-and-so?" is a statement of the person's purpose in doing so-and-so—"in order to bring about such and such." Also, in a different but no doubt derivative sense, mere things can be said to "have purposes" too. Thus the purpose of a pen (to write) is not the conscious aim of the black and white plastic pen in my hand, for an inanimate object can have no purpose of its own. Rather, it is the purpose in the mind of the person who designed and manufactured the pen and the purpose of the one who uses it.

Here, with this sense of purpose, we have clearly related purpose to *function*. But function, purpose, and meaning cannot be taken as synonymous. For example, in the case of a machine such as an automobile, the function of a component part usually but not necessarily corresponds with its purpose—that is, with the job it was consciously designed to do—its function. On the other hand, a biologist might interpret the question, "What is the function of human life?" as a request for or an

account of the role our species plays in the larger ecological environment of which it is a part. But neither of these corresponds to what we normally intend when we ask for "the meaning of life."

VALUE/WORTHWHILENESS

For most of us, when we inquire about the meaning of life, we are referring to the value and worthwhileness of life, either in particular or in general. Most would agree that if life or a life has meaning and purpose, then it has value and worthwhileness; but sociologists today writing about "a lost generation," or about "revolution rock," or even about "new individualism" find a generation of young people who are questioning that life has meaning. George Panichas says, "Our moral response is perhaps the most serious casualty of the spirit of our time, making us impervious to our condition of shipwreck. Unable to respond critically or morally to a Woodstock, and to everything it stands for, we perpetuate the structure of life we have been furiously fashioning. Woodstock, in the end, recreates our spiritual emptiness, our social disorientation, our moral obtuseness."

Perhaps Woodstock II, to which Panichas was referring, was a flash in the pan, a temporary and obscure pimple on the historic cultural landscape. Or perhaps, as Panichas thinks, it symbolizes a break with a system of moral values that has not ushered in the "moral community" so *idealistic* in the mind of our youth. The nihilism displayed at Woodstock I and II is played out in a million smaller cases each day in communities all over the world. Ours is a culture, a civilization in search of meaning, of self, of value, of "the permanent things." Some doubt that these so-called permanent things were ever there, but in the minds of every adolescent, this search is real and begins with a break with the past—the values of traditional religion, the public schools, and the authority of parents. Western civilization itself began its adolescent search for meaning and value soon after World War II, perhaps stimulated by racial, ethnic, and gender unrest and dissatisfaction and sped up by the Vietnam War. From Baby Boomers and their new individualism to the rockers and post-rockers (*alternative music* is now the term), with their Woodstock nihilism, and now to scholars who are searching for signs in what they call "postmodernism," one sees traditional values and ethics in disarray, religion drawing into itself and becoming even more authoritarian, and public education searching for quick fixes in therapeutic programs that are quickly replacing a traditional emphasis on academics in order to stem the tide of violence, drug use, and absenteeism.

By living in an environment of shifting values, all seems relative and nothing appears dangerous, wrong, or sinful. As Panichas observes, "any spontaneous urge, however flagrant, is acceptable." And although values and virtues seem to have vanished—at least the traditional ones—we can ask as did Keats, "Was it a vision, or a waking dream?" Was Woodstock—the Woodstock in ourselves—illusion, or is it reality? Have we overreacted or misinterpreted? Perhaps we have matured through an ordered consent to the passion stirred in us by desire for meaning, for worthwhileness, and so might our civilization.

As we approach the new millennium, we find the moral, intellectual, and spiritual crisis of our time is visible most plainly in the arts. The postmodern cultural establishment is, in the words of Frederick Turner, philosophically empty and esthetically corrupt. In his *Culture of Hope*, Turner argues that the changes in scientific thought and a new esthetic synthesis arising from the unexpected convergence of religion, art, and science will restore a hopeful vision of the universe (one of meaning, value, and worthwhileness) as intelligent, creative, and self-ordering and provide the missing ground for the recovery of classical values in the arts, such as beauty, order, harmony, and meaning. Turner comments:

As machines take over the drudgery, the labor basis of value is being replaced by an information basis of value; and this in turn will be replaced, perhaps, by an emergent kind of value which is hard to define but has a kind of embodied grace. . . . Freedom is what our bodies were designed to produce, if they are properly taught, disciplined, loved, and nurtured by a culture that has not forgotten its roots. Freedom is not a condition but a unique personal achievement, reached through submission to one's culture's best traditions and one's body's demand for training in what it does best.

Although Turner's analysis focuses on the arts, his insights into modern sociological conditions are profound. He sees a new movement—what he calls the *Radical Center*—evolving in the arts that rejects the ethnocentrism of the right and the demonization of the West by the left that perhaps gives us hope that a common vision is possible and that our moral fiber has not been so frayed as to leave us empty and meaningless.

SOURCES

Baier, Kurt. "The Meaning of Life." Inaugural Lecture, Canberra University College. 1957.

Balfour, Arthur. *Foundations of Belief*. New York: Longmans. 1919.

Panichas, George A. "The Woodstock in Our Selves." *Modern Age* 37:3 (Spring 1995).

Turner, Frederick. *The Culture of Hope: A New Birth of the Classical Spirit*. New York: Free Press. 1995.

MEDICAL ETHICS

The physician's code embodies ideas that have been in the process of formation since ancient times. The laws of Hammurabi (2500 B.C.) dealt with fees paid to physicians and with punishment when injury was done. During the fifth century B.C. in Greece, the "Oath of Hippocrates" set forth the duties of the medical man. Although physicians generally have been men and women of character and integrity and have made outstanding advances in medicine, current books and articles on health problems and medical ethics—many of which have been written by doctors and other health specialists—leave one with the impression that there are numerous problems and much to be done to maintain and improve the health of the people of the world as a whole. Controversies surround such matters as fees and charges, insurance and prepayment plans, fee splitting, "ghostsurgery," group practice, experimenting with patients, transplanting organs from healthy to diseased persons, and so on.

There are a number of conditions responsible, at least in part, for the new problems: (1) the rapid increase of medical knowledge and new laboratory techniques, with the creation of numerous specialties and subspecialties, which has changed the nature of the doctor-patient relationship and has brought various forms of "multiple practices" and the use of nondoctors or physician assistants on an ever-widening scale; (2) the growing demand for some method of payment that distributes the cost of medical care more evenly over the years; (3) the growing demand for more preventive medicine; and (4) the fact that both government and industry are employing doctors on a salary basis to provide medical service for their employees or members.

The American Medical Association (AMA) was organized in 1847 and immediately became concerned with a code of ethics and with setting minimum standards for medical education and practice. In 1955 the AMA published *Principles of Medical Ethics*, which establish the purpose of the medical association in addition to the patient's right to choose his or her physician; the physician's right to choose whom he or she will serve; free competition among doctors; and a "fee commensurate with the service rendered and the patient's ability to pay."

The *Principles* clearly condemn certain practices as unethical. These include fee splitting—the secret division of fees among doctors for referring patients to them;

"ghost surgery," in which one doctor passes his patient over to another in the operating room to perform the operation; advertising or the solicitation of patients; accepting rebate on prescriptions and appliances or commissions from those who aid in the care of patients; taking a patent on a surgical or diagnostic instrument so as to retard research or restrict its use; association with or assistance of cultists, optometrists, and medical organizations controlled by groups of laymen; and criticism of other doctors in the presence of patients.

Problems facing the medical profession include the following:

- The uneven distribution of doctors. A more even distribution of medical personnel and resources, and of the cost of medical care, would partially remedy many unsatisfactory conditions.
- Experiments with patients. What risks in experimenting with humans, rather than animals, may legitimately or ethically be taken? Organ transplants are a case in point: Who is to decide who is to live and who is to die?
- Can practices such as sterilization, abortion, and artificial insemination ever be morally justified?
- Can euthanasia ("mercy killing") be justified? If so, how?
- Does an individual have a right to know the truth about the condition of his or her health? There are times when a patient is emotionally unable to cope with the full knowledge of his or her illness, and this knowledge could be detrimental to his or her well-being; yet, without knowledge of one's condition and the freedom to choose on the basis of the known facts, patients are little more than puppets.
- Finally, what ethical issues arise in meeting medical costs? Are insurance companies dictating the type and longevity of certain medical servic-

es—even what doctors one can see—and is this in the patient's best interest? Are patients denied certain medical procedures or drugs because of their inability to pay, or because insurance companies think them too expensive, or because of age?

When considering these problems in particular cases, the interests of the physician and his or her fellow practitioners as well as the larger interests of humanity have to be considered and adjusted—and not just from a practical point of view, but from a moral point of view as well. The harmonizing of practice and ideals in a changing society is an ever-present problem.

See also Abortion; American Medical Association; Ethics, Theory of; Euthanasia; Hippocratic Oath.

SOURCES

American Academy of Political and Social Science. "Medicine and Society." *The Annals* 346 (1963).

"Ethical Aspects of Experimentation with Human Subjects." *Daedalus* (Spring 1969).

Ferre, Frederick. *Philosophy and Technology.* Athens: University of Georgia Press. 1995.

Nozick, Robert. *Philosophical Explanations.* Cambridge, MA: Harvard University Press. 1981.

Vaux, Kenneth. *Who Shall Live? Medicine, Technology, Ethics.* Philadelphia: Fortress Press. 1970.

MENTAL HEALTH

Certainly one of the things we prize the most is our health. Most of us think about our health in physical terms. Either we are sick or we are healthy, and we know which state we are in on the basis of the cues we get from our bodies. However, health is a psychological issue as well as a physical one. The psychological study of health considers four main areas: (1) promoting and maintaining health; (2) preventing and treating illness; (3) identifying the causes and correlates of health, illness, or other dysfunctions; and (4) improving the health care system and the formation of health policy.

Another important lesson of health psychology is that health is not a purely physical matter, but rather a *biopsychosocial state.* According to the biopsychosocial model, a person's state of health is a complex interaction among several factors: *biological factors* such as genetic predisposition to a particular disease or exposure to a certain virus; *psychological factors* such as the experience of stress; and *social factors* such as the amount of social support one receives from one's friends and family. Once we view health and illness in this way, it becomes clear that good health is something that everyone achieves by engaging in a healthy lifestyle.

SOURCES

Gatchel, R. J., and A. Baum. *An Introduction to Health Psychology.* Reading, MA: Addison-Wesley. 1983.

Taylor, S. G. *Health Psychology.* New York: Random House. 1986.

MERCY KILLING

See Euthanasia.

METAETHICS

Ethics and the study of ethics are generally divided into two broad categories: *normative ethics* and *metaethics*. Normative ethics asks what is morally right, wrong, or obligatory; what is morally good or bad; when are we morally responsible; and what is desirable, good, or worthwhile. Normative ethics seeks to arrive at acceptable principles of obligation and general judgments of value in order to determine what is morally right, wrong, or obligatory, and what or who is morally good, bad, or responsible.

On the other hand, metaethics does not propound any moral principles or goals for action, except possibly by implication. Thus, its role is entirely philosophical analysis: clarifying and understanding the language and propositions of normative theory; e.g., "A Linguistic Analysis of the Question 'Why Be Moral?'" (a 1972 doctoral dissertation topic). Metaethics, observes William K. Frankena, asks the following questions: (1) What is the meaning or definition of ethical terms like *right*, *wrong, good*, or *bad*? That is, what is the nature, meaning, or function of judgments in which these and similar terms occur? What are the rules for the use of such terms and sentences? (2) How are moral uses of such terms to be distinguished from nonmoral ones, or moral judgments from other normative ones? What is the meaning of *moral* as contrasted with *nonmoral*? (3) What is the analysis or meaning of related terms or concepts like *action, conscience, free will, intention, promising, excusing, motive, responsibility, reason*, and *voluntary*? Finally, (4) Can ethical and value judgments be proved, justified, or shown valid? If so, how and in what sense? Or, what is the logic of moral reasoning and of reasoning about values?

Bernard Williams, when writing about "styles of ethical theory," says that the most helpful use of the expression "ethical theory" can best be caught by a rather complex definition: "An ethical theory is a theoretical account of what ethical thought and practice are, which either implies a general test for the correctness of basic ethical beliefs and principles or else implies that there cannot be such a test. It is the first kind of ethical theory, the positive kind." This is the classic definition of metaethics. Williams comments: "The first [normative] made substantive claims about what one should do, how one should live, what was worthwhile, and so on. The

second concerned itself with the status of these claims: whether they could be knowledge, how they could be validated, whether they were (and in what sense) objective, and so forth."

From the end of World War II to the early 1970s, metaethics seemed to be the only avenue for philosophers interested in ethics because of the newly emerging emphasis on language and language analysis. By the mid-1980s, this distinction was considered less significant, or convincing, than it had been. According to Williams, the most obvious and most relevant of these reasons is "that what one thinks about the subject matter of ethical thought, what one supposes it to be about, must itself affect what tests for acceptability or coherence are appropriate to it; and the use of those tests must affect any substantive ethical results. Conversely, the use of certain tests and patterns of argument can imply one rather than another view of what ethical thought is. A theory that combines views on what ethical thought is and how it should be conducted, with substantive consequences of conducting it in that way, is a positive ethical theory."

Frederick Ferre notes: "Ethical theory is not, however, designed to remove disagreements altogether. It may illuminate vital questions for responsible choice, but it will not finally by itself single out a uniquely ethical policy for action. It can push our preferences back to our fundamental convictions about what is real and worthwhile, and thus require us (insofar as we are rational) to acknowledge the implications of our choices, but it is not designed to guarantee moral behavior or even to guarantee unanimity or exactly what moral behavior requires."

See also Justification of Ethical Principles.

SOURCES

Ferre, Frederick. *Philosophy and Technology*. Athens: University of Georgia Press. 1995.

Frankena, William K. *Ethics*. 2d ed. Englewood Cliffs, NJ: Prentice-Hall. 1973.

Hester, Joseph P. "A Linguistic Examination of the Question 'Why Be Moral?'" Doctoral dissertation. Athens: University of Georgia. 1972.

Williams, Bernard. *Ethics and the Limits of Philosophy.* Cambridge, MA: Harvard University Press. 1985.

———. *Making Sense of Humanity.* New York: Cambridge University Press. 1995.

MONOGAMY

See Marriage.

MONROE DOCTRINE

The Monroe Doctrine, which grew out of conditions in Europe (the Holy Alliance of three leading absolute monarchies: Russia, Austria, and Prussia) and threatened to put an end to the system of representative government, was set forth by President James Monroe in a message he delivered to the Congress of the United States on December 2, 1823. It supported the independent nations of the Western Hemisphere against European interference "for the purpose of oppressing them, or controlling in any other manner their destiny." Also specified in the doctrine was that the American continents were "henceforth not to be considered as subjects for future colonization by any European powers." This statement was as important in 1823 as in 1962, with the Cuban missile crisis, for it would not allow new colonies to be created in the Americas, nor would it permit existing colonies to extend their boundaries.

SOURCES

Hofstadter, Richard, ed. *Great Issues in American History.* Vols. 1–3. New York: Vintage. 1958.

Schwartz, Bernard. *The Roots of the Bill of Rights.* Volumes 1–5. New York: Chelsea House. 1971.

MORAL OBLIGATION

Morality is a particular development of ethical thought, one that has special significance in modern Western culture. It particularly emphasizes certain ethical values over others, developing specifically a special kind of *obligation.* As a matter of fact, if we think of ethics as a rather broad system of values, we can define morals as a special use of ethical value, one that falls within a certain notion of obligation resting—as Immanuel Kant reminded us—at a deep level, in a person's *will.* To act morally is to act autonomously, not as a result of social pressure. In morality, a moral obligation is expressed in one especially important kind of deliberative conclusion—a conclusion that is directed toward what to do, governed by moral reasons, and concerned with a particular situation (for example, whether to keep a person hooked up to a machine that keeps the otherwise brain-dead person breathing). A moral obligation does not say that a person *may* do something, but that the person *should* or *ought to* or *must* do it, if the action is one that is in one's power and ability to perform: "Ought implies can." Another feature of moral obligations is that they cannot conflict ultimately. This follows from the assumption that what I am obliged to do must be in my power, if one also grants the principle *(the agglomeration principle)* that if I am obliged to do X and obliged to do Y, then I am obliged to do both X and Y.

Stephen David Ross invented a terminology, still sometimes used, for discussing the conflict of obligations that distinguishes between prima facie and actual obligations. A *prima facie obligation* is a conclusion supported by moral considerations that is a candidate for being one's *actual obligation.* It will be the proper conclusion of one's moral deliberation if it is not outweighed by another obligation. For example, if I have good and compelling reasons for breaking a promise, I many not be under an actual obligation to compensate the person who has been let down. The actual obligation has been broken because other considerations "outweigh" the prima facie, promise-keeping one. It is mistaken to blame or reproach oneself for not doing the rejected action: self-reproach belongs with broken (actual) obligations, and, it has turned out, there was no actual obligation broken.

As we inquire more deeply, we find that moral obligation is inescapable. Once we place ourselves under an actual moral obligation or find that we are under a moral obligation that was not our personal choice, there is no escaping it. The sense that moral obligation is inescapable, that what I am obliged to do is what I *must* do, is the first-personal end of moral obligation—that moral obligation applies to people even if they do not want it to. The third-personal aspect is that moral judgment and blame can apply to people even if, at the most, they want to live outside morality altogether. From the perspective of morality, there is no "where" outside the system, or at least, no "where" for a responsible person outside the system. As Kant wrote, moral obligation is categorical.

SOURCES

Ross, Stephen David. *The Nature of Moral Responsibility.* Detroit: Wayne State University Press. 1973.

Williams, Bernard. *Ethics and the Limits of Philosophy.* Cambridge, MA: Harvard University Press. 1985.

MORAL RELATIVITY

Moral relativity sets itself against claims of moral objectivity, the claim that moral views can be rationally justified or validated in the sense of holding up against all rivals through an impartial and informed examination. Moral relativism argues that moral objectivity is simply mistaken and must be given up. There are three forms of moral relativism: (1) *descriptive relativism* says that the basic ethical beliefs of different people and societies are different and even conflicting; (2) *metaethical relativism* holds that, in the case of basic ethical judgments, there is not an objectively valid, rational way of justifying one against another; consequently two conflicting basic judgments may be equally valid; and (3) *normative relativism,* which puts forth a normative principle (whereas descriptive relativism makes an anthropological or sociological assertion and metaethical relativism makes a metaethical one). That is, what is right or good for one person or society is not right or good for another, even if the situations involved are similar, meaning not merely that what is thought right or good by one is not thought right or good by another, but that what is really right or good in the one case is not so in another. This seems to violate requirements for consistency and universalization, but one can be a relativist of either sort described in (1) and (2) above without believing that the same kind of conduct is right for one person or group and wrong for another.

SOURCES

Frankena, William K. *Ethics.* 2d ed. Englewood Cliffs, NJ: Prentice-Hall. 1973.

Givertz, Harry K. *Beyond Right and Wrong.* New York: Free Press. 1973.

THE MORAL POINT OF VIEW

Ethics, as Aristotle points out, is a socialization process and aims at producing social individuals, imbued with their culture. Yet it is maintained that, although ethical behavior is fundamentally social, the purpose of ethics is not to deny individuals their personalities, aims, and aspirations. This latter thought is well contained within the definition of the moral point of view presented by Kurt Baier. Baier argues that the moral point of view looks and treats all people as "equally important centers of craving, impulses, desires, needs, aims, and aspirations; as people with ends of their own, all of which are entitled, prima facie, to be attained. From this point of view, every one of those individuals is required to modify his impulsive behavior, his endeavors and his plans by observing certain rules, the genuinely moral rules."

In Baier's view, ethics embodies both an individual and a social purpose, including principles of modification and exception. These two principles are called by Baier *principles of differentiation and priority. Differentiation* means that ethical rules governing societies and persons will differentiate between individuals only on morally relevant grounds. These include the following: (1) breaking a moral rule may result in a loss of protection by other moral rules; (2) special effort by someone on another's behalf may result in special considerations; (3) greater or less need may result in fewer or more tasks, duties, jobs, and obligations; and (4) special undertakings freely entered into may result in special obligations to carry these out.

The *principle of priority* says that when two moral or social rules clash, the moral person ought to observe the more important rule and break the less important one. Importance will be determined by the short- and long-range consequences of the behavior chosen, the number of people affected by the behavior, its effect on the self, and its consistency or lack of consistency with the principle of nondiscrimination. For Baier, the point of view of morality embodies no absolutes. Reason, prudence, and contextual considerations will involve individuals in the process of moral deliberation, of moral decision making. We should note that in Baier's view, the principle governing moral thinking is *nondiscrimination* or *fairmindedness*, the essence of the moral point of view. *Nondiscrimination*, when used as a moral guide, implies that

moral considerations and their subsequent responsibilities will be applied to everyone alike, and will only differentiate between individuals and circumstances on morally relevant grounds.

SOURCES

Baier, Kurt. *The Moral Point of View: A Rational Basis of Ethics.* Ithaca, NY: Cornell University Press. 1958.
――――. "The Point of View of Morality." *Australasian Journal of Philosophy* 32 (1954).
Frankena, William K. "The Concept of Morality." *Journal of Philosophy* 63 (1966).

MORALITY: THREE SCHOOLS OF CONTEMPORARY ETHICS

In revolt against traditional concepts of the good, three theories have come to dominate contemporary ethics: *utilitarianism, deontology,* and *communitarianism.* Each begins by denying reason's ability to prescribe directly authoritive ends and actions, and each claims exclusive validity for its own alternative. Although all three go on to absolutize a different determination of ethics, the diversity of their positions reflects a differentiation inherent in moral life.

UTILITARIANISM

Utilitarianism claims that reason's failure to dictate what goals and activities should be performed renders all claims of ethical validity ultimately matters of preference. Whatever ends and actions may be assigned moral significance are given moral status because they are objects of personal desire whose attainment, as such, provides pleasure. Feeling and desire are thus not just evidence for practical judgments, but the only evidence by which conduct can be judged. All things and actions are thereby deprived of instrinsic value, obtaining worth only by being of use in satisfying the extraneous end of given desire. At the same time, reason's inability to rank ends prevents the content of desires from being rationally ordered. If any goals and activities are to be assigned primacy, it can only be on the quantitative ground that their achievement likely offers a greater aggregate of pleasure. This provides the *utility principle*, whereby the good is nothing but the greatest satisfaction of the interests of the greatest number. On this accounting, moral freedom is the liberty of following desire that every individual enjoys by nature, and reason is relegated to a slave of passions, calculating the best means for promoting this empirically determined end.

DEONTOLOGY

In reaction to utilitarianism, deontology takes reason's incapacity to prescribe ends and actions to signify not that ethics is left to calculate aggregate satisfactions of desire, but that the formal character of intended action is the source of its validity. However this formal standard is defined, be it as the universalizability of intentions or as conformity to a privileged choice procedure certifying approval by all concerned, it offers a paradigm of *rational willing* that distinguishes the moral from the immoral without making any prior commitment to particular goals and activities, nor to any institutional framework they might sustain, nor, for that matter, to the privileged authority of preference calculation.

Deontology rejects the utilitarian principle as a dogmatic hypothesis that is hopelessly unworkable because of the incommensurability and contingency of desires and their satisfactions, and blind to any alternative solutions. In rendering all conduct instrumental to the maximization of pleasure, utilitarianism must face the question of why that goal can have exclusive legitimacy and not be itself instrumental to some further end. If, then, neither the content of ends and actions nor the pleasure that attends their achievement can

provide legitimacy for conduct, what else can render action conformable to moral principle than the forms of the willing that underlies it? So long as the person's intention has a lawfulness satisfying the normative requirement of universality, the quality of conduct's motivation can give it a moral character independent of desires and consequences. In accepting this as the only alternative, deontology may depart from the consequentialism of utilitarianism, but it still joins utilitarian thought in providing an ethic whose standard applies to persons irrespective of what community ties they have, to the exclusion of any other norms. In this respect, deontology offers a vision of morality without community in which a self-defining, disengaged individual agency is the force for determining ethical norms.

COMMUNITARIANISM

Communitarianism, on the contrary, rejects all such notions of a morality without community. It thinks reason's incapacity to dictate the goals and activities of the good life renders ethical standards internal to forms of community whose own character is historically given rather than rationally prescribed. The utilitarians' and deontologists' options are dismissed on the grounds that the deontologists' formal criterion is as arbitrary as utilitarianism's appeal to aggregate pleasures, and that its privileged form can no more unequivocally identify valid conduct than the principle of utility. The universalizability of the intentions of an action may, for instance, be a necessary condition of morality, but it is not a sufficient condition that allows for differentiating moral from immoral conduct. Instead, communitarianism maintains that ethical standards only have an identifiable validity for persons who belong to a community within which membership entails a pursuit of common ends and activities by which members reproduce the bonds that unite them to one another and the roles they exercise. This means not simply that moral persons are inherently in relationship to each other, but that the forms of their activities and the content of their purposes are predicated upon the existing institutional framework to which they constitutively belong. Thus, the communitarian vision of obligation binds people to reproduce the very mode of community that determines their moral identity and common duties. The ethical is thus inherently actual, for ethical norms are now seen to operate only within a context where their pursuit both assumes and sustains an existing community embodying their realization.

Upon reflection, we must recognize that utilitarianism, deontology, and communitarianism reflect essential aspects of ethics that are not mutually exclusive and that, subject to proper reformulation, each captures dimensions of a unitary ethic dictated by reason independently of appeals to their old formulations. A full discussion of this idea can be found in Richard Dien Winfield's *Freedom and Modernity*.

See also Ethics, Theory of.

SOURCES

Foster, M. B. *The Political Philosophies of Plato and Hegel*. Oxford: Oxford University Press. 1968.

Taylor, Charles. *Philosophy and the Human Sciences: Philosophical Papers 2*. Cambridge: Cambridge University Press. 1985.

Winfield, Richard Dien. *Freedom and Modernity*. Albany: State University of New York Press. 1991.

———. *The Just Economy*. New York: Routledge. 1988.

———. *Reason and Justice*. Albany: State University of New York Press. 1988.

N

NATION OF ISLAM

The Nation of Islam is a religious movement in the United States. For 45 years—1930 to 1975—the Nation of Islam accepted only blacks as members and thought of whites as "Devils." They also supported the separation of blacks and whites, combining some teachings of the Islamic religion with doctrines of black nationalism. After 1975, the movement turned toward Sunni Islam and began accepting people regardless of ethnic background. Today, the Nation of Islam prefers not to use the designation *Black Muslim*.

Leaders of the Nation of Islam and Black Muslim movements included W. D. Fard, who taught his followers that their true religion was not Christianity, but the Islamic religion of the blacks of Asia and Africa; Elijah Muhammad, who claimed that Fard was Allah and that he was Allah's messenger, and who taught (1) the need for blacks to establish a separate nation in the United States, (2) the need to recover an acceptable identity, and (3) the need for economic independence; Malcolm X, who converted to the movement while in prison; and Louis Farrakhan, who has continued the black separatist and nationalist teachings of Elijah Muhammad.

See also Black Power.

SOURCES

Lincoln, C. Eric. *The Black Muslims in America*. Westport, CT: Greenwood Press. 1982.

Lomax, Louis E. *When the Word Is Given: A Report on Elijah Muhammad, Malcolm X, and the Black Muslim World*. Westport, CT: Greenwood Press. 1979.

Marsh, Clifton E. *From Black Muslims to Muslims: The Transition from Separatism to Islam, 1930–1980*. Metuchen, NJ: Scarecrow Press. 1984.

NATIONALISM

Nationalism is the belief that one's own country is the best or that one's own national group (ethnic or racial group) is the best in the world. At its best, nationalism may be a healthy pride in one's country or national group. At its worse, it may cause one nation or ethnic group to try to dominate others.

The feeling of nationalism is not uncommon. In ancient times, one's allegiance was to the city-state. In the middle ages, one's chief loyalty was to the church or social class or even tribe, rather than to the nation (if there was one). As trade and communication took hold in Europe, city-states became countries and mercantilist interests replaced social class. Nationalism, defined in terms of wealth and power, replaced old loyalties such as those to the church or ethnic group. At the end of the

Enlightenment in Europe, the American Revolution and the French Revolution strengthened nationalism—and along with it, trade, wealth, and an emphasis on representative government. People were now united in the common causes of winning freedom, defending their nation against foreign enemies, and strenthening their nation through trade and commerce. Even in the 1990s, news broadcasts seldom fail to mention the *balance of trade* in terms of dollars between the major industrial countries.

Nationalism and national pride are reinforced by threats from the outside and from practices of discrimination. Discrimination reminds victims of the need for meaningful forms of group identification and expression. Although many ethnic and racial groups come to the United States because of promises of freedom, fraternity, and equality, poverty and cultural inequality and the emotional drive to unite with others have drawn many into the hundreds of fraternal societies that flourish throughout the country. On coming to the United States they were faced by rebuff and sought the security of renewed identification with their own ethnic, racial, or former national groups. Without quite knowing it, they longed to hear speech that was familiar to their ears and smell food like the food that they were accustomed to eating. As in other societies, these impulses strengthened their ethnic identification rather than their national identification.

It was under the economic threat of the Great Depression of the 1930s and the military threat of Nazism that new meanings were given to liberty and fraternity in the United States. With the New Deal, ethnic groups in America attempted to square their individual cultural heritage with the requirements of the larger society. That redefinition of liberty and fraternity was joined with assertions of rights of citizenship and equality before the law. Socially and culturally, America slowly began to acquire a more definitive persona wrapped in openness, acceptance, and pluralism. This idealism cast in the form of nationalism has continued through the civil rights movement, antiwar demonstrations, the coming of age of Baby Boomers, movements for gender equity, and efforts to develop a multicultural, politically correct society. One wonders if some of these activities are not having a negative effect on the growth of nationalism and a positive effect on learning about individual differences and developing respect for them.

See also Ethnocentrism.

SOURCES

Handlin, Oscar, and Lilian Handlin. *Liberty and Equality: 1920–1994*. New York: Harper Collins. 1994.

Lappe, Frances Moore. *Rediscovering America's Values*. New York: Ballantine. 1989.

Reich, Robert B. *Tales of a New America*. New York: Times Books. 1987.

NATIVE AMERICANS

The Native Americans were the first inhabitants of North America and the first to be subordinated to the Europeans. The Native Americans who survived contact with the white people were removed from their ancestral homes, often far away. The government weakened tribal institutions through a succession of acts beginning with the Allotment Act of 1884, and efforts to strengthen tribal autonomy, such as the 1934 adoption of white society's lifestyle. The modern period of Native American-white relations is characterized by government programs (Employment Assistance Program and the Termination Act) that encouraged Native Americans to assimilate. But the *Red-Power* and *Pan-Indian* movements speak of a diverse native people with many needs: settlement of treaty violations, increased employment opportunities, control over natural resources, improved educational programs, and greater self-rule, to name a few.

Research shows that both black Americans and Native Americans are more likely to have lower incomes than whites, to suffer from poor health, and to experience prejudice and discrimination. Both of these minority groups have protested these injustices for centuries. Beginning in the 1960s, these civil rights protests gained a new sense of urgency. But there the similarities between the nearly 29 million African Americans and the 1.4 million Native Americans in the United States end. For example, the Indian reservation is not a ghetto. It is economically depressed, but the reservation is their home—if not physically, then ideologically. Also, the reservation's isolation means that frustrations of reservation life and violent outbursts do not alarm large numbers of whites as disturbances in black ghettos do. The federal government, since the Bureau of Indian Affairs was created in 1824, has had much greater control over Native Americans than any other civilian group in the nation.

THE INDIGENOUS ENVIRONMENTAL NETWORK

By 1995 the Indigenous Environmental Network (IEN) was staking out a new position in the histories of both the Native movement for sovereignty and the environmental movement for a cleaner earth. The IEN was founded in 1990 at the village of Dilkon, on the Dine (Navajo) Nation in Arizona. It was hosted by Dine Citizens Against Ruining Our Environment (CARE), a reservation group opposed to toxic waste storage, incineration, and clearcutting. The network has six primary goals:

1. Educate and improve Indigenous grassroots people to address and develop strategies for the protection of the environment;
2. Reaffirm our traditional and natural laws as Indigenous peoples;
3. Recognize, support, and promote environmentally sound lifestyles and economic livelihoods;

4. Commit to influence all politics that affect our people on a local, regional, national, and international level;
5. Include youth and elders in all levels of activities; and
6. Protect our rights to practice our spiritual beliefs.

In 1991, the IEN established an Environmental Code of Ethics: "As Indigenous Peoples, we speak for ourselves; no one is authorized to speak on our behalf. Environmental groups have no rights to represent Indigenous Peoples. We will not make accommodations for or deals with polluters." According to the IEN, among threats to native lands are the following:

- Commercial nuclear wastes
- Military pollution (nuclear wastes/weapons)
- Oil (spills, drilling)
- Logging (clearcutting)
- Toxics (chemical waste storage)
- Dams (flooding indigenous lands)
- Mining (of sacred sites)
- Harvesting rights

In association with environmental concerns and the defense of natural resources, the IEN has blended native sovereignty. This is a new environmentalism that includes supporting the survival of endangered cultures and putting the protection of nature in a larger social, cultural, and economic context. The IEN's strategies come strictly from the grass roots. In workshops and meetings, many indigenous people prefer to talk about building an ecologically appropriate economic base in their local communities. While they continue to gain strength from within their own societies, they also have unique perspectives on the twenty-first-century capitalist society. Their views tend to put less naive faith in the ability of the powers-that-be to protect the earth, and more trust in the power of local communities that are resisting the modern technological-capitalistic society in their own political, cultural, and spiritual ways.

SOURCES

American Indian Policy Commission. Washington, D.C.: U.S. Government Printing Office. 1976.

Deloria, Vine, and Clifford M. Lytle. *American Indians, American Justice.* Austin: University of Texas Press. 1983.

Grossman, Soltan. "Native and Environmental Grassroots Movements." *Z Magazine* (November 1995).

IEN National Office. P.O. Box 485, Bemidji, MN 56601.

Josephy, Alvin Jr. *Now That the Buffalo's Gone: A Study of Today's American Indians.* New York: Alfred A. Knopf. 1982.

NATURAL LAW

The term *natural law* refers to a wide variety of theories attempting to outline a moral basis of law and justice. Although doctrines of natural law exhibit a remarkable diversity of content, a few basic shared features can be isolated. Generally, natural law is understood in opposition to *positive, existing law,* which—as enacted from the Marxist perspective—expresses the interests of the ruling class in a class society. Unlike doctrines of natural law, positive law theories hold that no element of law preexists as an act of the state. Consequently, the test of the validity of the law is not moral but procedural. Unlike positive law, which varies according to time and place, natural law is based upon invariant fundamental principles that provide norms for justice.

According to Herbert Spiegelberg, there are three different species of cognitive concepts of natural law—that is, among those that distinguish nature as the *mentor* of justice. First, there is *innate natural law,* which is to be found in everyone and of which everyone may demand satisfaction. Second, there is *obvious natural law,* which, though not innate, can be recognized with

natural reason by everyone. Finally, there is *revealed natural law,* which, without being innate and without having to be deduced by reason, is communicated to man by nature, which teaches it to him as a voice. Spiegelberg comments that in valid natural law, we find a sense of law that provides the standard for all of nature, a law that is inscribed in nature or constitutes it.

Since the Sophists in ancient Greece sharpened the distinction between manmade *(thesis)* and natural *(physis)* laws, the fundamental presupposition of all natural law has been that there is an essential unity between what is right and what is the highest expression of nature. All natural law theories hold that there is some natural standard independent of and above life as we know it that provides the normative basis and free space for any legitimate critique of existing conditions. The metaphysical models for these normative principles have ranged from physical nature to God, to reason, to human nature, and the nature of the cognitive approach to these principles varies as well. In every case, natural law theories have represented their principle as universal and immutable. Here we find the postulates of "inalienable" rights and the normative ideals of the just society.

SOURCES

Bloch, Ernst. *Natural Law and Human Dignity.* Cambridge, MA: MIT Press. 1986.

Harris, James F. *Against Relativism: A Philosophical Defense of Method.* LaSalle, IL: Open Court. 1992.

NATURALISTIC FALLACY

The idea that ethics should pay special attention to definitions was greatly encouraged by G. E. Moore. In his *Principia Ethica* (1903), Moore advanced a set of views about *goodness* as a nonnatural, simple quality that could not be defined. Those who attempted to define goodness were said to commit the *naturalistic fallacy*. Moore's central point is that although pleasure, self-regulation, happiness, and the like may be goods or consequences of action on which goodness may be predicated, they do not define the nature of or constitute goodness itself. The identification of good with other properties of an object or action Moore called the "naturalistic fallacy."

It is hard to think of any other widely used phrase in the history of philosophy that is such a misnomer as *naturalistic fallacy*. In the first place, it is not clear why those criticized were committing a *fallacy* (which is a "mistake in inference") as opposed to making an error, or simply redefining a word. Moreover, the application of the word *naturalistic* to a misconceived purpose is misleading. A naturalistic view of ethics was previously contrasted with a supernaturalistic view, and it simply meant that ethics was to be understood in worldly terms, without reference to God or any transcendental authority. It meant the kind of ethical view that stems from the general attitude that humans are a part of nature. Views that are naturalistic in this broad sense do not necessarily commit the "naturalistic fallacy." What causes even more confusion is that not everyone who was accused by Moore of committing this fallacy was a naturalist. Some were antinaturalistic, such as those who defined goodness in terms of what is commanded or willed by God.

Easily, there is more than a problem of definition involved in Moore's conceptualization. If the fallacy is a significant error, what exactly are we required to avoid? There is not simply a ban on defining *good* in naturalistic terms; it also bans definitions that are nonnaturalistic. So perhaps it just bans a definition of *good* in terms of anything? This was Moore's own position, but he was prepared to define *right* in terms of "good," which is also confusing. Thus, the naturalistic fallacy is not a ban merely on defining *good;* it was taken as setting up two classes of expressions: *evaluative* (containing such terms as *good* and *right*) and *nonevaluative* (statements of fact and mathematical truth) terms. The naturalistic fallacy was developed as the attempt to define any concept that belongs to the first class entirely by using terms that belong to the second. The fallacy also includes any attempt to deduce an evaluative conclusion from premises that are entirely nonevaluative. The ban on definitions is a special case of this, since a definition is a kind of logical equivalence or two-way implication. This wider attempt not only excludes attempts to derive *good;* it also excludes something that David Hume found suspect—the attempt to derive *ought* from *is*. Hume remarked that a change from propositions containing *is* to others containing *ought* "is of the last consequence. For as this *ought*, or *ought not*, expresses some new relation or affirmation, 'tis necessary that it shou'd be observ'd and explain'd; and at the same time, that a reason should be given, for what seems altogether inconceivable, how this new relation can be a deduction from others, which are entirely different from it." Bernard Williams (*Ethics and the Limits of Philosophy*) doubts whether Hume himself meant by this passage what has subsequently been made of it. He mentions that attention to this point would "let us see, that the distinction of vice and virtue is not founded merely on the relations of objects, nor is perceived by reason," but the relation of that kind of conclusion to matters of definition and logical deduction is not entirely clear.

Although the phrase *naturalistic fallacy* is today used for breaches of this ban on deriving *ought* from *is*, some additional explanation is needed to explain why a ban involving *ought* will equally yield a ban involving *good*. If we are convinced that there must be two classes of expressions, one related to value and the other to fact, it is natural to see one member of the value class as basic (such as *ought*), while others are to be defined in terms of it. One should note that ethical theories accepting this view *(intuitionism* and *prescriptivism)* have created their own set of problems that require analysis and explanation. We might view the naturalistic fallacy as a logical outcome of modernism and its faith in scientific propositions, while shunning all else. Historically, the reductionism at work in the modernist movement was to reduce it to the "is/ought problem," to which hundreds of philosophers have contributed their time. Now that the basic tenets of modernism are being questioned and a postmodern era is dawning, it may be that the naturalistic fallacy will itself disappear and be relegated to the realm of a pseudoproblem.

SOURCES

Hudson, W. D., ed. *The Is-Ought Question.* New York: St. Martin's. 1969.

Hume, David. *A Treatise on Human Nature.* (Originally publ. in 1739, III.i.i.) Oxford: Clarendon Press. 1968.

Moore, G. E. *Principia Ethica.* Cambridge: Cambridge University Press. 1959.

Williams, Bernard. *Ethics and the Limits of Philosophy.* Cambridge, MA: Harvard University Press. 1985.

NEO-ORTHODOXY

Religious ethics, like philosophical ethics, are of many kinds and varieties. Neo-orthodoxy is one of these varieties. Neo-orthodoxy emerged in the middle decades of the twentieth century as an important force in religion, bridging the gap between a liberalism that tried to remain consistent with modernism and its scientific method and the literalism of the conservative movement. As such, neo-orthodoxy accepted the historical approach to biblical literature and the results of modern historical scholarship but sought revelation in the events the Bible relates. The content of neo-orthodox ethics, consistent with this view, became a matter of ascertaining what God expects one to do or how one is to live one's life—and then obeying God's commands.

Neo-orthodoxy's ethical framework can thus be defined as "the ethics of duty or the right." It requires obedience apart from the goodness of the act (behavior) and is sometimes called *deontological* ethics (from *deon,* or "duty," and *logos,* or "science"). It stresses obligation or duty as opposed to *teleological* or *axiological* ethics, which places emphasis on some goal or end that is considered good, right, or proper.

The ethics of duty asks what is required by the moral law, or by the Great Lawgiver, God. What is right is obedience to some authority—God, the Bible, conscience, the church, etc. This type of ethic attempts to keep ethics strictly theological by refusing to seek or mimimize other reasons as a justification for right acts. Ethical duties stand out by themselves with no reason or justification except that they follow the authority or the "code." Another form of this ethic is found in *fundamentalism,* which differs from neo-orthodoxy with its biblical or creedal literalism.

Historically, in Protestant Christianity, the ethics of duty appealed to the Reformation leaders, especially Luther, and is referred to as the *ethics of faith, of revelation, and of obedient love.* In the twentieth century, Emil Brunner, Karl Barth, and Paul Lehmann have been among its defenders. The right or the good in this view is not to be found in some moral system or set of principles, or in some intrinsic value. Reason sees what is human but not what is divine. Ethics in this view involves reflection upon life and upon morality from the standpoint of certain theological principles. For example, Lehmann speaks of this as the ethic of *koinonia* (the fellowship or body of believers). Koinonia emerged from a fellowship of Christians, although Lehmann maintains that the ethical content of this fellowship cannot be stated as a rational generalization or general principle. This approach has sometimes been referred to as the *ethics of self-renunciation,* in contrast to the *ethics of good* or the *ethics of self-fulfillment*. It is *antinomian* (*anti*, or "against," and *nomos*, or "law/norm") because it stressed freedom from law and all external regulation of human life. The emphasis is on faith and on the inner or spiritual person.

SOURCES

Corkey, R. *A Philosophy of Christian Morals for Today.* London: George Allen & Unwin. 1961.

Herberg, Will. *Protestant, Catholic, Jew: An Essay in Religious Sociology.* New York: Doubleday. 1955.

Lehmann, Paul L. *Ethics in a Christian Context.* New York: Harper & Row. 1963.

NEO-NAZISM

A number of small neo-Nazi (or "new-Nazi") parties have been founded in Germany since the end of World War II whose purpose is to reestablish Nazi principles. Nazi principles included *fascism*, which tightly restricted personal freedom but permitted private ownership of property; aggressive nationalism, militarism, and glorification of Aryans (northern Europeans) over those they considered inferior (Jews, Slavs, and other minority groups); and opposition to democracy, communism, socialism, feminism, and any other political systems that favored equality. In Germany, these neo-Nazi groups worked to reunify East and West Germany, have promoted anti-Semitism, and denied that the Holocaust occurred. After Germany's reunification in 1990, neo-Nazism grew in popularity and its adherents began to make frequent attacks on foreigners. In the United States since 1980, neo-Nazi ideas have been supported by Ku Klux Klan members, by the Nazi Party, by the Aryan Nation, and by other white-supremacist groups. These individuals and organizations promote racism and anti-Semitism and use violence against Asian Americans, blacks, homosexuals, and Jews.

SOURCES

Information Finder. World Book. 1994.

Cheney, Lynne V. *Telling the Truth.* New York: Simon & Schuster. 1995.

Turner, Frederick. *The Culture of Hope: A New Birth of the Classical Spirit.* New York: Free Press. 1995.

NIHILISM

Nihilism holds that there are no objective values at all; no ethical truths that hold, apart from our opinion. If, as the nihilist maintains, no ethical standards are rationally justifiable, we are on our own, for there exist no values or true ethical principles. James Harris reminds us that *radical relativism* (Willard Van Orman Quine, for example) claims that "no statement is immune to revision" and "ontology recapitulates philology"—or that questions of reality can be reduced to questions of language.

In ethics a normative theory of rights can only be built on a foundation of universal principles, or principles that are derivable from generalized individual ideas of right, or upon relations between persons that contain their own nonderivative rights and duties. Nothing less can chase nihilism from ethics and morals. In this respect, the nurturing of individual freedom, equality, and responsibility through the maintenance of moral norms among persons and groups of persons can appear as the highest ethical good—indeed, as the entire end of justice.

SOURCES

Hamilton, Alexander. "The Federalist, No. 7." In *The Federalist.* Edited by Jacob E. Cooke. Middletown, CT: Wesleyan University Press. 1982.

Harris, James F. *Against Relativism: A Philosophical Defense of Method.* LaSalle, IL: Open Court. 1992.

Strauss, Leo. *The City and the Man.* Chicago: University of Chicago Press. 1978.

Winfield, Richard Dien. *Freedom and Modernity.* Albany: State University of New York Press. 1991.

OBSCENITY

Obscenity and *pornography* are terms used to designate written, recorded, or pictorial material—including motion pictures—that many people consider indecent and thus find offensive. The term obscenity can also refer to language or behavior believed to corrupt public morals. Some people consider violence and war obscene. Pornography refers chiefly to printed or pictorial material intended primarily to cause sexual stimulation. The terms obscenity and pornography are often used interchangeably.

Most states and cities in the United States have laws against publishing, distributing, or selling obscene materials. But these laws have been hard to enforce because judges, juries, lawyers, and the public interpret them differently. Thus, the nature of obscenity and pornography and the laws governing them have been a continuing source of controversy. Some believe that obscene and pornographic material corrupts public morals. Others believe that antiobscenity laws violate the rights of free speech and freedom of the press guaranteed by the First Amendment to the U.S. Constitution.

The U.S. Congress passed the first federal law against obscenity as part of the Tariff Act of 1842. This law made it illegal to bring what it called "indecent and obscene" material into the country. In 1865, Congress passed legislation prohibiting the mailing of obscene material. By 1900, at least 30 states had passed laws to control distribution of such material. In 1957, in the case of *Roth v. United States*, the Supreme Court ruled that freedom of the press as guaranteed by the First Amendment does not apply to obscenity. However, the court provided only loose guidelines for determining what can be considered obscene.

During the 1960s the public debate over obscenity intensified, and in 1967 Congress created a national Commission on Obscenity and Pornography to study the matter. In 1970, the commission reported that it found no reliable evidence that pornography caused crime among adults or delinquency among young people. The commission recommended the repeal of all laws prohibiting the sale of pornography to consenting adults, but not to young people.

In 1973, in the case of *Miller v. California*, the Supreme Court went on to develop guidelines for judging whether material is obscene. According to these guidelines, material can be considered obscene if the average person, applying contemporary community standards, finds that the material taken as a whole appeals to the *prurient* ("sexually arousing") interest; if the material shows, in a clearly offensive way, sexual conduct specifically defined as obscene by law; and if the material lacks serious literary, artistic, political, or scientific value. States and cities were expected to use these guidelines in enforcing their own antiobscenity laws and in framing new legislation.

See also Censorship.

SOURCES

Adler, Mortimer J. *We Hold These Truths: Understanding the Ideas and Ideals of the Constitution*. New York: Macmillan. 1987.

Thomson, Judith Jarvis. *Rights, Restitution and Risk: Essays in Moral Theory*. Edited by William Parent. Cambridge, MA: Harvard University Press. 1986.

OMNIPOTENCE

Omnipotence, when applied to the theistic conception of God, has traditionally meant "all-powerful, all-knowing, supremely wise, and all-loving." This is a basic belief in Judaism, Christianity, and Islam. Although theists hold to this conceptualization, usually without question, it causes the reflective theists some difficult logical problems. Consider the following:

- If God has a plan for the universe that is implemented as a part of his omnipotent will, why does He not simply create a deterministic universe in which the goal of the plan is inevitable? Or better still, create it with the plan achieved? If the universe is indeterministic, however, does that not mean that God's power is limited because of His inability to predict or decide what the outcome will be?
- It could also be argued that God— being all-powerful—is free to relinquish some of his power if he wishes. He can give us free will to act against His plan if we so desire, and He can

give atoms the quantum factor to turn His creation into a cosmic game of chance. But, can a truly omnipotent God relinquish some of His omnipotent power?

- The idea of freedom implied by omnipotence is quite different from the sort of freedom that humans enjoy. You may be free to choose coffee or tea, but only so long as the supply lasts. You are not free to do anything you please—to turn the moon into blue cheese or to fly like a bird by flapping your arms. Human power is limited and only a small range of desires are capable of being fulfilled. By contrast, the power of an omnipotent God is without limit, and such a being is free to have whatever He chooses.
- Omnipotence also raises some awkward theological questions. Is God free to prevent evil? If the answer is yes, then why doesn't He do so? Does this mean that God is neither all-wise nor all-good? This devastating argument was used by David Hume: If the evil in the world is from the intention of God, then God is not benevolent. If the evil is contrary to God's intention, then God is not omnipotent. God cannot be both omnipotent and benevolent for evil to exist in the world.
- We can respond to this problem by saying that evil is due entirely to human action; because God has given us freedom, we are free to do evil and thus frustrate God's plan. Still, if God is free to prevent us from doing evil, must He not share some of the responsibility if He fails to do so? Must we therefore conclude that evil is all part of God's plan? Or is God not free after all to prevent us from acting?

The problems associated with omnipotence and evil seem insurmountable, as they are intertwined with the long-standing enigma of free will and determinism. We can turn to the new physics of *quantum theory* and the theory of relativity for help, for here we discover the possibility of multiple realities and a universe of extended time as well as space. Of course, this does not solve the problem of free will and determinism, but challenges us with a new set of problems and difficult questions worth our exploration.

SOURCES

Capra, Fritjof. *The Tao of Physics.* 3d ed. (updated). Boston: Shambhala. 1991.

Davies, Paul. *God and the New Physics.* New York: Simon & Schuster. 1983.

OYAJI GIRL

Since the enactment of Japan's 1986 Equal Employment Opportunity Law, professional women have become one major symbol of Japanese womanhood, although the symbol can be a caricature, as Barbara Molony observes:

> Her gestures, her dress, and her office destination are modeled on those, deeply embedded in Japanese imagination, of the male *sarariman* ("salaryman"), a catch-all designation for employed white-collar workers in private business and the public sector. She is a creature of the press, inspired by but only tangentially related to the new professional women who have begun to enter the previously all-male ranks of *sogo shoku*—"comprehensive employees" who enjoy the implicit though conditional promise of lifetime employment and seniority-based promotions.

The woman in the caricature is called an *oyaji girl*—an "old chap, one of the boys"—crossing gender boundaries. The creators of this image seem to welcome the entry of young women into professional ranks, although these women must become "manlike" in the process. One should notice that this image demands no change in the workplace and does not question the equation of male behavior and professionalism, although it does suggest that male behavior or work behavior is not limited to the male sex. (Traditionally, in the United States before 1960, any work outside the home was thought of as "man's work." World War II and the employment of women in the defense industry helped to destroy this image, but it took the radical 1960s to finish it off.) It is interesting that we find gender stereotypes cutting across cultural barriers, although one might argue that the Americanization of Japan after 1945 helped destroy these barriers and introduce some of American culture into the Japanese mainstream.

SOURCES

Bergeson, Jan M., and Kaoru Yamamoto Oba. "Japan's New Equal Employment Opportunity Law: Real Weapon or Heirloom Sword?" *Brigham Young University Law Review* 3 (1986).

Molony, Barbara. "Japan's 1986 Equal Employment Opportunity Law and the Changing Discourse on Gender." *Signs: Journal of Women in Culture and Society* 20:2 (1995).

Smith, Robert J. "Gender Inequality in Contemporary Japan." *Journal of Japanese Studies* 13 (1987).

P

PARENT TEACHER ASSOCIATION

Parent-teacher organizations are volunteer groups that work to improve the education, health, and safety of children and youth in local communities. They encourage close cooperation between home and school to achieve this goal. Parent-teacher organizations may be local or connected to a larger state or national body such as the Parent Teacher Association (PTA) and its governing body, the National Congress of Parents and Teachers (NCPT). There are approximately 27,000 local PTAs throughout the United States, with about 7 million members. Most local PTA units function in public and private schools, draw up their own constitutions using the rules of the NCPT as a guideline, and develop programs to suit the needs of their schools and communities. These programs must also fit the basic goals of the NCPT. These goals, called "Objects of the National Congress," urge cooperation between parents and educators to give students all possible advantages in mental and physical education. The "Objects" call for improvement of the environment of children and youth in their home, school, and community.

SOURCE
Information Finder. World Book. 1994.

PATRIOTISM AND PIETY

Two sources of moral integration compete for preeminence as foundations of community: civility and piety. Civility governs diversity, protects autonomy, and upholds toleration. On the other hand, piety expects devotion and demands integration (compare this with Durkheim's distinction between organic and mechanical solidarity: Organic solidarity generates rules of civility, whereas mechanical solidarity is based on a shared history and identity). The norms of civility are impersonal, national, and inclusive, whereas piety is personal, passionate, and particularistic. The conflict between these very different aspirations generates troublesome issues of morality and community. Their reconciliation is an important object of theory, policy, and politics.

Modern thought is not comfortable with the idea of piety. The democratic and secular person is likely to associate it with sanctimonious devotion to ritual and uncritical subordination to religious authority. But piety has a broader and more attractive connotation, perhaps best expressed by George Santayana, who commented, "Piety, in its nobler and Roman sense, may be said to mean man's reverent attachment to the sources of his being and the steadying of his life by that attachment." This so-called nobler idea treats piety as an aspect of human nature, a reflection of the need for coherence and attachment. The distinctive virtues of piety are humility and loyalty. As Philip Selznick observes, "Not only patriotism but every object of piety—friendship, kinship, parental love, institutional participation, religious faith—contemplates a relatively unconditional bond."

John Dewey voiced a similar conception and found "natural piety" in human nature as a cooperating part of a larger whole. Natural piety is an attitude of reverence and respect for human interdependency and for continuation between humans and nature. The root experience is a sense of connectedness or common meaning. Like Santayana, Dewey could think of piety as a pervasive human experience and as having an enduring value.

Thus understood, piety is an attitude that strives for "a working union of the ideal and the actual" and at the same time takes into account human finitude and dependency. To recognize an enveloping world beyond ourselves is to know that our achievements are not ever alone. In truth, says Dewey, "our successes are dependent on the cooperation of nature." Among piety's connotations are those of faithfulness to the duties owed to parents and relatives and loyalty and respect. These attachments have a claim to fidelity because they play a vital part in the formation of our selves. They are sources of our beginning. In that sense, piety is ultimately an affirmation of self; a sign of psychological coherence; a foundation of self-respect. Thus, piety exhibits a healthy disposition toward individuality and rootedness in a larger society.

A classic form of piety is patriotism. It is a virtue, and a highly effective one at that, capable of creating a potent union of self and place, self and history. Patriotism extends the reach of fellowship, enlarges the meaning of self-interest, and reinforces morality by securing it to a particular heritage. Like other forms of piety, patriotism claims unconditional devotion as necessary to its power; it is also a main source of moral failing. Therefore we are normally driven to invoke a higher patriotism—one that retains devotion but legitimates criticism. Piety has corrupt forms that resist criticism, condemn apostasy, and create outcasts. These forms are self-righteous, intolerant, and unforgiving. This "lower" aspect of piety undercuts its moral worth. Therefore, patriotism, as a form of piety, needs a complementary principle of order—the principle of civility.

SOURCES

Dewey, John. *A Common Faith*. New Haven: Yale University Press. 1934.

Santayana, George. *The Life of Reason*. New York: Scribner's. 1954.

Selznick, Philip. *The Moral Commonwealth: Social Theory and the Promise of Community*. Berkeley: Univeristy of California Press. 1992.

Sills, Edward. *The Intellectuals and the Powers and Other Essays*. Chicago: University of Chicago Press. 1972.

PERSONHOOD

The concept of integrity goes to the heart of what is meant by *person* and *personhood*, especially "person as a moral agent." In Western philosophy, theology, and social theory, *person* used as a term of *art* has reappeared again and again since ancient times. Although frustratingly vague and elusive, the idea persists because it contains a core of meaning that seems indispensable to moral thought and judgment.

Many analysts have found it helpful to distinguish between the words *individual* and *person*. This is so because, in the doctrine of modernity, individuals tend to lose their distinctiveness. They become interchangeable, ahistorical units within a political, legal, or economic scheme of things. The driving ideals of liberal capitalism—national unity, the rule of law, political democracy, free enterprise—have the effect of identifying people by general categories rather than by the concreteness of selfhood, connection, and context. As the category is abstract, so too is the individual; hence the phrase *abstract individual,* which is one of the more barren and dehumanizing legacies of modern nationalism.

Such an outcome was certainly not intended. The architects of the Enlightenment wanted to enhance and vindicate, not diminish, the moral worth of the individual person. They therefore stressed the importance of moral autonomy and freedom, including freedom from unchosen obligations and from the fetters of the past. Rationalists took for granted much in traditional society, especially individualism, family, and rural life. They did not foresee the moral and cultural attenuation that would stem from an ethos of individualism set loose in a world of industrial and urban expansion.

From the point of view of morality, the image of a self-distancing individual is hardly a convincing or attractive picture of what participation in a moral order should entail. When the human being is abstracted from history and context, we lose the value of what it means to be a multidimensional moral person who is concerned morally for his or her fellow humans. The texture of the moral society is lost.

The concepts of personhood and person are conceived in our moral vocabulary to retrieve that texture. The *individual as person* is rediscovered, protected, and fulfilled only in a specific historical setting. The point is to vindicate the general idea of human dignity and worth. Although the value at stake is necessarily abstract, it is realized in each individual person (through concreteness). This union of the general and the particular distinguishes the person from the abstract individual.

In etymology and social theory, *person* suggests particularity, coherence, and responsibility. The Latin and Greek terms *(persona, prospon)* refer to the masks used in classical drama and, by extension, the part or character represented by the actor. This identification of person with role takes an ethical meaning in the Stoic tradition. It is the duty of moral persons to "play well" the roles they are assigned. The Stoic ideal presumes a moral order largely founded on assigned roles and fixed statuses. In a rank-society, role and person are closely congruent. To be a person is to be defined by one's place in the moral order.

These overtones of hierarchy and discipline are also found in what used to be called the law of persons. Historically, this branch of Anglo-American law dealt with all those relations that could be said to create a legal identity: slave, serf, master, servant, ward, infant, husband, wife, cleric, king. All these were statuses recognized by law, affixing to the individual salient, identity-fixing privileges or disadvantages. Thus the law of persons was the law of status, rooted in a society where kinship, locality, religion, and social rank were the great parameters of belonging.

By the middle of the nineteenth century, it was clear that the law of persons would soon become an anachronism. In 1861, Henry Summer Maine conceived his famous "law of progress." He said, "The movement of the progressive societies has hitherto been a movement *from status to contract.*" Maine perceived that contract was the preferred form of legal relation in modern society. Persons in the modern era are now reduced to individual units of investment, labor, or consumption. Their special identities are lost in the egalitarian, free-market imagery of "economic man." The group becomes an aggregate or a composite of freely chosen individual arrangements. This transition brings to mind the fact that the historical reality of personhood is closely related with status and subordination. With this fact it is easy to appreciate how important is the appeal of the new individualism and the contract model. As it developed in the nineteenth century, the law of contract embodied values of freedom, equality, and self-government. Contract law was liberating and facilitative; a powerful tool for defining rights and enforcing accountability. All this weighed heavily against the received morality of role and status.

The lesson of history is that our understanding of personhood should give full weight to *self-affirming* participation in a moral order. As Steven Lukes reminds us, respect for individuals as persons requires "that we regard and act toward other persons in their concrete specificity, that we take full account of their specific aims and purposes and of their own definitions of their life situations." And as Jacques Maritain reflects, the person as an object of moral concern can never be an abstraction, never wholly subordinated to social needs, never dissolved into a group process. This is the meaning of personhood. The moral unity of the person is a counterweight to demands for sacrifice to the common good. Here we develop meaning in life, autonomy, and selfhood, but, as Bernard Williams says, not ungoverned choice. An unspoken condition of moral individuality is that one's activities and commitments must meet a threshold standard of moral justification. Also, although the claims of personhood assert that each life is unique, this does not mean that all are acceptable. It is not moral autonomy to do as I please regardless of outcomes for my own character and integrity. Rather, self-determination is the freedom to find one's proper place within a moral order, not outside it. In doing so one takes account of the qualities of that order—its legitimacy and the propriety of its demands.

SOURCES

Lukes, Steven. *Individualism*. Oxford: Blackwell. 1973.

Maine, Henry Summer. *Ancient Law*. Boston: Beacon Press. 1963.

Maritain, Jacques. *The Person and the Common Good*. New York: Scribner's. 1947.

Selzick, Philip. *Law, Society, and Industrial Justice*. New York: Russell Sage. 1969.

Williams, Bernard. *Morality: An Introduction to Ethics*. New York: Harper. 1972.

PLEASURE PRINCIPLE

See Epicureanism; Happiness.

POLITICALLY CORRECT

Politically correct or gender-free (also ethnic-free, racial-free) language has been a controversial policy on college campuses for over a decade. In late 1990 and early 1991, there was a period of immense media interest in political correctness. *Newsweek* magazine ran a cover story on "thought police" that detailed issues and situations covering politically correct forces on campuses trying to enforce a "new" orthodoxy. *New Yorker* magazine also put political correctness on its cover, and writer John Taylor called its proponents "the new fundamentalists." The purposes of higher education were called into question as professors and students advanced the cause of "correct" viewpoints: Is it to pursue the truth or advance inoffensive viewpoints?

Among those campaigning for political correctness was the Modern Language Association, whose policy statements, publications, and conventions had epitomized the politicalization of teaching and learning. Other groups, Teachers for a Democratic Culture and the Union of Democratic Intellectuals, claimed that conservatives were behind the criticism of college teaching and curricula for the purpose of reversing the advances made by women and minorities.

Not only did groups and individual students exert control over the content and language of curricula and professors, but, in time, many professors controlled curricula and students using the same tactics. But when some voices and inclinations are banned in the classroom, it becomes virtually impossible for participants to doubt, debate, question, revise, and find ways of working within culture without being dominated and enslaved by it.

See also Politics in the Classroom.

SOURCES

Cheney, Lynne V. *Telling the Truth*. New York: Simon & Schuster. 1995.

Fine, Melinda. *Habits of Mind: Struggling over Values in America's Classrooms*. San Francisco: Jossey-Bass. 1995.

Goodlad, John I., and Pamela Keating. *Access to Knowledge*. New York: College Entrance Examination Board. 1994.

Grossman, Lawrence K. *The Electronic Republic*. New York: Viking. 1995.

POLITICS IN THE CLASSROOM

The concept of political correctness, of ethnic neutrality, and of avoiding gender bias defines how politics has reached into the classroom at both the college and public school levels. Consider:

- A Massachusetts educator warns teachers about using *The Story of Babar* because it "extols the virtues of a European, middle-class lifestyle and disparages the animals and people who have remained in the jungle" (Ramsey 1987).
- A teacher of "radical math literacy" warns against bombarding students with "oppressive ideology." Among the practical applications of mathematics that she says should be avoided is totaling a grocery bill, since such an exercise "carries the non-neutral message that paying for food is natural" (Frankenstein 1990).
- The author of a textbook for future teachers urges skepticism for the idea that the people now known as American Indians came to this hemisphere across the Bering land bridge. Indi-

an myths do not tell this story, she writes. Moreover, she observes, the scientific account has nothing "except logic" to recommend it. A committee of parents and teachers in Berkeley, California, subsequently offers this argument or reason for rejecting a fourth-grade history text (Bennett 1990).

Lynne V. Cheney (1995) draws the conclusion that the people in these examples have a common goal: "They want to be sure that American schools show no favor to—and, indeed, positively downgrade—ideas and practices associated with the United States and its Western heritage, including, in the last instance, the Enlightenment legacy of scientific thought." This goal marks a growing trend for politics to control the education of the young in the United States, very often at the expense of truth or the search for truth. Instead of encouraging students to *search* for a complicated truth, students are increasingly presented with oversimplified versions of the American past that focus on the negative, such as presenting Columbus not as the "discoverer" of America, but as a "greedy" man and a "murderer" who "stole" it.

In 1991, Sandra Stotsky, a researcher at Howard University, reviewed teaching materials being used in a Brookline, Massachusetts, high school and concluded that there was "one major theme" running through the course outlines and examinations for social studies: "the systematic denigration of America's Western heritage." For example, a ninth-grade examination on ancient history asked students to identify the "Hellenic epic which established egotistical individualism as heroic." Almost all questions on Greece and Rome emphasized negative aspects, while "all items about ancient China were worded positively or drew attention only to China's positive features, such as 'Chinese belief in pacifism and relativism.'" According to Stotsky, not a word was written about "the existence of slavery in ancient China and the thousands of slaves who built, and died building, the Great Wall."

Another example of this phenomenon is the National History Standards developed at the University of California at Los Angeles and released in the fall of 1994, which encourages students to take a benign view of the failings of other cultures while being hypercritical of the one in which they live. These standards pay little attention to scientific and technological achievement because feminists argue that science represents destructive male thinking (Harding 1986).

Charlotte Crabtree and Gary Nash (1994) point out that in the World History Standards, the fact that women generally had different roles from men in the ancient world is seen simply as a matter of gender "differentiation"; that is, until it happens in Athens, Greece, the birthplace of Western civilization. Then it becomes a matter of "restrictions on the rights and freedoms of women." Both sexism and ethnocentrism are introduced in the context of Greek civilization, but not in the study of either Asia or Africa.

These "adjustments" to the study of history are a part of the politically correct movement in the United States in the 1990s. For example, the Cold War is viewed as a deadly competition between two equally culpable superpowers, each bent on world domination. Nothing is said of communist totalitarianism in the Soviet Union on the one hand, and U.S. freedom and liberty on the other hand. Crabtree and Nash wonder whether one could conclude from reading the Standards that it would have made very little difference in terms of human freedom how the Cold War ended.

Associated with these "value" movements is also that of multiculturalism, which stresses the faults of the United States (and thereby undermines patriotism) and the virtues of other nations. For example, Martha Nussbaum (1994) says that patriotism is "morally dangerous."

She writes, "To give support to nationalist sentiments subverts, ultimately, even the values that hold a nation together, because it substitutes a colorful ideal for the substantive universal values of justice and right." Although there is much truth in the negative value of rigid ethnocentrism (as a form of patriotism), she does seem to ignore the emphasis the American democratic system has placed on the nurturing of justice and natural rights. Cheney comments, "The principles of freedom and liberty that have inspired our political system have also informed our economic arrangements and made the United States a beacon of opportunity to people everywhere." For example, the idea conceptualized in the Declaration of Independence that all men are created equal has been a driving force behind the changes made in the United States to achieve a greater degree of equality than exists anywhere else in the world for racial, ethnic, religious, and gender minorities.

There has been some significant reaction to efforts to politicize the school curriculum and the words of textbooks and teachers. In 1994, the school board in Lake County, Florida, complied with state directives to teach multiculturalism with the following statement:

> This instruction shall also include and instill in our students an appreciation of our American heritage and culture such as: our republican form of government, capitalism, a free enterprise system, patriotism, strong family values, freedom of religion and other basic values that are superior to other foreign or historic cultures (1994 Basic Instructional Program).

Of course, America and Americans are far from perfect. Students should learn of their country's shortcomings, but a true understanding of history is important so that students will know what Americans have done very well.

One way of viewing the phenomena of multiculturalism, political correctness, ethnic and gender neutrality, and even

America-bashing, is as an overreaction to a problem that requires fixing: the accurate reporting and chronicling of history of all races, all nations, both genders, including the good, the not-so-good, and the really bad. But out of the cloud of turmoil caused by these reactions have come some positive effects: recognition of the contribution of women, in the past and in the present; a "gender equity" bill introduced in the Congress in 1993, which became part of the Elementary and Secondary Education Act; and a concerted emphasis on multiculturalism. To more completely understand the contemporary issues and wide diversity of this phenomenon, one must study the cellular movements that form this larger movement to reform American education:

GENDER EQUITY

The Civil Rights Act of 1964 reads in part: "It shall be an unlawful employment practice for an employer—(1) to fail or refuse to hire or to discharge any individual or otherwise to discriminate against any individual with respect to his compensation, terms, conditions, or privileges of employment, because of such individual's race, color, religion, sex, or national origin." Although justice is supposed to be blind to both race and gender, in the 30 years or so since the origin of this law, we have given race and gender a preeminent place through affirmative action, quotas, and entitlements. In 1995, Republican legislators have made this an issue once again with the emphasis on individual merit rather than group power.

VERTICAL THINKING

Peggy McIntosh (1992) says that schools must stress the "lateral" thinking typical of women and minorities and deemphasize the "vertical" thinking that white males exhibit. Lateral thinking aims "not to win, but to be in a decent relationship with the universe. Vertical thinking, on the other hand, is what

makes "our young white males dangerous to themselves and the rest of us—especially in a nuclear age."

MERITOCRACY

Meritocracy (Rita Kramer 1991) has come under assault in the schools as part of the repressive "masculine world of technology [and] competition." According to others, meritocracy teaches that success comes from "deferred gratification, hard work, and an achievement orientation." These qualities or values give way to "sensitive, emotional, and relational qualities.

MULTICULTURALISM

Multiculturalism, the objective teaching about other cultures, has both its positive and negative effects. On the positive side is an understanding of other cultures, nations, habits, and customs. On the negative side, this understanding may decrease patriotism and disunite the nation. On the positive side is the inclusion of other cultures in the social studies curriculum. On the negative side is the presentation of American culture and Western civilization in a negative light while ignoring the negative and, perhaps, immoral practices of other nations and cultures.

AFROCENTRISM

Also having impact on the public school curriculum are the ideas of Afrocentrists. School districts across the nation have introduced Afrocentric curricula, and a primary source for them is the *African-American Baseline Essays* developed for Portland, Oregon, under the direction of Asa Hilliard III, a professor from Georgia State University who served on the One Nation, Many Peoples committee. The problem discovered about the *Baseline Essays*, says Cheney, is that they "purport to detail African contributions to history and knowledge; but in all too many instances what they actually do is make ill-founded claims" (See Hunter Havelin Adams III 1990).

MALE DOMINANCE

Establishing the victimhood of women and keeping it in the forefront is crucial in order to give the cause of women precedence over the cause of other groups (Catherine A. MacKinnon 1987). According to this view, male dominance historically caused a reality that encouraged women to be submissive. MacKinnon, the leading exponent of this view, and perhaps its driving force, has effected legislation to prevent violence against women and pornography that uses images of women. Although feminists do not totally agree with MacKinnon's position, one must agree that racial and sexual harassment are wrong and that we (ethically) should make the workplace, schoolrooms, and the home harassment free.

See also Gender Equity; Politically Correct.

SOURCES

Adams, Hunter Havelin III. "African and African-American Contributions to Science and Technology." Portland, Oregon: Portland Public Schools. 1990.

"Basic Instructional Program: Related Curriculum Issues, Policy 10." Tavares, Florida: Lake County Schools. 1994.

Bennett, Christine I. *Comprehensive Multicultural Education: Theory and Practice.* Boston: Allyn and Bacon. 1990.

Cheney, Lynne V. *Telling the Truth.* New York: Simon & Schuster. 1995.

Cohen, Richard. "To Multiculturalism." *Washington Post* (May 19, 1994): A21.

Crabtree, Charlotte, and Gary Nash. *National Standards for United States History: Exploring the American Experience, Grades 5–12.* Los Angeles: National Center for History in the Schools, UCLA. 1994.

Frankenstein, Marilyn. "A Different Third R: Radical Math." In *Politics of Education: Essays from Radical Teachers.* Susan Gushee O'Malley, Robert C. Rosen, and Leonard Vogt, eds. Albany: State University of New York Press. 1990.

Kramer, Rita. *Ed School Follies: The Miseducation of America's Teachers.* New York: Free Press. 1991.

MacKinnon, Catherine A. "Difference and Dominance: On Sex Discrimination." In *Feminism Unmodified: Discourses on Life and Law.* Cambridge: Harvard University Press. 1987.

McIntosh, Peggy. *How Schools Short Change Girls.* Washington, D.C.: American Association of University Women. 1992.

Nussbaum, Martha. "Patriotism and Cosmopolitanism." *Boston Review* 3 (October/November 1994).

Ramsey, Patricia G. *Teaching and Learning in a Diverse World: Multicultural Education for Young Children.* New York: Teachers College Press. 1987.

Stotsky, Sandra. "Multicultural Education in the Brookline Public Schools: The Deconstruction of an Academic Curriculum." *Network News & Views* (October 1991).

PORNOGRAPHY

See Obscenity.

PRAGMATISM

Pragmatism is a method of inquiry and a theory of meaning and truth derived from the natural sciences and designed to promote the clarification of the meaning of conceptions and propositions by employing the maxim: *What practical consequences might conceivably result by necessity from the truth of that conception?*

Late in his career, Charles Sanders Peirce adopted the term *pragmatism,* a name "ugly enough to keep it from kidnappers," in order to distinguish his doctrine from other versions of pragmatism. William James also developed a theory of pragmatism from his effort to "move" British philosophy from the aberration of absolute idealism and call it back to its empirical roots. What James found lacking in absolute idealism (as espoused by Hegel), John Dewey found to be a positive contribution: a sense of life, process, and the concreteness of experience itself. Dewey said in 1930: "Hegel's treatment of human culture, of institutions and the arts, involved the same dissolution of hard-and-fast dividing walls, and had a special attraction to me." What Dewey took from Hegel formed the heart of his own pragmatic outlook. It was a sense of the dynamic and fluid interaction of life, its organic quality, and the ways in which all philosophic distinctions and dichotomies were "dissolved" and properly understood as functional distinctions within the context of experience that Dewey discovered in Hegel and attempted to integrate into his own naturalism and pragmatism.

Historically, pragmatism arose out of Hegelianism, but not Hegel only; there was both a negative and positive reaction to Hegel that arose in the latter part of the nineteenth century, one of the most creative and fruitful periods of philosophic activity in the United States. Peirce, James, and Dewey benefited from their involvement in this philosophical activity. Peirce was a practicing scientist most of his life, James was trained as a medical doctor, and Dewey's interests were in the social sciences and education. Each of these men was saved from the provincialism that can so easily affect an academic discipline such as philosophy. They each exhibited in their work traits that they took to have cosmic significance—novelty and openness.

For Dewey, the role was to reconstruct philosophy so that it would become a guide to enlightened action. Peirce, although suspicious of this practical turn, explored and articulated a new conception of inquiry that became so fundamental to Dewey as to guide his own views on social reconstruction. Peirce was concerned primarily with logical issues and with coming to grips with what he called the "experimental habit of mind." For both Peirce and Dewey the role of human conduct and action became central and provided the basis for an understanding of the place of humans in the world.

From these beginnings, pragmatism became manifest in the works of many practicing twentieth-century philosophers. It was a new approach to knowledge, inquiry, and conduct. We can understand pragmatism best by focusing on what has been called the *foundation metaphor* of knowledge and the *spectator* view of the knower. The conception of knowledge that Peirce criticizes as mistaken is one that claims that knowledge does have a basic fixed foundation. The character of this foundation is an issue that has divided many modern thinkers—whether it consists of impressions, simple matters of fact, sense data, universals, a priori truth, and so on. In such diverse views as rationalism and empiricism, there is an underlying conviction that there is such a rock-bottom foundation. The task is to find out what this foundation is or ought to be, and then to show precisely how more complex knowledge rests on it. If we can do this, we will be in a position to "legitimize" our knowledge claims. We will have criteria for distinguishing what we know from what we do not know, or to distinguish what is meaningful from what is meaningless. From this perspective too, humans as knowers are *spectators*. That is, as humans we view the world aright or have "legitimate" knowledge when we penetrate the vagueness, indeterminacy, and confusion of ordinary thought and see clearly the foundation of legitimate knowledge. The primary elements of knowledge cannot be inferred or deduced from other elements—for then they would not be primary. Instead, they must be grasped directly or rationally intuited. It is this cardinal doctrine of immediate knowledge or knowledge by intuition that Peirce attacked in 1868.

Peirce argues that the quest for such an epistemological foundation is misguided. Knowledge and inquiry neither have nor need such a foundation. It is certainly true that in any inquiry there are starting points, procedures, methods, and rules that are taken as fixed and unquestioned. But this does not mean that there are absolute, logical starting points that are grasped directly by some intuitive faculty. In Peirce's view, inquiry is a self-corrective process that has no absolute beginning or ending points and in which any claim is subject to further rational criticism, although we cannot question all claims at once. Our claims to knowledge are legitimized not by their origins, but rather by the norms and rules of inquiry itself. These norms and rules are also open to rational criticism.

The fallibility of all knowledge means that every knowledge claim is open to further interpretation and has consequences that are to be publicly tested and confirmed. In the continuous process of inquiry, we may be called upon to revise our knowledge claims no matter how indubitable they may appear. Knowledge, therefore, is essentially social in character. The very meaning of our concepts depends on the role that they play in a social context of rules and norms. Humans as inquirers, as participants in a community of inquiry, are no longer viewed as *spectators*, but rather as *active participants* and *experimenters*. Human agency is the key to understanding all aspects of human life, including inquiry and knowledge. This is the heart of pragmatism. Pragmatism cannot be fully understood without understanding humans as active inquirers.

SOURCES

Dewey, John. "The Development of American Pragmatism." In *Philosophy and Civilization*. New York: Bolch. 1931.

Hartshorne, Charles, and Paul Weiss, eds. *Collected Papers of Charles Sanders Peirce: Vols. I–VI, 1931–1935*. Also *Vols. VII–VIII*, Edited by Arthur W. Burks, Cambridge, MA: Harvard University Press. 1958.

James, William. *A Pluralistic Universe*. London: Longmans, Green. 1909.

PRAXIS

The Greek term *praxis* has an ordinary meaning that roughly corresponds to the ways in which we now commonly speak of "action" and "doing," and it is usually translated into English as "practice." As Nicholas Lobkowicz points out, "the verb prassw [prasso] has a number of closely related meanings such as 'I accomplish' (e.g., a journey), 'I manage' (e.g., a state of affairs), 'I do or fare' (e.g., well or ill), and, in general, 'I act, I perform some activity.'"

While these uses are common in Greek, praxis takes on a distinctive and quasi-technical meaning in Aristotle. Aristotle continues to use the expression in a general way to refer to a variety of biological life activities, but he also uses praxis to designate one of the ways of life open to a free person, and to signify the sciences and behaviors that deal with the activities characteristic of human ethical and political life. In this context, the contrast that Aristotle draws is between *theoria* and praxis, where the former expression signifies those sciences and activities that are concerned with knowing for its own sake. In modern times, this idea gave rise to the distinction between *theory* and *practice* that has been central to Western philosophical and scientific thought.

On occasion Aristotle introduces a more refined distinction between *poesis* and praxis. The point here is to distinguish activities and disciplines that are primarily a form of *making* (building a house, writing a play, etc.) from *doing* proper, where the end, or *telos*, of the activity is not primarily the production of the artifact, but rather performing the activity in a certain way, such as performing the activity well: *eupraxia*.

Praxis in this more restricted sense signifies the disciplines and activities predominant in human ethical and political life. These disciplines, which require knowledge and practical wisdom, can be contrasted with theoria because their end is not knowing or wisdom for its own sake, but doing—living well. When we add that for Aristotle, individual ethical activity is properly a part of the study of political activity—activity in the *polis*—we can say that praxis signifies the free activity and the discipline concerned with activity in the polis.

For Aristotle, theoria—which signifies contemplation and reason—and praxis—free political and ethical activity—emerge as two dimensions of the truly human and free life. When we consider the role that praxis and action have played in Marxist thought and analytic philosophy respectively, they appear to indicate two independent and unbridgeable intellectual concerns. With Marx, praxis was developed into a comprehensive theory that is a key to understanding his early philosophic speculation and his detailed analysis of the structure of capitalism. As Marx reflects, "The chief defect of all previous materialism is that the object, actuality, sensuousness is conceived only in the form of the *object or perception [Anschauung]*, but not as *sensuous human activity, practice [Praxis]*, nor subjectively. Hence in opposition to materialism the *active* side was developed by idealism—but only abstractly since idealism naturally does not know actual, sensuous activity as such" ("Theses on Feuerbach"). Praxis thus provides the perspective for grasping Marx's conception of man as "the ensemble of social relationships" and his emphasis on production; it is the basis for comprehending what Marx meant by "revolutionary practice." In Marx we find a unity of theoria and praxis, a harmony, in the sense that theoria is a rational ingredient in praxis, the comprehension of praxis—praxis is the self-activity of theoria.

In analytic philosophy, praxis becomes action, which was the focal point of Wittgenstein's investigations. *Action* in this context came to signify a complex web of issues in understanding *intention, motive, purpose, reasons*, and *teleological explanation* (or purpose). Ironically, although the meanings of praxis and action are very close, few have raised the question of the connection between Wittgenstein's concept of action and Marx's idea of praxis.

SOURCES

Arendt, Hannah. *The Human Condition.* Chicago: University of Chicago Press. 1958.

Bernstein. Richard J. *Praxis and Action.* Philadelphia: University of Pennsylvania Press. 1971.

Lobkowicz, Nicholas. *Theory and Practice: History of a Concept from Aristotle to Marx.* Notre Dame: University of Notre Dame Press. 1967.

PRAYER IN THE PUBLIC SCHOOLS

Stephen L. Carter of Yale University has noted that it has become common in our culture to perceive of parents who complain about school curricula on religious grounds as "backward, irrational, illiberal fanatics." Many of these same parents also ask for prayer to be permitted in the school, that creationism be taught along with evolution, and that certain books be banned or censored for religiously offensive content or language.

Some also argue that religious fundamentalists have a perfect right to their beliefs—but no right to control the teaching of science or literature or even have open, organized prayer in the schools. The Bill of Rights's separation of church and state is often cited for justifying the exclusion of religion from the public schools in any normative form. But we must ask ourselves how many times *belief* rather than *fact* has actually entered the curricula of schools—and ask what is being taught or not taught in the name of feminism or in the name of multiculturalism or of minorities, for example. Lynne V. Cheney observes: "If the principle that ideology should not dominate what children learn in public schools is a sound one—and generations have held it to be—then surely it deserves the widest possible application." Again, one must ask about the purpose of schooling in the United States and if education and the promotion of certain views to the exclusion of others, or the practice of religions, can coexist.

SOURCES

Carter, Steven L. *Culture of Disbelief.* New York: Basic Books. 1993.

Cheney, Lynne V. *Telling the Truth.* New York: Simon & Schuster. 1995.

Sykes, Charles J. *Dumbing Down Our Kids*. New York: St. Martin's. 1995.

PREDESTINATION

In Christian theology, predestination is a doctrine that sets forth the belief that the eternal destiny of humans is determined by God. The word *predestination* comes from Latin and means "determined beforehand." Belief in predestination is based on Paul's words in Romans 8:28–30, which reads:

> We know that in everything God works for good with those who love him, who are called according to his purpose. For those whom he foreknew he also predestined to be conformed to the image of his Son, in order that he might be the firstborn among many brethren. And those whom he predestined he also called; and those whom he called he also justified; and those whom he justified he also glorified.

Saint Augustine (A.D. 354–430) and Saint Thomas Aquinas (A.D. 1224–1274) also helped make this doctrine a part of Christian theology. John Calvin, too, emphasized predestination as a part of Protestant theology. We also must note that predestination is an essential part of Islam, which teaches that humans are predestined to goodness and happiness, as well as to evil and misery.

The theological issue covered by predestination is raised by the question, "Is final resistance to God possible?" To answer this question in the affirmative presents a delicate mystery for the theist. On the one hand, the theist says that we have the freedom and power to resist God, but—for the theist—this does not mean that such people really escape God ("the devils also believe, and tremble," James 2:19). Yet the theist is forced to take the view that apparently God does not overtake everybody. To the theist this is a mystery because in the divine encounter, God uniformly presents Himself as infinitely loving and superabundantly powerful. How then do humans resist being overpowered by God?

The following three interpretations (or solutions) are available for the theist: (1) God is unable to overtake or save everybody; His power is limited so that either He is forced to restrict Himself to certain persons or else in certain cases He fails; (2) God does not *intend* to overtake (save) everybody; that is, He purposely restricts His love to certain persons to the exclusion of others; or (3) God makes His love available to everyone, but allows them the free choice to choose or not to choose his love.

All three interpretations present serious difficulties. The first seems inconsistent with the theist's own experience, for if God can overpower one's resistance to Him, it seems incredible that He could conceivably fail with anyone else who is of the same human nature. There is nothing in one that deserves the infinite love that confronts one in the encounter; it comes as a pure, unmerited gift. The second interpretation, that God does not *intend* to "save" everybody, means that He deliberately restricts His gift to an elect number of individuals. This is the view that has been taken not only by Paul, Augustine, and Calvin, but embodies the predestination view of God, embraced by many, that God "saves" only those whom He chooses, leaving the others to the consequences of their unresolved anguish. The third interpretation is not really very different from the second, because if God permits some to resist Him, He is still refraining from loving or saving them as He might.

The reason this problem arises is because of the seemingly inescapable fact that an experience of God claimed by some is not enjoyed by all; that some even stake a claim to a "special" revelation of God and that others are excluded by design. To some devoted theists, predestination and its concommitant problem—the problem of evil—remain a mystery. Of course, others see this not as a problem of God's, but a problem of humans who make claims that might not be true and who delight in claiming that God has "chosen" them and excluded others.

SOURCES

MacGregor, Geddes. *Introduction to Religious Philosophy.* Boston: Houghton Mifflin. 1959.

Tillich, Paul. *Perspectives on 19th and 20th Century Protestant Theology.* New York: Harper & Row. 1967.

PREJUDICE

Prejudice and discrimination are related concepts, but not the same. Prejudice is a negative attitude toward an entire category of people. The two important components of this defintion are *attitude* and *entire category.* Prejudice involves attitudes, thoughts, and beliefs, not actions. Frequently, prejudice is expressed through the use of *ethnophaulisms,* or ethnic slurs, which include derisive nicknames. A prejudicial belief leads to categorical rejection. Prejudice is not disliking someone you meet because you find his or her behavior objectionable. It is disliking an entire racial or ethnic group, even if you have had little or no contact with them.

Unlike prejudice, discrimination is an action. Discrimination involves behavior that excludes all members of a group from certain rights, opportunities, or privileges. Like prejudice, discrimination must be categorical. Prejudice does not necessarily coincide with discriminatory behavior. Sociologist Robert Merton, in exploring the relationship between negative attitudes and negative behavior, has identified four major categories, to which is added a folk-label for identification:

1. The unprejudiced nondiscriminator (all-weather liberal)
2. The unprejudiced discriminator (reluctant liberal)
3. The prejudiced nondiscriminator (timid bigot)
4. The prejudiced discriminator (all-weather bigot)

Merton's typology points out that attitudes should not be confused with behavior. People do not always act as they believe. Beliefs or actions exist in the context of social norms.

SOURCES

Allport, Gordon, W. *The Nature of Prejudice.* Reading, MA: Addison-Wesley. 1954.

Glazer, Nathan. *Affirmative Discrimination: Ethnic Inequality and Public Policy.* New York: Basic Books. 1975.

Merton, Robert K. "Discrimination and the American Creed." In Robert M. MacIver, ed. *Discrimination and National Welfare.* New York: Harper & Row. 1949.

PRESS, FREEDOM OF

Moral freedom means the capacity to choose and act on one's choice, and finds expression in the issue of freedom of the press. Moral freedom involves the power to choose between alternative courses of action and the power to act as a causal agent in the process of behaving. Moral freedom is freedom of the *will,* the person's ability to perform voluntary acts; the *will* is the person expressing himself or herself in action. Freedom of the will is the freedom to choose, to make decisions, to express an opinion, and to report facts openly and objectively. Thus, by proliferation of free thought and differing opinions, freedom of the press is an expression of freedom of the will, of moral freedom.

In the mid-1950s Nathan M. Pusey, while recognizing that the climate of opinion may change from time to time, said that "the predominant pressures in our culture" have been moving for some decades with increasing force in the direction of conformity. We see this clearly as more "fundamentalistic" factions have gradually taken over the Southern Baptist Convention and forced more moderate or even liberal groups within the convention either to move out and form new alliances or to stay within guidelines established by the dominant group. Literature such as state Baptist newspapers and educational material is being coerced to conform. Writing in the early 1960s, a member of the U.S. Supreme Court expressed a view similar to Pusey's: "The trend to conformity has possessed us since World War II. The causes are numerous, some of them reflecting no more than a conservative outlook that is usually reflected in an affluent society."

Certainly in the 1990s, this scene has not changed significantly. With the conservative victories in the U.S. Congress in 1994, the movement toward conformity has continued. Many newspapers, news magazines, and radio and television news shows, in their effort to capture "readership," "listenership," and "viewership" (and the profits they bring), have not taken clear stands on issues, but remain in a muddled middle-road position. Tabloid magazines, political talk shows, and televised shows that masquerade as news broadcasts are phenomena that have arisen with persuasive power and influence. All of these claim to be "the press," and to possess both moral and political freedom. Yet, truth and fact seem to be in short supply when their content is analyzed; and when pushed for objectivity, most of them claim to be "entertainment shows."

The growth of this mass media of communication has given us powerful new instruments for creating public opinion. Through them we are manipulated and controlled by the work of propagandists and advertisers. The cry, "They're just doing their job," permeats the airways and seems to forgive them of any dedication to truth, fact, and ethics. Although the Fifth Amendment to the U.S. Constitution protects freedom of the press, the Fourth Amendment recognizes the right of privacy. Also, from a moral perspective, the "press"—or mass media—is obligated to act diligently and honestly on their knowledge. Yet, we know that those who have money also have power to influence politicians and use the media to their advantage. Trying to eliminate wealth as a factor in influencing public opinion would mean even more interference with

personal freedom, and this paradox simply will not disappear.

The spirit of freedom requires a certain amount of trust. It also requires that citizens have access to the widest possible range of viewpoints and outlets for expressing their own views and learning about the views of others. Thus, freedom questions the constitutionality of the movement toward media monopoly—media outlets controlled by fewer and fewer people. The United States has the freest press in the world and is one of the few nations in which the government does not heavily control the press. But government can control information and stifle free expression without owning the media—by greater secrecy, by intimidation, and by barring dissenting views from being aired or spoken. To expose this kind of control, we need competitive news sources—with no vested interests—and that is what we are losing.

SOURCES

Bagdikian, Ben H. *The Media Monopoly.* 4th ed. Boston: Beacon Press. 1987.

Nozick, Robert. *Anarchy, State, and Utopia.* New York: Basic Books. 1974.

PRIMARY GROUP

Charles Horton Cooley, in 1909, was the first to use the term *primary group* to describe such groups as families, neighborhoods, and children's play groups. Such groups were, in Cooley's view, "a necessity of human nature" where the essential sentiments of group loyalty and concern for others could be learned. Cooley was not creating an entirely new concept, but he contributed the word *primary* along with a sensitive description of the meaning of *primary group relationships.*

The characteristics of the primary group Cooley described are those of face-to-face interaction, sentiments of loyalty, identification, emotional involvement, close cooperation, and concern for friendly relations

COOLEY'S PRIMARY GROUP CONCEPT

Primary Group	
Examples:	family, children's play groups, close-knit neighborhood
Traits:	Emotional involvement, close cooperation, face-to-face interaction, identity, psychological security, belonging an end in itself
Secondary Group	
Examples:	Giant corporation, state university, U.S. Army
Traits:	Unemotional, competitive, less intimate, identity less relevant, economic efficiency, belonging a means to an end

SOCIETAL TYPES SIMILAR TO PRIMARY-SECONDARY RELATIONSHIPS

Tonnies:	*Gemeinschaft* (person-centered) / *Gesellschaft* (business-centered)
Durkheim:	Mechanical solidarity (members all alike as though turned out of a machine) / Organic solidarity (members all different, held together by interdependence)

as an end in themselves, not as a means to an end. The primary group is usually rather small, but size is much less important than sentiment. The primary group gives the individual his or her "first acquaintance with humanity." For Cooley, "human nature is not something existing separately in the individual, but a group-nature or primary phase of society." Human nature, he reflects, "comes into existence through fellowship and decays in isolation." Primary groups are thus a great source of emotional and psychological security. Cooley concluded that the positive and affectionate characteristics of the human being grow in families, neighborhoods, and children's play groups in all societies and that hatred, bigotry, and intolerance are, to a great extent, features of these sentiments that spread beyond the small group.

GROUP RELATIONS AND SOCIETAL TYPES

The first diagram above illustrates Cooley's primary group concept. The second diagram (see Litwak and Szeleny) illustrates societal types similar to primary-secondary relationships.

SOURCES

Cooley, Charles Horton. *Social Organization.* New York: Free Press. 1958.

Litwak, E., and Ivan Szeleny. "Primary Group Structures and Their Functions: Kin, Neighborhood, and Friends." *American Sociological Review* 34:4 (August 1969).

PRIVACY, RIGHT TO

Any list of human rights will need to be restated from time to time as conditions of life change. One of these is the right to privacy. We live in a technological age when our phone numbers and addresses are sold on the open market to retail vendors and when we are overwhelmed by telephone solicitations in the privacy of our homes and our mail boxes are constantly full of what we commonly call "junk mail." Ours is also a day of the tabloid press, which seems to take freedom of the press very seriously but not the responsibility that goes with it, thus leaving private individuals at the mercy of reporters and cameras. The right to privacy, guaranteed by the Constitution, is a principle that most of us value highly but that seems to fall in a legal/moral fuzzy area between the individual and the society's so-called right to know.

The right to privacy is a part of a much larger group of values classified under the topic of the *right to freedom*. The right to freedom includes the freedom of expression (which generates the advantages of education and democracy), freedom of opinion, of speech, and of the press. Intellectual freedom and the right to considerable privacy are essential parts of the Bill of Rights: "The right of the people to be secure in their persons, houses, papers, and effects, against unreasonable searches and seizures, shall not be violated, and no Warrant shall issue, but upon probable cause, supported by Oath or Affirmation, and particularly describing the place to be searched, and the persons or things to be seized."

SOURCES

Kennedy, C., and E. Alderman. *In Our Defense.* New York: William Morrow. 1991.
———. *The Right to Privacy.* New York: Alfred A. Knopf. 1995.

PRO-CHOICE, PRO-LIFE

With regard to abortion, pro-choice is the right to make one's own choice as the highest moral priority, so that it matters little what the effects of that choice are upon others. On the other hand, pro-life defines abortion as murder, and murder of any type is taboo. Different political action groups have been formed promoting each of these points of view, lobbying state and federal lawmakers, and using the media to gain members.

See also Abortion.

SOURCE

Van Horne, Harriet. "A Commentary by Harriet Van Horne: The Sexual Revolution—in Living Color." *McCalls* 95 (October 1967): 46.

PROFESSIONAL ETHICS

Whenever a group of people organize for some special purpose or function, they create an institution. We can possibly do together what we cannot do alone, and so we organize all sorts of groups-for-doing-things. In the modern world, institutions have multiplied rapidly and are related to important human purposes: recreation, education, religion, science, the professions, government, business, and so on. Institutions are able to collectively influence cognitive development and moral (or immoral) outlook.

An institution set up for a specific purpose may change in its outlook as time goes on, or even lose its original purpose. Such an institution may continue and become an end in itself, and its members may see their main task as that of keeping the institution in existence even though its original purpose may have been accomplished or is no longer needed (one should note that state and federal governments create bureaucracies for certain programs, but when those programs have completed their mission, the bureaucracies—many times—remain in place (e.g., subsidies for the production of honey is a case in point). Excessive loyalty to institutions has led some to break the law and undermine the moral code they profess to follow, as we discovered in the 1973 Watergate break-in. Some people who have been honorable and pillars of their communities have been put in prison for practices carried out in connection with their professional and business activities. Such persons have had multiple moralities and loyalties as they have moved from group to group or institution to institution.

Arnold Toynbee, who studied a score or more of civilizations that have existed in the past, tells us that over periods of time institutions tend to be captured by "collective self-centeredness" and thus often come to serve "anti-social and anti-human ends." A professional person or a business person could use any methods or tactics he or she can "get away with." On the other hand, he or she may be interested primarily in the development of persons and in social welfare, and, if this is the case, plan to make a living in the service of mankind, not merely in servitude to the profit motive. This person will follow the law and practice his or her business or profession with a moral end in mind, to benefit not only self but society as well.

MORALS, LAWS, AND PROFESSIONAL ETHICS

What is the relationship between morals, law, and professional ethics? The term *morals* is the broadest term; it includes any form of voluntary human activity where the judgment of right and wrong may enter. The *law,* on the other hand, is a command of the state. It is usually set forth in some statutory provision; it applies to all individuals in a specific territory and gen-erally provides penalties for disobedience. Morals are basic, and laws tend to follow the moral ideals of the community and to change with the development of the moral consciousness. Thus, morals are slow to change and are—strictly speaking—not necessarily relative, but may possess a universal strain. Since obedience to the law is usually considered a part of moral behavior, all laws may be included in the moral realm.

Professional ethics, as distinct from morals and from the law, gives attention to certain additional ideals and practices that grow out of a person's professional privileges and responsibilities. Professional ethics—professional ethical codes—crystallize moral opinion and define behavior in these specialized professional fields. Professional ethics is therefore the expression of the attempt to define situations that would otherwise remain indefinite and to direct the moral consciousness of the professional member to its peculiar problem.

Function

There are three basic functions of professional ethics: (1) The dignity and standing of the particular profession is dependent on the confidence the public has in it. Thus, professional ethics is a means of social control, defining professional conduct for new members. (2) Professional ethical codes, if effective, prevent control or interference by the government or by society. Groups that maintain high standards are seldom interfered with by the government or other watchdog groups. (3) Ethical codes can be important in developing higher standards of conduct. Professional ethical codes bring together what are usually the best opinions and judgments of the profession; tend to eliminate misunderstanding and conflict; and enable groups to bring pressure to bear on those who would lower the standards of the group or cast negative reflection on its good name. Thus, we find in the 1990s many professions requiring high standards in regard to harassment and drug abuse, and providing personnel development training for understanding and clarification.

Criteria

When evaluating professional ethical codes, the following criteria have been established that provide insight and assistance:

1. Does the code refer to the service the profession provides for society?
2. Is the code clear and definite, or merely the expression of a vague idealism open to varied interpretations?
3. Does the code represent only a small conscientious minority within the profession, or do the rank and file members respect and attempt to follow it?
4. Are there effective means of enforcing the code? Are delinquent members of the profession called to account or penalized in some way?
5. Is there some plan and effort to keep the code up to date as conditions change?

See also Business Ethics.

SOURCES

Hall, Cameron P., ed. *On-the-Job Ethics.* New York: National Council of Churches. 1963.

MacIver, R. M. "The Social Significance of Professional Ethics." In *Ethical Standards and Professional Conduct* 297. Philadelphia: The Annals of the American Academy of Political and Social Science. 1955. (See also volume 343.)

Smith, Page. *Killing the Spirit.* New York: Viking. 1990.

PROMISE KEEPING

Intuitionists have argued that what is right—such as promise keeping—needs no justification. That is, no argument supporting moral goodness, what is right, what is our duty, or obligation is necessary. For example, in 1912, H. A. Pritchard wrote an article entitled "Does Moral Philosophy Rest on a Mistake?"—a question he answered in the affirmative. Since early Greek times, it has been assumed by most students of moral thought that a *moral judgment* called for a defense of the *good* of the individual and of society. From this point of view, moral judgments sought to show that the act of being considerate, of promise keeping, was conducive to human welfare. Pritchard claimed that this is a mistake. No justification is necessary or possible. What is right, he claimed, is not necessarily good. The reason most of us keep a promise is that it is self-evidently right and obligatory. The act may be right even though there is no discernible good to be had as a result, or even if some evil may be the result.

Sir David Ross (1930), an outstanding proponent of the school of twentieth-century British intuitionists, said that in practice there may be exceptions where duties conflict or where an act or event has a diversity of obligations. Immanuel Kant took a more extreme position and pushed the principles of duty and obligation to the point where there were no exceptions. For Ross, the good act is self-evidently good, just as a mathematical axiom or the validity of a form of inference is self-evident. Certain prima facie duties have a direct claim on us and they grow out of the situation we are facing. Ross named seven of these duties: promise keeping was the first to be mentioned, along with reparation for injuries, duties of gratitude, duties of justice, beneficence, self-improvement, and not injuring others. In this view, the person who does not realize that a solemn promise lays him or her under an obligation to respect it is morally blind.

During the past 150 years, moral thinkers have sought some unifying principles that underlie acts that are right and obligatory. Some have suggested that a quality called *fittingness* may serve this purpose—and that all behavior that we can call "right" has this quality. That is, it is *fitting* that we keep our promises and it is *fitting* that each individual add to the sum total of human good. Fittingness is a judgment or intuitive induction matching the duty to the particular situation that calls its forth.

According to many ethical thinkers, therefore, promise keeping has a rightness of its own that is to be denied only under rather exceptional conditions. G. E. Moore said that "it seems to me self-evident that knowingly to do an action which would make the world, on the whole, really and truly worse than if we had acted differently, must always be wrong." In concluding his book, *Rightness and Goodness*, O. A. Johnson comments: "If it is true that rightness and goodness are so independent of each other that a person may have fulfilled his duty even though his action leaves the world a worse place than it would have been had he not acted, then, I should say, moral action becomes irrational and ethics, as an attempt to provide a theoretical interpretation of moral life, impossible." Promise keeping, we can conclude on this account, is both right and good, for it produces long-range good for both individuals and society.

SOURCES

Johnson, O. A. *Rightness and Goodness*. The Hague: Mortinus Nijhofl. 1959.

Moore, G. E. *Ethics*. New York: Henry Holt. 1912.

Pritchard, H. A. "Does Moral Philosophy Rest on a Mistake?" *Mind* 21 (1912).

PROTESTANTISM

BACKGROUND

The sixteenth century saw religious reform take hold and change the face of religious faith and practice throughout Europe. Beginning as reforms "within" the Catholic Church by pointing out faults and making a vigorous protest, the *protestants* soon found themselves outside the church. Thereafter, the pattern became more and more common of first breaking away and then obtaining reform, until Protestants began breaking away from Protestants. The only general reform of the church from within occurred by way of reappraisal, redefinition, and renewal; this was the Catholic Reformation.

The Protestant Reformation split Western Christendom into two apparently irreconcilable groups. It was long in preparation, and with the rise of the middle class to economic and cultural self-sufficiency during the fourteenth and fifteenth centuries, the stage was set. The rise of towns, the development of capitalism, and the relaxation of the domination of the lords and princes brought the development of true individualism. Therefore, it is not surprising that the common person of Europe began to want his or her religious competence recognized too, whether in the use of reason or in the exercise of conscience. In the sixteenth century we see the rise of Lutheranism in Germany, the Zwinglian and Calvinistic reformations in Switzerland, the rise of the French Huguenots, Calvinism in the Netherlands, the Church of England, and Presbyterianism in Scotland, to name the major Protestant groups of that time. Martin Luther (*see* Hulme 1914) goes to the heart of the issue when he observes: "I say, then, neither pope, nor bishop, nor any man whatever has the right of making one syllable binding on a Christian man, unless it be done with his own consent. Whatever is done otherwise is done in the spirit of tyranny. I cry aloud on behalf of liberty and conscience, and I proclaim with confidence that no kind of law can with any justice be imposed on Christians, except so far as they themselves will; for we are free from all."

In the first half of the seventeenth century, wars of religion broke out on the continent of Europe. The emperor and the pope, subscribing to the decisions of the

Council of Trent (1545), sought Catholic recovery of lost ground, while Protestants fought for freedom from suppression and for dominance in central Europe. The Thirty Years War, which decimated central Europe, changed little territorially. In it the Catholics regained some ground, and the Protestants established their right to exist independently of the pope or emperor. The Treaty of Westphalia (1648) granted the Calvinists and Lutherans the right to certain territories with no further interference by emperor or pope, and recognized Catholic dominance in other—largely southern—areas of central Europe. The seventeenth century saw the rise of the Puritans, the Congregationalists, the Baptists, the Unitarians, and the Quakers.

THE MODERN PERIOD

Methodism, actually not a reformation movement, was the one major Protestant development of the eighteenth century, and was born as a response to new conditions created by the development of science and the rapid rise of industrial capitalism. Methodism stands at the beginning of the shifts and changes characteristic of modern times. During the eighteenth-century Enlightenment in Europe, Western science established itself among thinking/reflective individuals and compelled religion to justify its case inductively. The whole structure of revealed religion was abandoned by those thinkers, and before the "iron laws" of the beautifully running mechanical universe, it came tumbling down. "Causality" was now thought of not in terms of God's providence but in terms of the physical frame of nature. The Deists came to terms with modern science by separating God from his creation and conceiving that the latter ran by itself, like a clock, and therefore could be a separate object of study.

THE MISSIONARY MOVEMENT

The nineteenth century may be thought of as a Protestant century. It opened with

what was called a "great awakening" in the United States—a series of revivals that increased the number of Baptists and Methodists in the midwestern states. In Great Britain the Church of England was powerfully moved by a pietistic Evangelical Movement, which in later decades brought in the Tractarian Movement, the formation of the Young Men's Christian Association (YMCA, 1844), and the organization of the Salvation Army (1865). In Germany the theologians Schleiermacher (1768–1834) and Ritschl (1822–1889) gave a liberal turn to Protestant theology. But perhaps the two most significant developments of the century were the organization of worldwide Protestant missions and the rapid expansion of the Sunday School movement and religious education. By the turn of the twentieth century, a better-informed leadership reformed Christian education by applying the principles and techniques of secular public instruction. No more serious and sustained educational effort to bring Christianity into the lives of individuals as a discipline for the whole of human life has ever been attempted in any period of the history of the Christian Church than the Sunday School or Church School Movement.

REACTIONS AND BELIEFS

Before the end of the nineteenth century, a momentous struggle began between orthodox religion and a naturalism bred by science. David Strauss and Ernest Renan radically rewrote the life of Jesus. Lower (textual) criticism and higher (historical and literary) criticism of the Bible demonstrated that its books were the work of many different authors at many different times. Violent controversies erupted over these movements and their conclusions (still evidenced in the 1970s, and 1980s, and in the 1990s we continue to see and hear these eruptions and are witnessing a split in Southern Baptist ranks). Fundamentalists rejected Biblical criticism and held to five basic beliefs:

- The verbal inspiration of the Bible
- The virgin birth of Jesus
- The substitutionary atonement of Christ
- The bodily resurrection of Christ
- The second coming of Christ

The fundamentalist movement became identified with the National Association of Evangelicals in 1942. Members of another branch of fundamentalism that prefers to put more emphasis upon the personal experience of conversion are known as "born-again" Christians.

On the other side, liberal Protestants saw no problems between science and religion. In the view of Henry Drummon in Scotland and John Fiske in New England, the Bible is nothing more than prescientific theorizing and has to be taken poetically; its form requires reinterpretation. With this beginning, the liberals proceeded confidently to reconstruct and demythologize the Bible. For them, the Christian faith is unshaken in its major assumptions. The liberal view was confident and optimistic in its faith in God and in humanity.

Severely shaken by World War I, liberalism emerged thereafter as a neoorthodoxy that accepted the findings of science and of historical criticism, insisting that God is not in nature and history in the way previously proposed, but is transcendent, existing quite apart from nature and humanity. Indeed, God became the *Wholly Other* who must break through the wall of human error and self-contradiction that separates Him from humans in order to appear in human history. Without such breaking through, humans are lost.

Recent theological trends in Protestantism include the counterculture "Death of God" theology of the 1960s, where the emphasis is on the death of meaningless God talk and the death of transcendence: Christianity is about humans, not God; after the cross God was born again as here-and-now imminence. In Europe, theologians such as Jurgen Moltmann and Wolfhart Pennunberg responded to secularism and the collapse of traditional values by reinterpreting the eschatological dimensions of the Gospels: the coming One, who is also present, offers the hope of the future. This theology of hope anticipated and paralleled some new developments in the Americas, where particular facets of oppression and attendant forms of hoped-for redress came to be the focal points of black theology, liberation theology, and feminist theology.

SOURCES

Hulme, E. M. *The Renaissance, the Protestant Reformation, and the Catholic Reformation.* 2 vols. New York: Century House. 1914.

MacKintosh, H. R. *Types of Modern Theology.* New York: Scribner's. 1937.

Noss, David S., and John B. Noss. *Man's Religions.* 7th ed. New York: Macmillan. 1984.

Rouse, R., and S. C. Neill, eds. *A History of the Ecumenical Movement, 1517–1948.* New York: Westminster Press. 1954.

RACISM

Before the eighteenth century, the upper classes in England and France, as everywhere else, developed a vague theory that the "lower classes" were inferior by nature. This belief that both biological and cultural traits are socially significant, making one group or race superior (or inferior) to others, is called racism.

Throughout human history is found an emergent doctrine of racial supremacy. The Egyptians of the Middle Kingdom, chiefly the Twelfth Dynasty (2000–1800 B.C.) and the New Kingdom or Empire, Eighteenth through Twentieth Dynasties (1570–1090 B.C.), held slaves from their conquered territories about whom they felt racially and culturally superior. The Hebrews in their conquest of Palestine labeled the native Canaanites living there *gentiles*. In the biblical drama there are three *dramatis personae:* God, the nations, and Israel. The word *nations* is variously translated as "gentiles," "heathens," and "pagans." Considering themselves the "holy people" among the nations, Israel considered her whole history and calling to be spreading the word of Yahweh (*ya'w*) to all nations. A caste system was established in India (about 3,500 years ago, when Aryans came into India) to control the Indians and keep them separate (*kast,* from the Portuguese word that means "family," "strain," or "race"— usually referring to groups into which the people of India are divided by religious laws, but in a general sense, it means a hereditary division of any society into classes on the basis of occupation, color, wealth, or religion). In the seventeenth century, white Europeans institutionalized slavery, finding that the African culture did not fit their three-tiered caste system. They therefore labeled Africans as inferior and subhuman, permitting them to be bought and sold as chattel or property. More recently, in the 1930s, the German-American Bund (Amerika-Deutscher Volksbund) sought the intellectual and spiritual reform of Americans of German extraction, whose influence, politically activated, would tip the balance in the struggle against communism and Jews and in favor of an "independent Aryan-governed United States of America."

DISCRIMINATION

The outgrowth of racism is discrimination, which favors one group or one race while denying equal rights and opportunities to individuals and groups of other races. Before 1920 in Europe and America, scientific theories of race were developed that generated the belief that only certain types of individuals were fit to run a society. This discriminatory action was fueled by prejudice, the preconceived opinion about certain groups of people formed without knowledge, thought, or reason. Discrimination happens when people approach one another focusing primarily on their genetic, cultural, and social differences as decisive. About discriminatory practices, Milton Friedman has observed, "No one who buys bread knows whether the wheat from which it is made was grown by a Communist or a Republican . . . a Fascist or . . . a Negro or a white . . . an impersonal market separates economic activities from political views and protects men from being discriminated against."

The secondary labor market affecting many members of social and ethnic minorities has come to be called the *irregular economy*. This describes the nature of work in many inner-city neighborhoods, in sharp contrast to the rest of the marketplace. Workers are employed in the irregular economy either seasonally or infrequently. According to the dual labor market model, the irregular economy is that to which minorities have been relegated. This model emphasizes that minorities fare unfavorably in the competition between dominant and subordinate groups.

The life of the ghetto black seeking employment has been portrayed accurately in Elliot Liebow's study of lower-class black men, *Tally's Corner: A Study of Negro Streetcorner Men* (1967). Liebow, an anthropologist, conducted participant-observation research on a street corner in Washington, D.C., of which the following excerpt documents the problem of working in the irregular economy:

> The streetcorner man is under continuous assault by his job experience and job fears. His experiences and fears feed on one another. The kind of job he can get—and frequently only after fighting for it, if then—steadily confirms his fears, depresses his self-confidence and self-esteem until finally, terrified of an opportunity even if one presents itself, he stands defeated by his experiences, his belief in his own self-worth destroyed and his fears a confirmed reality.

PREJUDICE

Prejudice—the prejudging of persons, groups, and behaviors—is a social phenomenon. Children learn prejudice before they exhibit it. Prejudice and discrimination are related concepts, but they are not the same. Prejudice is a negative attitude toward an entire category of people. Prejudice involves thoughts, attitudes, and beliefs, but not actions. Discrimination is an action.

Frequently, prejudice is expressed through the use of *ethnophaulisms,* or ethnic slurs, which include derisive nicknames such as "honkie," "nigger," or "wetback." Ethnophaulisms also include speaking about or to members of a particular group in a condescending way—"Jose does well in school for a Chicano." A prejudiced belief leads to categorical rejection. It is disliking an entire racial or ethnic group, even if you have little or no contact.

Discrimination involves behavior that may exhibit the prejudiced attitude or feeling one holds. But prejudice does not necessarily coincide with discriminatory behavior. Sociologist Robert Merton has identified four major categories of negative attitudes and negative behaviors:

1. The unprejudiced nondiscriminator;
2. The unprejudiced discriminator;
3. The prejudiced nondiscriminator;
4. The prejudiced discriminator.

Interestingly, Merton's typology points out that attitudes should not be confused with behavior. People do not always act the way they believe.

Racial prejudice is frequently involved to justify keeping a group in a subordinate position, like a lower social class. Racial and social hostility are ways the dominant group keeps its position of status and power intact. Even the less affluent white working class uses prejudice to minimize competition from upwardly mobile minorities.

Related to this exploitation form of prejudice is the caste approach that is found in the United States. The caste approach is a system of social inequality in which status is inherited and there is little if any opportunity to change one's social position. The caste explanation for racial subordination sees race and social class as closely related, because blacks and other nonwhite minorities are destined by the social structure to occupy a caste-like position.

Closely related to prejudice is the *authoritarian personality,* which social scientists have isolated. They do not find prejudice an isolated trait that anyone can have. Several efforts have been made to detail the prejudicial personality, but the most comprehensive effort culminated in a volume entitled *The Authoritarian Personality* by T. W. Adorno et al. (see also James W. Vander Zanden's *American Minority Relations*).

The basic characteristics of the authoritarian personality include adherence to conventional values, uncritical acceptance of authority, and concern with power and toughness. With obvious relevance to development of intolerance, the authoritarian personality is also characterized by aggressiveness toward people who do not conform to authority or conventional norms. These authors find that this personality type develops from an early childhood of harsh discipline. A child with an authoritarian upbringing obeys and later treats others as he or she has been treated. Although these studies have been highly criticized since their publication, Richard T. Schaefer points out that the very existence of criticism indicates the impact of a study.

HISTORICAL PERSPECTIVE: CAPITALISM, SLAVERY, AND REPUBLICAN VALUES

Racial discrimination became wedded to economic policies after the English Civil War and settlement in 1688. When James II abdicated, Tories and Whigs put aside their bitter and often peptic differences to draw up a declaration of rights. This bill of rights effectively transferred sovereignty from king to Parliament and shifted the balance of power accordingly. The newly empowered Parliament was itself principally composed of landed property owners, whether aristocrats or gentry. The

revolution was successful over the monarch's feudal conservatism because significant numbers of the dominant landed classes had been making a steady but gradual economic transformation to capitalist practices.

Private property won victories at the expense of both royalty and labor. The differences that had softened between Tories and Whigs were actually overcome by economic similarities. Now Parliament began passing legislation that became the legal foundation on which the economic edifice of the eighteenth century was built. Of all the laws passed by Parliament during the early days of the Industrial Revolution, the *enclosure acts* are the most revealing. In issuing these orders of expropriation (dispossession), Parliament dismantled the ancient rights of Englishmen and replaced them with the natural rights of *homo oeconomicus.* By the time England entered the nineteenth century it had become the classic model of capitalist development. Unlike the rest of Europe, England had uprooted and "pauperized" its peasantry and created a new three-tiered society of capitalists, landlords, and workers that claimed to be grounded in nature's moral *principia.*

Land (property) was now a condition of freedom and citizenship, justified by an appeal to natural law, and compatible with commercial enterprise so long as that enterprise was land based. Enclosure contributed to the formation of the working class and in so doing impoverished the English laboring classes (*see* G. E. Mingay's "The Transformation of Agriculture" in R. M. Hartwell et al., *The Long Debate on Poverty: Eight Essays on Industrialization and the "Condition of England."* London: Institute of Economic Affairs, 1972; and J. D. Chambers's "Enclosure and Labour Supply in the Industrial Revolution" in *Economic History Review,* 2nd series: 5, 1953).

Both mercantile and landed interests agreed that trade was the main condition of freedom and that it necessitated the triad of classes. In the United States, the triad of classes that was linked to wage labor and capital in classical political economy also determined voting rights and became the justification for slavery (*see* Eric Williams, *Capitalism and Slavery*. Chapel Hill: University of North Carolina Press, 1949). Virtue was now practically synonymous with property (land or human), which provided the common interest for citizens. The antifederalists accepted commerce as a legitimate pursuit, and Jefferson suggested territorial expansion as a solution to satisfy this need.

By 1830, many believed a natural unity existed between Northern and Southern propertied classes. Southerners warned the Northern property owners that their endorsement of abolitionist demands was actually an endorsement of majoritarian tyranny, for if the abolitionists could legislate against the property rights (make slavery illegal) of the Southern slave owners, a majority could eventually outlaw private property altogether. From this perspective slavery became the immediate issue historically, while theoretically it assumed secondary consideration as only one particular form of property.

There is a footnote to this discussion of racism. It was in the summer of 1836 that the William and Mary College Board of Visitors chose Thomas Roderick Dew as college president. Dew was a senior professor at the college and had distinguished himself both as a scholar and a spokesperson for Southern interests. His inaugural address was a display of erudition and dedication to Southern property rights—pointedly, the right to hold slaves as chattel. Dew argued that slavery was more than compatible with the ideals of the American Revolution; that it was virtually indispensable to their realization. Dew went on to assert that future slaveholders bore a considerable responsibility in plotting the future of republicanism. His years spent at William and Mary would be for the purpose of training property owners in the intellectual skills needed to fulfill their historic duty.

SOURCES

Adorno, T. W., Frenkel-Brunswik, Levinson, and Sanford. *The Authoritarian Personality*. New York: Wiley. 1950.

Buttrick, George Arthur, et al., eds. *The Interpreter's Dictionary of the Bible*. Vol. R–Z. New York: Abingdon Press. 1962.

Carroll, Peter N., and David W. Noble. *The Free and the Unfree: A New History of the United States*. 2d ed. New York: Penguin. 1987.

Davis, David B. *The Problem of Slavery in the Age of Revolution*. Ithaca: Cornell University Press. 1975.

Friedman, Milton. *Capitalism and Freedom*. Chicago: University of Chicago Press. 1963.

Grant, Frederick C. *Hellenistic Religions: The Age of Syncretism*. New York: Merrill. 1953.

Handlin, Oscar, and Lilian Handlin. *Liberty and Equality 1920–1994*. New York: Harper Collins. 1994.

Kaufman, Allen. *Capitalism, Slavery, and Republican Values: American Political Economists, 1819–1848*. Austin: University of Texas Press. 1982.

Lappe, Frances Moore. *Rediscovering America's Values*. New York: Ballantine. 1989.

Liebow, Elliot. *Tally's Corner: A Study of Negro Streetcorner Men*. New York: Little, Brown. 1967.

Locke, Mary S. *Anti-Slavery in America*. Gloucester: Peter Smith. 1965.

Rose, Arnold. *The Negro in America*. Boston: Beacon Press. 1961.

Schaefer, Richard T. *Racial and Ethnic Groups*. 2d ed. Boston: Little, Brown. 1984.

Sobel, Mechal. *The World They Made Together*. Princeton: Princeton University Press. 1989.

Swami Nikhilananda. *The Upanishads*. New York: Harper Torchbooks. 1963.

Vander Zanden, James W. *American Minority Relations*, 3d ed. New York: Ronald Press. 1972.

RAINBOW CURRICULUM

An uproar occurred in 1992 when New York City Chancellor Joseph A. Fernandez endorsed the multicultural "Children of the Rainbow" curriculum, which included among its over 600-book bibliography three picture books for young children encouraging a tolerant attitude toward homosexuals. The sensationalizing of the controversy by the media and the reactions of the new right groups, including the Christian Coalition, helped fan the flames of homophobia. In reaction local parent groups were organized to oppose the books and the curriculum itself. In 1993, Fernandez was removed by the New York City Board of Education because of his support for the curriculum, which advocated tolerance for diverse social groups as well as initiatives that included AIDS education and condom distribution. According to Carol Ann Gresser, the board's chairperson, parents were upset by Fernandez's promotion of a "social agenda" in the schools. "You can't bring into the classroom issues that haven't even been decided by the society," she said.

SOURCES

Kirp, David. *Learning by Heart: AIDS and School Children in America's Communities*. New Brunswick, NJ: Rutgers University Press. 1989.

Ryan, Kevin. "Mining the Values in the Curriculum." *Educational Leadership* (November 1993).

Sharpe, Rochelle. "Efforts to Promote Teaching of Values in Schools are Sparking Heated Debate Among Lawmakers." *Wall Street Journal* (May 10, 1994).

REFLECTIVE MORALITY

Reflective morality consists not only of forming judgments but of setting forth the reasons for one's moral judgments. When a moral problem confronts a person, the morally mature will examine and carefully consider the motives, means, and consequences involved in the selection of each of the possible lines of action. In the light of the person's comparison of the values involved, he or she will make a decision. Reflection will bring to one's attention values and considerations that would have been overlooked had the person merely followed impulse and blind custom.

In a rapidly changing world, there is the continuous need to bring our morals up to date and close the gap between principles and practices. As knowledge and understanding have increased, we have shifted more and more from external to internal guidance, from smaller to more inclusive circles of friends included in the in-group, and from external forms to a consideration of the present and long-range effects of acts on persons. There is a need in a world of conflicting values for an adventurous, inquiring morality that is concerned with both principles and all the available facts or evidence relating to the questions under consideration.

We should understand that reflective morality will take place within a frame of reference or within a structure of beliefs and agreements. These are usually taken for granted, rest on past experiences, on both explicit and implicit commitments of various kinds, and on faith in certain principles and assumptions: that life is worth living; that there is some meaning in the universe; that it is better to be rational than irrational; and that the world can be made better. But to always remain in a critical mood may mean failure where success is possible. Reflective morality means we must respect the agreements and commitments into which we have entered, since the deepest and richest experiences of life arise only when we have trust and confidence.

SOURCE

Schwartz, Tony. *What Really Matters: Searching for Wisdom in America*. New York: Bantam. 1995.

RELIGION AND MORALITY

In our schools and in our communities where social popularity, athletic acclaim, and perhaps classroom accomplishments are thought to be the reigning values, many students—and this is surprising—are joining in the journey, asking profound questions and proceeding along a path of spiritual growth. With our schools anchored in pluralism, multiculturalism, and rationalism (or scientific-mathematical thought processing), how much room is there for religious belief? But religious belief is flourishing among our young people. It is not a new movement and it is not just that old-time religion, or just an enduring force of habit. Rather, something profound is occurring among our youngsters. In a society that seems starved of meaning, more and more students—young and old—are creating a "wider frame of reference" than what secular study allows.

In the 1950s, modernity was going to open up the world and explain everything to us. But rather than broadening the scope of human concerns, the modern scientific mind has created a demystified, flattened universe, cut down to our size, dissected to its smallest parts, that, contrary to the claims of science, are never capable of explaining the whole. What we should understand, historically anyway, is that our basic understanding of moral values is rooted in and connected to the Judeo-Christian tradition that has dominated and formulated much of how Western civilization views the world, the Muslim traditions, religious beliefs from Africa and Asia, and from indigenous people around the world. Ideas such as *respect* and *honesty, truthfulness* and *integrity,* although secular terms to many of us today, were formed in religion and embellished with religious meaning and imagery.

Religious experience solidifies individual commitments to ethical values and energizes people to perform moral tasks. Supporting the expression of ethical values in a secular world, religion builds community among like-minded persons. In a diverse, multicultural society, bridge-building through shared ethical values is an important part of both schooling and parenting. In one's spiritual journey, a person goes through times of difficult self-probing. The modern world has made it difficult to find a meaningful pattern of living, one that is purposeful and ethical to the core, but faith and discovery help many put their values in some kind of meaningful and understandable order. In the lives of many people we find that we cannot separate faith and values, morals and belief, or commitment to ethical principles and commitment to God.

SOURCES

Berdyaev, Nicolas. *The Destiny of Man.* New York: Harper & Row. 1960.

Bultman, Rudolf. *Existence and Faith.* New York: Living Age. 1960.

Sadler, William A. *Existence and Love.* New York: Charles Scribner's Sons. 1969.

THE RELIGIOUS RIGHT

The Christian Right is a confusing phenomenon; every time it does itself in, it rises from its own ashes in an even more virulent strain. Neither the death of Jerry Falwell's Moral Majority, the scandals of television preachers Jimmy Swaggart and Jim Bakker, nor the failure of Pat Robertson's absurd 1988 presidential candidacy have managed to finish it off. The history of evangelical Christianity in America predates even the founding of the republic, and its influence on our society cannot be exercised without unraveling the very fabric of our culture. Born of the Great Awakening in the 1730s, Christian evangelicalism is a product of the American soil, an outgrowth of Massachusetts Puritanism, conceived in answer to the terrors of wilderness life in territories inhabited only by a people thought of as "heathen" Indians.

After the Constitution and the secular state it created became the law of the land, America's revivalist religion preached a doctrine advocating "separation from the world," which all but forbade involvement in such a worldly pursuit as politics. But 200 years after the signing of the Declaration of Independence, Jimmy Carter heralded a new age when he ran for president. His description of himself as "born again" in the 1976 campaign won him the votes of Southern evangelicals. There the Right saw its opening!

It was the secular players of the New Right—Paul Weyrich, Richard Viguerie, and Howard Phillips—who turned the religious right into a political force in the 1970s and 1980s. Over the next 25 years, Weyrich earned credit for being the New Right's principal architect. Viguerie became the resident expert at a new technique, direct-mail fundraising, creating the lists that formed the backbone of the New Right's support. And Phillips aimed his energies at grassroots organizing. It was Weyrich who, foreseeing the break-up of the Soviet Union's "Evil" Empire, first used social issues as a cause to rally the forces of the New Right. Being a conservative eastern Catholic, he was sensitive to the abortion issue. Viguerie, managing George Wallace's third-party campaign, walked away at the campaign's end with Wallace's list of angry whites from which to launch his own efforts. And Phillips, after a short stint in the Nixon administration, began building the Conservative Caucus in 1974. Viguerie did the direct-mail work, while Phillips visited all 435 of the nations' voting districts in search of grassroots support.

In 1979, at the urging of Ed McAteer of the Religious Roundtable, Weyrich and Phillips engineered the Moral Majority and pushed Jerry Falwell to front the first organization that built a mass following for conservative religious politics. Weyrich, meanwhile, managed to tap the Coors Beer fortune to fund his newly founded Heritage Foundation. He and Viguerie also built the Committee for the Survival of a Free Congress, which evolved into Weyrich's present-day Free Congress Foundation, training future leaders in Eastern Europe and running National Empowerment Television, the right-wing, tax-exempt network that broadcasts House Speaker Newt Gingrich's made-for-TV college course, "Renewing American Civilization," as well as several Christian Right shows. Weyrich also inspired the formation of the Christian Coalition in 1984, and many of the themes sounded in the Coalition's "Contract with the American Family," from school vouchers to the elimination of the Department of Education and the National Endowment for the Arts. Other conservative causes, such as withholding welfare benefits from unmarried women, also came from Weyrich and his associates.

THE CHRISTIAN COALITION
The Christian Coalition comprises the most visible component of the religious right, made up of conservative Catholics and Protestant evangelicals. The Coalition has essentially created its own party within the GOP by encouraging its members to run for the grunt jobs in the local, county, and state Republican committees. The Christian Right by 1994 dominated the GOP organizations of some 18 states and is an important force in another 13 states. No Republican presidential candidate can win the nomination without the support of the Coalition and its allies.

But the Christian Coalition is not "merely" a religious group. In 1995, the Coalition spent more than $1 million toward the passage of Gingrich's "Contract with America." With Gingrich by his side, Ralph Reed, executive director of the Religious Coalition, unveiled his own "Contract with the American Family." Pat Robertson told the media in 1979 that "sometimes the perception of power is equal to the reality of it." That is, the Christian Coalition claims some 1.7 million supporters, but its newspaper, *Christian American,* has only 450,000 subscribers, and although it says it is a 501(C)(4) tax-exempt organization, by the end of 1995 the IRS had not granted it that status.

Through the Coalition's lobbying efforts, key provisions of the Coalition's "contract" are on their way to becoming law, including reductions in federal welfare programs, education, arts, and humanities—while providing "family-friendly tax relief." Certain abortion procedures, if the Coalition has its way, will be recriminalized; there is an erosion strategy on a woman's right to choose abortion; and the Religious Equality Amendment to the Constitution, if passed, would expand the legal allowance for prayer and other religious expression in public settings.

REACTIONS

Rabbi Arthur Hertzberg, of the Interfaith Alliance, a coalition of clergy formed to oppose the religious Right, sees the Right exploiting a religious impulse felt by the economically strapped middle class to further an agenda that will only fill the coffers of the rich. "They are putting on the magic act of family values," says Hertzberg, "while the pickpocket in league with them goes through the crowd and steals their wallets."

Dominion theology, espoused by Robertson, claims that Christians have the duty to rule and reign—while awaiting Jesus' second coming—in His absence in order to prepare the world for his return. Dominion theology of this kind derives from a movement known as Christian Reconstructionism, which emphasizes the Ten Commandments and the law of the *Pentateuch*, which calls for death by stoning for adulterers, practicing homosexuals, and insubordinate children. According to *Mother Jones* magazine, "Whatever its theological underpinnings, the Christian America envisioned by the New Right is enough to chill the soul."

WHO'S WHO

- *Paul Weyrich*, the New Right's strategic architect, founded the powerful Heritage Foundation (1973), helped start the Moral Majority (1979), and inspired the founding of the Christian Coalition. He now runs the Free Congress Foundation.

- *Richard Viguerie* has raised millions for New Right causes and candidates with the most lucrative direct-mail operations this side of L. L. Bean. "Direct mail," he says, "is like having a water moccasin for a watchdog. Silent but deadly."

- *Howard Phillips*, with Weyrich and Viguerie, forms the New Right's trinity. He founded the Conservative Caucus, helped start the Moral Majority, and now heads the U.S. Taxpayers Party, which hopes to draft Pat Buchanan for president.

- *Pat Buchanan*, presidential candidate in 1995–1996, announced a "cultural war" and ignited the religious right at the 1992 GOP convention. "Just wait until 1996," he promised; "then you'll see a real right-wing tyrant."

- *Pat Robertson* made a failed presidential bid in 1988 and founded the Christian Coalition. His 1991 book, *The New World Order*, charged that a cabal of Freemasons and Jewish bankers is leading the Western world into ruin.

- *Ralph Reed*, the boyish executive director of the 1.7-million-member Christian Coalition, has been Robertson's front man since 1989. Reed once boasted, "I do guerrilla warfare. You don't know it's over until you're in a body bag."

- *James Dobson's* daily radio program "Focus on the Family" has 5 million listeners per week. "People in Washington don't know those people are out there," he says. "They don't realize that it's probably the majority of Americans."

- *Phyllis Schlafly*, one of the religious right's few female leaders despite its large number of women, led fights against the Equal Rights Amendment and a nuclear freeze, once saying, "The atomic bomb is a marvelous gift that was given to our country by a wise God."

TIMELINE

- *1960:* William F. Buckley founds Young Americans for Freedom (YAF). Future New Right leaders meet in YAF, which takes off after Lyndon Johnson defeats conservative Barry Goldwater in the 1964 presidential race.
- *1961:* Pat Robertson launches the Christian Broadcasting Network on TV.
- *1963:* The 21st Ecumenical Council (Vatican II) "absolves" Jews for the crucifixion of Jesus Christ.
- *1964:* Richard Viguerie hand-copies Goldwater's campaign donor list and turns it into a highly successful direct-mail fundraising base by the early 1970s. Phyllis Schlafly's book, *A Choice Not an Echo,* sounds future New Right themes.
- *1966:* Nixon hires Pat Buchanan as speechwriter; Howard Phillips hired by Republican National Committee; Pat Robertson's "700 Club" goes on the air.
- *1967:* Paul Weyrich hired as Senate aide. He will be one of the first on the right to focus on abortion.
- *1968:* Nixon elected on "silent majority" theme, prefiguring the Moral Majority.
- *1972:* Schlafly founds Stop ERA, a precursor of the Eagle Forum.
- 1973: *Roe v. Wade* affirms abortion rights; Weyrich founds Heritage Foundation, which becomes an influential conservative think tank.
- *1974:* Nixon forced out by Watergate; Phillips founds Conservative Caucus and visits all 435 congressional districts to get support for conservative causes.
- *1976:* Jimmy Carter becomes first elected president to describe himself as a born-again evangelical.
- *1977:* James Dobson founds Focus on the Family; Weyrich founds Free Congress Foundation (then the Committee for the Survival of a Free Congress); Robertson creates the Family Channel.
- *1979:* Weyrich helps found Moral Majority with Jerry Falwell as head; they help elect Ronald Reagan president in 1980.
- *1982:* ERA fails; two Florida abortion clinics are firebombed; the owner of an Illinois abortion clinic and his wife are kidnapped and held for a week by the "Army of God."
- *1984:* Abortion clinics are firebombed or burned by arsonists 24 times.
- *1987:* Televangelist Jim Bakker caught in sex and financial scandals.
- *1988:* Televangelist Jimmy Swaggart caught in sex scandal; televangelist Robertson fails in Republican nomination bid.
- *1989:* Falwell disbands Moral Majority after several years of decline; Robertson founds Christian Coalition, hires wunderkind Ralph Reed to be its director.
- *1992:* Buchanan calls for "cultural war" in failed presidential bid; George Bush campaigns on "family values" platform.
- *1994:* GOP wins House and Senate with Christian Coalition help; Christian Right gains majority in 18 state parties.

SOURCES

Institute For First Amendment Studies. P.O. Box 589, Great Barrington, MA 01230.

Political Research Associates. 678 Massachusetts Avenue, Suite 704, Cambridge, MA 02139.

Stan, A. M. "Power Preying." *Mother Jones* (December 1995).

RESPECT

Respect is a part of the inner language we use to explain the real commitments of our lives. It is acknowledging and living a life that views other humans, the environment, and our communities as extensions of ourselves. Like love, respect is a cornerstone of our moral attachment and responsibility to others. Thus, respect does not mean thinking about what you can get out of your friends and family, but what you can give to them that might enhance and improve their lives and, in turn, your life as well. Respect is that ethical value that recognizes that each person is precious and has intrinsic worth. The value we discover in each other, when respected, becomes the foundation for dialogue and for the morally coherent life.

SOURCES

Bloom, Allan. *Love and Friendship*. New York: Simon & Schuster. 1993.

Douglas, Susan J. *Where the Girls Are: Growing Up Female with the Mass Media*. New York: Times Books. 1994.

RESPONSIBILITY

Responsibility means that we should take the development of our own lives in hand with the purpose of not just preserving the integrity of human life, but of modifying our lives by improvements of our own doings. The simple recognition of our responsibility to self and others, and to the future that is yet to be, awakens us to the fact that we are not completely our own masters, but rather trustees of a heritage.

SOURCES

Adler, Mortimer J. *Six Great Ideas*. New York: Collier. 1981.

————. *We Hold These Truths: Understanding the Ideas and Ideals of the Constitution*. New York: Macmillan. 1987.

RESTITUTION

Moral theory should be simple: the moral theorist attends to ordinary human action to explain what makes some acts right and others wrong, and we need no microscope to observe a human act. Yet, no moral theory that is simple captures all of the morally relevant acts.

Judith Jarvis Thomson, in a set of vivid examples, stories, and cases *(Rights, Restitution & Risk)*, shows just how an array of moral considerations has bearing on all but the simplest of problems. She brings new depth of understanding to the most difficult question: What is it to have a moral right to life, or any other right? What is the relation between the infringement of such rights and restitution? How is rights theory to deal with the imposition of risk?

By restitution, Thomson means "compensation." She says, "compensation is repayment for a wrong." Through example and by argument she explains when, where, and why restitution is required and when it is not. Her analysis includes "payment to reduce loss," "for right infringement," "for enrichment," "for past discrimination," "for joint liability," and "for damages." Her lengthy analysis also illuminates consent and compensation, waiving rights, and certain personal risks one takes in complying with compensation requirements, or accepting them. Thomson's is a definitive work. Any serious study of restitution and its concommitant issues will include this book.

SOURCES

Ross, Stephen David. *The Nature of Moral Responsibility*. Detroit: Wayne State University Press. 1973.

Thomson, Judith Jarvis. *Rights, Restitution & Risk: Essays in Moral Theory*. Cambridge, MA: Harvard University Press. 1986.

RIGHT AND WRONG

The question, "Why is *right* right?" takes us to the center of the moral problem: distinguishing right from wrong and then using conceptualizations of right to define the point of view of morality. The starting place of ethics is a return to the basic moral postulate of the worth of persons. This fundamental value has been stated, restated, and interpreted hundreds of times in ways that include the dignity of persons, reverence for life, respect for persons, the integrity of human life and its environment, and the like. When we accept these postulates we have a basis not only for distinguishing between right and wrong, good and evil, but a basis for defending a doctrine of human rights, including freedom, equality, and charity—the ingredients of a democratic society.

When right is understood in this way, we discover that it is person-affirming; wrong is person-denying or degrading. Likewise, evil denies the good and destroys persons and human welfare. From this perspective, some things are naturally good because they are based on natural human needs. Some things are wrong or evil because they inflict pain, injury, and death. Some other things are good or evil by convention and may differ from society to society, like marriage customs, the training of children, and dietary regulations.

Common sense tells us that some things are better than others, that some are good and others bad. For example, health is better than illness; knowledge and understanding are better than ignorance; love and goodwill are better than hate and ill will; friendship is better than loneliness; freedom is better than slavery; some wealth is better than deprivation; living an enriched, fulfilling life is better than merely living.

We take persons and the worth of persons as our basic moral postulate because it finds its source in our normal psychological needs and reactions. If those things we deem as right and good are denied us, then we naturally resist. There is almost universal indignation and resistance against pain and injury. All living creatures, including humans, have a will to live, to seek fulfillment, and resist things that impair life.

Finally, the concept of the worth and dignity of persons is based on the unique and distinctive qualities of selfhood. Only in persons do we find those qualities that are universally recognized as valuable:

1. Self-consciousness
2. Abstract thought and the power of reflective thinking
3. Ethical discrimination and some freedom of choice
4. Aesthetic appreciation
5. Religious aspiration and commitment
6. Transcendence of particular conditions of space and time
7. Development fulfilled through community living
8. Unique powers of creativity

Thus, to be moral is to observe the facts and principles of personal and social welfare as these are discovered through our search for a more satisfying life. To deny the criterion of the worth and welfare of persons would seem to lead eventually to the elimination of both life and reason.

SOURCES

Kessler, Gary E., ed. *Voices of Wisdom: A Multicultural Philosophy Reader.* Belmont, CA: Wadsworth. 1992.

Radhakrishman, S., and P. T. Raju, eds. *The Concept of Man: A Study in Comparative Philosophy.* London: George Allen and Unwin. 1960.

Schwartz, Tony. *What Really Matters: Searching for Wisdom in America.* New York: Random House. 1995.

ROCK 'N' ROLL

Rock 'n' roll had its beginnings in the early 1950s as a combination of jazz and the blues found in the black community. By the 1960s rock became a form of social protest and then, by the early 1970s, evolved into the mainstream as the Baby Boomers aged. By the mid-1980s and into the 90s, with the alternative sounds, rock was reinvented as a form of social protest to which many Baby Boomers were unable to relate.

According to the reports of the mass media, Kurt Cobain and his band, Nirvana, were the mouthpiece of disillusioned, emotionally damaged young people born of dysfunctional families. But although the suicide of Cobain ignited an enormous amount of media hype, to the vast majority of people above the age of 30, his social and musical influence hardly mattered. Certainly, most Boomer-age rock fans could not identify with the sounds or emotions coming from a generation of younger bands like Nirvana. Sociologist Deena Weinstein reflects: "The sense of impending doom—ecological, economic, political, educational, and social—has replaced a sense of progress and of hope for a future world that is better than the current state of affairs. Much of the distinctively youth-based music, especially thrash metal, cogently and emotionally articulates this view. Against the commercial music's message of 'Don't Worry, Be Happy,' young people belonging to youth subcultures worry a lot."

The prevailing wisdom from the media is that grunge rock is what happens to children of divorced parents, but reducing post-punk rock to family breakdown recalls the psychobabble absurdities of the 1960s that identified student radicalism as a by-product of permissive parenting. But, according to Sandy Carter, "while much of the angst and aggression of younger bands clearly reflects family pain, the punk-metal dissonance of our times is wired into fundamental contradictions of society. No less than the music of the 1960s, rock in the 1990s is a music of social protest. And, no doubt surprising to many progressive elders who view contemporary rock as a lot of whining nihilism, this protest is often infused with idealism and left-wing political radicalism."

See also Ethics, Theory of.

SOURCES

Carter, Sandy. "Revolution Rock." *Z Magazine* (November 1995).

Furstenberg, F., and A. Cherlin. "Children's Adjustment to Divorce." In A. S. Skolnick and J. H. Skolnick, eds. *Family in Transition.* 8th ed. New York: HarperCollins. 1994.

Weinstein, Deena. "Expendable Youth: The Rise and Fall of Youth Culture." In L. Cargan and J. Ballantine, eds. *Sociological Footprints.* 6th ed. Belmont, CA: Wadsworth. 1994.

SANCTITY OF LIFE

See Abortion; Ethics, Theory of.

SATANISM

Satanism, or devil worship, is an anti-Christian movement that has a small number of followers in Europe and North America. It is the practice of worshiping demons or other evil spirits. Its chief ceremony is the Black Mass, a distorted version of a Christian church service in which the worshippers praise Satan and ridicule God.

See also Devil Worship.

SOURCE
Ellwood, Robert S. "Devil Worship." From *Information Finder*. World Book. 1994.

SCHWEITZER, ALBERT

Albert Schweitzer (1875–1965) was a brilliant German philosopher, physician, musician, member of the clergy, missionary, and writer on theology. He was educated in both France and Germany, and at the age of 21 decided to spend his next nine years on science, music, and preaching. He decided that at the age of 30 he would devote the rest of his life to serving humanity directly. Before the age of 30, he had won an international reputation as a writer on theology, as an organist and an authority on organ building, as an interpreter of the works of Bach, and as an authority on Bach's life.

In 1902, Schweitzer became principal of St. Thomas Theological College at the University of Strasbourg. He was inspired to become a medical missionary, and studied medicine from 1905 to 1913 at the university. He raised money for a hospital at Lambarene, French Equatorial Africa (now Gabon) by giving concerts for the Paris Bach Society, which he had helped found. In 1913, he began serving at Lambarene. Over the years, he built a large hospital and a medical station where thousands of Africans were treated yearly. He used his Nobel Prize money to expand the hospital and set up a leper colony.

In 1949, Schweitzer visited the United States to speak at the Goethe Bicentennial Convocation at Aspen, Colorado. In 1955, Queen Elizabeth II conferred Great Britain's highest civilian award, the Order of Merit, on him, and in 1957, Schweitzer went on record as opposing further atomic weapons tests because of the danger of radioactive fallout to mankind.

SOURCE

Christian, James L. *Philosophy: An Introduction to the Art of Wondering.* 4th ed. New York: Holt, Rinehart and Winston. 1986.

SELF-IMPROVEMENT AND A SENSE OF WORTH

A major condition determining the quality of life is the feeling one develops about oneself. In general, if things go right for us, then we develop positive feelings: self-worth, self-esteem, self-love. Whatever the terms, we are referring to a cluster of *constructive* feelings that we develop about the self and the things the self does. A person who develops himself or herself and, thus, has these positive feelings, feels privileged to be who he or she is; the person enjoys living with himself or herself. Eric Fromm *(The Art of Loving)* comments: "The member of a primitive clan might express his identity in the formula 'I am we'; he cannot yet conceive of himself as an 'individual,' existing apart from his group. When the feudal system broke down, this sense of identity was shaken and the acute question 'who am I?' arose."

Self-development occurs as we seek the guidance of others who have made decisions and developed skills and attitudes that work for them. As we develop and perfect certain skills for ourselves and are successful at using them in society, we are recognized for these accomplishments. It is impossible to escape the fact that we are completely dependent upon the feelings and reflections of others during our early stage of development.

A person who has been loved during his or her formative years develops a love of self. Arthur Combs *(Perceiving, Behaving, Becoming: A New Focus for Education)* observes: "The self concept, we know, is learned. People learn who they are and what they are from the ways in which they have been treated by those who surround them in the process of their growing up." Self-love is not selfish love, nor a narcissistic obsession with one's physical or intellectual qualities, nor egotism. One should note that *self-interest* is a generic term that manifests itself in at least four different ways: (1) *selfish-interest* places the self above and before all others; (2) *self-centered-interest* places the self first some of the time (when making a living or taking care of one's bodily needs), but also considers others' needs and aspirations; (3) *unselfish-interest* considers the needs of others on a par with the needs of the self; and (4) *selfless-interest* places the needs of others before the needs of the self.

Finally, a person who is in a positive state of development, whose self-worth is constantly being improved, is—in the words of Abraham Maslow—a "self-actualizing person"; in the words of Carl Rogers, a "fully functioning and creative person"; and in the thought of S. I. Hayakawa, a "genuinely sane person." These three mention six distinct characteristics shared by all such people:

1. Actualized individuals are not well adjusted in the sense that they conform to social norms; but neither are they rebellious against society.
2. They are unusually open to what is going on inside themselves. They experience fully their own thoughts and feelings. Self-awareness is great; self-deception is minimal.
3. They are not bothered by the unknown. They can be comfortable with disorder, indefiniteness, doubt, and uncertainty. They don't have to know all the answers. They can accept what is without trying to organize and label neatly all of life's contents.
4. They are remarkably existential: they enjoy the present moments of life more fully, not as means to future ends, but as ends in themselves. Their lives are not a perpetual prepa-

ration for the future; they enjoy living now.

5. They are creative individuals, not merely in customary roles such as painters or musicians, but in all that they do. Their own distinctive style touches everything they do.

6. They are ethical in the deepest sense. They rarely follow the superficial, conventional norms of moral behavior. They consider the majority of so-called moral issues to be trivial. Their ethical concern is expressed in a positive, constructive attitude toward all people and all things. Their caring is the wellspring of their ethical nature.

SOURCES

Combs, Arthur W., ed. *Perceiving, Behaving, Becoming: A New Focus for Education.* ASCD 1962 Yearbook. Washington, D.C.: Association for School Curriculum Development. 1962.

Frankl, Vicktor E. *Man's Search for Meaning.* New York: Washington Square. 1963.

Fromm, Eric. *The Art of Loving.* New York: Harper & Row. 1963.

Hayakawa, S. I. *Symbol, Status, and Personality.* New York: Harcourt, Brace & World. No Date.

Hester, Joseph P., and Philip F. Vincent. *Philosophy for Young Thinkers.* 2d ed. Monroe, NY: Trillium Press. 1988.

Rogers, Carl. *On Becoming a Person.* Rev. ed. New York: Houghton Mifflin. 1966.

SEX DISCRIMINATION

See Gender Equity.

SIN

Sin in Judeo-Christian scripture is "no less than a condition of dreadful estrangement from God, the sole source of well-being. They knew that apart from God, man's a lost sinner, unable to find himself or find true happiness" (Buttrick et al. 1962). Even in early times, the Hebrews had at least the beginnings of a genuine awareness of the theological meaning of sin. As their understanding of God's being and personality developed, their recognition of the seriousness of sin increased. The prophets preached the tragic reality of the nation's sin, and the people learned it by experience, particularly in the events leading up to the exile. The New Testament put sin in an even darker light as it simultaneously demonstrated God's amazing way of dealing with it in Christ.

MEANINGS

In the Old Testament:

- A deviation from what is good and right ("miss," "fail," "fault," or "error")
- Theological terms, indicating sin as defiance against God ("to revolt," "rebel," or "transgress")
- Terms describing a sinner's inner state expressing conscious and intentional badness ("be or act wrongly, pervertedly")
- Terms in which the ethical aspect is prominent ("be bad," "be wicked," and "treat violently or wrongly")
- Terms indicating the baneful results of sin ("toil," "trouble," "mischief," and "evil")
- Terms for guilt (generally the Hebrews did not distinguish between the sin and its resultant guilt; thus, all the leading words for "sin" also express "guilt")

There are major differences in the meanings of sin found in the New Testament when compared with the Old Testament. The work of Jesus Christ significantly deepened and transformed the meaning of sin, but with a difference: the assurance that Christ has come to conquer it. Thus, whatever is said to emphasize sin's deadliness and seriousness serves to magnify the greatness of the salvation from sin that Christ has obtained. New Testament meanings include:

- "deviation from good"
- "lawlessness," which is an attitude or condition of contempt for and violation of the law, such as "iniquity" and "wickedness"
- Terms indicating spiritual badness ("bad" and qualitative and moral evil)
- Ethical and juridical terms ("injustice" and "unrighteousness")

REMEDY

In the New Testament, the very purpose of the stern teaching about sin is to convince humans of their need for the remedy that they know so well. God's affective answer to sin is Christ: "For God has done what the law, weakened by flesh, could not do: sending his own Son in the likeness of sinful flesh and for sin, he condemned sin in the flesh, in order that the just requirement of the law might be fulfilled in us, who walk not according to the flesh but according to the Spirit" (Romans 8:3–4). All this puts the problem of sin into an entirely different light. The question is no longer how to obtain righteousness (that is God's free gift) or how to rid oneself of guilt (Christ has taken this upon himself), but how to live consistently in this new sphere of life.

SOURCE

Buttrick, George Arthur, et al., eds. *The Interpreter's Dictionary of the Bible*. Vol. R–Z. New York: Abingdon Press. 1962.

SITUATION ETHICS

Those who claim that morality is situational have brought forth both secular and religious versions. Joseph Fletcher says that "the situationist enters into every decision-making situation fully armed with the ethical maxims of his community and its heritage, and he treats them with respect as to illuminators of his problem. Just the same he is prepared in any situation to compromise them or set them aside in the situation if love seems better served by doing so." According to Fletcher, situation ethics accepts reason as the instrument of moral judgment, while rejecting the idea that the good is "given" in the nature of things, objectively.

FLETCHER'S PROPOSITIONS

1. Only one thing is intrinsically good; namely, love: nothing else at all.
2. The ruling norm of Christian decision is love: nothing else.
3. Love and justice are the same, for justice is love distributed, nothing else.
4. Love wills the neighbor's good whether we like him or not.
5. Only the end justifies the means; nothing else.
6. Love's decisions are made situationally, not prescriptively.

Both Fletcher and Bishop J. A. T. Robinson *(Honest to God)* ascribe to a Christian situational ethic. Robinson says, "Nothing can of itself always be labelled as wrong." He goes on to comment that "because it is an act of love" states a good reason why an act ought to be done. Robinson seems to think we can look at situations and ask, "What would love do here?" and perceive the answer.

Robert L. Cunningham notes:

Situationism is worth serious effort, for it appeals to a great many for a variety of reasons. It is congenial to the atheistic existentialist who denies that man is morally nature-bound, to the secular humanist who gives primacy to personal values, to the "practical" men who emphasize the actual facts of the case, to the "scientific-minded" who demand full use of the personal and impersonal sciences in ascertaining the facts of the situation, to some Protestants who see the Christian moral decision as a response to a call by God in the actual situation, and to some Catholics who, especially in continental Europe, are disenchanted with traditional natural law theory and who wish to emphasize the role of Christian love.

W. D. Hudson criticizes situation ethics for failing to make a distinction between (1) hard-and-fast principles, appeal to which is made a substitute for thinking by the morally insensitive ("God says," "The Bible says"), and (2) reasons that must be given where moral thinking is rational and that are reasons only because they invoke principles or rules. Cunningham adds, "To an equally broad spectrum of critics, situationism appears to be a chaotic antinomian wasteland in which the role of reason and principle is minimized almost to the vanishing point, in which moral acts consist of virtually nothing but circumstances, 'a wage packet with nothing but deductions,' and in which there is excessive reliance on intuitive, quasi-mystical responses to the facts of the situation."

In the field of metaethics, deontological theories *deny* that the right, the obligatory, and the morally good are wholly—whether directly or indirectly—a function of what is nonmorally good or of what promotes the highest balance of good over evil for self, one's society, or the world as a whole. Instead, they assert that there are other considerations that may make an action or rule right or obligatory besides the goodness or badness of its consequences—certain features of the act itself other than the value it brings into existence.

William K. Frankena observes that deontological theories are also of different kinds, depending on the role they give to general rules. *Act-deontological theories* maintain that the basic judgments of obligation are purely particular or situational, as in "In this situation I should do so-and-so," and that general ones like "We ought always to keep our promises" are useless, or at best derivative from particular ones. *Rule-deontologists* hold that the standard of

right and wrong consists of one or more rules, such as "We ought always to tell the truth," and/or "It cannot be right for A to treat B in a manner in which it would be wrong for B to treat A, merely on the ground that they are two different individuals, and without there being any difference between the natures or circumstances of the two that can be stated as a reasonable ground for difference of treatment." People who take "conscience" to be their guide or standard in morality are usually either act-deontologists or rule-deontologists, depending on whether they think of conscience enabling a person to make particular judgments in particular situations, or providing a person with particular rules.

SOURCES

Cunningham, R. L. *Situationism and the New Morality.* New York: Appleton-Century-Crofts. 1970.

Davitt, Thomas E. *Ethics in the Situation.* New York: Appleton-Century-Crofts. 1970.

Fletcher, Joseph. *Situation Ethics.* Philadelphia: Westminster Press. 1966.

Frankena, William K. *Ethics.* 2d ed. Englewood Cliffs, NJ: Prentice-Hall. 1973.

Hudson, W. D. *Modern Moral Philosophy.* Garden City, NY: Anchor Books. 1970.

Robinson, J. A. T. *Honest to God.* Philadelphia: Westminster Press. 1963.

SPECIESISM

Peter Singer has long been the philosophical moral voice for animal rights and species equality. In his *Animal Liberation: A New Ethics for Our Treatment of Animals,* he comments: "To end tyranny we must first understand it. As a practical matter, the rule of the human animal over other animals expresses itself in practices like the slaughter of wild animals for sport or for their furs. These practices should not be seen as isolated observations. They can be properly understood only as the manifestations of the ideology of our species—that is the attitudes which we, as the dominant animal, have toward the other animals."

The argument identifying *speciesism* has the following three steps:

1. The fundamental moral principle of equality of consideration of interests ought to govern our relations with all beings, including nonhumans.
2. Humans inflict suffering on nonhumans for trival purposes that have been defended by Western thinkers—that humans have a right to do this.
3. In light of premise one, the advancement of premise two is speciesism—the ruthless exploitation of nonhumans for human ends.

Those interested in this topic should consult chapter 6 in Singer's book, "Speciesism Today: Defenses, Rationalizations, and Objections to Animal Liberation." A thorough study of this issue and Singer's argument, especially premise one above, will help clarify the problem and put it in the light of "normal" human moral arguments and discussions. The parallels will be enlightening. Especially, one should inquire what is meant by "nonhuman moral equality" and by the "equality of consideration of interests" as they pertain to humans and to nonhuman beings.

See also Animal Rights.

SOURCES

Brandt, Richard B., ed. *Social Justice*. Englewood Cliffs, NJ: Prentice-Hall. 1962.

Carson, Gerald. *Cornflake Crusade*. New York: Rinehart. 1957.

Godlovitch, S., R. Godlovitch, and J. Harris, eds. *Animals, Men and Morals*. New York: Taplinger. 1972.

Melden, A. I., ed. *Human Rights*. Belmont, CA: Wadsworth. 1970.

National Humane Review. "The American Humane Association." (November 1974).

Singer, Peter. *Animal Liberation: A New Ethics for Our Treatment of Animals*. New York: Random House. 1975.

STATES RIGHTS

When the delegation to the Continental Congress declared American independence in 1776, its members had to decide what sort of national government would bind the 13 states together. The former colonists were loyal to their own states and feared most a powerful national government. Yet the delegates knew the new nation needed a government to act for it.

With the delegates trying to protect the rights of their individual states, it took a year and a half for the Continental Congress to agree on a final draft of the nation's first constitution. Known as the Articles of Confederation, this constitution was not ratified until 1781. With abuses by the British Parliament fresh in their memories, the states were wary of giving too much power to a central authority. To ease this concern, a clause in the Articles guaranteed that each state would retain its "sovereignty, freedom, and independence" and keep "every power, jurisdiction, and right" not given directly to Congress. This strong *reserved powers* clause protected the rights of the states and made it more likely that the state legislatures would approve the document.

By the spring of 1787, many Americans realized that the Articles of Confederation needed to be changed if the young republic was to survive. The threat of foreign intrigue, economic disruptions, and armed rebellion revealed the weaknesses of the Articles of Confederation. Central to these debates was the question of sovereignty, the source of the government's power or authority. The debate over sovereignty resulted in a system known as federalism, in which governmental authority was divided between national and state governments. Power was divided into national or delegated power, power reserved for the states or reserved powers, and powers shared by the states and the national government or *concurrent powers*. The system of federalism established a new relationship between the states and national government and between the people and the national government. The Constitution stated that it and any national laws passed under it were the supreme law of the land. All people had to abide by them, and state legislatures could not change or violate them. Voters elected members of the House of Representatives. State legislatures no longer served as intermediaries.

SOURCES

Hofstadter, Richard, ed. *Great Issues in American History*. Vols. 1–3. New York: Vintage. 1958.

Knefel, Don, ed. *100 Essays from Time*. Boston: Allyn and Bacon. 1992.

Lappe, Frances Moore. *Rediscovering America's Values*. New York: Ballantine. 1989.

STEINEM, GLORIA

As a writer and leading supporter of the women's liberation movement, in 1968 Gloria Steinem campaigned for women's rights in employment, politics, and social life. In 1972, she founded *Ms.*, a magazine published and edited by women. A year before, Steinem helped found the National Women's Political Caucus, which encourages women to seek political office and to work for women's rights laws. In 1971, she also helped establish the Women's Action Alliance, which fights discrimination against women. Steinem authored the following books: *Outrageous Acts and Everyday Rebellions* (1983), *Marilyn* (1986), and *Revolution from Within: A Book of Self-Esteem* (1992).

See also Feminism.

SOURCES

Douglas, Susan J. *Where the Girls Are: Growing Up Female with the Mass Media*. New York: Times Books. 1994.

Knefel, Don, ed. *100 Essays from Time*. Boston: Allyn and Bacon. 1992.

McKee, Charlene, ed. *Women of Power* 24 (Summer 1995).

SURVIVAL OF THE FITTEST

Charles Darwin argued that the individual owes his or her strength as a social animal to his or her individual weaknesses in the struggle for existence as a solitary physical animal. To make up for these weaknesses, the individual had to develop intelligence and cooperative habits. Lacking natural weapons, the individual had to invent tools and to use group strategies. Intelligence, cooperation, and toolmaking also allowed the human to move from climate to climate and environment to environment. With these increased adaptive powers, the improvement of the individual's physical capacities became less needed for survival.

Darwin felt that an evolutionary ethic, which has been overlooked in other ethical theories, has to do with the inherent worth of other life and that it would—on this account—be arbitrary to recognize only human life as of value. Why should humans use other life as a mere means to their own interests? Kenneth Hunt supports this view in the development of his conception of a biocentric community, and Herbert Spencer's elaborate and influential interpretation of evolutionary ethics in the nineteenth century posited the notion that the natural laws of the evolutionary process lead in the direction of the good. Spencer theorized that as the individual improved physically, he or she was moving from a crude gregariousness to conscious sympathy and intelligent cooperation. The laws of nature gradually bring harmony, so that behaviors that bring pleasure, cause personal adaptation, and preserve the group and the race tend to coincide in one grand harmony. Spencer notes that individual sacrifice for the good or preservation of the species is sometimes necessary, but he truly felt that the opposition between individual good and social good was becoming less and would eventually disappear. The chief duty of the individual is to stand aside and avoid interference with the processes of nature. Biological changes in the constitution of the individual tend to eliminate evils and to bring happiness and progress. Thus, according to Spencer, a system of morality should be founded on the laws of the evolution of life.

See also Natural Law.

SOURCES

Darwin, Charles. *The Descent of Man*. Princeton, NJ: Princeton University Press. 1981.

———. *The Origin of Species*. New York: Modern Library. 1937.

Hunt, Kenneth. "A Biocentric Concept." *Unity* 146 (March 1960).

T

TAOISM, ETHICS OF

Among the ways of looking at the world and of acting within the world, two great traditions—Confucianism and Taoism—attempt to include all explanations of the universe under one set of principles. Confucianism found the key to the meaning of things in human relations, while Taoism found it in the workings of nature.

The term *Taoism* is ambiguous. It has been used to signify either the type of thought or philosophy found in the *Tao Te Ching* and known by Chinese scholars as *Tao-chia (Dao-jia)*, or as a Taoist philosophy that is a mixture of magic and religion with deep roots in the past known as *Tao-chiao (Dao-jiao)* or Taoist religion. Within either, Taoism has been a powerful influence both in China and neighboring countries.

The ethics of the *Tao Te Ching* can be stated positively: one must exhibit within oneself the procedure of the Tao and be characterized by its quietude of power, its production without possession, action without self-assertion, development without domination—and on the negative side, do not meddle with the smooth course of nature going on her blessed way. As the *Tao Te Ching* says, it is wise to practice *wu-wei* (quietism, nonaggression, nonmeddlesome action). It is possible to achieve without doing:

"Therefore, the sage carries on his business without action, and gives his teaching without words" (see Duyvendak, L7). The sage also says:

Without going out of the door
One can know the whole world;
Without peeping out of the window
One can see the Tao of heaven.
The further one travels
The less one knows.
Therefore the sage knows everything
    without traveling;
He names everything without seeing it;
He accomplishes everything without doing it.

There is affirmative power in the quietism of *wu-wei*; its attendant virtues in human life are kindness, sincerity, and humility. If one does not meddle with others, human relations will fall as the Tao brings them to pass naturally and simply. There will be a spontaneous birth of true love, real kindness, simplicity, and contentment in the lives and relationships of humans. Just the restraint of self from anger, ambition, and meddlesome action is never merely negative in its consequences; power *(Te)* is in it, power for the good.

SOURCES
Blakney, R. B. *The Way of Life: Lao Tzu*. New York: Mentor Books. 1955.
Chang Chung-Yuan. *Creativity and Taoism: A Study of Chinese Philosophy, Art, and Poetry*. New York: Julian Press. 1963.
Duyvendak, J. J. L., Translator. *Tao Te Ching: Lao Tzu*. London: John Murray. 1954.

TOTALITARIANISM

Totalitarianism is the view that the state is supreme and its interests take precedence over those of individuals and of all other groups—political, economic, scientific, cultural, or religious. For those who accept a totalitarian view of the state, rights tend to disappear entirely. From this point of view, the individual's sole duty (not right) is to the interest of the state; the state is an end unto itself.

See also Ethics, Theory of.

SOURCES

Kimball, Bruce A. *Orators and Philosophers: A History of the Idea of Liberal Education.* New York: College Entrance Examination Board. 1995.

Murphy, Jeffrie G. *An Introduction to Moral and Social Philosophy.* Belmont, CA: Wadsworth. 1973.

TRUTHFULNESS

See Honesty.

UNITED NATIONS CHARTER

The United Nations (UN) has two major goals: peace and human dignity. The Charter of the United Nations has 19 chapters divided into 111 articles that explain the purposes (goals), principles (basic beliefs), and operating methods of the UN. The charter lists four purposes and seven principles of the UN. The purposes are to preserve world peace and security; to encourage nations to be just in their actions toward each other; to help nations cooperate in trying to solve their problems; and to serve as an agency through which nations can work toward these goals. The principles are the following: (1) all members have equal rights; (2) all members are expected to carry out their duties under the charter; (3) all members agree to the principle of settling their disputes peacefully; (4) all members agree not to use force or the threat of force against other nations, except in self-defense; (5) All members agree to help the UN in every action it takes to carry out the purposes of the charter; (6) the UN agrees to act on the principle that nonmember states have the same duties as member states to preserve world peace and security; and (7) the UN accepts the principle of not interfering in the actions of a member nation within its own borders, but these actions must not hurt other nations.

SOURCE
Information Finder. World Book. 1994.

UNIVERSAL DECLARATION OF HUMAN RIGHTS

Article 23 of the United Nations Charter sets forth a "Universal Declaration of Human Rights," adopted on December 10, 1948. This declaration sets forth the basic civil, economic, political, and social rights and freedoms of every person. This declaration states that all people are born free and equal in dignity and rights and that this declaration is meant to serve "as a common standard of achievement for all peoples and all nations." Among other things, it proclaims that:

1. Everyone has the right to work, to free choice of employment, to just and favorable conditions of work, and to protection against unemployment.
2. Everyone, without any discrimination, has the right to equal pay for equal work.
3. Everyone who works has the right to just and favorable remuneration

ensuring for himself and his family an existence worthy of human dignity, and supplemented, if necessary, by other means of social protection.

4. Everyone has the right to form and to join trade unions for the protection of his interests.

SOURCE
Information Finder. World Book. 1994.

UTILITARIANISM

Utilitarian considerations have been advanced to guide our moral choices and refer to the effects of actions, or contemplated actions, on the happiness or unhappiness of the person likely to be affected by them. The person who does the action, of course, will be affected, as in the case of killing someone. The victim is also affected. Then there are the "third parties"—spouses, siblings, children, friends and dependents, colleagues, customers, neighbors, and the like. Insofar as these persons have love for the victim, or interests in his or her continued existence, they are harmed by the victim's death and will be saddened by it.

Utilitarianism can be defined as the view that ultimately only considerations of utility have relevant application to moral decisions. When another kind of reason appears to be relevant, the utilitarian argues, it is only because that reason points to a feature of actions in virtue of which they tend, in the vast majority of cases, to have an effect on human happiness. For example, utilitarians might condemn killing or robbery on the ground that it is a deliberate act of taking human life or depriving a person of something that is rightfully theirs, but only because they believe that such actions tend on balance to have very adverse effects on human happiness. In the very case where utilitarians think that killing or stealing or cheating will lead to a net gain in happiness over unhappiness, they will—in all consistency—approve of the killing, stealing, or cheating.

See also Ethics, Theory of.

SOURCES
Gouinlock, James, ed. *The Moral Writings of John Dewey.* Rev. ed. Amherst, NY: Prometheus. 1994.

Norris, Christopher. *Uncritical Theory: Postmodernism, Intellectuals, and the Guild War.* Amherst, NY: The University of Massachusetts Press. 1992.

Rorty, Richard. *Objectivity, Relativism, and Truth.* Cambridge: University of Cambridge Press. 1991.

VALUES

The word *value* refers to that property of a thing or person for which it is esteemed, desirable, or useful; or of worth, merit, or importance. Value implies an intrinsic excellence or desirability. In humans, worth/value implies moral excellence. When we refer to certain moral values that are held in esteem by most or all human beings, we normally mention cleanliness, freedom, education, self-esteem, and such virtues as honesty, good manners, promise keeping, fairness, and duty.

Frances Moore Lappe (*Rediscovering America's Values*) puts it this way:

> To be an American has always meant to take pride in more than the grandeur of our natural endowment, the strength of our armed forces, or the genius of our Nobel laureates. More than anything, we are proud that *America stands for something,* a set of enduring values that have given us a common identity in the midst of incredible diversity—values that have made us one people. These values are the common language of our commonwealth, without which we could not talk to each other and be understood. Freedom, democracy, and fairness are certainly three such values, but most of us would also likely agree on a host of other closely connected ones—responsibility, productivity, community, family, and work itself—as central to our national identity.

Walter Lippman, in *A Preface to Morals,* wrote:

> But if civilization is to be coherent and confident it must be known in that civilization what its ideals are. There must exist in the form of clearly available ideas an understanding of what the fulfilment of the promise of that civilization might mean, an imaginative conception of the good at which it might, and, if it is to flourish, at which it must aim. That knowledge, though no one has it perfectly, and though relatively few have it at all, is the principle of all order and certainty in the life of that people. By it they can clarify the practical conduct of life in some measure, and add immeasurably to its dignity.

Our values are not "fixed," but as Lappé says, are a "common language" by which we learn to live with each other. Thus, our values continually emerge, change, and produce offshoots that must in turn be evaluated by tradition, by principle, and by utility. Engaging in this dialogue, we learn who we are and what we hold dear and are able to test new ideas within the process. Values-growth implies being drawn into the debate and inspired to reexamine our most deeply held assumptions about life and living.

See also Ethics, Theory of.

SOURCES

Bellah, Robert N., et al. *Habits of the Heart: Individualism and Commitment in American Life.* Berkeley: University of California Press. 1985.

Kemmis, Daniel. *The Good City and the Good Life: Renewing the Sense of Community.* Boston: Houghton Mifflin. 1995.

Lappe, Frances Moore. *Rediscovering America's Values.* New York: Ballantine. 1989.

Lippman, Walter. *A Preface to Morals.* New York: Macmillan, 1929

Selznick, Philip. *The Moral Commonwealth: Social Theory and the Promise of Community.* Berkeley: University of California Press. 1992.

Turner, Frederick. *The Culture of Hope: A New Birth of the Classical Spirit.* New York: Free Press. 1995.

WHITE SUPREMACY

See Ku Klux Klan; Racism.

WIDE REFLECTIVE EQUILIBRIUM

We can begin moral deliberation by beginning where we are with what we have—our own prereflective judgments about what is right and what is wrong. Thus, we begin with our own ethical judgments or intuitions about the rightness or wrongness of some particular behavior and about certain general principles, such as "all human beings have a right to life," "one should try to keep one's promises," or "gratuitous cruelty to animals is wrong." People will have considered judgments at all levels of generality. They reflect and make judgments about situations, institutions, standards, and principles.

These considered judgments will always be open to revision, according to proponents of Wide Reflective Equilibrium (WRE). As such, they are merely the starting point of a coherent moral perspective. Still, a person must acknowledge that these starting points are historically, culturally, and personally relative. We cannot stop here, however; most move forward to offer reflective justification of our moral point of view, and, according to WRE, to consider all values because someone thinks they are true and equally significant.

Critics of moral principles remind us that moral intuitions are learned at home, where what is taught is biased, unreflective, and inconsistent. Some will argue that many forms of morality are derived from religious systems, warped views of society, and/or customs necessary for the survival of the group. They are neither culturally nor personally neutral. Because of this inner subjectivity, it is suggested that a person's moral intuitions be subjected to a wider examination. This requirement tells one that what is needed is informed individuals with a wide variety of personal experiences. WRE is a metamoral process involving three steps: (1) The first step is to reconsider, compare, and evaluate one's moral intuitions with other relevant and different moral theories. (2) The second step is to make sure that personal moral adjustments are internally consistent. (3) The third step is to take into account relevant information from both the social and human sciences to consider the effects on this reconsidered moral view. This process will help a person make moral judgments externally consistent with relevant information about humans and human environments.

This reflective process will come to a close when reason and filtering tell a person that one moral judgment, one moral perspective, is rationally preferable to others. Instead of trying to squeeze moral principles from moral definitions, WRE insists that one must focus on the social nature and purposes of morality. Thus, by carefully considering the human and social function of a moral code, a person may be able to advance reasonable and objective grounds for preferring some moral principles over others. WRE is a method of justifying or evaluating moral principles and their applications. It assumes that moral thought should stand up to reflection and that moral principles and their applications should be rendered in a coherent and objective fashion.

See also Justification of Ethical Principles.

SOURCES

Hester, Joseph P., and Philip F. Vincent. *Philosophy for Young Thinkers*. 2d ed. Monroe, NY: Trillium Press. 1987.

Nielsen, Kai. *Ethics without God*. Rev. ed. Amherst, NY: Prometheus. 1990.

WISDOM

James Christian says: "Man has a need that (we think) goes beyond the deer and the dolphin: the need for meaning. For man a meaningless existence is a contradiction. Intuitively we have known that the well-lived life—the meaning-full life—results from what we humans call wisdom. By definition wisdom *is* the understanding of life and how to live it; and for as long as men have sought wisdom it has been apparent that wisdom is correlated to our capacity to *perceive more* and *understand more*."

C. G. Jung observes that "When a speculative philosopher believes he has comprehended the world once and for all in his system, he is deceiving himself; he has merely comprehended himself and then naively projected that view upon the world." To be sure, life is a puzzle and the goal of seeing the whole of life clearly, unmistakably, and realistically has come to very few individuals. The contemporary quest for wisdom may itself be a selection of the best metaphor through which and from which we are able to understand the world. In the West, the dominant metaphors are to be found in science: observation, calculation, and logic. In the East, we can select from dreams ("My young men shall never work. Men who work cannot dream, and wisdom comes in dreams:" Smohalla, Indian prophet); from simplicity; and through contemplation and sacrifice ("He who knows does not speak; He who speaks does not know:" *Tao Te Ching*). Christian proposes a synthesis between East and West. He says: "Synoptic synthesis focuses specifically on our thinking habits. It helps each person develop the habit of erasing imaginary boundaries; it tears down mental walls that hamper free access to needed fields of information. This means reconditioning ourselves to think through arbitrary barriers, to turn to all disciplines for data, and to ask interdisciplinary questions."

SOURCE

Christian, James. *Philosophy: An Introduction to the Art of Wondering*. 4th ed. New York: Holt, Rinehart and Winston. 1986.

Jung, C. G. *Psychology and Religion*. New Haven, CT: Yale University Press. 1938.

Nozick, Robert. *The Examined Life: Philosophical Meditations*. New York: Simon & Schuster. 1989.

Turner, Frederick. *The Culture of Hope: A New Birth of the Classical Spirit*. New York: Free Press. 1995.

WOMEN

See Discrimination; Feminism; Gender Equity.

WOMEN'S SUFFRAGE

The year 1995 marked the seventy-fifth anniversary of women winning the right to vote in the United States. The suffragists' long and courageous campaign won the right of half our citizens—the women—to vote through the ratification of the Nineteenth Amendment, also referred to as the Susan B. Anthony Amendment. The editors of *Women of Power* comment:

> Throughout the course of seventy-two years, thousands of determined women circulated countless petitions and gave speeches in churches, convention halls, meeting houses, and on street corners for suffrage. They published newspapers, pamphlets, and magazines, and they were harassed and attacked by mobs and police. Some women were thrown into jail, and when they protested with hunger strikes they were brutally forcefed. Still they persevered. Finally, on August 26, 1920, women won the right to vote with the ratification of the 19th Amendment to the United States Constitution.

But this is only part of the story. By 1815, large segments of the population—religious minorities, propertyless workers, frontier settlers—were demanding the rights of republican (representative democracy) government. Such pressures culminated in the summoning of state constitutional conventions to propose reforms of the existing political system. James Kent of New York complained: "It is not to be disguised that our governments are becoming downright democracies. The principle of universal suffrage, which is now running a triumphant career from Maine to Louisiana, is an awful

power, which, like gun powder, or the steam engine, or the press itself, may be rendered mighty in mischief as well as in blessings."

But even these democratizing reforms presented limitations to the concept of "universal suffrage." There were qualifications of age, and of sex. Women were excluded, and so were minors. Blacks and Native Americans were also denied the right to vote. "They are a peculiar people," said an opponent of black suffrage, "incapable of exercising that privilege with any sort of discretion, prudence, or independence. They have no just conceptions of civil liberty" (Carroll and Noble). Nor did anyone defend the rights of Native Americans. American political leaders—being conservative—feared democracy and political parties. By accepting the idea of interest politics, suffrage was expanded and political parties were encouraged, but this idea came slowly in the nineteenth century and only grew with some fury during Reconstruction. For example, in the 1880s and 1890s, black voters in Virginia and North Carolina formed alliances with low-income whites and challenged the power holders in the state Democratic parties. In response, white politicians painted such a negative picture of blacks that interracial alliances were systematically destroyed, creating an atmosphere of racial hysteria marked by a rapid rise in lynching.

The right to vote is therefore marked by a trail of blood that not only stains the American soil, but gives the idea of participatory democracy strength and a historical foundation. Thus, the hope for the future may be the shared logic of the people whose U.S. citizenship has only recently been recognized. American history is, in one way, an unfolding of the understanding of the interconnectedness of all its diverse peoples and the appearance of liberation movements of Americans once considered worthless —Africans, Hispanics, Asians, women, the religiously different, and the sexually unorthodox. As these people are freed to develop themselves, the "old" American history may be finished as the "new" American history is being written. At the end of the twentieth century, Americans may well be standing at the beginning of a new era.

SOURCES

Carroll, Peter N., and David W. Noble. *The Free and the Unfree: A New History of the United States.* 2d ed. New York: Penguin. 1987.
"Celebrating Suffrage—The Diamond Jubilee." *Women of Power* 24 (Summer 1995).

WORLD ORDER (PEACE)

Many social, political, and religious groups/institutions have voiced opposition to war and have actively promoted world order and peace. Buddhism, Hinduism, Confucianism, Christianity, and the Baha'i Faith have proclaimed the importance of the unification of humans the world over in some kind of peaceful order. Organizations such as the North Atlantic Treaty Organization and the United Nations have taken the promotion and maintenance of world order and peace as their primary purpose.

In ancient times, some prophets among the Hebrews looked forward to a time when men would mold their spears into pruning hooks and their swords into plowshares. Among the early Greeks, the Stoics opposed war and the early Christians stressed nonviolence and refused to bear arms. Among Roman Catholics, twentieth-century popes have called for men and nations to seek peace.

The ethics behind this call for world peace and order is expressed clearly by the Universal House of Justice, the supreme governing body of the Baha'i Faith, which

> enjoins upon its followers the primary duty of an unfettered search after truth, condemns all manner of prejudice and superstition, declares the purpose of religion to be the promotion of amity and concord, proclaims its essential harmony with science, and recognizes it as the foremost agency for the pacification and the orderly progress of human society. It unequivocally maintains the principle of equal rights, opportunities and privileges for men and women, insists on compulsory education, eliminates extremes of poverty and wealth, abolishes the institution of priesthood, prohibits slavery, asceticism, mendicancy and monasticism, prescribes monogamy, discourages divorce, emphasizes the necessity of strict obedience to one's government, exalts any work performed in the spirit of service to the level of worship, urges either the creation or the selection of an auxiliary international language, and delineates the outlines of those institutions that must establish and perpetuate the general peace of mankind.

SOURCES

Gross, Ernest. *The United Nations: Structure for Peace.* New York: Harper and Brothers. 1962.
The Universal House of Justice. *The Promise of World Peace to the Peoples of the World: A Statement by the Universal House of Justice.* Wilmette, IL: Baha'i Publishing Trust, 1985.

AUTHORITARIANISM
The belief that knowledge is validated by the will of a source entitled to unquestioning obedience, rather than by independent or competing efforts to discover what is true or false.

AXIOLOGY
The study of values.

CATEGORICAL IMPERATIVE
A command or requirement that holds regardless of circumstances or of the desires and inclination of persons, and regardless of the findings of experience. Hence, it is an unconditional demand. In Kant's writings, the categorical imperative states the requirements that must be met by a maxim if it is to be regarded as morally binding, as moral law.

CIVIL LIBERTIES
Those rights whose enjoyment does not depend on a person's political status; in the United States, rights such as those of freedom of thought, speech, press, assembly, worship, and conscience.

DEONTOLOGICAL ETHICS
This type of ethics holds that some acts are morally obligatory regardless of their consequences for human welfare.

DETERMINISM
This is the view that any event is entirely caused by previous events and conditions.

According to determinism, the realm of nature, including humans, is an unbroken chain of cause and effect.

DUE CARE
The care that a person should exercise in choosing and acting in order to have reasonable grounds to expect his or her action to have results in accord with his or her intention and with his or her obligations to other people.

DUTY
The conduct or action required of a person on moral grounds.

EMOTIVIST THEORY OF ETHICS
This view claims that the chief function of ethical terms is to convey emotions, feelings, and moods that lead to attitudes and action rather than to truth and knowledge.

ETHICAL NATURALISM
The system of theories that explains the meaning of ethical terms by reference to human nature, the satisfaction of human interests, or experiences of worth that make their appeal for justification of ethical judgments to observation and experience.

ETHICAL OBJECTIVISM
The view that holds that the truth of an ethical judgment is independent of the person who makes the judgment and of the time and place it is made.

ETHICAL RELATIVISM
The view that there are no universally applicable ethical standards but that their applicability is dependent on historical, cultural, or other conditions.

ETHICS
The study of good and bad, right and wrong in human conduct. Ethics comes from the Greek *eqos* (way of life) and is applied to the study of moral conduct. While some persons use the terms *morals* and *ethics* synonymously, among philosophers *morals* and *morality* usually refer to the conduct or behavior pattern, whereas *ethics* and *ethical* refer to the study of these matters or to a system of ideas about them.

EUTHANASIA
Mercy killing or the deliberate putting to death of persons suffering from pain and incurable diseases.

EXISTENTIALISM
The attitude and outlook that stresses the human predicament and emphasizes human existence and the qualities distinctive of individuals, rather than of "man" in the abstract, or nature and the world in general.

FATALISM
The belief that events are irrevocably fixed so that human effort cannot alter them, although sometimes things appear otherwise; the idea that "what is to be, will be."

FORMALISM
Adherence to prescribed forms. In ethics, it has meant the view that certain types of acts follow fixed moral principles, so that circumstances do not alter cases.

FREEDOM OF CHOICE, FREE WILL
The doctrine that humans have some genuine power of alternative choice: the power of self-determination.

GOLDEN RULE
The principle "do unto others as you would have them do unto you."

GOOD
The term applied to a thing or an experience that is of worth, possesses desirable qualities, or satisfies some need. Goods are of two kinds: *intrinsic* goods, which are valuable in and of themselves, and *extrinsic* goods, which are a means to something else.

HEDONISM
The doctrine that pleasure or happiness is the chief good in life and that we ought to seek that good.

HUMANISM
A doctrine that emphasizes distinctively human interests and ideals.

INDETERMINISM
The theory that personal choices in some cases are independent of antecedent events.

INDIVIDUALISM
The theory that stresses individual rights or self-direction by individuals opposed to growing regulation and governmental control, and the idea that the interests of the individual should be paramount in determining right and wrong.

INSTRUMENTALISM
The view (formulated by John Dewey) that the experimental use of intelligence in actual problematic situations is a necessary condition for converting them into consummatory experience. Instrumentalism is based on inquiry whose purpose is liberative, not prescriptive. In Dewey's ethics (to be distinguished from *pragmatism*), instrumentalism is completely unsentimental (not based on nor used for emotional satisfaction): the liberating function of ideas in conduct can only be realized when we unflinchingly recognize nature's instrumentalities and limitations; for example, the scientific inquirer deals with problematic situations—he or she may seek a cure for cancer or the means to land a person on the moon, and in either case, his or her problematic situation

is not resolved until such ends-in-view are achieved.

INTUITIONISM
The view that knowledge can be gained by direct apprehension, in contrast with the view that reliable knowledge can only be gained by the use of reasoning, sense perception, or a combination of these means.

JUSTICE
The impartial adjudication of conflicting claims, implying giving every person his or her due; also implied is a distribution of the products of society so that all persons have equal or equitably determined opportunity; ethical justice stresses the right of persons to fair treatment in all respects.

LIBERALISM
A social and political philosophy favoring a growth of civil liberties or greater freedom in political and religious matters.

MELIORISM
The view that the world is neither entirely good nor entirely evil but can be made better through our efforts.

METAETHICS
The study of ethical theories, as distinguished from the study of moral and ethical conduct itself.

METALANGUAGE
The language that we use to talk about a language itself, in contrast with an *object language* that we use to talk about the world.

MORALS
The term comes from the Latin *moralis* (the custom or way of life) and means the conduct and codes of conduct of individuals and groups. *Moral judgments* refer to the actions of human beings insofar as they are considered right or wrong. The adjective *moral* is used in three different ways: in contrast to *immoral;* in contrast to *nonmoral*

when referring to all actions about which there is a question of right or wrong; and often in the plural, when one refers to the behavior pattern of a particular group.

NATURALISM
The theory that accepts the experienceable world as the whole of reality, as opposed to *supernaturalism.*

NORMATIVE ETHICS
The ethics that set forth norms or standards by which people may judge what is the morally best way to live.

OBJECTIVISM IN ETHICS
An objective moral judgment is one that a rational agent will accept if he or she reasons disinterestedly and has available the relevant facts.

OBLIGATION
That which a person is morally bound to do because of some promise, agreement, duty, or law.

POSITIVISM
The belief that only empirically verifiable or analytic propositions are meaningful, and that metaphysics is meaningless.

POSTULATES
Fundamental assumptions used as a basis for developing a system of proofs, but not themselves subject to proof within the system. All *axioms* (self-evident truths) are postulates, but not all postulates (presuppositions that are not necessarily self-evident) are axioms.

PREDESTINATION
The doctrine that all events in man's life have been decreed or determined from the beginning of time by the sovereign will of God.

PRIMARY GROUPS
The intimate, face-to-face groups (family, play groups, friends, etc.) where persons meet not just for one specific purpose, but for informal and personal relationships.

RATIONALISM
The view that the mind has the power to know some truths that are logically prior to experience and yet not analytic.

REDUCTION
The analysis of a whole into its parts or units, and the equating of the whole with the aggregate of the parts. The "fallacy of reduction" arises when we attempt: (1) to equate the value or character of the whole with those of the simple parts; (2) to explain the later stages entirely by the earlier stages; and (3) to take something that is commonly thought to be of a novel character or value and reduce it to an appearance of something else.

RELATIVISM
The view that truth depends on time, place, and the thinking and point of view of the observer, and that there is no interpersonally valid truth.

RIGHT
Conforming to moral standards. The term is used when speaking of acts.

RIGHTS
Those things to which people have a just claim.

SECONDARY GROUPS
The institutionalized groups where people meet on only one plane of life for a specific purpose, normally based upon more formal and impersonal relations than those contacts within primary groups.

SKEPTICISM IN MORALS
An attitude that may vary from uncertainty, doubt, and the questioning of all assumptions until they are confirmed, to the claim that knowledge is impossible and therefore the quest for truth is in vain.

SUBJECTIVE
That which pertains to the subject, the self, or the knower; that which exists in consciousness but not apart from consciousness. The term stands in contrast to *objective*.

SUBJECTIVISM
The view that reality consists of only conscious beings and their mental states; that all we can know is the subject and his or her sensory and mental states; and that value statements are about the attitudes or feelings of the person who makes the statement.

TELEOLOGY
The theory of ends or purposes; the doctrine that there is design or purpose operating in the universe as a whole and that this principle is needed to supplement other types of explanations.

TELEOLOGICAL ETHICS
The ethics that judges conduct as right or wrong in relation to its results as assessed in relationship to some end or goal that is considered good.

TOTALITARIANISM
The view that the state is supreme and its interests take precedence over those of individuals and of all other groups.

UTILITARIANISM
The ethical theory that claims that utility, in the sense of the greatest happiness of the greatest number, should be the aim of acts and the criterion by which we judge them.

VALUE
That which has worth or is desirable.

BIBLIOGRAPHY

Adams, Bert N. *The Family: A Sociological Interpretation.* 5th ed. New York: Harcourt Brace. 1995.

Adams, Hunter Havelin III. "African and African-American Contributions to Science and Technology." Portland, Oregon: Portland Public Schools. 1990.

Adler, Mortimer J. *Six Great Ideas.* New York: Collier. 1981.

———. *The Paideia Proposal: An Educational Manifesto.* New York: Macmillan. 1982.

———. *We Hold These Truths: Understanding the Ideas and Ideals of the Constitution.* New York: Macmillan. 1987.

Adorno, T. W., Frenkel-Brunswik, Levinson, and Sanford. *The Authoritarian Personality.* New York: Wiley. 1950.

Ahrons, C. R., and R. H. Rogers. *Divorced Families: A Multidisciplinary View.* New York: Norton. 1987.

Aiken, H. D. *Reason and Conduct.* New York: Alfred A. Knopf. 1962.

Albright, W. F. *From the Stone Age to Christianity.* 2d ed. New York: John Hopkins Press. 1957.

Alexander, Elizabeth. "'We Must Be About Our Father's Business': Anna Julia Cooper and the Incorporation of the Nineteenth-Century African-American Woman Intellectual." *Signs, Journal of Women in Culture and Society* 20 (Winter 1995).

Allport, Gordon W. "Attitudes." In C. Murchison, ed. *A Handbook of Social Psychology.* Worcester, MA: Clark University Press. 1935.

———. *The Nature of Prejudice.* Reading, MA: Addison-Wesley. 1954.

"Alternative Medicine." *Consumer Reports* 59, 1 (January 1994).

American Academy of Political and Social Science. "Medicine and Society." *The Annals* 346 (1963).

American Association of School Administrators. "Teaching Thinking and Reasoning Skills: Problems and Solutions." *AASA Critical Issues Report* no. 20. Arlington, VA: American Association of School Administrators. 1987.

American Civil Liberties Union. "Freedom through Dissent." In *42nd Annual Report, July 1, 1961 to June 30, 1962.* New York: ACLU. 1963.

———. "To Secure: To Use: These Rights." In *43rd Annual Report, July 1, 1962 to June 30, 1963.* New York: ACLU. 1964.

American Indian Policy Commission. Washington, D.C.: U.S. Government Printing Office. 1976.

Ames, Roger T. *Thinking Through Confucius.* New York: State University of New York Press. 1987.

Anderson, Patrick. *High in America: The True Story Behind NORML and the Politics of Marijuana.* New York: Random House/Viking. 1981.

Anderson, Robert T., and Peter B. Fischer. *An Introduction to Christianity.* New York: Harper & Row. 1966.

Andrae, Tor. *Mohammed: The Man and His Faith.* Translated by Theophil Menzel. London: George Allen & Unwin. 1936.

Aquinas, Saint Thomas. *Summa Theologica, I–II.* New York: Random House. 1944.

Arberry, Arthur J. *The Koran Interpreted.* (Combined in one volume). New York: Macmillan. 1955.

Ardvey, Robert. *The Territorial Imperative.* New York: Atheneum. 1966.

Arendt, Hannah. *Crises of the Republic.* New York: Harcourt, Brace, and Jovanovich. 1972.

————. *The Human Condition.* Chicago: University of Chicago Press. 1958.

Arieti, Silvano. *The Intrapsychic Self: Feeling, Cognition, and Creating in Health and Mental Illness.* New York: Basic Books. 1967.

Arkes, Hadley. *Abortion Politics: Principle and Paradox.* New York: The Wall Street Journal. 1995.

ASCD Panel on Moral Education. "Moral Education in the Life of the School." Report. Alexandria, VA: ASCD. 1988.

Asimov, Isaac. "The 'Threat' of Creationism." *New York Times Magazine* (June 14, 1981).

Atlee, Tom. *Thinkpeace.* 6622 Tremont, Oakland, CA, 94609.

"Attack on the Conscience." In *Bridges and Borders: Diversity in America. Readings from Time Magazine, 1923–1994.* New York: Time Warner Books. 1994.

Augustine. *Confessions.* London: F. J. Sheed. 1943.

————. *The City of God.* London: Everyman. 1945.

Avioli, P. S. "The Labor-Force Participation of Married Mothers of Infants." *Journal of Marriage and the Family* 47 (1985).

Ayer, A. J. *Philosophical Essays.* New York: St. Martin's. 1954.

Ayers, M. R. *The Refutation of Determinism.* London: Methuen. 1968.

Baber, K. M., and P. Monaghan. "College Women's Career and Motherhood Expectations: New Options, Old Dilemmas." *Sex Roles* 19 (1988).

Bagdikian, Ben H. *The Media Monopoly.* 4th ed. Boston: Beacon Press. 1993.

Baier, Kurt. "The Meaning of Life." Inaugural Lecture, Canberra University College. 1957.

————. *The Moral Point of View: A Rational Basis of Ethics.* Ithaca, NY: Cornell University Press. 1958.

————. "The Point of View of Morality." *Australasian Journal of Philosophy* 32 (1954).

Balfour, Arthur. *Foundations of Belief.* New York: Longmans. 1919.

Barry, Brian. *Theories of Justice.* Berkeley: University of California Press. 1989.

"Basic Instructional Program: Related Curriculum Issues, Policy 10." Tavares, Florida: Lake County Schools. 1994.

"Battered Parents." *Society* 15, 5 (July/August 1978): 54–55.

Beauchamp, Tom L., William T. Blackstone, and Joel Feinberg. *Philosophy and the Human Condition.* Englewood Cliffs, NJ: Prentice-Hall. 1980.

Beck, Lewis White, ed. *18th-Century Philosophy.* New York: Free Press. 1966.

Becker, Gary S. *The Economics of Discrimination.* 2d ed. Chicago: University of Chicago Press. 1971.

Bedau, Hugo, ed. *The Death Penalty in America.* Garden City, NY: Doubleday. 1964.

Beene, K., and S. Tozer, eds. *Society as Educator in an Age of Transition: Part II.* Chicago: National Society for the Study of Education. 1987.

Bell, R. *Introduction to the Qur'an.* Edinburgh: Edinburgh University Press. 1953.

Bellah, Robert N., et al. *Habits of the Heart: Individualism and Commitment in American Life.* Berkeley: University of California Press. 1985.

Bem, S. L. "Sex Role Adaptability: One Consequence of Psychological Androgyny." *Journal of Personality and Social Psychology* 31: 634–643.

Bennett, Christine I. *Comprehensive Multicultural Education: Theory and Practice.* Boston: Allyn and Bacon. 1990.

Bennett, William J. *The De-Valuing of America.* New York: Summit Books. 1992.

Berdyaev, Nicolas. *The Destiny of Man.* New York: Harper & Row. 1960.

Berger, Peter L. *The Noise of Solemn Assemblies.* Garden City, NY: Doubleday. 1961.

Bergeson, Jan M., and Kaoru Yamamoto Oba. "Japan's New Equal Employment Opportunity Law: Real Weapon or Heirloom Sword?" *Brigham Young University Law Review* 3 (1986).

Bergson, Henri. *The Two Sources of Morality and Religion*. Garden City, NY: Doubleday. 1951.

Berlin, I. *Karl Marx: His Life and Environment*. London: Oxford University Press. 1948.

Bernstein, Richard J. *Praxis and Action*. Philadelphia: University of Pennsylvania Press. 1971.

Berry, George R., and James Strong. *Interlinear Greek-English New Testament with a Greek-English Lexicon and New Testament Synonyms and a Greek Dictionary of the New Testament*. Grand Rapids, MI: Baker Book House. 1981.

Bickeo, Alexander. *The Supreme Court and the Idea of Progress*. Cambridge, MA: Harvard University Press. 1970.

Birkerts, Sven. "The Advent of the Computer." In *The Gutenberg Elegies*. Boston: Faber and Faber. 1994.

Birnbaum, Jeffrey H. "The Gospel According to Ralph." *Time* (May 15, 1995).

Black, Jim Nelson. *When Nations Die*. Wheaton, IL: Tyndale House Publishers. 1996.

Blackham, H. J. *Humanism*. Baltimore: Penguin. 1968.

Blakney, R. B. *The Way of Life: Lao Tzu*. New York: Mentor Books. 1955.

Blanshared, Brand. "The Case for Determinism." In *Determinism and Freedom in the Age of Modern Science*. Edited by Sidney Hook. New York: New York University Press. 1958.

Blauner, Robert. *Racial Oppression in America*. New York: Harper & Row. 1972.

Bloch, Ernst. *Natural Law and Human Dignity*. Translated by Dennis J. Schmidt. Cambridge, MA: MIT Press. 1986.

Bloom, Allan. *The Closing of the American Mind*. New York: Simon and Schuster. 1987.

———. *Love and Friendship*. New York: Simon & Schuster. 1993.

Boas, George. *The Limits of Reason*. New York: Harper and Row. 1961.

Bochenski, I. M. *Contemporary European Philosophy*. Berkeley: The University of California Press. 1966.

Boetcher, Ruth-Ellen, et al., eds. *Signs, Journal of Women in Culture and Society* 20 (Winter 1995).

Bogardus, Emory S. *The Development of Social Thought*. 4th ed. New York: David McKay. 1960.

Boorstin, Daniel J. *The Americans: The Democratic Experience*. New York: Random House. 1973.

———. *The Image*. New York: Macmillan. 1961.

Boswell, T. D., and J. R. Curtis. *The Cuban-American Experience*. Totowa, NJ: Rowman and Allanheld. 1984.

Bouquet, A. C., ed. *Sacred Books of the World*. Baltimore: Penguin. 1967.

Boyer, R. W., et al. *Apache Mothers and Daughters: Four Generations of a Family*. Norman: University of Oklahoma Press. 1992.

Bradley, F. H. *Ethical Studies*. London: Oxford University Press. 1970.

Brandt, Richard B., ed. *Social Justice*. Englewood Cliffs, NJ: Prentice-Hall. 1962.

Bravermon, Harry. *Labor and Monopoly Capital: The Degradation of Work in the Twentieth Century*. New York: Monthly Review Press. 1974.

Braxton, Joanne M. "Afra-American Culture and the Contemporary Literary Renaissance." In *Wild Women in the Whirlwind: Afra-American Culture and the Contemporary Literary Renaissance*. Edited by Joanne M. Braxton and Andree N. McLaughlin, xxi–xxx. New Brunswick, NJ: Rutgers University Press. 1990.

Breham, S. S. *Intimate Relationships*. New York: Random House. 1985.

Brehier, Emile. *The History of Philosophy: The Hellenistic and Roman Age*. Translated by Wade Baskin. Chicago: The University of Chicago Press. 1965.

Bridge, T. P., A. F. Mirsky, and F. K. Goodwin, eds. *Psychological, Neuropsychiatric, and Substance Abuse Aspects of AIDS*. New York: Raven Press. 1988.

Bronowski, Jacob. *Science and Human Values.* New York: Harper & Row. 1965.

Broom, Leonard. *The Transformation of the American Negro.* New York: Harper and Row. 1965.

Brown, Rexford G. *Schools of Thought.* San Francisco: Jossey-Bass. 1991.

Brunner, Emil. *Justice and the Social Order.* London: Lutterworth Press. 1945.

Buber, Martin. *Between Man and Man.* Boston: Beacon Press. 1955.

———. *Good and Evil.* New York: Charles Scribner's Sons. 1953.

———. *I and Thou.* 2d ed. New York: Charles Scribner's Sons. 1970.

Bultman, Rudolf. *Existence and Faith.* New York: Living Age. 1960.

Bureau of the Census. "Historical Statistics of the United States: Colonial Times to 1970." *Population Bulletin* 35 (January 1981): 4.

———. *Current Population Reports,* Series P-25, no. 704. "Projections of the Population of the United States: 1977–2050." *Statistical Abstract of the United States 1987.* Washington, D.C.: Government Printing Office. 1987: 34.

Burks, Arthur W., ed. *Collected Papers of Charles Sanders Peirce: Vols. VII–VIII.* Cambridge, MA: Harvard University Press. 1958.

Burtt, E. A. *In Search of Philosophic Understanding.* New York: New American Library. 1965.

Butler, Joseph. "Sermon XI, Preached on Advent Sunday, from Fifteen Sermons upon Human Nature." London, 1726. Printed in Robert Paul Wolff. *Philosophy: A Modern Encounter.* Englewood Cliffs, NJ: Prentice-Hall. 1971.

Buttrick, George Arthur, et al., eds. *The Interpreter's Dictionary of the Bible.* 4 vols. New York: Abingdon Press. 1962.

Capra, Fritjof. *The Tao of Physics.* 3d ed. (updated). Boston: Shambhala. 1991.

Capra, Fritjof. *The Turning Point.* New York: Bantam Books. 1982.

Cargan, Leonard, and Jeanne H. Ballantine, eds. *Sociological Footprints: Introductory Readings in Sociology.* 6th ed. Belmont, CA: Wadsworth. 1994.

Carnegie Forum on Education and the Economy. *A Nation Prepared: Teachers for the 21st Century.* New York: Carnegie Corporation. 1986.

Carroll, Peter N., and David W. Noble. *The Free and the Unfree: A New History of the United States.* 2d ed. New York: Penguin. 1988.

Carson, Gerald. *Cornflake Crusade.* New York: Rinehart. 1957.

Carson, Rachel. *Silent Spring* (1962). New York: Houghton Mifflin. 1987.

———. *Under the Sea Wind.* New York: Dutton. 1991.

Carter, Hugh, and Paul C. Glick. *Marriage and Divorce: A Social and Economic Study.* Cambridge, MA: Harvard University Press. 1970.

Carter, Sandy. "Revolution Rock." *Z Magazine* (November 1995).

Carter, Steven L. *Culture of Disbelief.* New York: Basic Books. 1993.

"Celebrating Suffrage—The Diamond Jubilee." *Women of Power* 24 (Summer 1995).

Ch'en, Kenneth K. S. *Buddhism: The Light of Asia.* Woodbury, NY: Barron's Educational Series. 1968.

Chadwick, Douglas H. "Dead or Alive: The Endangered Species Act." *National Geographic* 187:3 (March 1995).

Champion, Selwyn Gurney, and Dorothy Short, eds. *Readings from World Religions.* Greenwich, CT: Fawcett. 1951.

Chang Chung-Yuan. *Creativity and Taoism: A Study of Chinese Philosophy, Art, and Poetry.* New York: Julian Press. 1963.

Chartrand, S. "Experts Assess a Decade of In Vitro Fertilization." *New York Times* (April 11, 1989): C5.

Cheney, Lynne V. *Telling the Truth.* New York: Simon & Schuster. 1995.

Chopra, Deepak. *Ageless Body, Timeless Mind.* New York: Harmony Books. 1993.

Christian, James L. *Philosophy: An Introduction to the Art of Wondering.* 4th ed. New York: Holt, Rinehart and Winston. 1986.

Clark, Barbara. *Growing Up Gifted.* 2d ed. Columbus, OH: Charles E. Merrill. 1983.

Clark, Homer. *Domestic Relations.* St. Paul: West. 1968.

Clark, John, ed. *The Students Seek an Answer.* Waterville, ME: Colby College Press. 1960.

Cleveland, Harlan. *The Knowledge Executive: Leadership in an Information Society.* New York: E. P. Dutton. 1985.

Cloninger, C. Robert. "A Systematic Method for Clinical Description and Classification of Personality Variants." *Archives of General Psychiatry* 39 (1987): 1242–1247.

Cloud, P. "Scientific Creationism—A New Inquisition Brewing." *The Humanist* 37:1 (1977).

Cohen, Edmond. *The Predicament of Democratic Man.* New York: Macmillan. 1961.

Cohen, Jerry S. *America, Inc.: Who Owns and Operates the United States.* New York: Ideal Press. 1971.

Cohen, Richard. "To Multiculturalism." *Washington Post* (May 19, 1994): A21.

Combs, Arthur W., ed. *Perceiving, Behaving, Becoming: A New Focus for Education.* ASCD 1962 Yearbook. Washington, D.C.: Association for School Curriculum Development. 1962.

Commission on Civil Rights. *Twenty Years after Brown: The Shadows of the Past.* Washington, D.C.: U.S. Government Printing Office. 1974.

Commoner, Barry. *The Closing Circle.* New York: Knopf. 1971.

Compton's Encyclopedia. Chicago: Compton's Learning Company. 1994.

Compton's Online Encyclopedia. Chicago: Compton's Learning Company. 1995.

"Concern over AIDS Changed Sexual Behavior among One Third of Unmarried United States Women." *Family Planning Perspectives* 23 (1991): 234–235.

Cone, James. *Black Theology and Black Power.* New York: The Seabury Press. 1969.

Cook, E. P. *Psychological Androgyny.* New York: Pergamon. 1988.

Cooley, Charles Horton. *Social Organization.* New York: Free Press. 1958.

Cooper, Anna Julia. *A Voice From the South.* (Introduction by Mary Helen Washing-

ton.) New York: Oxford University Press. 1988.

Corkey, R. *A Philosophy of Christian Morals for Today.* London: George Allen & Unwin. 1961.

Council on Environmental Quality. In *Environmental Quality—1980.* Washington, D.C. 1980.

Crabtree, Charlotte, and Gary Nash. *National Standards for United States History: Exploring the American Experience, Grades 5–12.* Los Angeles: National Center for History in the Schools, UCLA. 1994.

Creation/Evolution 7 (Winter 1982).

Cross, Theodore. *The Black Power Imperative.* New York: Faulkner Books. 1984.

"Cross-Race Adoption: Not a Black and White Issue." *USA Weekend* (March 17–19, 1995).

Cuber, John F., and Peggy B. Harroff. *The Significant American.* New York: Hawthorn. 1965.

Culp, D.W., ed. *Twentieth Century Negro Literature.* Atlanta: J. L. Nichols. 1902.

Cunningham, R. L. *Situationism and the New Morality.* New York: Appleton-Century-Crofts. 1970.

Current Biography 53:9 (September 1992).

Curry, Thomas. *The First Freedom: Church and State in America to the Passage of the First Amendment.* London: Oxford University Press. 1986.

Daly, Mary. *The Church and the Second Sex.* Rev. ed. New York: Harper & Row. 1975.

Damon, William. *The Moral Child.* New York: Free Press. 1988.

Darnton, Nina. "Committed Youth: Why Are So Many Teens Being Locked Up in Private Mental Hospitals?" *Newsweek* 14, 5 (July 31, 1989): 66–72.

Darwin, Charles. *The Descent of Man.* Princeton, NJ: Princeton University Press. 1981.

Darwin, Charles. *The Origin of Species.* New York: Modern Library. 1937.

Davies, Paul. *God and the New Physics.* New York: Simon & Schuster. 1983.

Davis, David B. *The Problem of Slavery in the Age of Revolution.* Ithaca: Cornell University Press. 1975.

Davitt, Thomas E. *Ethics in the Situation.* New York: Appleton-Century-Crofts. 1970.

Dawiclowicz, L. S. *The Golden Tradition: Jewish Life and Thought in Eastern Europe.* New York: Holt, Rinehart and Winston. 1967.

———. *The War Against the Jews.* New York: Holt, Rinehart and Winston. 1975.

de Beauvoir, Simone. *The Coming of Age.* New York: Warner Paperback Library. 1973.

DeFleur, M. L., et al. *Understanding Mass Communication.* 4th ed. New York: Scholastic College Division. 1991.

Delfattore, Joan. *What Johnny Shouldn't Read: Textbook Censorship in America.* New Haven, CT: Yale University Press. 1992.

Deloria, Vine, and Clifford M. Lytle. *American Indians, American Justice.* Austin: University of Texas Press. 1983.

Denzinger, H. J. D. *The Sources of Catholic Dogma.* B. Herder. 1957.

Desmond, Edward W. "Playing Catchup in Cyberspace." *Time* (March 6, 1995).

Dewey, John. *A Common Faith.* New Haven: Yale University Press. 1934.

———. *Democracy and Education.* New York: Macmillan. 1916.

———. "The Development of American Pragmatism." In *Philosophy and Civilization.* New York: Bolch. 1931.

———. *Reconstruction in Philosophy.* New York: Henry Holt. 1920.

Dewey, Robert E., and James A. Gould. *Freedom: Its History, Nature, and Varieties.* New York: Macmillan. 1970.

Dichter, Ernest. *The Strategy of Desire.* Garden City, NY: Doubleday. 1960.

Douglas, Susan J. *Where the Girls Are: Growing Up Female with the Mass Media.* New York: Times Books. 1994.

Douglas, William O. *Freedom of the Mind.* Chicago: American Library Association in cooperation with the Public Affairs Committee. 1962.

Du Bois, W. E. B. *The Philadelphia Negro: A Social Study.* New York: Schucken Books. 1967.

Dubos, Rene. *The Torch of Life.* New York: Pocket Books, 1962.

Durkheim, Emile. *The Division of Labor in Society.* Translated by S. A. Solovay and J. H. Mueller. Glencoe, IL: Free Press. 1960.

Duyvendak, J. J. L., Translator. *Tao Te Ching: Lao Tzu.* London: John Murray. 1954.

Dworkin, Ronald. *Law's Empire.* Cambridge, MA: Harvard University Press. 1986.

———. *Taking Rights Seriously.* Cambridge, MA: Harvard University Press. 1978.

Dyer, Wayne. *Real Magic: Creating Miracles in Everyday Life.* New York: HarperCollins. 1992.

E, The Environmental Magazine 6: 5 (Oct. 1995).

"Eavesdropping Devices." Grolier Electronic Publishing. 1992.

Eckland, B. K. "Theories of Mate Selection." *Eugenicu Quarterly* 15 (1968).

Edel, Abraham. *Ethical Judgment: The Use of Science in Ethics.* London: Free Press of Glencoe. 1955.

Edel, Mary, and Abraham Edel. *Anthropology and Ethics.* Springfield, IL: Charles C. Thomas. 1959.

Educational Research Service. "Asian Students and Desegregation." *ERS Bulletin* (January 1995).

Edwards, Paul, and Richard H. Popkin, General eds. *Readings in the History of Philosophy.* (An eight-volume paperback series.) New York: Free Press. 1969.

Edwards, Rem B. *Reason and Religion.* New York: Harcourt Brace Jovanovich. 1972.

Ehrlich, Paul Ralph, et al. *Human Ecology: Problems and Solutions.* San Francisco: W. H. Freeman. 1973.

Ehrlich, Paul Ralph, and Anne H. Ehrlich. *Population/Resources/Environment: Issues in Human Ecology.* 2d ed. San Francisco: W. H. Freeman. 1972.

Eibl-Eibesfeldt, Irenaus. *Human Ethology.* New York: De Gruyter. 1989.

Eisenhower, Dwight D. (Address at Dartmouth College, June 14, 1953.) Quoted in *The Freedom to Read.* Chicago: American Library Association. 1953.

Eitzen, D. Stanley, and Maxine Baca Zinn. *Social Problems.* 4th ed. Boston: Allyn and Bacon. 1989.

Ellwood, Robert S. "Devil Worship." From *Information Finder*. World Book. 1994.

Encyclopaedia Britannica. Chicago: Encyclopaedia Britannica. 1990.

Encyclopedia Americana. Danbury, CT: Grolier Incorporated. 1993.

Erickson, Kai T. *Wayward Puritans: A Study in the Sociology of Deviance*. New York: Wiley. 1966.

Ernest, J. F. *Patterns of Ethics in America Today*. New York: Collier. 1962.

"Ethical Aspects of Experimentation with Human Subjects." *Daedalus* (Spring 1969).

Etzioni, Amitai. *Capital Corruption: The New Attack on American Democracy*. New York: Harcourt Brace Jovanovich. 1984.

"The Familiar Faces of Fascism." *Utne Reader* 72 (November-December 1995).

Farrell, Warren. *The Myth of Male Power*. New York: Simon & Schuster. 1993.

"Feminism." Grolier Electronic Publishing. 1992.

Ferre, Frederick. *Philosophy and Technology*. Athens: University of Georgia Press. 1995.

Fine, Melinda. "Collaborative Innovations: Documentation of the Facing History and Ourselves Program at an Essential School." *Teachers College Board* 94:4 (1993).

———. *Habits of Mind: Struggling over Values in America's Classrooms*. San Francisco: Jossey-Bass. 1995.

Finkelstein, L., ed. *The Jews: Their History, Culture, and Religion*. New York: Harper & Brothers. 1960.

Fishman, Joshua, ed. *The Rise and Fall of the Ethnic Revival*. Berlin: Mouton. 1985.

Fiss, Owen M. *Information Finder*. World Book. 1994.

Fletcher, Joseph. *Situation Ethics*. Philadelphia: The Westminster Press. 1966.

Foster, M. B. *The Political Philosophies of Plato and Hegel*. Oxford: Oxford University Press. 1968.

Foucault, Michel. *The History of Sexuality: An Introduction*. Translated from the French by Robert Harley. New York: Vintage Books. 1990.

Frankena, William K. "The Concept of Morality." *Journal of Philosophy* 63 (1966).

———. *Ethics*. 2d ed. Englewood Cliffs, NJ: Prentice-Hall. 1973.

Frankena, William K., and John T. Granrose, eds. *Introductory Readings in Ethics*. Englewood Cliffs, NJ: Prentice-Hall. 1974.

Frankenstein, Marilyn. "A Different Third R: Radical Math." In *Politics of Education: Essays from Radical Teachers*. Susan Gushee O'Malley, Robert C. Rosen, and Leonard Vogt, eds. Albany: State University of New York Press. 1990.

Frankl, Vicktor E. *Man's Search for Meaning*. New York: Washington Square. 1963.

Franklin, John Hope. *From Slavery to Freedom: A History of Negro Americans*. 5th ed. New York: Alfred A. Knopf. 1980.

Freeman, Howard E., and Norman R. Kurtz, eds. *America's Troubles: A Casebook on Social Conflict*. Englewood Cliffs, NJ: Prentice-Hall. 1969.

Freeman, Jo. *The Politics of Women's Liberation*. New York: David McKay. 1975.

Friedan, Betty. *The Feminine Mystique*. 10th Anniversary ed. New York: Norton. 1974.

"Friedan, Betty." Grolier Electronic Publishing. 1992.

Friedman, M. *Martin Buber: The Life of Dialogue*. New York: Harper & Row. 1960.

Friedman, Milton. *Capitalism and Freedom*. Chicago: University of Chicago Press. 1963.

Fromm, Eric. *The Art of Loving*. New York: Harper & Row. 1963.

Furstenberg, F., and A. Cherlin. "Children's Adjustment to Divorce." In A. S. Skolnick and J. H. Skolnick, eds. *Family in Transition*. 8th ed. New York: HarperCollins. 1994.

Futuyma, Douglas J. *Science on Trial*. New York: Pantheon Books. 1983.

Gaines, James R., et al., eds. *Bridges and Borders: Diversity in America*. New York: Time Warner. 1994.

Galbraith, John Kenneth. *The New Industrial State*. 2d ed. Boston: Houghton Mifflin. 1971.

Gardner, Robert W., Bryant Robey, and Peter C. Smith. *Asian Americans: Growth, Change, and Diversity.* Washington, D.C.: Population Reference Bureau. 1985.

Garfinkel, I., and S. S. McLanahan. *Single Mothers and Their Children.* Washington: Urban Institute. 1986.

Gatchel, R. J., and A. Baum. *An Introduction to Health Psychology.* Reading, MA: Addison-Wesley. 1983.

Geertz, Clifford. "The Uses of Diversity." *Michigan Quarterly Review* 25 (1986).

Giddings, Paul. *When and Where I Enter.* New York: William Morrow. 1985.

Gill, S.. et al. "Measuring Gender Differences: The Expressive Dimension and Critique of Androgyny Scales." *Sex Roles* 17 (1987).

Gilligan, C. *In a Different Voice: Psychological Theory and Women's Development.* Cambridge, MA: Harvard University Press. 1982.

Ginsberg, Morris. *On the Diversity of Morals: Approaches to Ethics.* London: Heinemann. 1962.

Girvetz, Harry K. *Beyond Right and Wrong.* New York: Free Press. 1973.

Glazer, Nathan. *Affirmative Discrimination: Ethics Inequality and Public Policy.* New York: Basic Books. 1975.

Godlovitch, S., R. Godlovitch, and J. Harris, eds. *Animals, Men and Morals.* New York: Taplinger. 1972.

Goldwin, Robert A., ed. *Left, Right and Center: Essays on Liberalism and Conservatism in the United States.* Chicago: Rand McNally. 1967.

Goode, Erich. *Drugs in American Society.* 2d ed. New York: Alfred A. Knopf. 1984.

Goodlad, J., ed. *The Ecology of School Renewal: Part I.* Chicago: National Society for the Study of Education. 1987.

Goodlad, John I., and Pamela Keating. *Access to Knowledge.* New York: College Entrance Examination Board. 1994.

Gordon, Milton M. *Assimilation in American Life: The Role of Race, Religion, and National Origins.* New York: Oxford University Press. 1964.

Gouinlock, James, ed. *The Moral Writings of John Dewey.* Rev. ed. Amherst, NY: Prometheus. 1994.

Grant, Frederick C. *Hellenistic Religions: The Age of Syncretism.* New York: Merrill. 1953.

Grene, Marjorie. *Introduction to Existentialism.* Chicago: Phoenix Books. 1963.

Grobstein, C., M. Flower, and J. Mendeloff. "External Human Fertilization: An Evaluation of Policy." *Science* 222: 127–133.

Gross, Ernest. *The United Nations: Structure for Peace.* New York: Harper and Brothers. 1962.

Grossman, Lawrence K. *The Electronic Republic.* New York: Viking. 1995.

Grossman, Soltan. "Native and Environmental Grassroots Movements." *Z Magazine* (November 1995).

Guilford, J. P. "Creativity." *American Psychologist* 5:444–454. 1950.

Habermas, Jurgen. *Postmetaphysical Thinking: Philosophical Essays.* Translated by William Mark Hohengarten. Cambridge, MA: MIT Press. 1992.

Halberstam, David. *The Fifties.* New York: Villard Books. 1993.

Hall, Cameron P., ed. *On-the-Job Ethics.* New York: National Council of Churches. 1963.

Hall, Thomas S. *Ideas of Life and Matter, Studies in the History of General Physiology 600 B.C. to 1900 A.D.* Vols. 1–3. Chicago: University of Chicago Press. 1969.

Hamilton, Alexander. "The Federalist, No. 7." In *The Federalist.* Edited by Jacob E. Cooke. Middletown, CT: Wesleyan University Press. 1982.

Hampden-Turner, Charles. *Maps of the Mind.* Edited and designed by Mitchell Beazley. New York: Macmillan. 1981.

Handlin, Oscar, and Lilian Handlin. *Liberty and Equality: 1920–1994.* New York: HarperCollins. 1994.

Harris, James F. *Against Relativism: A Philosophical Defense of Method.* LaSalle, IL: Open Court. 1992.

Hartshorne, Charles, and Paul Weiss, eds. *Collected Papers of Charles Sanders Peirce: Vols. I–VI, 1931–1935.* Cambridge, MA: Harvard University Press. 1958.

Harvard University Press. "Perspectives on Inequality." *Harvard Education Review Reprint Series* No. 8. Cambridge, MA: Harvard University Press. 1976.

Hayakawa, S. I. *Symbol, Status, and Personality*. New York: Harcourt, Brace & World. No Date.

Hechinger, Fred M. "Storm Over the Teaching of Sex." *New York Times* (September 1969): Education Section, 7.

Hegel, Georg W. F. *Reason in History*. Translated with an introduction by Robert S. Hartman. New York: The Liberal Arts Press. 1953.

Heilbronner, Robert L. *The Future Is History*. New York: Harper & Row. 1960.

Helmer, William J. "New York's 'Middle-Class' Homosexuals." *Harpers Magazine* (March 1963), 85–92.

Hendrick, C., ed. *Close Relationships*. Newberry Park, CA: Sage. 1989.

Herberg, Will. *Protestant, Catholic, Jew: An Essay in Religious Sociology*. New York: Double-day. 1955.

Herskovits, Melville J. *The Myth of the Negro Past*. New York: Harper Brothers. 1941.

Hertzler, J. O. "The Sociology of Anti-Semitism Through History." In Isacque G. Raeber, ed. *Jews in a Gentile World*. New York: Macmillan. 1942.

Hester, Joseph P. *Bridges: Building Relationships and Resolving Conflicts*. Carrboro, NC: New View. 1995.

———. "A Linguistic Examination of the Question 'Why Be Moral?'" Doctoral dissertation. Athens: University of Georgia. 1972.

———. "Subjective Commitment and the Problem of Moral Objectivity." *Philosophy and Phenomenological Research* 25:4 (June 1975).

———. *Teaching for Thinking*. Durham, NC: Carolina Academic Press. 1994.

Hester, Joseph P., and Philip F. Vincent. *Philosophy for Young Thinkers*. 2d ed. Monroe, NY: Trillium Press. 1987.

Hills, Stuart. *Demystifying Social Deviance*. New York: McGraw-Hill. 1980.

Hobart, C. "How They Handle It: Young Canadians, Sex, and AIDS." *Youth and Society* 25 (1992): 411–433.

Hochschild, A. R. "Disengagement Theory: A Critique and Proposal." *American Sociological Review* 40 (1975).

Hofstadter, Albert, and Richard Kuhns, eds. *Philosophies of Art and Beauty: Selected Readings in Aesthetics from Plato to Heidegger*. Chicago: University of Chicago Press. 1964.

Hofstadter, Richard, ed. *Great Issues in American History*. 3 vols. New York: Vintage. 1958.

Hospers, John. *Human Conduct: An Introduction to the Problem of Ethics*. New York: Harcourt, Brace & World. 1961.

Hudson, W. D. *Modern Moral Philosophy*. Garden City, NY: Anchor. 1970.

Hudson, W. D., ed. *The Is-Ought Question*. New York: St. Martin's. 1969.

Hulme, E. M. *The Renaissance, the Protestant Reformation, and the Catholic Reformation*. 2 vols. New York: Century House. 1914.

Hume, David. *A Treatise on Human Nature*. (Originally publ. in 1739, III.i.i.) Oxford: Clarendon Press. 1968.

Hunt, Kenneth. "A Biocentric Concept." *Unity* 146 (March 1960).

Hunt, Morton. *The Universe Within: A New Science Explores the Human Mind*. New York: Simon and Schuster. 1982.

IEN National Office. P.O. Box 485, Bemidji, MN 56601.

Information Finder. World Book. Chicago: Field Enterprises Educational Corporation. 1994.

Institute For First Amendment Studies. P.O. Box 589, Great Barrington, MA 01230.

Irving, J. A. "Towards Radical Empiricism in Ethics." In *American Philosophy: Today and Tomorrow*. Edited by H. M. Keller and S. Hook. New York: L. Furman. 1935.

Isaksen, Scott G., ed. *Frontiers of Creativity Research*. Buffalo, NY: Bearly. 1987.

Jackson, K. *Crabgrass Frontier: The Suburbanization of the United States*. New York: Oxford University Press. 1985.

James, William. *A Pluralistic Universe*. London: Longmans, Green. 1909.

Jaynes, Julian. *The Origin of Consciousness in the Breakdown of the Bicameral Mind*. Boston: Houghton Mifflin. 1976.

Johnson, J. T. *Mothers of Incest Survivors*. Bloomington: Indiana University Press. 1992.

Johnson, O. A. *Rightness and Goodness*. The Hague: Mortinus Nijhofl. 1959.

Johnson, Paul. *Intellectuals*. New York: Harper & Row. 1988.

Jonas, Hans. *Philosophical Essays: From Ancient Creed to Technological Man*. Englewood Cliffs, NJ: Prentice-Hall. 1974.

Jones, B. *Health of Americans*. Englewood Cliffs, NJ: Prentice-Hall. 1970.

Jones, F. H. *Positive Classroom Discipline*. New York: McGraw-Hill. 1987.

Jones, H. M. *The Pursuit of Happiness*. Ithaca, NY: Cornell University Press. 1953.

Jones, Kenneth L., et al. *Health Science*. New York: Harper & Row. 1971.

Jones, W. T. *The Classical Mind: A History of Western Philosophy*. 2d ed. New York: Harcourt, Brace & World. 1969.

Jordan, Barbara C., and E. D. Roston, eds. *The Great Society*. Austin: LBJ School of Public Affairs, University of Texas. 1986.

Josephy, Alvin Jr. *Now That the Buffalo's Gone: A Study of Today's American Indians*. New York: Alfred A. Knopf. 1982.

Jung, Carl G. *Psychology and Religion*. New Haven, CT: Yale University Press. 1938.

Kafka, Franz. *The Complete Stories*. New York: Schocken. 1988.

Kahn, Theodore C. *An Introduction to Hominology: The Study of the Whole Man*. Springfield, IL: Charles C. Thomas. 1972.

———. *Hominology: The Study of the Whole Man*. Springfield, IL: Charles C. Thomas. 1972.

Kamer, Samuel N. *Sumerian Mythology*. New York: Harper Torchbooks. 1961.

Kant, Immanuel. *Critique of Practical Reason*. Translated by Louis White Beck. New York: Bobbs-Merrill Library of Liberal Arts. 1956.

Kaplan, Harold. *Power and Order: Henry Adams and the Naturalist Tradition in American Fiction*. Chicago: University of Chicago Press. 1981.

Kart, Cary S. *The Realities of Aging*. Boston: Allyn and Bacon. 1981.

Kaufman, Allen. *Capitalism, Slavery, and Republican Values: American Political Economists, 1819–1848*. Austin: University of Texas Press. 1992.

Kaufman, Allen. *Capitalism, Slavery, and Republican Values: American Political Economists, 1819–1848*. Austin: University of Texas Press. 1982.

Kaufmann, Walter, ed. *Religion from Tolstoy to Camus*. New York: Harper Torchbooks. 1961.

Kelley, J. N. D. *Early Christian Doctrines*. New York: Harper & Brothers. 1958.

Kelley, Kathryn, and Donn Byrne. *Exploring Human Sexuality*. Englewood Cliffs, NJ: Prentice-Hall. 1992.

Kemmis, Daniel. *The Good City and the Good Life: Renewing the Sense of Community*. Boston: Houghton Mifflin. 1995.

Kennedy, C., and E. Alderman. *In Our Defense*. New York: William Morrow. 1991.

———. *The Right to Privacy*. New York: Alfred A. Knopf. 1995.

Kennedy, John F. *A Nation of Immigrants*. New York: Harper & Row. 1964.

Kenny, Anthony, ed. *Aquinas: A Collection of Critical Essays*. Garden City, NY: Doubleday. 1969.

Kerr, Peter. "Rich vs. Poor: Drug Patterns Are Diverging." *New York Times* (August 30, 1987).

Kessler, Gary E., ed. *Voices of Wisdom: A Multicultural Philosophy Reader*. Belmont, CA: Wadsworth. 1992.

Killian, L. M. *The Impossible Revolution, Phase 2: Black Power and the American Dream*. New York: Random House. 1975.

Kimball, Bruce A. *Orators and Philosophers: A History of the Idea of Liberal Education*. New York: College Entrance Examination Board. 1995.

Kirp, David. *Learning by Heart: AIDS and School Children in America's Communities*.

New Brunswick, NJ: Rutgers University Press. 1989.

Klaysbrun, Frances. *Married People: Staying Together in the Age of Divorce*. New York: Bantam. 1985.

Knefel, Don, ed. *100 Essays from Time*. Boston: Allyn and Bacon. 1992.

Knight, Harold V. *With Liberty and Justice for All: The Meaning of the Bill of Rights Today*. Rev. ed. Dobbs Ferry, NY: Oceana Publications. 1968.

Kohlberg, L. *Essays on Moral Development: The Psychology of Moral Development*. 2 vols. San Francisco: Harper & Row. 1981.

Koller, John. *Oriental Philosophies*. 2d ed. New York: Charles Scribner's Sons. 1985.

Kramarae, Cheris, and Paul Treichler. *A Feminist Dictionary*. Boston: Pandora Press. 1985.

Kramer, Rita. *Ed School Follies: The Miseducation of America's Teachers*. New York: Free Press. 1991.

Krech, D., and R. A. Crutchfield. *Theory and Problems of Social Psychology*. New York: McGraw-Hill. 1948.

La Barre, Weston. *The Ghost Dance: The Origins of Religion*. Garden City, NY: Doubleday. 1970.

Lacy, Dan. *The White Uses of Blacks in America*. New York: McGraw-Hill. 1976.

Lamont, Corliss. *The Philosophy of Humanism*. New York: Frederick Ungar. 1971.

Lancaster, Lane W. *Masters of Political Thought*. Vol. 3. Boston: Houghton Mifflin. 1966.

Langer, M. *Motherhood and Sexuality*. Translated by Nancy C. Hollander. New York: Guilford Press. 1992.

Lappe, Frances Moore. *Rediscovering America's Values*. New York: Ballantine. 1989.

Larrabee, Mary Jeanne, ed. *An Ethic of Care: Feminist and Interdisciplinary Perspectives*. New York: Routledge. 1993.

Lawrence, Nathaniel, and Daniel O'Connor. *Readings in Existential Phenomenology*. Englewood Cliffs, NJ: Prentice-Hall. 1967.

Lawson, Don. *The Long March: Red China Under Chairman Mao*. New York: Harper. 1983.

Le Vine, Robert, and Mary White. "The Social Transformation of Childhood." In J. B. Lancaster et al., eds. *Parenting Across the Life Span*. New York: Aldine de Grater. 1987.

Leff, Gordon. *Medieval Thought, St. Augustine to Ockham*. Baltimore: Penguin. 1958.

Lehmann, Paul L. *Ethics in a Christian Context*. New York: Harper & Row. 1963.

Leinberger, Paul, and Bruce Tucker. *The New Individualists*. New York: HarperCollins. 1991.

Leone, Richard C. "Foreword. " In L. K. Grossman. *The Electronic Republic*. New York: Viking. 1995.

Leuba, C. *The Natural Man*. Garden City, NY: Doubleday. 1954.

Levine, Art. "The Uneven Odds." *U.S. News & World Report* (August 17, 1987).

Leviton, Richard, ed. *Alternative Medicine Digest*. P.O. Box K, Milton, WA 98354.

Lewinson, Paul. *Race, Class, and Party: A History of Negro Suffrage and White Politics in the South*. New York: Universal Library. 1965.

Lewis, Anthony. *Gideon's Trumpet*. New York: Random House. 1964.

Liebow, Elliot. *Tally's Corner: A Study of Negro Streetcorner Men*. New York: Little, Brown. 1967.

Lincoln, C. Eric. *The Black Muslims in America*. Westport, CT: Greenwood Press. 1982.

Lippman, Walter. *A Preface to Morals*. New York: Macmillan, 1929

Lisitzky, G. *Four Ways of Being Human*. New York: Bantam. 1963.

Litwak, E., and Ivan Szeleny. "Primary Group Structures and Their Functions: Kin, Neighborhood, and Friends." *American Sociological Review* 34:4 (August 1969).

Lobkowicz, Nicholas. *Theory and Practice: History of a Concept from Aristotle to Marx*. Notre Dame: University of Notre Dame Press. 1967.

Locke, Mary S. *Anti-Slavery in America.* Gloucester: Peter Smith. 1965.

Lomax, Louis E. *When the Word Is Given: A Report on Elijah Muhammad, Malcolm X, and the Black Muslim World.* Westport, CT: Greenwood Press. 1979.

Luker, Kristin. *Abortion and the Politics of Motherhood.* Los Angeles: The University of California Press. 1984.

Lukes, Steven. *Individualism.* Oxford: Blackwell. 1973.

Lyotard, Jean-Francois. *The Post Modern Explained.* Translated from the French by Don Barry, Bernadette Maher, Julian Pefanis, Virginia Spate, and Morgan Thomas. Minneapolis: University of Minnesota Press. 1992.

————. *The Postmodern Condition: A Report on Knowledge.* Translated from the French by Geoff Bennington and Brian Massumi. Minneapolis: University of Minnesota Press. 1993.

MacGregor, Geddes. *Introduction to Religious Philosophy.* Boston: Houghton Mifflin. 1959.

MacIver, R. M. "The Social Significance of Professional Ethics." In *Ethical Standards and Professional Conduct* 297. Philadelphia: The Annals of the American Academy of Political and Social Science. 1955. (See also volume 343.)

MacKinnon, Catherine A. "Difference and Dominance: On Sex Discrimination." In *Feminism Unmodified: Discourses on Life and Law.* Cambridge, MA: Harvard University Press. 1987.

MacKintosh, H. R. *Types of Modern Theology.* New York: Scribner's. 1937.

Madden, Edward H., and Peter H. Hare. *Evil and the Concept of God.* Springfield, IL: Charles C. Thomas. 1968.

Madison, James. "Extend the Sphere": The Federalist No. 10. In *The Federalist Papers by Alexander Hamilton, James Madison, and John Jay.* New York: Bantam. 1982.

Maine, Henry Summer. *Ancient Law.* Boston: Beacon Press. 1963.

Mandel, B., and B. Mandel. *Play Safe: How To Avoid Getting Sexually Transmitted Diseases.* Goster City, CA: Center For Health Information. 1985.

Margolis, Joseph. *Values and Conduct.* New York: Oxford University Press. 1971.

Maritain, Jacques. *The Person and the Common Good.* New York: Scribner's. 1947.

Marsh, Clifton E. *From Black Muslims to Muslims: The Transition from Separatism to Islam, 1930–1980.* Metuchen, NJ: Scarecrow Press. 1984.

Martin, L., and S. Kerry. *Anti-Rock: The Opposition to Rock'n'Roll.* Hamden, CT: Archon. 1988.

Marx, Karl. "Capital Punishment." In *Marx and Engels: Basic Writings on Politics and Philosophy.* Edited by F. Feuer. Garden City, NY: Doubleday. 1959.

————. *A Contribution to the Critique of Political Economy.* Translated by N. I. Stone. Chicago: Charles Kerr. 1904.

————. *Writings of the Young Marx on Philosophy and Science.* Edited by Loyd D. Easton and Kurt H. Guddat. Garden City, NY: Anchor Books. 1967.

Marx, Karl, and Friedrich Engels. *Manifesto of the Communist Party.* Revised (English Edition). Moscow: Foreign Language Publishing House. 1888.

Maslow, Abraham. *Toward a Psychology of Being.* New York: Van Nostrand Reinhold. 1968.

May, Rollo. *The Courage To Create.* New York: Norton. 1975.

Mayer, Robert N. *The Consumer Movement: Guardians of the Marketplace.* Twayne, 1989.

McCallum, R. B., ed. *On Liberty, Considerations on Representative Government.* London: Oxford University Press. 1946.

McCord, William, and Arline McCord. *American Social Problems.* Saint Louis: C. V. Mosby. 1977.

McGoldrick, Monica. "Women through the Family Life Cycle." In McGoldrick, Monica, et al., eds. *Women in Families: A Framework for Family Therapy.* New York: Norton. 1989.

McGoldrick, Monica, et al., eds. *Women in Families: A Framework for Family Therapy.* New York: Norton. 1989.

McIntosh, Peggy. *How Schools Short Change Girls*. Washington, D.C.: American Association of University Women. 1992.

McKee, Charlene, ed. *Women of Power* 24 (Summer 1995).

McLeod, A. *Management Information Systems* (Casebook). Chicago: Science Research Associates. 1987.

McLuhan, Marshall H. *Understanding Media*. Cambridge, MA: MIT Press. 1994.

Mead, Walter Russell. *Mortal Splendor*. Boston: Houghton Mifflin. 1987.

Mehrabian, A. "The Development and Validation of Measures of Affiliation Tendency and Sensitivity to Rejection." *Education and Psychological Measurement* 30 (1970): 417–428.

Melden, A. I., ed. *Human Rights*. Belmont, CA: Wadsworth. 1970.

Merton, Robert K. "Discrimination and the American Creed." In Robert M. MacIver, ed. *Discrimination and National Welfare*. New York: Harper & Row. 1949.

Mill, John Stuart. "On Liberty." In *The Range of Philosophy*. Edited by Harold H. Titus and Maylon H. Hepp. New York: American Book. 1964.

Miller, David. *Social Justice*. Oxford: Clarendon Press. 1976.

Mills, C. Wright. *Power, Politics, and People*. Edited by Irving Louis Horowitz. New York: Balantine Books. 1963.

Molony, Barbara. "Japan's 1986 Equal Employment Opportunity Law and the Changing Discourse on Gender." *Signs: Journal of Women in Culture and Society* 20:2 (1995).

Montagu, Ashley, ed. *Man and Aggression*. New York: Oxford University Press. 1968.

Moore, Charles A., ed. *Philosophy and Culture: East and West*. Honolulu: University of Hawai'i Press 1962.

Moore, G. E. *Ethics*. New York: Henry Holt. 1912.

———. *Principia Ethica*. Cambridge: Cambridge University Press. 1959.

Moorehead, W. K. "Ghost-Dances in the West." *Illustrated American* 5:48 (1891).

———. "The Indian Messiah and the Ghost Dance." *American Antiquarian* 13 (1890).

Morris, Aldon. *The Origins of the Civil Rights Movement: Black Communities Organizing for Change*. New York: Free Press. 1984.

Muelder, Walter G. *Moral Law in Christian Social Ethics*. New York: John Knox. 1966.

Muller, Herbert J. *The Children of Frankenstein: A Primer on Modern Technology and Human Values*. Bloomington, IN: Indiana State University Press. 1970.

Mumford, Lewis. *The Pentagon of Power*. Volume 2: *The Myth of the Machine*. New York: Harcourt Brace Jovanovich. 1970.

Murphy, Jeffrie G. *An Introduction to Moral and Social Philosophy*. Belmont, CA: Wadsworth. 1973.

Murray, Gilbert. *The Five Stages of Greek Religion*. Oxford: Clarendon Press. 1925.

National Commission on Excellence in Education. *A Nation At Risk*. Washington, D.C.: U.S. Government Printing Office. 1983.

National Council of Teachers of English. "The Students' Right To Read." Champaign, IL: NCTE. 1962.

National Humane Review. "The American Humane Association." (November 1974).

National Women's History Project. *Women Win the Vote*. Windsor, CA: National Women's History Project, 1995.

Natural Health. P.O. Box 7440, Red Oak, IA 51591.

Niebuhr, Reinhold. *Moral Man and Immoral Society*. New York: Charles Scribner's Sons. 1932.

Nielsen, Kai. *Ethics without God*. Rev. ed. Amherst, NY: Prometheus. 1990.

Noll, Elizabeth. "The Rippling Effect of Censorship: Silencing in the Classroom." *English Journal* 83 (December 1994).

Noonan, John T. *The Morality of Abortion*. Cambridge, MA: Harvard University Press. 1970.

Norris, Christopher. *Uncritical Theory: Postmodernism, Intellectuals, and the Guild*

War. Amherst, NY: The University of Massachusetts Press. 1992.

Noss, David S., and John B. Noss. *Man's Religions*. 7th ed. New York: Macmillan. 1984.

Nozick, Robert. *Anarchy, State, and Utopia*. New York: Basic Books. 1974.

———. *The Examined Life: Philosophical Meditations*. New York: Simon & Schuster. 1989.

———. *Philosophical Explanations*. Cambridge, MA: Harvard University Press. 1981.

Nussbaum, Martha. "Patriotism and Cosmopolitanism." *Boston Review* 3 (October/November 1994).

Nygren, A. *Agape and Eros*. Revised English Translation by P. S. Watson. Philadelphia: Westminster. 1953.

Oakley, Ann. *Social Support and Motherhood*. Cambridge: Blackwell. 1993.

Odum, Eugene P. *Fundamentals of Ecology*. Philadelphia: W. B. Saunders. 1971.

Packard, Vance. *Our Endangered Children*. Boston: Little, Brown. 1983.

Page, Clarence. "Counting by Race." *The Charlotte Observer* (September 13, 1995): 13A.

Pahel, Kenneth, and Marvin Schiller, eds. *Readings in Contemporary Ethical Theory*. Englewood Cliffs, NJ: Prentice-Hall. 1970.

Palmer, Donald. *Looking at Philosophy*. Mountain View, CA: Mayfield. 1988.

Panichas, George A. "The Woodstock in Our Selves." *Modern Age* 37:3 (Spring 1995).

Parenti, Michael. *Democracy for the Few*. 5th ed. New York: St. Martin's Press. 1983.

Patterson, Gerald R. *Coercive Family Practices*. Eugene, OR: Castilio. 1982.

Patterson, Orlando. *Slavery and Social Death: A Comparative Study*. Cambridge, MA: Harvard University Press. 1982.

Paul, Richard. *Critical Thinking Handbook, K–3*. Rohnert Park, CA: Center for Critical Thinking and Moral Critique. 1986.

Pearson, Carol, and Catherine Pope. *The Female Hero in American and British Literature*. New York: R. R. Bowker. 1981.

Peck, M. Scott. *The Road Less Traveled*. New York: Simon & Schuster. 1978.

Pegis, Anton C., ed. *Basic Writings of St. Thomas Aquinas*. Vols. 1 and 2. New York: Random House. 1945.

Peirce, Charles Sanders. *Collected Papers of Charles Sanders Peirce*. Vols. I–VI. Edited by Charles Hartshorne and Paul Weiss. Cambridge, MA: Harvard University Press. 1931–1935.

People for the American Way. "Attacks on the Freedom To Learn: Report." Washington, D.C. 1994.

Peters, Tom, and Nancy Austin. *A Passion for Excellence*. New York: Random House. 1985.

Pike, Nelson. *God and Evil*. Englewood Cliffs, NJ: Prentice-Hall. 1964.

Plamenatz, J. D., ed. *Mill's* Utilitarianism, *Reprinted with a Study of the English Utilitarians*. London: Oxford University Press. 1949.

Plummer, Joseph T. "Changing Values." *The Futurist*. January-February 1989.

Pollard, Spencer D. *Science News* (April 8, 1972): 228.

Popkin, Richard H. *The Philosophy of the 16th and 17th Centuries*. New York: The Free Press. 1966.

President's Committee on Civil Rights. "To Secure These Rights." Washington, D.C. 1947.

Pritchard, H. A. "Does Moral Philosophy Rest on a Mistake?" *Mind* 21 (1912).

Pritchard, James B. *Ancient Near Eastern Texts Relating to the Old Testament*. 3d ed. Princeton: Princeton University Press. 1969.

Pryse, Marjorie. "Zora Neale Hurston, Alice Walker and the 'Ancient Power' of Black Women." In *Conjuring: Black Women, Fiction and Literary Tradition*. Edited by M. Pryse and H. Spellers. Bloomington: Indiana University Press. 1985.

Purdom, P. Walton, and S. H. Anderson. *Environmental Science*. 2d ed. Columbus, OH: Charles E. Merrill. 1983.

Quale, G. A. *A History of Marriage Systems*. Westport, CT: Greenwood. 1988.

Quinney, Richard. *The Social Reality of Crime*. Boston: Little, Brown. 1970.

Quittner, Joshua. "Cracks in the Net." *Time* (February 27, 1995).

———. "Unmasked on the Net." *Time* (March 6, 1995).

Radhakrishman, S., and Charles Moore, eds. *Source Book in Indian Philosophy*. Princeton, NJ: Princeton University Press. 1957.

Radhakrishman, S., and P. T. Raju, eds. *The Concept of Man: A Study in Comparative Philosophy*. London: George Allen and Unwin. 1960.

Ramsey, Patricia G. *Teaching and Learning in a Diverse World: Multicultural Education for Young Children*. New York: Teachers College Press. 1987.

Rawick, George P. *From Sundown to Sunup: The Making of the Black Community*. Westport, CT: Greenwood Press. 1972.

Rawls, John. *A Theory of Justice*. Cambridge, MA: Belknap Press of Harvard University Press. 1971.

Reader's Digest. "Consumer Adviser: An Action Guide to Your Rights." Rev. ed. 1989.

Redfield, Robert. *Human Nature and the Study of Society*. Chicago: University of Chicago Press. 1962.

———. *Tales of a New America*. New York: Times Books. 1987.

Reich, Robert B. *The Next American Frontier*. New York: Times Books. 1983.

Research and Forecasts, Inc. "The Connecticut Mutual Life Report on American Values in the '80s: The Impact of Belief." Hartford, CT: Connecticut Mutual Life Insurance Company. 1981.

Richardson, Laurel W. *The Dynamics of Sex and Gender: A Sociological Perspective*. Boston: Houghton Mifflin. 1981.

Rigden, Diana W., and Susan S. Waugh, eds. *The Shape of This Century: Readings from the Disciplines*. New York: Harcourt Brace Jovanovich. 1990.

Riesman, David, and N. Glazer. *Faces in the Crowd: Individual Studies in Character and Politics*. New Haven, CT: Yale University Press. 1952.

Robinson, J. A. T. *Honest to God*. Philadelphia: Westminster Press. 1963.

Rogers, Carl R. *On Becoming a Person: A Therapist's View of Psychotherapy*. Boston: Houghton Mifflin. 1961.

———. *On Becoming a Person*. Rev. ed. Boston: Houghton Mifflin. 1966.

Rorty, Richard. "On Ethnocentrism: A Reply to Clifford Geertz." In Rorty, Richard, ed. *Objectivity, Relativism, and Truth*. New York: Cambridge University Press. 1991: 203–210.

———. *Objectivity, Relativism, and Truth*. New York: Cambridge University Press. 1991.

Roscoe, B., and T. L. Krugere. "Aids: Altering Adolescents' Knowledge and Its Influence on Sexual Behavior." *Adolescence* 25 (1990): 39–48.

Rose, Arnold. *The Negro in America*. Boston: Beacon Press. 1961.

Rose, T. L. "The Corporal Punishment Cycle: A Behavioral Analysis of the Maintenance of Corporal Punishment in the Schools." *Education and Treatment of Children* 4 (1981): 157–169.

Rosenzweig, L. W. *The Anchor of My Life: Middle-Class American Mothers and Daughters, 1880–1920*. New York: New York University Press. 1993.

Ross, Stephen David. *The Nature of Moral Responsibility*. Detroit: Wayne State University Press. 1973.

Rossi, A. "Transition to Parenthood." *Journal of Marriage and the Family* 30 (1968): 26–39.

Rothenberg, David. *Is It Painful To Think? Conversations with Arne Naess*. Minneapolis: University of Minnesota Press. 1993.

Rouse, R., and S. C. Neill, eds. *A History of the Ecumenical Movement, 1517–1948*. New York: Westminster Press, 1954.

Royce, Joyce R. *The Encapsulated Man*. Princeton, NJ: Van Nostrand. 1964.

Rubin, Lillian B. *Erotic Wars: What Happened to the Sexual Revolution?* New York: HarperCollins. 1990.

Ryan, Kevin. "Mining the Values in the Curriculum." *Educational Leadership* (November 1993).

Sadler, William A. *Existence and Love.* New York: Charles Scribner's Sons. 1969.

Sadoff, Dianne F. "Black Matrilineage: The case of Alice Walker and Zora Neale Hurston." *Signs* 11 (1985).

Santayana, George. *The Life of Reason.* New York: Scribner's. 1954.

Schaefer, Richard T. *Racial and Ethnic Groups.* 2d ed. Boston: Little, Brown. 1984.

―――. *Racial and Ethnic Groups.* 3d ed. Boston: Scott, Foresman and Co. 1988.

Schedler, Norbert O. *Philosophy of Religion.* New York: Macmillan. 1974.

Schermerhorn, R. A. *Comparative Ethnic Relations: A Framework for Theory and Research.* New York: Random House. 1970.

Schlafly, Phyllis. *Child Abuse in the Classroom.* Illinois: Pere Marquette Press. 1980.

―――. *The Phyllis Shlafly Report*

Schlechty, P. C. *Schools for the 21st Century: Leadership Imperatives for Educational Reform.* San Francisco: Jossey-Bass. 1990.

Schlick, M. *Problems of Ethics.* New York: Prentice-Hall. 1939.

Schmitt, Lois. *Smart Spending: A Young Consumer's Guide.* New York: Charles Scribner's Sons. 1989.

Schulte, Brigid. Observer Washington Bureau. *The Charlotte Observer* (Feb. 23, 1995): Carolinas, 1C.

Schutz, William C. *FIRO: A Three-Dimensional Theory of Interpersonal Behavior.* New York: Rinehart and Winston. 1958.

Schwartz, Bernard, ed. *The Roots of the Bill of Rights.* 5 vols. New York: Chelsea House. 1971.

Schwartz, Tony. *What Really Matters: Searching for Wisdom in America.* New York: Random House. 1995.

Sears, David O., Letitia Anne Peplau, Jonathan L. Freedman, and Shelley E. Taylor. *Social Psychology.* Englewood Cliffs, NJ: Prentice-Hall. 1988.

Seliger, V. A. *Pricing the Priceless Child.* New York: Basic Books. 1985.

Sellin, T., ed. *Capital Punishment.* New York: Harper & Row. 1967.

Selznick, Philip. *Law, Society, and Industrial Justice.* New York: Russell Sage. 1969.

―――. *The Moral Commonwealth: Social Theory and the Promise of Community.* Berkeley: Univeristy of California Press. 1992.

Senge, Peter. *The Fifth Discipline.* New York: Doubleday. 1990.

Shaffer, Carolyn R., and Kristin Anundsen. *Creating Community Anywhere.* New York: Putnam. 1993.

Shapiro, Herman, ed. *Medieval Philosophy: Selected Readings.* New York: Modern Library. 1964.

Sharpe, Rochelle. "Efforts to Promote Teaching of Values in Schools are Sparking Heated Debate Among Lawmakers." *Wall Street Journal* (May 10, 1994).

Siegel, Bernie S. *Love, Medicine & Miracles.* New York: Harper & Row. 1986.

Signs: Journal of Women in Culture and Society 20:2 (1995).

Sills, Edward. *The Intellectuals and the Powers and Other Essays.* Chicago: University of Chicago Press. 1972.

Simon, Reynolds. "Woodstock for the Lost Generation." *New York Times* (August 4, 1991): Section H, 22.

Simon, S., and H. Kirschenbaum. *Values Clarification.* New York: Hart Publishers. 1972.

Simon, S., H. Kirschenbaum, and B. Fuhrmann. *An Introduction to Values Clarification.* New York: J. C. Penney, 1972.

Singer, Peter. *Animal Liberation: A New Ethics for Our Treatment of Animals.* New York: Random House. 1975.

Skinner, B. F. *Beyond Freedom & Dignity.* New York: Alfred A. Knopf. 1971.

Skolnick, Arlene S., and Jerome H. Skolnick, eds. *Family in Transition.* 8th ed. New York: HarperCollins. 1994.

Smith, Adam. *The Theory of Moral Sentiments.* London: Bohn. 1853.

Smith, Page. *Killing the Spirit, Higher Education in America.* New York: Viking Press. 1990.

Smith, Robert J. "Gender Inequality in Contemporary Japan." *Journal of Japanese Studies* 13 (1987).

Sobel, Mechal. *The World They Made Together*. Princeton: Princeton University Press. 1989.

Sprague, Elmer, and Paul Taylor, eds. *Knowledge and Value*. New York: Harcourt, Brace and World. 1967.

Stace, W. T. *The Concept of Morals*. New York: Macmillan. 1962.

Stan, A. M. "Power Preying." *Mother Jones* (December 1995).

Stengel, Richard. "The Changing Face of AIDS." *Time* (August 17, 1987).

Sternberg, Robert. "A Triangular Theory of Love." *Psychological Review* 93 (1986): 119–135.

Sternburg, R., and M. L. Barner, eds. *The Psychology of Love*. New Haven: Yale University Press. 1988.

Stevenson, C. L. *Ethics and Language*. New Haven, CT: Yale University Press. 1944.

Stotsky, Sandra. "Multicultural Education in the Brookline Public Schools: The Deconstruction of an Academic Curriculum." *Network News & Views* (October 1991).

Strauss, Leo. *The City and the Man*. Chicago: University of Chicago Press. 1978.

Strom, Margot S., and William S. Parsons. *Facing History and Ourselves: Holocaust and Human Behavior*. Watertown, MA: Intentional Educations. 1982.

Struhl, Karsten J., and Paula R. Struhl, eds. *Ethics in Perspective*. New York: Random House. 1975.

Swami Nikhilananda. *The Upanishads*. New York: Harper Torchbooks. 1963.

Sykes, Charles J. *Dumbing Down Our Kids*. New York: St. Martin's. 1995.

Taylor, Charles. *Philosophy and the Human Sciences: Philosophical Papers 2*. Cambridge: Cambridge University Press. 1985.

Taylor, Richard. "Fatalism." *The Philosophical Review* 71 (January 1962): 56–66.

Taylor, S. G. *Health Psychology*. New York: Random House. 1986.

Terrell, Huntington. "Moral Objectivity and Freedom." *Ethics* 76 (1965).

Thilly, Frank, and Ledger Wood. *A History of Philosophy*. New York: Henry Holt. 1959.

Thomson, Judith Jarvis. *Rights, Restitution, and Risk: Essays in Moral Theory*. Edited by William Parent. Cambridge, MA: Harvard University Press. 1986.

Tillich, Paul. *Perspectives on 19th and 20th Century Protestant Theology*. New York: Harper & Row. 1967.

Time Magazine. Special Issue (Spring 1995).

Titus, Harold H., and Morris T. Keeton. *Ethics for Today: Social Theory and the Promise of Community*. 5th ed. New York: Van Nostrand. 1973.

Toner, Robin. "Bible Is Being Translated into a Southern Coastal Tongue Born of Slavery." *New York Times* (March 1, 1987): 18.

Tonnies, Ferdinand. *Community and Society*. East Lansing, MI: Michigan State University Press. 1957.

Torrance, E. Paul, and R. E. Myers. *Creativity Learning and Teaching*. New York: Dodd-Mead. 1970.

Toulmin, Stephen E. *Cosmopolis: The Hidden Agenda of Modernity*. Chicago: The University of Chicago Press. 1990.

———. *The Place of Reason in Ethics*. Cambridge: Cambridge University Press. 1950.

Toynbee, Arnold. *An Historian's Approach to Religion*. London: Oxford University Press. 1956.

Turner, Frederick. *The Culture of Hope: A New Birth of the Classical Spirit*. New York: Free Press. 1995.

Twining, Mary Arnold. "Movement and Dance on the Sea Islands." *Journal of Black Studies* 15 (June 1985): 463–479.

U.S. Department of Health, Education, and Welfare, 1968. "Proceedings: Symposiums on Human Ecology." Washington, D.C. 1968.

U.S. Environmental Protection Agency, 1973. "The Quality of Life Concept." Washington, D.C. 1973.

Universal House of Justice. *The Promise of World Peace to the Peoples of the World: A Statement by the Universal House of Justice*. Wilmette, IL: Baha'i Publishing Trust, 1985.

Van Horne, Harriet. "A Commentary by Harriet Van Horne: The Sexual Revolution—in Living Color." *McCalls* 95 (October 1967): 46.

Vander Zanden, James W. *American Minority Relations*. 3d ed. New York: Ronald Press. 1972.

Vaux, Kenneth. *Who Shall Live? Medicine, Technology, Ethics*. Philadelphia: Fortress Press. 1970.

Ver Steeg, Clarence T., and Richard Hofstadter, eds. *Great Issues in American History*. 3 vols. New York: Vintage. 1969.

Vincent, Philip F. *Character Education: A Primer*. Chapel Hill, NC: New View. 1994.

Vogel, Lawrence. *The Fragile "We" Ethical Implications of Heidegger's "Being and Time."* Evanston, IL: Northwestern University Press. 1994.

Walhout, Donald. *Interpreting Religion*. Englewood Cliffs, NJ: Prentice-Hall. 1963.

Walker, Alice. *In Search of Our Mothers' Gardens*. New York: Harcourt Brace Jovanovich. 1984.

Walker, Williston. *A History of the Christian Church*. New York: Charles Scribner's Sons. 1918.

Wallace, A. F. C. "Revitalization Movements." *American Anthropologist* 58 (1956).

Waller, Douglas. "Spies in Cyberspace." *Time* (March 20, 1995).

Warburg, James. *The West in Crisis*. Garden City, NY: Doubleday. 1959.

Watson, Steven. *The Harlem Renaissance*. New York: Pantheon. 1995.

Watt, W. M. *Islam and the Integration of Society*. London: Routledge & Kegan Paul. 1961.

Webster, Donovan. "Shrink to Fit." *Men's Health* (April 1995): 76–81.

Weil, Jonathan S. "Dealing With Censorship: Policy and Procedures." *Education Digest* 53 (January 5, 1988).

Weinberg, Meyer. *A Chance to Learn: A History of Race and Education in the United States*. Cambridge: Cambridge University Press. 1977.

Weinstein, Deena. "Expendable Youth: The Rise and Fall of Youth Culture." In L. Cargan and J. H. Ballantine, eds. *Sociological Footprints*. 6th ed. Belmont, CA: Wadsworth. 1994.

———. *Heavy Metal: A Cultural Sociology*. New York: Macmillan/Lexington. 1991.

Wells, Donald A. *God, Man, and the Thinker*. New York: Dell. 1962.

Wilden, A. *Systems and Structure: Essays in Communication and Exchange*. 2d ed. London: Tavistock. 1980.

Williams, Bernard. *Ethics and the Limits of Philosophy*. Cambridge, MA: Harvard University Press. 1985.

———. *Making Sense of Humanity*. New York: Cambridge University Press. 1995.

———. *Moral Luck*. Cambridge: Cambridge University Press. 1981.

———. *Morality: An Introduction to Ethics*. New York: Harper & Row. 1972.

Williams, F. E. "The Valilala Madness." Port Moresby, Territory of Papua: Anthropology Report #4. 1923.

Williams, J. E., and D. L. Best. *Measuring Sex Stereotypes: A Multinational Study*. Newberry Park, CA: Sage. 1990.

Wilson, James Q. *The Moral Sense*. New York: Free Press. 1993.

Wilson, William J. *The Declining Significance of Race: Blacks and Changing American Institutions*. 2d ed. Chicago: University of Chicago Press. 1980.

Winfield, Richard Dien. *Freedom and Modernity*. Albany: State University of New York Press. 1991.

———. *Reason and Justice*. Albany: State University of New York Press. 1988.

Winfield, Richard Dien. *The Just Economy*. New York: Routledge. 1988.

Wippel, J. F., and A. B. Wolter. *Medieval Philosophy from St. Augustine to Nicholas of Cusa*. New York: Free Press. 1969.

Wittgenstein, Ludwig. "A Lecture on Ethics." *The Philosophical Review* 74 (January 1965).

Wolff, Robert Paul. *Philosophy: A Modern Encounter.* Englewood Cliffs, NJ: Prentice-Hall. 1971.

Wolff, Robert Paul, ed. *Kant: A Collection of Critical Essays.* Garden City, NY: Doubleday. 1967.

Wolgast, Elizabeth. *Ethics of an Artificial Person.* Stanford, CA: Stanford University Press. 1992.

Women of Power, A Magazine of Feminism, Spirituality, and Politics. Charlene McKee, ed. Orleans, MA (published bi-annually).

Women of Power: A Magazine of Feminism, Spirituality, and Politics. Charlene McKee, ed. Orleans, MA (published bi-annually).

Woodson, Carter G. *The African Background Outlined.* New York: Negro Universities Press. 1968.

Woodward, C. Vann. *American Counterpoint: Slavery and Racism in the North-South Dialogue.* Boston: Little, Brown. 1971.

———. *The Strange Career of Jim Crow.* New York: Oxford University Press. 1974.

World Book Encyclopedia. Chicago: Field Enterprises Educational Corporation. 1993.

World Book Encyclopedia Yearbook 1980. Chicago: Field Enterprises Educational Corporation. 1980.

Worsley, Peter. *The Trumpet Shall Sound: A Study of "Cargo" Cults in Melanesia.* London: Macgibbon and Kee. 1957.

Wright, P. H. "Self-Referent Motivation and the Intrinsic Quality of Friendship." *Journal of Social and Personal Relationships* 1 (1994): 115–130.

Yankelovich, Daniel. "Restoring Public Trust." *Mother Jones* (November/December 1995).

Zachner, R. C., ed. *The Concise Encyclopedia of Living Faiths.* New York: Hawthorn Books. 1959.

INDEX